William Blake and
Impossible History

William Blake and the

Impossible History

of the 1790s

Saree Makdisi

The University of Chicago Press
Chicago and London

SAREE MAKDISI is associate professor of English and comparative literature at the University of Chicago. He is the author of *Romantic Imperialism: Universal Empire and the Culture of Modernity*. He has also written extensively on the cultural politics of the contemporary Arab world.

The University of Chicago Press, Chicago 60637
The University of Chicago Press, Ltd., London
© 2003 by Saree Makdisi
All rights reserved. Published 2003
Printed in the United States of America
11 10 09 08 07 06 05 04 03 02   1 2 3 4 5

ISBN: 0-226-50259-7 (cloth)
ISBN: 0-226-50260-0 (paper)

Library of Congress Cataloging-in-Publication Data

Makdisi, Saree.
   William Blake and the impossible history of the 1790s / Saree Makdisi.
      p. cm.
   Includes bibliographical references and index.
   ISBN 0-226-50259-7 (alk. paper)—ISBN 0-226-50260-0 (pbk. : alk. paper)
   1. Blake, William, 1757–1827—Political and social views.   2. Politics and literature—Great Britain—History—18th century.   3. Political poetry, English—History and criticism.   4. Blake, William, 1757–1827—Religion.   5. Antinomianism in literature.   6. Imperialism in literature.   7. Economics in literature.   8. Slavery in literature.   9. Liberty in literature.   I. Title.
   PR4148.P6 M35 2002
   821'.7—dc21
                                                                                    2002002545

⊚ The paper used in this publication meets the minimum requirements of the American National Standard for Information Sciences—Permanence of Paper for Printed Library Materials, ANSI Z39.48-1992.

For Christina

 CONTENTS

List of Illustrations   ix
Preface and Acknowledgments   xi

1. INTRODUCTION — 1
2. FIERCE RUSHING: WILLIAM BLAKE AND THE CULTURAL POLITICS OF LIBERTY IN THE 1790S — 16
3. LABORING AT THE MILL WITH SLAVES — 78
4. WEARY OF TIME: IMAGE AND COMMODITY IN BLAKE — 155
5. BLAKE AND ROMANTIC IMPERIALISM — 204
6. IMPOSSIBLE HISTORY AND THE POLITICS OF LIFE — 260
7. CONCLUSION: STRIVING — 313

Notes   325
Bibliography   369
Index   385

ILLUSTRATIONS

1. Blake, *America: A Prophecy*, copy E, plate 5 — 18
2. Blake, *The Dance of Albion (Glad Day)* — 36
3. Blake, *The Accusers of Theft, Adultery, Murder (War)* — 37
4. Blake, *The Marriage of Heaven and Hell*, copy L, plate 1 — 51
5. Blake, *The Book of Urizen*, copy G, plate 17 — 82
6. Blake, *The Book of Urizen*, copy G, plate 9 — 84
7. Blake, advertisement for Moore & Company — 109
8. Blake, *Songs of Innocence and of Experience*, copy C, plate 23 — 166
9. Blake, *Songs of Innocence and of Experience*, copy Z, plate 10 — 167

Following page 188
10. Blake, *America: A Prophecy*, copy E, plate 6
11. Blake, *The Marriage of Heaven and Hell*, copy D, plate 21
12. Blake, *Unknown Subject (Let Him look up into the Heavens and laugh in the bright air)*
13. Schiavonetti after Blake, *Death's Door*
14. Blake, white-line etching of *Death's Door*
15. Blake, *At Death's Door*
16. Blake, *For Children: Gates of Paradise*, copy D, plate 17
17. Blake, *America: A Prophecy*, copy E, plate 14

18. Eugène Delacroix, *Combat of the Giaour and Hassan* — 210
19. Eugène Delacroix, *La Mort de Sardanapale* — 211
20. Prospect of Balbeck, in Henry Maundrell, *A Journey from Aleppo to Jerusalem* — 221
21. Fallen ruins, in *Ionian Antiquities* — 223
22. Blake, *Oeconomy and Self Denial*, in Mary Wollstonecraft, *Original Stories from Real Life* — 228
23. Blake, frontispiece, in Mary Wollstonecraft, *Original Stories from Real Life* — 229
24. Blake after King, *A Family of New South Wales* — 253

ILLUSTRATIONS

25. Blake, *The Execution of Breaking on the Rack*, from John Gabriel Stedman, *Narrative of a Five Years Expedition Against the Revolted Negroes of Surinam* — 254
26. Blake, *Europe Supported by Africa and America*, from John Gabriel Stedman, *Narrative of a Five Years Expedition Against the Revolted Negroes of Surinam* — 255
27. Blake, *Laocoön* — 264
28. Garnet Terry, frontispiece, in *Prophetical Extracts*, no. 5 — 305

PREFACE AND ACKNOWLEDGMENTS

> You have no feeling for the fact that prophetic human beings are afflicted with a great deal of suffering; you merely suppose that they have been granted a beautiful "gift," and you would even like to have it yourself. But I shall express myself in a parable. How much many animals suffer from the electricity in the air and the clouds! We see how some species have a prophetic faculty regarding the weather: monkeys, for example (as may be observed even in Europe, and not only in zoos—namely, on Gibraltar). But we pay no heed that it is their *pains* that make them prophets. When a strong positive electrical charge, under the influence of an approaching cloud that is as yet far from visible, suddenly turns into negative electricity and a change of the weather is impending, these animals behave as if an enemy were drawing near and prepare for defense or escape; most often they try to hide: They do not understand bad weather as a kind of weather but as an enemy whose hand they already *feel*.
> —Friedrich Nietzsche

Ignored by the art world, marginalized in the engraving world, essentially unknown in the world of poetry, William Blake—one of the finest poets in the English language, one of the world's most accomplished engravers, and one of its most unusual and talented artists—may have had his moments of despair and even of outrage, and somehow one feels that he was entitled to them. Most Blake scholars are familiar with those expressions of Blake's rage in, for example, his *Public Address*, or in his furious marginal comments on the works of Sir Joshua Reynolds and other "generalizing Idiots," or in his private ruminations about Robert Cromek ("Bob Screwmuch") and Louis Schiavonetti ("Assassinetti"). Far too much has been said about those comments, however, and far too much has been abstracted from them; since few people would have been able to tolerate the gradual deterioration into the common grave that Blake experienced without the occasional expression of resentment, such expressions are, to my mind, hardly surprising. What *is* surprising, however, when we look back over the writing from a career that spanned over forty years, of which the last thirty were spent in a gradual decline of fame and recognition—in inverse relation to the growing brilliance and complexity of the artist's work—is not how *much*, but rather how *little* outrage, how little bitterness and resentment there is, and on the contrary, how much generosity, kindness, and humanity one notes in Blake, and not only in his work but also in those few remaining recollections of him from those who knew him.

Samuel Palmer knew Blake late in the latter's life and remembers him partly for the resilience of his spirit in the face of his decline into poverty and obscurity. In his dress, there was a kind of "triumph of the man over his poverty," Palmer notes; "indoors, he was careful, for economy's sake, but not slovenly: his clothes were threadbare, and his grey trousers had worn black and shiny in front, like a mechanic's. Outdoors, he was more particular, so that his dress did not, in the streets of London, challenge attention either way. He wore black knee breeches and buckles, black worsted stockings, shoes which tied, and a broad-brimmed hat. It was something like an old-fashioned tradesman's dress. But the general impression he made on you was that of a gentleman, in his own way." Palmer once accompanied Blake on a visit to the Royal Academy (in which Blake had been denied membership by virtue of his status as an engraver, since the academy, reflecting society's prejudices, considered engraving a trade rather than an art, and its practitioners mere common tradesmen, like hosiers or shoemakers, rather than true artists). During the visit, Palmer recalls, Blake "pointed to a picture near the ceiling, by Wainwright, and spoke of it as 'very fine.' It was a scene from Walton's *Angler*. While so many moments better worthy to remain are fled, the caprice of memory presents me with the image of Blake in his plain black suit and rather broad-brimmed but not quakerish hat, standing so quietly among all the dressed-up, rustling, swelling people, and thinking to myself, 'How little you know who is among you.'"

And so Blake passed from this world, essentially robbed of recognition, despite all his effort and despite all his brilliant works, which still dazzle us when we encounter them today in libraries or museums. Yet he apparently never allowed himself to let resentment, anger, or hate rule his reaction to his decline. "If a man is master of his profession, he cannot be ignorant that he is so," Blake ruminated once his fall into obscurity had been confirmed following his falling out with Cromek, the editor of an illustrated edition of Robert Blair's *Grave* who withdrew Blake's engraving commission from him; "and, if he is not employed by those who pretend to encourage art, he will employ himself, and laugh in secret at the pretences of the ignorant, while he has every night dropped into his shoe—as soon as he puts it off, and puts out the candle, and gets into bed—a reward for the labours of the day, such as the world cannot give; and patience and time await to give him all that the world can give." Yes, in the reference to the "secret laughter" at the "pretences of the ignorant," we get a taste of Blake's resentment, a sense of his battered pride, even his arrogance (the very same kind of arrogance which we admire in that probably apocryphal story about Beethoven, in not dissimilar circumstances, telling a now obscure prince that there had been and would be countless princes, but there was only one Beethoven); but in the rest of the passage we also get the sense that there is a faith much deeper and more profound than mere resentment, a faith that kept Blake going, a faith that manifested itself not only in the way he lived his life but also in the kinds of things he drew and wrote—a faith based on joy rather than resentment, on love rather than hate. This is the very kind of faith that had led Spinoza, again in not entirely dissimilar circumstances, to write decades earlier that "Hate is increased by being returned, but can be destroyed by love."

Indeed, it seems to me that the overriding emotions in Blake's work are not bitterness and resentment, but rather love and joy, themes which dominate his poetry from the earliest of the poetical sketches to the closing moments of *Jerusalem* ("joy," in fact, is one of the most frequently used words in Blake's work). And about the persistence, the growth, the celebration, of love and joy in Blake far, far too little has been written, or even acknowledged, in modern scholarship. As a result, contemporary scholarship is in a much better position to address the theme of despair in *London*, or the theme of exploitation in either of the chimney sweeper poems, or even the theme of revenge in *A Poison Song*, which is actually quite anomalous in Blake's oeuvre; and it finds itself all but stripped of the critical capacity and the conceptual language with which to make much of the joys and desires of *The Garden of Love*, or *Ah! Sun-Flower*, or *A Little Girl Lost*, or Oothoon's cries of "Love! Love! Love! happy happy Love!" in *Visions of the Daughters of Albion*. Thus, for example, the latter is far more frequently read as a poem about slavery, trickery, deceit, infidelity, and repression than as a poem about joy. Scholars have never really known what to do with the joy in—and of—Blake's work. Such joy has been left for the private appreciation of individual readers, rather than for public scholarly or critical understanding, unless it can somehow be tamed into one of those pseudo-Jungian narratives of transhistorical drives and abstract ethereal passions that sometimes make their way into Blake criticism—drives and passions so abstract that no living human being could possibly experience them. However, the opposition between public and private is just one of the many of binary oppositions that Blake's work undermines, and it turns out that joy in Blake is not the property of a private self sealed off from an outside public sphere. It is, or rather it ought to be, the basis of community—and hence it has an immediately political character and is intimately tied up with all those things that are ordinarily understood to be appropriate to the world of history and politics.

This is a book about many things having to do with history and politics and the resistance to mass conformity, to the brutality of capitalist monoculture, to modern imperialism, to the beginnings of what we now call "globalization," which Blake identified over two hundred years ago as a tendency toward "universal empire." But it is also a book about the kinds of joy and love that we encounter in Blake's work. Sometimes, as Wordsworth once wrote, "we murder to dissect." I can only hope that having offered a scholarly framework for understanding joy and love in Blake's work, I will not have murdered them in the process. For in a world still dominated by hate, and ruled by oppression, by exploitation, by conquest and brutal military occupation, I think we might still have things to learn from Blake, as we search for all those rewards that the world cannot give, as well as the rewards that it certainly can.

I could not have written this book without the support, encouragement, and criticism of colleagues, friends, and my family.

My colleagues in the Departments of English and of Comparative Literature at the University of Chicago provided me with a supportive and stimulating environment in which to work and think. I am grateful to Lauren Berlant, Homi Bhabha, Bill Brown, James Chandler, Bradin Cormack, Miriam Hansen, Elizabeth Helsinger, Paul Hunter, Françoise Meltzer, Mark Miller, Tom Mitchell, Janel Mueller, Michael Murrin, Larry Rothfield, Lisa Ruddick, Joshua Scodel, Eric Slauter, Richard Strier, Katie Trumpener, Robert von Hallberg, Kenneth Warren, and Anthony Yu for their time and patience in reading and commenting on earlier drafts of this project, and in sharing their criticisms with me. I am especially grateful to Homi Bhabha, Bill Brown, Tom Mitchell, and Michael Murrin, who were particularly supportive during some of the difficult passages this book took me through over the past two or three years; and to James Chandler, for his wisdom and encouragement over the years, without which this project probably would not have survived. I would also like to thank my colleagues Moishe Postone and Dipesh Chakrabarty for many illuminating conversations, which helped me to think through particular moments in my overall argument; indeed, the work of Dipesh, as well as our discussion many years ago of the relationship between Blake and Tagore, has been more of an inspiration than he realizes. Edward Said took the time to read drafts of two early chapters and his insights and criticisms have proved invaluable: I am very grateful to him for his comments, and for always reminding me of the importance of audience.

I was able to write this book with the institutional support of the University of Chicago, and I am grateful to the current and previous chairs of the English and Comparative Literature Departments—Jay Schleusener, Elizabeth Helsinger, Michael Murrin, and Françoise Meltzer—and to the current and former deans of humanities, Philip Gossett and Janel Mueller, for their encouragement of my research and writing, and particularly for the generous allocation of leave time and research support, without which this book could not have been written.

The students at Chicago, both graduate and undergraduate, have proved to be stimulating and thoughtful interlocutors, and I am glad to have had the chance to develop my thinking on Blake in dialogue with them, inside the classroom and outside it, over the past several years. I am grateful to all the students in my seminars on Blake and on radical culture in the 1790s, and I am particularly grateful to Stefani Engelstein, Noel Jackson, Michael Robertson, Hilary Strang, and Eirik Steinhoff, with whom I have discussed this project and who have read parts of it and shared their criticisms with me.

The Franke Institute for the Humanities at the University of Chicago provided me with an atmosphere conducive to work during my fellowship year there, and the Huntington Memorial Library very generously provided me with a fellowship to study its marvelous collection, including several copies of Blake's illuminated books: I am greatly indebted to these institutions and their librarians and staffs, as well as to the librarians and archivists at the British Library, the print room of the British Museum, the Goldsmiths Collection at the University of London Library, the United Kingdom Public Records Office in Kew, the Dr. Williams Library of Dissent, and the Westminster City Archives, where I spent a great deal of time researching 1790s London. Catherine Haskins and Jay Satterfield at the University of Chicago Library have also been very helpful. I would also like to thank Steven Connor of Birkbeck College at the University of London, who provided much invaluable assistance in getting my feet on the ground during a research year there.

This book would not have taken the form it has without its illustrations, and I would like to thank the various collections which have generously supplied me with these images and granted permission to reproduce them here, including the University of Chicago Library, the Library of Congress, the

Preface and Acknowledgments

British Library, the British Museum, the National Gallery of Art in Washington, the Carnegie Museum of Art in Pittsburgh, the Art Institute of Chicago, and the Musée du Louvre (with particular thanks to M. Jacques Foucart, conservateur général at the Louvre, who kindly supplied me with the photograph of Delacroix's *La Mort de Sardanapale*). I would also like to thank Robert Essick for allowing me to reproduce images from his personal collection, and the editors of the on-line Blake Archive (Robert Essick, Morris Eaves, and Joseph Viscomi) for supplying me with image files for items in the Essick Collection and the Library of Congress; Joseph Viscomi and Robert Essick have both gone out of their way to help me with these images, and I am indebted to them for all their assistance. Alan Thomas and Randy Petilos at the University of Chicago Press deserve special thanks for magically transforming this project, images and all, from a manuscript into a book, and I am grateful to Erik Carlson for his help with the manuscript.

I am thankful for the many opportunities over the years to have presented my work in lectures, meetings, and conferences, at venues including the Huntington Library, the Blake Society in London, Tate Britain, the Centre for Eighteenth Century Studies at the University of York, the University of Groningen in Holland, University College Cork in Ireland, the University of Minnesota, and Rice University; I am very grateful to all those responsible for the generally thankless tasks of organizing such events. It has, of course, been a wonderful and enriching experience to have learned from scholars and colleagues in the field, among whom I can now count many friends. Conversations over the years with John Barrell, David Worrall, Steve Clarke, Michael Phillips, Ann Bermingham, Jon Mee, Kevin Gilmartin, Michael Ferber, Annie Janowitz, Christopher Hobson, Bob Patten, D. W. Dörrbecker, Robert Essick, Frances Ferguson, Andrew Lincoln, Iain McCalman, Anne Mellor, Peter Otto, Alan Liu, Marilyn Butler, Morris Eaves, and Joseph Viscomi have all helped to nourish the intellectual project that culminated in this book. I am particularly grateful to Robert Essick for his hospitality and generosity, for his patience in reading and rereading earlier drafts of the book—and many loose passages and fragments in between—and for sharing his wisdom and knowledge, as well as for saving me from being "awarded" the dreaded Essick-Viscomi Prize for the Worst Description of Relief Etching (for which I believe I may have been in the running at one point). Moreover, his comments as one of the press readers for the manuscript were of immense value. Kevin Gilmartin also read the manuscript for the press, and his suggestions and criticisms proved extraordinarily helpful.

I am also thankful to the late Robert F. Gleckner, whose teaching and love of Blake were formational parts of my graduate school experience and whose continued support and criticism over the years was without parallel. He had read some of the following chapters; I am sorry that he did not see the whole book before he passed away in the summer of 2001.

The relationship between base and superstructure may not be as evident as it once was in cultural theory, but one can still say that no intellectual project would be possible without a wide base of support—intellectual, social, cultural, political, alimentary, and otherwise. I know for a fact that I could not have written this book without the company, the hospitality, the generosity and the friendship of Mona and Rashid Khalidi, Mario Santana and Elisa Martí-Lopez, Vincenzo Binetti and Heidi Busch, Wissam and Shermine Boustany, and Tariq Dajani. Jon Mee may have been identified as the "fun face of Blake criticism," which he undoubtedly is—and for which we should be thankful, for it is a field of criticism that otherwise takes itself all too seriously—but our conversations over the years, and the examples set by his own tireless explorations of the plebeian radical underground of the 1790s and Blake's dangerous enthusiasm, have been an important source of inspiration to me. Over the years, Richard Dienst has been both a friend and a source of intellectual support, but his work on the question of the image was truly foundational for me as I was making my way through this book: I am lucky to have been able to turn to him for help when thinking through Blake's complicated use of images. The thought and friendship of Cesare Casarino have almost literally been absorbed into the fabric of this study: among many other things, he is responsible for reminding me always of the significance of joy—a question far too often overlooked in scholarship—and none of the references to joy in the following pages (of which there are surprisingly many) would really be complete without some acknowledgement of Cesare: they are the traces of his presence in the book.

I must also acknowledge the support of my parents, Samir and Jean Makdisi, and my brothers Ussama and Karim, all of whom have been subjected to enough Blake and Blakeana to last several lifetimes and yet still somehow manage expressions of encouragement and enthusiasm years into the project! I am especially grateful to Ussama, who, despite having had to put up with Blake's many jabs against "reasoning historians," has always been willing to share with me his discipline's sense of the past, and in a book that is at least in part about history that has proved invaluable. My aunt and uncle Rosemarie Said Zahlan and Tony Zahlan have always provided me with hospitality when research or conferences took me to London, and I am grateful to them, as I am to Wissam and Shermine Boustany, who have hosted me in their London home on more occasions than they probably care to remember. When the newest member of the family, baby Samir, arrived in the world as I was supposed to be finishing the draft of this book in January of 2001, his arrival may have delayed the completion of this project in one terribly mundane sense but in another sense he lent it altogether new meaning: he has never stopped reminding me of why Blake expressed such faith in children and such joy in their presence, and of why such faith and such joy are—or should be—the keys to living our lives and interacting with others.

Above all others, however, I want to thank Christina Beyrouti Makdisi. She has not simply watched this book mature (or at least change) over the years from a scattering of wild and loose ideas to its present form: she made this transformation possible, with encouragement, with patience, with support, with love. Without Christina, this book would not have been possible; which is why it is to Christina that it is dedicated.

Material from earlier versions of chapters 4 and 5 appeared in my contributions to *The Cambridge Companion to Blake* and *The Cambridge History of Romanticism*, respectively, and it has been much revised and expanded for this book.

 CHAPTER ONE

Introduction

All a poet can do today is warn.
—Wilfred Owen

"The history of all times & places," William Blake once wrote, "is nothing else but improbabilities and impossibilities; what we should say, was impossible if we did not see it always before our eyes."[1] In these astonishing lines, Blake is at once pointing out the difference between the way we experience historical transformation and the way in which that transformation is recorded and pointing to the gap between historical experience and history itself: that is, the tools and concepts, the paradigms and discourses, the rules and regulations—the laws—according to which historical experience is recorded and narrated. He is also, however, implicitly raising the very question of how and by whom the possible is distinguished from the impossible, the probable from the improbable; and in so doing he is pushing us to consider why it is that the impossible and the improbable seem to triumph, for better or for worse, over the categories and regulations designed to exclude them and cordon them off. These are important questions because Blake's work, his art, his poetry, his political, philosophical, religious, and aesthetic beliefs, even he himself, were in his time understood—and indeed they usually still are—as both improbable and impossible.

For Blake's work invokes a world of spirits and of imaginative power, a sense of time as fractured and unevenly heterogeneous, a sense of sharing and being in common that requires that we take seriously the propositions that "God only acts & Is, in existing beings or Men,"[2] and that "the Eternal Body of Man is THE IMAGINATION. that is God himself," the "Divine Body" of which "we are his Members."[3] According to such propositions, which we should consider not simply as articles of faith but rather as attempts to think through and interpret historical experience, freedom should be understood

1

CHAPTER ONE

not in terms of the negative freedom enshrined in the liberal tradition—consolidated through the struggles of the 1790s—but rather in creative, affirmative, positive terms, as the power to constitute "the eternal body of man"; as the power to imagine, and to create through imagining; as the power to affirm life as being in common, and art as the making of that "divine body" of which we are all "members." If such a world and such propositions seem impossibly alien to us, improbably fantastic, uncomfortably dependent on what looks like a worn-out and outmoded religious language (which they undoubtedly are), that is precisely the point. Having said that, we could either go on reading Blake as an improbable oddity from another time (quaint, strange, a bit mad), or we could take seriously the challenge to think through—and indeed to rethink, to unthink if need be—the ways in which the probable and the possible are defined, and the ways in which these and similar discourses have come to regulate not only how we experience historical transformation, and hence the ways in which we approach and think of history itself, but also the very ways we live our lives and interact with others.

In this book, I explore the ways in which Blake's illuminated books of the 1790s allow and even compel us to reconsider the "impossible history" of the turbulent decade in which they emerged as a moment in which the cultural logic of modernization was fully articulated. Too often in Blake scholarship, issues and questions in Blake's work that seem, according to a modern political idiom, not to be readily identifiable as political in nature—his understanding of being, his views of art, his sense of love, his conception of the imagination—are assumed to mark a departure into some other realm: the mythic, the cosmic, the universal, the spiritual—all of which are assumed to be somehow opposed to or irreconcilable with the historical, the political, and the real. Moreover, a great deal of what cannot be immediately explained—and of what does not make immediate sense—in the work is also consigned to the realm of the ahistorical and the nonpolitical. Much of what Blake wrote, as E. P. Thompson once pointed out, is "altogether too disturbing: it is either wrong, or mad, or it requires the rewriting of history."[4] Blake, Thompson tells us, requires the latter. However, what the present book proposes is that the history whose rewriting Blake requires is not only the history of revolution and political transformation which his work has often been taken to depict, but also the conceptual history of modernity itself, its sense of possibility and impossibility, and its fundamental conceptual categories, above all the stable unitary subject, the sovereign individual essential to the newly emergent world of liberalism, republicanism, and commodity culture.

Introduction

Clearly, Blake's language of imagination, of power, of sharing and being in common—that is, the language of radical antinomian enthusiasm, which he, like others, inherited from older currents of thought and modified for the exigencies of his own time—was already considered obsolete by the 1790s. But it was obsolete only in the sense that it was allowed no room in the historicist discourse of modernity, and in the culture of modernization, which had to purge itself of such enthusiastic tendencies. For the language of enthusiasm refused the concept of empty homogeneous time which would prove foundational not just for modernity, but for the very sense of history according to which—as I argued in *Romantic Imperialism*—other cultures, other narratives, other peoples can be seen as "obsolete," irrecuperable, unhistorical, or altogether "impossible."[5] Such a sense of history was essential to much (but not all) of the radicalism of the 1790s, as well as to the strands of romanticism and the modern form of imperialism that emerged along with it, all of whose exponents would have regarded someone like Blake as an outsider, an other—as other, indeed, as all those other others so frequently denigrated in radicalism, aestheticized in romanticism, and vilified in imperialism: the restless urban mob, the languorous Oriental harem girl, the fanatical Asiatic warrior, the "mad-headed" enthusiast. Hence, the language of enthusiasm—and Blake was by no means alone in using such a language in the 1790s—had to be denied a place not only in the progressive revolutionary narratives developed by many (though not all) of the radicals of the 1790s, but also the narratives that have been inherited and sustained by subsequent historians and literary critics.

Partly as a result of this, most historically oriented studies of Blake's work have situated him primarily and often exclusively in the political context defined by the culture of modernization itself, effectively assimilating him into a culture in which he did not really belong, a culture that regarded him as alien, a culture whose premises he bitterly contested. Thus, in most scholarship Blake has been scripted into history as a participant in the radical struggle for liberty and the "rights of man" against the hereditary religious and political order of the old regime: a struggle associated with the work of Tom Paine, John Thelwall, Mary Wollstonecraft, and others. As a result, much modern scholarship has also—whether consciously or unconsciously—identified Blake with the champions of an emergent modern consumer culture, which, through the rhetoric of rights and choices, shared the key conceptual and philosophical assumptions of the radical discourse of liberty (primarily the celebration of the secular freedom of the sovereign individual) and would in fact prove to be inseparable from it. For much of the period's radical discourse—notably the discourse generally best preserved

3

CHAPTER ONE

and most foregrounded in modern scholarship, as opposed to the proliferating "other" discourses forgotten, downplayed, and pushed to the margins both by certain radicals themselves and by scholars ever since—this sovereign individual ought to be free to exercise choice in politics as in commerce, free to develop a sense of moral virtue and indeed moral superiority precisely through the practice of choice, and hence not only free to regulate him- or herself, but to cherish freedom itself as the ability to regulate, control, police oneself.

However, the relationship among moral virtue, choice, freedom, and self-regulation that was developed in much of the radical discourse of the 1790s, and in romanticism itself, was profoundly Orientalist in nature—to an extent that has hitherto gone almost entirely unrecognized in scholarship. As much in the work of Wordsworth or Coleridge as in that of Paine or Thelwall, this discourse sought to authorize a modern Western set of values, a modern Western sense of citizenship, above all a modern Western sense of *self*, as against what it perceived to be an Oriental culture supposedly incompatible with and hostile to all those values. In celebrating the moral virtue of the modern self, much of the radical and romantic writing of the 1790s necessarily celebrated the modern self's superiority to the Oriental other.

As we shall see in greater detail in chapter 5, however, such Orientalism turns out to be the key not only to the radical culture of the 1790s—as well as to the culture of romanticism that emerged with it—but also to Blake's divergence from both. For, as against what he called the "philosophic and experimental" knowledge of Paine or Wordsworth, with its class- and race-defined requirements for what must be recognized as a stable Western subject (adequately learned, prepared, disciplined, and cultivated), and with its quest for moral virtue and domination over the other, Blake proposes the prophetic power of the poor and unlearned, of Asians and Africans, of his "fellow labourers,"[6] and of children. Jesus, Blake writes, "supposes every Thing to be Evident to the Child & to the Poor & Unlearned Such is the Gospel." For, he adds, "the Whole Bible is filld with Imaginations & Visions from End to End & not with Moral virtues that is the baseness of Plato & the Greeks & all Warriors The Moral Virtues are continual Accusers of Sin & promote Eternal Wars & *Domineering over others*."[7] Thus, rather than the imperial "warrior" discourse essential to the dominant strand of 1790s radicalism as well as to at least a major strand of romanticism—a discourse obsessed with sovereign power and domination of the other—Blake proposes an opening out away from the discourse of sovereign power and toward a mode of being which recognizes that "God is Man & exists in us & we in

4

him" and that "all must love the human form, / In heathen, turk or jew. / Where Mercy, Love & Pity dwell, / There God is dwelling too."[8]

In the chapters that follow, then, I will argue that Blake's sympathy with what has become the familiar radical attack on hereditary aristocratic government did not prevent him from questioning the political and cultural assumptions of the best-known radicals (most famously Tom Paine) with whom he has often been associated, as well as the liberal spirit of commercial, consumerist, and political freedom being championed in their writings and struggles. For, as I will demonstrate, the sovereign individual whose political and commercial rights constituted the ultimate objective of the dominant radical movement of the 1790s (though not, as we shall see, other varieties and strands of radicalism) is profoundly destabilized and rendered inoperative in Blake's work of the same decade. Blake found this conception of rights far too limited and restrictive, especially in its reliance on the notion of individual selfhood, which for Blake represented the worst form of confinement and restriction. Decades later, expressing the anxieties of the individual selfhood, or the so-called centered subject, the great writers and artists of twentieth-century modernism would, according to Fredric Jameson, dramatize "the unhappy paradox that when you constitute your individual subjectivity as a self-sufficient field and a closed realm, you thereby shut yourself off from everything else and condemn yourself to the mindless solitude of the monad, buried alive and condemned to a prison cell without egress."[9] Writing at the moment marking the cultural, political and economic consolidation of the monad, Blake was already warning of the dangers of such a burial alive. In so doing, he was, however, not exactly anticipating the modernist critique of bourgeois culture that would develop in the work of T. S. Eliot, James Joyce, Virginia Woolf, Edward Munch, Gertrude Stein, Wyndham Lewis, Filippo Marinetti, or Vincent van Gogh. Blake was, rather, expressing a cultural and political standpoint that bourgeois culture would first have to eradicate in order for the modernist critique, as it developed in the early twentieth century, to become possible in the first place. Blake, then, was not simply a modernist *avant la lettre* (for such a proposition would be sustainable only in grossly ahistorical and apolitical terms). If certain of his cultural, political and aesthetic positions sometimes resemble those of modernism, that is because he shared with the twentieth-century modernists a common enemy in the rationalizing, alienating, mechanizing, quantifying, modernizing, and empire-building culture of the nineteenth century. The latter oriented the world around the rational, alienated, mechanized, quantified, modern, and imperial subject, whose anxieties and pathologies may have been more or less successfully repressed

CHAPTER ONE

through the nineteenth century but would emerge and be given their fullest expression in modernism. Such expressions would intensify after the Great War of 1914–1918, which revealed the frailty of the individual selfhood for what it was in the trenches of the Somme and Verdun and the mud of Gallipoli.[10] If the cultural trauma of the Great War may be said to have brought the "long" nineteenth century to its end, however, it was in the context of the revolutionary wars of the 1790s—which are often taken to mark the beginning of the "long" nineteenth century—that Blake produced his own seemingly forgotten warning against the political, economic, cultural and psychical centralization that would necessarily accompany the bourgeois domination of both self and others.

What I propose is that Blake's illuminated books of the 1790s—including *Songs of Innocence and of Experience*, *The Marriage of Heaven & Hell*, *Visions of the Daughters of Albion*, *America: A Prophecy*, and *The Book of Urizen*—undermine the conceptualizations of sovereignty and reification that were essential to the logic of consumer culture and the free market, as well as to the logic of the republican movement and liberal democracy. In Blake's work, for example, we very rarely see characters that are sovereign in the sense required by the conception of freedom demanded by Paine. Attempts at such sovereignty, as, for example, in the figure of Urizen, invariably turn into new forms of oppression, both of the other and of the self supposed to be rendered free. In linking the constitution of Urizen's body to the constitution of the chains of linear time, for example, Blake reminds us of the extent to which the "fallen" human body anticipates, even complements, the modern assembly line, so that the sovereign subject—with all his supposed freedom and liberty—is revealed to be the mirror image, the necessary correlate, of the factory drone; hardly free at all.

In the illuminated books, the supposed freedom of the sovereign individual is shown to be compromised by the extent to which selves and others exist in a dispersed and mutually dependent network that is not really compatible with a discourse of identity and difference. Thus, the world of the illuminated books never really coheres into—in fact it precludes altogether—the simple juxtaposition of self and other in an atomized social space, which was the presupposition, the ground, of both consumerism and liberal republicanism. The world of Blake's books is characterized instead by a series of links and synapses in which selves and others are shown to be made up of common and shared elements, and in which meanings are generated immanently rather than by reference to transcendent and transparent or "self-evident truths"—such as the ones invoked by the American Declaration of Independence —which provided the inspiration for much of the radical movement in London, though they are broken down beyond repair in the world of the illuminated books.

Such a dispersed network, I argue, is not only figured in the "content" of Blake's prophecies, but also embodied in their form and even in their very materiality. As I argue in chapter 4, the illuminated books should be seen as an open network of verbal and visual texts which share many verbal and visual elements, none of which can really be said to function in a genuinely sovereign sense, that is, as self-governing and independent from others. Certain elements of *America* (1793), for example, are shared with *Visions of the Daughters of Albion* (1793) and *The Marriage of Heaven & Hell* (1790–93), and hence, as I argue in chapter 4, their meaning cannot be figured independently, but depends instead on the network of interactions among those texts. Even a "single" work, such as *America*, cannot be said to have a sovereign existence, as it exists in a series of nonidentical "copies" with no prior referent or prototype, whose very lack of homogeneity stands out in the context of a drive toward ever greater homogenization of products—and producers, consumers, citizens—in the emergent consumer culture of the late eighteenth century.

What the following chapters will reveal is that in his work Blake elaborated a very different conception of being—and hence a very different conception of politics, as well as of aesthetics—from the one that would rise to hegemony in the radical struggle of the 1790s. For Blake can be seen to locate the foundation of both his aesthetics and his politics, as well as his sense of being, in desire, which was taken to be the great scourge of the radical culture of the period, the morally virtuous self's means of differentiating itself not only from passionate Orientals but also from the unruly mob and decadent aristocrats (since, as Mary Wollstonecraft writes, virtue is understood as the conquest of passion by reason).[11] "The desire of Man being Infinite," Blake writes, man is "himself Infinite."[12] However, if for Blake our being is defined by our desire, we are not fixed in definite (and intermeasurable) forms, as unitary, self-contained, and self-regulating individuals; indeed, we do not exist as definite forms at all, but rather as ever-changing bundles of relations articulated by our (infinite) desires. Here Gilles Deleuze's reading of Spinoza—who elaborated a similar sense of desire, though in much more formidable philosophical language—offers a great deal of potential for our understanding of Blake as well. "The important thing," Deleuze writes, "is to understand life, each living individuality, not as a form, but as a complex relation between differential velocities, between deceleration and acceleration of particles," which is why, he adds, if we are true Spinozists "we will not define a thing by its form, nor by its organs and its functions, nor as a substance or a subject"; rather, we will define it "by the affects of which it is capable."[13] Certainly, for Blake at least as much as for Spinoza, the ultimate horizon of our affective relations and our infinite desires—and hence the ultimate horizon of our being—is not a narrow formal selfhood, a self as opposed to others, but rather our participation in the common body of God, the "divine body" of which "we are his members."

The extent to which the illuminated books contest the logic of self-regulation and disciplinary necessity in any of its forms must be seen in terms of Blake's deep and abiding commitment to radical antinomian principles. Stemming from a sense that all living things together immanently constitute God (so that, in a line that Blake reiterates in many of the books, "every thing that lives is holy"), Blake's antinomian principles gave him a basis from which to question those juridical or disciplinary processes which might be seen to approximate the moral law of the Old Testament. "All Penal Laws court Transgression & therefore are cruelty & Murder," Blake writes, adding that the moral commandments of the Old Testament are "the basest & most oppressive of human codes, & being like all other codes given under pretence of divine command were what Christ pronounced them, The Abomination that maketh desolate, i.e., State Religion, which is the source of all Cruelty."[14] From such a standpoint, any attempt to contest the cruelty of the moral law must surely contest the authority of the state, and vice versa. Thus, whereas much of the radical struggle for liberty in the 1790s was aimed exclusively at the apparatuses of the state, Blake's challenge to tyranny requires a social, economic, and cultural dimension as well, and recognizes that a struggle for freedom must go beyond the strictly political-representational issues raised in the writings of activists like Paine, to challenge not only the forms of identity taken for granted by Paine, but also the radical faith in the law and competition. The contrast here, as in much of Blake's work, is between the iron codes of disciplinary cruelty—in economic and cultural instantiations as well as political ones—and a deep and abiding antinomian faith in the "everlasting gospel," the unwritten gospel which according to Blake "is forgiveness of Sins & has No Moral Precepts."[15]

That Blake's work articulates such an antinomian stance suggests that we can see in it a joyous form of freedom—which I believe needs to be considered seriously as a political formulation—utterly incompatible with the doctrine of individual rights. This possibility has not yet received the critical attention that it deserves, partly because we have been trying to make Blake conform to a political culture which his work disrupts. In reading

Blake, then, it is important to try to question or to step outside the conceptual parameters imposed by the dualisms we have (sometimes uncritically) inherited from Locke, which were enshrined in the culture of modernization whose hold over life Blake so passionately contested. For if these parameters were indeed challenged in Blake's work, it would have to be in ways that would necessarily remain inaccessible to criticism ultimately derived from Locke himself. More often than not, this critique would be registered as bizarre, inexplicable, mysterious, even dangerous; a breakdown of the conceptual language through which the fundamental ideologemes[16] of modernity were articulated—a language out of which Blake developed his own subversive slang.

For in the illuminated books, Blake must be seen to be tinkering with and disrupting these ideologemes, the basic conceptual and ideological building blocks of modernization, in effect rewriting the conceptual language of modernization for alternative political and aesthetic purposes. That Blake was tinkering with the very same concepts that were so essential to the economic and political discourse of the time—in which, as we shall see, he was immensely interested, though from a subversive position—cannot be a coincidence. Both scholars and amateur Blakeans have wondered what Blake could possibly have known about modern industrial production and modernity itself. It will, however, become clear through the course of this book that Blake found himself in a privileged location to think through the economic and political concerns of a rapidly modernizing society—its transition to a consumer society—from his standpoint as a *producer*. As we will see in greater detail in chapter 3, when Charles Babbage, one of the greatest early theoreticians of the modern assembly line, was looking for the conceptual ancestor of the modern factory, he found it neither in the steam engine nor in the textile mill, but rather in Blake's trade: in copperplate engraving. According to Babbage, the efficient modern factory should ideally reiterate the logic of copperplate engraving by producing a stream of identical copies based on the same original "impression." The industrially produced commodity, or copy, thus represents a kind of "image" of the prototype, and the image itself is for Babbage the core concept of industrial society. Thus, the art to which Blake was apprenticed from his youth, and by which he made his living as an adult, was the perfect location for understanding modern industrial production, first because it was among the earliest forms of production to deploy what can be recognized as an industrial process based on the division of labor, and second because it was concerned with the reproduction of the image: the concept which, according to theo-

CHAPTER ONE

rizations of modern society from Babbage and Marx to Guy Debord, Jean Baudrillard, Gilles Deleuze, Fredric Jameson, and Richard Dienst lies at the very heart of modern (capitalist) culture.

If, therefore, Blake's illuminated books do not conform to our understanding of history, it is not because they are apolitical (let alone ahistorical), but rather because they pose a fundamental challenge to our understanding of history and modernity itself. For if Blake questions the status of narrative and representation, for example, he does so partly in order to question conventional understandings of history, especially history considered as a narrative of development supposedly recounting the story of the "universal empire" of modernization.[17] In posing this challenge, however, Blake is confronting not just a certain type of historicism, but also the political culture, the forms of narrative and representation, the modes of subjectivity and temporality, the forms of production and exchange, which it simultaneously presupposes and enables—by all of which the impossible and the improbable are either excluded or else broken down, assimilated and absorbed into the real. What the illuminated books allow us to question is the very status of the possible; and what they so often seem to propose instead is a history of the impossible and the improbable rendered without that saving transformation into the real, and specifically into the normative reality of modernity.

Many, even most, of the politically and historically oriented examinations of Blake tend to place greater emphasis on the history of political *events* than they do on the history of the *concepts* that we rely upon to understand those events. What I offer here instead is something like an archaeology of the conceptual and political parameters of Blake's illuminated books. This has required me to move between and connect together a number of areas addressed in Blake's work but usually divided into separate spheres of scholarly activity: art history, the status of the engraving industry, the logic of image reproduction in capitalist culture, the antinomian religious and political tradition, the radical culture of the 1790s, the socioeconomic history of the period, literary criticism and interpretation, and of course the "composite art" and mode of production introduced by the illuminated books themselves. As a result, this book will be primarily concerned not so much with the representational practice of the illuminated books as with concepts and the ways in which particular concepts—having to do with identity, singularity, sovereignty, exchange, production, reproduction—are deployed, challenged, altered, and recombined in Blake's work in relation to the ways in which they were deployed, challenged, altered, and recombined in the wider discursive context (political, economic, religious, ideological, and material) of the 1790s and shortly afterward.

The book is divided into seven chapters, including this one.

Chapter 2 presents an overview of the radical culture of the 1790s and considers the ways in which Blake's illuminated books mark a series of ruptures and departures from what emerged through the decade as a hegemonic radical position, which was centered on the commercial and political liberty of the individual. Through a reading of key passages of *America* and *The Marriage of Heaven & Hell*, I propose that while Blake participated in the radical attack on authoritarian priestcraft and kingcraft, he also developed in his illuminated books a very powerful critique of the epistemological and conceptual basis of the dominant radical agenda. I argue that Blake's interest in the antinomian tradition going back at least to the seventeenth century offered him a set of concepts with which to contest the cultural and political primacy of the individual, which allowed him to produce a conception of freedom that went far beyond the narrow scope of liberty sanctioned by the hegemonic radical position, in which political equality was sharply distinguished from socioeconomic egalitarianism.

Chapter 3 proposes an investigation of some of the socioeconomic contexts of Blake's work. Here I continue to explore the suggestion in the preceding chapter that Blake was unwilling to accept the hegemonic radical notion that the individual could have ontological priority outside human history and could hence be taken for granted as the transcendental and transhistorical basis for liberty. I suggest that in the illuminated books we see an ongoing relationship between political, cultural, economic, and social institutions—castles, palaces, hospitals, workhouses, churches—and the subjective categories, the psychobiological modes of existence, produced and organized by them. In other words, we see here a seamless continuity between social, legal, economic, and political organizations and the psychological and physiological organisms inhabiting the world defined by them. Individuals here are not given for all time, but are defined through a social and historical process of production. I suggest that in his critical interest in such forms of organization, Blake must be seen to be tinkering with the basic conceptual and ideological building blocks of modernization, in effect rewriting the conceptual language of modernization for alternative political and aesthetic purposes. In particular, I argue that Blake has discovered in the logic of organization one of the conceptual cores both of industrial production and of unitary psychobiological subjectivity in an expanded social, political, and cultural domain well outside the gates of the earliest factories. In other words, the dark satanic mill here is a figure not just of the organization of production in early industrial society, but also of the social, political, and religious constitution of the individual psychobiological subject. The illu-

CHAPTER ONE

minated books allow us to see the extent to which the division of labor in manufacture and the seemingly opposing logic of bourgeois subjectivity are not as opposed as they might seem and, even if they are not quite identical, share the very same political and epistemological basis, amounting to two sides of the same coin. The individual human subject—rather than being something that has always already had a self-evident existence as defined by reason, nature, and nature's god, and so on—is a product like any other, an assemblage, a machine: a making machine, a consuming machine, a desiring machine, a living machine.

Chapter 4 begins with a reading of one of the central plates from *America* and considers the temporal structure of Blake's illuminated books, which ultimately break down the teleology associated with the hegemonic or mainstream radical position and force us to reconsider cultural and political discourses assuming a sense of linear time. Blake's texts, I argue, rarely move either "backward" or "forward," and open up instead into a kind of eternal time of repetition. Much of the chapter is taken up with the consideration of a widely recognized phenomenon in Blake's work—the repetition of the same verbal and visual images and texts in different works—in terms of Blake's relationship to his craft of engraving, which was itself based on a logic of repetition, albeit of material images rather than simply figural ones. I propose that just as Blake tried to subvert the reproductive machinery of commercial engraving in his illuminated books, using it to produce a number of dazzlingly heterogeneous "copies" that have no "original" to refer back to, he did so figurally as well, by using repetition to expand and elaborate meanings rather than simply to reproduce them. Later sections of the chapter turn from *America* to some of the other works with which it shares repeated phrases and images and asks us to consider how Blake's logic of generating variability through repetition might problematize certain modern concepts of production and exchange as well as the notions of identity and community associated with them.

Chapter 5 argues that Blake conceived of a very different way of inhabiting and sharing the world from that of the "universal empire" of modernization which was consolidated during his lifetime. The chapter examines in detail Blake's relationship to the cultural politics of imperialism emergent in both hegemonic 1790s radicalism and Wordsworthian romanticism. The first part of the chapter consists of a reading of the Orientalism that sometimes latently and sometimes manifestly informs and sustains 1790s radicalism and Wordsworth's aesthetic of otherness. The second part reflects on Blake's own attitudes toward imperialism and the romantic aesthetic of otherness and demonstrates the extent to which his work contests and subverts that aesthetic and the cultural politics from which, as I argue here—and in my earlier book *Romantic Imperialism*—it is inextricable. In this sense, this chapter, and indeed the book as a whole, acts as a kind of sequel to *Romantic Imperialism*.

Chapter 6 provides a detailed examination of the process of subjective organization in the illuminated books. Beginning with close readings of the verbal and visual images in *The Book of Urizen*, *The Book of Ahania*, and *The Book of Los*, which are all deeply concerned with the generation of individual identity as a punitive restriction from the infinite world beyond the confines of the self, I consider the relationship between Blake's conceptualizations of individual identity and contemporary theories of subjectivity. I also investigate in greater detail than in the other chapters the nature of the relationship between Blake's understanding of identity, belonging, and community and certain philosophical, religious, and political traditions going back to at least the middle of the seventeenth century.

Chapter 7, finally, draws the various subarguments of the book together and proposes some conclusions which will hopefully have significance not only for our understanding of Blake, but also for our understanding of the period in which he worked and, indeed, for our understanding of the culture of modernization itself.

It may seem at first glance that what I offer here is a series of readings of *America*, since plates from that text feature centrally in chapters 2, 3, and 4. But, as I explain in detail in chapter 4 itself, it is not my intention here to produce a consistent sustained reading of *America* or of any of the other prophecies. On the contrary, I think it is often much more useful to read elements of *America* alongside elements of *The Marriage of Heaven & Hell* or *Visions of the Daughters of Albion* than it is to try to invent an overall organizing schema to contain a single reading of *America* itself. It has always been difficult for critics to devise a way to organize more or less coherently their readings of Blake's illuminated books, since it is a daunting task to try to contain these books with any of the organizing rubrics of modern scholarship without severely distorting their somewhat anarchistic tendency. For if we accept, even provisionally, that Blake's work might propose a break with the modern political aesthetics of identity, then the organizing principles of modern scholarship—the book, the author, the work, the subject—might actually prevent us from seeing what is most significant about Blake's work. In the chapters that follow, I will try to question such organizing principles in order to propose a method of reading Blake's work in terms of his conceptual and material practice. Moreover, the illuminated books are not just partly verbal and partly visual: as the rich variety of Blake scholarship demonstrates, Blake's work occupies a node that reaches out to a number of different discursive formations (literary criticism, art history, social history, the craft of engraving, economic production, etc.), and it is very difficult to devise a way to address all of these different domains coherently.

My own way of negotiating these familiar dilemmas has been to alter the scale of my discussions of Blake's verbal and visual texts, offering readings aimed at different textual levels for the different chapters, and sometimes even for the different sections of each chapter, each of which calls upon a distinct archive requiring a distinct mode of scholarship. In some places, I will concentrate on very detailed textual analysis; in others I will work through much broader questions in political or economic history; in still others I will integrate my reading of Blake's poetry with his visual art. Thus, at times I will center my readings of particular plates in one or more of the illuminated books, and at other times, I will recalibrate the level at which I am operating and will focus instead on particular phrases or images as they reappear through Blake's work. If many of the plates and phrases or images that ground my readings here are taken from *America*, that is because the prophecy provides an important occasion to frame, orient, and discuss the questions that I am most interested in. This is due to *America's* pivotal location in Blake's corpus, as the first prophetic book, one which was produced at a crucial moment of transition in the revolutionary politics of the 1790s, and as the book where Blake most clearly distinguishes his version of radicalism from the hegemonic one. Also, of course, America itself—the place—was a crucial organizing reference point for the radical struggle in London (which was in certain respects inspired by the American War of Independence).

Indeed, America's special status in the modern world had already been recognized in the late eighteenth and early nineteenth centuries. Hegel was not alone in thinking that the basic character of American society "is marked by the private person's striving for acquisition and profit and by the predominance of a private interest which devotes itself to the community for personal benefit alone."[18] But if for Hegel and others such a recognition would explain why America is to be considered "the land of the future," for Blake, it inspired a fierce rush to understand *how* such a history could come to pass—and to do whatever possible to produce an alternative history of the future, one premised on the hope of freedom incompatible with the highly restricted and bounded private liberty of the isolated individual. "The bounded," as Blake once wrote, "is loathed by its possessor. The same *dull round* even of a universe would soon become a mill with complicated wheels."[19] If weakly organized historians "cannot see either miracle or prodigy," Blake wrote two decades later, that is because "all is to them a *dull round of probabilities and possibilities*."[20] But if, with Blake, we recognize that the history of all times and places is improbable and impossible, that preserves the hope of an as yet unimaginable history of freedom, one not restricted the dull round of individual rights and duties and allowing instead the participation in a community open to all. After all, "what is now proved was once, only imagin'd."[21]

CHAPTER TWO

Fierce Rushing: William Blake and the Cultural Politics of Liberty in the 1790s

> If commerce were permitted to act to the universal extent it is capable, it would extirpate the system of war, and produce a revolution in the uncivilized state of governments. The invention of commerce has arisen since those governments began, and is the greatest approach towards effecting universal civilization, that has yet been made by any means not immediately flowing from moral principles.
> —Thomas Paine

> Commerce, the boasted glory of our isle—Commerce, who from her very essence should be free as air, is to groan in manacles!
> —John Thelwall

> First Trades & Commerce, ships & armed vessels he builded laborious
> To swim the deep; & on the land, children are sold to trades
> Of dire necessity, still laboring day & night till all
> Their life extinct they took the spectre form in dark despair;
> And slaves in myriads, in ship loads, burden the hoarse sounding deep,
> Rattling with clanking chains; the Universal Empire groans.
> —William Blake

1. Introduction: London Radicalism in the 1790s

"*America*," wrote Henry Crabb Robinson in an 1811 essay, "appears in part to give a poetical account of the [American] Revolution, since it contains the names of several party leaders. The actors in it are a species of guardian angels. We give only a short example, nor can we decide whether it is intended to be in prose or verse." Like its sister book *Europe: A Prophecy*, Robinson concluded, *America* is a "mysterious and incomprehensible rhapsody, which probably contains the artist's political visions of the future, but is wholly inexplicable."[1] Having read *America* some twenty years later, the art critic and biographer Alan Cunningham concluded that "with much freedom of composition and boldness of posture," Blake "was unmeaning, mystical, and extravagant, and that his original mode of working out his conceptions was little better than a brilliant way of animating absurdity."[2]

Reading *America* a little later in the nineteenth century, Blake's first major biographer, Alexander Gilchrist, found himself dazzled by the "unquestionable power and design" of the plates: "Turning over the leaves, it is sometimes like an increase of daylight on the retina, so fair and open is the effect of particular pages. The skies of sapphire, or gold, rayed with hues of sunset, against which stand out leaf or blossom, or pendant branch, gay with bright plumaged birds; the strips of emerald sward below, gemmed with flower and lizard and enamelled snake, refresh the eye continually."[3] But even Gilchrist found the text "hard to fathom; with far too little Nature behind it;—the fault of all this class of Blake's writings; too much wild tossing about of ideas and words." Although he found *America* dazzling in some respects, Gilchrist concluded that it was a profuse scattering of "unhewn materials of poetry and design," the product of a "loose and rudderless" genius. Part of what Gilchrist found so puzzling about the prophecy was the uncanny combination and jarring contrast of Blake's "Ossian-like" mythical names and "those of historic or matter-of-fact personages occasionally mentioned in the poem, whom, notwithstanding the subject in hand, we no longer expect to meet with, after reading the *Preludium*." Through the chaotic storm clouds of prophecy, he writes, "the merely human agents show small and remote, perplexed and busied in an ant-like way."

Given the perplexed early reception history of Blake's *America*, it is striking that this prophecy, of all of Blake's work, is the one around which a fairly clear consensus has emerged in modern scholarship, a consensus which has only in the past few years faced systematic questioning.[4] There has been much discussion of the various divisions in Blake studies, but on the question of *America* there has been a rare convergence of the conflicting strands of scholarship.[5] Although it is often argued that it was the unfinished piece *The French Revolution*, due to have been printed in 1791 by Joseph Johnson—the publisher of William Godwin, Tom Paine, Mary Wollstonecraft, Joseph Priestley, and other well-known radicals—that confirmed Blake's position in the 1790s struggle for "liberty," according to the critical consensus it was in *America* that Blake produced his most political work.[6]

This view has largely developed from a tendency to see Blake, in Gilchrist's words, as "an ardent member of the New School, a vehement republican and sympathiser with the Revolution, hater and contemner of kings and king-craft.... To him, at this date, as to ardent minds everywhere,

17

Figure 1. William Blake, *America: A Prophecy*, copy E, plate 5. Lessing J. Rosenwald Collection, Library of Congress. Copyright © 2001 the William Blake Archive. Used with permission.

the French Revolution was the herald of the Millennium, of a new age of light and reason." Blake has often been made to fit seamlessly into a respectable company of rational, sensible, judicious, and essentially (if not actually) secular intellectuals, for whom revolution was first and foremost a matter for ardent minds. His class position—that of a small tradesman, an independent artisan—has been repeatedly invoked as a more or less sure indicator of the extent to which he must have conformed to the standards of secular radicalism, as they supposedly filtered down from the ideologues who attended Johnson's dinner parties to the cadres of the London Corresponding Society (LCS), which was made up largely of tradesmen and artisans occupying the same social stratum as Blake. Radicalism in this context has often been taken to imply a mobilization of light and reason to peer into the dark recesses and gloomy mysteries of the old regime. This, of course, is explicitly the Enlightenment role that Tom Paine and Mary Wollstonecraft claimed for themselves in their confrontations with Edmund Burke, and many modern scholars have taken their position for granted as definitive of all radicalism in the period, including Blake's. As a result, the complex political positions of both Blake's early work and his later work have often been read reductively, either—in the case of the early work—as a conformist celebration of "liberty," or—in the case of the later work—as a kind of apolitical quietism.[7] Thus, Blake has been configured as a soft liberal who was buoyed by the false hopes of a foreign revolution only to soften into respectable quietism in later years when that revolution supposedly revealed its true nature.

What I want to propose in the present chapter is that *America* is indeed concerned with Blake's commitment to the radical struggles of the 1790s, as well as with the relationship between the events that unfolded in the American War of Independence and the events defining London radicalism in the 1790s. However, as I understand it, Blake's concern has nothing to do with a gratuitous celebration of either the American War or the notion of liberty being heralded by Tom Paine and his followers. While I concur with David Erdman's reading of Blake as a "prophet against empire" and as a constant opponent of the forces of tyranny and what he would call oppressive codes (such as the iron laws of "State Religion, which is the source of all Cruelty"),[8] I am not convinced that there is much evidence of Blake's sharing the fundamental conceptual and political assumptions of the advocates of liberty. For it will be my contention here that *America*, which was written at a crucial turning point during the political struggles of the 1790s, confirms both Blake's attack on the old regime *and* his disruption of the philosophical, conceptual, and political narratives underlying the discourse of "lib-

CHAPTER TWO

erty," and in particular his critique of the narrow conception of freedom animating much of 1790s radicalism. Blake would hardly have been alone in articulating a radical position that was critical both of the old regime and of the struggle for what he took to be a very limited understanding of freedom.[9] What I will show in this chapter and in the ones to follow is the extent to which Blake's illuminated books, not only *America*, must be understood in terms of this engagement in ways that have yet to be specified—and on a scale that has yet to be recognized—in Blake scholarship.

The academic understanding of the 1790s as a crystalline moment of struggle between two highly polarized forces—on the one hand, the defenders of the old regime (e.g., Edmund Burke, Hannah More, Patrick Colquhoun), and on the other, the rational and secular advocates of a newfound liberty (e.g., Tom Paine, Mary Wollstonecraft, William Godwin)—has been complicated in recent scholarship. Iain McCalman, Jon Mee, David Worrall, Mark Philp, E. P. Thompson, and others have demonstrated the extent to which the decade of the 1790s was characterized, especially among radicals, by a complex and heterogeneous network of forces and tendencies, making such straightforward polarizations difficult to plot. In particular, critical attention has been drawn to the resurgence during the 1790s of forms of popular enthusiasm and radical antinomianism, explicitly reaching back to the writers and activists of that earlier moment of revolutionary crisis in the seventeenth century, many of whose tracts were reprinted in fresh editions during the 1790s.[10] Richard Brothers, the ex–Navy officer who in 1792 began prophesying earthquakes and revolutions and the fall of monarchies (as well as a quasi-colonialist fantasy in which he, the Nephew of God, would lead the Hebrews to Palestine, where they would "rebuild" Jerusalem) until he was arrested and declared to be insane and consequently locked up from 1795, is only one of the many colorful figures of late-eighteenth-century London radicalism of whom we are now more aware.

The activities and publications of Brothers, as well as Thomas Spence, Robert Wedderburn, William Sharp, Richard Lee, Garnet Terry, Thomas Bentley, William Blake (who could easily have been arrested for violating the very same Elizabethan laws against prophecy under which Brothers was charged),[11] and many others who drew to a greater or lesser extent on the antinomian heresies of the seventeenth century—in addition to the persistence of often politically charged practices in alchemy, astrology, mysticism, magnetism, and illuminism in the London from which the great Cagliostro had only recently departed[12]—complicate the often-invoked polarization between the educated spokespersons of a secular and rational radicalism on the one hand and the tradition-bound defenders of the old regime on the other. There was clearly a bubbling variety of radicalisms, often popular, unrespectable, semiliterate, or downright "dangerous," that drew on religious or at any rate mystical faith but could nevertheless ally themselves—up to a point—with the teachings of sophisticated and formally educated secular rationalists in a common fight against the established order. And, as Jon Mee argues, even in the work of Paine himself we can at times discern references to "a submerged millenarianism, built up through biblical allusions," alongside Paine's "sturdy rationalism."[13] Thus, the dangerous enthusiasm of plebeian radicals could, at least provisionally, coexist with more "sophisticated" versions of Jacobin rationalism, together constituting what Iain McCalman—drawing on the confessions of William Hamilton Reid, a former radical himself—calls "a mélange of blasphemy, millenarianism and sedition."[14] Indeed, Reid's 1800 *Rise and Dissolution of the Infidel Societies in this Metropolis* provides an insider's account of the genealogical relationships, going back to the seventeenth century, between religious enthusiasm and infidel secular organizations such as the London Corresponding Society; for, as Reid writes, "to suppose the late inclination to infidelity, to have been the result of cool inquiry, or rational conviction, would be a gross libel upon the good sense of the country."[15]

The fact that various seventeenth-century currents had resurfaced in 1790s London allows us to more fully appreciate the extent to which Blake (whose antinomian affiliations had been recognized as early as 1958 by A. L. Morton and were amplified in Michael Ferber's 1985 study, before being further elaborated by E. P. Thompson and Jon Mee)[16] was not alone in his faith in the "everlasting gospel," that key concept in antinomian thought linking Blake and other 1790s enthusiasts to seventeenth-century heretics like Abiezer Coppe and Laurence Clarkson.[17] "For all his individual genius," McCalman points out, "William Blake was a more typical figure in his day than many scholars have realized."[18]

However, the recent scholarly emphasis on the heterogeneity of 1790s radicalism, and on the extent to which popular enthusiasm could be combined with secular rationalism in a pungent revolutionary blend, should not prevent us from discerning the presence of a strand of radicalism that sought to rise above the fray and to assert its own legitimacy, partly by making its own claims on "respectable" political discourse, partly by denying, excluding, and disassociating itself from other forms and subcultures of radicalism (which it regarded as inarticulate, unrespectable, unenlightened, and hence illegitimate), and partly by working to assimilate as many grievances as possible into its own agenda for reform, rearticulating them when necessary—

and thereby exercising, in effect, a form of hegemony, albeit one whose dominance was still very much in question at the time and would fade altogether amid the deepening crises of 1796–97, only to return early in the nineteenth century. This strand of radicalism enjoyed the allegiance of many of the best-known radical intellectuals as well as relatively broad-based popularity among the artisan class whose members constituted the core of London's radical culture. Its hegemony has been extended by scholars ever since, many of whom have lost sight of other varieties of radicalism and now read the radical activity of the period in a unidimensional, almost reductive way, in the very terms proposed by this hegemonic tendency, which was centered almost exclusively on what are by now familiar ideas, namely, demands for universal (male) suffrage and annual parliaments, or in other words for an extension of the political franchise through more adequate representation in parliament. These demands would reemerge in modified form after the end of the Napoleonic Wars and would gather strength under the banner of Chartism.[19] The persistence of what may usefully be thought of as this liberal-radical tendency is what tied together, for example, the great open-air meetings organized by the London Corresponding Society at Copenhagen Fields in October and November 1795 (which according to some drew up to two hundred thousand participants) and the now more famous Peterloo gathering of 1819. For John Thelwall's tireless reiterations through the mid-1790s of the argument that "there is no redress for a country situated as we are, but by restoring to the people their right of universal suffrage and annual parliaments: rights which nature dictates, and which no law can take away" would be adopted unchanged by the later organizers.[20] As James Chandler points out, "the plan for the great assembly at St. Peter's Field in Manchester [in 1819] was to have been a key action in the campaign led by Henry 'Orator' Hunt and others to organize working people in London, in the north of England, and in Scotland under what Hunt called 'the watchwords of freemen: Annual Parliaments and Universal Suffrage.'"[21]

Both in the 1790s and in the early nineteenth century, however, the spokesmen of this liberal-radical tendency had to articulate their own position, and reinforce their claims to legitimacy, by focusing attention on certain questions—principally those concerning political representation—and suppressing those questions that were seen to be incompatible with their own epistemological and philosophical foundation. For this strand of radicalism was motivated by and articulated in terms of that form of philosophy (identified by C. B. Macpherson as "the political theory of possessive individualism") which, following its emergence in the seventeenth century, "had discovered individual man as the irreducible basic unit of the social world," as Günther Lottes points out, and "had applied this principle mercilessly to one field of knowledge after the other: to philosophy and psychology, to religion and ethics, to social philosophy and economics."[22] Although other notions of rights, and other ways of imagining identity, belonging and community, and even freedom itself, were certainly present in the great panoply of 1790s radicalism, they were disavowed not only by the repressive apparatuses of the state, but often by the liberal-radicals themselves, as they tried to extend their hegemony over London's fractious, disunited, and heterogeneous radical movements. Just as the more radical antinomians and communists (for whom political and economic egalitarianism—popular sovereignty and the abolition of private property—went hand in hand against what was perceived as the oppressive order of king and market) had been suppressed as the seventeenth-century revolution consolidated its political program, and had been forced underground long before the Restoration itself, the most prominent radical intellectuals, such as Paine and Thelwall, as well as the early (pre-1797) leadership of the London Corresponding Society, repeatedly denounced "levelling," with all the seventeenth-century connotations of that word, as part of their program for political reform, and they disassociated themselves from those radicals whose political demands or revolutionary methodologies went far beyond what was envisaged by their own liberal-radical position.[23]

Indeed, if Christopher Hill is right to distinguish two revolutions in seventeenth-century England, one that succeeded (and established and protected property rights and gave political power to those with property) and another that failed (which, according to Hill, "might have established communal property, a far wider democracy in political and legal institutions, might have disestablished the state church and rejected the protestant ethic"), then perhaps we can discern a similar dynamic, along similar lines, in two revolutions in 1790s England, *both* of which failed (though the cause of one would later be resurrected in the early nineteenth century).[24] For, as I will discuss at greater length in later sections of this chapter, what emerged as the hegemonic position in the struggle for liberty in the 1790s was centered on a set of carefully limited demands for political representation, and most assuredly not on demands for socioeconomic "levelling."

Thus, the liberal-radical position very carefully distinguished the political rights of the property-owning and individual from collective or communal rights of any kind. "Assured that man, Individual man, may justly claim Liberty as his birthright," one of the earliest declarations of the London Corresponding Society begins, "we naturally conclude that, as a member of Society, it becomes his indispensable duty to preserve inviolate that Liberty for the benefit of his fellow citizens and of his and their posterity."[25] In reiterating this claim and trying to extend its hegemony, the early leadership of the LCS had to wage two continuous struggles: on the one hand, against the state, and, on the other, against those radicals and enthusiasts, some of whom drew on seventeenth-century traditions in order to formulate very different—and far more "excessive"—political demands, and, moreover, far more excessive means to achieve them. Political arguments here merged with philosophical, religious, and epistemological ones, for these different political demands grew out of different conceptual frameworks, different understandings of identity, being, and community. Hence, what might on one level seem like a narrowly political gesture often had an epistemological or conceptual motivation. The LCS, for example, publicly renounced any association with the likes of Richard Lee, who according to Jon Mee was "the purveyor of the most flagrantly seditious literature in London," and ejected him from its membership lists (according to Reid, this happened because Lee refused to sell Constantin Volney's *Ruins* and Paine's *Age of Reason*, which he found too liberal and deistical).[26] Thomas Spence, for his part, condemned the liberal-radical reformers, including Paine, Thelwall, and the LCS leadership, for being too compromising; but then, as he wrote in one of his many pamphlets, "They have no chance of being Kings, but many of them are already, and the rest foolishly and wickedly hope to be sometime or other Landlords, lesser or greater."[27] And when Spence, true to the spirit of Gerrard Winstanley, called for the collective ownership of the land, his views were considered so unacceptable to the liberal-radical position that Francis Place, the best-known spokesman of that position in the nineteenth century, would later write—in what must be recognized as a defensive gesture even twenty years on—that they "were so directly opposed to those which prevailed, that even the eccentric few who are almost always ready to adopt any new doctrine, never shewed any desire to adopt his."[28]

In fact, Place's generally sympathetic reading of Spence should prompt us to be wary of the extent to which such a liberal-radical hegemony might be at least partially a retrospective construction, that is, one assembled at least in part by historians rather than by actual circumstances. While it is true that figures like Thelwall and Paine had a kind of prominence that was apparently unavailable to someone like Spence (though Spence was prosecuted at least as vigorously by the state and repeatedly arrested and imprisoned), we today also happen (or choose) to know more about the optimistic commercial liberalism of Paine and Thelwall than we do about the proto-communism of Spence, or for that matter the insurrectionism of Colonel Edward Despard; and so the former liberal-radical position seems to enjoy even more prominence and hegemonic authority in hindsight than it may have had at the time, while figures like Spence and Despard (and countless others) fade into the colorful background of plebeian revolutionary activity. The work of Paine and Thelwall is readily available in modern paperback editions, for example; the work of Spence is almost impossible to get hold of.

Similarly, while we know more today about the black abolitionist Olaudah Equiano than we do about the equally active mulatto abolitionist Robert Wedderburn—who attempted to tie together Caribbean slave revolutions with a working-class revolution in England itself—that may in part have do with the ways in which Equiano's rags-to-riches narrative of enlightenment and self-improvement (however mediated by his conversion to Methodism) fits more closely with modern tastes than does Wedderburn's rough, unapologetic, and at times enthusiastic plebeian radicalism; and again this disparity in our knowledge might also have to do with the fact that Equiano's work is currently available in an inexpensive paperback edition, and Wedderburn's is not. As Iain McCalman reminds us, neither Wedderburn nor Spence made much of an effort to accommodate themselves to the lofty requirements of respectable society. "Having himself been reduced from schoolmaster to ragged street vendor, Spence was indifferent to the usual credentials of respectability," McCalman points out; "his boozy alehouse free-and-easies gathered up immigrants, petty criminals and other members of the outcast poor, along with struggling artisans and a sprinkling of marginal middle-class clerks, surgeons, journalists and lawyers. His propaganda matched this social diversity, ranging from literary periodicals and tracts to street ballads, wall chalkings and metal tokens intended to appeal to the less literate."[29] Plenty of radicals at the time were, however, much more eager to differentiate themselves from the unrespectable, the poor, and the illiterate and much more willing to make an effort to accommodate themselves to respectable society. We need to be wary of the extent to which those figures who loom large in our conception of the 1790s may do so for reasons other than their actual status at the time, for the hegemony of the liberal-radical tendency has been extended, wittingly or unwittingly, by modern scholarship. In this context, however, it is worth at least mentioning a point we will return to later on, which is that William Blake, for his part, noted that "Christ & his Apostles were Illiterate Men," whereas "Caiphas Pilate & Herod were Learned," adding that "the Beauty of the Bible is that the most Ignorant & Simple Minds Understand it Best."[30]

Chapter Two

Clearly, Blake was not interested in trying to conform to the tastes and standards of a learned and refined audience, a fact which undoubtedly contributed to his decline into poverty and obscurity, as well as his inaccessibility to educated audiences ever since, despite the efforts of scholars who have worked so hard to make him conform to the aesthetic and political standards of commercial liberalism.

Clearly, then, the combination to a certain extent of "rational" and "enthusiastic" radicalisms in a "mélange" of seditious activity in the 1790s did not prevent the emergence of what can be specified (and not only in hindsight) as a hegemonic strand of radicalism, which was continually challenged both by other radicalisms—more extreme, more subversive, more dangerous—and of course by the overwhelming power of the state. In considering the 1790s, then, we need to keep sight of distinctions among varieties of radical ideology, some of which would not only ultimately rise to respectability, but would develop into the very bases of the modern liberal democracy and the free market that we presently inhabit, while others would continue—and still continue—to be thought of as mad, bad, and dangerous to know. The spokesmen of the former position tended to formulate their arguments around the concept of the sovereign individual (the modern subject first systematized by Locke),[31] they tended to draw on rationalist arguments and natural law for their justification, and as a result they were to a certain extent, as Lottes observes, "unable to break free from the political language of the established system in which their political consciousness had been formed."[32] The advocates of the latter position, often though not always drawing their strength and inspiration from an older radical subculture, sought to question the primacy of individual rights and the very status of the individual as a transcendent metaphysical category, a unit granted ontological privilege as the alpha and omega of all historical processes and political developments.

As I will explain in greater detail in another section of this chapter, the distinction between the finite and strictly representational rights of the individual called for by the liberal-radical tendency and other kinds of rights and demands not only expresses a very particular philosophical position, it also expresses a class valence. For, even when articulated by the artisans and small tradesmen who constituted the core of 1790s radicalism, this distinction expresses the difference between, on the one hand, an emergent bourgeois notion of political rights and private property that was still in the process of consolidation and, on the other, certain forms of sovereignty and power that, rightly or wrongly, would sometimes be associated with the disenfranchised and the "working class." In the 1790s, as Craig Calhoun has observed, a modern "working class," like the modern "middle class," was still very much in the process of formation, rather than a category that could be taken for granted.[33] In the writings of that decade, in fact, one rarely encounters the phrase "working class"; instead, one more often sees references to the "numerous class," "the uneducated," "the unlettered," "the people," the "ordinary vulgar," "the lower class," "the poor," and of course "the swinish multitude," as opposed to "the respectable," "the reflecting part of society," "men of property," "the polite," and "persons of rank." As one anonymous pamphlet from the 1790s summed up the distinction, "THE RICH . . . are *named* but not *numbered*," while "THE POOR . . . are *numbered* but not *named*."[34]

In the era of the French Revolution, the amorphous assemblage that was still in the process of making itself into "the English working class" could—depending on who was articulating it—include not only artisans and tradesmen, but also "sansculottes" and "the mob," abstractions who carried an ideological charge that far outweighed their actual existence. The leaderships of the various radical societies tried to steer a determined course away from the spectacle of mob violence and levelling so often imputed to them by conservative and reactionary writers, for whom "republicanism" and "levelling" were the same thing, both equally reminiscent of the madness of the seventeenth century; and hence they had to steer away from more enthusiastic and plebeian forms of radicalism. Whether real or imagined, actual or potential, this tension between what the organized radical movements repeatedly declared themselves to be—movements for political equality in a properly bourgeois sense, and hence for strictly individual representational rights—and what in the eyes of some they threatened to become—movements for economic equality, and hence collective rights, mob rule, sansculotte levelling, and so on—was a highly significant feature of the 1790s radicalism and the conservative response to it.[35]

Even if it is taken as a heuristic device, the significance of the distinction between "bourgeois" and "sansculotte" radicalisms should not be underestimated. The hegemonic liberals and radicals had constantly to reiterate their claim to "bourgeois" reforms while distancing themselves from more radical socioeconomic redistributions identified with the sansculotte "mob." In the 1790s, as Calhoun points out, "political liberties, not fundamental social reforms, were the key to the popular program. In London, politics and economics were separate enough for workers (of the better sort) to be invited into a political union of 'members unlimited' without economistic cavil."[36] Nevertheless, through the decade (and especially, as we shall see, after 1793), the propertied and educated reformers—fearing its supposed leveller tendencies—began to pull away from the movement, increasingly leaving it in the hands of artisans and tradesmen. The artisans, while rejecting the sansculotte position they were constantly accused of, appealed to a protobourgeois position from which they would come to be excluded by virtue of the realignment of class structures in the early industrial period, which sharply distinguished between mental and manual labor, or conception and execution (terms which we shall return to in later chapters). In other words, the artisan radicals ended up in an impossible situation, articulating the position of a class that they did not belong to—largely because it pertained to a modern social formation in which the figure of the artisan would be altogether anomalous—while at the same time disassociating themselves from a class that they thought of as "below" them, when in fact they were about to be absorbed into it.[37] Their invocation of individual rights not only had to take for granted the existence of the individual as a discrete unit; it was meant to concern all individuals constituting a society in their capacity as individuals rather than as members of a particular class. This is a peculiar form of class discourse, perhaps the only one if its kind, because it tends to erase its own class affiliation in its appeal to "natural" and "universal" truths, which are framed in terms of the individual ("We hold these truths to be self-evident, That all men are created equal, that they are endowed by their creator with certain unalienable rights; that among these are life, liberty & the pursuit of happiness").[38]

However, as we have seen, not all radicals, and not all artisans, clung so tightly to the class discourse associated with individual political rights. Particularly from a radical antinomian stance, it was possible to propose both a levelling of political and economic power and a sense of minute particularity that need not be hardened into the reified—and even imprisoning—form of identity articulated by Locke and his politicophilosophical progeny. As against the Lockean position which affirms bounded subjectivity (according to which "Man" is "only a natural organ subject to Sense,"[39] "Reasoning upon its own Dark Fiction / In Doubt which is Self Contradiction"),[40] Blake, for example, repeatedly stresses an immanent conception of God, and hence a human potential for the infinite: "He who sees the Infinite in all things sees God. He who sees the Ratio only sees himself only. Therefore God becomes as we are, that we may be as he is."[41] The extent to which these lines articulate an antinomian stance seen in much of Blake's work has been suggested by numerous scholars. What has not yet received the critical attention that it deserves is the degree to which, with such lines in mind, we can see in the illuminated books a joyous form of freedom—that is, a political formulation—utterly incompatible with the doctrine of individual rights and opening up a radically different set of concepts concerning subjectivity, temporality, identity, and community. What I want to propose is that older philosophical, political, and religious traditions—including antinomianism—offered Blake not only an ample reservoir of striking themes and images (as some scholars have suggested), but also a pool of conceptual and political formulations that would have been indispensable to any sustained critique of the struggle for liberty, and that must be understood not merely as a thematic feature of the poetry, but as a much more profound concern throughout Blake's work, both in terms of verbal and pictorial "content" and in terms of the unique "form" of the illuminated books from which that content is ultimately inseparable (as I will show in chapter 4).

Michael Ferber points out that Blake may have shared certain political goals with the advocates of "liberty," but few epistemological and theological positions.[42] E. P. Thompson argues that Blake's antinomian inheritance allowed him to question and to resist certain aspects of Enlightenment epistemology "represented by the blunt, humane ultra-radicalism of Paine and Volney," which "collided with an older antinomian tradition, co-existed in Blake's heart and argued matters out inside his head."[43] But while Blake, like Spence, Daniel Isaac Eaton, Lee and others, may indeed have cobbled together arguments and beliefs from a variety of different positions into what Jon Mee calls a bricolage all his own, that should not prevent us from seeing the consistent critique of the hegemonic position of 1790s radicalism and its underlying conceptual and epistemological framework which emerged in Blake's work, in what Robert Essick argues was at times "a critique of liberal ideology broader and deeper than Burke's *Reflections*."[44] All this does not automatically make Blake an antinomian or a communist, of course (though Ferber is not alone in identifying Blake as the heir of Winstanley).[45] But an antinomian stance, and the immanent conceptual and philosophical positions associated with it, did provide Blake with an articulate standpoint from which—even if he was by no means alone in this regard—the discourse of "liberty" could be seen threatening to replace one kind of tyranny with another, one class of rulers with another, one set of oppressive codes with another, while offering at the same time a kind of freedom compatible only with its most effective and productive forms of coercion.

2. Life, Liberty, and the Pursuit of Representation

One difficulty with the straightforward allegorical readings of *America* inspired by the work of David Erdman is that they often tend to become

Chapter Two

direct and somewhat uncritical extensions of the rhetoric of Joel Barlow, Richard Price, and Tom Paine, all of whom saw the American War of Independence as the first spark of a potentially global struggle for liberty.[46] The latter term is often deployed by modern critics without pausing to ask what it might mean, as though we could take for granted that what Barlow or Paine defined as freedom (freedom of the individual and freedom of commerce, i.e., the sort of freedom by which "pity is become a trade, and generosity a science, / That men get rich by")[47] would have been accepted without hesitation by Blake. Echoing Price—and anticipating Shelley—Paine wrote in 1792 that "from a small spark, kindled in America, a flame has arisen, not to be extinguished."[48] He had already suggested in the first part of *Rights of Man* that "Government founded on *a moral theory, on a system of universal peace, on the indefeasible hereditary Rights of Man*, is now revolving from west to east, by a stronger impulse than the government of the sword revolved from east to west. It interests not particular individuals, but nations, in its progress, and promises a new era to the human race."[49] Blake may have supported the French Revolution, but, much as he may have opposed priestcraft and the aristocratic state, it is not clear that he necessarily sympathized with all of the rhetoric or the logic of the progressive revolutionaries, with all their zeal for moral virtue and superiority over the aristocratic or Oriental other (notions which Blake, for his part, always regarded as destructive). For it is not clear that what Paine and Barlow (or for that matter the London Corresponding Society) took liberty to mean is exactly what Blake took it to mean as well, or that he was satisfied with their understanding of liberty and its philosophical foundation in natural law and the freedom of commerce. As early as the satirical piece *King Edward the Third*, Blake had developed a parody making fun of the bland commercial faith in "Liberty, the charter'd right of Englishmen."[50] In many critical accounts, however, Blake's own project has been seen in terms of liberal and Paineite rhetoric; moreover, because of the extent to which *America* has been assimilated by critics into the conceptual and epistemological apparatus relied upon by Paine and the hegemonic liberal-radical position, the prophecy's conceptual and political divergence from that position has also been assimilated into narratives with which it is quite incompatible.

Thus, scholars working in the tradition established by Erdman have argued that Blake would have seen the outbreak of revolutionary activity in London as he was writing *America* as the seamless continuation of the outbreak of the struggle for liberty that began in the American war. Stephen Behrendt, for example, argues that, "in *America*, Blake in effect suggests that the official English opposition in 1793 to the flames of Liberty tangibly represented in the French Revolution in fact merely repeats the retrogressive and socially destructive response to *inevitable* and *irresistable progress* that had characterized English response to the American movement for independence." Thus, Behrendt continues, Blake "implies that just as England was devastated emotionally, economically, and morally by that earlier attempt to stifle the *natural growth* and dissemination of Liberty in the New World, so will the nation again suffer from its renewed opposition to the forces of Liberty at work in the Old."[51] This kind of reading has been readily extended from *America* itself to the rest of the so-called continental prophecies (*Europe* as well as *Asia* and *Africa*, and the two parts of the *Song of Los*), along with suggestions that we read the progress of liberty across and between the continents unfolding in a unilinear sequence.[52]

The problem here is that the very logic of progressivism—above all the language of natural and inevitable growth and moral superiority—associated with Price, Paine, and Barlow, as well as with much contemporary scholarship, is radically inconsistent with what Blake was doing in *America* and in the other prophecies, in which anything resembling a unilinear, progressive, or developmental temporality is undermined and subverted, both in terms of form and in terms of content. Furthermore, even if it were to be taken as a kind of narrative, the story of Orc as a revolutionary figure is severely problematized in Blake's prophecy, and ultimately it is the intercontinental migration of Orc and his revolutionary flames that is taken by most critics to represent Blake's celebration of the apparently unilinear—west-to-east—movement of the struggle for liberty. Helen Bruder points out that the triumphant phallogocentrism of the progressivist rebels in *America* (beginning with the rape scene of the preludium), and especially the figure of Orc himself, is cast in very doubtful terms by Blake, who "introduces violent allusions and associations which were very rarely employed by revolutionary sympathizers in Britain in the 1790s."[53]

America's often explosive combination of historical and geographical references and indecipherable mythic and prophetic energies is undoubtedly its most striking characteristic. Gilchrist and the other nineteenth-century readers are quite right to ask how we can make sense of this combination, or even whether such sense is possible. Quite apart from the visual elements, the swirling lettering, the proliferating spirals and serpents, the clouds and blasts of flame and smoke, the text is difficult to follow precisely because of the presence of historical and geographical references, which often seem to defamiliarize and destabilize the reading. Every step that one takes toward pinning down some specific concrete reference to the historical realities or events of the American War of Independence seems ironically to make the prophecy that much more difficult to interpret. For all the scholarly consensus that *America* tells a straightforward progressive story, such a unilinear narrative would have to develop in precisely the sort of temporal sequence that it is difficult or impossible to find anywhere in the work of William Blake, from the most innocent of the *Songs of Innocence and of Experience* to the miasma of *Milton* and *Jerusalem*.

Thus, it is quite difficult to read *America* simply as a straightforward narrative of the American war. All the essential elements of narrative—or at least of a relatively straightforward narrative—are absent. Apart from momentary and highly localized bursts, there is no sense of temporal flow in the prophecy. Even where it does take place, such flow invariably disrupts and doubles back on itself, so that the "events" return to a suspended moment in which the distinctions between past, present, and future have collapsed, leaving little or no room for narrative development, especially the sort of development that could allegorically retrace the course of historical events.[54] With very few exceptions, the visual and textual elements of the prophecy are neither synchronized nor predictably syncopated (to use Northrop Frye's terminology).[55] If we "multiply" rather than "add" visual and textual elements, the confusion is further heightened until, as W. J. T. Mitchell observes, it becomes clear that Blake "has little interest in attempting to construct his compositions as narrative texts."[56]

Quite apart from the bewildering panoply of mythic figures, the apparently easily identified human "characters" seem to bear little relation to their historical counterparts. In any case, these historical figures—"perplexed and busied in an ant-like way," as Gilchrist puts it—for the most part stand around in declamatory poses whose absurd severity makes them almost comical. If, as has recently been suggested, we look to the sulfurous heavens as the scene of the "real action," we will still find little to allow us to pin down anything resembling a developing story.[57] As Peter Middleton has argued, in Blake's prophecies "the recurrence of names is not a guarantee of an existing entity, successfully named and located, able to unify the appearances of its names in the text." Even when Blake's characters speak, Middleton adds, "the speech is not a demonstration of character as in traditional poetic drama, but a further dimension or boundary or fragmentation that cannot be assimilated into a coherent, localisable narrative illusion. These characters are not, we might say, quite in the same play or on the same stage or even quite all there."[58]

America's disruption of straightforward narratives is not the prophecy's only challenge to the 1790s discourse of liberty. The opening speech that seems to come from Washington is striking not because it conforms to the rhetoric of Paine or Barlow and the progressivists (let alone George Washington himself), but because it marks a significant disruption of the discourse of liberty as that term was used by the hegemonic liberal-radicals in the 1790s. Blake pushes to the foreground in this speech at the beginning of the prophecy the one question that, with very few exceptions, the radicals of his own time preferred not to ask—though, as I will show at greater length in the next chapter, it is one that obsessed Blake—namely, the question of labor:

> Washington spoke: Friends of America look over the Atlantic sea:
> A bended bow is lifted in heaven, & a heavy iron chain
> Descends link by link from Albions cliffs across the sea to bind
> Brothers & sons of America, till our faces pale and yellow;
> Heads deprest, voices weak, eyes downcast, hands work-bruis'd,
> Feet bleeding on the sultry sands and the furrows of the whip
> Descend to generations that in future times forget.

The most striking thing about Blake's American rebels is that they are crushed by the hardships of physical labor, battered and torn by their work. Chains and whips, work-bruised hands and furrowed scars, bleeding feet on hot sands—these are not the images that one typically associates with the genteel work or the political struggles of Washington and Benjamin Franklin and Horatio Gates and Joseph Warren. These are images of the hardship of physical labor, and of slave-labor in particular. We are, then, not only *not* dealing here with the work performed by Washington and Thomas Jefferson and company, but on the contrary with the work performed by the slaves *owned* by them and the other leaders of the American war.

It could be, of course, that Blake is simply deploying here the familiar trope by which political oppression is metaphorically transformed into slavery. All of London's radical societies and writers, beginning with Price, resorted to this tactic at one time or another in their condemnation of "the slough of Corruption and Slavery" and their calls for fellow Britons to "cast away our bondage."[59] Michael Ferber even suggests that all the rulers in Blake's poetry are tyrants and all the subjects slaves.[60] It could also be, of course, that Blake took the American War of Independence and all of its leaders' declarations at face value and is simply parroting them here. But both these possibilities would have been singularly uncharacteristic of Blake, who was never given to idle imitation. It seems hard to believe that Blake could have given the American Declaration of Independence (which Erdman says Blake "paraphrases" in one plate of *America*)[61] his unflinching admiration, saturated and defined as it is, to its very core, by the discourse

33

of natural and commercial rights derived from John Locke, which Blake vehemently contested throughout his career. It would, for example, be very difficult to find a "self-evident truth" anywhere in Blake's work—especially in *America*—let alone an invocation of "the laws of nature and of nature's God." With his knowledge of slavery (he was by the mid-1790s engaged in a series of engravings for John Gabriel Stedman's *Narrative of a Five Years' Expedition against the Revolted Negroes of Surinam*), Blake may have been struck by the callous hypocrisy of the words "All men are created equal," collectively authored, after all, by a gathering of slave owners who did not mean them to include blacks (not to mention women).[62] And the Declaration's aggressive imperial depiction of "merciless Indian savages" presumably would not have pleased our "prophet against Empire." Especially insofar as they concern Blake's volatile temperament, all these questions must remain speculative, of course. But they compel us to ask just how close Blake's prophecy could have been to a straightforward celebration of the rhetoric of the American War of Independence, as well as the attendant discourse of liberty, which, largely via the more or less professional revolutionaries, such as Tom Paine and Joel Barlow, who commuted across the Atlantic, was picked up by radical reformers in 1790s London—who, according to H. T. Dickinson, admired the way in which the Americans had demonstrated how "the determination, the co-operation, and the moral virtue of the people could erect a new form of government," one that supposedly "protected the interests of all the people."[63] Not all the radicals in London, however, shared such a view of the outcome of the American war, nor of the supposedly inherent "moral virtue" of the American people (nor, for that matter, of "moral virtue" as a general political principle).[64]

3. Fierce Rushing

In this context, it becomes all the more important to consider what it means that the only revolutionary "action" that can properly be said to take place in *America* is carried out not by Washington, Franklin, and company (and their revolutionary army, with whom the sacred cause of liberty celebrated by the hegemonic radicals of the 1790s is to be associated), but by ordinary citizens: "Fury! rage! madness! in a wind swept through America / And the red flames of Orc that folded roaring fierce around / The angry shores, and fierce rushing of th'inhabitants together." For the decisive scene in *America* is this collective action of a crowd of angry citizens surging through city streets in precisely the sort of spectacle of urban mayhem which the radicals in London were at the time of the prophecy's appearance desperate to avoid, and which they avoided all the more desperately the more the situation in Paris got out of control.

In *America* it is only "the fierce rushing of th'inhabitants together," who "all rush together in the night in wrath and in raging fire,"[65] and not the frozen and almost comical posturing of the revolution's "real" leaders (who never come to power in Blake's prophecy), that apparently could keep Earth from "losing another portion of the infinite." Afterward, "the millions sent up a howl of anguish and threw their hammerd mail / And cast their swords & spears to earth, & stood a naked multitude."[66] It should be clear by now that the fierce rushing toward the end of *America* is quite inconsistent with those readings of the prophecy which, following David Erdman's magisterial account, see it either as a narrative of the American War of Independence, as it unfolded following the intervention of the colonial elite into what had begun as a mass uprising, or as a more or less straightforward celebration of the radical struggle for liberty in 1790s London as articulated in the work of Tom Paine or the LCS.

Erdman, Jacob Bronowski, and others have also suggested that this passage in *America* might be read not simply in terms of 1790s London, but in terms of the 1780 Gordon riots, the very kind of uprising from which Paine and other hegemonic radicals were careful to distinguish their own project for reform. Paine thought of the urban mob as an existential category which had simply reared its ugly head in 1780. "There is in all European countries," Paine writes, "a large class of people of that description which in England is called the '*mob*.' Of this class were those who committed the burnings and devastations in London in 1780, and of this class were those who carried the heads upon spikes in Paris. . . . in the commencement of a Revolution, these men are rather the followers of the camp than of the standard of liberty, and have yet to be instructed how to reverence it."[67] But in 1790s London "the mob" was, as I suggested earlier, an ideological category, and George Rudé reminds us that the 1780 storming of Newgate Prison—an event in which William Blake was either a participant or an observer[68]—may be taken as evidence of the way in which eighteenth-century revolutionary crowds were impelled by specific grievances and were movements of social protest, in which "the underlying conflict of poor against rich (though not yet of labor against capital) is clearly visible beneath the surface."[69]

Erdman argues that the apocalyptic language of the "fierce rushing" scene in *America* resembles contemporary accounts of the 1780 Gordon riots, which dwelt at length on the flames rising from burning buildings and the participants' "howls of anguish."[70] He also suggests that the famous print *The Dance of Albion*, which Blake first conceived in 1780, the year of the

Figure 2. William Blake, *The Dance of Albion (Glad Day)*. Rosenwald Collection, National Gallery of Art, Washington. Photograph © 2001 Board of Trustees, National Gallery of Art, Washington.

Figure 3. Blake, *The Accusers of Theft, Adultery, Murder (War)*. Rosenwald Collection, National Gallery of Art, Washington. Photograph © 2001 Board of Trustees, National Gallery of Art, Washington.

Gordon riots, but actually etched only in 1793, the year he printed *America*, should be read alongside the apocalyptic scenes of "fierce rushing" in *America* (see fig. 2). Pointing to the inscription beneath the image of the rising youth, "Albion rose from where he labourd at the Mill with Slaves / Giving himself for the Nations he danc'd the dance of Eternal Death," Erdman suggests that we see this as a picture of "the people of England" rising up in 1780 "in a demonstration of independence, dancing the dance of insurrection."[71] More recently, Robert Essick has elaborated Erdman's connections between the "fierce rushing" scene of urban insurrection in *America* and the drawing of *Albion rose*, which might be seen in effect as the latter's illustration. In the very next passage of the prophecy after we see "the millions" throw off their vestments of war and stand "a naked multitude," Blake "describes rulers shuddering with fear when confronted by this image of revolution, and concludes on the final plate of *America* that 'their end should come.'"[72] The same reaction, according to Essick, is pictured in a print closely related to *Albion rose*, called *Our End is Come*, and in a subsequent color-printed version of the same picture called *The senses are shaken*, as well as another version called *The Accusers of Theft, Adultery, Murder* (see fig. 3). Like *Albion rose*, these pictures seem to have been etched by Blake in 1793 and color printed in 1795–96; they depict a terrified king flanked by two equally terrified guards. Essick suggests that "when the revolutionary spirit of Albion's people arises," as depicted in *Albion rose*, and in the related "fierce rushing" passage of *America*, monarchs and their guardians "huddle in terror," as depicted in *Our End is Come*.

However, while Erdman's and Essick's elaborations of the insurrectionary scene are persuasive, their reading of the importance of the revolutionary crowd does not exhaust that passage's significance. For a very complicated conceptual movement develops toward the end of the prophecy. Here the scene of "fierce rushing" serves to break open the *conceptual* and *philosophical* as well as the merely tactical and organizational politics—and the aesthetic norms—of the dominant radical movement. What is at stake here for Blake is not merely a matter of how to run an urban revolution, but something much more profound—namely, the micropolitics of revolution, and in particular the micropolitics of subjectivity. If the register in which we have been operating so far has not yet exhausted the significance of this passage, that is because the passage demands that we shift registers into—and between—the domains of biology, epidemiology, physiology, psychology, sexuality, and subjectivity, and to investigate the ways in which these domains intersect with political transformation.

It is well known that the hegemonic 1790s liberal-radicals contested the view most memorably expressed in Edmund Burke's famous assertion that society is "a permanent body composed of transitory parts; wherein, by the disposition of a stupendous wisdom, moulding together the great mysterious incorporation of the human race, the whole, at one time, is never old, or middle-aged, or young, but in a condition of unchangeable constancy, moves on through the varied tenour of perpetual decay, fall, renovation, and progression." In Burke's view, the rights of the state must supersede the rights of its transitory parts, its individual members, for, he argues, an assertion of individual rights would lead the permanent body of society to "crumble away, be disconnected into the dust and powder of individuality, and at length dispersed to all the winds of heaven."[73] Those 1790s radicals who followed Paine and were inspired by the struggle for American independence adopted as their conceptual and philosophical foundation the Lockean formula of the transhistorical individual (which Rousseau and the Enlightenment would confirm as "born free but everywhere in chains"), whose eternal liberty Paine's *Rights of Man* would in one stroke confirm and guarantee for all time. While Blake accepted the radical attack on the ancien régime, and on priestcraft and kingcraft and patriarchal tyranny in general, he was very far from accepting the radical notion that the Paineite/Lockean individual—developing autonomously through the progressive linear time of modernity—could possibly be the basis for genuine freedom, or even that such an individual could be assumed to have a eternal validity, an ontological priority outside human history, to be taken for granted as it was by Paine and others, as an eternal reference point for all human struggles.

In order to see this, we need to reexamine the scene of fierce rushing. In that scene, the individuals are absorbed into the crowd that they constitute, not simply losing but altogether detonating their prior individuality. For the fierce rushing collective is sharply distinguished from "the citizens of New York" who "close their books & lock their chests," the "mariners of Boston" who "drop their anchors and unlade," the "scribe of Pennsylvania" who "casts his pen upon the earth," and "the builder of Virginia" who "throws his hammer down in fear." The condition of possibility for the constitution of the rushing multitude is, in other words, the loss—the annihilation—of the individual specificity of the little units, the citizens, who together make up the revolutionary crowd. It is only when they cease ("close," "drop," "cast," "throw") their individual occupations, which are figured here as their hastily abandoned occupational materials and tools, that the fierce rushing collective is brought into being. And, in another, quite different, sense, the rushing multitude—the urban revolutionary crowd par excellence—might be seen to challenge the sturdy independence and frugal individuality of the craftsmen who drop their tools in fear. This collective is much more than the sum of its little constituent parts. It is a form of belonging—a community—whose very existence is predicated upon the annihilation of those parts as self-sufficient, independent, sovereign units (i.e., citizens). While these sovereign units are being broken up and dissolved into a collective body whose parts have no ontologically prior existence, "fierce desire" and "lusts of youth" also dissolve the "bonds of religion." Now with "the doors of marriage open," these reborn sprits, who are depicted as largely female, "Run from their fetters reddening, & in long drawn arches sitting, / They feel the nerves of youth renew."[74]

In its uniquely Blakean slippage between political and biological language, this moment in the prophecy highlights the mutually constitutive relationship between political forms and the subjective categories—literally, the psychological and biological forms of identity—to which they correspond. Here, the breakdown of the one is inseparable from the breakdown of the other. For what seems to take place toward the end of the prophecy is the dissolution of one mode of existence, that of the property-owning individual, as well as the political institutions associated with it; and the constitution of a new mode of being, a new sense of community that is no longer commensurate with the political, psychological, or even biological units that brought the transformation about. The "fierce desire" associated with the "fierce rushing" is productive of the surging energy of the revolutionary crowd. This fierce energy is quite incompatible with the discourse of liberty associated with Paine. Indeed, it is reminiscent instead of that "wild democratical fury that leads nations into the vortex of anarchy, confusion and bloodshed,"[75] which most radical activists of the 1790s were as desperate to avoid as their seventeenth-century forebears William Walwyn and John Lilburne had been to dodge accusations of being "wild, irrational dangerous creatures."[76] The advocates of liberty, both in the seventeenth century and in the 1790s, believed fervently in the sovereign individual whose "rights" defined the basis of all forms of political, cultural, and economic activity. Richard Overton's insistence in 1646 that "to every individual in nature is given an individual property by nature not to be invaded or usurped by any," so that "all men are equally and alike born to propriety, liberty, and freedom," is exactly replicated in Paine's insistence that the "Liberty, property and security" of the individual define the fundamental natural basis of the rights of man."[77] This property-owning and sovereign individual is shown to be detonated in the fierce rushing of the closing lines of *America*.

Indeed, it seems odd that this unequivocal challenge to the very concept of the sovereign individual should ever have been read as a celebration of that individual and his supposedly god-given rights to life, liberty, and the pursuit of happiness.

This specific case allows us to make a more general point. If the psychosocial terrain that the modern reader of *America* and the other prophecies stumbles across is alienating and confusing—if it does not make sense—that is because it does not conform to the cognitive apparatus through which it is perceived. In other words, the prophecy not only depicts a psychosocial dissolution and reconstitution: it embodies and enacts that dissolution in its fragmentary form as well as its often incomprehensible content. (There were forty million British soldiers in colonial America? George Washington talked about the hardship of manual labor and the horrors of slavery? The American War of Independence opened the doors of marriage and dissolved the bonds of religion?). The history whose rewriting Blake requires is not only the history of revolution and political transformation, which his work has often been taken to depict, but above all the history of the sovereign self. For the individual whose political and commercial rights constituted the ultimate objective of the hegemonic liberal-radical movement is profoundly destabilized and rendered inoperative in Blake's work of the 1790s.[78] Readings of the prophecies that rely upon the modern epistemological and political paradigms and conventions which were being heralded by the hegemonic radicals of Blake's own time—and challenged by Blake—may offer plenty of meaning, and plenty of valid observations; but I believe that they will have only a loose and tentative grasp on the urgent cultural and political project that these works embody.

In all of Blake's prophetic writings from the 1790s, the most persistent form of oppression is not exactly the disciplinary authority of the state, but rather the process by which the "infinite" is bound, limited, and restricted by organ-ization into simultaneously physiological and psychological entities, limited into units defined by the five physiological senses, "barr'd and petrify'd against the infinite."[79] As I will argue at greater length in later chapters, it cannot be a coincidence that this is one—perhaps the only—feature that *The Marriage*, *Visions of the Daughters*, *America*, *Europe*, *Africa*, *Asia*, and the books of *Urizen*, *Ahania*, and *Los* certainly have in common. Each includes at least one moment in which we see this punishing and restricting process of organ-ization taking place: a process that literally embodies and organizes, produces psychophysiological units, defined and constituted by body parts—"shapes screaming flutter'd vain / Some combin'd into muscles & glands / Some organs for craving and lust"[80]—growing or congealing or

Chapter Two

being transformed into solitary units—"Branchy forms. organizing the Human / Into finite inflexible organs"[81]—that can only then be subject to the rule of law. When we read that Urizen is at a certain point a "disorganiz'd Immortal,"[82] we should take that literally; until his organ-ization takes place, "Effluvia vapor'd above / In noxious clouds; these hover'd thick / Over the disorganiz'd Immortal, / Till petrific pain scurfd over the Lakes / As the bones of man, solid & dark / The clouds of disease hover'd wide / Around the Immortal in torment / Perching around the hurtling bones / Disease on disease, shape on shape, / Winged screaming in blood & torment."[83]

There is, as far as I can tell, no other way to read these lines but in terms of a unification—which to us is perhaps inevitably confusing and even maddening—of the same physiological, psychological, and political language that we have already seen at work elsewhere in *America*. But *America* is about an escape from the finitude of the five senses—the "five windows" that "light the cavern'd Man"[84]—to the infinite, whereas many of the other books are about the process by which "Humans" are organ-ized into "finite inflexible organs," so that "No more could they rise at will / In the infinite void, but bound down / To earth by their narrowing perceptions."[85] This is a question that I will discuss at length in chapter 6, and to some extent in chapter 3; but for now I want only to note that for Blake these psychobiological units—that is, sovereign individuals—are not given for all time but are produced by social and political institutions and laws: the "Churches: Hospitals: Castles: Palaces," which "Like nets & gins & traps . . . catch the joys of Eternity," "closing and restraining: / Till a Philosophy of Five Senses was complete / Urizen wept & gave it into the hands of Newton & Locke."[86] In other words, for Blake there is a seamless continuity between the social, legal, economic, and political institutions (organ-izations) and the organ-ized psychological and physiological units inhabiting the world defined by those institutions. Here the sovereign individual is not given for all time—and is far from the inevitable "natural" given asserted by Overton, Locke, and Paine—but is defined through a process of production. This is why for Blake freedom has to be understood in terms of the simultaneous destruction of those social institutions *and* the narrow, restricted, limited, bound, finite beings who "reptilize" and inhabit what Ahania calls "the World of Loneness."[87] This is also why the deliverance at the end of *America* involves the destruction of "the five gates" of the "law-built heaven," and an escape into the infinite, a dissolution of the political and psychobiological forms of being corresponding to them.

For by the very end of *America*, we are told, "the five gates were consum'd, & their bolts and hinges melted; / And the fierce flames burnt round the heavens, & round the abodes of men."[88] Throughout Blake's work from the 1790s (and later), of course, "the five gates," and almost any formula based on a quintet, invariably refers to what the narrator of *The Marriage of Heaven & Hell*, following his encounter with a mighty Devil in the first of the "Memorable Fancies," calls "the abyss of the five senses."[89] These are the five senses that define the perceptual and cognitive apparatus of the sovereign self championed by Locke and since him by Paine and his followers. "With corroding fires," the narrator says, "he wrote the following sentence now perceived by the minds of men, & read by them on earth: 'How do you know but ev'ry Bird that cuts the airy way, / Is an immense world of delight, clos'd by your senses five?'" Especially with the self-congratulatory irony by which "the following sentence," which is literally "now perceived by the minds of men, & read by them on earth" because Blake himself not only wrote it but etched it on copper and printed it, and so on, it is increasingly tempting to identify the narrator with Blake in one of his more playful modes. Even if this amounts partly to a certain ironic playfulness on Blake's part, it also addresses the passage's meaning, and particularly its method of highlighting the process of its own production (precisely as happens with the harp smashing at the beginning of *America*).

A little later in *The Marriage*, the narrator announces: "The ancient tradition that the world will be consumed in fire at the end of six thousand years is true, as I have heard from Hell. For the cherub with his flaming sword is hereby commanded to leave his guard at [the] tree of life; and when he does, the whole creation will be consumed and appear infinite and holy, whereas it now appears finite and corrupt." This, the narrator promises, "will come to pass by an improvement of sensual enjoyment. But first the notion that man has a body distinct from his soul is to be expunged; this I shall do by printing in the infernal method, by corrosives, which in Hell are salutary and medicinal, melting apparent surfaces away, and displaying the infinite which was hid." Finally, the narrator tells us, "If the doors of perception were cleansed every thing would appear to man as it is, infinite. For man has closed himself up, till he sees all things through the narrow chinks of his cavern."[90]

The deliverance of "another portion of the infinite" that takes place at the end of *America*—the prophecy whose verbal and visual elements were indeed "revealed" by Blake's use of corrosive aqua fortis on the copperplates he had previously drawn upon with acid-resistant varnish—is precisely the kind of deliverance that the narrator of *The Marriage* had promised. This is a deliverance not only into the infinite, but also from the finitude of individuality, from the monadic prison of the individual self governed by the five

43

CHAPTER TWO

senses so dear to Locke and the advocates of liberty. It is, moreover, a liberation enabled by and associated with two primary considerations. First, it involves a collective "fierce rushing together," in which the lineaments of occupational identity and even individual citizenship and sovereignty, far from being affirmed and glorified as they were by the advocates of the rights of man (and of woman), are altogether dissolved and annihilated. And, second, just as the narrator of *The Marriage* had promised, it comes "to pass by an improvement of sensual enjoyment." Hence, it involves an all but orgasmic deluge of sensory, sensual, and indeed sexual excess, delight, appetite, and pleasure.

The hegemonic liberal-radical writers of 1790s London would have found Blake's orgasmic excesses not merely shocking but typical of the degeneracy and voluptuousness of European palaces and Oriental seraglios, which had already been designated the targets of radical activism in the 1790s by Paine, Wollstonecraft, and others.[91] "Passions are spurs to action," Mary Wollstonecraft admits, "and open the mind; but they sink into mere appetites, become a personal and momentary gratification when the object is gained, and the satisfied mind rests in enjoyment."[92] This, according to Wollstonecraft, is why sensual pleasure is so very dangerous, and why, as far as she is concerned, virtue is the product of the conquest of passion by reason.[93] This is also why, "in order to fulfil the duties of life, and to be able to pursue with vigour the various employments which form the moral character, a master and mistress of a family ought not to continue to love each other with passion. I mean to say that they ought not to indulge those emotions which disturb the order of society, and engross the thoughts that should be otherwise *employed*."[94] Wollstonecraft's main point here is that women should not be reduced to the playthings of pleasure-seeking men, as she supposes they are, not only among lounging aristocrats but also of course among all those luxuriating Arabs, Turks, and Indians (particularly the ones inclined to Islam). But if Wollstonecraft seems to throw the baby out with the bathwater, this is for reasons that go far beyond her protofeminist agenda. Paine and Volney, who had little to say about the rights of women, shared Wollstonecraft's hostility toward the passions, which they also regarded as the chief characteristic of idle aristocrats and profligate Asiatics alike, beneath the contempt of industrious citizens and hardworking "middle-class" men and women.[95] Indeed, as we will see at much greater length in chapter 5, the extent of the radical hostility to supposed Oriental degeneracy has for far too long been either overlooked or understated in modern scholarship, although it forms a central feature of the radical culture of the period—and marks the area where Blake's divergence from that culture can most clearly be established.

For this Orientalist hostility contributes to the continuity between the emergence of the discourse of individual and commercial liberty in the 1790s and the institutionalization of the very same discourse in the commercial, industrial, and moral evangelism underlying Victorian imperialism. The dominant or hegemonic radical writers and activists—in sharp distinction from their more enthusiastic comrades—shared an abiding hostility toward "those emotions which disturb the order of society, and engross the thoughts that should be otherwise employed," or in other words unproductive pleasure, which Volney for his part denounced as "the insatiable thirst of enjoyment" maintained by "sterile labours."[96] What they evoked instead was a sense of industrious and *productive* virtue and sober work discipline, in which desire could be subject to control. Moreover, the earliest disciplinarian industrialists—such as Josiah Wedgwood—were, via such institutions as the Lunar Society, fully integrated into the intellectual circles of the hegemonic radicals and liberals such as the Joseph Johnson circle (e.g., Paine, Priestley, Erasmus Darwin, Price, Richard and Maria Edgeworth, Godwin, Wollstonecraft).[97] This, indeed, will turn out to be the key that will gradually enable us, through the course of the present study, to understand how Blake refused their kind of liberty, even while sympathizing with the radical attack on the abusive authoritarianism of aristocratic government and state religion. It will also allow us to explain how he was able to produce an enduring critique of the new kind of authoritarianism associated with the radical cause—an authoritarianism of sober work and productive labor, in which the rational maintenance of productive order and useful employment is defended against the potential for degeneration posed by excessive pleasure, delight, and energy, or for that matter even simple leisure.[98]

4. Fierce Rushing Reconsidered

The fierce rushing toward the end of *America* is wholly inconsistent with a straightforward reading of the prophecy as a simple celebration of the colonies' achievement of political independence under the aegis of Washington, and of the subsequent eruption of the struggle for liberty in 1790s London. The latter was a struggle for the affirmation—not the annihilation—of the sovereign individual endowed with rights. The fierce rushing suggests a rupture between the official leadership of the movement for liberty, both in America and in England, and the naked multitude, the revolutionary crowd who according to Blake preserve "another portion of the infinite" from being lost and whose interest in freedom goes far beyond the narrow set of rights supposedly handed down to us by "nature and nature's god."

Although this "rushing together" of an insurgent urban crowd has little to do with the set-piece battles of Lexington and Concord, it does bear a striking resemblance to the early stages of the popular struggle for American independence, which Blake may well have known about. Urban crowds played a major role in the initiation of the American struggle against the British empire, at least until the appropriation and redirection of popular energies by Jefferson, John Adams, John Hancock, Washington, and company—a redirection which some have likened to an American Thermidor and whose end result was that politics would be moved from the street and "into legislative chambers, in which the propertyless would have no vote and no voice."[99] Alfred Young points out that in their resistance to British policies, the colonial elites were "preoccupied with harnessing, mobilizing, or suppressing the energies of the crowd," and their frequent warnings, such as "No violence or you'll hurt the cause," or "No mobs, no confusions, no tumults," would, as we shall see, be echoed by the proclamations of Thelwall and the London Corresponding Society in the 1790s.[100] American leaders such as James Madison expressed their fears of their people's "levelling spirit" and their worries about a resurgence of calls for agrarian law such as those that had proliferated during the English revolution of the seventeenth century (which would resurface in Spence and others in the 1790s).[101] And when the American elites finally got around to establishing their republic, they were very careful in drafting its constitution (held forth by Paine as the ideal constitution) to protect the rights of property owners—not least the rights of slave owners—and also to exclude and limit as much as possible any potential fierce rushing together of the people. According to the framers of the U.S. Constitution, after all, the people's "violent passions," so very threatening to "personal security and the rights of property," must be blocked by "some temperate and respectable body of citizens, in order to check the misguided career, and to suspend the blow meditated by the people against themselves, until reason, justice, and truth can regain their authority over the public mind."[102] America's constitutional hostility to the multitude is one reason why we can think of the scene of "fierce rushing" in *America*, in which the people's energy accomplishes what their leaders' empty postures cannot, as marking a significant departure from the naive celebration of American liberty that so many scholars have taken it to represent.

Whatever role they may have played in the American War of Independence, the weapons of an insurgent crowd—especially pikes—had long been recognized in England as the ideal arms for rebels, and particularly urban rebels such as the ones we see in Blake's prophecy: the only effective means by which untrained but determined militiamen could resist a regular army's heavy cavalry without firearms, for the simple reason that pikes do not require much training to use, and cavalry horses will not charge into a thicket of well-placed pikes.[103] Several issues of Daniel Isaac Eaton's journal *Politics for the People* included articles stressing the usefulness of pikes in a general popular arming, as well as the role of pikes as the people's weapon: cheap to make, easy to use—and effective only when deployed by a multitude, that is, by the people armed and mobilized as a mass, as the "proper counterpoise to the enormous power of their standing armies."[104] In fact, some of the more radical offshoots of the London Corresponding Society were rumored to have ordered pikes from Sheffield in anticipation of an urban revolt in London.[105] One of the two neighborhood LCS splinter groups that attracted government surveillance for arming and practicing military drill met at Thomas Spence's house in Holborn. But the other met in Lambeth, close to where Blake was at the same time composing his prophecies.[106] Blake may or may not have known about these preparations (though in any case the newspapers were full of such stories in those paranoid days, and the LCS, which Burke called "the Mother of all Conspiracies," was repeatedly depicted by the *Times* as a gang of armed ruffians intent on overthrowing the government).[107]

Historians have debated the significance and even the reality of these and other episodes of arming and insurrectionary activity.[108] The much-anticipated urban revolt—however exaggerated the fear of it may have been—never materialized, perhaps because of the tight network of surveillance and the state's extraordinary crackdown on radical activity: Britain in the 1790s was, as David Worrall puts it, a spy culture.[109] On the other hand, as Roger Wells argues, even if only a small minority of radicals did commit themselves to armed struggle, the sheer volatility of the population during this period rendered the potential outcome of any armed revolt unknown, and this in itself lends the question of insurrectionary activity much greater significance. "Which historian," asks Wells, "dares to assume that the bulk of the masses would have rallied to the government, or obeyed the dictates of the local representatives of the establishment, whatever the nature of a crisis?"[110] Elsewhere Wells points out the extent to which a fear of popular agitation was all pervasive during the decade; not only was the king's coach bulletproofed after one memorable incident, but his outings required huge numbers of armed guards and occasioned impromptu street protests. "Parts of London, notably but not exclusively St. Giles," Wells adds, "were virtually beyond the pale of normal policing, and on occasion the Volunteers were mobilized to throw a cordon sanitaire around the aristocratic West End."¹¹¹ Clive Emsley points out, similarly, that the final months of 1792 witnessed what he calls the "great fear" of the men of property and constituted a moment when Pitt's government may well have expected a popular armed disturbance.¹¹²

Whatever the reality of the arming and insurrectionary planning in mid-1790s London, what mattered above all was the very possibility—and at times the seeming inevitability—of such an uprising, armed or otherwise. Such a possibility haunted the hegemonic liberal-radicals at least as much as the government itself, and it certainly caused great concern among the more "polite" reformist elements in England. The tension between the two possible directions to be taken by antiaristocratic radicalism in England (reform or revolution) became most palpable following the bloody transition in France from Girondin to Jacobin control in 1792–93, the period from the September massacres to the Terror. Even as early as the first part of *Rights of Man*, however, the Girondin-associated Tom Paine had denounced the kind of mob that had stormed Newgate in 1780, although this did not prevent "polite" reformers like Christopher Wyvill from continually distancing their projects from the "extremism" of Paine.¹¹³ The demise of the more liberal and reformist Girondists in France (including ultimately the imprisonment and near execution of Paine himself, who was by then a member of the National Assembly) had a major effect on radical organizing in England. It caused many erstwhile radicals, and almost all the "polite" reformers (like Wyvill) to retreat from the antiaristocratic reform movement, staying out until at least the advent of Chartism. This panic directly enabled the government's alarmism from 1793 on, after which, as Gwyn Williams observes, the serious repression, "in particular the cat-and-mouse arrest, release, re-arrest of poor men," began. This is why, according to Williams, "for the British popular movement, the French Revolution which counted was that of August 1792," and why, according to J. Ann Hone, the mid-1790s marked the beginning of the end of the popular movement's momentum.¹¹⁴

No matter how much or how often the London Corresponding Society and other artisanal organizations made it clear that "reform and not riot" or "reform not revolution" or "liberty not equality" was their purpose,¹¹⁵ and no matter how many times they expressed their disapproval of levelling and tumult,¹¹⁶ by the time of the Terror in Paris, the more "respectable" reformers had nearly totally withdrawn their support from the radical cause in England, fearing that their liberty might be challenged by a popular struggle that would transcend it. It is for this reason that when splinter groups of the LCS were rumored to have started arming themselves by 1792–93, they were very careful to keep their plans secret not only from the state, but above all from the "many Men of Property among them, who had been rather ashamed of the Excesses committed by the French, and had kept back on that account."[117] By 1797, however, even the LCS leadership (now directed, following the withdrawal of Thomas Hardy and Thelwall, by the much more radical Spencean, Thomas Evans) saw that it had little to lose by contemplating armed struggle. Evans helped to form the United Englishmen, an armed underground group that, as John Belchem points out, was able to attract many of those unattracted to the earlier Jacobin societies, including the impoverished weavers, spinners, and laborers of the north of England, and was committed to a revolution in England in coordination with a French invasion and the United Irishmen's planned uprising in Ireland.[118] The United Englishmen coordinated their insurrectionary planning with the United Irishmen, on whom they were modeled—and both groups may have been connected to the great 1797 mutinies in the Royal Navy. By 1801 the United Englishmen had merged into the United Britons, some of whom were involved in Colonel Despard's plan to stage a coup and take control of London (a plan which ended in 1803 with the execution of Despard and his comrades on a charge of "imagining the death of their king").[119]

It was, then, simply the *possibility* of an urban insurrection—armed or otherwise—that terrified the government, the propertied classes, and the polite reformers, as well as the liberal-radicals themselves, but this terror expressed not only a fear of armed insurrection as such but also a fear of the multitude in general: the fear of its assuming an agency of its own, of taking matters into its own hands, of learning, writing, speaking, acting, and rushing.[120] For example, the written work most feared and hence most hunted down by the government was that with the highest potential for circulating among "the people," according, of course, to "the common acceptance of the term *people*," as the prosecutor of Daniel Isaac Eaton put it during the latter's 1794 trial for seditious libel (Eaton was arrested six times between 1792 and 1795).[121] Even a cheap price was taken to be damning evidence of popular appeal, and one of the reasons for the 1792 prosecution of Paine—along with Eaton, Spence, and others, who were actually imprisoned for selling or publishing *Rights of Man* while Paine fled the country—was precisely the price of part 2 of the *Rights of Man*, published that year at a mere six pence; part 1, like Burke's *Reflections*, had been priced at three shillings.[122]

49

pies and informers always placed great emphasis on certain popular *reach*, quite apart from their appeal, as their greatest rmer wrote to the solicitor general, "While you are fooling ...s nonsense and such stuff Eaton is selling *Ecce Homo—Age of Reason* &c and *Paine's* works by thousands."[123] And when in 1794 Eaton was again tried for sedition for publishing *Politics for the People*, the low price (two pence), was the main element in the prosecution's argument. According to the crown, the price, as well as the subtitle *Hog's Wash*—an ironic invocation of Burke's phrase "a swinish multitude"—immediately and manifestly demonstrated that Eaton's intent was "to render the people ferocious, to render them bloody, to render them cruel."[124]

What most frightened—and often surprised—government informers and spies was the dissemination of *articulate* arguments among the supposedly illiterate classes. As early as 1792 Joel Barlow recognized that the success or failure of revolution would depend on the mass mobilization of "the class that cannot write; and in a great measure, on those who cannot read."[125] When a spy attended one of Thelwall's political lectures in 1794, he said that he was "expecting to be treated with the low jargon of some illiterate scoundrel in the language & addressed to the passions of the most ordinary vulgar." Instead, what really frightened him was his surprise "to hear a most daring & biting Philippic against Kings, Ministers, & in short all the powers that be, delivered in bold energetic terms, & with a tone & manner that perfectly astonished me; calculated, I may venture to affirm, to produce the most pernicious effect in these very critical times upon the *numerous class of Society*, & in fact to turn them against the ruling powers of the Country."[126] The key to the government's strategy of repression was to distinguish, as another spy put it, "instruction to the lower class" from "appeal to the reflecting part [of society]," and hence to separate the literate from the illiterate, the articulate from the inarticulate, and the working class from its organic intellectuals. David Worrall argues that this continuous pressure actually helped to define the contours of "low cultural" discourse. "In London in the early 1790s," Worrall writes, "the act of writing and speaking was squeezed, shaped and misshaped by the immediate agency of the State."[127] Working-class and artisanal articulacy—let alone literacy—was therefore a primary target of the state, and the government sought to stifle it, partly by splitting the literate from the illiterate, those for whom knowledge is entertaining from those for whom knowledge and above all articulacy are dangerous.

Blake's illuminated works, of course, were not cheap reproductions, and at ten shillings *America* might not have been worth prosecuting, even if any-

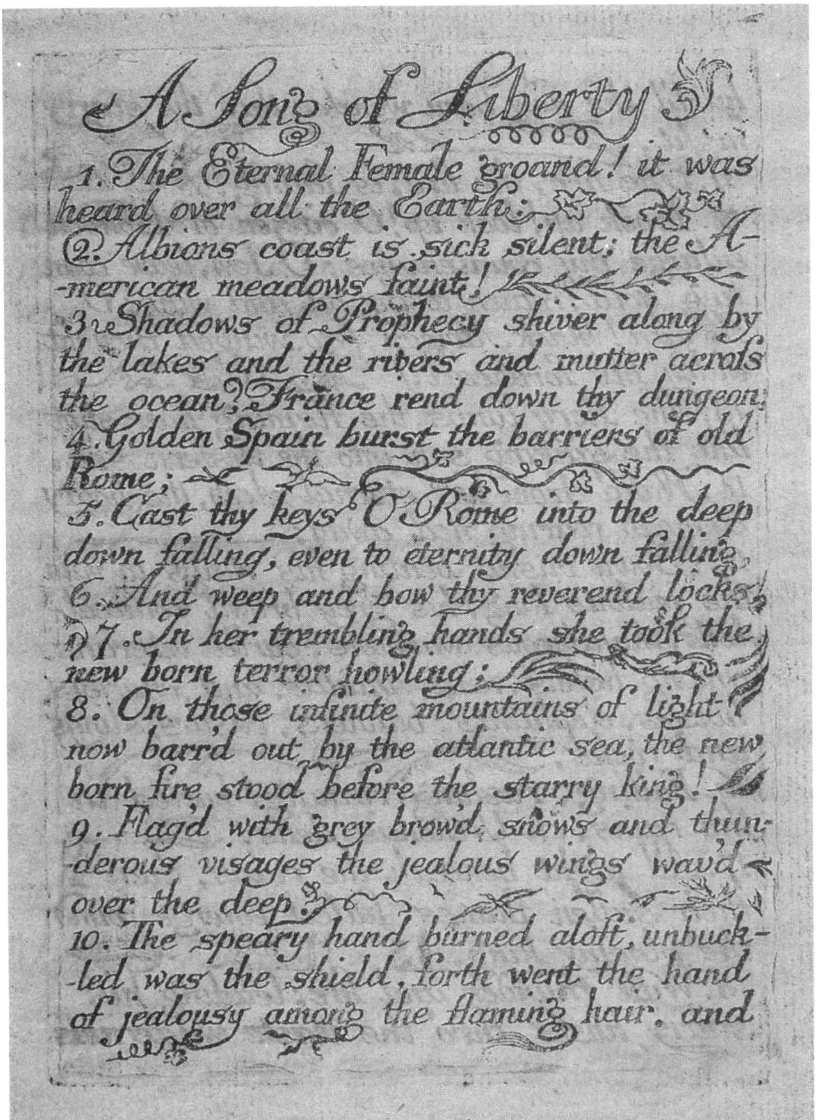

> A Song of Liberty
> 1. The Eternal Female groand! it was heard over all the Earth:
> 2. Albions coast is sick silent; the American meadows faint!
> 3. Shadows of Prophecy shiver along by the lakes and the rivers and mutter across the ocean? France rend down thy dungeon;
> 4. Golden Spain burst the barriers of old Rome;
> 5. Cast thy keys O Rome into the deep down falling, even to eternity down falling,
> 6. And weep and bow thy reverend locks.
> 7. In her trembling hands she took the new born terror howling:
> 8. On those infinite mountains of light now barr'd out by the atlantic sea, the new born fire stood before the starry king!
> 9. Flag'd with grey brow'd snows and thunderous visages the jealous wings wav'd over the deep.
> 10. The speary hand burned aloft, unbuckled was the shield, forth went the hand of jealousy among the flaming hair, and

Figure 4. Blake, *The Marriage of Heaven and Hell*, copy L, plate 1. Robert N. Essick Collection. Copyright © 2001 the William Blake Archive. Used with permission.

one had understood it. Michael Phillips has suggested, however, that copy L and copy M of *The Marriage of Heaven & Hell*—which are both actually stand-alone versions of *A Song of Liberty* appended to *The Marriage*, printed monochrome in the manner of cheap pamphlets rather than one of Blake's more lavishly decorated books (see fig. 4)—as well as a separate intaglio etching of *Our End is Come*, are evidence of the fact that Blake could easily have printed more of these rough-and-ready pamphlets cheaply and in relatively large numbers, though there is no record of Blake's actually having done so.[128] Though he would later (1803) be arrested and tried for sedition—he was also arrested on a different occasion, along with a friend, for "spying" when in fact they were sketching—and though he would in any case have had good reason to be paranoid, the structural and formal complexity, and hence the price, of *America* actually offered Blake some measure of protection, though he may not have taken much comfort in that. "I say I shant live five years," Blake wrote in a notebook entry of June 1793; "and if I live one it will be a Wonder."[129] Still, as Keri Davies has shown, *America* and the other illuminated books were publicly offered for sale in Joseph Johnson's bookshop.[130] They were also advertised in Blake's prospectus *To the Public* of 13 October 1793—long after the radical movement in London had started to break up as respectable reformers and many liberal-radicals began to withdraw from the struggle, and as the state and nongovernmental conservative forces were accelerating their crackdown on radical writing and activism. On the very date of Blake's prospectus, as Michael Phillips reminds us, a loyalist meeting—the sort of gathering that could easily degenerate into a neighborhood witch-hunt—was held in Lambeth itself.[131]

Thus, the very moment when Blake started to produce his most explicitly revolutionary and even insurrectionary work was precisely the moment when "respectable" reformers were abandoning the cause of reform and the liberal-radicals were beginning to reconsider their own approach to the question of reform, while on the other hand the participants in other strands of the radical struggle were beginning to harden their strategies, and some were even beginning to prepare themselves for armed struggle, urban insurrection, and hence sociopolitical upheaval on a scale not witnessed since the seventeenth century. That *America* is not about polite reform and rational individualism ought to be clear by now; but the prophecy's affirmation—however conspiratorially secretive it may have been—of the insurrectionary politics of the multitude takes on new meaning and has added significance in this dangerous and unstable context. Moreover, the discrepancies between different political sensibilities—as well as different understandings of liberty, different understandings of the modalities of political transformation—are not only evident throughout *America*, they are among its defining and constitutive features. And so it becomes harder than ever to read the prophecy simply as a naive celebration of the American struggle for independence or the beginning of what was supposed to be a universal struggle for liberty and bourgeois reform. The prophecy cracks open the discourse of liberty along the latter's fault lines and contradictions, between reform and revolution, between polite and plebeian, between the respectable and the disrespectable; and it locates itself and the striving for the infinite firmly on one side of this divide.

Indeed, as we have seen, one of the dividing lines between the class elements into which society was being divided during the 1790s was that between the respectably articulate and the unrespectably inarticulate. Artisans were caught in between, and while some of them deployed the discourse of liberty in order to lay claim—by virtue of their status as sovereign individuals—to a class position "higher" than the one the emergent social economy would actually allow them, given its strict division between mental and manual labor, Blake never did so, and in fact in his only references to his ideal audience he refers explicitly to the poor, the unlettered and unlearned, and children (see chapter 6).[132] Quite apart from how expensive or unfathomable his works would have been, had they been read in the first place, Blake the engraver, steeped in antinomian traditions and artisanal activism, producer of extraordinarily wild and dangerously incoherent, not to say inarticulate, illuminated works, would have belonged firmly on one side of this line. "Coming from the class of urban artisans and trained through the traditional system of apprenticeship," Robert Essick points out, "Blake was inevitably placed in a class below that of the university educated authors whose books he illustrated."[133] These issues are important for an understanding of Blake in general, but since they are were among the structuring principles of the cultural politics of the 1790s, they here become utterly indispensable. Jon Mee has argued that "Blake's writing and designs were caught up in a process in which a culture was defining itself as bourgeois, sorting itself out both from the patrician culture above and the unrespectability of those below. . . . Blake's vulgar enthusiasm functioned as the mark of an unrespectability which excluded him from this emergent public sphere."[134] Given the all-important distinction between tradesmen and artists which was essential to the emergent social order (as I will discuss at greater length in the next chapter), this is an especially important point.

In this context, of course, Blake can hardly be seen as merely a casual observer of the so-called Revolution controversy. Even if we agree with Essick's observation that "the Johnson circle was at once too secular in its liberalism and not radical enough in its revolutionism to satisfy Blake,"[135] Blake's work expresses much more than mere dissatisfaction. To the extent that his work produces a critical disruption of the revolutionary rhetoric and paradigms of the advocates of liberty—above all the doctrine of the sovereign individual, which was central not only to the discourse of liberty but to the political and cultural self-definition of an emergent middle class—this disruption takes on new meaning in the biographical context elaborated by Mee and lends interpretive authority to it in turn. Blake the engraver differed from the emergent bourgeois artistic circle gathered around Joseph Johnson for reasons other than whatever differences may have been registered by the distinction between his "low-cultural" or plebeian antinomianism and their polite deism. For his scathing critique of their conceptual paradigms can hardly be abstracted from their locations—whether actual or merely imagined—in the social hierarchy. While one version of artisan activism in the 1790s, as we have seen, tended toward an imagined inclusion in an emergent bourgeois class—precisely via the all-inclusive discourse of individual liberty—Blake, in rejecting that discourse, also rejected the class logic that went along with it. Given this, it is wholly inadequate to suggest, as Terry Eagleton does, that Blake was simply "a mythologer of bourgeois revolution."[136] To see why, we have to consider the nature of the hegemonic liberal-radical program into which so many scholars, including Eagleton, have tried to assimilate Blake, not to mention the other heterodox radicals of the 1790s.

5. Paine and Thelwall: London Radicalism Revisited

Here it is worth pausing to consider briefly the arguments proposed by two of the most prominent radical intellectuals of the 1790s. The hegemonic liberal-radical understanding of liberty was heavily influenced by Tom Paine, and the logic of Paine's notion of liberty was based firmly on the sovereignty of the individual—and what was for him the corollary freedom of sovereign units to compete and exchange on an open market. Such freedom would supposedly bind the members of society together into a reciprocally harmonious and self-regulating equilibrium in which, as Gregory Claeys observes, there would ideally be little or no need for government.[137] For Paine, the hereditary aristocratic-monarchical form of government poses an unnatural blockage in the free circulation of politics, just as the relatively immobile and often hereditary monopolies of land and commerce pose unnatural blockages in the free circulation of goods and services. "We must shut our eyes against reason," Paine declares, "we must basely degrade our understanding, not to see the folly of what is called monarchy. Nature is orderly in all her works; but this is a mode of government that counteracts nature. It turns the progress of the human faculties upside down. It subjects age to be governed by children, and wisdom by folly." A free representative government, on the other hand, "is always parallel with the order and immutable laws of nature, and meets the reason of man in every part."[138] Paine's ideal in both cases is a transparent "natural" system in which no blockages are tolerated, permitting the smooth and even circulation of commodities (the basic units of commerce) and citizens (the basic units of politics), leaving the system to find its own rational and harmonious balance. "In the representative system," he writes, "the reason for everything must publicly appear. Every man is a proprietor in government, and considers it a necessary part of his business to understand. It concerns his interest because it affects his property."[139]

For Paine, the primal foundation of all politics and philosophy is that of the sovereign property-owning individual. Moreover, the movement from the level of the individual citizen to that of society as a whole is simply a matter of scale. "Commerce," says Paine, "is no other than the traffic of two individuals, multiplied on a scale of numbers; and by the same rule that nature intended the intercourse of two, she intended that of all."[140] Thus, left to its own devices, commerce is as easily the guarantor of peaceful (and mutually profitable) relationships between sovereign states as it is between sovereign individuals. In a world free of military conquests—a world unified into one commercial space, a global market—commerce would serve on its own as "a pacific system, operating to cordialize mankind, by rendering nations, as well as individuals, useful to each other."[141]

Of course, some will be better at the game of commerce than others, and hence it is natural in Paine's view that society will consist of richer and poorer people. Nevertheless, an open and natural system would balance things out far more evenly than they were in England at the close of the eighteenth century. Claeys points out that in *Rights of Man* Paine also introduces a sense of government welfare support for the poor into an otherwise laissez-faire system.[142] Paine's scheme of an extremely sharply graded income tax would, for example, serve to redistribute vast inheritances so that all citizens would begin the rat race of life on a more or less equal footing, even if through life some would do better than others. (Actually, Volney, who produced a remarkably similar vision of an ideal society in *The Ruins*, obviates the need for such a redistributive mechanism with his faith that under ideal circumstances rich people would simply give up their excesses because excess itself is "unnatural.") According to this vision, class division and the distinction between rich and poor, master and servant, would remain intact, but it would operate synchronically within generations as opposed to diachronically between generations: individuals, rather than families, would clamber over each other to become rich or poor. But if Paine's understanding of political economy was defined to its deepest levels by a clear and deliberate distinction between political and economic egalitarianism, this was justified by his fervent faith in the ability of commerce to bring all members of society to a kind of happy middle.[143]

The extent to which Paine's understanding of liberty rose to dominance among London reformers is striking. Even some of those who were skeptical of mass action and distrustful of the "numerous classes," such as Wyvill, could accept the Paineite emphasis on the freedom of the sovereign individual and of commerce while at the same time maintaining their distance from the "swinish multitude" and even from Paine himself (whose name they sometimes deliberately misspelled "Pain"). Partly as a result of this, from at least the publication of *Rights of Man* onward, a rigid distinction between political and economic equality became sacrosanct among the hegemonic London radicals. Even John Thelwall, who privately declared himself "a downright *sans culotte*,"[144] was careful in his articles and lectures to steer the radical cause toward legislative reform rather than economic egalitarianism, and from mass action and "fierce rushing" to the sober petitioning of Parliament and reasoned expostulation with the respectable classes.[145]

Thelwall's position is significant because it is generally taken to mark the most extreme position in the cause of liberty, with which Blake has so long been identified. E. P. Thompson argues that although Thelwall's radicalism "was generally confined within the area defined by Paine . . . his emphasis, far more than Paine's, was on economic and social questions." According to Thompson, "Thelwall took Jacobinism to the borders of Socialism; he also took it to the borders of revolutionism."[146] Thelwall blamed society itself, rather than the idleness and debauchery of workers, for the creation and maintenance of the miserable living conditions experienced by the poor and the working people of England.[147] Like Paine, Thelwall argues that these conditions are the result of unnatural circumstances rather than the result of a kind of Malthusian inevitability. However, Thelwall is even more vehement than Paine in insisting that these unnatural conditions are produced by monopolistic blockages which disrupt the free circulation of property. He is also more vehement than Paine in asserting that the root cause of economic disequilibrium is political imbalance, and hence in asserting that an open commercial system is the only way to guarantee the natural rights of the individual. According to Thelwall, the aristocratic-monarchical system of government allows the proliferation of barriers "to prevent the free progress of mercantile intercourse," so that as a result "the first great maxim in the communion of nations ('Let the abundance of each be exchanged, that the scarcity of each may be removed!') is to be violated;—and commerce, the boasted glory of our isle—Commerce, who from her very essence should be free as air, is to groan in manacles!"[148] Political monopoly (in government) and economic monopoly (in the marketplace) maintain each other against the salutary competition that would be generated by the free circulation that such monopolies seek to suppress.[149] The appalling living conditions of the laboring classes, according to Thelwall, are the direct consequences of this monopolistic stifling of competition. Freed of such monopolistic blockages, an open commercial system would eliminate the appalling injustices characteristic of British society and restore it to a wholesome equilibrium. Mark Philp suggests that Thelwall's views are more homegrown and less universalist than Paine's.[150] In discussing the virtues of free trade, however, Thelwall expresses his own great faith that through the work of merchants in a global commercial system we might discover a means toward the "happiness and welfare of the whole universe."[151] For Thelwall as for Paine, then, commerce—or at least commerce freed of unnatural monopolistic blockages—would also guarantee a regime of pacific exchange on a global scale, which would in turn abolish the "artificial" distinctions between nations and allow the creation of a universal world market with no exterior.

According to Thelwall, a restoration of political freedom would do away with the unnaturally extreme distinctions between rich and poor. Thus left to their own individual abilities, most people would gravitate around a warm and happy middle. An individual's misery would be the product of his or her laziness and inability, rather than the unnatural creation of a perverted social system. On the other hand, another individual's success and wealth would be the result of his or her own extraordinary skill and individual merit, not an arbitrary inheritance from fortunate ancestors. Thelwall's endless refrain, that "there is no redress for a country situated as we are, but from a fair, full, and equal representation of the people in the Commons House of Parliament," thus becomes the ultimate objective of his political agitation, offering the solution to all problems because it would allow the breakdown of monopoly and the restoration of "natural" individual and commercial freedom.[152] Any further move beyond reforming Parliament and ending monopoly—that is, any move toward economic levelling and what we might call "fierce rushing," would, Thelwall says, be catastrophic. "Whatever calamities may result to society, from the present enormous inequality in the distribution of property," he writes, "all tumultuary attacks upon individual possession, all attempts, or pretences of levelling and equalization, must be attended with massacres and assassinations, equally destructive to the security of every order of mankind; and, after a long struggle of afflictions and horrors, must terminate at last, not in equalization, but in a most iniquitous transfer, by which cut-throats and assassins would be enabled to found a new order of nobility, more insufferable, because more ignorant and ferocious, than those whom their daggers had supplanted."[153]

It is in this sense, of course, that the British struggle for liberty in the 1790s did indeed draw its inspiration from the American independence movement, which had already enshrined the sovereign and propertyowning individual's god-given rights to "life, liberty, and the pursuit of happiness." American independence had eliminated certain political inequalities while leaving economic inequalities intact; and, as Spence and others warned, this would be the result of Paineite radicalism in Britain as well.

6. "No Tumult! No Levelling!"

However, no matter how comprehensively the views of radical intellectuals such as Paine and Thelwall rose to prominence and came to guide the movement for liberty, animating not only the "polite" reformers (the Johnson circle, the Society for Constitutional Information, the Friends of the People), but also the artisanal organizations (most famously the London Corresponding Society), there were other approaches to the question of freedom which contested this hegemonic position. "Reformism or radicalism in the 1790s is protean stuff," as Mark Philp cautions; "it resists a simple definitive classification of its nature and objectives, and it demands a more complex understanding of its ideology and political objectives than is often offered."[154] Daniel Isaac Eaton and Richard Lee, for example, consistently exceeded in their writings and publications the scope for movement allowed by a strictly Paineite rhetoric. Thomas Spence went far beyond Paine and Thelwall and called for the popular dissolution, by force of arms if necessary, of what he called "the mother of all monopolies"—the monopoly of land ownership—and the collective ownership of the land.[155] In addition to the movements inspired by Paine, organizations such as the United Irishmen had their own agendas, which culminated in their case in the abortive rebellion of 1798, though they were also connected to the 1797 mutinies in the Royal Navy. Jon Mee and David Worrall point out that there were many other radicals who transcended the claims of the liberal reforming writers and societies—and we will return to them in chapter 6.[156] Garnet Terry, for example, reprinted copies of works by the seventeenth-century antinomians John Saltmarsh and Samuel How and published a series called *Prophetical Extracts; Particularly such as Relate to the Revolution in France, and the Decline of Papal Power in the World.* Morton Paley reminds us that these, not just the Johnson gatherings, were the circles that Blake moved in. His friend the engraver William Sharp, for example, who followed Richard Brothers until the latter's imprisonment for insanity and then switched to the entourage of the prophetess Joanna Southcott, tried, albeit without success, to convert Blake to the cause.[157]

Even if we agree with Philp that it is misleading to think of "the reform movement" as a discrete entity, however, we can locate—even if only heuristically—a hegemonic notion of radical reform and liberty during the 1790s, as articulated by the dominant radical intellectuals such as Paine and Thelwall.[158] This notion of liberty, essentially the liberty of the rights-endowed and virtuous individual, had to be secured against other understandings of rights and duties, only some of which—for example, the notion of a moral economy—could be appropriated and included in the hegemonic understanding of freedom. "Alternative notions of community and different visions of rights and duties confronted one another in Britain during the late eighteenth and early nineteenth centuries," Lynn Lees argues; "Law, custom, rhetoric, and the graphic arts, as well as the brute facts of relative power, were brought into play in the struggles for legitimacy."[159] The extension of this emergent hegemonic understanding of freedom was therefore far from an easy task: it faced many challenges (some of which we will return to in later chapters). Despite internal dissension, however, this notion was, for example, adopted by the leadership of organizations such as the London Corresponding Society (Thelwall became the intellectual leader of the LCS, especially after the deportation of the first LCS leaders, Gerrald, Margarot, and Skirving, following the Scottish treason trials of 1793, and he remained so until the LCS hardened its position and moved closer to insurrectionism under the leadership of Evans in 1797).[160] This is not to underestimate the courage of the radical writers and organizations in confronting the repressive apparatuses of the state, or for that matter the impact and significance of their claims, or the deadly seriousness with which the government and its conservative allies took these claims and ferociously tried to counter them. After all, Tom Paine was convicted of seditious libel in 1792, and Thomas Hardy, John Horne Tooke, John Thelwall, and other radical leaders were arrested and tried for high treason in 1794 (though they were acquitted by a London jury). These radical claims, however intellectually circumscribed they may have been, were indeed revolutionary. They represented the demands not only of the nascent bourgeoisie, but of the ignored and disenfranchised to be included in the institutions of government and civil society, to be recognized as beings capable of autonomous intelligence, not merely beasts of burden.[161]

In articulating such a demand, however, the hegemonic liberal-radical position expanded and modified—rather than detonated—the tradition of civic humanism, appropriating its principles for potentially universal application to all men (and, just possibly, women) rather than merely men of the ruling class—in other words, to all men in their capacity as virtuous, rational, sovereign individuals. Hence, as Anna Clark has argued, this position was articulated on the basis of individual rights, and in particular on a notion of virtuous masculine citizenship (which, at least theoretically, might allow room for the rights of women as well, insofar as they are also capable of exercising rational civic virtue).[162] From this standpoint, virtually all political and economic problems could be addressed by allowing all citizens to exercise their own moral and civic virtues; or in other words, insofar as men are prevented from exercising this god-given right, all problems are seen as political problems and susceptible to a political solution. Indeed, this position may be understood as hegemonic precisely in that it attempted to assimilate all problems and all struggles into this one matrix, as political rather than economic, social, or cultural problems, and in particular as problems for the politics of the sovereign individual. Although many of the radical writers—such as Thelwall—were genuinely concerned with the increasingly appalling living and laboring conditions of the working poor in the metropolis, they sought to invoke these awful conditions as evidence of the urgent need for parliamentary reform rather than as the products of a system of economic exploitation; that is, they saw economic exploitation as the manifestation of a political imbalance, rather than a problem in itself.

Thus, the distinction between political and economic justice—or rather, the assimilation of economic struggle into the cause of a strictly political reform—became not only explicit, but also a significant part of radical intervention ("no tumult!" "no levelling!"). With some notable exceptions, the radical writers and organizations working in the struggle for political reform under the rubric of "liberty" distanced themselves not only from economic questions—except insofar as they could be read as symptomatic of underlying political ills and hence assimilated into the cause of political reform—but also from any notion of interfering in economic relationships and dispositions. "The Equality insisted on by the friends of Reform," declared one of the best-known LCS pamphlets, "is an EQUALITY OF RIGHTS; or, in other words that *every person* may be equally entitled to the protection and benefits of society; may *equally* have a voice in the election of those who make the laws by which he is affected in his *liberty*, his *life* or his *property*; and may have a fair opportunity of exerting to advantage any talents he may possess." Reproducing in precise detail the arguments of Paine and Thelwall, pamphlet concludes that "The rule is not '*Let all mankind be perpetually equal*;' GOD and nature have forbidden it—but '*Let all mankind start fair in the race of life.*' The *inequality* derived from labour and successful enterprise, the result of superior industry and good fortune, is an *inequality essential to the very existence of society*; and it naturally follows, that the property so acquired should pass *from a father to his children*. To render property insecure would destroy all motives to exertion, and tear up public happiness by the roots."[163]

Indeed, there was among the hegemonic radicals of the 1790s a remarkably widespread acceptance of the notion of private property as one of the sacred and inviolable natural rights of man and an equally widespread acceptance of the inevitable differences in property ownership and the consequent existence of a class hierarchy among sovereign individuals.[164] The LCS even had to have lengthy debates concerning the admission of apprentices to the society, for fear that it would undermine the essential distinction between master and servant. H. T. Dickinson points out that 1790s radicals rejoiced that American independence had demonstrated that "a more equal representation of the people did not inevitably lead to social revolution," and that "political equality could in fact be reconciled with the defence of property."[165] Thus, it was clear that the economic distinction between master and servant need not be challenged by the eradication of political distinctions between them, leaving each open to self-improvement through the race of life. It should be clear that the philosophical foundation of this hegemonic notion of liberty—hegemonic in that it sought to absorb and reconcile all struggles into its own project for reform—was the property-owning, rights-endowed individual. Grounded on this formulation of rights, the goal of the radical cause was the freedom of each individual, rich and poor alike, to exercise his own rational, self-governing, civic virtue. As Anna Clark has shown, the radical notion of citizenship appropriated and modified the masculinity of the older model of civic humanism. Clark points out that with the notable exception of Mary Wollstonecraft and a few others interested in women's rights as well as those of men, such a masculine orientation perpetuated the exclusion of women from the civic public sphere.[166] As a result, this notion of citizenship and rights was articulated in extraordinarily moralistic—masculine, homophobic, and even racial—terms: it praised the manly virtues over feminine indulgence, sobriety and rationality over sensuality and pleasure, and masculinity itself over both femininity and effeminacy.

In chapter 5, we will explore the ways in which this approach to citizenship and rights contributed to the emergence of a modern notion of imperialism, that is, an imperial project imagined and justified as a worldwide crusade against excess, laziness, voluptuousness, degeneration, unnaturalness, sodomy, effeminacy, pleasure—that is, all the things that the sober, rational, manly, Western citizen is *not*—whose greatest locus was of course taken to be the Orient. Here, however, we must note that this manly logic of citizenship (for even Wollstonecraft thought women, or at least middle-class women, were capable of exercising "manly" virtues)[167] was articulated in terms of moral virtue. Acquiring and exercising rights in this sense involved not merely demonstrating one's civic virtue but above all demonstrating that one possessed a moral virtue unavailable to certain others—women, aristocrats, the mob, lunatics, enthusiasts, Orientals, sodomites, degenerates, brutes. The hegemonic notion of rights was in other words inseparable not only from a discourse of sovereignty, but above all from a sense of moral virtue articulated against a series of others who were seen to be incapable of such virtue. For, as Blake would point out, "The Moral Virtues are continual Accusers of Sin & promote Eternal Wars & Domineering over others";[168] and indeed Christopher Hobson points out that Blake was very critical of contemporary moralistic attitudes toward the otherness of, for example, homosexuality; but we will return to Blake shortly.[169] Hence, the agenda for reform was very clear: what was needed was a political reform that would allow each man as a free individual to exercise his civic and moral virtues. Higher and lower, richer and poorer would thus be distinguished not according to chance and inherited privilege, but rather according to the distribution of virtue, ability, and merit in the society—and according to whether one either worked hard or else succumbed to moral degeneration, depravity, luxury.

Given this extraordinary faith in individual rights, the hegemonic form of radicalism appropriated the older conservative belief in the perpetual necessity of the existence of "innumerable servile, degrading, unseemly, unmanly, and often most unwholesome and pestiferous occupations, to which by the social oeconomy so many wretches are inevitably doomed."[170] But unlike Burke the radicals fervently believed in the principle of opening up all careers (not least, of course, their own) to individual merit and ability, so that, as Thelwall puts it, "not accident of birth, but worthlessness, indolence, depravity, should doom the individual to an abject state."[171] These radicals agreed with a now outmoded form of conservatism that the market operated upon certain natural principles which cannot be violated (and hence with Burke's dictum that it is "pernicious to disturb the natural course of things, and to impede, in any degree, the great wheel of circulation which is turned by the strangely directed labour of these unhappy people").[172] In its purest form, the hegemonic radical argument sought to restore the commercial system to its "natural" rhythm and to protect the principle of private property by reforming the system of parliamentary representation. They recognized that, in addition to virtue and reason, discipline and the laws of economic necessity underlying property relations—and hence class relations—could be *reinforced* by a widening of the political franchise.[173]

In conceiving of politics strictly in terms of the rights of the property-owning individual, properly economic questions were thus removed not only from the realm of politics, but from the realm of human agency altogether and reified into a system of abstract laws and principles which human beings are seen to be powerless to correct, modify, or question. The purest distillation of the radical argument—and its accompanying moralism, its call for exercising and judging moral restraint on an individual rather than a social level, and hence for also paying the price of the lack of restraint on an individual level, not intervening as an impoverished worker watches his children die of starvation, because it is the worker who failed to exercise moral restraint in fathering new children when he should have known better, who should not have let his desires get the better of his rational and moral restraint—would be found, however, not in Thelwall or Paine but in Thomas Malthus, whose first *Essay on the Principle of Population* was published by Joseph Johnson's radical press in 1798.[174] In Malthus, "the economic system and its accompanying rights and duties, as well as the divinely inspired population principle itself, now took priority over the Christian duty of charity," Gregory Claeys argues. "The terrain onto which Malthus as well as Smith had brought the debate about poverty was one in which the operations of natural economic laws seemed the supreme arbiter of all questions of social welfare," he continues, adding that "in the twenty years between 1790 and 1810 this became an overwhelmingly persuasive notion which deeply influenced the outlook of popular radicalism as well as other reform proposals."[175] Not all the radicals of 1790s London agreed with such an argument, and though it would exercise considerable influence over the radical struggle, other conceptions of rights and freedoms would, as we shall see, continue to be elaborated, though the commercially oriented liberal-radical hegemony would at times overwhelm them.

Increasingly, then, the questions of financial exploitation, economic inequality, and above all the hardship of necessary labor were evacuated from

CHAPTER TWO

the discourse of liberty and the struggle for reform in 1790s London (at least to the extent of the radicals' quasi-religious faith in the ability of a naturally free commerce to prevent gross extremes in wealth and poverty). And at the same time—though there were, again, many exceptions—when workers organized in this early industrial period, a renunciation of political motivation and above all a denial of Jacobinism was often, though not always, a part of their demand for workplace reform.[176] Strikes, illegal combinations of workmen, refusal to work at particular times or places, demands for increased wages, attempts to break engines and machines (including the brand-new steam engines at a colliery in Liverpool in 1792 and most famously the steam engines installed by Matthew Boulton and James Watt in the Albion Flour Mills in Lambeth, which were burned down in 1791), and bread riots took place all over Britain during this turbulent decade, as E. P. Thompson has so richly described. John Belchem argues, however, that the food riots of 1795–96 were not indebted to the political agitation of the English Jacobins; moreover, he adds, when by 1799 what had begun as food riots turned into more radical political movements, the terms of their radicalism far exceeded those of the LCS and included "popularly elected committees of the people, local 'dictatorships of the proletariat' which enforced justice in the marketplace."[177] On the other hand, among striking textile workers in Manchester in July 1791,[178] among striking carpenters in Liverpool in April 1792,[179] among Liverpool dockworkers in May 1792,[180] among cutlers in Sheffield in June 1792,[181] among colliers in Bristol in August 1792,[182] among colliers in Liverpool in October 1792,[183] among sailors in Yarmouth in October 1792,[184] and among sailors in South Shields in November 1792[185]—and in countless other cases—the economic demands of petitioning and striking workers were frequently clearly delineated and distinguished from political demands and sometimes even accompanied by denunciations (whether rhetorical or genuine) of "that wild democratic fury that leads nations into the vortex of anarchy, confusion and bloodshed."[186] In a printed letter addressed to "the Nobility, Gentry, and People of Great Britain," aggrieved cotton workers insist, for example, that "frequent attempts have been made to prejudice the public mind against us, by insinuating that we were connected with Seditious Societies: we hereby solemnly declare, that such insinuations are founded upon the grossest misrepresentations; that we have no connections with Political Societies of any description, being a body of Labouring People, subject to such Impositions as, we presume, were never borne by any other in Britain; surrounded on every side by designing men, who daily endeavour to calumnate and misrepresent us."[187]

The political agitations by the London Corresponding Society and other radical movements and writers were thus often distinguished from the seething agitations, strikes, demonstrations, and petitions of workers who were demanding economic redress for their deplorable circumstances. Roger Wells argues that the LCS used the metropolitan unions' organizations to distribute its propaganda.[188] But in most cases we may see this as an attempt to extend the hegemony of liberal-radicalism by incorporating workers' economic demands into the LCS's strictly political program for representational reform. Sometimes political and economic struggles did unify. Among the most notable examples of this was the great mutiny in the Royal Navy's North Sea and Channel fleets at Spithead and the Nore in 1797, where the striking sailors led by the sailor-citizen Richard Parker declared themselves a "floating republic." What the admiralty found most disturbing about this mutiny in the middle of the war against France was that it had to confront not merely rebellious sailors, but among them "a number of Seamen, calling themselves Delegates,"[189] the term used in the organizational structure of the LCS and other movements (actually there were a number of United Irishmen and United Britons—and probably a number of ex-LCS men—among the mutinous sailors, so this was not a coincidence). Many weeks after the mutiny broke out, it was with great relief that Admiral Duncan could write to Evan Nepean that "the Mutiny and Rebellion which for some time past have prevailed amongst the Crews of His Majesty's Ships at the Nore, have at length been happily suppressed, and . . . Richard Parker with others of the Ringleaders were under confinement in the Garrison of Sheerness."[190] Shortly afterward Parker and the other leaders were hanged.

The explicit distinction between political and economic reform—or at least the assimilation of economic questions to the agenda of political reform—among the radicals was shrewdly exploited by conservatives and the government. On the one hand, every attempt at political reform was denounced as a move toward social anarchy and economic instability and as an assault on private property.[191] On the other hand, every claim by workers for increased wages or reduced work time was denounced as an incipient case of seditious Jacobin agitation and hence as a threat to the monarchy and Parliament.[192] Indeed, in fighting on both sides of this bifurcation at once, the conservatives and reactionaries were well able to amplify their power precisely because they were aware—and able to make use—of the underlying connections between political and economic questions, particularly as these affected the laboring poor. From the conservative standpoint, it seemed obvious that republicanism and levelling go together (which is why it is striking that so many radicals should have disavowed levelling precisely in the name of republicanism, breaking a continuum uniting political and economic questions that had been in place since the seventeenth century). However, the split between political and economic questions introduced by the hegemonic radicals was amply taken advantage of by the partisans of the established order. In both cases, the conservatives—from Edmund Burke to Hannah More, from the Association for the Preservation of Liberty and Property from Republicans and Levellers to the Church of England— invoked the importance of obeying and respecting patriarchal authority and discipline in all of its forms, whether political, economic, religious, or simply paternal (indeed, the patriarchal figure, whether king, master, or father, became in the conservative documents of the day a central image, and it is no coincidence that Blake's Urizen may be seen as the father of all patriarchs).[193] Especially during and after the panic of 1792-93, this unity drew together otherwise irreconcilable interests, such as the landed aristocracy and the emergent industrialists, against both economic and political reform.[194]

The power and authority of state religion—which synthetically drew together the endless calls for sobriety, tolerance, piousness—was the most important unifying rallying cry on both fronts at once. Indeed, the authority of religion served as *the* essential ideological buttress of the repressive institutions of the state all through this critical period. The combined patriarchal authority of state and religion—with king and God playing the role of father—was deployed in the conservative attempt to maintain both political order in the streets and economic order in the early industrial workplace. Viewing political and economic agitation as a single source of disease and contagion, Richard Watson, the bishop of Llandaff, exclaimed in a 1795 sermon that "this impious fever of the mind, this paralysis of human intellect, originated in a neighbouring nation; it's contagion has been industriously introduced, and is rapidly spreading in our own; it becomes us all in our several stations to endeavour to stop it's progress.... For of this we may all be well assured," adds the bishop: "that when religion shall have lost it's hold on men's consciences, government will lose it's authority over their persons, and a state of barbarous anarchy will ensue."[195] The bishop continued his crusade against the advocates of liberty in his famous *Apology for the Bible in a Series of Letters addressed to Thomas Paine*, essentially a critique of Paine's *Age of Reason*.[196] It was on the basis initiated by Bishop Watson— elaborating the seamless continuity of the authority of religion and the authority of the state with the harsh discipline of the early industrial workplace—that Burke would argue, in the face of the appalling conditions experienced by the working poor particularly after the bad harvest of 1795, that "Patience, labour, sobriety, frugality, and religion, should be recommended to them; all the rest is downright *fraud*."[197]

7. Antinomianism, Patriarchal Power, and Work Discipline

No matter what difficulties he may have had with the discourse of liberty, Blake had no hesitation whatsoever in joining the radical attack on the patriarchal institutions of state religion and the political authority of the government: it is of course the established church where the little chimney sweeper's parents "are gone to praise God & his Priest & King, / Who make up a heaven of our misery."[198] This is where Jon Mee's notion of Blake's *bricolage* becomes essential to our understanding of his work. Even if in many important ways Paine could, and should, be configured as Blake's philosophical and indeed political opponent, Blake rose to Paine's defense against none other than the bishop of Llandaff himself. He did so privately, of course—for like Wordsworth[199] he never published his attack on the bishop, though apparently unlike Wordsworth he withheld it not just from a simple practical fear of prosecution for seditious libel, but because "I have been commanded from Hell not to print this, as it is what our Enemies wish."[200]

However, Blake's counterattack on state religion at a time when, he says, "the Beast & Whore rule without control" far transcends that of Paine and the advocates of liberty. Blake takes much more seriously than they do the continuity elaborated by the bishop of Llandaff between political and socioeconomic order and insists that a full critique of the behavioral codes imposed by "manuscript-assumed authority" and autocratic power would have to take on economic, religious, philosophical, and political issues at once. To Watson's assertion in defense of class hierarchy that "God made both Rich and Poor," Blake writes, "God made Man happy & Rich, but the Subtil made the innocent, Poor. This must be a most wicked & blasphemous book."[201] Indeed, the great significance of Blake's annotations to Watson is not the fact, occasionally remarked upon by scholars (including Thompson)[202] that Blake finds "Tom Paine is a better Christian than the Bishop," but rather the sheer scale of Blake's critique of authority, governmentality, and the moral virtues in these woefully underread notations. What the annotations confirm is that the continual reiteration of the formula for patriarchal power, "God & Priest & King," which occurs throughout Blake's work as the signifier of autocratic authority, is a denunciation of the power of authoritarian discipline and behavioral codes *in any form*, and not merely the highly restricted and narrowly conceived state-political authority of aristocratic government which was the target of the advocates of liberty.

For Blake's withering attack on the bishop of Llandaff—which he regarded with the utmost seriousness not as one of life's "trifles, sports of time," but rather as the "business of Eternity"[203]—is a denunciation of the logic of disciplinary necessity and moral virtue as such, and a rejection of the dictatorial imposition of this logic in any of its forms, as well as an assault on the authority of written codes and manuscript authority. It is, in short, an attack on cruelty itself, cruelty understood, in Blake's terms, as the enforcement of disciplinary necessity and moral virtue according to behavioral codes—including the very kinds of codes that, as we have seen, so animated the hegemonic form of radicalism. In Blake's account the ultimate such code is of course the moral law of the Old Testament. "All Penal Laws court Transgression & therefore are cruelty & Murder," writes Blake; "The laws of the Jews were (both ceremonial & real) the basest & most oppressive of human codes, & being like all other codes given under pretence of divine command were what Christ pronounced them, The Abomination that maketh desolate, i.e., State Religion, which is the source of all Cruelty."[204] The moral law and commandments of the Old Testament here become the basic forms of state religion and are seen to provide a basis for all other behavioral and penal codes as well as codes of moral behavior and superiority over others. State religion and the state itself may, in narrowly political terms, serve as the practical limit for the enforcement of disciplinary necessity in any form; but the moral law of the Old Testament serves as a kind of ultimate disciplinary horizon, a master source for all forms of cruelty.

The realm of state politics—the realm in which the advocates of liberty were interested to the exclusion of any and all other considerations—is superseded in Blake's critique of authority by his elaboration of a disciplinary network of commandment and obedience that is simply not reducible to questions of taxation and representation (in which Blake was not particularly interested). Hence, from Blake's standpoint, a critique of state politics that does not confront the broader issue of disciplinary necessity, moral virtue, and the logic of commandment in a broader sense—including an economic sense—misses the point. Moreover, a narrow critique of state politics in isolation from the network of disciplinary necessity and moral virtues with which it is tied up is doomed to failure precisely by virtue of its limited scope. If Blake agrees with Paine that "The Bible is all a State Trick, thro' which tho' the People at all times could see, they never had the Power to throw off,"[205] one reason they never had the power to throw it off is that this "state trick" and the other repressive apparatuses of government are tied up with networks of coercion and disciplinarity—moral, religious, sexual, economic—that both constitute them and are reciprocally constituted by them in turn. Even if the state forms a central node in the network of oppression, it cannot be successfully challenged on its own or in isolation from the rest of the network, which ties together other areas of life and work beyond that of the state. For Blake, as we have seen, the binding and limiting "finite forms of existence" inhabiting the state are the products of social and legal institutions (hospitals, churches, palaces); abolishing or reforming the state while leaving those finite forms intact does nothing to achieve freedom, which in Blake's terms must, as we will see in chapters 3 and 6, be a freedom into the infinite, and away from the finitude of the "world of loneness." Moreover, the logic of disciplinary authority and of unalterable commandment is in Blake's critique also the logic of the sovereign text. The definite and unalterable—the reified—text lies in this sense at the heart of the network of disciplinary control. That Blake seeks to undermine the sovereignty of the text, and indeed sovereignty as such—something I have already remarked upon and will return to at greater length in chapter 4—can in this context no longer amount simply to a certain playfulness with words, but must also be recognized as a profoundly political activity.

"To me, who believe the Bible & profess myself a Christian," Blake declares, "a defence of the Wickedness of the Israelites in murdering so many thousands under pretence of a command from God is altogether Abominable & Blasphemous."[206] In reading Blake's annotations to Watson, it is absolutely essential to bear in mind that Blake's attack on state religion and on the invocation of divine right is, as Michael Ferber has suggested, an attack made in simultaneously religious, political, and philosophical terms.[207] If we do not keep this in mind, we will, I believe, be unable to understand either Blake's political beliefs or his religious ones, which are, it turns out, much more difficult to separate than much of the scholarship from the past five decades has led us to believe (indeed, Jackie DiSalvo's study of Blake and the politics of religion makes this linkage especially clear, along with the ways in which Blake distances himself from the rather antiplebeian politics of Milton).[208] The bishop of Llandaff draws Blake's fire for his defense of political and military oppression as well as his defense of economic and moralistic dogmatism, both of which are incompatible with Blake's own sense of his faith.[209] If Christ "died as an unbeliever," it was, according to Blake, not because he lacked the kind of love that would animate the gospel, but because he refused to believe in the moral law and the commandments of God. "Was not Christ murder'd," Blake writes, "because he taught that God loved

CHAPTER TWO

all Men & was their father & forbad all contention for Worldly prosperity?" The operative contrast here, as in much—perhaps all—of Blake's work, is between the iron codes of disciplinary cruelty and a deep and abiding faith in that love which cancels out selfhood (this is not the self-love of Paine and Volney), as well as in the everlasting gospel.

In *Witness against the Beast*, E. P. Thompson illustrates "the ubiquity and centrality of antinomian tenets to Blake's thinking, to his writing, and to his painting." Throughout Blake's work, Thompson writes, "there will be found this radical disassociation and opposition between the Moral Law and that gospel of Christ which is known—as often in the antinomian tradition—as 'the Everlasting Gospel.'"[210] Thompson, like A. L. Morton, also notes the proliferation and circulation of antinomian tracts in London in the 1780s and 1790s, all of which, as Jon Mee has also recently corroborated, would have been readily available to Blake.[211] The force of Mee's and Thompson's arguments (and also Ferber's and Morton's) is that we can no longer afford to regard Blake simply as a lonely visionary or cranky mystic, as a brilliant oddity. Blake's writing, Thompson insists, "is writing which comes out of a tradition. It has a confidence, an assured reference, very different from the speculations of an eccentric or a solitary. It also assumes," Thompson adds, "something like a radical constituency, an 'us' of 'the People' or of 'every man' as against the 'them' of the State, or of Bishops or of the servitors of 'the Beast and the Whore.'"[212] Such a subversive and even conspiratorial standpoint is evident, for example, in Blake's almost whispered admission at the beginning of the annotations to Watson that he has been "commanded from Hell not to print this, as it is what our Enemies wish." Thus, the great lesson of Thompson's book is that Blake was working not off in the deep space of a private lunacy, but "within a known tradition, using terms made familiar by seven or eight generations of London sectaries."[213] To what Thompson, Morton, Ferber, and more recently Mee have so thoroughly elaborated—that is, the antinomian basis of Blake's beliefs and its resonances in the popular culture of the 1780s and 1790s as well as an underground tradition going back to the middle of the seventeenth century—there is not much that I can directly contribute, though we will explore these issues at greater length in chapter 6.

It might, however, be useful to place alongside Mee's and Thompson's elaborations some reflection not only on the persistence of several strands of antinomianism at the end of the eighteenth century—as well as the explosion of popular apocalyptic enthusiasm, in the writings of Richard Brothers, Richard Lee, Garnet Terry, and many others—but also on the attacks on antinomian belief by those who sought to defend the established religious order. Indeed, it is quite impossible to separate such a sudden resurgence of attacks on antinomianism—unprecedented since the days of the Ranters and Muggletonians in the seventeenth century, "that fertile age for the propagation of new religions"[214]—from the perceived need for a defense of the established political and economic order as well.

"Society and law presuppose religion," one conservative wrote in the early 1790s, anticipating the bishop of Llandaff's anti-Jacobin crusade; "they acknowledge it to be their foundation and support: men are not to be governed but by it, and become monsters without it."[215] I have already mentioned the conservative awareness of the importance of religion in reinforcing patriarchal authority in whatever form the latter takes—religious, political, sexual, economic. In some cases, this centered on the kind of transubstantiation by which the father figures of God and king became one with each other and in which the body of the father became more than merely a symbol for the social body—so that the state itself became seen as a kind of father. We should, Burke writes in the *Reflections*, "approach to the faults of the state as to the wounds of a father, with pious awe and trembling solicitude." He adds, with obvious reference not merely to France but to the antiaristocratic radicals in London itself, "By this wise prejudice we are taught to look with horror on those children of their country who are prompt rashly to hack that aged parent in pieces, and put him into the kettle of magicians, in hopes that by their poisonous weeds, and wild incantations, they may regenerate the paternal constitution, and renovate their father's life."[216]

The only form of authority the harried and panicked conservatives of the 1790s felt they could rely on was patriarchy. This, of course, frames Blake's many visual and verbal depictions of patriarchal power, including the figures of Urizen and Old Nobodaddy (the famous frontispiece of *Europe* is perhaps the most striking visual example of this), in a very significant political context. However, in addition to the transubstantiation of father and state, during the 1790s it also became routine for conservatives to explicitly link together filial obedience to God and filial obedience to the power of all other social institutions. The patriarchal authority of God thus became identifiable with socioeconomic and political authority in any form. "Ye must needs be subject, not only through fear of wrath, but ye must be subject to those civil powers that are of God," thundered William Huntington, "or you cannot *keep a conscience void of offence toward God.*"[217] The radical political agitators, chief among them Tom Paine, thus became guilty of an offense toward God, not merely an offense toward parliament and the state. "Therefore, reader," Huntington concludes, "cease to hear the instruction that causeth thee to err from the words and ways of wisdom. Pay no regard to any preacher, either in church or meeting, who kindles the flames of rebellion, and breathes out rage, malice, and slaughter, against the civil rulers of the earth; for as sure as God communicates his spirit by the preaching of his gospel, so sure does the devil, that old rebel, traitor, and murderer, enter the hearts of men, by the reading of Tom Paine's books, and by the inflammatory discourses of such preachers."[218]

Far more than the "Jacobinism" of someone like Paine, however, antinomian belief seemed to be so very threatening to the representatives of authority in all its forms because it apparently constituted not only a threat to the established political order (the monarchy, the parliament of wealthy landlords), but a threat to *any* kind of authority—above all patriarchal authority such as was relied upon by the defenders of state religion—and even to the very principle of authoritarian discipline itself. For it was all too apparent to defenders of the established order that a popular disregard for the moral law could easily turn into a disregard for *any* law and any disciplinary process. Thus, it is but a small step from the position marked by Maria de Fleury's assessment that "the Antinomian thinks that the moral law is not to be considered as the rule of a believer's conduct; that sorrow for sin is unnecessary; that God never chastises his people upon the account of sin, or hides from them the light of his countenance"[219] to that taken by the anonymous author of another denunciation of antinomianism, "They are *against* the law, as the term signifies, and it is certain that some are against it in *principle*, others in *practice*, and some in *both*."[220] In fact, antinomianism was seen to constitute a threat not only to the law, but to duty of any kind. William Hurd argues that "the sanctions of all religions are obligations to duty; and the word duty implies three things, namely, our duty to God, to our neighbour, and to ourselves." He adds that "All these things are, however, despised by the Antinomians, and they teach, that men may sin as much as they please; because however God may hate sin, yet he takes pleasure in forgiving it."[221]

It would in fact be difficult to account for the number of attacks on what by the mid-1780s constituted a religious minority so small it would not be worth bothering about (according to Hurd, "these people have not above two or three meetings in England"), unless this minority was somehow seen to pose a cultural or ideological threat to the established order, potentially infecting the wider culture with its "barbaric" disregard for sobriety, discipline, authority, and hard work. In other words, we can best make sense of the discourse of antinomianism in the 1780s and 1790s not as a strictly religious matter but rather in broader cultural and political terms, as a discourse naming a kind of cultural and political stance that would prove unassimilable to the requirements of a market economy and a properly modern mode of socioeconomic organization. Such a deep-rooted cultural-political threat would far outweigh the strictly state-political threat posed by the hegemonic form of liberal-radicalism. This was, I think, due not only to the links which Mee has demonstrated between popular antinomianism and radical political enthusiasm,[222] but also to the early recognition of the potential threat that the antinomian *cultural* disregard for discipline and sobriety would pose to a new regime of labor that relied on coercive necessity and patriarchal power for its very existence and well-being. From disrespect for discipline to outright drunken depravity and debauchery was of course but a small step. "Consistent with the nature of their practices, and indeed the practices of all those who believe in such sentiments," Hurd writes contemptuously of the antinomians, "they discuss their religion in public houses. As morality is an unnecessary thing, and as holiness, say they, can be no evidence of faith, so some of them meet in a room in a public house every Sunday evening, having before them that much despised book the Bible. Every member pays for a pot of beer, which is drank by the company in a social manner. Then a text of the sacred scripture is read, and every one in his turn is called to deliver his opinion concerning it. A great deal of jargon with no meaning ensues, and every thing is said that can possibly be thought of against holiness or good works. The sacred scriptures are debased to the worst of purposes, namely, to set open the flood-gates of profaneness; and youth are corrupted under the prostituted name of religion."[223] It is in response to arguments such as this that Blake presumably wrote the "Song of Experience" *The Little Vagabond*, in which a young child tells his mother that he prefers the "healthy & pleasant & warm" alehouse to the cold church:

> But if at the Church they would give us some Ale,
> And a pleasant fire, our souls to regale:
> We'd sing and we'd pray all the live-long day:
> Nor ever once wish from the Church to stray.
>
> Then the Parson might preach & drink & sing,
> And we'd be as happy as birds in the spring:
> And modest dame Lurch, who is always at Church,
> Would not have bandy children nor fasting nor birch.[224]

Antinomianism in this sense could readily be regarded as a manifestation of the "idleness and debauchery of our manufacturing people," which, according to the anonymous author of the *Essay on Trade and Commerce* (published in 1770), "is a many-headed monster, which every one should oppose, because every one's property is endangered by it; nay, the riches, strength, and glory of this kingdom, must ever be insecure whilst this evil remains unchecked."[225] In other words, antinomian belief could pose as much of a problem for industrial discipline (and what Max Weber would call the Protestant work ethic) as it would for the established political order. "If a proper subordination is not kept up," the author ominously warns, "riot and confusion will take the place of sobriety and order."[226]

Ultimately, however, the gap between Bishop Watson's decree that "God made both Rich and Poor" and Blake's insistence that "God made Man happy and Rich," signifies not only the distance between Blake and the established order, but also the yawning abyss between his position and that of the hegemonic liberal-radical tendency, with its strident emphasis on the moral virtue and moral superiority of the manly citizen. Blake's stress on love, community, forgiveness, and freedom, his revulsion at "contention for Worldly prosperity," is radically inconsistent with many of the liberal-radicals' deep and abiding faith in the necessity of free competition on an open market (open both to competition and to the whole world), the exercise of moral virtue over dominated others, and the consequent persistence of a class hierarchy based on the accumulation of private property. Even more important, however, we can find in Blake's work an explicit renunciation of both the political oppression generated by the ancien régime and the economic oppression of the logic of the free market and commerce and its attendant discourse of the disciplinary necessity of labor. These were together beginning their rise to worldwide dominance in the 1790s as some of the radical arguments driving Paine and Thelwall reached their full fruition in the work of people like Malthus and Bentham, who, as Dickinson points out, would inspire the philosophical and political radicals of the nineteenth century.[227] In fact, by the 1820s, John Belchem argues, Paineite radicalism would be inherited by the likes of Richard Carlile, a "doctrinaire individualist" and "the proselyte of laissez-faire political economy." Belchem notes that the Carlile-Place radical utilitarianism of the 1820s took for granted the freedom of market forces.[228]

Against such tendencies in radicalism, antinomianism comes to name not a particular religious belief as such but rather a plebeian cultural and political refusal of subordination, just as enthusiasm itself would by the end of the eighteenth century cease to be a strictly or properly religious discourse and would come to name a general condition, the potentiality of the multitude to be swept by supposedly irrational crazes.[229] "Enthusiasm" would ultimately be identified with the creative potential of the multitude, its ability to generate other modes of social, economic, cultural, aesthetic, religious, and political organization than the ones recognized by both the established authorities and the hegemonic liberal-radical reformers. For, as we have seen, both statesmen and would-be reformers would ultimately come to share a discourse predicated on the dual sanctity of, on the one hand, the rational sovereign Western bourgeois subject and, on the other hand, private property itself, both of which would be challenged by what was thought of as plebeian enthusiasm and antinomianism. Enthusiasm and antinomianism threaten to undermine the sanctity, the stability, the moral virtue, the sovereign imperviousness of the unitary subject, just as they threaten the sanctity of private property and the political norms and orders of the state. Antinomianism thus comes to stand not merely for a particular religious persuasion (which could hardly be homogenized in any case), but in a far more general sense for all that had to be excluded from the realm of bourgeois aesthetics, bourgeois subjectivity, bourgeois politics and economics—and bourgeois history itself.

We will explore the implications of this argument at greater length in the chapters that follow. For now I want to point out only the extent to which Blake's abiding antinomian faith allowed him to draw upon a powerful cultural tradition in his rejection not only of "the simplicities of mechanical materialism and Lockean epistemology," on which, as E. P. Thompson argues, "the revolutionary impulse was to founder,"[230] but also of the logic of industrial labor and the tendentially global commercial network of productive exploitation—the universal empire—with which, "rattling with clanking chains" (or, as Marx would later put it, "dripping, from head to toe, from every pore, with blood and dirt),"[231] it came into the world. For Blake's faith gave him a standpoint from which to challenge not only the advocates of the landed aristocratic government, but also the cultural and political beliefs of the hegemonic liberal-radicalism. "If we consider the actual assumptions of the 'Age of Reason,'" Thompson points out, "then the antinomian stance acquires a new force, even a rationality. For it struck very precisely at critical positions of the hegemonic culture, the 'common sense' of the ruling groups, which today can be seen to be intellectually unsound and sometimes no more than ideological apologetics."[232] What needs to be qualified here, though, is precisely the fact that the hegemonic culture and ruling groups that Thompson refers to are not those of the ancien régime, but above all those of an emergent new regime which was then only coming into being. Thompson is not sufficiently precise here. Blake's most important criticisms—simultaneously and inextricably religious, political, economic, philosophical, conceptual, and material—were levelled not only at an actually ruling class, but at a future ruling class; not only at a current mode of

CHAPTER TWO

production, but at a future mode of production which was in the 1790s only in its infancy; not only at the reactionary defenders of the state religion, but at the radicals who espoused the sacred cause of individual liberty.[233] Blake's sense that he was living in a world in which what matters "is not whether a Man has Talents & Genius . . . But whether he is Passive & Polite & a Virtuous Ass: & obedient to the Noblemens Opinions in Art & Science," though written from the standpoint of one who spent "the Vigour of [his] Youth & Genius under the Oppression of Sr Joshua & his Gang of Cunning Hired Knaves Without Employment & as much as could possibly be Without Bread," also can be seen to spill into his work. In *The Four Zoas*, in which Blake began to pull all these questions together, Urizen explains the ruling principles of his own commercial-political order, the universal empire:

> Compell the poor to live upon a Crust of bread by soft mild arts
> Smile when they frown frown when they smile & when a man looks pale
> With labour & abstinence say he looks healthy & happy
> And when his children sicken let them die there are enough
> Born even too many & our Earth will be overrunn
> Without these arts If you would make the poor live with temper
> With pomp give every crust of bread you give with gracious cunning
> Magnify small gifts reduce the man to want a gift & then give with pomp
> Say he smiles if you hear him sigh If pale say he is ruddy
> Preach temperance say he is overgorgd & drowns his wit
> In strong drink tho you know that bread & water are all
> He can afford Flatter his wife pity his children till we can
> Reduce all to our will as spaniels are taught with art.[234]

Some of the ways in which Blake attacked the ruling state religion have been discussed by scholars. But there has been far too little consideration of his critique of the hegemonic radical position and of the cause of liberty, as well as the commercial system of the universal empire, and it is to this question that much of the remainder of this study will be addressed. Blake would, as we shall see, define a form of freedom that went far beyond the notion of liberty celebrated by Paine. He would develop the crushing tyrrany of Urizen fully in *The Four Zoas* by 1797, where we see Urizen constructing a simultaneously political, religious, legal, and commercial system, where the double movement of "Trades & Commerce ships & armed vessels" allow the sale of children "to trades / Of dire necessity still laboring day & night." Here the full power of Urizen's laws are put to use in order "To perplex youth in their outgoings & to bind to labors / Of day & night the myriads of Eternity. that they might file / And polish brass & iron hour after hour laborious workmanship." But if the connection between patriarchal moral and legal restraint on the one hand and work discipline on the other becomes especially obvious in *The Four Zoas* (and would be further elaborated in *Jerusalem*), even in the earlier illuminated books we can see the form of freedom that Blake seems to be interested in. This is a form of freedom incompatible with restriction and confinement of any kind, especially the confinement marked by individual identity. Any attempt to restrict, contain, define, identify—as for example with the priests in black gowns walking their rounds in *The Garden of Love*, "binding with briars" our "joys and desires"—is incompatible with this notion of freedom. Blake, in other words, searches for a notion of freedom for which even individual selfhood can be seen as punishing and as restrictive as any other kind of disciplinary incarceration; what this suggests is a further exploration of the relationship between individual identity and those other forms of incarceration and discipline—above all the work discipline of early industrial capitalism—that I will take up more fully in later chapters.

No "fierce rushing" took place in London's streets in the 1790s, and the closest things to mass mobilization were the quite peaceful though very well attended open-air demonstrations organized by the LCS in 1794–95. *America* concerns itself not with a celebration of the cause of liberty, but rather with a critique of its conceptual and practical limitations with regard to popular politics and the question of labor. If it subverts the discourse of liberty with questions that most London radicals and reformers preferred not to discuss, Blake's prophecy does not do so because this discourse goes too far, but because it does not go far enough. The prophecy utterly resists being made to conform to the grand narrative of bourgeois revolution, in which critics have attempted to locate it. Much of the significance of Blake's prophecy is derived from its capacity to disrupt a certain kind of logic, a certain kind of philosophy, along with its attendant politics, temporality, subjectivity, and epistemology. What *America* opens up is the confusion and "animated absurdity" of history, rather than the reassurance and order often provided by historians and critics. For it is in just such "animated absurdity" that *America*'s prophetic power lies. "Strange" indeed, as Gilchrist himself points out, "to conceive that a somewhile associate of Paine producing these 'Prophetic' volumes!"[235]

CHAPTER THREE

Laboring at the Mill with Slaves

> An hour's labour lost in a day is a prodigious injury to a commercial state.
>
> —Anonymous
>
> His profitable labour has given the English mechanic the means of getting a watch. Machinery, used in every possible way, has made this watch cheap. The labour formerly employed in turning the hour-glass, or in running to look at the church-clock, is transferred to the making of watches. The user of the watch obtains an accurate register of time, which teaches him to know the value of that most valuable possession, and to economize it; and the producers of the watch have abundant employment in the universal demand for their valuable machine.
>
> —*The Working-Man's Companion*

1. Introduction

A vast Spine writh'd in torment
Upon the winds; shooting pain'd
Ribs, like a bending cavern
And bones of solidness, froze
Over all his nerves of joy.[1]

The globe of life blood trembled
Branching out into roots;
Fib'rous, writhing upon the winds;
Fibres of blood, milk and tears;
In pangs, eternity on eternity.
At length in tears & cries imbodied
A female form trembling and pale.[2]

And his world teemd vast enormities
Frightning; faithless; fawning
Portions of life; similitudes
Of a foot, or a hand, or a head
Or a heart, or an eye, they swam mischevous
Dread terrors! delighting in blood.[3]

Then the Inhabitants of those Cities:
Felt their Nerves change into Marrow
And hardening Bones began
In swift diseases and torments,
In throbbings & shootings & grindings
Thro' all the coasts; till weaken'd
The Senses inward rush'd shrinking,
Beneath the dark net of infection.[4]

The shapes screaming flutter'd vain
Some combin'd into muscles & glands
Some organs for craving and lust
Most remain'd on the tormented void:
Urizens army of horrors.[5]

He arose on the waters, but soon
Heavy falling his organs like roots
Shooting out from the seed, shot beneath
And a vast world of waters around him
In furious torrents began.
Then he sunk, & around his spent Lungs
Began intricate pipes that drew in
The spawn of the waters. Outbranching
An immense Fibrous form, stretching out
Thro' the bottoms of immensity raging.[6]

In Blake's illuminated books, organs and body parts, even whole organisms, do not work the way they are supposed to. What language do we have—other than that of madness—to talk about spines writhing in the wind? Spines do not normally writhe in the wind. Ribs do not normally freeze over nerves of joy. Feet, hands, heads, hears, and eyes do not normally swim mischievously (or otherwise, for that matter); they do not usually delight in blood. The body may grow organically, but we do not normally associate that with throbbings & shootings & grindings as felt by the body itself.

Chapter Three

Scholars have never really known what to do with this rush of blood-drenched body parts, screaming organs, diseased fibers of blood, milk, and tears shooting and writhing: it seems mad, disgusting, even nauseating—but above all hard to figure out. F. B. Curtis pointed out long ago that in many of these passages Blake was drawing on contemporary medical and physiological terms, which he may have encountered in books in Joseph Johnson's shop, such as Aitken's *Essays on Several Important Subjects in Surgery* of 1771, or Osborn's *Essays in the Practice of Midwifery*, which Johnson published in 1792.[7] Blake did produce some illustrations for James Earle's *Practical Observations on the Operation for the Stone*, and John Brown's *Elements of Medicine* (1795).[8] As Stefani Engelstein has shown, he was also closely engaged with much of the medical and physiological discourse of the late eighteenth century, partly through his training at the Royal Academy.[9] But while some of the vocabulary (fibers, nerves, bones) may indeed be derived from medical discourse, the uses to which it is put are clearly no longer strictly physiological and mark instead a convergence—which we have already encountered in the previous chapter's discussion of *America*—in which physiological and biological language has merged into the psychological, the socioeconomic, and the political. Here, organs are combined into organisms, and those organisms in turn inhabit the appropriately organized cities and nations of the "world of Loneness" ruled by Urizen, "the great Work master," where they are subject to his iron laws, "laws of peace, of love, of unity: / Of pity, compassion, forgiveness." The process of organ-ization here is dictated by necessity and the law. Ironically, Blake is actually somewhat closer here to early conceptualizations of evolution (e.g., Erasmus Darwin, whose *Botanic Garden* Blake engraved after Henry Fuseli)[10] than to the kind of political creationism relied upon by Paine and his followers, according to whom a particular human organization—a form of identity, a sovereign political-economic unit—was given by "nature and nature's god" once and forever.

In the world of Blake's illuminated books, no form of organ-ization can be taken for granted. Just as we see the fibrous forms in *The Book of Los* being re-organized to adapt to a new set of tasks—producing, fabricating, a new body in the process—the closing chapter of *The Book of Urizen* is one of the many places in the illuminated books in which the process of organ-ization is described in simultaneously physiological and sociopolitical terms, as the Inhabitants of the world of Urizen—following Urizen himself—are re-organ-ized to adapt to the world that they must inhabit (see fig. 5). Just as Urizen becomes oblivious to the "myriads of Eternity: / All the wisdom & joy of life," which "Roll like a sea around him, / Except what his little orbs /

Of sight by degrees unfold," their own organs of perception are appropriately narrowed and ossified, their nerves hardened into marrow and bones, and they find themselves "bound down / To earth by their narrowing perceptions," unable to "rise at will / In the infinite void." Then they "form'd laws of prudence, and call'd them / The eternal laws of God." As I discussed in the previous chapter (and we will return to this point at greater length in chapter 6), the law here is a code that enables sociopolitical and economic production precisely by determining psychobiological production. Disciplinary codes, psychobiological constitution, socioeconomic production are thus coordinated and systematized by the discourse of the law.

This is only a more elaborate description of the same process we see over and over again in the illuminated books, where the very point of departure of Locke's philosophy—that the five senses, "the Windows by which light is let into this dark Room"[11] of the self, permanently establish both how we can see and indeed who we are—is contested by Blake, who reveals such confinement to be the result of political circumstances rather than inevitable, natural, or divine givens (as they are for Locke). "Man has closed himself up, till he sees all things thro' narrow chinks of his cavern," the narrator of *The Marriage* explains; "five windows light the cavern'd Man," mocks the fairy at the beginning of *Europe*; "They told me that the night & day were all that I could see; / They told me that I had five sense to inclose me up; / And they inclos'd my infinite brain into a narrow circle," laments Oothoon in *Visions of the Daughters*. The world inhabited by its "inclosed" and "cavern'd" inhabitants takes on a certain appearance because it is seen through the chinks of the cavern. Without the cavern, the world would take on a totally different appearance; and such an escape would also allow a different way of being, living, inhabiting. What once appeared finite would now appear infinite. "If the doors of perception were cleansed every thing would appear to man as it is: infinite." This, the narrator of *The Marriage* promises, "will come to pass by an improvement of sensual enjoyment; but first the notion that man has a body distinct from his soul, is to be expunged; this I shall do, by printing in the infernal method, by corrosives, which in Hell are salutary and medicinal, melting apparent surfaces away, and displaying the infinite which was hid." As we saw in the previous chapter, the ending of *America*, with the fierce rushing and fierce desire breaking open the "five gates" of the "law-built heaven" and allowing an opening into the infinite expanse of energy, marks the very sort of deliverance promised in *The Marriage of Heaven & Hell*. Freedom here is understood in terms of the simultaneous destruction of both the sociopolitical institutions and the narrow, restricted, limited, bound, finite beings who inhabit what Ahania calls

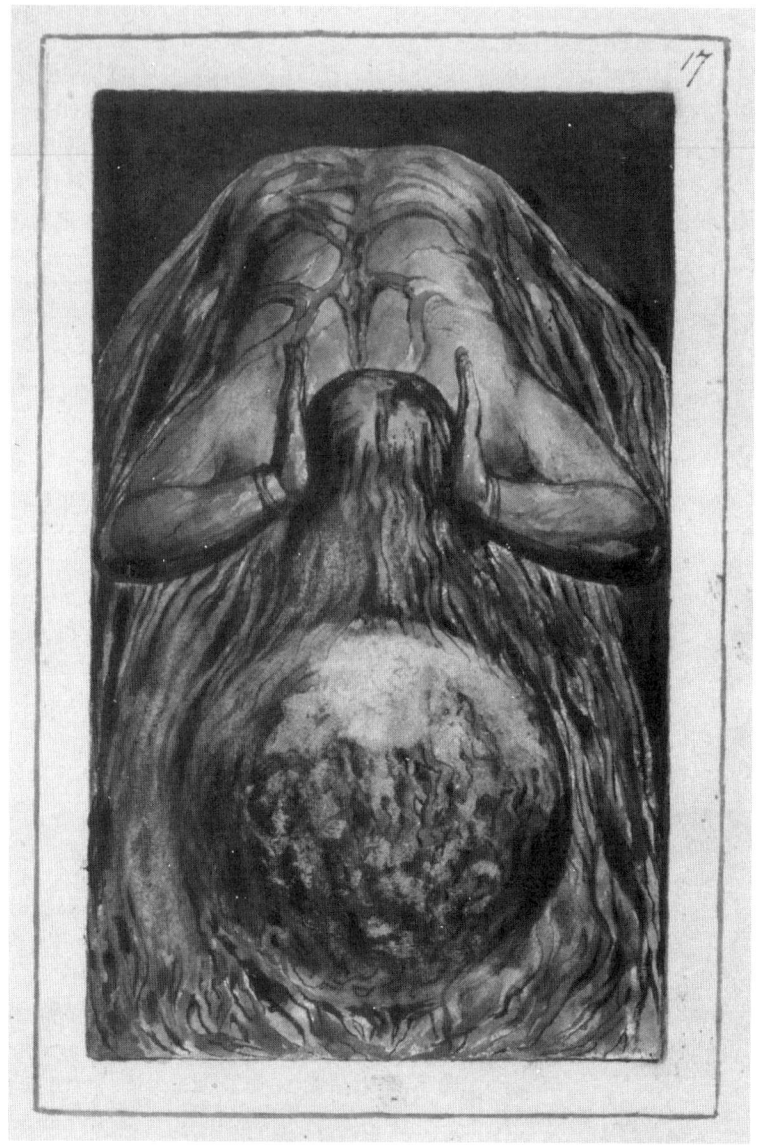

Figure 5. Blake, *The Book of Urizen*, copy G, plate 17. Lessing J. Rosenwald Collection, Library of Congress. Copyright © 2001 the William Blake Archive. Used with permission.

"the World of Loneness"; it marks an escape into the infinite as a simultaneous dissolution of political formations and the psychobiological modes of existence which correspond to them. Thus, an escape from the cavern of the five senses would enable not a new combination of organs (which would amount to a new form of confinement and restriction), but an escape from the determining discourse of organs and organisms into a freedom enjoyed by bodies without organs.[12]

While Blake may have accepted the radical attack on the priestcraft and kingcraft of the old regime, he was, as we saw in the previous chapter, very far from accepting the hegemonic radical notion that the sovereign individual—as formulated by Locke and reiterated by Paine—could be taken for granted as the transcendental and transhistorical basis for human freedom. For Blake, there is a relationship, which simply cannot be taken for granted, between political, cultural, economic, and social institutions—castles, palaces, hospitals, workhouses, churches—and the subjective categories, the psychobiological modes of existence, which correspond to them.[13] In other words, there is a seamless continuity among social, legal, economic, and political organizations and the organisms inhabiting the world defined by them. The world's inhabitants are not given for all time, but are produced according to the requirements of a political and economic network that generates—fabricates, assembles—the inhabitants appropriate to it. Blake's illuminated books synthesize the philosophical and the material, the biological and the political, the cultural and the economic, the religious and the epidemiological, constitution and production. What is made, and how it is made, and the circumstances under which it is made, and who makes it here become coextensive, codetermining processes.

Thus, although we are used to thinking of organs within a particular discursive domain (the physiological, the medical, the anatomical), in Blake's work they cannot be contained within that domain. They force us to move between—and link together—different discourses: physiology, psychology, economics, religion, politics. They compel us to operate at the intervals between discourses, rather than in a single register which might contain and explain them to us, or allow us to make sense of them according to the sanctions of a particular discipline. Blake's use of the language of organization defamiliarizes the terms he is working with: it allows him to construct concepts with a language that was not designed to handle those concepts. Perhaps he felt the need, skilled craftsman as he was, to cannibalize from the parts—the linguistic and conceptual parts—he had at hand to put together these new concepts he was so interested in, so he could devise a way to write about the relationship of parts to wholes that would allow him more poetic

Figure 6. Blake, *The Book of Urizen*, copy G, plate 9. Lessing J. Rosenwald Collection, Library of Congress. Copyright © 2001 the William Blake Archive. Used with permission.

and conceptual flexibility than some other more readily available language. In doing so, Blake was actually returning to the archaic meaning of terms such as "organization," which was originally used to refer not to preexisting entities but rather to the *process* of coordinating living—that is, biological (organic)—parts into wholes for particular functions.[14] Here, however, he deploys such terms to discuss the relationship between psychobiological organization on the one hand and sociopolitical organization on the other; processes which in the illuminated books are indistinguishable.

What I want to propose in the present chapter is that Blake's seemingly arcane tinkerings with organs and body parts must be elaborated in terms of a much broader set of social and cultural discussions of organ-ization that were taking place all around him as he crafted the illuminated books, and particularly in—and between—the newly developing discourses of politics and economics.

For within these still emerging discourses, two competing narratives of organization can be located in the 1790s, one principally among conservative and reactionary writers addressing the realm of politics, and the other principally among the analysts and prophets (but also the critics) of the new industrial mode of production addressing the realm of economics. The former narrative is concerned with the best way to organize society (and hence politics), and the latter, with the best way to organize a new system of production (and hence economics). Here we should take note of an essential contradiction: namely, that organ-ization was being discussed in nearly identical ways in both politics and economics, but for what would ultimately turn out to be dramatically opposite—and indeed opposing—purposes. This contradiction expresses the transitional nature of the late eighteenth and early nineteenth centuries, in which properly modern discoveries, institutions, and practices (of production, of representation, of political organization) were still coming into being, often as disruptions of older modes of practice and organization.

For in this transitional moment, the language, the concepts, and the very terminology being used by the conservative writers of the 1790s to discuss the organ-ization of society into "various classes of labour and opulence" (which for them was "not a rule of our government, but a law of our nature"), by which each person in the social order must be seen as "but an engine in the great mechanism of circulation,"[15] was being adapted and modified by economists and philosophers of industrialization—many of them, including Bentham, participants in radical political discourse themselves— to talk about the organization of factory workers into what Andrew Ure would later identify as "a vast automaton, composed of various mechanical and intellectual organs, acting in uninterrupted concert for the production of a common object, all of them being subordinated to a self-regulated moving force."[16] However, whereas the conservative writers were obsessed with the way in which society, as a kind of factory, produced the little organs constituting the social organism (that is, the individuals of whom society is composed—individuals clearly lacking genuine individuality), the *economic* discourse that began to appropriate this same terminology in the 1790s ultimately drew a sharp distinction between economic production (the factory) on the one hand and social, cultural, and political organization on the other. Whereas the factory came to be regarded as the appropriate site of disciplinary authority, society itself would be recognized as a realm of freedom, above all of the freedom of choice pertaining to the individual whose rights were celebrated by Paine—as transhistorical givens, true for all time.

Blake's poetic tinkerings, as we shall see, are located on the border between politics and economics. But another supervening discourse can be located here as well, in the explosion through the 1790s of writings concerning the production—the organization—of a stable, uniform, standardized workforce, ready for industrial labor, from the uneven and potentially explosive raw material made available by the ravages of an industrializing society; that is, the "human resources" teeming through the streets of London and other cities. The preeminent authority in this domain was Patrick Colquhoun, though in our own time the figure of Jeremy Bentham is, presumably because of the work of Foucault, more familiar to us. What Colquhoun, Bentham, and others proposed was a way to absorb into a number of disciplinary institutions a heterogeneous flow of poor people (especially children) and to generate at the other end of the process a stream of disciplined, sober, industrious workers, who could be put to use in a number of productive occupations.

I will clarify these issues in later sections. Here I want to point out one or two other things by way of introduction. Although some of the sections that follow will consider in detail the ways in which, for example, the prophets of the assembly line conceived the production process, or the ways in which certain conservative writers conceived the production of useful members of society, or the ways in which workers in the 1790s were combined together to make consumer goods, the primary concern of this chapter will be to explore the *concepts* that are in play here, which emerge from and structure all these different discourses. This is what will differentiate my work here from the work of the social historians of this period, whose concern is primarily empirical and experiential rather than theoretical. The work of economic and social historians, including Richard Brown, E. P. Thompson, Anna

Clark, Lynn Lees, John Belchem, David Green, Peter Linebaugh, Deborah Valenze, Maxine Berg, and others, is of course invaluable in understanding this period, and I am deeply indebted to it. By drawing on my own readings of late-eighteenth- and early-nineteenth-century sources, I hope to supplement their work by closely pursuing the conceptual language that emerged in those decades—a conceptual language through which the fundamental ideologemes[17] of modernity were articulated; a language out of which Blake developed his own subversive slang.

For in the illuminated books, Blake must be seen to be tinkering with and disrupting these ideologemes, the basic conceptual and ideological building blocks of modernization, in effect rewriting the conceptual language of modernization for alternative political and aesthetic purposes. That Blake was tinkering with the very same concepts that were so essential to the economic and political discourse of the time—with which, as ought to be clear by now, he was immensely interested, though from a subversive position—cannot be a coincidence. Both scholars and amateur Blakeans have wondered what Blake could possibly have known about modern industrial production and modernity itself. It will, however, become clear through the course of this chapter that Blake was indeed in a privileged location to think through the economic and political concerns of a rapidly modernizing society—its transition to a consumer society—from his standpoint as a producer. As we will see in greater detail in the last section of this chapter, when Charles Babbage, one of the greatest early theoreticians of the modern assembly line, was looking for the conceptual ancestor of the modern factory he found it neither in the steam engine nor in the textile mill, but rather in Blake's trade: in copperplate engraving. According to Babbage, the efficient modern factory should ideally reiterate the logic of copperplate engraving by producing a stream of theoretically identical copies based on the same original "impression." The industrially produced commodity thus represents an "image" of the prototype, and thus, the image itself is for Babbage the core concept of industrial society, essential to modern understanding of production, exchange, equivalence, identity. Thus, the art to which Blake was apprenticed from his youth, and by which he made his living as an adult, was the perfect location for understanding modern industrial production, first, because it was among the earliest forms of production to deploy a recognizably industrial process based on the division of labor, and second, because it was concerned with the reproduction of the image: the concept which, according to theorizations of modern society from Babbage and Marx to Guy Debord, Jean Baudrillard, Gilles Deleuze, Fredric Jameson, and Richard Dienst, lies at the very heart of modern capitalist culture. For

87

CHAPTER THREE

if we can think of the wealth of societies in which the capitalist mode of production prevails appears as an "immense collection of images," and if the image would prove essential to the logic of capitalism, we must recognize that Blake was thinking and working with the image in an entirely new way, taking it in directions whose full potential has yet to be explored.

2. Organ-isms

> The morning comes, the night decays, the watchmen leave their stations;
> The grave is burst, the spices shed, the linen wrapped up;
> The bones of death, the covering clay, the sinews shrunk & dry'd
> Reviving shake, inspiring move, breathing! awakening!
> Spring like redeemed captives when their bonds & bars are burst;
> Let the slave grinding at the mill, run out into the field:
> Let him look up into the heavens & laugh in the bright air;
> Let the inchained soul shut up in darkness and in sighing,
> Whose face has never seen a smile in thirty weary years,
> Rise and look out, his chains are loose, his dungeon doors are open.
> And let his wife and children return from the oppressors scourge;
> They look behind at every step & believe it is a dream,
> Singing, The Sun has left his blackness & has found a fresher morning
> And the fair Moon rejoices in the clear & cloudless night;
> For Empire is no more, and now the Lion & Wolf shall cease.[18]

These joyous lines from *America* stand uneasily within the turbulent pages of Blake's prophecy. This plate is not just out of order within a narrative of the American war, and not just out of place as part of that narrative. Rather, it confirms the disruption of the order of whatever narrative might take place in the prophecy, and even of the logic of unilinear, determining, exclusive narrative itself. For the freedom being celebrated here is precisely a freedom from narrative determination, linking together freedom from the narrative of the labor process, from the narrative of unilinear time, and from the narrative of individual subjectivity.[19] Once again, labor is brought to the foreground in this plate, especially labor considered as a process that unifies and *produces* subjectivity and temporality as much as it produces simple material commodities—that is, a process that in effect creates both its producers and their products.

The highly alliterative fifth line ties together and makes sense of the previous unevenly metered lines of broken and fragmentary description. Only after this key line do we see the recognizably human figures of the slave and his family. Here the freedom of the slave is not merely symbolized or allegorized by the gradual awakening of his bones, flesh, and muscles. Rather, the freedom of body parts is literally transmuted into the freedom of the organism. It is not the organism that unilaterally controls and determines the action of the organs;[20] it is the organs that recombine to produce a new organism, for in becoming free (reviving, inspiring) themselves they produce freedom for the organism that they constitute (reviving and inspiring it). It is literally these organs themselves, not the recombined organism, that spring like redeemed captives when their bonds and bars are burst. Once they are free—free to produce new connections, to recombine, develop, reconnect, overlap, reformulate, adapt, and intersect—they produce the freed slave.

Thus, the usual relationship between "organ" and "organism" is here broken down, either because organs can combine together to form organisms, or because apparently whole organisms turn out to be merely combinations of organs held together in some subjective or bodily assemblage larger than themselves. An easy and familiar opposition between the parts and the whole does not work here. Any one part can as easily be made up of other parts (of which it represents a whole) exactly at the same time as it plays the role of a mere part in some larger whole that transcends itself. At the same time, any one part could presumably be connected to—be part of—any number of different wholes. There is no ultimate horizon, no final determining instance, no grand authority, no limit to the extent of fluid combinations and recombinations and the contingencies that the parts can produce in this vision of freedom from external direction and power.

The slave's freedom is at once material and immaterial. But the relationship between "body" and "soul" is not easy to determine. Read metonymically, the freed slave is himself the soul who can now run out laughing in the open air. But in another, quite different, sense, the soul is now free from the body of the slave within which it had been *in*chained. Once again, these two readings are not necessarily mutually exclusive: the slave's freedom from the mill could involve the same process by which his soul is freed from his body. The most obvious—but not the only—possibility here is death. But this begs the question: death from what, death into what? If the slave's sinews and muscles are reviving themselves *from* death, what would it mean for the slave himself to be reviving *into* death? *Reviving* into *death?* My point here is not simply to play games with words, but to show how many contingent possibilities are inherent in this portentous passage, with its typically Blakean grammar, and to make it clear that these are not all mutually exclusive possibilities.

CHAPTER THREE

The context of the plate within the larger prophecy now becomes particularly important for understanding its significance. For if this plate in *America* somehow projects an image of freedom and liberation, it also confirms Blake's departure from the master narrative of liberty, not only because it is inconsistent with master narratives of any kind, but because it is utterly inconsistent with the discourse of liberty as this term was understood and deployed by those radical writers during the 1790s who saw their struggle as a continuation of the republican independence movement in America (see chapter 2). For this plate of *America* reintroduces the question of social and economic freedom, and it does so, clearly, by insistently locating the site of liberty in what is preeminently a workplace: the mill. Scholarly accounts of *America* that have tried to reconcile Blake's vision with the more general radical narrative of liberty tend to overlook the central importance of the fact—already anticipated in Washington's speech in one of the early plates—that the figure celebrating his freedom here is specifically a slave, who is now free from his labors at the mill.

Several new questions, and a new wave of contradictions and inconsistencies, now present themselves. Once slavery has been removed from a purely rhetorical realm, in which it can be deployed to signify oppression and injustice of all kinds, it refers to a particular mode of productive labor, and in this late-eighteenth-century context to a global commercial network connected to an imperial world system centered on the so-called triangular trade across the Atlantic. And yet, even if Blake seeks to rescue the term "slavery" from a merely rhetorical usage, it is immediately clear that he is not exclusively interested in, for example, the slave labor of the British colonies in America and the West Indies (though, to be sure, he is also interested in that as well). For it is a peculiar feature of Blake's work that weary and time-measured labor is almost always associated with rumbling mills. Blake would later write in *Jerusalem*: "When winter rends the hungry family and the snow falls / Upon the ways of men hiding the paths of man and beast, / Then mourns the wanderer: then he repents his wanderings & eyes / The distant forest: then the slave groans in the dungeon of stone, / The captive in the mill of the stranger, sold for scanty hire. / They view their former life: they number moments over and over, / Stringing them on their remembrance as on a thread of sorrow."[21] Far from being solely associated with the agony of slave labor in the American cotton and sugarcane fields, Blake's dark satanic mills would seem to be more readily associated with the manufactories of the early industrial period in England, in which strangers sold for scanty hire labor their weary lives away (typically, during the 1790s, for fourteen hours a day, six days a week, "employed, by turns," as Sir Frederick

Morton Eden wrote in 1797, "during the greater part of the night, and robbed of that rest which, though indispensable to us all, is most required by the young").[22] Here, even the memories of a prior freedom are defined and measured by the numbered moments of work time, and the thread of sorrow on which these moments are miserably numbered is time itself.

In this context, it is probably not a coincidence that this passage in *America* in which the slave rises from his labors at a mill (rather than a cotton field) is strikingly reminiscent of a passage at the very beginning of Milton's *Samson Agonistes* (1671), a text which Blake knew well. In the argument of that play, Milton writes, "Samson, made Captive, Blind, and now in the Prison at Gaza, there to labour as in a common work-house, on a Festival day, in the general cessation from labour, comes forth into the op'n Air, to a place nigh, somewhat retir'd, there to sit a while and bemoan his condition." A little way into the play, Samson himself emerges and cries out:

> Why was my breeding ordered and prescrib'd
> As of a person separate to God,
> Design'd for great exploits; if I must dye
> Betray'd, Captiv'd, and both my Eyes put out,
> Made of my Enemies the scorn and gaze;
> To grind in Brazen Fetters under task
> With this Heavn'n-gifted strength? O glorious strength
> Put to the labour of a Beast, debas't
> Lower then bondslave! Promise was that I
> Should *Israel* from *Philistian* yoke deliver;
> Ask for this great Deliver now, and find him
> Eyeless in Gaza at the Mill with slaves,
> Himself in bonds under *Philistian* yoke.

Samson's bondage at the mill—in particular his bondage during what is supposed to be a day of rest—clearly stands here for compelled labor in general, that is, the necessity of labor itself, rather than specifically colonial plantation labor. Particularly once it has been "translated" from Milton's time to the 1790s, the mill here functions not as a particular site of production (of grains or of textiles) but as a site of compelled labor in general, and the slave held captive in the mill of the stranger is a worker, sold for scanty hire, laboring under compulsion. I will return to this issue a little later on and elaborate it more fully, with reference to the general issues raised in Blake's texts as well as to those issues raised by Blake's life and work.

Here, however, we must contend with another inconsistency that has often been pointed out (but seldom explained) in Blake scholarship. For all the bewildering variety of mills that one encounters in Blake's work, there is hardly ever a concrete description—much less a visual image—of the mill. This absence suggests that the mill, which plays a vital role in Blake's work, is not so much a simple location (i.e., a textile mill, a corn mill), but rather a process. Thus, one labors at the mill to the extent that one labors in the process identified as the mill, and the mill is a conceptual space defined by practice or, more specifically, a conceptual space in which imagination and even life itself have been harnessed to the material requirements of a certain kind of productive process. In a later section of this chapter, I will try to suggest how we can account for the often bewildering variety of mills that one encounters in Blake's work. For now, I want to further examine the more immediate question of slavery itself.

Blake produced his most extended meditations on slavery in the period 1793–94, not only in *America*, but also in *Visions of the Daughters of Albion*, which he was working on at the same time. Stephen Behrendt has stressed the mutual interdependence of the so-called continental prophecies, and he is quite right to argue that *America* should be read alongside *Europe* and *The Song of Los* (*Africa & Asia*).[23] But we should be careful not to overstate the unity of the continental prophecies as a closed constellation, since *America* is at least as closely related to *Visions of the Daughters of Albion* (and also *The Marriage of Heaven & Hell*) as it is to *Europe*. Especially with regard to their central concern—slavery—*America* and *Visions* need to be read even more closely than merely *alongside* each other, as they seem at times to link together the very same "glittering fragments" in different ways.

The first and most striking image of slavery in *Visions* comes in the very first line: "Enslav'd, the Daughters of Albion weep: a trembling lamentation / Upon their mountains; in their valleys, sighs towards America." For although there are references to the "voice of slaves beneath the sun," and Bromion, apparently a slavemaster, says "Stampt with my signet are the swarthy children of the sun," the enduring reference to slavery is not, or not only, that of African slavery in the sunburned fields of the Americas, but rather the slavery of the daughters of Albion in the gloomy mountains and valleys of England itself. Oothoon (whose transatlantic cries the daughters of Albion "eccho back") is identified repeatedly not simply as a slave, but rather as a harlot, much like the female figure who appears throughout Blake's songs and prophecies as an object of commercialized desire. The sexual dynamics of Oothoon's relationships to Bromion and Theotormon (not to mention to herself) have been read in various ways, particularly suggestively in terms of late-eighteenth-century understandings of female eroticism.[24] But Bromion's rape of Oothoon has also been read by Erdman and others (in a different political-economic register) as that of a master raping his slave to impregnate her and thus increase her market value. Bromion refers to Oothoon as "this harlot here," while all along Oothoon herself cries out that she is a "virgin fill'd with virgin fancies." What is happening here, then, is not that the harlots or the spinning daughters—the spinsters—of England are being compared with slaves in America (as in the radical trope mentioned in the previous chapter), but rather the reverse. What remains unclear, however, is just what "slavery" means in this context, and for that matter just what kind of slave Oothoon herself really is.

Helen Bruder has produced a detailed and compelling reading of *Visions* in terms of the changes in the discourses and practices of female sexuality at the end of the eighteenth century, and particularly the increasing subjection of female eroticism to patriarchal control. Countering the tendency within Blake scholarship to read the prophecy as a meditation on purely mental desire and repression, Bruder insists that the enslavement of both the daughters of Albion and their sisterly Oothoon "is *literal*, not purely mental as so many Blake critics have argued."[25] In reading Oothoon's cries of joy and desire, which are either repressed or ignored by Theotormon and Bromion, Bruder suggests that Blake is attempting "to find a place for the unfettered expression of women's desires at a historical moment when the controlling discourses of patriarchy were attempting, with much more effectiveness, to silence the voices of female eroticism."[26] According to Bruder, "slavery" may be taken to connote a "literal" subjection of female sexuality and indeed female bodies to male desire and control (for example, in pornography, which was enjoying a boom in the late eighteenth century), as well as the nearly complete repression of female desire as such. However, it might be possible to extend Bruder's understanding of slavery, especially if one seeks to generate an account of slavery that might link together not only Oothoon and the daughters of Albion, but also the male slave of *America*.

The turning point of Bruder's argument concerns her opposition between the expression and the repression of a specifically female sexual desire (this is how she materializes what has been a tendency in other scholarship to read this in terms of the expression and repression of desire in purely emotional terms). Oothoon's cries of love are thus taken as an expression of female eroticism—even autoeroticism—in defiance of patriarchal repression and the latter's specifically male-oriented eroticism. Even if we grant this, the other recurring contrast in *Visions* (and elsewhere in Blake's work), which immediately requires further elaboration in this context, is that between "virgin" and "whore" or "harlot." Once again Blake goes beyond conventional uses of these terms. Virginity here does not imply merely a tech-

93

nical condition prior to sexual experience, while the figure of the harlot is a woman whose sexuality has been confined, objectified and, above all, rendered *productive*. Sexual pleasure and desire (rather than a kind of chaste sterility) belong to the virgin, whereas the harlot is stripped of pleasure and freedom and ultimately reduced by necessity to the status of a productive organ, a womb. Here we should consider Oothoon's speech in plates 6 and 7 of *Visions:*

> Infancy, fearless, lustful, happy! nestling for delight
> In laps of pleasure: Innocence! honest, open, seeking
> The vigorous joys of morning light; open to virgin bliss.
> Who taught thee modesty, subtil modesty, child of night & sleep?
> When thou awakest wilt thou dissemble all thy secret joys,
> Or wert thou not awake when all this mystery was disclos'd?
> Then com'st thou forth a modest virgin, knowing to dissemble,
> With nets found under thy night pillow, to catch virgin joy,
> And brand it with the name of whore; & sell it in the night,
> In silence, ev'n without a whisper, and in seeming sleep,
> Religious dreams and holy vespers, light thy smoky fires:
> Once were thy fires lighted by the eyes of honest morn.
> And does my Theotormon seek this hypocrite modesty,
> This knowing, artful, secret, fearful, cautious, trembling hypocrite?
> Then is Oothoon a whore indeed! and all the virgin joys
> Of life are harlots, and Theotormon is a sick man's dream;
> And Oothoon is the crafty slave of selfish holiness.
> But Oothoon is not so: a virgin fill'd with virgin fancies.
> Open to joy and to delight where ever beauty appears;
> If in the morning sun I find it, there my eyes are fix'd
> In happy copulation; if in evening mild, wearied with work,
> Sit on a bank and draw the pleasures of this free born joy.[27]

Here, as elsewhere throughout *Visions*, the figural opposition is between freedom and necessity, and in particular the unfettered freedom of innocence as opposed to the productive necessity of enslavement (and ultimately procreative marriage). Oothoon thus hovers between her status as an innocent, loving "virgin"—open to and delighting in happy copulation and "free-born joys"—and her potential enslavement as a "whore" bound by religious laws to a strictly reproductive procreation.

For here, the figure of the "whore," far from being a sinner and an outcast, is produced and sustained by religious laws, for all she might "blight with plagues the marriage hearse."[28] The virgin and the whore are not exactly mutually exclusive categories, but rather contingent identities. This is why Oothoon can at certain moments alternate between virgin and whore. Virginity in this sense amounts not to something that is lost once and forever, but rather to a condition of freedom—freedom from a reification into the productive status of the whore. This is also why innocence, as well as childhood and even infancy, are not exactly desexualized (on the contrary, infancy clearly has its own "lusts"). What makes them "free" is their freedom from restraint and from the necessity of reproduction—and above all their capacity for multiplicity as opposed to a restricting reduction to a single purpose. Thus, it is only as a free virgin that Oothoon can call out in plate 7, "Love! Love! Love! happy happy Love! free as the mountain wind!" Here, however, Blake must be seen to be operating in the discursive continuum established in the heterogeneous antinomian tradition.

For various antinomian writers—including Abiezer Coppe, Laurence Clarkson, and Jacob Bauthumley, who achieved such notoriety during the seventeenth-century revolutionary period that their works were burned and they themselves thrown into jail, Bauthumley after having had his tongue bored through—the deliverance from sin sanctified in the everlasting gospel ("to the pure all things are pure") is not simply a license to "kisse and hug Ladies, and love my neighbours wife as my selfe, without sin," as Coppe writes. Rather, love is to be understood simultaneously in physical and spiritual terms as an ecstatic joy celebrating that unity "infinitely beyond expression" which is God ("my love my dove is but one, thou one, not two, but only one, my love: Love is God, and God is Love," Clarkson writes in *A Single Eye*).[29] When Blake writes in *The Marriage of Heaven & Hell* that "Man has no Body distinct from his Soul," the "Eternal Delight" that he refers to there may be "from the Body," as he indicates, but it opens up into a joyous sharing and being in common in God. Thus "the improvement of sensual enjoyment" that he turns to later on allows us to "cleanse" the "doors of perception" by opening out from the confines of one body into "the infinite which was hid." Read in such an antinomian sense, those proverbs of hell that have sometimes been taken as celebrations of a selfish hedonism ("Sooner murder an infant in its cradle than nurse unacted desires"; "He who desires but acts not, breeds pestilence"; "The road of excess leads to the palace of wisdom") may be seen to stand at the farthest possible distance from a celebration of selfishness, for they point toward that "Blood-life-spirit-communion" that Coppe writes of: an escape from selfishness into universal love.

If love may be thought of as a way to celebrate common infinite unity, a way to escape from the narrow confined finitude of self-ish existence, these

CHAPTER THREE

perhaps are the terms in which we should consider Oothoon's otherwise inexplicable celebration of happy and free love. The unselfishness of her virginal innocent love, which is not restricted in either a bodily or a subjective sense to a single identity, is opposed to the selfish love and indeed the self-love that enables—and requires—reproduction in order to sustain itself:

> Can that be Love that drinks another as a sponge drinks water.
> That clouds with jealousy his nights, with weepings all the day,
> To spin a web of age around him, grey and hoary, dark,
> Till his eyes sicken at the fruit that hangs before his sight?
> Such is self-love that envies all, a creeping skeleton
> With lamplike eyes watching around the frozen marriage bed.[30]

Selfishness here, then, denotes not only a kind of blinding greed, but above all a literal *self*ishness, a reduction into, a confinement as, a single, limited, unitary self, "clos'd up" and cut off from the "infinite." For, when threatened with being transformed from "virgin" to "harlot," what Oothoon most fears is just such a reduction into a single subjective selfhood, by which she would become a "slave of selfish holiness" who is tied to "the frozen marriage bed":

> They told me that the night & day were all that I could see:
> They told me that I had five senses to inclose me up,
> And they inclos'd my infinite brain into a narrow circle,
> And sunk my heart into the Abyss, a red round globe hot burning
> Till all from life I was obliterated and erased.[31]

It is not a coincidence that the language of this passage is reminiscent of the language of *America*, for once again the oscillation that takes place throughout *Visions* is between an open-ended freedom and the contrary reification of the self, a restricted organism enclosed in the narrow circle of the five senses so dear to the theorists of natural law and natural rights from John Locke to Tom Paine. Here the reduction to a singular bodily and subjective organism—an individual identity or self—is imagined as the worst of all confinements; Oothoon thus anticipates Tharmas's agonized speech in *The Four Zoas* ("I am like an atom / A Nothing left in darkness yet I am an identity / I wish & feel & weep & groan Ah terrible terrible"). Just as in *America*, this identifying confinement moves rapidly and contingently between organism and organ. For if the virgin's sexuality is one of happy and open copulation (open not merely because it involves multiple lovers, but above all because it involves multiple *selves*), the sexuality of the "whore" has been confined, objectified, and turned into a productive mechanism. The

96

crippling finitude of reproductive sexuality in the service of monadic identity may be read against the blissful infinity that would be opened up by the fierce rushing, the ecstatic dis-organ-ization, seen at the end of *America* (see chapter 2). That scene in *Visions* in which Oothoon offers to selflessly catch virgins for Theotormon's pleasure has been read as an expression of Blake's supposed "sexism," but it must also be read in terms of the question of subjectivity; for if Oothoon is free from the confines of unitary subjecthood, the pressures of jealousy and possession need not weigh her down.

Again, especially given the discourse of "adulterous" love that they implicitly raise, such scenes in *Visions* need to be considered in the context of antinomian belief. For example, through his contrapuntal reading of Romans 8:23 ("we ourselves groan within ourselves, waiting for the redemption"), Clarkson justifies his claim that true freedom involves that form of love which allows an escape from unitary embodiment and into an infinite community. For Clarkson and Coppe, as well as for Blake, such restrictive embodiment was understood in terms of the five senses. "Whereas before thou wast alive to five, dead to one, and dead to one," Clarkson writes, "now thou shalt be dead to five, and alive to one, that lovely pure one who beholds nothing but purity, wheresoever it goeth, and what soever it doth, all is sweet and lovely." Here, supposedly transgressive sins like adultery are no longer to be considered sinful because they mark a union not only of bodies but of souls. Indeed, as Clarkson writes (speaking for God), "till flesh be made Sprit and Spirit flesh, so not two but one [cf. Blake's "man has no body distinct from his soul"], thou art in perfect bondage; for without vail, I declare that whosoever doth attempt to act from flesh, in flesh, to flesh, hath, is, and will commit Adultry; but . . . for my part, till I acted that, so called sin, I could not predominate over sin; so that now whatsoever I act, is not in relationship to the Title, to the Flesh, but that Eternity in me; So that with me, all Creatures are but one creature, and this is my form, the Representative of the whole Creation: So that see what I can, act as I will, all is but one most sweet and lovely."[32] Carnal pleasures, Coppe's "base impudent kisses," are here not ends in themselves, but means to unite bodies and souls in an infinite community. Read in this context, the confining reduction dreaded in Oothoon's speech at this moment of *Visions* is not merely that of a single confined and restricted organism—that is, confined and restricted precisely by a reduction to a single definite identity—but even more specifically that of a mere organ for reproduction, a restriction by which, as Oothoon says, "she who burns with youth, and knows no fixed lot, is bound / In spells of law to one she loathes." Fearing just such enslavement, Oothoon asks in plate 5:

CHAPTER THREE

> And must she drag the chain
> Of life, in weary lust? must chilling, murderous thoughts obscure
> The clear heaven of her eternal spring; to bear the wintry rage
> Of a harsh terror, driv'n to madness, bound to hold a rod
> Over her shrinking shoulders all the day, & all the night
> To turn the wheel of false desire, and longings that wake her womb
> To the abhorred birth of cherubs in the human form,
> That live a pestilence & die a meteor, & are no more?[33]

The reproductive function of the womb that we see here is revisited in the preludium of *America*, where the victim of Orc's rape is not exactly the "dark virgin," but rather "the terrific loins" and especially "the panting struggling womb" that he violently "seizes."[34] For it is not that the womb or the loins figure here as metonymical references to the woman. Rather, by the act of rape itself, the "nameless shadowy female" has literally *become* merely a womb: she has no other existence outside or beyond this organ-ic and reproductive capacity. Indeed, the violence of the rape consists in this very reduction, this confinement to a particular reproductive function. What is most striking about Oothoon's impassioned speeches in *Visions* is that she makes it clear that this reduction to organ is not only not worse than a reduction to organism: it is the same thing, and is produced by the same process. In this sense, the "joys and desires" repeatedly celebrated in Blake's work—especially in that they must be rescued from the "priests in black gowns, walking their rounds, binding with briars," as in the *The Garden of Love*—involve both a freedom from a restriction to reproductive labor (as an organ) and a freedom from confinement into a singular selfhood (organism). The productive process identified in the preludium of *America* as rape generates and reifies both a certain result and also the very organs and organisms that will literally produce it. This suggests once again that a simple opposition between part and whole does not work and is irrelevant (and, hence, that returning to a prelapsarian "whole" is not just impossible but quite beside the point).

The most significant opposition here, then, is between contingency and fluidity and multiplicity on the one hand, and a rigid unilateral reification and identification on the other. For having been defined and classified according to function in this productive process, one exists and is identified merely as a reified organ within a larger assemblage. In the process of reification one is cut off from all the other possibilities of life. Enslavement thus involves two interchangeable and mutually constituting elements: isolation as an organism with a fixed and reified identity, and isolation as a reified organ within a productive process. The language of plate 5, in which the bringing forth of a series of "abhorred births" is likened to the weary turning of a wheel, night and day, reminds us once again of the "complicated wheels" that are invariably associated with Blake's rumbling mills. *Visions* is clearly not solely preoccupied with sexual reproduction, but at least one sort of enslavement to which the daughters of Albion are subjected is their function as reproductive organ(ism)s. There are recurring images throughout *Visions* of women lying in deathlike postures, as for example in plate 3, where a woman in a prone position is being torn by an eagle (reminiscent of the image of the woman giving birth to a crying infant in plate 3 of *The Marriage*). It is absolutely essential to bear in mind that it is not sexual reproduction as such—or even reproduction in general—that is being stigmatized here, but rather objectifying women as merely reproductive organs: in other words, reifying them.

In more general terms, it is not production or even work as such that is being stigmatized in *America*, but rather a particular process of production that requires a minute and highly orchestrated social division of labor and the reification of particular laboring roles within that division. Once again, enslavement has to do with confinement and restriction to a particular identity and a particular role within a productive process. This process generates the role and location within itself of the slave whose labor it requires for its own sustenance. The vision of slavery here is one in which a certain kind of labor both produces and is produced by a certain form of subjectivity, so that the laborer's very identity is commensurate with his or her labor and has no ontological independence from labor, potential or actual. Outside of such work time, labor not only has no value: it has no existence. As in literal slavery, labor is compressed into the body that provides it, a body whose social existence is registered only by virtue of its capacity to do work. Were it not productive, or were it to cease being productive, this form of labor and the identity commensurate with it would not be tolerated for a moment, and if at all possible, it would be exterminated without a trace.

The extent of Blake's departure from the assumptions of the hegemonic form of liberal-radicalism in the 1790s—by which his work draws attention to issues that might otherwise be forgotten or set aside in the struggle for liberty—is greatly amplified here by the ways in which these early prophetic books insist on the irreducible organic connections among political, economic, social, religious, biological, and psychological processes of organization. In later chapters I will return to a broader elaboration of the questions of subjectivity and temporality that have already been introduced here. For now, however, I want to continue the exploration of the connection

CHAPTER THREE

between individual identity and the laboring process at the end of the eighteenth century that the illuminated books elaborate, or in other words the ontological relationship between labor and the laborer: that process of reification by which the free worker would be transformed in the prophetic books into a "slave."

3. Producing Workers

Blake was by no means alone in exploring the dynamic relationships between the requirements of a protoindustrial process of production and the social being of the worker in a society that was increasingly being defined both by, and according to the needs of, this process. For even if the radical champions of liberty were not particularly interested in this question—for reasons to which we will have to return later on—other writers in the 1790s were obsessed with it. Patrick Colquhoun (perhaps best known for his *Treatise on the Police of the Metropolis* of 1797), Sir Frederick Morton Eden (author of the gigantic study *The State of the Poor*, published in 1797), George Dyer, Hannah More, Robert Young, Thomas Ruggles, William Young, Jeremy Bentham (best known for his *Panopticon* of 1791), Samuel Bentham (Jeremy's brother, who carried out in the 1790s a detailed study of the labor practices in the royal dockyards), and many others produced enormous volumes during the decade from 1790 to 1800. This sudden explosion of interest in the social and psychological conditions of Britain's and especially London's workers, in addition to the proliferation of miscellaneous reports (governmental, philanthropic, reactionary, and otherwise) concerning the poor, the indigent, orphan children, asylums, workhouses, industry schools, poor laws, early factory workers, vagrants, ex-soldiers, dockyard laborers, chimney sweepers, spinners, and weavers anticipated Mayhew's celebrated Victorian study by several decades, rivalling and often exceeding it with regard to both scale and detail.

Several things are impressive about the sheer volume of this explosion of interest in the social conditions of London labor. First of all, apart from the work of a few benevolent individuals, it was almost entirely produced by conservative and often reactionary writers, whose primary concern was keeping labor productive ("industrious") and above all under control. Lynn Lees has examined the "widespread faith in social engineering to be found among the disciplinarians of the poor" in this period.[35] Ironically, the discourse in the 1790s that came closest to Blake's interest in the relationship between sociopolitical or socioeconomic organizations on the one hand and psychobiological organizations (organ/isms) on the other, was the work of those interested in organ-izing labor for strictly productive purposes—that is, in what Lees calls social engineering—and in linking wherever possible that process of organization to those forms of political domination and control from which Blake sought to escape. Since the hegemonic radicals were for the most part content to assume that the worker, like the citizen, has an independent existence and hence certain "inalienable" rights, they were not concerned with the sort of detailed psychosocial investigations of workers being produced by conservative writers, whose overriding concern was discipline rather than liberty, and in particular the appropriate method for literally *producing* the right kind of disciplined worker and eliminating all the other kinds.

The point of departure for most of the period's studies in social engineering is invariably an extraordinary system of classification according to which the underclass could be divided into more or less desirable groups, ranging from the "industrious poor" and "the useful poor" through the "indigent poor," the "gin-drinking poor," and the "idle poor" to, finally and calamitously, the "criminal poor."[36] With very few exceptions, these studies, and the subscription plans or philanthropic institutions with which they were often associated, had as their primary objective not the alleviation or elimination of poverty as such (poverty was seen not only as inevitable but as actually desirable so long as it could be controlled), but rather the productive management of the poor, and in particular what might be called the yield management of the labor power of the poor. This approach, according to which poverty provided the ideal raw material for producing useful laborers, was already prevalent by the early part of the 1790s, but it became much more systematic as the decade wore on. In fact, insisting that "nothing but necessity will enforce labour and industry," the author of an *Essay on Trade and Commerce* could conclude as early as the 1770s that "A person must have a very imperfect knowledge of human nature, to suppose mankind would labour from any other motive."[37] It is for this reason, the same author argues, that "the idleness and debauchery of our manufacturing people is a many-headed monster, which every one should oppose, because every one's property is endangered by it; nay, the riches, strength and glory of this kingdom, must ever be insecure whilst this evil remains uncheck'd."[38] Blake, of course, was interested in the possibility of wresting a realm of freedom away from the realm of necessity; so, however much they may share his interest in the logic of organization, these conservative efforts to eliminate the realm of freedom in the name of an overriding productive necessity take exactly the opposite direction from the one taken by Blake, with his great faith in "Rest before Labour" (the phrase that appears as the epigraph of *The Four Zoas*).

Patrick Colquhoun, the most prolific of the investigators of poverty, writes in his early studies simply of the desirability of encouraging "virtue, industry, and sobriety" while at the same time discouraging "vice and idleness." Hence, his early schemes tended to exclude "the idle gin-drinking poor." But by the time he published *The State of Indigence* in 1799, his approach had hardened. Now the "corruption of morals" was to be regarded as a "gangrene" that needed to be "healed" by "a correct system of Police, calculated to reach the root and origin of the evil."[39] This is largely because of Colquhoun's developing understanding of poverty. "By *the Poor*," he writes in his 1799 study, "we are not to understand the whole mass of the people who support themselves by labour; for those whose necessity compels them to exercise their industry, become by their poverty the actual pillars of the State." Thus, Colquhoun continues: "Labour is absolutely requisite to the existence of all Governments; and as it is from the Poor only that labour can be expected, so far from being an evil they become under proper regulations, an advantage to every Country, and highly deserve the fostering care of every Government. It is not *Poverty*, therefore, that is in itself an evil, while health, strength, and inclination, afford the means of subsistence, and while work is to be had by all who seek it.—The evil is to be found only in *Indigence*, where the strength fails, where disease, age, or infancy deprive the individual of the means of subsistence, or where he knows not how to find employment when willing and able to work."[40] The problem then becomes how to control or eliminate indigence, while maintaining a desirable level of poverty and hence encouraging the production of useful labor power, which depends on poverty for its very existence. Colquhoun argues that "the great art, therefore, in managing the affairs of the Poor, is to establish Systems whereby the poor man, verging upon indigence, may be propped up and kept in his station."[41] It is because of this remarkably frank approach that, as Peter Linebaugh argues, "if a single individual could be said to have been the planner and theorist of class struggle in the metropolis," it would have to be Colquhoun.[42]

This approach to the question of labor led to the unprecedented proliferation during the 1790s of carceral and disciplinary institutions—foundling hospitals, asylums for industry, charity schools, shelters for girls, orphanages, workhouses, houses of industry—whose main objective was the careful production, from the raw material of the children of the indigent and poverty-stricken classes, of "industrious" laborers.[43] Whenever possible, this process was to begin with infants and children, so that, as one writer put it, "the rising generation would be educated in more regular habits of industry."[44] Such disciplinary training would enable the children of even the most dissolute parents to be rescued and reformed, "by proper education, forming to moral principles, and to habits of industry," and hence might enable the elimination of the class of criminal poor while maintaining a sufficiently large pool of the productive or "useful poor."[45] Thus, as Colquhoun would later argue, the existence of poverty itself could be exploited and maintained as a perpetual source of the raw material for labor.

From this standpoint, however, poverty itself does not produce useful workers: it presents only the raw material in a chaotic and potentially explosive form—for, quite apart from the political agitations associated with the cause of liberty, English and particularly London workers were notorious for their turbulence and lack of deference. These disciplinary institutions can therefore be seen as factories for processing this potentially dangerous raw material and filtering out the wasteful and undesirable while producing a continuous stream of useful, regular, uniform, tame workers. Indeed, the key features of this production process, to be started at as early an age as possible, are regularity and uniformity.[46] While the intake might consist of an irregular flow of "the abandoned and depraved,"[47] who are used to "riotous intemperance"[48] and are characterized by their sheer "ignorance and gross immorality,"[49] or even of children who might "mix in mobs" or "play at any unlawful games,"[50] the output would assuredly consist of a steady flow of "useful labourers,"[51] people with "a habit of labour, of cleanliness, and of decency,"[52] who have been "gradually accustomed to regular and early habits of order and attention"[53] and instructed in "true Humility and Obedience to their superiors, and such necessary Qualifications as may make them of Benefit to the Community, and honest and useful Servants."[54] Thus, for example, could the Lambeth Asylum for Girls boast, "trained to habits of industry and regularity, a *supply of diligent and sober domestics* is formed."[55] The Lambeth Asylum was located just around the corner from Hercules Buildings, where Blake was at the time producing the illuminated books. Indeed, to *The Song of Los*'s many references to contemporary sociopolitical concerns, such as the price of labor and cutting off bread from the city, we should certainly add its interest in the "Churches: Hospitals: Castles: Palaces," which appear "Like nets & gins & traps to catch the joys of Eternity," which in Blake's work are invariably associated with the joys of children. Here, once again, Blake should be seen to be engaging oppositionally in the discourse of carceral and disciplinary institutions used for organizing productive labor.

CHAPTER THREE

Due to their easily adaptable homogenization—and above all their adaptation to time standards and routine schedules—such newly produced workers could be put to use not only as domestic servants, but anywhere in the production process.[56] Thomas Simons reassures the housekeepers of London, on behalf of the parochial industry schools, that these schools produce not merely useful children, but workers *for life*, a whole new class of the "useful" poor. "A willing obedience and a reform will never take place among them until they are taught what the duty of subjection means," Simons argues, and "when by these helps they are more civilised, then more cheerfully will they labour."[57] In its most effusive and ambitious form, this attitude, which rose to dominance through the 1790s, sought not only to define and hence to control the individual worker—and the working class collectively—through actual work, but if at all possible to continue this project even in times of leisure. For, as one writer puts it, "it would be a better policy that the mass of the people should be employed in the useless task of building Pyramids, than suffered to contract habits of idleness."[58] What we can see in such projects, however, amounts not just to a kind of social engineering—as Lynn Lees has called it—but far more specifically to an ontological project of *individual* engineering, the production of useful individuals.

Indeed, while the eighteenth-century emergence of commercialized leisure has long been recognized,[59] it is important to remember that this commercialization has to do not only with the creation of a swarm of consumers with enough appetite to swallow up the products of the early factories, but also with keeping those consumers under a kind of regulative control increasingly similar to the discipline of the workplace itself. Thus, the ultimate dream was to turn leisure into a quantified system of discipline, so that even outside of work, idleness, identified as early as 1770 as a "many-headed monster," would never be allowed to challenge the "habits of industry and regularity" which were apparently so essential to the economy of the late eighteenth century, and so that, as Richard Dienst has argued in a different context, "non-work time" could become "subject to the same kinds of antagonisms that cut across labor time."[60] Indeed, at their most extreme, the advocates of the disciplinary system saw the laborer's free time as the greatest problem and argued that if time itself could somehow be regulated throughout the day and not just at work, the manufacturing populace would not be at leisure to irregularly consume their free time, "the most fatal of all their consumptions."[61]

Not all the writers of the period, of course, were completely in favor of such disciplinary incarceration and enforced labor for children in these "gaols without guilt," this "legalized system of prisons."[62] Many were concerned with the awful conditions of health and sanitation inside the asylums and workhouses. "I must avow," writes George Dyer, "that I have visited several prisons, in which I had rather be lodged, with a view to health, than in some workhouses in London."[63] And many more were concerned with the effect on the national character of producing nothing but an endless series of standardized drones ready for doing any work which is presented to them. "It may happen," writes William Young, "that by long habits of submission to toil, without reward, under the lash of a task-master, and in confinement without any freedom of action, the freedom of mind may finally be subdued, and the British spirit broken." Thus, Young fears, "a succeeding generation spawned in a work-house, may be fitted for slaves, not only from depression of mind and spirit, but from enfeeblement of the race begotten in misery, born in a goal [sic], and losing the health and spring of youth in contagion and restraint."[64]

It is significant for our purposes here that one of the debates surrounding the social ontology of labor throughout the 1790s concerned a type of labor whose effects on the individual worker were visible not only in mental or psychoaffective ways, but tangibly and physically, in his very body. This debate concerned a figure very dear to Blake and immediately familiar to even the most casual reader of any of his works, from *Songs of Innocence and of Experience* through to *Jerusalem*: the chimney sweeper. Even beyond a series of laws concerning the duration and regulation of the work performed by these "climbing boys" (e.g., they were not supposed to "call the streets" without the supervision of one of their master's journeymen, and then "only" from five in the morning until midday, six days a week),[65] there was by the late 1780s and early 1790s a great deal of concern for the diseases and deformations to which their work subjected them.[66] In addition to the perpetual filth and darkness in which they worked and lived, their continual inhalation of smoke and soot, their being forced—sometimes by scorching—up narrow and twisted chimneys, and their inability to secure adequate rest and cleanliness, all of which subjected them to terrible scars, burns, scratches, and diseases (including ulcerous growths and "a peculiar disease" of the scrotum), there was also a great deal of worrying about the long-term effect of their labor on their very bodies. For, typically beginning work at around the age of five, by the age of twelve or thirteen a chimney sweeper, now grown too large for this cramped work, would inevitably be a broken and stunted cripple, finished for life.[67] The chimney sweepers who populate Blake's works, invariably crying and weeping, are the ultimate evidence of the extent to which work could literally form the worker, at once mentally, emotionally, and physically.

In this context, Blake's meditation on the relationship between the ontology of the worker and the miserable conditions of work suddenly seems much less mystical, and—however oppositional and counterhegemonic—much more the product of a certain moment in social and economic history. What distinguishes Blake from social engineers such as Colquhoun, of course, is that his primary concern is freedom rather than discipline. What distinguishes him from the hegemonic radicals is that he is unwilling to take for granted the relationship of work and the worker as a simple practical relationship of a reified product to its ontologically independent owner or seller. Indeed, it is essential to bear in mind the extent to which Blake's broader understanding of both labor and freedom (from coercive labor) marked a departure from the discourse of liberty that one normally associates with London political radicalism of the 1790s. He is not interested in the freedom of an individual whose social ontology can be taken for granted, the natural producer of a reified capacity to work which he merely sells like any other product in a jostling marketplace ideally free of monopolistic perversions and disruptions. Blake locates the ways in which the individual is literally identified—given an individual identity—by his or her labor, and hence the ways in which one's individual identity is inextricably associated with and generated by a certain mode of social production, both in the workplace and in society at large, rather than being simply an inevitable natural "given." Thus, freedom for Blake meant something altogether different from the liberty of the hegemonic form of liberal-radicalism: freedom here involves a liberation from formation into individuality, not the freedom associated with a life of individuality. Those comments in Blake's writing that have often been taken by scholars as expressions of either artisan resentment or of his supposed elitism and arrogance—that is, as expressive of his supposed bourgeois attachment to individual liberty and self-determination—must be reconsidered in this light.

Blake's urban figures of the whore and the chimney sweeper offer particularly striking cases of the reduction of human beings to reified organs for work. For during the 1790s it was becoming increasingly clear that the disfiguration and agony of such marginalized and indeed preindustrial figures were no longer so exceptional, as all of society was gradually beginning to turn into a factory, with the utterly catastrophic results for working people already evident in London's streets. "Those pale famished countenances, those tattered garments, and those naked shivering limbs, we so frequently behold, are striking testimonies of these melancholy truths," one shocked London observer wrote in the middle of the 1790s.[68] Even by the beginning of the decade, the Blakean whore and chimney sweeper can be seen not as oddities, but, paradoxically, as prototypes for the social factory. Perhaps this is why they are so central to the prophecies.

Blake was certainly not alone in pondering the question of the relationship of the worker to his or her work. "It may, perhaps, be worthy [of] the attention of the Public, to consider," Sir Frederick Morton Eden wrote in 1797, "whether any manufacture, which, in order to be carried on successfully, requires, that cottages and workhouses should be ransacked for poor children; that they should be employed, by turns, during the greater part of the night, and robbed of that rest which, though indispensable to us all, is most required by the young . . . will add to the sum of individual, or national, felicity."[69] Indeed, the newly defined ontological relationship of organism to organ is particularly clear in the properly industrial process of manufacturing, in which "the captive in the mill of the stranger" is "sold for scanty hire." This process was, of course, growing rapidly during the 1790s and could be found in Blake's time not just in the production of bulk goods such as textiles (with which it is usually identified), but in the manufacture of other things as well, from pins and watches to clothes and artwork.

There were certainly many highly visible innovations associated with the total reorganization of textile manufacture, with the introduction through the 1780s of the spinning jenny, the water frame, the mule, the new carding machines, and around 1790 the first application of steam power to the new spinning machines. As Anna Clark and Deborah Valenze remind us, these new devices enabled the mechanization of a largely female and juvenile workforce—the daughters of Albion indeed—of spinners supplying a predominantly male workforce of handloom weavers with spun cotton.[70] (The mechanization of weaving in the nineteenth century was a separate process, with well-known catastrophic results for the weavers themselves.)[71] The increasingly enormous and powerful new machines, which moved the site of labor from the home to the new mills, and the increasing use of child labor to serve the machines are probably what made the changes in the textile industry so dramatically visible and so very disturbing to the moral and cultural patterns of preindustrial society (see fig. 7).[72] In his chapter "Under the Great Work Master," David Erdman explores in rich detail the many references in Blake's work to early industrial factories.[73] In these "dark satanic mills," the new machines and the unskilled female and juvenile workforce serving them could be combined together for increased efficiency and productivity.[74] They were made to work for up to fourteen hours a day, six days a week (plus another six hours on the seventh day for cleaning and maintaining the machines), even if they were "too often treated in the most barbarous and unfeeling manner,—worked night and day,—ill-fed, ill-clothed,—

CHAPTER THREE

reduced to decrepitude by excessive labour,—exposed to a variety of afflicting accidents by the machinery."[75] As early as the mid-1790s, in fact, there was grave concern for "the untimely labour of the night, and the protracted labour of the day," among the women and especially the children in the spinning factories, "these human beings [who] are only regarded as parts of the machinery which they set in motion."[76] Because of the dramatic deterioration of working conditions in the textile mills, it was as early as 1802 that the first act was passed in Parliament to regulate the working day in the new factories.

John Belchem points out, however, that the relentlessness of factory discipline was in place long before the arrival of what we now think of as industrial production.[77] Indeed, the immensely important innovations in textile production—whose effects were so highly visible because of the use of machinery and child labor—should not obscure the fact that similar innovations were taking place through the 1790s in other industries as well, above all in those areas of manufacturing catering to the nascent consumer culture. "Contrary to popular impression," Colin Campbell writes, "the manufacturing industries most closely associated with the Industrial Revolution were those producing consumer rather than capital goods, and among these, those which produced objects for 'luxury' consumption predominated."[78] The new consumer goods were tied in from the very beginning to geared seasonal changes in patterns and fashions, which kept up a steady demand for new fabrics, clothes, gardening materials, toys, and even dolls with their very own sets of interchangeable clothes, houses, furniture, and other items, including engravings.[79] "The future," as Fernand Braudel put it, "belonged to societies which were trifling enough, but also rich and inventive enough, to bother about changing colours, materials and styles of costume."[80]

Thus, even though the 1790s may not have been the moment of the great boom in heavy industry, an increasingly industrialized process of manufacturing was firmly in place by the beginning of the decade—motivated by what David Green identifies as less technologically driven strategies for the intensification of work[81]—particularly in the consumer-oriented industries. And with the intensification of the new manufacturing process there emerged a growing awareness that the worker thrown into this new process without any social or legal recourse or defense, without any adequate preparation (which, obviously, a preindustrial age could not provide), would be almost entirely consumed by it, reduced to a miserable existence as a "poor, wretched, o'er-toiled, half-starved, ill-clad and worse-lodged labourer of Britain; who, in the midst of surrounding luxury, splendour, and refinement,

LABORING AT THE MILL WITH SLAVES

Figure 7. Blake, advertisement for Moore & Company. © Copyright The British Museum.

rears his half-naked children in savage ignorance, and hears them cry for bread, when bread is not his to give them."[82] Pointing to the extent to which "the labouring man must find extreme difficulty to preserve his family from the miseries of real want, not only of the comforts, but even of the necessaries of life," one London writer asks in astonishment how "a poor man,

CHAPTER THREE

with half-a-guinea a week, feeds and clothes a family, pays rent for his apartment, buys a few coals, and contrives to exist. This wonder will be increased, if [we] take into consideration, that by exposure to all weather sickness often supervenes, and every resource is, in a moment, annihilated."[83]

Such wonder aside, for better or for worse, the new process of manufacturing and its associated technologies and techniques—but also subjections and miseries—were spreading rapidly throughout the country, including London. As early as 1786, Boulton and Watt had already installed one of the first of their new steam engines in the great Albion Flour Mill on the Blackfriars Road in Lambeth—which, as a symbol of the new age of industrial labor, was burned down by rioters in March of 1791, just a few months after the Blakes moved to Lambeth, in the autumn of 1790 (the burned-out hulk remained there until 1809).[84] By the 1790s, the silkweavers of Spitalfields and Bethnal Green in London's East End were already facing great difficulties due to a massive deterioration in wages associated in part with the machine production with which they were forced to compete (for, as the Society for the Diffusion of Useful Knowledge would later point out triumphantly, "the moment the machine comes into competition with human labour, the wages of that labour begin to adjust themselves to the lesser cost of production by the machine").[85] One observer wrote in the mid-1790s that "The labouring People and Mechanics in the Eastern Quarter of the Metropolis, have been reduced to the greatest Distress during the late severe Season." Many workers, this writer added, must now "resort to the miserable Alternative of pledging their Household Goods, and even their Childrens' Wearing Apparel, for the Purpose of raising Money to obtain the Necessaries of Life."[86]

The process of imposing the strict discipline of wage labor on even the nonindustrial workers of London was also well under way by the 1790s, as Green and Belchem remind us. By the middle of the decade, wages were simply not keeping up with the cost of eking out even the most miserable existence. Except for the one sanctioned day a week, customary work stoppages were gradually uprooted and a new sense of time discipline was imposed on the workforce.[87] In Josiah Wedgwood's porcelain factory, for example—which Blake would have known about through his friend John Flaxman, who worked for Wedgwood—the old preindustrial work habits were slowly eradicated through the 1780s and into the 1790s; workers who had been accustomed to the uneconomical waste of time and materials were gradually formed to the new work discipline of the modern era, "the punctuality, the constant attendance, the scrupulous standards of care and cleanliness, the avoidance of waste, the ban on drinking."[88] As Gerhard

Dohrn–Van Rossum points out, "the new concept of the 'economy of time' [to which, Marx would say, 'all economy ultimately reduces itself'] that arose along with workshops and factories did not concern primarily the length of work time, but above all its regularity and intensity, and thus the preconditions for its efficient economic use."[89] This new time discipline was particularly evident in factories, of course—by the 1790s Wedgwood's porcelain factory was referred to as the "bell-works" because of the way in which the central administration signaled time shifts—but whenever possible it was also imposed on labor outside the factory.

At the same time, taking customary nonpecuniary forms of compensation, such as the cuttings, sweepings, spillings, and trimmings of the materials of production, which were formerly understood to constitute a legitimate part of a worker's payment, was first criminalized and then vigorously prosecuted—punished by hanging and transportation—as rationalizing employers in pursuit of the maximum efficiency sought to substitute more readily accountable and quantifiable, and hence controllable, money wages instead.[90] Again, while perhaps most obvious in the early factories, this mode of efficiency emerged in other trades as well, such as the burgeoning river trade at the very heart of the global commercial system centered on the port of London (which may have accounted for up to a third of London's adult workforce).[91] Samuel Bentham's 1790s project to make the London dockyards more efficient—by introducing more rigorous weekly paybooks, by eliminating workers' appropriation of sweepings or "chips," by introducing night shifts to keep work going around the clock—is a notable example of this.[92]

The strict monetization of clock time toward the end of the eighteenth century really made sense of the way in which not labor, but labor *power*— the capacity to do work—became a commodity to be bought and sold on the open market. Both the hegemonic radicals and the conservatives in the 1790s came to agree on this central point: "labour," Burke insists, is "a commodity, and as such, an article of trade"; while Thelwall writes that "the most inestimable of all property is the sweat of the poor man's brow:—the property from which all order is derived, and without which grandeur must starve in the midst of supposed abundance."[93] At times, workers were able rhetorically to turn the conservative defense of the sanctity of property to a defense of their rights as laborers. "The Legislature has wisely provided laws for the protection of property," aggrieved mechanics in Glasgow point out, "and surely the time, ingenuity, and industry of a Mechanic, which must be considered his property, has an equal right to legal protection."[94] The difference, of course, lies in their analyses of what should happen when, because

CHAPTER THREE

of the introduction of machinery or other reasons, the price of labour power cannot keep up with the cost of life itself, and this is perhaps the key distinction between conservatives and radicals during the 1790s.

In *Thoughts and Details on Scarcity*, Burke sums up the emergent view of a political and cultural system increasingly seen—by liberal radicals and by conservatives alike—to be driven by abstract and inhuman laws and principles: "Labour must be subject to all the laws and principles of trade, and not to regulations foreign to them, and that may be totally inconsistent with those principles and those laws. When any commodity is carried to market, it is not the necessity of the vender, but the necessity of the purchaser that raises the price. The extreme want of the seller has rather (by the nature of things with which we shall in vain contend) the direct contrary operation. If the goods at market are beyond the demand, they fall in their value; if below it, they rise. The impossibility of the subsistence of a man, who carries his labour to market, is totally beside the question in this way of viewing it. The only question is, what is it worth to the buyer?"[95] Thus, Burke insists, "Whenever it happens that a man can claim nothing according to the rules of commerce, and the principles of justice, he passes out of that department, and comes within the jurisdiction of mercy."[96] This is because, according to Burke, the market alone can determine the price of labor: "The balance between consumption and production makes price. The market settles, and alone can settle, that price. Market is the meeting and conference of the *consumer* and *producer*, when they mutually discover each other's wants. Nobody, I believe, has observed with any reflection what market is, without being astonished at the truth, the correctness, the celerity, the general equity, with which the balance of want is settled. They who wish the destruction of that balance, and would fain by arbitrary regulation decree, that effective production should not be compensated with by encreased price, directly lay their *axe* to the root of production itself."[97]

For Thelwall and the radicals, however, such an "antinomy, of right against right, both equally bearing the seal of the law of exchange," but producing an unacceptable result, suggests not a fault in the market as such, but rather an unnatural distortion in this particular market, and an abuse of a natural right.[98] "Notwithstanding the scandalously inadequate price of labour—wages being, in many instances, rather a mockery than a support," Thelwall insists, "*every* man, and every *woman*, and every *child*, ought to obtain something more, in the general distribution of the fruits of labour, than food, and rags, and a wretched hammock, with a poor rug to cover it: and that without working twelve or fourteen hours a day, six days out of seven, from six to sixty. They have a claim, a sacred and inviolable claim, growing out of the fundamental maxim, upon which alone all property can be supported, to some comforts and enjoyments, in addition to the necessaries of life; and to some 'tolerable leisure for such discussion, and some means of such information,' as may lead to an understanding of their *rights;* without which they can never understand their *duties*."[99] For Thelwall (as I suggested in the previous chapter), the distortion in the labor market is the result of the monopoly of politics and the monopoly of commerce, held by the landed and aristocratic classes. It is as a result of these monopolies, he insists, that "there are but three classes of men left among us—the monied speculators, among whom may be classed the great farmers I have been describing; the proud high towering drones, who hum, and buz, and make a noise in the hive; but who never brought a morsel of honey into the cells; and the poor hard-working drudges, who toil from day to night, and almost from night to day, and receive for their useful and important services the bitter inheritance of unpitied poverty."[100] It is on this basis that Thelwall insists that if the monopolies on commerce and politics were relinquished, the natural rhythms of the market, including the market for labor, would be restored, and all would be well once more. Thus the "sacred compact, implied in the very distinction of labourer and employer," would be restored according to terms which, he says, "are to be decided, not by the power of the one and the wretchedness of the other, but by the reason of the thing, and the rules of moral justice."[101]

These questions are very important for measuring the distance between Blake and the hegemonic tendency in 1790s radicalism. For the latter, as indeed for the conservatives themselves, "laborer" and "employer" are categories to be taken for granted; whereas for Blake, they are socio-bio-psychological organisms, the products of a particular social organization. As we have seen, in the economic discourse emerging in the 1790s, the buying and selling of labor power in a process of exchange had to assume the prior and independent existence of the identities involved in the exchange. But for Blake production and exchange have to be understood as parts of a larger sociopolitical continuum, and in particular, the very organisms transacting these exchanges have to be understood as the organized products of the social, economic, and political organizations by which they are determined and in whose terms their actions and exchanges are defined. Who works, how he or she works, and the conditions under which he or she works are all inextricable questions for Blake. Rather than being ascribed to natural or divine causes, all are processes to be understood in social and political terms, just as we see the inhabitants of the world of Urizen at once forming "laws of prudence" themselves and calling them "The eternal laws of God."[102]

Especially given the position that Blake was articulating in his illuminated books, the contrary faith among radicals and conservatives alike in the adjudicating powers of the market as a force beyond human control—as a force seen to be standing beyond or outside of society and culture, like God and Nature one of those "things with which we shall in vain contend"—is astonishing.[103] It was in large measure as a result of this unanimity that, by the end of the eighteenth century, the worker came to be recognized as a being offering and selling on an open market an undefined *potential* (to do work). In other words, in the alienation of labor power from the laborer, what was bought and sold was a capacity to work. Having been reified and purchased at an agreed price, this capacity could be put to use in whatever form the purchaser specified; it could be combined in quantities and measures and with an intensity and efficiency altogether unimaginable when considering the particular abilities of discrete workers. In short, it made it possible to combine the labor power of workers and groups of workers in ways—both quantitative and qualitative—that had previously been literally unthinkable, and that made it imperative to come up with a new understanding of the relationship of the laborer to his or her alienated labor.

By the 1790s, such labor power had to be understood in terms of average ability, rather than in terms of exceptional individual ability, skill, and training characteristic of artisanal labor, with its seven-year apprenticeship and hierarchies of masters and journeymen. An early industrial manufacturing process had to be established on the basis of a given flow over a certain duration of a certain intensity of *average* labor power. Exceptional ability and individuality were here no longer a benefit, as they were in artisanal labor, but an obstruction in the regulation of an otherwise smooth flow premised on averages rather than exceptions. In artisanal or handicraft labor, a workman would complete all stages of the process of production of a particular finished commodity himself. In the flow of early industrial manufacturing, the process itself must allocate a certain intensity and duration of abstract labor to perform each of the various stages of production, some requiring more strength, some more dexterity. "The commodity," as Marx observes, "from being the individual product of an independent craftsman, becomes the social product of a union of craftsmen, each of whom performs one, and only one, of the constituent partial operations."[104] The intellectual management of the process, which is now the role of the supervisor or master, is therefore distinguished from the merely physical aspect of literally doing the work, which is now the role of the simple workers.[105]

Of course, the earliest resistance to this new process of production came from artisans, whose whole way of life was threatened by the replacement of their skilled, independent craftsmanship by the smooth but highly regulated and controlled flow of unskilled abstract labor power characteristic of the new manufactories. David Green argues that artisans did what they could to defend their customary privileges against the implementation of an industrial culture.[106] And, as Anna Clark observes, one of the hallmarks of artisan ressentiment in this period involved an attempt to strengthen the patriarchal status of the male artisan within his family as well as bolstering other paternalistic privileges.[107] However, although there were many outbursts during this period against the new rhythm of production and its deleterious social and cultural consequences—from food riots to the burning of the Albion mills to the first waves of Luddism and frame breaking in the 1810s—sustained and broad-based nationwide political and economic resistance to industrialization would emerge during the 1820s and 1830s, in the Chartist movement as well as the struggles of a properly industrial working class. "Before the 1820s," Craig Calhoun writes, "artisans had dominated the popular radicalism of England. They felt the industrial revolution largely negatively, as a disruption of or threat to their ways of life and their livelihoods." By the 1830s, Calhoun continues, "the predominance of the artisans had passed. Factory workers and others who were the products of the industrial revolution, not its victims, were the mainstay of Chartism."[108] The new working class that emerged in the 1830s was "properly" industrial in that it was the creation of the new conditions as much as their creator, not merely the first victim of those new conditions, which is how the artisan movements of the early nineteenth century saw themselves.

4. Automaton and Panopticon

As we have seen, the new process of production was one in which a flow of undifferentiated labor could be applied in varying degrees. Again, what counted was averages, rather than exceptions. "Unquestionably, there is a good deal of difference between the value of one man's labour and that of another, from strength, dexterity, and honest application," writes Edmund Burke. "But I am quite sure, from my best observation, that any given five men will, in their total, afford a proportion of labour equal to any other five within the periods of life that I have stated; that is, that among such five men there will be one possessing all the qualifications of a good workman, one bad, and the other three middling, and approximating the first and last. So that in so small a platoon as that of even five, you will find the full complement of all that five men *can* earn. Taking five and five throughout the kingdom, they are equal."[109] Blake would express the results of this formulation a decade later: "Commerce Cannot endure Individual Merit its insatiable Maw must be fed by What all can do Equally well at least so it is in England as I have found to my Cost these Forty Years."[110] Such expressions have generally been taken by scholars to represent a kind of artisan ressentiment—if not merely arrogant elitism—on Blake's part. But most of what Anna Clark tells us are the key features of artisan ressentiment, such as a bitter recourse to patriarchal authority, are absent in Blake, who, as we saw in the previous chapter, associated patriarchal power with tyranny—as in the figure of Urizen. This is not to say that Blake did not feel resentment, but it would be naive to dismiss his critical elaborations of the emergent industrial culture as mere resentment; even worse than naive, it would be misleading, as we would then be tempted to see Blake as a figure of petty bourgeois egotism—a reading which would miss the point entirely. For Blake, as we shall see, the two most destructive processes institutionalized in the modern industrial forms of production were, first, its absolute reliance on a smooth flow of average labor, and second, the structuring distinction between conception and execution, that is, the distinction between (intellectually) planning and directing production and (materially) carrying it out.

The latter principle is also evoked by Burke, who argues that "In all things whatever, the mind is the most valuable and the most important" and who hence insists that "In this scale the whole of agriculture is in a natural and just order; the beast is as an informing principle to the plough and cart; the labourer is as reason to the beast; and the farmer is as a thinking and presiding principle to the labourer. An attempt to break this chain of subordination in any part is equally absurd."[111] The manufactories of the 1790s (and even earlier) extended this same principle from agriculture to industry, intensifying it in the process and rigorously enforcing the distinction between mental and manual labor within the production process. "Many mechanical arts, indeed, require no capacity," Adam Ferguson observed as early as the 1760s; "they succeed best under a total suppression of sentiment and reason; and ignorance is the mother of industry as well as of superstition." Ferguson adds that "reflection and fancy are subject to err; but a habit of moving the hand, or the foot, is independent of either"; this is why, he suggests, "Manufactures, accordingly, prosper most where the mind is least consulted."[112] Neither the industrial reliance on average unskilled labor nor the early factories' strictly enforced distinction between conception and execution escaped Blake's notice.

Thus, Blake's *Public Address* to the Chalcographic (copper-engraving) Society may in one sense be read as the expression of artisan outrage—indeed, Blake himself admits that "Resentment for Personal Injuries" has "some share" in what he writes.¹¹³ But it is also an extraordinarily coherent analysis of some of the key features of modern industrial production, which Blake vehemently opposed on what I think should be taken as principled political grounds, not merely on the basis of personal outrage, much less the bourgeois sentiment that many scholars have detected in some of the text's twists and turns. In seeing that the "Maw of Commerce" must be "fed" by "what all can do equally well," Blake recognized that a modern industrial process of production had to operate on the basis of averages, in which exceptions would be targeted as disruptions to be excluded at all costs, which is why, as Blake quite accurately notes, "Individual Merit" is the "Great hatred" of commerce. Blake's attack on the "Monopolizing Trader" of the era of John Boydell and Rudolph Ackermann, "who Manufactures Art by the Hands of Ignorant Journeymen till at length Christian Charity is held out as a Motive to encourage a Blockhead & he is Counted the Greatest Genius who can sell a Good for Nothing Commodity for a Great Price," is certainly motivated *in part* by his outrage at the principles of industrial manufacture being applied to the art world—especially to the art of engraving.

As we shall see, however, this does not mean that Blake's account cannot and did not *also* function as a critique of the early industrial manufacturing process in general. Readings of *Public Address* as the outraged response of someone who cared to distinguish the "useless arts" from the "productive arts" can all too easily configure Blake as a conservative, like Martin Shee a defender of bourgeois or aristocratic artistic integrity. Certainly, Blake responds with anger to "the destruction of all true art" by the supervention of not merely monopolizing traders but specifically "Picture traders, Music traders & Rhime Traders," who have thereby transformed poetry and music as well as the visual arts into processes for the production of "good for nothing Commodities." But what I want to propose is that Blake's outrage has to do with his skeptical attitude toward commerce in general; for, rather than stopping at a denunciation of the incursion of commerce into areas where it does not belong, much of Blake's work denounces commerce as such, mourning the pitiful condition of "Britannias Isle / Round which the Fiends of Commerce smile."¹¹⁴

Especially by the time of *The Four Zoas*, what Blake develops in his poetry is a full-scale critique of the conditions of labor under the disciplinarian rule of Urizen, "the great Work master," who absolutely dominates an industrial and commercial mode of productive organization in which "each took his station, & his course began with sorrow & care / In sevens & tens & fifties, hundreds, thousands, numberd all / According to their various powers. Subordinate to Urizen." Here, Urizen's role as "work master" is quite inseparable from his self-proclaimed role as god ("Am I not God said Urizen. Who is Equal to me"). After he claims for himself the status of "A God & not a Man a Conqueror in triumphant glory," Urizen builds his universal empire:

> First Trades & Commerce ships & armed vessels he builded laborious
> To swim the deep & on the Land children are sold to trades
> Of dire necessity still laboring day & night till all
> Their life exctinc they took the spectre form in dark despair
> And slaves in myriads in ship loads burden the hoarse sounding deep
> Rattling with clanking chains the Universal Empire groans.

Now, the "arts of life"—the archaic "simple workmanship" of the hourglass, the plowman, the waterwheel, the shepherd—are "contemnd," and the "arts of death" are introduced instead, "wheels invented Wheel without Wheel / To perplex youth in their outgoings & to bind to labours / Of day & night the myriads of Eternity. that they might file / And polish brass & iron hour after hour laborious workmanship / Kept ignorant of the use that they might spend the days of wisdom / In sorrowful drudgery to obtain a scanty pittance of bread / In ignorance to view a small portion & think that All." When in *Public Address* Blake denounces the art of William Woollett and Robert Strange for being "the Lifes Labour of Ignorant Journeymen," and contrasts "Journeymens undecided bungling" with "the firmness of a Masters Touch," and "Manual Labour" with work of "Genius," we can certainly detect—as Morris Eaves so richly documents—the anger of a highly skilled craftsman facing the dire and very real threat of being reduced to an unskilled or deskilled industrial laborer. Indeed, it would hardly be surprising if Blake felt that his depiction of laboring under the despotism of Urizen was not merely a matter of the poetic imagination, but a lived experience for himself and "fellow labourers," in whose "Approbation" he writes that he has Enough; "this is my glory & exceeding reward I go on & nothing can hinder my course."[115] But for all the immediacy of this threat as it is digested in *Public Address*, it is hardly as though Blake thought the industrial and commercial system would be fine if left to its own proper sphere of activity in the "useful" arts, since it is clear from his writings long before *Public Address* that he regarded a despotic (Urizenic) system of organization—whether political, economic, artistic, or religious—as damnable in itself.

What Blake condemns here, in other words, is the despotism of any mode of organization that hierarchically separates leaders from followers, priests from laymen, kings from subjects, masters from workers, and hence subordinates obedience to regulation, belief to doctrine, execution to conception, physical practice to mental process, organ to organism, copy to original. Blake's denunciation of "servile copying" has often been read in strictly aesthetic terms, like his rejection of the subordination of engraving to painting; but it should also be considered as an economic, a religious, and a political matter as well, in the same sense that Urizen's role in the univeral empire is simultaneously and inextricably political, religious, and economic. What is being denounced here, in short, is that coercive and yet productive combination of despotism and discipline which was essential at once to absolute monarchy, to state religion and the organized church, and to the industrial mode of production emerging so catastrophically in Blake's own lifetime. As I discussed toward the end of the previous chapter, from Blake's standpoint, any despot—"God or Priest or King," Urizen, Nobodaddy, overseer, taskmaster, boss—is much like any other; any code of conduct or disciplinary mechanism or punitive apparatus is much like any other—"All Penal Laws court Transgression & therefore are cruelty & Murder"—and all tend toward the moral law of the Old Testament, the Ten Commandments which are the "most oppressive of human codes, & being like all other codes given under pretence of divine command were what Christ pronounced them, The Abomination that maketh desolate, i.e., State Religion, which is the source of all Cruelty."[116]

For any disciplinary system, whether political, religious, or economic, virtue is primarily understood in terms of obedience. In economic terms, for example, as Blake notes in *Public Address*, "Obedience to the Will of the Monopolist is calld Virtue." Blake recognized that he was living in a world in which increasingly what mattered "is not whether a Man has Talents & Genius . . . But whether he is Passive & Polite & a Virtuous Ass: & obedient to the Noblemens Opinions in Art & Science." Hence it is of some interest to turn to that "Memorable Fancy" in *The Marriage of Heaven & Hell* in which some of the principles of antinomian faith are stated most explicitly. In response to the smiling Angel who rhetorically asks, "has not Jesus Christ given his sanction to the law of ten commandments and are not all other men fools, sinners, & nothings?" the Devil there retorts, "If Jesus Christ is the greatest man, you ought to love him in the greatest degree; now hear how he has given his sanction to the law of ten commandments: did he not mock at the sabbath, and so mock the sabbath's God? murder those who were murderd because of him? turn away the law from the woman taken in adultery? steal the labor of others to support him? bear false witness when he omitted making a defence before Pilate? covet when he pray'd for his disciples, and when he bid them shake off the dust of their feet against such as refused to lodge them? I tell you, no virtue can exist without breaking these ten commandments: Jesus was all virtue, and acted from impulse: not from rules." Clearly, the kind of obedience demanded by authoritarian organizations, whether religious, economic, or political, would be quite incompatible with even the most basic principles of antinomian faith in love and community. Now perhaps we are better able to understand why in the late eighteenth century antinomianism was repeatedly denounced as a threat to the law, and even to duty of any kind. "The sanctions of all religions are obligations to duty," William Hurd writes in his history of religion; "and the word duty implies three things, namely, our duty to God, to our neighbour, and to ourselves." He adds that "All these things are, however, despised by the Antinomians, and they teach, that men may sin as much as they please; because however God may hate sin, yet he takes pleasure in forgiving it."[117] Clearly, however, an antinomian rejection of religious obedience did not stop at religion, but went on to a disregard for any kind of moral or disciplinary authority; it was incompatible with any form of authoritarianism, whether religious, political, or economic.

This is significant for our purposes because what I want to suggest in the following sections of this chapter is that Blake's critique of early industrial production, in the illuminated books and *The Four Zoas*, as well as in *Public Address*, draws together simultaneously economic, religious, and political concerns. What Blake is concerned with is any form of organization that generates and disciplines its constituent organs, that organ-izes disciplined, subservient constituents. In this respect, Blake must be seen to be articulating two sets of discursive and material practices—the political and the economic—which were beginning to be treated quite separately in the 1790s and in the decades immediately afterward, and increasingly distinguished into the separate discursive domains of politics and economics. Our investigation of Blake's work now requires that we consider the development of this distinction, and hence the emergence of two discourses of sociopolitical and economic organization (i.e., organization of society and of the factory), in order ultimately to see how Blake's illuminated books not only mediate between the two but subject them to a common critique. We need first to consider the development through Blake's lifetime of a properly modern industrial mode of production, as well as a new form of discourse defining and articulating it; then we will turn to the domain of sociopolitical organization.

The manual labor required for the production of any manufactured commodity involves a series of steps akin to the stages of a unilinear narrative. Notwithstanding outside hardships and pressures, a preindustrial or independent craftsman or artisan would in principle control not only each step of the process, but the overall production "narrative" through which the separate steps are strung together into a continuous sequence resulting in the finished product.[118] Here, both the intellectual and physical aspects of production distinguished by Ferguson and Burke are united in the craftsman, who exercises mental control over his own manual labor, determining its speed, intensity, rhythm, and flow. This was the case, for example, with Blake's own mode of producing his illuminated books. As Marx points out, "a craftsman who performs the various partial operations in the production of a finished article one after the other must at one time change his place, at another time his tools. The transition from one operation to another interrupts the flow of his labour and creates gaps in his working day, so to speak."[119] Marx puts this tentatively because the very notion of such gaps in time depends upon a modern conception of time as an independent continuous flow, rather than time identified with and defined by a series of events, as it often is in premodern temporal conceptions.[120] The transition between successive stages of the production process would amount to a temporary disruption of the production narrative stream, "so to speak," to the extent that this stream is seen to take place on a flow of time that goes on with or without production. In other words, this could be understood as a "loss of time" only to the extent that time itself is understood or imagined as a continuous homogeneous flow, the units of which are either made use of as they flit by or are lost forever in "innumerable short pauses, separately of little account, but great when added together."[121] After all, as one factory inspector noted later in the century, "moments are the elements of profit."[122]

If, on the other hand, instead of being unified as they are in the artisan's labor, the different stages of the production of a particular commodity are divided up so that each is executed by a different worker, these "gaps" in the working day are closed, and the production process becomes at once more intensive, more efficient, and more productive.[123] The flow of narrative time and work time can thus keep up with the perpetual flow of empty homogeneous time itself—especially if labor takes place continuously around the clock, as was already becoming increasingly common during the 1790s.[124] In Blake's lifetime this kind of intensity of labor, in which workers were pushed beyond their limits, was perhaps most evident in the textile industry because of its widespread use of machinery. "Whilst the engine runs the people must work," observes Sir James Kay of the Manchester mills; "men, women, and children are yoked together with iron and steam. The animal machine—breakable in the best case, subject to a thousand sources of suffering—is chained fast to the iron machine, which knows no suffering and no weariness."[125] He adds, "the operatives are congregated in rooms and workshops

CHAPTER THREE

during twelve hours in the day, in an enervating, heated atmosphere, which is frequently loaded with dust or filaments of cotton, or impure from constant respiration, or from other causes. They are engaged in an employment which absorbs their attention, and *unremittingly employs their physical energies*. They are *drudges* who watch the movements and assist the operations of a mighty, material force, which toils with an energy ever unconscious of fatigue. The *perservering labour* of the operative, must rival *the mathematical precision*, the *incessant motion*, and *the exhaustless power of the machine*."[126] Working at the relentless rhythm of the machine—even in industries, such as Boulton's toy-making factory or Wedgwood's porcelain factory, where the machinery was much less sophisticated and dramatic, but where the identical principle of the division of labor into its constituent elements ("animal machines") was still deployed for increased productivity and efficiency—the precious flow of time is thus conserved rather than disrupted. As Charles Babbage observes, the time that would otherwise be lost in having a single worker change from one task to another is saved.[127]

Babbage, a member of the Royal Society and a founder of the Analytical Society, is best known as the inventor of the card-punching analytical engine (which, although he never actually completed it, was the conceptual forerunner of the modern digital computer). But with *The Economy of Machinery and Manufacture* (1832), in which he argues that "the arrangements which ought to regulate the interior economy of a manufactory, are founded on principles of deeper root than may have been supposed," he was also among the earliest theoreticians of the modern industrial production process.[128] Drawing on what were already three or four decades of industrial and protoindustrial experience, and seeking the maximum economy of time, Babbage argues that the most efficient manufacturing process would be one in which the stages of the production "narrative" could be simplified and broken up into its constituent elements or stages. Once each stage is defined according to a particular action and "reduced to the use of some simple tool,"[129] it can be assigned to one particular worker to perform continuously. By the 1790s, in Wedgwood's porcelain factory, for example, the workers "were not allowed to wander at will from one task to another as the workmen did in the pre-Wedgwood potteries," Neil McKendrick points out. Instead, "they were trained to one particular task and they had to stick to it."[130] This was partly a result of Wedgwood's firm belief that "the same hands cannot make *fine, & coarse — expensive & cheap* articles so as to turn to any good account to the Master."[131] But it was also, clearly, the result of a quest for improved efficiency and productivity.[132]

Drawing on Babbage's researches much later on, Marx would observe that the result of this arrangement for the worker "who performs the same simple operation for the whole of his life" is that he "converts his body into the automatic, one-sided implement of that operation. Consequently, he takes less time in doing it than the craftsman who performs a whole series of operations in succession."[133] But Babbage, writing in the early 1830s, sees the result, from another perspective, in terms of the more efficient purchase and application of a quantified stream of abstract labor power. "The master manufacturer," he points out, "by dividing the work to be executed into different processes, each requiring different degrees of skill and force, can purchase exactly that precise quantity of both which is necessary for each process; whereas, if the whole work were executed by one workman, that person must possess sufficient skill to perform the most difficult, and sufficient strength to execute the most laborious, of the operations into which the art is divided."[134] Because of the considerable savings in time and labor power and the resulting increase in efficiency and productivity, Babbage concludes that, when "the number of processes into which it is most advantageous to divide [the manufacturing process] is ascertained, as well as the number of individuals to be employed, then all other manufactories which do not employ a direct multiple of this number, will produce the article at a greater cost."[135]

At least according to these early theorists of factory production, it is evident that in the division of labor within a factory the intellectual function of supervision and decision making—the determination of and control over the narrative process of production—no longer resides with the workers, each of whom now performs what Jeremy Bentham identifies as "one single operation of such perfect simplicity, that one might defy the awkwardest and most helpless idler that ever existed to avoid succeeding in it."[136] Instead, the intellectual control of the narrative process, and of the flow of space and time by which it is constituted, resides with a supervisory power that stands outside and above the narrative flow itself. "When each process has been reduced to the use of some simple tool, the union of all these tools, actuated by one moving power, constitutes a machine," Babbage writes, adding that, "in contriving tools and simplifying processes, the operative workmen are, perhaps, most successful; but it requires far other habits to combine into one machine these scattered arts."[137] The control and management that can indeed draw together these scattered arts now pertain to the factory owner or supervisor.

"The cooperation of wage-labourers is entirely brought about by the capital that employs them," Marx points out, echoing Babbage. "Their unification into one single productive body, and the establishment of a connection between their individual functions, lies outside their competence. These things are not their own act, but the act of the capital that brings them together and maintains them in that situation." Hence, Marx adds, "the interconnection between their various labours confronts them, in the realm of ideas, as a plan drawn up by the capitalist, and in practice, as his authority, as the powerful will of a being, who subjects their activity to his purpose."[138] The concentration of control in the supervisory power is literalized by the way in which discipline is enforced and the pace of work set, whether by machines or supervisors, whether by the rhythm of the line or the sounding of bells and whistles, and by the way in which the workers are arranged "in sevens & tens & fifties, hundreds, thousands, numberd all / According to their various powers." Indeed, the authoritarian despotism of Blake's Urizen must be understood not only in religious and political terms, but in economic terms as well. Urizen is not just a figure of God & Priest & King, but of a supervisory regulating power as well; a power distinguishing mental from manual labor by concentrating intellectual power in itself and delegating brute physical labor to its remoter appendages—human machines—according to a centrally determined rhythm and intensity. This is the kind of organized despotism resolutely attacked in Blake's work.

The earliest factories operated to extremely rigorous—even fanatical—temporal standards, with a rigid series of times by which certain functions had to be performed, and a long series of fines and punishments for cases when they were not. Again, in Wedgwood's factory, for example, there were precise times when the bell of the bell works should be rung: first at 5:45 A.M. ("or a quarter of an hour before [the men] can see to work"), then for breakfast at 8:30, again at 9:00 to resume work, and so forth until "the last bell when they can no longer see."[139] The factory owners took their obsession with time to what might seem to be pathological extremes, "snatching a few minutes" here and "nibbling and cribbling at meal-times" there. But they were quick to point out that five minutes cut from lunch or breakfast and multiplied by a number of workers added up to a great deal of time—and a great deal of money, since, as one owner pointed out to the factory commissioners, for even one worker, "five minutes a day's increased work, multiplied by weeks, are equal to two and a half days of [unpaid] produce in the year."[140]

The sweeping and comprehensive concentration in the Urizenic supervisory power of the intellectual principles of the narrative of production (to which, as Burke points out, the manual principles must be held subservient) is reinforced by the greatest possible evacuation of skilled knowledge from the workforce. "On the handicraft plan, labour more or less skilled, was usually the most expensive element of production," as Andrew Ure observes; "but on the automatic plan, skilled labour gets progressively superseded, and will, eventually, be replaced by mere overlookers of machines."[141] However, it is not merely that skilled labor is regarded here as unnecessary and useless because the intellectual functions and knowledge of production and narrative control have been appropriated by a supervisory power. Rather, skill, talent, training, ability, are regarded as principles of interference and disruption to the process, if only because they present an unevenness, an irregularity in the smooth dispersion of average labor power. "By the infirmity of human nature it happens," Ure argues, "that the more skilful the workman, the more self-willed and intractable he is apt to become, and, of course, the less fit a component of a mechanical system, in which by occasional irregularities, he may do great damage to the whole."[142] The principle already posited by Burke and Ferguson—and angrily recognized by Blake—here becomes absolute. It was a matter not just of outrage but of insight on Blake's part when he recognized that this form of organized production really cannot endure individual merit; "its insatiable Maw must be fed by What all can do Equally well." Individual merit is its "Great Hatred" because in industrial production, not merely must skill, knowledge, power, control, and determination of the narrative of production reside with the supervisory power: any expression of will on the part of the worker is taken to pose a threat to the smooth flow of the process and must be suppressed by means of fines and punishments.

Thus, not only is the rhythm and pace of the work not determined by the workers themselves. For the purposes of this form of production, the workers must be evacuated not just of skill but also—to the greatest possible extent—of any sense or expression of will, even of independent movement. All of their actions and motions must be determined by the authors of the narrative process: hence Wedgwood's fervent desire "to make such *machines* of the *Men* as cannot err."[143] The workers are therefore divided up and assigned to tasks not as individual organisms, but rather as subservient organs, "animal machines" linked to iron machines and driven by an outside power. In Ure's rather fanciful version of this process, the space of the factory becomes one in which workers are nearly totally relieved of the necessity of thought and voluntary action. "In those spacious halls," he writes of the textile mills driven by steam power, "the benignant power of steam summons around him his myriads of willing menials, and assigns to each the regulated task, substituting for painful muscular effort on their part, the energies of his own gigantic arm, and demanding in return only attention and dexterity to correct such little aberrations as casually occur in this workmanship."[144] However, as the Hammonds remind us, the early factory worker "was summoned by the factory bell; his daily life was arranged by factory hours; he worked under an overseer imposing a method and precision for which the overseer in turn had to answer to some higher authority; if he broke one of a long series of minute regulations he was fined, and behind all this scheme of supervision and control there loomed the great impersonal system."[145]

The opposition posited by Ferguson and Burke between mental and physical operations is, again, taken to its furthest extreme, and—as is evident from the language of Wedgwood, Fielden, Ure, Babbage, Kay and others—even in this early industrial moment the ideal factory would be the one in which the workers are transformed into simple machines devoid of their own will and intellect and wholly subservient to the will of the supervisory power, just as the arms and legs of a man are to his mind. Proudly announcing in 1791 the virtues of his Panopticon—a disciplinary space designed with factories in mind at least as much as prisons—Jeremy Bentham exclaims, "What hold can any other manufacturer have upon his workmen, equal to what my manufacturer would have upon his? What other master is there that can reduce his workmen, if idle, to a situation next to starving, without suffering them to go elsewhere? What other master is there, whose men can never get drunk unless he chooses they should do so?"[146] Indeed, embodied both in the sternly enforced behavioral and temporal codes keeping the manufactory under control (the panopticon is an extreme version of this, of course) and also in the tools and machines of labor as well, with their often unrelenting pace and rhythm, the disciplinary authority held by this power now begins to assume an intensity akin to that of an omniscient god. Again, Urizen with his iron books of laws is the great example of this, and it is difficult not to see the same kind of despotic pride evoked by Bentham in Urizen's gloating boast that with such power it is easy to "reduce the man to want a gift & then give with pomp / Say he smiles if you hear him sigh If pale say he is ruddy / Preach temperance say he is overgorgd & drowns his wit / In strong drink tho you know that bread & water are all / He can afford Flatter his wife pity his children till we can / Reduce all to our will as spaniels are taught with art."[147] The principle at stake in such reduction to "our will" is the separation of mental direction from manual labor in an organized hierarchy. "The separation of the intellectual faculties of the production process from manual labour, and the transformation of those faculties into powers exercised by capital over labour," Marx argues, would by the late nineteenth century be "finally completed by large-scale industry erected on the foundation of machinery. The special skill of each individual machine-operator, who has now been deprived of all significance, vanishes as an infinitesimal quantity in the face of the science, the gigantic natural forces, and the mass of social labour embodied in the system of machinery, which, together with those three forces, constitutes the power of the 'master.'"[148]

However, as is clear, for example, in Bentham's celebrated project of the panoptic "inspection house," already in the late eighteenth century, this principle was, as Green and Belchem point out, evident in the newly intensified manufacturing process characteristic of the early industrial age, even in factories not dominated by machines. Again, Wedgwood's porcelain factory provides an ideal example of the way in which "moral machinery" could be combined with "mechanical machinery" for efficient production.[149] When the control over time and space is fully established, the production narrative is amplified, and the industrial manufactory is at its most efficient and productive. "It is clear that the direct mutual interdependence of the different pieces of work, and therefore of the workers, compels each one of them to spend on his work no more than the necessary time," Marx writes. He adds, "this creates a uniformity, a regularity, an order, and even an intensity of labour, quite different from that found in an independent handicraft or even in simple co-operation."[150]

Indeed, at its most efficient, with the workers properly disciplined and orchestrated, the factory with all its workers functions as kind of extended machine. This is the case not only in that, as Sir Frederick Morton Eden worries, each worker would be "made to perform the office only of a machine, or, in other words, where he can exercise no intellectual faculties, nor display a single virtue, besides that of patient submission"; and not only in that, as Fielden says, the worker is merely "a living machine and not a free agent"; and not only in that, as an early parliamentary committee on factories pointed out, the workers taken together "are only regarded as parts of the machinery which they set in motion." Rather, even apart from whatever mechanical machinery (i.e., mechanisms made of iron and wood) might be in use, the group of orchestrated workers itself functions collectively as a machine, so that, as Ferguson anticipated long before the deployment of steam, "the workshop may, without any great effort of imagination, be considered as an engine, the parts of which are men."[151]

In even the early industrial manufactory, the distinction between human and nonhuman parts really does break down altogether, so that what we are left with are simply different kinds of machines working in concert—a fusion of human task workers and their metal tools—the union of which, "actuated by one moving power, constitutes a machine," according to Babbage.

However, Babbage makes it clear that the existence and operation of such a machine is not confined to workshops in which mechanical devices are used along with human labor. Rather, just as he says "the division of labour can be applied with equal success to mental operations, and that it ensures, by its adoption, the same economy of time," the machine we are considering here is clearly a mode of work and practice that is not by any means confined to the manufactory as such.[152] This kind of machine is simply a process linking a number of interchangeable human organs together into a larger organism. Such machines may be found in all areas of society, especially insofar as society is itself thought of as a kind of assemblage, "a fictitious *body*," as Bentham puts it, "composed of the individual persons who are considered as constituting as it were its *members*."[153]

This conception becomes even clearer in the work of Andrew Ure (with Babbage another of the earliest prophets of the modern assembly line). Ure also conceives that the factory, "in its strictest sense, involves the idea of a vast automaton, composed of various mechanical and intellectual organs, acting in uninterrupted concert for the production of a common object, all of them being subordinated to a self-regulated moving force."[154] What is particularly striking about the language that Ure uses here, of course, is that he introduces precisely the same conceptual slippage between the mechanical and the organic that Blake himself was tinkering with in his illuminated books. Neither purely mechanical nor purely organic, an automaton could be both a mechanism that seems to be an organism—and an organism that behaves as though it were a mechanism. In other words, long before the appearance of the cyborg in the twentieth century, the automaton represents the convergence of the organic and the mechanical, the human and the machine—that point at which the human becomes a machine, and the machine a human. As Ure describes it, then, the factory constitutes an automaton in which not only have the human and nonhuman elements combined imperceptibly, but both sets of elements have surrendered their will to that of the automaton as whose "mechanical and intellectual organs" they serve. Almost exactly like the inhabitants of the world of the illuminated books, adaptively organ-ized to the finite Urizenic world, Ure's automaton is an assemblage, a simultaneously mechanical and organic monster brought to life by the elements that constitute it.

In his theorization of cooperative production long before the advent of heavy industry as we generally understand it, Marx takes Ure's argument one conceptual step further in his all-important distinction between what he calls the "specialized" worker and the "collective" worker. On the one hand, the specialized worker, according to Marx, performs what Bentham refers to as "one single operation of . . . perfect simplicity." The collective worker, on the other hand, represents for Marx the gathering together of a number of these specialized workers into a larger subjective assemblage. More than merely an automaton, Marx's collective worker constitutes a genuine subject, an identity, even a gendered "he." Articulated together and animated by a common logic and narrative, the specialized workers become "special organs of a single working organism that acts only as a whole and therefore can operate only by the direct cooperation of all."[155]

Endowed with a subjective and gendered identity as an assemblage of the specialized workers and their tools and implements, Marx argues, "the collective worker now possesses all the qualities necessary for production in an equal degree of excellence, and expends them in the most economical way by exclusively employing all his organs, individualized in particular workers or groups of workers, in performing their specialized functions." Thus, Marx concludes, "the one-sidedness and even the deficiencies of the specialized individual worker become perfections when he is part of the collective worker. The habit of doing only one thing converts him into an organ which operates with the certainty of a force of nature, while his connection with the whole mechanism compels him to work with the regularity of a machine."[156] Here too, especially insofar as he is describing a mode of cooperative production already evident in the late eighteenth century, Marx is working in very much the same conceptual continuum that Blake was working with in the illuminated books; and for Marx as for Blake, the most oppressive feature of this despotic form of organization—which would be taken to new extremes in the modern factory—is the way in which it restricts and confines its constituent elements to particular identities: organic identities which have been generated as a result of an overall productive and organ-izational logic.

In identifying not only the collective worker but also the production process itself as "a productive mechanism whose organs are human beings," Marx reintroduces the same slippage already seen in Ure, between the mechanical and the organic. What is evidently most "natural" about the collective worker is his human organs, the little specialized workers—human beings stripped of their own agency and acting now merely as moving parts for a machine-like assemblage larger than themselves. And what is evidently most "mechanical" about the collective worker is ironically his very own sense of identity and subjectivity, which "compels him to work with the regularity of a machine." The organic and the mechanical have become virtually interchangeable here. The human being is at his most organic when serving merely as an integral part of a larger mechanism; and the machine is at its most mechanical when endowed with life as a virtual human subject—again, like the subjects we see assembled both organically and machinically in Blake's illuminated books.

This of course takes us full circle back to where we began with the constitution of the laboring subject (fictive or otherwise—indeed, here the point is that such a "subject" is always fictive, rather than given once and for all time as was supposed in the liberal tradition that Blake was contesting). The "whole" that is approximated by the collective worker is no more—but also no less—real than the "whole" approximated by each of the specialized workers in turn. The binary opposition between organ and organism breaks down as each such "whole" turns out to be an assemblage of a number of parts. The distinction between organ and organism is not absolute. Neither is reified except as a contingent result of the process of production, a process that generates its own identical and interchangeable producers as well as the stream of identical and interchangeable finished products which is spewed out as a result of their labor.

Ultimately, then, two great lessons may be derived from theorizations (and experiences) of the early or manufactory. The first is that what is a machine can be recognized as a kind of organism; and in precisely the same way, what is organic or natural can be understood in mechanical terms. In this context, in other words, an organism, including a human organism, can be thought of as a machine with various parts—a thought anticipated long before such factories in Hobbes's *Leviathan*—and a machine as an organism constituted by various organs.

The second lesson, however, is that such an approach does not involve a simple binary opposition between a whole and its constituent parts. Parts and organs are defined and constituted according to their assigned function, to which they are forced to adapt—they have little or no "meaning" or identity on their own. Far from being reified, their meaning is in other words entirely contingent on their location within the organism or the machine itself, a location which changes from assemblage to assemblage. The overall logic that unifies them and makes sense of them—endows them with a sense of selfhood, purpose, and identity—is evident only at the level of the organism or the machine, once all the parts and organs are united and are working together for a common purpose, which in the case of the manufactory is the production of a stream of identical commodities according to a certain narrative scheme. Imploding the binary, we have again come full circle: identity and meaning, and even subjectivity itself, are here the products of contingency and location, even of function, instead of a priori reifications whose existence can be taken for granted as the products ⌐ and nature's god."

This is the very logic that we have already seen at work (at the beginning of this chapter) in *America*, in which the various organs, sinews, tissues, and so on, of the freed slave spring in freedom from the dark oppression of the mill. Blake's slave with all his body parts is not, however, merely an allegorical representation of an industrial laborer, nor is the plate discussed above simply a mimetic replication of the hierarchical organizing logic of industrial labor. Blake can certainly be seen to be tinkering with exactly the same concepts that were being used in his lifetime to think through (and to organize) an industrial logic of production, a form of authoritarian despotism that he contested in the illuminated books and other writings including the *Public Address*. But that plate of *America*, like Oothoon's impassioned speeches in *Visions of the Daughters*, also hovers at the liminal moment uniting the logic of the organization of labor in industrial production and the generation of unitary (bourgeois) subjectivity. If in the conceptual continuum elaborated in the illuminated books, as we have seen, both organs and organisms are determined by an external supervisory power, neither can be taken for granted as autonomous or transcendent entities, given once and for all time.

Thus, the most significant point here is not simply that Blake has discovered in the logic of organization one of the foundational ideologemes of industrial production; it is that in the illuminated books this logic is also shown to be foundational for conceptualizations of unitary psychobiological subjectivity in an expanded social, political, and cultural domain well outside the gates of the earliest factories. In other words, the dark satanic mill here is a figure not just of the organization of production in early industrial society; it is a figure of the social, political, and religious constitution of the individual psychobiological subject, determined—produced—by social and political circumstances, rather than being given by the laws of nature and nature's god. Moreover, the subject can also be recognized as a form of imprisonment, confinement, and restriction as deleterious as occupational confinement in a productive industrial organization. In contrasting the deskilled journeyman with the skilled craftsman, in other words, Blake was contrasting two forms of social, political, and religious organization, not just two levels of productive skill or two ways of producing art (which is generally how critics read those lines). Art, society, economics, politics, and religion must be seen here as one continuum, not segregated areas of activity. Blake's condemnation of the threat to "individual merit" is not an expression of bourgeois individualism, but rather an expression of a desire for

CHAPTER THREE

freedom from domination and confinement into a restricted role, whether as organ or organism.

Perhaps the most striking figuration of this process in Blake can be seen in way in which the constitution of Urizen's body is inseparable from the constitution of the chains of linear time: thus, the "fallen" human body anticipates, even complements the assembly line, so that the sovereign subject—with all his supposed freedom and liberty—is revealed to be the mirror image of the factory drone. Indeed, the mechanico-organic automaton that we encounter in contemporaneous theorizations of industrial production appears in Blake's illuminated books as a figure of the individual subject as well as of the deskilled industrial laborer. For example, both the individual subject (organism) and the individual laborer (organ) embody the forms of confinement that Oothoon dreads in her speeches in *Visions*. The slave rising from his labors at the mill in *America* can be seen on the one hand to be escaping the despotic confines of the site of organized production; but on the other hand, he can also be seen to be escaping the equally despotic confines of individual selfhood. Freedom in either case involves an escape from the confines of reified finitude and into a joyous and unrestricted form of being (a premise that we shall investigate in greater detail in the following chapters). In other words, the dark satanic mill in Blake's illuminated books describes not just a place of labor (though it certainly is that as well); it also describes a form of organized restriction, confinement, limitation: of action, of belief, of thought, of imagination, of desire, of activity; of religion, politics, economics, and art—practices and discourses that it is difficult to meaningfully separate in the work of Blake. "The bounded is loathed by its possessor," Blake wrote in one of his very first independently printed texts; "The same dull round even of a univer[s]e would soon become a mill with complicated wheels." But, he continues, "Less than All cannot satisfy Man," and against the dull confined restriction of the mill—the individual subject, the monad, the dedicated taskworker—we have to remember that in Blake's terms, "the desire of Man being Infinite the possession is Infinite & himself Infinite." From such a standpoint, as I suggested earlier, it becomes possible, even necessary, to see the transition from the basic antinomian claim that "He who sees the Infinite in all things sees God" to another basic claim, that "God becomes as we are, that we may be as he is," as the expression of an extremely serious and potent *political* desire utterly incompatible both with the logic of industrial organization and with the logic of individual bourgeois subjectivity.

If this is so, however, it is surely no longer the case that the most appropriate deliverance from a despotic division of labor is a "return" to a more unified consciousness that, perhaps through a Schillerian play-drive,[157] would reunify the subject. In other words, the best way to challenge one form of division (in labor) is to invoke not another form of division (in society), but rather an end to such arbitrary divisions altogether. The unified bourgeois consciousness, the romantic artist, the genius, are identities as limiting and constraining as that of the simplest taskworker, their necessary counterpart in bourgeois society. Indeed, what becomes clear in the illuminated books is that the division of labor in manufacture (with its extreme subdivisions and limitations, pertaining to the "organ") and the seemingly opposite logic of bourgeois subjectivity (with its emphasis on the unity and coherence and will and desire of the unified "organism") are not as opposed as they might seem, and instead share the very same political and epistemological basis, amounting to two sides of the same coin. The production generated by the "organs" enables the pleasurable consumptions of the "organism," for example. It is no coincidence that bourgeois pleasures are based on consumption, and even that bourgeois identity is largely predicated on self-expression through consumption. Again, this is the very logic that Blake is getting at in *America*, which enables our recognition that the human subject—rather than being something that has always already had a self-evident existence as defined by reason, nature, and nature's god, and so on—is a product like any other, an assemblage, a machine: a making machine, a consuming machine, a desiring machine, a living machine.[158] This requires much further elaboration, which I will turn to partly in the conclusion of the present chapter and partly in the chapters that follow.

5. The Chains of Subordination

The key to the industrial manufacturing process—a feature that would persist in large-scale machine production and through the period of Taylorism and Fordism well into the twentieth century—is that it is a form of production which is a form of re-production. That is, the products emerging from any given industrial production narrative (at least until the regime of "flexible accumulation" of our own time) are at least theoretically identical, produced in a *linear* stream generated by a *cyclical* process of continuous and uninterrupted repetition. If "uniformity and steadiness in the rate at which machinery works, are essential both for its effect and its duration," Babbage was already noting in the 1830s, "nothing is more remarkable, and yet less unexpected, than the perfect identity of things manufactured by the same tool." Thus, he concludes, the key principle "which pervades a very large portion of all manufactures, and is one upon which the cheapness of the articles produced seems greatly to depend," is "that of COPYING, taken in its most extensive sense."[159] In other words, the division of labor in manufacturing finds its perfection in a means of production that consists of the generation of an endless series of theoretically if not always actually uniform copies of a prototype. If the industrial commodity is always by definition a copy rather than an original, the "mechanical and intellectual organs" of the factory may be seen more than ever as reproductive organs, bringing forth a series of "abhorred births" into the world. Here we are reminded once again of the passage in *Visions of the Daughters of Albion* in which the reproductive labors of the "whore" are likened to a nightmarish version of factory labor with its rods and wheels, in which the woman-womb is forced "all the day, & all the night / To turn the wheel of false desire" and bring into the world "cherubs in the human form, / That live a pestilence, & die a meteor, & are no more." Again, this suggests a continuity between the logic of factory production and the logic of sexual reproduction when women are instrumentalized, treated like machines (this need not rule out other forms of production and generation, of course).

The key to mass production, in turn, is of course mass consumption, and the mass consumption of the late eighteenth century was already characterized by a striking degree of conformity and homogeneity. "A larger and more homogeneous market was the basis of mass-produced factory output," Neil McKendrick argues, adding that by the late eighteenth century "the pattern of change was now more uniform, and more than ever at the behest, and for the convenience, of commerce."[160] The relatively simple reproductive capacity of the early factories could not accommodate too much or too rapid flexibility and change, and hence—particularly with luxury consumer products such as the articles of fashion which drove the early consumer revolution—thus required a fairly consistent demand for a certain homogeneous product in order to produce it economically (and profitably). McKendrick argues that entrepreneurs like Boulton and Wedgwood "needed to ring the fashion changes in order to keep up and inflate even further the buoyant home demand of the late eighteenth century, but having set their production machines to meet its fickle needs, they needed to be able to control and 'fix' its fugitive character for long enough to profit fully from its potentialities before its successors were, in turn, allowed their fleeting fashion life-cycle."[161] Thus, the widespread conformity of late-eighteenth-century tastes, anchored in London, was particularly suited to the standardized output of the early factories.[162] Moreover, the consumption of these articles of fashion and leisure, which drove the consumer revolution, was taken to be the basis of the emulative self-fashioning denounced in 1795 by the

Rev. Edward Wilson for the way in which it introduced "habits of luxury and expense universally disproportionated to income, which greatly increase the number of the indigent, and contribute to their degeneracy and debasement."[163] In this moment of the emergence of what Bill Brown has identified in a different context as a material unconscious, self-fashioning and even self-recognition were increasingly produced and sustained by patterns of consumption and display.[164]

Another striking aspect of this system of re-production, of which we have already taken note, was the extent to which the principle of homogeneity extended from the endless re-production of homogeneous and interchangeable products to the generation of un- and even deskilled laborers to serve the production process as its organs. Such laborers may perform certain particular functions within the productive machine that they help to constitute, but they themselves are stripped of their own will, and hence, however particularized they may be as "organs" of production, they are interchangeable as autonomous "organisms." It is ironic that a system of production catering to the desires and wills and needs of a population of consumers—who even in Blake's time were being encouraged to express their individuality through their consumption—should depend for its very operation on the cooperative labor of a number of people altogether stripped of the possibility of individuality and self-expression, at least during their working hours (which of course often consumed their entire lives). In distinguishing "servile copying" from "determined Execution," Blake can be seen to distinguish not just two ways of producing art, but also two ways of constituting the art worker himself. In other words, for Blake the separation of "invention" from "execution" depends as much on a despotic hierarchy of labor as it does on two ways of sitting down to produce a drawing.

Marx would later note in a similar context that the despotism of the factory provides a striking contrast with the anarchy of the modern social system with which it is reciprocally caught up—a contrast that forms one of the most profound structural contradictions of modern society. For in the relationship of consumption and production, or consumer and producer—Blake would call them the devourer and the prolific[165]—there exists a contradiction which defines the relationship of society to factory. By Marx's time, this contradiction was glaring and obvious. "The same bourgeois consciousness which celebrates the division of labour in the workshop, the lifelong annexation of the worker to a partial operation, and his complete subjection to capital, as an organization that increases its productive power, denounces with equal vigour every conscious attempt to control and regulate the process of production socially, as an inroad upon such sacred things as the rights of property, freedom, and the self-determining 'genius' of the individual capitalist." Thus, Marx points out, "it is very characteristic that the enthusiastic apologists of the factory system have nothing more damning to urge against a general organization of labour in society than that it would turn the whole of society into a factory."[166]

When it first began to emerge in the discourse of liberty, however, the challenge to the despotism of the social order of the ancien régime would initially be inseparable from a certain sociocultural (rather than economic) challenge to the logic of factory production itself. "Foul befal the government," warned Thelwall, "that considers the great mass of the people as brute machines; mere instruments of physical force; deprived of all power, and destitute of all right of information; and doomed, like the dray-horse, or the musquet, to perform, mechanically, whatever task of drudgery, or murder, a few 'counsellors and deliberators' may command."[167] For reasons that lie outside the scope of the present study, those challenges would later separate into the contradiction noted by Marx, in which the social anarchy of the market is seen to be fully compatible with the despotic form of production which sustains it, so that the supposed freedom of the former is distinguished from the actual submission of the latter—and, indeed, so that the supposed freedom of the former can be fantasized as a kind of genuine liberty in the first place, a liberty independent of any social or historical constraints, given for all time as one of the "laws of nature and of nature's god."

It could be argued that bourgeois cultural and ideological norms emerged out of an initial rejection of this logic of mass conformity, which was already evident in the slowly industrializing society of the late eighteenth century.[168] The middle class and the new system of production emerged with each other in a continuous relationship. However, a recognition that mass production and mass consumption entailed each other, that the homogeneous consumer and the homogeneous producer ("organism" and "organ") were two sides of the same coin, was unacceptable—even unimaginable—to certain bourgeois writers, who were keen to rescue the cultural originality and sovereignty of the individual subject from subjection to economic conformity and interchangeability. The middle-class cultural revolution consolidated during the romantic period, which was given its clearest expression in the doctrine of liberty, involved the rejection of this principle of homogeneous equivalence, which was, as we have seen, the fundamental basis of modern economic and political systems and the production techniques that emerged with them.

For whereas the elaboration of this seamless continuity lies at the heart of Blake's illuminated books, from at least the time of Tom Paine and the advocates of liberty and the rights of man, as I suggested in the previous chapter, the bourgeois cultural revolution was founded on a tireless insistence on the sanctity of the individual with certain inalienable rights and with origins extending back to the earliest prehistoric times. These ideological principles—and bourgeois culture itself—were therefore premised, founded, and grounded on the rejection of the social and historical creation and location of the individual subject, on the insistence that the individual subject is given for all time as both the point of departure and the final culmination of social "progress," rather than as a kind of automaton like the ones we see assembled in a mechanico-organic process in Blake's work. The concept of the sovereign individual which defined the very core of the discourse of liberty may be considered "ideological" in the narrow sense to the extent that—as a matter of definition—it denies and covers over the social and historical conditions of its own existence and coming into being and imagines itself as a force beyond social and political contingency and cultural location.

In any case, during the 1790s, even if the contradiction between social anarchy and despotism in production was already visible to some as a potential, a very different pattern of acceptance and denial—and a very different sense of threat—emerged, and it opened up possibilities for critical insight that would be rendered ideologically more difficult later on in the nineteenth century. For in the 1790s, society was itself thought of, at least by some, precisely as a kind of factory, as a kind of organic whole, a continuous moral-mechanical organism like the ones we see at work in Blake's books. For whatever ideological and cultural reasons, in the later part of the nineteenth century such an insight would become more difficult to articulate, when, as Marx observes, however machine-like the production process made people, they were regarded as autonomous individuals outside work. But in the late *eighteenth* century, the production process already spewing out a stream of homogenized products (with which it would later "batter down all Chinese walls") could be imagined as extending beyond the increasingly homogenized and interchangeable producers themselves to encompass society as a whole. The order and hierarchy of the factory could be seen to be fully compatible with the reigning cultural and ideological norms and standards of an as yet still strictly hierarchical society that was still not defined by the fantasies of individual fluidity and self-expression that would be associated with the middle class (whose very "middleness" is by definition potentially all-encompassing and all-inclusive rather than being definitive and exclusive like the aristocratic residuum of the ancien régime that it eventually supplanted).[169]

CHAPTER THREE

In the 1790s, there did not seem to be much contradiction between the despotism of the factory and the anarchy of the social order, because that order was itself still largely despotic and, if anything, was seen by some to be *threatened* by the anarchy of the market ("in a nation of gamesters," as Burke cautioned, "the many must be the dupes of the few who conduct the machine of these speculations").[170] As I suggested in the previous chapter, the despotism of the factory emerged seamlessly out of a social order which was itself founded upon principles of patriarchal hierarchy and power; both of which are contested by Blake. This enabled a certain discourse of social production in which "useful" workers were seen to be generated by various social institutions. But it also made it possible to imagine all of society as a kind of machine, or a continuous organism. This is why it is generally the case, according to conservative writers, that the inevitable result of the disruption of the subordination of servant to master would be the disruption of the subordination of subject to king, and hence why from this standpoint economic and political revolution are inseparable. For here political and economic subordination and hierarchy—both regulated by seemingly unquestionable political and economic laws and backed by a religious faith in patriarchal power—are seen to be continuous, inside the manufactory and outside it as well.

According to this conservative standpoint, the relationship of the different members of society to each other once again functions much like the relationship of a number of organs to the organism that they constitute, adapted here for social and political rather than simply economic purposes. The difference is that in this case there is a strict hierarchy of these "organs," which are by no means interchangeable or equivalent, and which are not capable of even a momentary existence as autonomous organisms. Here, as we shall see in greater detail in chapter 6, the movements of the social organism itself are strictly determined by the higher (mental) organs, even if they are executed by the lesser (manual) ones which carry the weight of the burden. The "gentleman" in one of the dozens of 1790s political dialogues sponsored by the Association for the Preservation of Liberty and Property from Republicans and Levellers insists to his interlocutor, a mechanic (i.e., a worker in a manufactory), that "every order in society is instituted for the common good of every other order; that no one particular rank can exist without tending to produce that general effect." Hence, the gentleman adds, "the distribution of men, into various classes of labour and opulence, is not a rule of our government, but a law of our nature. Some are appropriated to mental, some to bodily activity." Each person, he concludes, "is but an engine in the great mechanism of circulation."[171] In such discourse, the Urizenic despotism of the factory can be seen to be operating in an expanded social and political setting; the dark satanic mill can be recognized as a figure for modern society in general and not merely for industrial production in particular.

From a conservative standpoint, the hierarchical discipline of the manufactory was therefore continuous with that of the social system itself, which is precisely why a threat to the one always constitutes from this perspective a threat to the other. One way to think of this is to see the conservative vision as in fact more logically rigorous and straightforward—and even, at some basic level, more honest and self-reflexive—than the liberal one. As I argued in the previous chapter, the advocates of liberty in the 1790s claimed that it ought to be possible to distinguish political equality from economic equality, and to enable the former while preventing the latter. Thus, one might work as a mere "organ" in the economic realm, as a *producer*, but enjoy the rights and pleasures of an independent "organism" in the political and cultural realm, as a *consumer*, so that, as Marx would later observe, economic despotism could be seen to coexist with political and even cultural freedom, if only under the banner and the rubric of consumer choice. Here the all-important distinction is between one's status as a producer caught up with the dictates of an economic process and one's status as a consumer free to choose from the products of that process.

For conservatives, however, economic subordination and political subordination—and hence one's status as both producer *and* consumer—go hand in hand. Economic inequality is therefore simply a necessary and inevitable correlate of political and cultural inequality. "We cannot all be masters or all servants," one pamphlet of the Association for the Preservation of Liberty and Property from Republicans and Levellers pointed out in 1792: "wealth will be the lot of some, and labour and poverty of others. Those distinctions will arise from the unconquerable nature of things, which promote the union, and form the security of social life."[172] Another pamphlet from around the same time notes, "by this happy Inequality, and dependence of one man on another, employment is found for all, in their several vocations to which they have been called by design or accident."[173] Moreover, John Bowles claims, "the Inequalities of Society are really calculated for the benefit of all," for "these very Inqualities," he hastens to add, "tend as much as human means can do to promote an Equality of happiness."[174]

Here the principle of the division of labor that is at work in the manufactory, as well as the subordination of manual to mental labor with all its consequent inequalities, is seamlessly extended into society as a whole. "It is vastly better, for us *all*," Richard Hey argues, "that there should be one set of men to make Shoes, another to make Coats, and another to make Laws; rather than that all these should be both Shoe-makers, Taylors, and Lawmakers. It would not be at all convenient or good for us, that Men of all Educations, Trades and Professions, should break off their employments, every one a little now and then, to make a few Laws, and then return to their work."[175] What counts here, yet another conservative writer points out in 1792, is not simply the general inherited principle that "the rich inhabitants should be few, and the laborious many; and that the subordination of the different classes to each other, is the life and soul of every species of manufactory," but the far more specific organic principle that "the different members of the body are made for different functions, but it is the co-operation of all, in the respective discharge of them, that gives energy, effect, and indeed life to the system."[176] Quite explicitly, in producing such an argument, the conservative writers deployed—or, rather, appropriated—a specific reading of that memorable passage in *Corinthians* ("all the members of that one body, being many, are but one body; so also is Christ") of which the antinomian tradition, and Blake in particular, would produce an almost diametrically opposed reading (see chapter 6). The image that we have already encountered in *The Four Zoas* of an organized system in which constituent elements are distribiuted "in sevens & tens & fifties, hundreds, thousands, numberd all / According to their various powers. Subordinate to Urizen," is as appropriate as a figure of this despotic social and political system as it is as a figure of the despotism of factory labor.

Thus, for conservatives an insistence on the equality and equivalence of the organs of the social body, as of the organs of the manufacturing body of the factory, would be absurd, as absurd as confusing a simple organ with an independent organism, as absurd as supposing that the one could become the other. Such differences are to be maintained at all costs. Here the political logic and the economic logic—whose differentiation is paramount to the cause of liberty—become fully integrated and unified in the conservative cause. On the one hand (in the words of William Playfair), "any attempts to approach what is called a full and equal representation, must be attended, as they were in France, with anarchy and revolution, from which, I hope, the Providence that watches over England will long preserve this happy land."[177] And on the other hand, if we were to suppose, with the author of *A Word in Season*, that "the working manufacturers of Manchester or Birmingham should be so far inflamed by these new-fangled doctrines of the Rights of Man, as to say to their masters, 'We have toiled for you long enough, you shall now toil for us:—It is by our skill and industry that you are become rich, we will, therefore, have our rightful share of the wealth acquired by our means.' Of such an operation of the Rights of Man, what would be the consequence?" The answer, of course, is inevitable: "Ruin to all—to the rich, who would be despoiled of their property; and to the poor, who would, thereby, lose every means of future maintenance and support. Indeed, it appears to me, that, in places particularly devoted to trade, manufactures, and commerce, there can be no evil so much to be dreaded as popular commotions."[178] The "setting up Equality of Ranks, and Liberty without any bounds,"[179] such conservatives argued, would not only produce riots and commotions, but would be tantamount to the sudden seizure of the social body with a traumatic mental collapse, a breakdown in order and behavior as certainly calamitous for the nation as it would be for a person who had suddenly lost all control over his limbs and organs and degenerated into a total breakdown.

Clearly, such conservative arguments mobilized the logic of the social division of labor in order to justify social as well as political inequalities: because of the population's uneven and unequal distribution, this argument goes, the social body requires careful regulation and maintenance in order to maintain these distinctions, since they are the very source of the life and vitality of the social body. "If we compare the ruling members of the body politic, to the superior faculties in the human frame," writes William Hamilton Reid, "it will appear that there is a natural correspondence, and apposite relation between the lowest and worst passions in individual existence, and the tumultuous motions, the furor, or the panic fears of democracy in the great world, or organized society; while Aristocracy, from its stability, and the superior enlargment of its views, naturally approximates to Reason, and the cardinal virtues of Prudence, Justice, Temperance, and Fortitude."[180] Here the principle of governmentality is directed at the regulation of the social body, and in particular the kind of biopolitics of the social body which was the object of the work of writers such as Colquhoun and Burke, for whom the paramount question is how the form of the social body can be disciplined, cultivated, nourished, its diseased members and cancers either reformed and cured or cauterized and amputated, its resources enhanced, more productively and efficiently distributed, its population more effectively managed, channeled through a series of coercive and disciplinary institutions (hospitals, asylums, workhouses, prisons), or, when redundant, given the treatment appropriate to what Bentham called "an excrementitious mass" that should be projected "as far out of sight as possible," spewed out to the farthest reaches of the nascent empire.[181]

Both an economic revolt ("levelling") and a revolution in the political system ("republicanism") would be the equivalent of madness and insanity

CHAPTER THREE

for the social body in which all are organs—greater or lesser, some more "mental," others more "bodily," some more dignified, others less so—within the larger organism. This organism is identified by Burke not as civil society but precisely as the state, from which it was yet impossible to distinguish a civil society—that is, "a permanent body composed of transitory parts; wherein, by the disposition of a stupendous wisdom, moulding together the great mysterious incorporation of the human race, the whole, at one time, is never old, or middle-aged, or young, but in a condition of unchangeable constancy, moves on through the varied tenour of perpetual decay, fall, renovation, and progression."[182]

To enable the mobility and fluidity—to admit the independent will and subjectivity—of individual organs within this state would be to destroy its very basis as a continuous whole, so that "no one generation could link with another" and "men would become little better than the flies of a summer evening." The loss of rigid distinctions between the different organs constituting the social body—that is, an admission of their status as mere individuals, "flies of a summer evening," would according to Burke assuredly result in total anarchy. "No part of life would retain its acquisitions," he warns with the greatest urgency; "Barbarism with regard to science and literature, unskilfulness with regard to arts and manufactures, would infallibly succeed to the want of a steady education and settled principle; and thus the commonwealth itself would, in a few generations, crumble away, be disconnected into the dust and powder of individuality, and at length dispersed to all the winds of heaven."[183]

The "chain of subordination" that Burke imagines linking the laborer to his master certainly does not stop at the edge of the workshop, therefore, but rather continues in his depiction through the entire organically unified social body that he identifies as the state. In fact, the chain of subordination in the social body ought to be more powerful and compelling even than that of the workshop. "Society is indeed a contract," Burke writes in the most evocative passage of *Reflections on the Revolution in France*, which it is worth quoting here at length:

> Subordinate contracts for objects of mere occasional interest may be dissolved at pleasure—but the state ought not to be considered as nothing better than a partnership agreement in a trade of pepper and coffee, callico or tobacco, or some other such low concern, to be taken up for a little temporary interest, and to be dissolved by the fancy of the parties. It is to be looked on with other reverence; because it is not a partnership in things subservient only to the gross animal existence of a temporary and perishable nature. It is a partner-

ship in all science; a partnership in all art; a partnership in every virtue, and in all perfection. As the ends of such a partnership cannot be obtained in many generations, it becomes a partnership not only between those who are living, but between those who are living, those who are dead, and those who are to be born. Each contract of each particular state is but a clause in the great primeval contract of eternal society, linking the lower with the higher orders, connecting the visible and invisible world, according to a fixed compact sanctioned by the inviolable oath which holds all physical and all moral natures, each in its appointed place.... This necessity is no exception to the rule; because this necessity itself is a part too of that moral and physical disposition of things to which man must be obedient by consent or force; but if that which is only submission to necessity should be made the object of choice, the law is broken, nature is disobeyed, and the rebellious are outlawed, cast forth, and exiled, from this world of reason, and order, and peace, and virtue, and fruitful penitence, into the antagonist world of madness, discord, vice, confusion, and unavailing sorrow.[184]

For Burke, then, the reason and order of the social body depends upon all physical and moral "natures" accepting and respecting the positions appointed to them by fate. Such a submission to the rule of necessity is not simply the principle of the manufactory, clearly, but of the higher—social and political—existence compared to which the manufactory and the economy itself are matters of a gross and temporary nature. The admission of the principle of individuality—a chaos of elementary principles abstracted from the unified whole to which they belong—is itself the key to disaster, to the "antagonist world" of madness and confusion. The individual organs of the social body are not merely interdependent: as transitory parts they should have no independent existence at all, and the process in which they replace each other by emerging, growing, decaying and dying does not affect the "great mysterious incorporation," of which they are mere parts, an organic incorporation that exists "in a condition of unchangeable constancy."

One of the most striking things about this synthesis for our purposes is the extent to which the discourse of the manufactory (recall Ure and Babbage) seems like an uncanny replication of the political vision of someone like Burke, with the patient submission to the rule of necessity transposed from the social body to the body of the collective worker or the automaton. This is precisely the mediation effected—though in an oppositional way—by Blake's illuminated books, which anticipate the seamless continuity of these two forms of despotism, the political and the economic. In both cases, the subordinate (human) organs of the machine must be evacuated of their own will and purpose and submit to the direction imposed by the higher intellectual faculty, over which they have no control. In both cases, the paramount distinction between the manual and the mental, or the lower and the higher, or the permanent body and its transitory parts, completely overrides the distinctions among the transitory parts themselves. Each has its appointed place certainly—"numberd all / According to their various powers"—but each can easily be replaced by a similar unit; in fact, in Burke the replacement of such parts is so smooth as not to be noticed by the permanent body, in which it takes place in a process of "perpetual decay, fall, renovation, and progression."

The difference between the bourgeois discourse celebrating the manufacturing process and that of the conservatives of the old order is that the former imagines the opening up and development of a realm beyond production in which it ought to be possible to be free from the rule of necessity, whereas the latter does not. For bourgeois discourse, the realm of freedom is of course that of politics, and also that of culture—that realm in which an independent consumer can choose a unique mode of self-fashioning and hence self-identity—both defined by the logic of consumer choice (choice of products, choice of representatives). This depends upon the possibility of being able to open up just such a realm, in which autonomous organisms can make choices, in which, in fact, there can be not only an autonomous organism in the first place, but the possibility for making choices based on sensory input and the rational choices enabled by the regulation of the five senses.

But if, as Blake's work insists, the organism making these choices is seen as a product of the system which also produces the objects of consumption from which it chooses, what we are left with is no longer autonomy and freedom, but a closed circuit of production and consumption, producer and consumer, organism and organ, all generated by the same continuous process as parts subservient to the requirements of a larger whole composed by them. In other words, if the principle of homogeneous equivalence is extended from the products of this process—that is, commodities—to its producers, the exteriority fantasized by middle-class writers—and the fantasy of a realm of cultural and political freedom—is threatened with annihilation. If the logic of the reified object is extended to the logic of the reified subject, it becomes difficult to imagine a realm within this process which might avoid or evade the laws of the commodity and hence the rule of necessity; in other words, it becomes difficult or impossible to imagine genuine freedom within such a social system. If it is true, as Blake would write toward the end of his life, that "since the French Revolution Englishmen are all Intermeasurable One by Another, certainly a happy state of Agreement to which I for One do not Agree," freedom in the bourgeois sense becomes impossible to imagine, and liberty the sort of thing that Blake would surely have called a contemptible falsehood. Indeed, his very refusal to go along with the happy Agreement being consolidated during his lifetime should be read not—as it sometimes has been—as the expression of bourgeois intellectual autonomy but rather as the expression of an alternative political and cultural position, one antithetical to the argument centered on the liberty of the individual subject and the fantasy of a realm of freedom supposedly beyond or prior to the domain of social production. "To imagine that, sheltered from the omnipresence of history and the implacable influence of the social, there already exists a realm of freedom," Fredric Jameson argues, "is only to strengthen the grip of Necessity over all such blind zones in which the individual subject seeks refuge, in pursuit of a purely individual, a merely psychological, project of salvation. The only effective liberation from such constraint begins with the recognition that there is nothing that is not social and historical—indeed, that everything is 'in the last analysis' political."[185] Indeed, in articulating the sense in which everything must be situated within the domain of social, cultural, and economic processes, Blake is, in effect, arguing that there can be no escape from the determination of the social field and its rule of necessity (a question that we will explore at greater length in chapter 6). For what Blake offers is an alternative from both the inescapable organic and political hierarchy of the conservatives on the one hand, and the vision presented on the other hand by the advocates of liberty, in which the cultural and political freedom of the bourgeois organism is seen to be mutually compatible with the economic enslavement of the worker as an organ within the production process. Blake rejects the simple opposition of organ and organism, and with it the supposed freedom opened up with this opposition by the advocates of liberty. At the same time, he also rejects the tyrannical hierarchy called for by the conservative and reactionary writers and by various state apparatuses. What he proposes instead is a kind of freedom—into the infinite—that is ultimately incompatible with the unitary subject and with bourgeois society, as well as with the disciplinary "codes of cruelty" of both the ancien régime and the emergent cultural and political order which was to replace it.

6. Images of Truth

In the final pages of the present chapter I would like to raise the question of why Blake might have been a privileged observer of this process of historical and cultural transformation, and to return to the discourse of liberty from which Blake's prophetic books mark such a significant departure. To do that, of course, we must return once again to the site of labor.

First let us go to the site of Blake's own labor. As I have suggested already, it is significant that the prime example which Babbage would deploy to illustrate the logic of modern industrial production is neither the steam engine nor the textile mill but rather—of all things—copperplate engraving. In Babbage's analysis, as we have seen, the industrial factory operates according to a logic of production that has been transfigured into re-production through the generation of a series of theoretically identical commodities. Babbage locates the precursor—really the archetype—for this re-productive process in copperplate engraving, in which, he says, "the impressions from the same block, or the same copper-plate, have a similarity which no labour could produce by hand. The minutest traces are transferred to all the impressions, and no omission can arise from the inattention or unskilfulness of the operator."[186] According to Babbage, the efficient modern factory should ideally reiterate this very logic, producing a stream of identical copies based on the same original impression. The industrially produced commodity thus represents a kind of copy or indeed an "image" of the prototype.

Thus, the image becomes for Babbage the central concept driving the production process in even the earliest factories. The latter can now be thought of as machines re-producing material "images," replications of an original that stands outside the production process. Here the commodity can be thought of as a kind of image; or, to put it the other way around, the mass-produced and circulated image may be recognized as the ultimate commodity. Now, however, the industrial process with its division of labor into an assemblage machine made up of a number of deskilled taskworkers enjoys a decisive superiority over the original copperplate engraving, whose logic of image re-production the factory inherits and brings to perfection. The image copies generated in copperplate engraving are the results of a labor-intensive process. Moreover, as Babbage points out, most of this labor goes to waste in making what may be thought of as the prototype, since "an artist will sometimes exhaust the labour of one or two years upon engraving a plate, which will not, in some cases, furnish above five hundred copies in a state of perfection."[187] Eliminate the plate—eliminate the "original"—and you eliminate the waste of time and labor that goes into the making of a block or copperplate that is not itself to be put up for sale. One would then be left with nothing but the copies, which take comparatively little effort, and less skill, to stamp out. Thus, Babbage's factory appropriates the logic of the copperplate engraver, but it distributes the labor involved—originally embodied in the well-trained and highly skilled artisan toiling away on the surface of the copperplate—among the organs of the "collective worker," that is, the assemblage of all the specialized workers working together. And it does so by eliminating the need for a highly elaborated and unprofitable—uncommodified—original, and requiring the generation instead of nothing but the "copies," images with no real referent.[188]

Ironically, just as—or perhaps just before—copperplate engraving was recognized as the archetype of the modern industrial process, the art of engraving was in Blake's time being transformed by precisely the same principles of production efficiency and the division of labor that were already animating the early factory. Much of this transformation hinges on distinctions we have already touched upon, particularly those between mental and manual labor and between original and reproduction. Once again, these are issues that will be taken up at greater length in later chapters, but here it is important to recall the extent to which these transformations were taking place, as well as the extent to which they play a role in Blake's own work—in the conditions of his production, to be sure, but also in the work itself.

Morris Eaves, Robert Essick, and others have pointed out that by the late eighteenth century even the art of portrait painting was already anticipating the efficiency and the logic of the assembly line. Joshua Reynolds (who was, along with Francis Bacon, Isaac Newton and Locke, among Blake's favorite rhetorical targets) was the prime example of this tendency, since the various details of his portraits would be filled in by the taskworkers who specialized in hands, landscapes, animals, fashionable clothing, hats, backgrounds, and so on, and Sir Joshua would come along only to complete the face itself.[189] At around the same time, Rudolph Ackermann was using a similar process to mass produce colored prints in an assembly line set up according to a division of artistic labor.[190] Wedgwood, with his simultaneous mission to at once make "Artists" of "mere men," and "to make such machines of the Men as cannot err," was of course the inspiration for much of this.[191] The ideal worker in such schemes was indeed an "artist" who functioned as a machine in precisely the way that the earliest theorists of modern production system (e.g., Ure and Babbage) would later argue.

One of the most significant examples of such transformations was the Shakespeare Gallery project set up by Boydell to produce paintings and engravings for a mass market. "Boydell realized that engraving was more than another department of the arts," Morris Eaves argues; "it was the missing link with commerce: engraving, as it reproduces painting, makes painting commercial."[192] Boydell's approach—which aroused the anger of commen-

CHAPTER THREE

tators such as John Landseer and Martin Shee, as well as contemporary engravers such as James Barry and of course William Blake—was to distinguish the "mental" and "mechanical" aspects of art and engraving. In his art factory, he assigned the mental tasks of original conception and execution to painters and the mechanical tasks of mass reproduction to engravers, whose task was to generate a stream of identical copies—images both literally and in Babbage's sense—based on the "real" artists' original conceptions. These image-commodities were relatively inexpensive for the very reasons that Babbage would later identify with assembly line production, that is, because of efficiency and mass duplication.

Certainly, in such an engraving factory, the relationship of the various copyists, whose work was seen as mechanical rather than mental, would anticipate the division of labor within other kinds of factories. However, Boydell's scheme represented simply an intensification of processes already at work in the late-eighteenth-century art world. Long before the Shakespeare Gallery, the engraver James Barry (one of Blake's few heroes) had warned against the prevailing British tendency "to contract the art itself, to split it into pieces, and to portion it out into small lots, fitted to the narrow capacities of mechanical uneducated people."[193] Years later, as we have already noted, Blake himself would reiterate the same warning and say that the art of engraving was being lost in England as it was being transformed into "the Life's Labour of Ignorant Journeymen, Suited to the Purposes of Commerce no doubt, for Commerce cannot endure Individual Merit; its insatiable Maw must be fed by what all can do Equally well." Henceforth, there could be no art, Blake insists, but such as is "Subservient to the interest of the Monopolizing Trader," a figure "who Manufactures Art by the Hands of Ignorant Journeymen till at length Christian Charity is held out as a Motive to encourage a Blockhead, & he is Counted the Greatest Genius who can sell a Good-for-Nothing Commodity for a Great Price."[194]

My point here is not to explore the distinction between original artistic conception on the one hand and the process of "manufacturing art" on the other (a question to which we will return later on—though we should already be wary of the way it lends itself to misleading distinctions between the supposed originality and creativity of the bourgeois "organism" or genius and the merely manual labor of the productive "organs" in a factory).[195] It is, rather, to remind us of the extent to which art, and especially the form of art to which Blake had been trained and apprenticed and by which he earned a living, was by the 1790s already subject to the pressures of industrial production. Even in workshops not as efficiently commercial as Boydell's, engraving was by its reproductive nature more subject to commercial and industrial pressures than other art forms. Robert Essick points out the many tasks necessary for preparing a copperplate for printing. "Most of these operations," he adds, "were purely mechanical and, when repeated again and again on dozens of plates, tended toward monotony." In larger workshops, these tasks would be delegated by the highly skilled master to his apprentices and journeymen.[196]

The principles of standardization and uniformity which Babbage would (not coincidentally) emphasize later on were thus already essential to the accuracy and efficiency of engraving. These principles extended from the formal preparation of the copperplate to the content of the engraved or etched image itself, since "the demand for uniformity in copy engravings resulted in a repetition of the same linear patterns to represent similar objects, textures, and lighting in different prints." Thus, Essick argues, "a division of labor in the engraver's shop intensified standardization because the work of each man had to fit imperceptibly with all the others. The economic and artistic systems reinforced each other, for both demanded the division of the plate as well as the engraver's working hours into uniform, discrete, and infinitely repeatable units."[197] Morris Eaves suggests accordingly that the kinds of artistic products (engravings) generated by this quasi-industrial process were both quantitatively and qualitatively determined by the technologies and methods involved, so that, as he writes, "the artistic product of the machine becomes what the machine is able to behold."[198] We have already encountered a similar closed circuit of perception and imagination in Blake's depiction of subjectivity in *America*, to which we will return, and it is worth remembering here that the psychosocial terrain that the modern reader of *America* and the other prophecies encounters is alienating precisely because it does not conform to the cognitive apparatus through which it is perceived.[199]

Robert Essick observes that it was the ability of copperplates "to bear exactly repeatable images that gave them their primary importance in an age before photography."[200] This is certainly the case. But we know from our own engagement with Babbage that the concept of the minutely reproducible image is the key not only to techniques of graphic reproduction—the discursive history in which Essick and Eaves and others have very rightly situated Blake—but also to modern factory production in general. Thus, the form of art to which Blake was apprenticed from his youth, and by which he made his living as an adult, happens to be doubly privileged (not quite the right word in this context) for the understanding of modern industrial production, first because it was among the earliest forms of production to deploy what can be recognized as an industrial process based on the division

CHAPTER THREE

of labor, and second—at least as important—because it was concerned with the reproduction of the image, which lies at the very heart of modern capitalist culture.[201]

One immediate point to be registered here is that Blake experienced the cultural revolution of modernization not from the so-called margins, but from the privileged site at which the relentless logic of production merged with and was absorbed into the equally relentless logic of reproduction in the generation of identical image-commodities that lay at the heart of capitalist industrialization. Jacob Bronowski wrote long ago that "there is nothing odd in what happened to Blake; for it was happening to many thousand others. The fine London watchmakers were becoming hands in sweatshops. The learned societies of the Spitalfields silk-weavers were rioting for bread. The small owners were losing their place, and the skilled workers were losing their livelihood." This is a "murderous story," Bronowski adds, "and it is Blake's story. But it is not the poet's story, nor the painter's. It is the story of Blake the engraver."[202] Bronowski's argument may be seen as a useful corrective to those—far too many—readings of Blake that tend to disassociate Blake the poet or Blake the artist from Blake the engraver (though perhaps Bronowski here goes too far in the other direction). All three Blakes were grounded in the same set of material circumstances, and we can certainly see in all three something of the artisanal rejection of the new industrial order, given that the artisan radicals of the early industrial period in London were, as Craig Calhoun argues, "not only opposed to the free play of market forces, they were opposed to all forces which had the prospects of destroying the particular virtues of their trades."[203]

Blake certainly experienced the cultural revolution of modernization at one of its focal points, and this undoubtedly lends explanatory power to a great deal of his angry denunciations of commerce, monopolizing traders, ignorant hirelings, and above all the detestable Sir Joshua Reynolds, "a Man Hired to Depress Art."[204] After all, Blake himself is the first to admit that, "Having spent the Vigour of my Youth & Genius under the Oppression of Sr Joshua & his Gang of Cunning Hired Knaves Without Employment & as much as could possibly be without Bread," his readers must expect to find in his annotations to Reynolds's *Discourses on Art* "Nothing but Indignation & Resentment." He adds, in fairness, an explanation: "While Sr Joshua was rolling in Riches, Barry was Poor & Unemploy'd except by his own Energy; Mortimer was call'd a Madman, & only Portrait Painting applauded & rewarded by the Rich & Great. Reynolds & Gainsborough Blotted & Blurred one against the other & Divided all the English World between them. Fuseli, Indignant, almost hid himself. I am hid."[205]

Any interpretation of Blake's work that does not somehow acknowledge or take into consideration the basic fact that it was—all of it, the poetry and painting fully as much as the engraving—the product of a man who, although clearly "the master of his profession," was resolutely "not employed by those who pretend to encourage art," will face grave difficulties. For one thing, as is already clear, aesthetics and politics are genuinely inseparable in Blake's work, and he often designed his pieces—for aesthetic, conceptual, and political reasons—in ways that challenged all kinds of conventional norms. To anticipate the text that will be the focus of the next chapter, for example, his devastating rejection by Cromek for the designs for Blair's *Grave* (versions of which, as we shall see, he had already included in *America* and *The Marriage of Heaven & Hell*) was precisely due to the extent to which Blake flouted engraving conventions, though he did so for reasons that were motivated at least as much by political and conceptual considerations as they were by aesthetic ones.[206] One of the works that Blake includes in his *Descriptive Catalogue* was, he acknowledges bitterly, "painted in self-defence against the insolent and envious imputation of unfitness for finished and scientific art; and this envious imputation, most artfully and industriously endeavoured to be propagated among the public by ignorant hirelings." If, Blake promises, other artists, "more obedient to an employer's opinions and directions," have flourished while his own work has been "cried down as eccentricity and madness; as unfinished and neglected by the artist's violent temper," he is confident that "the works now exhibited will give the lie to such aspersions."[207] This, of course, they never did. For if Blake was "hid," it was at least as much because he categorically refused to go along with the standards driving his industry, and his world, as it was because he was callously ignored by the commercial art dealers for simple personal reasons.

However, no matter how important these points are, it would be equally shortsighted and mistaken to biographically reduce all interpretations of Blake's work to his status as a starving and resentful artisan caught in the remorseless Maw of Commerce. In fact, much of the meaning-generating power of his work may be derived—and may even only become evident—contextually, marked by the extent to which it contrasts with, and suggests such a significant departure from, the norms and assumptions of the free-market discourse of liberty. Indeed, in challenging the combined production and aesthetic standards to which the art world was gradually forced to conform by the end of the eighteenth century, Blake was at the same time challenging the political assumptions of the discourse of liberty and of his erstwhile companions among the hegemonic radicals.

CHAPTER THREE

If, after such a long excursus, this is no longer—or not already—clear, it ought to be, for we have returned full circle to the beginning of this chapter, to the slave rising in freedom from his labors at the mill. Far from being the rights-of-man individual envisaged by the advocates of liberty, this slave, we will recall, is not an ontologically sovereign whole, but is instead composed provisionally of a dynamic and highly contingent assemblage of "organs" and body parts acting together in a fluid process, rather than having been determined and yoked together as finite organs by an overarching discourse that tyrannically ties them together into a logical order driven by a "higher" reason. The freed slave of *America* hovers at a liminal surface between "organ" and "organism," so that his freedom consists in the fact that he is not limited by having been defined and reified as a particular identity, whether as an organ or as an organism. Freedom, according to this vision, is a freedom at once from the logic of the mere (proletarian) organ working machinically in a production process, and at the same time from the logic of the consuming (bourgeois) organism bound and trapped in the crushing limitations—so bemoaned by Oothoon—of unitary subjectivity. Freedom is in other words freedom from reification and limitation, both in terms of labor and in terms of identity itself. Hovering between the status of the virgin and the whore, Oothoon for her part celebrates the freedom of the virgin, whose pleasures are sustained not simply by multiple lovers, but by the eternal joy of multiple selves. She celebrates this "Love! Love! Love! happy happy love! free as the mountain wind!" which is "open to joy and to delight where ever beauty appears," in contrast to the "self-love that envies all, a creeping skeleton / With lamplike eyes watching around the frozen marriage bed." Love, as an ontological category, must be clearly distinguished from sexual freedom, however, and this passage should be recognized as a celebration of the freedom from individual selfhood rather than as an ode to free sex (which is how it is usually read). To accept her fate as a "whore," acting as a procreative womb, "turning the wheel of false desire" and churning out "the abhorred birth of cherubs in the human form" would also be to accept her fate as a unitary subject, with "five senses to inclose me up," her "infinite brain" now "inclos'd . . . into a narrow circle." If *America* offers any vision of freedom at all, it is a vision of freedom at once from necessity of labor, from the guardian angels of the state, and from the "five gates of their law-built heaven," which at the end of the prophecy are "consum'd, & their bolts & hinges melted," in a simultaneous dissolution of the limitations of unitary subjectivity and of the state that seems to go with it.

In forcing us—in such marked distinction from the writings of the advocates of commercial liberty—to think of freedom as freedom from individual identity and subjectivity as much as freedom from the entrapment of labor under the rule of necessity, Blake accomplishes several things.

First, the modern industrial labor process is seen to generate not only a stream of reified commodities, but also a stream of crippled and stunted organs that serve it, as well as a stream of essentially homogeneous consumers (self-fashioning subjects) that enjoy its products. Thus, the workplace is the site in which these three narratives—labor, commodity, and subject—converge. Second, the commodity and the subject are hereby very closely associated, so much so that they appear to be virtually indistinguishable. Both are literally the products of reification, confinement, and restriction, as opposed to multiplicity and freedom in Blake's sense of those terms (which we will elaborate at greater length in later chapters). Third, the mill must be seen as a process, rather than a location—a process that defines a particular mode of labor, as we have already seen; but also a process that defines a particular mode of thought and of imagination. This principle goes back in Blake's work to one of his first illuminated books, *There is No Natural Religion*, in which he argues against the Lockean tradition (in which the advocates of liberty had their conceptual basis) and insists that "Man's perceptions are not bounded by organs of perception; he perceives more than sense (tho' ever so acute) can discover," and that "Reason, or the ratio of all we have already known, is not the same that it shall be when we know more." This leads him to the declaration that "The bounded is loathed by its possessor. The same dull round, even of a universe, would soon become a mill with complicated wheels." The mill here is in other words that bounded and limited mode of thought, of imagination, of subjectivity, and indeed of life which is celebrated by the advocates of reason and of the rights of man, individuality, and liberty. The mill, whether as the designation of a mode of thought or as the designation of a mode of labor, is a process concerned with reification and limitation, with boundedness, as opposed to the boundless energetic freedom celebrated by Oothoon. The slave is at once the organ working within that process and the organism whose mode of thought and whose very identity is defined by this mill with its complicated wheels.

Perhaps the best way to conclude the present chapter is to anticipate the texts and discussions to be taken up in the next chapters. Most readers of Blake are familiar with one of his earliest prints, designed and dated 1780, of a smiling naked youth with outstretched arms hovering before an intensely illuminated sunburst. Although it was originally untitled (though sometimes loosely referred to as *Glad Day*), Blake added the following line at the bottom of the plate to later versions and thus made explicit concepts already present in the image in a visual register: "Albion rose from where he

CHAPTER THREE

labour'd at the Mill with Slaves: Giving himself for the Nations he danc'd the dance of Eternal Death." The figure (see fig. 2 in chapter 2 above) seems an appropriate enough image of freedom, but it is important to reflect on the nature of the freedom being celebrated here: freedom from labor at the mill. The print can be read at once as an icon of freedom from labor, and of freedom from unitary subjective existence, hence, perhaps, the otherwise inexplicable dance of "eternal death." If we add to what I have said Robert Essick's reading of the plate, new patterns emerge. Essick points out that in the etched image of the youth, and the engraving of the plate in general, Blake reverses one of the standard methods of copy engraving: normally, the engraved figure would be crosshatched against a background which provides contrast for its openness. But in *Albion rose*, it is the background that is densely crosshatched, providing a darkened background against which to see the figure of the youth celebrating his freedom. "By magnifying the least pleasing features of commercial technique," Essick argues, "Blake makes the figure standing before them seem all that much more liberated from their restraints." In this context, it is not a coincidence, as Essick makes clear, that the inscribed date (1780) takes on particular significance, for, he adds, "it was Blake's first full year of independent work after leaving James Basire's shop, the first year of his struggle to liberate his own life and art from the limitations of the copy engraver's craft."[208] Blake's struggle would go on through the rest of his life, of course, and he would succeed in finding such freedom only in his own work, rather than in the commissioned work by which he eked out an increasingly difficult living. Blake's graphic techniques, his aesthetic sense and political sentiments, all fuse together in his illuminated works, which must now be read as celebrations of freedom from the mill with all its deadening wheels, the mill of work, the mill of unitary subjectivity, the mill which threatens to consume life itself.

CHAPTER FOUR

Weary of Time: Image and Commodity in Blake

All men are alike (tho' infinitely various)
—William Blake

The more an image is joined with other images, the more often it flourishes.
—Spinoza

1. Introduction

> The morning comes, the night decays, the watchmen leave their stations;
> The grave is burst, the spices shed, the linen wrapped up;
> The bones of death, the covering clay, the sinews shrunk & dry'd
> Reviving shake, inspiring move, breathing! awakening!
> Spring like redeemed captives when their bonds & bars are burst;
> Let the slave grinding at the mill, run out into the field:
> Let him look up into the heavens & laugh in the bright air;
> Let the inchained soul shut up in darkness and in sighing,
> Whose face has never seen a smile in thirty weary years,
> Rise and look out, his chains are loose, his dungeon doors are open.
> And let his wife and children return from the oppressors scourge;
> They look behind at every step & believe it is a dream,
> Singing, The Sun has left his blackness & has found a fresher morning
> And the fair Moon rejoices in the clear & cloudless night;
> For Empire is no more, and now the Lion & Wolf shall cease.

With these momentous lines, Blake disrupts whatever narrative flow the reader of *America* might have chosen to associate with the American War of Independence, by challenging the sense of linear flow that enabled the hegemonic London radicals to fantasize the migration from America to Eu-

CHAPTER FOUR

rope of a continuous revolution (figured by Paine and others as the "flames of liberty"). According to this radical narrative, such a revolutionary movement would ultimately set the self-owning and self-conscious individual—the modern subject first systematized by Blake's great enemy Locke—free to exercise his natural and god-given rights of consumption ("life, liberty, and the pursuit of happiness") in a world devoid of commercial and political monopoly. *America*, as we saw in the previous chapters, subverts this narrative by challenging and undermining many of its conceptual and political assumptions, as well as its teleological force.

But if this disruption is produced by the prophecy's attempt to blast a hole in what the radicals (and generations of scholars since them) understood to be a continuous and progressive history, it also has the effect of bringing that narrative, and whatever might be understood as the continuum of history, to a sudden and grinding halt. In other words, a moment of clarity is achieved in this prophetic vision by bringing the flow of empty, homogeneous historical time to a momentary pause.[1] For the prophecy shifts our emphasis to a particular moment, and indeed to the time of the moment itself, and away from what had already been identified in Blake's age as the relentless march of progress (which in our own age has been said to culminate in the very end of history itself). Here the moment has a kind of fullness which could never be adequately recognized or addressed through the concept of clock time. For the logic of clock time, empty time, stresses the equivalence and even the quantifiable homogeneity of all of its measurable units, whereas Blake's emphasis on the moment suggests not so much that empty modern time abstracts uniqueness in the name of a relentless homogeneity (of products and producers, and of time itself), but rather that empty time is a mode of thought and of discourse that has no way of reconciling itself with its others, no way of accounting for difference other than in its own terms.

Even if "eternity is in love with the productions of time," time for Blake has no way to acknowledge either the existence of eternity or the uniqueness of the moments by which eternity is continuously constituted, an ever-changing constellation of interlocking, overlapping, sometimes complementary and often contradictory moments. If "the hours of folly are measur'd by the clock," no clock can measure "wisdom" because the unmeasurable, unquantifiable moment, and eternity itself—rather than the stream of empty time—are according to Blake the provenance of wisdom and of prophecy. If the commodity and the sovereign subject and the mode of production with which they came into the world, and hence the psychosocial terrain to which they correspond, are regulated by clock time, the persistence of the moment suggests not simply another way of counting time, but rather other ways of imagining the interaction and mutual constitution of subjects and objects, selves and others, bodies and souls, heavens and hells.

Once again, it will be useful to consider plate 6 of *America*, but in this chapter to move through and between various different discursive, material, and historical contexts in which the plate, and the prophecy itself, intervene, and in terms of which they must accordingly be read. Although these various contexts will be addressed in different sections, the argument presented here will develop out of the repetitions necessitated by returning to the same plate and resituating it in different historical and theoretical domains, some demanding close textual analysis, some requiring theoretical considerations, some taking us to an investigation of the historical and political circumstances surrounding the illuminated books, and some demanding consideration of the technical details of Blake's mode of artistic production. Many of the following sections will depart from *America* and will consider what I take to be closely related works, including *The Marriage of Heaven & Hell*, *Visions of the Daughters of Albion*, some of the *Songs of Innocence and of Experience*, and the illustrations that Blake produced for Robert Cromek's 1805 edition of Blair's *Grave*. If I make no attempt to present a consistent reading of *America* as such, that is because part of what I am trying to establish here is that it is just as productive, perhaps even more productive, to read plate 6 of the prophecy in the discontinuous and heterogeneous verbal and visual context provided by Blake's other works than it is to try to frame it strictly within the context of the prophecy, away from which it opens up so many lines of flight.

2. In Sync and Out of Time

Plate 6 of *America*—which we read in a different context at the beginning of the previous chapter—negates the smooth linear flow of time normally associated with radical discourse of the 1790s. The language of expectation, of the coming dawn of liberty and of deliverance from taxation and monopoly, is all here, but it is presented in such a way that its temporal (and hence its political) logic is collapsed. The plate's verbal component opens with just such expectant language, laden with the cyclical overtones of the coming of day, the end of night, and the changing of the guard, as well as the anticipation of some future and as yet undefined event. However, that expectation is undermined by the second and third lines, which at first seem to emphasize present conditions and then turn to the ambiguous—both physically

CHAPTER FOUR

and temporally inert—stockpile of bones and clay. That ambiguity in turn is succeeded by the sudden movement of the following line, in which the previously lifeless material is suddenly animated, though some afterglow of the ambiguity is retained by the unresolved mix of nouns and verbs, gerunds and participles. The next line also begins with a burst of movement, though its immediacy is shaken by the mixture of possible tenses in the rest of the line: not only does the spring forward take place with reference to a past in which the enabling redemption was made, it happens when—rather than after—the bonds and bars are burst.

The next few lines once again move back to the expectant mode with which the passage began, a series of imperatives with a view to a future moment (the slave is still grinding at the mill; the enchained soul is still shut up in darkness). But then the emphasis returns to the present (his chains are loose; his dungeon doors are open). The slave's wife and children are also the subjects of a biblical-sounding imperative ("let them . . ."), but already they are free and looking behind them at their former captivity, believing it to be a dream. Finally, the text ends as it began, with a set of at once expectant and cyclical references to the turn of night and day. Now, however, both linear and cyclical movement have broken down irreparably: the sun has left his blackness and has found a fresher morning *and* the moon rejoices in the clear night sky. The passage, which had begun at the liminal moment at which night is in the process of turning into day, ends in a kind of no-time in which night and day fully coincide.

This moment of rupture and of clarity marks an intervention in, and a disruption of, several narratives at once. There is the narrative of the struggle for liberty, which was seen to link seamlessly together the American War with the movements in 1790s London. There is the broader narrative of the world history of modernization and progress, of which the struggle for liberty was seen to be the prime mover. More locally, there is the narrative of the nameless freed slave, delivered—like Milton's Samson—from his labors at the mill (see chapter 3). And finally there is the narrative (such as it is) of *America*, the prophetic book in which all these other narratives seem to converge, in layers that many critics since the time of Erdman have taken to be interreferential and allegorical. Thus, the freedom of the slave has been seen by scholars to mark the independence of the United States, the independence of the United States has been taken to mark the emergence onto the world stage of the sovereign subject, and that emergence in turn has been taken to mark the origins of the struggle for parliamentary reform in 1790s London. In each of these cases, the empire that is declared to be "no more" is seen as a transcendent external threat whose dominance could be challenged and finally subdued after a long and arduous struggle, a road leading to what Aimé Césaire would (in a similar context) call the rendezvous of victory—only for Césaire there would be "room for all" at this rendezvous, whereas for the hegemonic radicalism of the 1790s only some are qualified for it.

However, there are problems with all of these interpretations, according to which deliverance from empire marks the telos of both historical narrative and political struggle. The plate is quite inconsistent with such teleological narratives. Although it opens with references to the decay of night and the coming of day—which do indeed lend themselves to teleological narratives—it concludes, as we have seen, with the breakdown of that cycle and of the sense of linear flow leading to a kind of deliverance. For deliverance here marks not the end point of such a narrative, but rather the dissolution and breakdown of narrative itself. Surely the most striking thing about the deliverance here is that it is far from apocalyptic and cosmic; there are plates later on in *America* that bear the hallmarks of such an apocalypse. This deliverance seems banal by contrast.

An examination of the significance of this moment must take into account its location in different temporal contexts. The immediate temporal framework introduced in the plate is the diurnal cycle of night and day, but we also have, especially with the (visual as well as verbal) reference to the grave, the related temporal scale suggested by the cycle of life and death. Finally, there is the temporal scale suggested by the working day, from which the freed slave has been delivered. The working day is of course cyclical, though here it is set against the scale of the working life ("thirty weary years"), which is linear. The different temporal frameworks introduced in the plate interact in a number of ways, both contradictory and complementary. In the case of the cycle of life and death, deliverance comes from death rather than from birth. Paradoxically, the grave here marks the source of life rather than its end. Initially, at least, this seems to be paralleled by the movement from night into day, so that the coming of a new life is symbolized by the coming of the new day. The relationship of the diurnal cycle of night and day and of death and life in this plate of *America*—and indeed all of its multiple overlapping and sometimes contradictory temporal frameworks—is strongly reminiscent of one of the *Songs of Experience*:

> Ah Sun-flower! weary of time.
> Who countest the steps of the Sun:
> Seeking after that sweet golden clime
> Where the travellers journey is done

Chapter Four

> Where the Youth pined away with desire,
> And the pale virgin shrouded in snow;
> Arise from their graves and aspire
> Where my Sun-flower wishes to go.

Here once again the diurnal cycle is closely related to the cycle of life and death. However, there is also the intruding alternate temporality of the working day, and of the journey with a definite end, by which the golden glory of the sunset is figured at once as the final resting place of the sun, and as the end of the sunflower's labor for the day. The weary monotony of linear time—figured in the second line's somber alliteration ("countest the steps of the sun")—is likened to a journey, like the thirty weary years of the slave's labor in *America*, and it cuts across the cyclical temporality by which the journey, and the sunflower's weary labor, will begin the very next day. The sunset, as the end point of each day's linear time, paradoxically marks both the location where the youth and virgin arise from their graves, and the location where they aspire (to go).

Thus there is a rupture between the linearity of daytime and the diurnal cycle, a disjuncture between the end of one working day and the certain knowledge that the flower's time-weary movement will begin all over again the next morning. The youth and the virgin exist precisely in this no-time, paradoxically aspiring (that is, both desiring and breathing)[2] to be in the place where they already are, a desire that can never be fulfilled because it cannot be conveyed in either linear time or cyclical time. It falls, rather, in the gap, the no-time in between, a no-time in which the distinction between past and present breaks down. Hence the indeterminacy of Blake's own grammar, whose very openness encourages multiple and even contradictory readings of the same passage; such grammatical and lexical indeterminateness lend his poetry its characteristic sense of restless vitality. For in that sweet golden clime, it is the youth who *pined* and the virgin *shrouded* in snow who *arise* and *aspire* where the sunflower wishes to go, which is where they already are. The paradoxical temporal doubling-back takes place in the last two lines, and also in the jarring gap between the last line of the first stanza and the last line of the second. "Where the travellers journey is done" is "where the Youth pined away with desire," and "where the Youth pined away with desire" is "where my sun-flower wishes to go." The diachronic movement from "where the travellers journey is done" to "where my sun-flower wishes to go" is intersected by the synchronic movement of "where the Youth pined away with desire / And the pale virgin shrouded in snow."

A similar slippage from diachronic to synchronic time takes place in plate 6 of *America*. If the plate begins with the cycle of night turning into day and if that can be said to parallel the emergence of a new life from the finitude of the grave, by the end of the plate the diurnal cycle has broken down, and sun and moon, day and night, fully coincide. This breakdown in turn calls for a closer examination of the cycle of life and death with which it seems to be so clearly associated at the beginning of the plate. In both *Ah! Sun-Flower* and plate 6 of *America* the figure emerging from the grave is a fully formed youth (or virgin). Ordinarily such figural poetic license might be of no particular interest, but here it takes on great significance because of the question of time with which it is so closely caught up. The fully formed figure who emerges from the grave into the exuberance of youth and beauty clearly precludes any narrative of development, whether the narrative of the newborn infant's growth from birth into adulthood or of the adult's decay into old age and ultimately death. The youth who emerges from the grave in both texts neither grows nor decays but is always already a fully formed figure at the peak of life, in between the growth into adulthood and the degeneration into death.

In this sense, the fully formed youth and the grave have a complementary and reciprocal relationship in these texts. Both mark synchronic moments of transition between the diachronic narrative of development on the one hand and the diachronic narrative of degeneration on the other. In both texts, the youth and the grave also mark moments of rupture in the cyclical movement of life and death, night and day, rest and leisure, departure and arrival. As a result, the cyclical and the linear undercut each other. Because of the diurnal framework with which the plate opens, the slave freed from his labors at the mill seems to be celebrating, like the sunflower, the end of a day's (or night's) labor. But as he celebrates his newfound freedom, the moment of deliverance suddenly shifts from the cyclical to the linear, so that his freedom comes not at the end of the working day, but at the end of a long and weary working life (of thirty years). Thus, freedom from the cyclical time of the working day is transfigured into freedom from the linear time of the working life. The moment of deliverance is located in the gap, the no-time in which repetition slides into interruption, and diachrony into synchrony—a no-time in which freedom is celebrated neither at the beginning nor at the end of a narrative (whether linear or cyclical), but in the disruption of narrative and the implosion or explosion of historical time. This, however, is only the first of many frames for the text on the plate.

CHAPTER FOUR

3. Change through Repetition

The breakdown of linear time and narrative in Blake's works, which we have been exploring so far, is part of what lends it its characteristic flavor. As a result, some people find Blake's work unappealing. Not seeing any immediately obvious meaning, not even recognizing in Blake's text any of the conventions and cues which normally guide readings, they find themselves repelled by the text's seemingly obscure words and bizarre images and ultimately find reading Blake a tiring and unrewarding activity, involving a great deal of effort and very little definite accomplishment. Other readers admire Blake's work for the very same reason: confronting the seemingly impenetrable wall of words and images, they arm themselves with formidable scholarly guides, dictionaries, and code books, writings of long-forgotten mystics and visionaries, and they seek out the text's buried treasures, relishing the extraction of what they take to be the mysterious knowledge contained within, access to which is seemingly barred to all but those who have passed certain (presumably secret) rituals of initiation.

However, neither of these approaches to the illuminated books is consistent with Blake's own assessment of his work and habits of reading. Blake had nothing but contempt for ritualistic mystery and hidden knowledge. Indeed, he recognized these as the essential features of priestcraft and the repressive power of what he called "state religion," which he associated with such notorious "state tricksters" as the bishop of Llandaff and with that version of the Bible which had been repeatedly deployed as "a State Trick, thro which tho' the People at all times could see they never had the power to throw off."[3] Against the closed texts and the careful regulation of knowledge and power which he took to be essential to state trickery, Blake offered a series of "open" texts, suggestive of a kind of reading that would open out from the text, rather than trying to seduce the reader into its hidden confines—a revolutionary model of reading better suited to the uninitiated and the uneducated, and hence to "the people," than to the servants of power.[4] But although Blake once pointed out to a dissatisfied customer complaining of his work's obscurity that "that which can be made Explicit to the Idiot is not worth my care," he explained that the best kind of writing and art is that which "rouzes the faculties to act." He also pointed out that his own work has been particularly well elucidated by children, who "have taken a greater delight in contemplating my Pictures than I even hoped."[5]

This suggests the need to devise a new approach to Blake's work, one that would involve "unlearning" whatever it is that makes us "learned," or taking seriously Blake's implicit suggestion that our very "learning" is what stands in the way of our reading his work with all the freshness of a child, whose "rouzing" faculties are uninhibited by paradigms of reading and by literary, aesthetic, and political conventions, and perhaps even by the regulations of "state trickery" itself. It may be, in other words, that the very way we have learned to read is precisely what prevents us from reading Blake properly, in which case, perhaps embracing—rather than recoiling from, or vainly trying to normalize—those aspects of his work that make it special or unusual might enable not merely greater appreciation for it, but also actual pleasure in reading it.

Of all the special characteristics of Blake's illuminated books, surely the most unusual is the way in which they are constituted by the dynamic relation of words and images. Here again, however, Blake's work pushes us to question whatever conventions might govern the ways we associate words and images, and even what we think of the nature of words, images, and narrative itself. As we have seen, the linear and sequential sense of time essential to narrative, even on those occasions when it is present, is undermined and subverted in Blake's work. This—as Blake's detractors have often pointed out in frustration—is exactly what so often makes them "impossible to follow."[6] Moreover, the pictures in Blake's books rarely simply illustrate the words that they accompany, and even when they do, such "simplicity" is often confounded. Most often, especially in the prophetic books, the words and images seem to operate more or less autonomously, more often than not pulling away from each other and tracing different trajectories.[7] It may be useful to think of the illuminated books not as finite texts, contained within a closed circuit of interpretation as defined by some cage of mutually illustrative (and hence reinforcing) words and images, but rather as *virtual* texts, constituted by, even suspended in, the indefinite and expansive gap between words and images—a gap kept resolutely alive by the open nature of Blake's work.

Thus, in reading the illuminated books, we necessarily find ourselves mediating between words and images, generating active and vital meanings from this very process of mediation. What I am proposing here is of course a very different mode of reading from that undertaken by those readers of Blake who, like archaeologists entering a tomb, try to recover what they take to be the text's inert and hidden meanings, which they presume to be buried and simply waiting to be discovered by someone sufficiently clever, educated, and erudite to find them. In our mode of reading, on the contrary, the "meaning" of Blake's text emerges from the process of reading itself—the kind of reading toward which the illuminated books "rouze" our faculties to act. Rather than resisting the open logic of Blake's work, our mode of read-

CHAPTER FOUR

ing accepts this logic and takes it as far as possible, by locating much of the meaning of the work in the very logic animating it, the kinds of connections it allows us to make, the freedom of thought and of energy that it enables.

Indeed, if we follow the open logic of the illuminated books far enough, we will quickly discover that reading Blake involves not just working with the words and images on a particular plate of one of the books—a kind of openness already daunting enough to some readers—but rather taking the openness even further, mediating between words and images on different plates of the same book and even between words and images in altogether different books. For, after all, if we are willing to follow the logic of Blake's work far enough to explore the possibility that our reading is located in the unmediated gaps between words and images, why should we foreclose interpretive possibilities by limiting our exploration of such gaps only to particular plates of a single book? Once we can accept that our reading of Blake's illuminated books necessarily takes place in the gaps between words and images, there is no particular reason to suppose that such gaps open and close only on a plate-by-plate basis. For if we can agree that the images on a particular plate often do not illustrate the words alongside which they appear, one possibility that we are left with is that they might actually relate more closely to words printed elsewhere. Thus, for example, the image accompanying plate 10 of *America* (a devilish youth rising in flames from the bottom of the page) seems to fit much more closely with the speech in plate 6 ("The terror answer'd: I am Orc") than with the text that appears in plate 10 itself ("Thus wept the Angel's voice")—which actually seems a much closer fit with the image in plate 6 (a mournful and godlike old man, Urizen, Orc's great antagonist).

Much of the experience of reading one of the illuminated books, then, involves alternating between reading words and reading images, and turning back and forth through the plates, tracing and retracing different interpretive paths through the gap between words and images. This is a kind of reading—really an ongoing rereading—that is essentially incompatible with the straightforward linear sense of time, and indeed the very habits of reading, to which we have been generally conditioned. In fact, since another part of the experience of reading one of Blake's books is that we seem to keep stumbling across words, lines of text, characters, figures, images, or even poems that we have seen before in other works by Blake, this process of tracing and retracing interpretive paths—that is, the process of reading Blake—can hardly ever be confined to a single text or book. Reading, for example, *The Little Black Boy* of *Songs of Innocence* alongside *The Chimney Sweeper* is an experience altogether different from reading *The Little Black Boy* on its own.

Skin color and identity are treated similarly in both, though in the former as a question of race and in the latter as a question of class and occupation. This relationship might lead us to question the conclusion drawn by certain critics that *The Little Black Boy* is an inescapably "racist" text, since *The Chimney Sweeper* reminds us that becoming "white" is not simply a matter of "race" in the narrow sense and, in any case, both need to be read with some measure of irony, since both subvert parental wisdom.[8]

Moreover, reading *The Chimney Sweeper* of *Songs of Innocence* alongside *The Chimney Sweeper* of *Songs of Experience* is a different experience, and generates different meanings, from reading either one on its own. This is by no means to suggest that one "version" alone is somehow less complete than the two together, but rather, quite simply, that to read both alters our reading of each. Similarly, what begins as a mediation between word and image in one plate can shift into a mediation between words and images in two different plates. This process is of course amplified by the way in which even reading different copies, of, say, *The Chimney Sweeper* of *Songs of Experience* on their own also offers us a different experience of the "same" plate. But perhaps this particular point will be better illustrated if we consider, for example, what might happen to our reading of *The Little Black Boy* if we try to take account of the fact that in some versions of the plate the little black boy is colored black or brown, and in others white or pink (see figs. 8 and 9). Does that alteration in *image*—between different versions of the "same" plate—in turn alter the meaning of the words themselves, given the multiple overlapping racial and colonial contexts in which the plate was produced? Can we any longer think of the words (which initially seemed, unlike the image in this case, to be constant rather than variable) as stable holders of meaning, or has something happened in our experience of reading the *images* to alter the way in which we think of reading the *words?* Are the same words really the "same" in the sense that they convey the same meaning? Or must we acknowledge that a seemingly identical imprint—whether verbal or visual—can be seen to generate multiple meanings according to the context in which it is read, a context constituted not only by various important cultural, historical, and political factors, but also by the path of reading that the reader has developed in tracing and retracing various paths between words and images through *Songs of Innocence*?

As a result of such rereadings, the "same" plate can become other to itself—that is, no longer identical to itself—in the sense that it gradually becomes much more difficult, even impossible, to think of it as a single, definite, stable entity. What we can think of as the gap between different plates (e.g., *The Chimney Sweeper* in *Innocence* and *The Chimney Sweeper* in *Experi-*

CHAPTER FOUR

Figure 8. Blake, *Songs of Innocence and of Experience*, copy C, plate 23. Lessing J. Rosenwald Collection, Library of Congress. Copyright © 2001 the William Blake Archive. Used with permission.

ence) can thus be compared to the gap within the same plate (e.g., two copies of *The Little Black Boy*) and, in turn, the gap within the same work (e.g., the multiple nonidentical copies of *Songs of Innocence and of Experience*). Thus, the stable self-containment of a single illuminated book is superseded by the wide virtual network of traces among different plates, different copies, different illuminated books—*virtual* because it is not always necessarily activated and, even when it is, not always activated in the same way. This is also

Figure 9. Blake, *Songs of Innocence and of Experience*, copy Z, plate 10. Lessing J. Rosenwald Collection, Library of Congress. Copyright © 2001 the William Blake Archive. Used with permission.

the case with the many images, phrases, and lines of text that we see repeated and recycled in Blake's work. When we encounter apparently the same line of text, or the same image, in multiple contexts (whether multiple versions of the same plate, or altogether different plates), our reading can expand to draw together these multiple appearances. Determining the meaning of a particular text (whether verbal or visual) involves reading it in an ever-expanding—though not unlimited—number of contexts.

In order to make our discussion a little less abstract, let us take some further examples from the illuminated books themselves. It has often been pointed out that the opening line of *America* ("The Guardian Prince of Albion burns in his nightly tent") reappears as the closing line of *Africa* in *The Song of Los*.[9] Most critics assume that this signals the continuity of the narrative of progress from the end of *Africa* to the beginning of *America*. But there is no need to impose progressive time—or cyclical time—on Blake's work just in order to make sense of such repetitions. For this appearance of an apparently identical line in *America* and *Africa* might suggest a very different relationship between the two works, an indication of their locations in a larger network of expansive relations. By undermining the autonomy of each work to tell its own story, such a connection does not merely occasion a one-time retroactive link to another work; it rather reminds us of the array of perpetually open channels, the network of continually firing synapses, linking Blake's works to each other. A similar movement occurs in plate 6 of *America*. The last line of the text ("For Empire is no more, and now the Lion & Wolf shall cease") also appears, slightly modified, in *A Song of Liberty* appended to *The Marriage of Heaven & Hell*.[10] In turn, the last line of *A Song of Liberty* ("For every thing that lives is Holy") reappears, once again slightly transformed, two plates later in *America* ("For every thing that lives is holy, life delights in life"), and again in the last plate of *Visions of the Daughters of Albion* ("Arise and drink your bliss. for every thing that lives is holy").[11]

Of course, any artist or writer can repeat and recycle images, characters, and concepts, and maybe even whole phrases and lines of text. But there is a consistency in the way Blake effects this kind of repetition which contributes to his work's characteristic flavor. And as someone who earned his living (such as it was) as a reproductive engraver—whose professional obligation was at least in principle to faithfully copy prior images into a new medium where they could be rapidly and accurately reproduced in print—Blake was used to thinking of repetition in a particular way. The logic of copying through repetition was essential to the reproductive engraving business.[12] However, as we saw in the previous chapter, it was essential not only to engraving, but also to the modern industrial form of production as a whole, to the logic animating each of those "dark Satanic Mills" which were already in Blake's lifetime dotting England's "green and pleasant land."[13] This is why when Babbage was looking for the conceptual ancestor of the modern factory, he found it in the logic of engraving. For if the industrially produced commodity represents a kind of "image," a copy, of a prior prototype, the image becomes for Babbage the central concept driving the production process in even the earliest factories, as we have seen.

We can probably see that these material considerations greatly increase the significance of the persistence of forms of repetition, including those of words and whole phrases, within Blake's own work. However, whereas the reproductive logic of copying essential to commercial engraving as celebrated by Babbage generates a series of more or less identical standardized replications faithful to a prior original, in the illuminated books the copying—the *reiteration*—of the "same" text or image in several different contexts changes the meaning not only of the reiterated text itself, but of the contexts in which it appears in each of its iterations. Such reiteration amplifies the meaning of the "same" text, and transforms it as it is channeled through a number of different circuits of signification. As a result, what we might cautiously refer to as the "usual" relationship of text and context, from which meanings are generated, is amplified by the process of reiteration—just as we have already seen with reference to some of *Songs of Innocence and of Experience.*

In principle, of course, there is actually nothing unusual about this aspect of Blake's work. Whenever a text of whatever kind is cycled through—read in—different contexts, its meaning changes; that, after all, is what reading is all about.[14] In this sense, all texts are "open" rather than "closed," all texts are "virtual" rather than definite, fixed, finite in meaning. Blake's work, however, literalizes this principle of reading: by reiterating the same texts or images in a variety of contexts it presents the principle in actual form rather than solely as potential, though in so doing it always reminds us of this potential. On the one hand, this paradoxically ends up looking like an attempt to circumscribe and limit the principle of reading, by anticipating, containing, and channeling the circuits of interpretation through a wide—but not unlimited—number of contexts. On the other hand, what is unusual about Blake's work is not just the text itself in a narrow sense, but rather the mode of reading, indeed the consciousness of reading, toward which the text "rouzes" us. Far more than most literary and artistic work, Blake's reminds us of the extent to which all texts are open and virtual; and hence, far more than most, it frees us from the determinism of those texts that pretend to be closed and definite—texts which are, for example, constitutive of "state trickery."

Thus, the kind of repetition we see in the illuminated books is quite distinct from repetition in any ordinary sense. It multiplies the text and amplifies its significance rather than merely replicating it. What might look like a process of reproductive copying or printing—which, through his rolling press, is how all of Blake's illuminated books came into the world—turns into one of transformation. Thus, any possible distinction between "origi-

CHAPTER FOUR

nal" and "copy" (no matter how fraught with difficulties those terms are) breaks down. Those lines, images, and fragments of text are all simultaneously copies and originals, and hence neither quite copies nor originals. Indeed, Blake's process of reiteration ends up subverting the fundamental basis of what Babbage and others identified as the industrial logic of reproduction, since the products of his printshop emerged in anything but a stream of identical copies, and since, after all, there is no real "original" or prototype of *Songs of Innocence* to distinguish from the various "copies." For the etched copperplate was merely one element or tool—and the initial printing itself only one step—in Blake's production process.

Perhaps we can find the closest aesthetic relative of Blake's work not in print or visual culture, but in performance, in music, and especially in jazz. This is a good point to recall some questions that have come up repeatedly in Blake studies: What, or where, is Blake's *America*? Is it all of the copies that exist? Is it the lost copperplates? Is it the concept underlying the seventeen surviving copies? Is it the lowest common denominator unifying all the copies? Is there one particular copy that is more original or more definitive than the others? Does *America* exist as a kind of multiple of the many variants that Blake produced, some with different inks, some with different color washes, some with missing elements, others with added elements, some with missing plates, others with extra plates? Or is *America* at one and the same time all of the copies and each of the copies, both one and many, constant and changing? Indeed, can *America* even be distinguished as such from the vast interlocking network of synapses and relays, both verbal and visual, linking it corporeally to *The Marriage of Heaven & Hell*, *Visions of the Daughters of Albion*, and other works, each of which in turn exists in multiple nonidentical copies? Such questions become even more difficult when we consider Blake's color-printed pages (for example, the title page of *The Song of Los*), in which separate prints are barely based on a permanent plate image and, by the time of the large color prints first executed in 1795, are either based on a lightly scratched outline or printed from unetched copperplates or millboards.[15]

Jerome McGann considers some of the implications of such questions in a particularly succinct way in order to generalize from them to broader aesthetic and political principles. "It was part of Blake's artistic project," writes McGann, "that each of his works *be* unique." Pointing out that fewer than ten original copies of *Jerusalem* survive, each of which is quite distinct, McGann argues that "to speak of the Text of *Jerusalem* . . . as if that term comprehended some particular concrete reality rather than a heuristic idea, is manifestly to talk nonsense." If Blake "strove so resolutely, even obsessively, to produce work that was wholly his own," McGann concludes, the result is that "each original copy of *Jerusalem is* unique, and in them Blake has achieved an extraordinary degree of artistic freedom."[16] According to McGann's account, what Blake as a great independent artist was able to accomplish with his method of publication was the production of a series of unique artworks. Indeed, this account emphasizes the status of the artwork as a material product as well as the relationship of the artwork to the artist who created it.[17]

For McGann, then, Blake is a kind of exception proving the rule of the social production and dissemination of art. What he calls Blake's "fierce individuality" would, he says, have been severely compromised by various social institutions had his work been published, distributed, and sold in the usual commercial manner; and hence what might otherwise seem to be Blake's "failure" can ironically be seen as a kind of "success."[18] From this standpoint, of course, Blake has been seen not only as the producer of and unique artworks—rather than merely the author of homogeneous, mass-produced books, where the processes of conception and execution are mediated by the book trade rather than the author or producer—but as the ultimate embodiment of romantic genius: a great individual struggling to find an authentic mode of self-expression. Morris Eaves approaches Blake from a similar angle, and he anticipates McGann's reading of the relationship between Blake as a "fierce individualist" and the unique products of his printing press. What Eaves proposes in his reading of Blake is essentially a Schillerian version of romanticism, in which, as Schiller had argued, "it must be open to us to restore by means of a higher Art the totality of our nature which the arts themselves have destroyed."[19]

For Eaves the unique artwork, the unique individual artist, and the aesthetics of originality all converge in a figure like Blake. "The restoration of wholeness to the personality restores identity," Eaves argues in *Blake's Theory of Art*, "and in doing so restores the possibility of originality to art. When Blake calls for originality we must understand that he means the complete self-expression of a complete self in imagination. Imagination is less the name of a specialized faculty that processes thoughts or images than a synonym for identity." Thus, Eaves concludes, considered as a process, the work of the imagination "is restoring thoughts and images to identity, that is, to wholeness."[20] Eaves continues his elaboration of this line of reasoning—in which romantic art is understood as self-expression—in his momentous study *The Counter-arts Conspiracy* (which is essentially an extended close reading of Blake's *Public Address* of 1809), in which he argues that Blake's critique of reproductive technologies develops precisely from his ferocious individualism. Here, indeed, Eaves's Blake is no longer merely a romantic genius struggling for self-expression but the producer of what Eaves refers to at times as "Christian-aristocratic" aesthetic and political positions, and at times as exercises "in middle-class self-construction." In this expression of ambition, Eaves argues, "a utopian Christian vision legitimizes the desire to penetrate the confederation of devouring upper, controlling middle and exploited lower classes at its mid-point to make economic room for autonomous middle-class artist heroes who see the possibility of combining in themselves the aesthetic judgment of an elite and the technical skills of a working class."[21]

From such a standpoint, Blake's blistering attacks on the "Arts of Trading Combination," the "Booksellers & Trading Dealers," and above all the "Monopolizing Trader" of the Boydell era ("who Manufactures Art by the Hands of Ignorant Journeymen till at length Christian Charity is held out as a Motive to encourage a Blockhead & he is Counted the Greatest Genius who can sell a Good for Nothing Commodity for a Great Price"), may be read, just as Eaves proposes, as the outraged responses of an isolated artist committed to producing self-expressive art, and hence to controlling the means of production as well as distribution of his unique—precisely because self-expressive—works.[22] Left to its own devices, the "counter-arts" system of commercial monopoly would on this account otherwise succeed in dividing production from distribution, and more importantly conception from execution.[23] What this account leaves us with is Blake the romantic artist, and perhaps above all Blake the craftsman, the petit bourgeois tradesman and artisan concerned with the sale of his goods: a natural exponent of the virtues of the free market (as against the tyranny of monopolizing traders) and what Eaves calls middle-class self-construction. This Blake—though Eaves does not take his argument so far—becomes almost an inevitable advocate of Paineite radicalism, a champion of the rights of the sovereign individual as celebrated in *Rights of Man*, and a natural candidate for the meeting rooms of the London Corresponding Society or for the ships carrying emigrants in pursuit of life, liberty, and the pursuit of happiness to the cities or the frontiers of America. Indeed, this version of Blake merges with the figure of the urban artisan elaborated in a similar context (early republican America) by Laura Rigal. Rigal's artisans are self-made men, skilled producers bridging "what a production-based political economy depended upon breaking apart: skill, or knowledge (sometimes called the "secrets" or "mysteries" of a craft), and labor, or the body's productive activity under the management of the mind."[24] Such artisans seek to concentrate in their own expanded sphere of activity all the processes of production and distribution that the modern social division of labor normally breaks apart. Blake himself has often been seen this way, as a paranoid crank trying to control and determine social processes no longer normally vested by a modern economy in individual producers, and hence as a kind of would-be superman.[25]

This version of Blake stems from considerations of a direct and unmediated relationship between artist and artwork—or, in other words, producer and product—in which the terms of analysis are provided by the unitary opposition between subject and object as distinguished in the kind of ontological dualism ultimately derived from the philosophy of Locke. Artistic production is in this view a process for the production of identity, especially the identity of the romantic artist. Based on these principles, the task of criticism has been seen as a matter of reuniting these units to rediscover the circuits of originality binding them together and guaranteeing their reproduction, or else investigating where these circuits have been broken by the intervention of social and political processes—or a public—hence leading to the well-known crises of romantic subjectivity and the romantic artist's withdrawal from the public sphere into a realm of imaginative interiority. Indeed, Eaves suggests that from this angle Blake "may seem to represent more completely than any of his English romantic contemporaries the artist in the phase of withdrawal."[26]

However, the line of argument elaborated by Eaves leads to certain conceptual and philosophical—not to mention political—difficulties. According to Eaves, Blake's individualism must be seen as an argument against a system of production in which the work of art "reproduces the class structure that produces it."[27] Blake's defense of "individual merit" against the "maw of commerce" thus alternates between a form of "bourgeois individualism" and a kind of quasi-aristocratic claim to spiritual nobility. There are several places in his complex and nuanced argument where Eaves points out that for Blake "the individual and the collective are on the same continuum," and that the ability to "see one in many and many in one" is characteristic of the "prophetic imagination."[28] Therefore, as Eaves says, we need to distinguish between what he calls originality$_1$ (historical specificity) and originality$_2$ (individual originality), whose uneasy and contradictory coexistence is explained in Eaves's account precisely by recourse to the "enthusiastic rhetoric of radical Protestantism." But in Eaves's argument this Protestant radicalism seems inevitably to slip into the kind of possessive individualism which would put Blake back into "the house of romanticism that individualizes and internalizes Christian discourse with increasing emphasis on psychology, the creative imagination, and the connection of art ('vision') with that mental faculty."[29] According to Eaves, this explains Blake's insistence on his artistic originality, a rejection of the separation of (mental) conception and (manual) execution in an essentially Schillerian romantic reunification of a divided self.

This could be understood as a kind of bourgeois individualism, but Eaves's recognition that Blake's individualism is "powerfully antipathetic" to the atomistic individual of Lockean philosophy leads him to suggest that the form of individualism celebrated by Blake is perhaps more adequately understood as one backed up "not by notions of mental development but by fantasies of the precedence of birth over technical education." To that extent, Eaves argues, Blake's individualism "adapts aristocratic values, hence his ready disdain for the supposed vulgarity of artists admired for their technical skills: mere copyists, he complains, envisioning a class that can only ape the manners of an authentic nobility that knows how to be original because it was born that way."[30] But this leads Eaves into what he ends up admitting is a kind of dead end to his argument, because, as he points out, "it would be rash to conclude that his nonconformist individualism spurns community." Eaves suggests that "the baffling union of individualism and communalism at the heart of [Blake's] thinking" is "no 'problem' that we can hope to 'solve,'" and so he chooses to leave his argument in this unresolved state. The lack of a definite conclusion to Eaves's account may not be a fault, of course, and there may indeed be no certain resolution to these questions. But, on the other hand, the apparent contradiction that Eaves, to his credit, prefers not to try to compress into a reductive resolution may emerge from the conceptual or epistemological basis of this argument, rather than from the argument itself. For Eaves understands radical Protestantism to lead willy-nilly to a form of individualism. There is, of course, a very strong tendency in Protestantism (the one elaborated by Max Weber, for example) to lead to just those forms of individualism that Eaves elaborates, culminating in notions of interiority and psychology so important—as Eaves points out—to romanticism itself. What this suggests, then, is that some of what we cannot account for in Blake with the dualistic concepts derived ultimately from the philosophy of Locke (which Blake contested) might well make more sense if considered from other philosophical and political standpoints. The conundrum that Eaves acknowledges may be the result of the philosophical and political gap between the tradition that Blake belonged to and the one that Locke articulated.

What would happen to Eaves's account if we were to try to step outside the conceptual parameters imposed by the ontological dualism we have inherited from Locke? The latter, after all, may well be challenged in Blake's work, albeit in ways that would necessarily remain inaccessible to criticism ultimately derived from Locke himself. If Blake's text were to be read as an activity and a practice, rather than as an inert object or set of objects, for example, the logic of live performance here might be taken to challenge that of the book understood as a fixed object. This question pushes us to reconsider whether in reading Blake's works we should set our conceptual and theoretical parameters in terms of the book (as a unitary and reified object) or instead in terms of a more open-ended process. Perhaps, in answer to the set of questions I raised earlier, *America* is most adequately thought of not as a book, nor even as a collection of dissimilar "copies," but rather as a virtual performance, since, as W. J. T. Mitchell points out, reading the illuminated books is less like viewing sequentially the items in a string of galleries than it is "synaesthetic, tactile, and phantasmagoric" and "more like watching a furious debate, in which the contestants are capable of projecting vast multimedia displays to demonstrate their arguments."[31] In this sense, the illuminated books can perhaps be thought of, even heuristically, as a performance to be repeatedly recreated without the intervention of a controlling principle designed to guarantee its outcome or meaning—or at least without *absolute* principles, since what we encounter in Blake's work is not really sheer dissemination but rather a series of repetitions through preexisting channels of reiteration. Through the pattern of possible repetitions, a new layer of "meaning" can emerge, a layer inaccessible and inscrutable at the level of text as object or the book as a "good for nothing commodity." In reading *America*, or any of the illuminated books, we should therefore keep an eye on the textual *process*—that is, the pattern of reiterations—as a kind of meaning-generating performance quite in addition to the sorts of sound-and-light shows described by Mitchell.

4. Identity and Exchange

In Blake's work, the question of identity merges with the question of repetition and exchange. Just as the process of commodity production in the modern economy takes for granted the identity of the commodities being produced, the process of exchange takes for granted the relatively stable self-identity of the objects of exchange, so that the value of stable equivalents can be transparently calculated and transacted on an open market. Thus, the value of different objects can be determined, rendering them intermeasurable and hence exchangeable. A form of production that breaks down the object's stable identity and singular reified existence in the stream of linear time would threaten to break down the process of commercial pro-

CHAPTER FOUR

duction and exchange, both of which rely conceptually and operationally on stable, reified, discrete objects. This difficulty becomes especially clear when one considers the matter of economic equivalence and its political correlate, equality—an issue that defined, as we have seen, the conceptual core of the 1790s discourse of liberty.

The context of *Visions* and *A Song of Liberty*, as well as *The Marriage* itself—to all of which plate 6 of *America* provides multiple synapses and relays—is particularly important in considering all these questions. A crucial element of the discourse shared by *The Marriage* and *Visions*, which also appears in *America*, involves, as we have seen in previous chapters, an extensive critique of reification and autonomous singularity. One of the many textual relays linking these works to each other appears in the slavemaster Bromion's speech in the middle of *Visions*:

> Ah! are there other wars, beside the wars of sword and fire!
> And are there other sorrows, beside the sorrows of poverty?
> And are there other joys, beside the joys of riches and ease?
> And is there not one law for both the lion and the ox?

What Bromion's speech asserts through these rhetorical questions is the stability of meaning and of identity, as well as the rules or laws by which meaning and identity are defined. War, sorrow, joy are here defined according to their respective meanings as provided in the speech, which anticipates Urizen's declaration in his book of brass that all life should be governed by

> One command, one joy, one desire,
> One curse, one weight, one measure
> One King. one God. one Law.

Such reified singularity is at odds with the textual politics of Blake's prophetic books, which preclude the possibility of stable identities—and hence the transparent exchange of equivalent values—at any level. This contradiction becomes evident in the dissenting speech that follows Bromion's declaration, in which Oothoon addresses Urizen (this is, significantly, the first time the latter is referred to by name in Blake's work):

> O Urizen! Creator of men! mistaken Demon of heaven!
> Thy joys are tears, thy labour vain to form men to thine image.
> How can one joy absorb another? are not different joys
> Holy, eternal, infinite? and each joy is a Love.
> Does not the great mouth laugh at a gift, & the narrow eyelids mock
> At the labour that is above payment? and wilt thou take the ape

> For thy counsellor, or the dog for a schoolmaster to thy children?
> Does he who contemns poverty and he who turns with abhorrence
> From usury feel the same passion, or are they moved alike?
> How can the giver of gifts experience the delights of the merchant?
> How the industrious citizen the pains of the husbandman?
> How different far the fat fed hireling with hollow drum,
> Who buys whole corn fields into wastes, and sings upon the heath!
> With what sense does the parson claim the labour of the farmer?
> What are his nets & gins & traps; & how does he surround him
> With cold floods of abstraction, and with forests of solitude,
> To build him castles and high spires, where kings & priests may dwell.

This speech counters the very notions of identity, equivalence, and exchange proposed by Bromion (and Urizen himself). It also undermines any concept of equality based on the logic of equivalence and exchange. Here each joy exists as a unique moment that could never be rendered or expressed in terms of any other joy. One joy cannot "absorb" another because each is "holy, eternal, infinite." Paradoxically, it is each joy's extension into the infinite that defines its particularity; its extension into eternity is what defines it as a particular moment. This notion of uniqueness is clearly incompatible with a discrete and definite—finite—existence, which is how uniqueness is normally understood in concrete and reified terms, and which is also how value is ordinarily determined so that exchange can take place.[32] Thus, the unique here rests in permanent contradiction with the finitude of singularity, and this contradiction precludes the possibility of the intermeasurability, and hence the equivalence and exchangeability, of particular joys. Whereas in *America* "pity is become a trade, and generosity a science / That men get rich by,"[33] here in *Visions*, Oothoon's joy is that which refuses the logic of trade altogether (perhaps because pity implies a relation of alterity, of self to other, and hence can be transformed into a currency for exchange, whereas joy opens out into the infinite, making exchange not just difficult or impossible but irrelevant).

This apparently oxymoronic form of infinite and eternal particularity is contrasted sharply with the forests of solitude and the singular spires and castles overseen by the parson and sustained by his appropriation of the farmer's labor. The lone castle, the single spire, the individual tree—and the forest of solitude made up of such singular entities—are each opposed to the dispersed network of the eternal and the infinite. Here and indeed throughout Blake's work, singular and isolated structures—spires, towers, and especially trees—tend to grow upward, to stretch out vertically and become images of hierarchy and oppression. Such images tend in other words to become approximations of the tree of mystery which we see in *The Human Abstract* being sown by "mutual fear" and "selfish love," that is, a tree that exists nowhere in nature, though "there grows one in the Human Brain."[34] (Indeed, the contrast between the tree as a symbol of oppression in Blake and the tree as a symbol of freedom, e.g., the tree of liberty, elsewhere in 1790s radicalism is striking).

In this context, the shoots and tendrils that we see throughout Blake's work provide a significant alternative to the generally lonely trees that often frame his plates. It would be all too tempting to identify this contrast as an opposition between arborescent and rhizomatic structures, or in other words structures whose "development" must be followed along a predetermined and hierarchical series of roots and branches as opposed to those which can connect, disconnect, and reconnect through a nonhierarchical variety of openings and nodal points enabling continually changing combinations of elements.[35] In any case, the basis of the opposition between the singular and the infinite is precisely that of the single definite object embodied in time and space as against that form of uniqueness which is defined by a combination of the one and the many, the simultaneously constant and changing, the momentary and the eternal. It is significant that what enables the parson's appropriation of the farmer's labor is not right or power or authority as such, but rather the logic of *sense*, or in other words the conceptual basis of the individual subject defined by the five senses and embodied in time and space as a particular definite person with inalienable rights.

A broader critique of exchange also emerges from the redefined notion of uniqueness proposed in Oothoon's speech. Rather than attempting to link together equivalent or commensurate values (both in terms of images and in terms of the plate's own language), much of the rest of this extraordinarily complex passage links together a series of incommensurate pairs. In the process, each pair is redefined in the obverse of the normal act of exchange: instead of equivalent being traded for equivalent, we have opposites juxtaposed to each other in such a way that their smooth and transparent exchange is precluded because their value in relation to each other cannot be determined. These are not opposites in a dualistic sense, but are rather simply incompatible with each other. As a result, even the logic of opposition breaks down, and each term of the pair bounces off the other, rather than trading places with it. The ape and the dog, the counselor and the teacher, the merchant and the giver of gifts, the citizen and the husbandman, the parson and the farmer cannot be reconciled to each other. If there is a division of labor here—as there seems to be—its logic is not immediately clear, and there is no sense that all of these disparate functions somehow work together to constitute a harmonious whole.

Such forms of incompatibility proliferate throughout Blake's work, especially when it comes to matters of instruction, or at least instruction that demands simple imitation. In Oothoon's speech here the absurd figures of the ape as counselor and dog as instructor have a resonance elsewhere in Blake's work as indicators of the futility of instruction by imitation or simple replication. "The eagle never lost so much time," one of the "Proverbs of Hell" suggests, "as when he submitted to learn of the crow." The "lesson" here is not merely that, as another proverb puts it, "the tygers of wrath are wiser than the horses of instruction." Rather, we seem to return precisely to the discourse of infinite minute particularity which defies not merely instruction but any form of mimesis, any form of simple replication or duplication, and hence by extension any form of production-as-reproduction. And since, after all, we never see in Blake images of crows teaching crows, or eagles teaching eagles, it would seem that here all forms of mimesis turn out to be mistaken almost by definition. Thus each particular form maintains its own particularity ("the apple tree never asks the beech how he shall grow, nor the lion, the horse; how he shall take his prey," another proverb has it).[36] At the same time, because they participate in and even collectively constitute the infinite, such particulars are not complete in themselves but together immanently constitute a kind of unity, just as God has been seen as immanent in all animate and inanimate forms, rather than being a transcendent force outside of those forms, as we are reminded, for example, in *A Divine Image*: "All must love the human form, / In heathen, turk or jew. / Where Mercy, Love & Pity dwell, / There God is dwelling too."

What emerges from this is a vision of the act of exchange as one of violence, as seen for example in the desolation generated by the fat fed hireling's purchases of land, where the act of exchange translates immediately into one of devastation (buying into waste). The joy of giving is contrasted with the delights of the merchant not merely because different joys are different, but because the concept of giving is incompatible with the logic of exchange that structures the merchant's, the hireling's, the parson's, and the usurer's activities. Labor can be "above" payment when it is given, rather than when it is appropriated by a violent act of exchange. What is given is by definition something that cannot be compensated for in the act of giving; its premise is difference, rather than equivalence; donation, rather than return; sacrifice, rather than gain; loss, rather than compensation; a moment, rather than a carefully regulated transaction in linear time.

What makes the act of exchange violent here is its fundamental reliance

CHAPTER FOUR

on the concepts of identity and intermeasurability underlying the concept of exchange value. Ironically, Bromion's most aggressive line is the one that might otherwise seem to be the most conciliatory: "Is there not one law for the lion and the ox?" In Bromion's speech, such a law reduces the lion and the ox to a kind of equality—an equality before the law, but one based on the logic of equivalence and self-identity, as well as interchangeability.

The notion of an equality based on the equivalence of discrete units is, of course, the notion of equality that was being preached by the advocates of liberty in the 1790s. Their notion of liberty was, as we have seen in previous chapters, based simultaneously on commercial and political freedom, on a vision of society as a perfectly transparent mechanical system in which no blockages are tolerated, permitting the smooth and even circulation of discrete commodities (the basic units of commerce) and unitary citizens (the basic units of politics). What enables this vision is the presumption that the circulating units must remain constant, quantifiable, and identical to themselves, their transactions and exchanges regulated in terms of the smooth flow of homogeneous time. Each unit here is governed by a sense of sovereignty and singularity, and what defines liberty—or this kind of liberty at least—is the freedom of sovereign subjects to exchange and consume discrete objects. "One law for the lion and the ox" ensures that the lion and the ox remain equal to each other in these terms, but also that the lion remains a lion and the ox an ox, with, on the one hand, each identical to itself and on the other, any lion being intermeasurable with any other.

Given all this, it is of some interest to look back at the very last line of *The Marriage of Heaven & Hell*:

One Law for the Lion & Ox is Oppression.

Because of the network of tendrils, synapses, and relays—not to mention the number of shared lines and images—linking *The Marriage* (1790–93) to *Visions* (1793), it is unlikely to be a coincidence that this momentous line happens to anticipate Bromion's thunderous declamation in the later work. What becomes clear here is that the logic of equivalence and exchange in the world of objects correlates to a certain logic of equality in the world of subjects, and hence that there is some ongoing relationship between the constitution of subjects and of objects. "Why is one law given to the lion & the patient Ox?" asks Tiriel; "Dost thou not see that men cannot be formed all alike."[37] What Tiriel, and for that matter *The Marriage of Heaven & Hell*, proposes as a critique of subjectivity, and indeed of liberal democracy as well, is at the same time a critique of the logic of industrial production, with which the notion of liberal democracy entered the world (see chapter 3).

What is being questioned in both cases is the very possibility of the untroubled self-identity through time of a singular, discrete, reified unit, which might be the basis of both politics and commerce, whose freedom of movement and circulation defined the discourse of liberty in the 1790s. If the mainstream understanding of democracy is one that is based on the constant identity of the bodies and subjects that are to be made both equal and equally represented ("since the French Revolution Englishmen are all Intermeasurable One by Another, certainly a happy state of Agreement to which I for One do not Agree," Blake wrote), what we have in these texts is profoundly undemocratic. Indeed, it defines this particular form of democracy precisely as oppression.

But what it opens up instead is the contrary possibility of a form of freedom and even of equality that is not derived from the philosophical politics of identity and exchange value. It is only according to this alternative concept of freedom that empire might be no more. How this might work at the level of the subject we will examine in later chapters. For now we must return to the status of the object, and how an object might be considered both one and many, both particular and infinite, both of the moment and of all eternity.

5. An Image That Flourishes

It turns out that our investigation of the "meaning" of Blake's work—the way in which we read it—must move between, on the one hand, an account of various textual contexts "within" the work and, on the other hand, the patterns of reiteration, including the material patterns of reiteration, linking those contexts together. For, as Nelson Hilton puts it, "how his [Blake's] text works is what it means"; or, as Paul Mann has argued very suggestively, "The 'meaning' of any Blake book is thus, first and foremost, that Blake made it, and made it *this way*, not just textually, not even only as a composite art, but fully, materially, as 'Itself & Not Intermeasurable with or by any Thing Else.'"[38] But while Mann and to a certain extent Hilton seek to shift critical attention toward the materiality of the object, I want to shift our attention beyond the object and instead toward the materiality of Blake's textual practice, the process of both textual and material reiteration in Blake's work. For Blake's work may be seen as the ideal site for a reunification of aesthetic and political-economic analysis. This would ultimately allow us to discuss simultaneously the poetic or artistic "vision" proposed in Blake's work and the material processes that articulated that vision (and were articulated by it in turn).

CHAPTER FOUR

With this in mind, let us take an example of the way in which reading the gap between image and words on a particular plate of one of the books ultimately refuses to be self-contained and instead pushes us toward an examination of the broader issues that have come up in our treatment of Blake's work. We will see how our reading of the relation between words and images on one plate pushes us beyond the edge of the plate, not only to other plates and books by Blake, but to the world beyond. For our example, let us turn again to plate 6 of *America* (see fig. 10).

Taking full advantage of the fluidity of his own technique—and demonstrating its profound differences from the conventional commercial combination of typographic print with separately engraved illustrations, whose political, economic, and aesthetic parameters and division of labor he contests in the prophetic books—Blake often unifies the plate's verbal text with its visual "background," especially where the ends of various letters adapt to and even merge with the roots or shooting vines that frame the text. Although the verbal text in plate 6 seems to be framed by the visual elements at the top and bottom of the plate—the gravelike mound on which the youth is resting and the undergrowth at the bottom of the plate—it can also be seen to open a new dimension in the space of the plate.

For it is not exactly the case that the verbal text here is depicted as lying "beneath" or "within" the space of the grave. Because of the flowers and animal life at the very bottom of the plate, which mark a location in the open air rather than either an underground scene or a merely stylized frame, the verbal text produces a distortion in the plate's visual field. Its effect is to push down (in the two dimensions of the printed page) what ought by rights to be extended toward the reader/viewer (in the multiple dimensions of the outside world). In other words, the plant and animal life that occurs on the bottom of the page is suggestive of a kind of foreground for the scene of the youth resting on the small mound, but here they are pushed vertically downward on the page by the presence of the verbal text. Just as the verbal text is contained by the preceding and successive plates (which frame and define the speech as Orc's), and is at the same time suggestive of an opening away from Orc and the narrative of the American War, the verbal text, though framed by the plate's visual elements, opens up a new moment by generating this distortion in the plate's visual field. In the fourth—temporal—dimension figured in this distortion of the visual field, the verbal text opens up into a moment that is out of synchrony with the visual elements surrounding and framing it. Much of the verbal text is taken up with action and movement (shaking, moving, awakening, springing, running, laughing, singing), but the visual image is one of rest, more suggestive of a pause than of strident (revolutionary) action. In this respect, of course, the visual imagery seems once again to mesh with the verbal imagery of momentary and eternal pauses.

The plate's verbal and visual texts are simultaneously integrated and disjointed. On the one hand, the words are literally woven into the plate's visual fabric. Moreover, there are many ways in which the verbal and the visual seem to correspond to each other (the line "the grave is burst," for example, seems to be illustrated here, and just as the text reads "let him look up into the heavens," we see a young man looking upward). On the other hand, the relationship between visual and verbal also suggests a certain kind of unevenness and lack of synchronization. Where is the mill that the text refers to? Are the mill and the grave the same? If so, why is the richness of the metaphor (if that is what it is) reduced to only one of its two terms? If this young man is the freed slave, he looks far too young to have been laboring for "thirty weary years." If he is supposed to be celebrating his freedom in the "bright air" and the "fresher morning," why is the sky here so cloudy, and why is the dark gloominess so accentuated in those copies that Blake went on to hand color? Where are the wife and children? Where is the open field? Where are the sun and moon, which play such important roles in the iconography of the verbal text?

What turns out to be the disjuncture of the verbal and the visual that we witness in plate 6 is enhanced by the fact that the relationship of design and text varies from copy to copy along with variations in inking and coloring. And the variation is vastly amplified by the fact that the image of the resting youth is by no means unique to this plate of *America* (figs. 10–17). In plate 21 of *The Marriage of Heaven & Hell*, which was composed and etched before *America*, we see the same figure, in a similar position (fig. 11); though again there are multiple copies of that plate as well, and hence extensive differences in inking, coloring, and background illustration. The same figure will also appear in plate 4 of *Jerusalem*, and finally, with some minor alterations in stance, as the top half of Blake's illustration for Blair's *Grave* (1805), as well as an initial white-line etching produced by Blake—which was rejected by the commissioning editor, Robert Cromek, and replaced by the more fashionable engraving (after Blake's own drawings) which Cromek subsequently commissioned from Louis Schiavonetti (figs. 13, 14).

The *Grave* illustrations open another series of relays which we must pursue through Blake's work. The figure of the old man entering "death's door," which constitutes the bottom half of Blake's *Grave* illustration, appears in a separate illustration (fig. 16) called *Death's Door* in Blake's own *For Children: The Gates of Paradise* (1793), as well as in a contemporaneous pencil drawing in his private notebook. This figure of the old man is also strikingly reminis-

CHAPTER FOUR

cent of the figure similarly robed, bearded, and on one crutch being helped through city streets by a small child in *London* and *Jerusalem*. The rising youth and the old man entering death's door were apparently first joined together in one image, precisely as they would later appear in the *Grave* illustration, in a much earlier pencil sketch which must have dated from around the time of *America*.[39] They would reappear in an undated pencil sketch later traced over in ink, with a pyramid background reminiscent of the pyramid in the background of plate 21 of copy D of *The Marriage* (fig. 15). Finally, of course, the old man appears on his own, still—as always—hovering at the entrance to death's door, in plate 12 of *America* itself (fig. 17).

Thus the passage in plate 6 acquires a new, and yet equally provisional and contingent, frame. Here it is set within the moment defining the gap between the youth's apparent emergence from the grave and the old man's hesitant entrance into the embrace of death. However, the parameters open up beyond the young man and the old man in their specific iterations within the body of *America* to embrace the rest of Blake's work. It is therefore at this continually provisional moment, at this point of contact between entrance and exit, that the speech rests. It is a moment—no longer contained by or within even the multiple copies of *America*—that is always on the brink of happening: a specific and yet highly variable moment that Blake would return to repeatedly through the corpus of his work. In this eternal and infinitely extended moment, the young man will never actually emerge from his expectant crouch, and the old man will never actually find his way into the grave that awaits him, even though all the tempests of time are pushing him toward it.

6. Images of Time

The visual play of the pictures that would constitute Blake's illustration for the *Grave* (that is, the old man and the youth in their various iterations) produces the same uncanny destabilizations of time that we have already witnessed in plate 6 of *America* and elsewhere, although it does so over a remarkable—and critical—ten-year span in Blake's career. The *Grave* drawing can be seen as an illustration of the dislocation in time also illustrated in plate 6 of *America*. As we have seen, the latter plate ends with the breakdown of diachronic time—which had been introduced earlier in the plate—and the crystallization instead of an alternative time of the moment. Similarly, the *Grave* illustration hovers at a closely related liminal moment. The picture is defined by the balance of the images of the old man entering the grave and the young man leaving it. If the yet-to-begin life story of the newly emergent youth is to be enabled by the conclusion of the about-to-conclude life story of the old man, there must clearly be a kind of synchronization of the birth of the former and the death of the latter, seen here in the way in which their figures are juxtaposed. On the other hand, the illustration is suggestive of the ways in which synchronic time is itself uneven, defined by rupture and suspension rather than seamless continuity. For the young man is shown emerging from the grave *before* the old man has actually crossed the literal threshold into death, and in this sense the continuity of their mutual life stories ("before" and "after") is disrupted by the lack of synchronization within the space of the grave.

The temporal displacement figured in the *Grave* illustration is amplified by the extent to which the images of the old man and the youth are dispersed in a wide network through so much of Blake's work. For just as Blake repeats the "same" line or verbal fragment in many different contexts (e.g., "every thing that lives is holy," "one law for the lion and the ox," "the Guardian Prince of Albion burns in his nightly tent"), he also repeatedly inserts the "same" pictorial image in several different contexts. This is significant because it affirms the extent to which Blake works with words and pictures in very much the same way, disrupting the commercial division of labor that separated typography (and hence words) from engraving (and hence pictures).[40] However, uniting words and pictures, as Blake does in his illuminated books, involves not only an aesthetic process but also a very specific form of cultural politics, and a challenge to a division of labor within the printing industry that was itself tied into a broader social division of labor. Hence, this aesthetic act directly generates a challenge to political formations that might otherwise seem to be far removed from the restricted world of reproductive engraving—though these are, of course, political formations that Blake happened to have also challenged within his work in other ways.

We must now further specify the ways in which the verbal and visual networks of Blake's work coincide with and amplify each other. Through the complex series of relays linking together Blake's different works, the verbal and pictorial elements and fragments of these works constitute a virtual text in which meaning should be understood in immanent rather than transcendent terms. While each textual fragment interacts with the particular context in which it happens to make an appearance, its meaning must be determined not only in terms of the immediate context of each such iteration, but *also* in terms of the context constituted through the broader network of verbal and visual reiterations running through the relays and synapses tying *America* to *Visions* to *The Marriage* to the *Grave* illustrations. The extent of this network of reiterations is amplified because of the ways in which most of these works exist in multiple discontinuous and nonidentical copies, many with their own unique finish, look, color, edition, sequence.

Blake's similar treatment of the verbal and visual components of the illuminated works now takes on new significance. Not only have both word and picture been painted together in his unique method, thereby uniting the separate realms of printing and illustration into what Mitchell identifies as a "composite art." They both also take on a kind of crystalline hardness literally grounded in the materiality of the copperplate from whose acid-washed surface they emerged together in Blake's material practice as an engraver. Nelson Hilton argues that Blake's work manifests "a vision of the word as object, as other, and as divine, that stretches our imagination to its limits." Thus, Hilton suggests, the words in the illuminated books often "strain to become pure graphic form, and sometimes they succeed." Similarly, he adds, we should learn to read some of Blake's marginal or interlinear graphic signifiers as "words."[41] Mitchell makes a similar argument, though he opens the way for us to push the point even further. He suggests that the distinction between "ideogrammatic seeing" and "pictorial seeing" is broken down in Blake's work, which "unites poem and picture in a more radical sense than simply placing them in proximity to one another."[42] Thus, he argues, "Blake's art does not just involve pushing painting towards the ideogrammatic realm of writing; he also pushes alphabetic writing toward the realm of pictorial values, asking us to see his alphabetic forms with our senses, not just read through or past them to the signified speech or 'concept' behind them, but to pause at the sensuous surface of calligraphic and typographic forms." In the body of his essay on Blake and visible language, Mitchell develops this important point with a discussion of the graphic nature of the letters constituting Blake's words.[43] However, in a highly suggestive though unelaborated footnote, he points out that his claim articulates the principle of graphic iterability in an even broader sense. "This principle," he writes, "links text and image, especially in the medium of engraving, and tends to subvert any perception of essential and necessary difference based in the supposed nature of the media, the kinds of objects they represent, or the kinds of perception they demand."[44]

What I want to propose here builds on the arguments provided by Hilton and Mitchell. For not only do Blake's words strain to become graphic forms while his calligraphic letters take on a graphic significance quite in addition to the other forms of signification in which they participate. What I want to add is that Blake's words function both as syntactical devices (however problematic) and—in addition to being the graphic objects that Hilton and

Mitchell describe—as full-fledged *images*, whose status we must now further specify. Just as the properly pictorial elements of the prophetic books demand reading in a textual sense—as both Mitchell and Hilton suggest—they *also* assume a nonpictorial function, as images whose significance, like that of their verbal counterparts, is derived from their contextual iterability, whether actual or merely potential. What I mean here is that the verbal phrases and components (such as "every thing that lives is holy") that we often encounter in multiple iterations throughout Blake's work function much like the pictorial images that we see similarly reiterated, repeatedly broken up and reunited from work to work. As I have already suggested, these images are reiterated in different contexts not according to the homogenizing process of industrial production—in which the image of the prototype is, according to Babbage, endlessly reproduced in a stream of uniform copies through the linear time of the working day—but rather in a way that disrupts the logic of that process and the spatiotemporal politics associated with it, by generating heterogeneity instead of sameness.[45]

Indeed, groups of words, sometimes single words, and either single or composite pictures all function as such images in Blake's illuminated work of the 1790s. These images are not mimetic or representational, or even pictorial in nature. Although their constituent elements may function in the pictorial and linguistic terms discussed by Mitchell and Hilton, they *also* function much like the images constituting both memory and matter according to Henri Bergson (whose concept of the image Gilles Deleuze would develop further in his philosophy of the cinema), that is, neither exactly representations nor objects but something in between.[46] At least in this instance, then, we need—as Hilton suggests—to move beyond reading "in symbols, metaphors or figurative language in general" in order to investigate the products of Blake's "literal imagination."[47]

What we encounter in Blake's prophetic books, then, is a number of actually or potentially reiterated images, both verbal and pictorial, and yet neither solely pictorial nor verbal: that is, similar but heterogeneous *graphemes* capable of—and subjected to—repeated iterability. In this sense, the verbal components of Blake's work function less as forms of representation than as images similar to the pictorial images that accompany them. The pictorial images in turn do not behave the way pictures are "supposed" to according to the aesthetic tradition from which they emerged, for, as with Blake's words, they no longer assume a strictly mimetic or representational operation. As graphemes, though, neither the pictorial nor the verbal images are particularly exceptional in this respect: the principle of iterability that they share, according to Derrida, "structures the mark of writing itself, no matter what particular type of writing is involved (whether pictographical, hieroglyphic, ideographic, phonetic, alphabetic)."[48] However, Blake's works literalize the process of iterability, both in that they literally reiterate the same verbal and pictorial images in different contexts, and in that Blake's mode of artistic production (etching and printing) is one of material reiteration. Blake's works tend to exaggerate what Derrida argues are the traits and processes underlying all forms of writing, making them stand out more.[49] One effect of this is to make other more traditional interpretive approaches—for example, those based on narrative, or allegory, or symbolism—more difficult because of the obscurity of the references in Blake's works and their general tendency toward inscrutability (which has frustrated many an encounter with the prophetic books).

But what is more significant and distinctive about Blake's work is the way in which it simultaneously takes advantage of the principle of iterability so central to his craft and tries to contain it; and above all the way in which the reiteration of images in his work is a simultaneously figural and material process, involving on the one hand the repetition of images among different works, and, on the other hand, the constitution of single works by the literal material "repetition" of images in his printing press as sheets of paper repeatedly made contact with inked or painted copperplates. Blake combines material practice and conceptual movement, by channeling the iterations of his network of images through a (nonsequential) series of relays and circuits. Here, the verbal and pictorial are played off against and alongside each other—not as marks of presence, but rather as marks of difference and deferral. These marks work together to constitute a heterogeneous and uneven network—visual and verbal, pictorial and linguistic—within which multiple iterations of the "same" image can take place. The units defining this syntax of images are, moreover, shown to be iterable either in whole or in part, and either verbally or pictorially, for the principle of iterability is, as Mitchell argues, always in play. And once again the process by which repetition turns into transformation characterizes both Blake's figural work and his material work. In this respect, the repetition of images and phrases between Blake's works may help us to think through the process of material repetition by which the illuminated books were produced, which is to say that scholars working on the materialist analysis of Blake's mode of production may turn out to have something to learn from those whose work is primarily oriented toward literary criticism, and not just the other way around, as has sometimes been suggested.

Figure 10. Blake, *America: A Prophecy*, copy E, plate 6. Lessing J. Rosenwald Collection, Library of Congress. Copyright © 2001 the William Blake Archive. Used with permission.

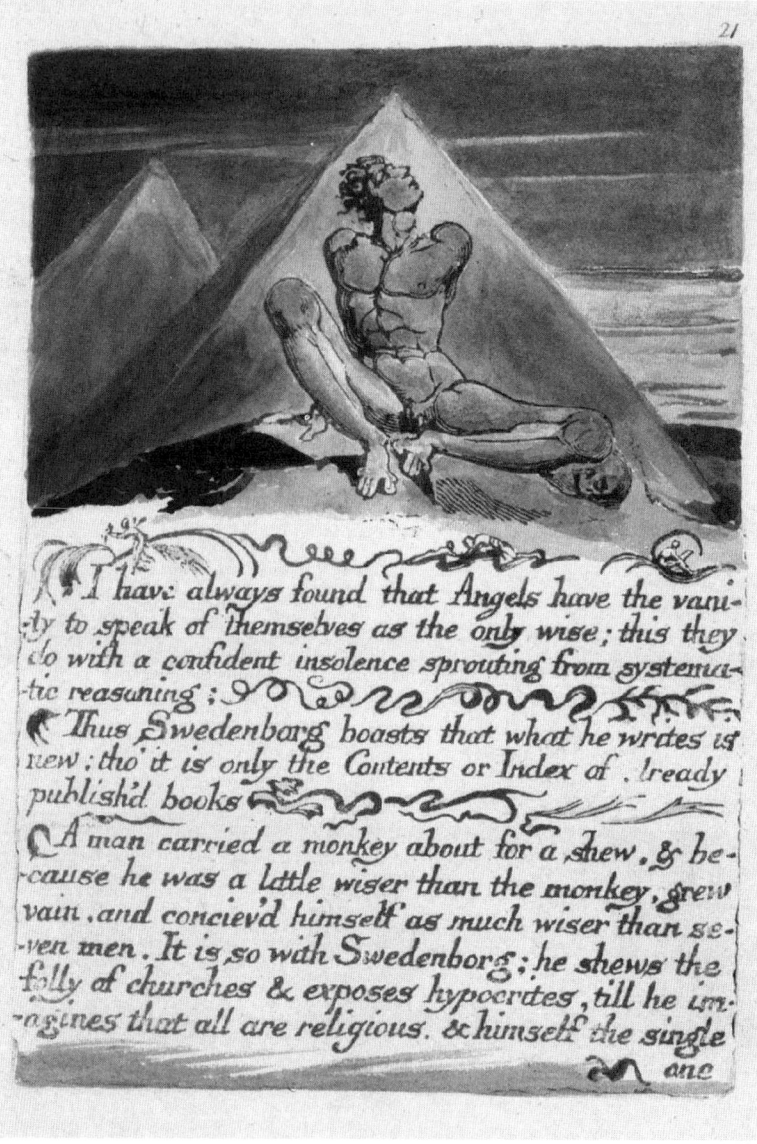

Figure 11. Blake, *The Marriage of Heaven and Hell*, copy D, plate 21. Lessing J. Rosenwald Collection, Library of Congress. Copyright © 2001 the William Blake Archive. Used with permission.

Figure 12. Blake, *Unknown Subject (Let Him look up into the Heaven and laugh in the bright air)*. Rosenwald Collection, National Gallery of Art, Washington. Photograph © 2001 Board of Trustees, National Gallery of Art, Washington.

Figure 13. Schiavonetti after Blake, *Death's Door*. Collection of Robert N. Essick. Reproduced with the kind permission of Robert N. Essick.

Figure 14. Blake, white-line etching of *Death's Door*. Collection of Robert N. Essick. Reproduced with the kind permission of Robert N. Essick.

Figure 15. Blake, *At Death's Door*. Carnegie Museum of Art, Pittsburgh; Bequest of Charles J. Rosenbloom.

Figure 16. Blake, *For Children: Gates of Paradise*, copy D, plate 17. Lessing J. Rosenwald Collection, Library of Congress. Copyright © 2001 the William Blake Archive. Used with permission.

Figure 17. Blake, *America: A Prophecy*, copy E, plate 14. Lessing J. Rosenwald Collection, Library of Congress. Copyright © 2001 the William Blake Archive. Used with permission.

7. Technicalities of the Infinite

It does not, I think, require much of an imaginative leap to consider how the figural cutting, folding, and repetition we encounter in Blake's work might be related to the material cutting, turning, folding, and printing of sheets of copper and of paper in Blake's workshop. For the figural movement here is intimately linked to the material process of production through which these images were generated in a number of different copies during Blake's etching and printing of the illuminated books. The production process used by Blake obviously had a certain sequential logic to it, as each Illuminated book had to go through a number of steps on the way to "completion." But the sequence of steps could vary enormously from one print run to the next, just as the sequence of plates in a particular book could also vary considerably from one copy to another (this is, as Mitchell demonstrates, particularly evident in *The Book of Urizen*, with its many nonverbal plates—and even some of its verbal plates, as we are reminded by the newly rediscovered copy E—inserted in different locations and sequences in the various copies).[50] This suggests a kind of relationship between the printing process and the finished products themselves, and it may not be a coincidence that Blake often printed more than one book at a time, which enabled him more readily perhaps to insert plates from one book into other books. Thus, what I have been discussing here as a question of reading and interpretation is also a question of Blake's own mode of production. What I want to suggest is that the relationship between the process and the products relates to the composition of the books as well as their figurative logic, since, as Joseph Viscomi and Robert Essick have argued, Blake's mode of composition is ultimately inseparable from his mode of production: drawing, and hence compositional "originality" in the act of production itself, rather than printmaking, with its logic of reproduction, was the defining aesthetic.

In the printing of *America*, Blake took full advantage of the special process of relief etching that he had invented. The conventional mode of etching in which Blake was trained—and by which he executed most of his commercial commissions—involved covering a copperplate with an acid-resist varnish and then using a sharp tool to scratch away lines in the resist so that the copper beneath could be exposed to an acidic aqua fortis (in engraving proper, as opposed to etching, the graver would be used to cut into the copper directly).[51] In intaglio printing, the grooves bitten into the copper by the aqua fortis would then be inked, the surface of the plate wiped clean, and the inked lines forced onto the paper by the pressure of the printing press. The resulting image could then be reproduced over and over, generating the

CHAPTER FOUR

series of identical copies which—theoretically if not actually—so interested Babbage in his analysis of industrial production (see chapter 3).

However, Blake's method of printing "in the infernal method" for his own work involved literally painting the acid-resist varnish (and later on, in color printing, paint and pigments) directly on the surface of the copperplate. This allowed him to smoothly integrate words and designs—which in conventional printing were divided into the separate realms and reproductive sequences of typography and engraving—in the same original composition. The plate would then be treated with corrosives ("which in Hell are salutary and medicinal, melting apparent surfaces away, and revealing the infinite which was hid"),[52] which would bite in the exposed surface of the copper so that the image to be printed would be exposed in relief. The raised surface—words and designs together—would then be inked and printed, and the subsequent print could be embellished with further designs and hand colored as well. It is important to note that both conventional typography and engraving were in Blake's time essentially reproductive activities, used primarily for the dissemination of a series of more or less identical copies of original, ontologically prior, texts and images. Blake's illuminated books were, as both Viscomi and Essick make clear, the result of original compositions and drawing on copperplates. What makes Blake's work distinctive is that it breaks down the logic opposing "original" and "reproduction" and leaves us instead with the oxymoronic logic of "original copies," or impressions that have no prototype, images that are *repeated*, but that remain *original* at the same time.[53]

Blake never used his own relief etching process for such reproductive work. "Blake was interested in a medium that permitted original composition in word and design," Essick notes; "harnessing his methods to the same type of commercial tasks burdening him as an intaglio copy engraver would have been antithetical to his basic intentions as one of the great technical innovators in the graphic arts."[54] This, indeed, is what marks Blake's departure from the logic of commercial reproductive engraving: different copies or editions of one of his illuminated books would not only combine words and designs from the beginning, they would differ from other editions and copies of the same book.[55] Despite the discipline and coordination that Blake and Mrs. Blake—he inking the plates and she printing them, according to Viscomi—needed to produce the illuminated books, from Blake's press would emerge not a stream of identical homogeneous products but rather a variety of different copies and editions of the "same" books. This was especially true when Blake turned to color printing in the mid-1790s, which ultimately did away with the need to etch in the outlines of a drawing, since Blake would paint directly on the copperplate and then pull through "copies" that could never have been made identically even if he had wanted to since each pull through the press lifted the pigment from the plate.

The logic of Blake's production process is important for our understanding of the multiple meanings of the illuminated books, since composition, execution, and production were (especially though not only in color printing) seamless activities for Blake, moments of an overall process which had to be repeated any time he wanted to issue new editions of his work. For it was never the case that the copperplates would serve merely as prototypes whose images would be (even more or less) identically replicated—like intaglio prints—at some point after composition and execution had taken place. Although, as Essick says, acid treatment of the etched copperplate "brings a sudden halt to free-wheeling composition and revision" characteristic of the earlier stages of production, even then printing surfaces could, in principle, be added (though with difficulty), and they could certainly be removed or even covered over.[56] Further alterations could, of course, be made during the final phase of production, in which Blake added finishing touches and sometimes water colors by hand. Moreover, by the time of Blake's experiments with color printing, the earlier production logic was taken a step further, and composition, execution, and production necessarily merged into a singular moment. For much of *The Song of Los*, *The Book of Los*, and *The Book of Ahania*, designs were printed from largely unetched plates, with Blake painting the pigments directly on the face of the copperplate, so that very considerable differences were inevitable among the different prints.[57]

Although the illuminated books emerged as "final" products from Blake's printshop, and were put up for sale as such, the unit of production and of the printing process itself was the plate, either individually or in pairs.[58] Thus, the plate—which could often be repeatedly altered, covered, erased, transformed, or augmented, in whole or in part, through any number of repetitions (though within limits)—bears the same relation to the illuminated book as a material product as the image bears to the illuminated book as a figural product, a text. Just as the text is constituted by a variety of images, the book as an object is constituted by impressions from a number of plates, that is, images in a literal sense. Both in the reading and in the making of the illuminated books—their "meaning" and their production—the category of the book as such seems almost an organizing fiction, a convenient rubric or packaging, a useful mode to try to contain what turn out to be uncontainable images.

CHAPTER FOUR

It is striking that in the printing process, the book as such seems almost (but not quite) an afterthought. It took shape as the various impressions were finally gathered together for packaging and sale, rather than as the organizing and guiding rubric for the process of production itself, which was based on different print runs, often including plates from more than one title (the great majority of printing sessions took place in the early to mid-1790s).[59] Even within a single printing session, variability was inevitable, as I have noted, but, "given the potential for variation," Viscomi notes, "the absence of more pronounced differences among copies within an edition is quite surprising and the differences themselves seem quite minor, the inevitable result of a mode of production involving two people printing and coloring numerous impressions by hand, before collation, without prototypes, and within broad parameters of what was visually acceptable."[60] Thus, the immanent variability of the material practice of production, rather than the transcendent logic of the "finished" product, determined the outcome of the printing process. Reification here is an afterthought, not the driving logic of the whole process: the resulting object is the outcome of a variable process, not the confirmation of a determining prototype, a copy based on a prior original. In other words, what does *not* happen in this process of production is the generation of a stream of identical products, homogeneous copies of a single master image, which Babbage said was the key to industrial production. Instead, the logic of Blake's production operates immanently rather than as a transcendent value; or, to use Viscomi's terminology, Blake has adopted the mechanisms of printmaking in order to produce drawings.

8. The Image and the "Good for Nothing Commodity"

I have been suggesting that there is some kind of relationship between the way Blake's illuminated works produce meaning and the way in which they were materially produced. Nelson Hilton, Paul Mann, and others have argued in different ways that how Blake's text works, and specifically how it was made, are significant parts of what it means. I agree. But what I am adding here is that what it means is also a significant part of how it works and how it was made. In other words, it is important to consider the concepts Blake was working with figuratively, as well as trying to empirically deduce them from the technical and material evidence deposited by the production process seen in isolation from the philosophical, textual, religious, and artistic dimension of the works themselves. The technical and material aspects of Blake's production practice are, in other words, inseparable from the conceptual matrix associated with them, which is also elaborated, even if in a different mode, in the books themselves.

In his *Public Address,* Blake presents an admittedly angry and at times inchoate account of his logic of production and its broader socioeconomic significance (which I touched on in the previous chapter). The immediate context of *Public Address* was the disastrous aftermath for Blake of a number of ventures into the commercial art market in the period 1805–9, a disaster which included the only contemporary reviews—uniformly dismal—of Blake's work. This calamitous period in Blake's career began with a commission from the publisher Robert Cromek to produce illustrations and etchings for an edition of Blair's *Grave,* and Cromek's decision soon afterward to take Blake's designs but have them etched by the more "fashionable" hand of Louis Schiavonetti—a decision which wounded Blake severely. The period ended with Blake's doomed exhibition of 1809 at his brother's house (where Blake had been born) at 28 Broad Street in Soho, whose centerpiece was a large painting, *Sir Jeffery Chaucer and the Nine and Twenty Pilgrims on their Journey to Canterbury,* a subject that had been treated in a very successful exhibition by Blake's soon-to-be-former friend Thomas Stothard two years earlier. Blake claimed that he had embarked upon his Canterbury project long before Stothard, who, according to Blake, had been given the idea by the maleficent Cromek and had stolen it.[61]

The acrimonious falling-out of Blake, Stothard, and Cromek—who appears in some of the more apoplectic passages of Blake's notebook as Bob Screwmuch, along with Blake's caricature of Louis Schiavonetti, who appears in the notebook as Assassinetti—is well documented, and I do not need to rehearse it here in any detail.[62] It is, however, worth bearing in mind that it is as a result of this whole debacle—recorded in angry exchanges of letters between Blake and Cromek, and also in Blake's furious and sometimes paranoid outbursts in his *Public Address,* which was directed to the Chalcographic Society (of which, as Dennis Read has pointed out, Cromek was then the secretary)[63]—that our conceptions of Blake the outraged and isolated artist are largely derived. It is also largely as a result of this calamitous period that Blake's reputation as a lunatic was formed. This reputation had to do not only with his artwork, but—something that most critics do not make much of—also with his expression of various antinomian concepts, which were received with ridicule and disdain by the progressive and secular reviewers (notably Robert Hunt) speaking for an enlightened, post-Paineite English society. In other words, it is not commonly recognized that Blake's reputation as a madman has to do with his religious and hence his political positions at least as much as with his odd paintings and bellicose behavior,

CHAPTER FOUR

and that those positions are ultimately inseparable from the form, content, and structure of his artwork as well as his illuminated books; moreover, those reviews, especially the one by Robert Hunt, can be seen as an index of the response of the secular progressive reform movement to the work of Blake, a measure of the enormous gap between Blake's religious, political, and conceptual stance and those of the mainstream public sphere. These are some of the questions that I would like to elaborate in the present section of this chapter.

Cromek transferred the *Grave* commission to Schiavonetti probably because he found Blake's initial white-line etching of *Death's Door*—which folds together the images of the old man and the youth from plates 6 and 12 of *America*—to be inappropriate, too bizarre and outlandish, for a profitable commercial venture. As even Blake's friend Flaxman confided, "I still very much fear his abstracted habits are so much at variance with the usual modes of human life, that he will not derive all the advantage to be wished from the present favourable appearances."[64] Blake broke with Cromek in early 1806 (after which, according to Bentley, he made no more commercial engravings for ten years).[65] The ugliness came to a head with the reviews of the *Grave*, many of which emphasized the bizarre and unseemly nature of the illustrations designed by Blake, though they generally praised Schiavonetti's etchings, and with the review of Blake's exhibition of 1809 (after which Blake began *Public Address*) by Robert Hunt.

All the reviews castigated Blake for what they took to be his absurd, nonsensical, and impossible combinations of the spiritual and the material. The early review of the *Grave* by Hunt in the *Examiner* praised Schiavonetti's work but condemned Blake, accusing him of trying "to perform impossibilities, to convert the pencil into a magical wand, and with it to work wonders, surpassing any recorded in the Tales of the Genii. How 'the visible and the invisible world' can be connected by the aid of the pencil without 'provoking probability,' nay even without outraging it, none but such a visionary as Mr Blake, or such a frantic as Mr Fuseli, could possibly fancy."[66] The reviewer in the *Antijacobin* in November 1808 wrote that "Mr Blake was formerly an engraver, but his talents in that line scarcely advancing to mediocrity, he was induced as we have been informed to direct his attention to the art of design." Exactly as Hunt had, this reviewer took issue with Blake's attempt to connect the material and immaterial worlds: "If it were really Mr Blake's intention 'to connect the visible and invisible world without provoking probability,' he should have done it with threads of silk and not with bars of iron. The beings of another world when depicted on the same canvas as earthly bodies, should be sufficiently immaterial to be veiled by the gossamer, and not, as they are here designed, with all the fullness and rotundity of mortal flesh."[67] The final calamitous review was not exactly of the *Grave* edition, but rather of Blake's exhibition of his paintings at 28 Broad Street and was published by Robert Hunt in the *Examiner* on 17 September 1809. "If beside the stupid and mad-brained political project of the rulers, the sane part of the people of England resquired fresh proof of the alarming increase of the effects of insanity," Hunt began, "they will be too well convinced from its having lately spread into the hitherto sober region of Art...."

> But, when the ebullitions of a distempered brain are mistaken for the sallies of genius by those whose works have exhibited the soundest thinking in art, the malady has indeed attained a pernicious height, and it becomes a duty to endeavour to arrest its progress. Such is the case with the productions and admirers of WILLIAM BLAKE, an unfortunate lunatic, whose personal inoffensiveness secures him from confinement, and, consequently, of whom no public notice would have been taken, if he was not forced on the notice and animadversion of the EXAMINER, in having been held up to public admiration by many esteemed amateurs and professors as a genius in some respect original and legitimate. The praises which these gentlemen bestowed last year on this unfortunate man's illustrations of Blair's *Grave*, have, in feeding his vanity, stimulated him to publish his madness more largely, and thus again exposed him, if not to the derision, at least to the pity of the public. That work was a futile endeavour by bad drawings to represent immaterially by bodily personifications of the soul, while it's partner the body was depicted in company with it, so that the soul was confounded with the body, as the personifying figure had done of the distinguishing characteristics of allegory, presenting only substantial flesh and bones. This conceit was dignified with the character of genius, and the tasteful hand of SCHIAVONETTI, who engraved the work, assisted to give it currency by bestowing an exterior charm on deformity and nonsense. Thus encouraged, the poor man fancies himself a great master, and has painted a few wretched pictures, some of which are unintelligible allegory, others an attempt at sober character by caricature representation, and the whole 'blotted and blurred,' and very badly drawn. These he calls an Exhibition, of which he has published a Catalogue, or rather a farrago of nonsense, unintelligibleness, and egregious vanity, the wild effusions of a distempered brain.[68]

It was in the context of these reviews that Blake wrote the *Public Address* and several other sections of his notebook. It must be noted, however, that Hunt's review addresses not just the paintings in the exhibition, but also Blake's *Descriptive Catalogue*. This piece of writing, which Hunt scornfully dismissed as "a farrago of nonsense," is, on the one hand, characterized by the perhaps inevitable resentment that Blake felt following the *Grave* fiasco; he writes, for example, "the painter courts comparison with his competitors, who, having received fourteen hundred guineas and more from the profits of his designs, in that well-known work, Designs for Blair's Grave, have left him to shift for himself, while others, more obedient to an employer's opinions and directions, are employed, at a great expense, to produce works, in succession to his [i.e., Stothard's Canterbury pilgrims], by which they acquired public patronage. This has hitherto been his lot—to get patronage for others and then to be left and neglected, and his work, which gained that patronage, cried down as eccentricity and madness; as unfinished and neglected by the artist's violent temper, he is sure the works now exhibited, will give the lie to such aspersions." On the other hand, though, the *Descriptive Catalogue* is a fairly cogent exposition not only of some of Blake's aesthetic principles, but of some of the key principles of antinomian enthusiasm, and it would undoubtedly have been recognized as such by the disdainful secular reviewers (see chapter 6).

Most accounts of Blake's critique of the commercial art industry are cast generally in terms of his resentment, as the denunciations of a commercial system by an isolated artist. Few pay sufficient attention to the profoundly significant politico-religious dimension of the damning reviews, or of Blake's work itself. Eaves does indeed include a whole chapter on the religious dimension of Blake's work, but, although he touches on *The Everlasting Gospel* and points out Blake's connections to Gerrard Winstanley—the seventeenth-century communist—Eaves's project is more concerned with the ways in which Blake introduces certain religious themes, largely having to do with the relation of copying and originality, into English-school discourse, and less concerned with the specifically antinomian tradition from which Blake's work emerged. As we saw earlier in the present chapter, Eaves's version of Blake's critique centers mostly on what Blake says about art, and what he documents is a counterhistory of art, and a history of the counterarts, narrated primarily from Blake's perspective. Much of Eaves's account is taken up with Blake's critique of copying, his denunciations of the "artistic machine" and of Joshua Reynolds, his claims to and on behalf of artistic integrity and originality, and the way in which he inverts the priorities of conception and execution and "tightens the sequence of the two to cancel the space that makes imitation possible."[69] The Blake that emerges from Eaves's account is "technologically regressive" and "given to notions of recovery and return," a kind of Luddite trying to stave off a "pincer-like alliance between a totalitarian body politic above and atomization below: the one a ruling class dominating the individual from above—allied, as it were, with the starry worlds—the other dividing the individual from below, at the level of intermeasurable constituents (atoms, Lockean impressions, interchangeable parts, interchangeable workers, money as the measure of all things)."[70]

As I pointed out in the previous chapter, however, Blake's challenge to a broader commercial and political system was formulated long before the *Grave* fiasco, which was only the culminating event in a long engagement. One potential problem with reading back from the resentful Blake of the *Public Address* is that we may end up becoming too preoccupied with the relationship of artist to artwork as one of holistic reunification and overlook the logic of a system based on division, multiplication, and exchange, reading Blake's denunciations of "ignorant journeymen" as the outrage of "an experienced artisan replaced by scab labor, a middle-class worker whose livelihood is threatened simultaneously by upper-class gullibility (to the outrageous appeal of empty fashions imposed by the merchant-traders) and lower-class encroachments (of the unskilled on the skilled)," that is, a resentful condemnation of a social division of labor as opposed to a principled critique of a mode of production (which is not quite the same thing).[71] In other words, there might be another way of framing Blake's opposition to a commercial system of intermeasurable and average and homogenizing exchange.

For if the illuminated books can be seen to break down the opposition between original and copy by subverting the emergent industrial logic of production as reproduction (by using what was recognized as a reproductive technology to generate productions rather than reproductions), then we can see the extent to which Blake's work poses a challenge not only to the logic of producing as copying, but to the much broader set of cultural, economic, political, and religious processes and concepts associated with it. This suggests that Blake's critique of industrial production is to be found not only in his late and resentful work (*Public Address*), but in the very method by which Blake, from his earliest work, distorted the relationship of copy and original which Babbage said was the conceptual heart of industrial production. In other words, Blake's critique of industrial production is both conceptual and practical—simultaneously philosophical and materialist—rather than solely rhetorical.

When reading the illuminated books (and associated prints), the principle of iterability and repetition must, as I have been saying, be considered as a simultaneously material and philosophical matter—at once a technical

CHAPTER FOUR

concern and an interpretive one. The figural reiteration of images *between* works in Blake is inextricably related to the material reiteration of images among versions of the "same" work. But the distinction I am making between figural and material reiteration is misleading because each act of reiteration is in fact both figural and material. For example, the line "every thing that lives is holy" not only had to be etched separately in the plates of *The Marriage* and *America* (and other plates as well); it had to be printed separately in different copies of *The Marriage* and *America*. Thus, what I first called the figural reiteration of an image between *The Marriage* and *America* also becomes a matter of material reiteration as the different editions of the two works were printed—which in turn enables figural comparisons between the two. Figural and material here repeat themselves as one slips into the other.

This is why there is more than a merely intuitive relationship between, on the one hand, reading *America* alongside *Visions of the Daughters* or *The Marriage of Heaven and Hell* and, on the other hand, reading copy G of *America* alongside copy D of *America* or copy A of *America*.[72] The philosophical principle of iterability by which a text assumes different meanings in different contexts—which holds true not just for Blake's texts, of course—is here enacted as a material principle as well. At the same time, the material practice by which the same image is repeatedly reproduced is transformed from a process generating identity to one generating multiplicity and variety.[73] For in the illuminated books, philosophical concept and material practice merge into each other and become inseparable. The aesthetic form of the illuminated books must be considered in terms of the combination of philosophical and material practices, not merely as derivative of material practice.

We are then faced with a very serious and potentially disabling dilemma. As long ago as 1985, Robert Essick pointed out what he calls the "fearsomely generative propensities" of the trend in Blake scholarship away from solely literary readings of the books and toward material as well as visual considerations.[74] Are we, he asks, now going to see the trend taken to its logical conclusion, so that scholarship on *Songs of Innocence and of Experience* as such would be altogether supplanted by scholarship based on different versions of different plates of different copies, and on comparisons between them? If so, he points out, only half jokingly, that we would be "offered the prospect of about nineteen hundred articles on just these two illuminated books." Essick's point is not that our critical concern with material questions—and especially our concern with variations among different versions or editions of the illuminated books—should disable scholarship with a breakdown into nothing but minute particularities, leaving us in effect unable to see the wood for the trees. His concern is, rather, to propose some chalcographic guidelines for interpretation. "That Blake permitted—perhaps even welcomed—chance as an intrinsic feature of his production methods is highly significant," Essick writes; "accordingly, its role must be taken into account by the interpreter of the images produced, particularly when they are seen in contradistinction to the vastly more uniform repeatability of typeset texts and intaglio prints." With perpetually variant impressions, he continues, "the relationship between print and plate becomes problematic, as do the very concepts of stability and ideality dependent upon repeatability. Are we to take each impression from a single plate as an independent work of art, or each as an imperfect representative of the image in the copper?" Both choices are problematic.

What Essick proposes—via a reading of several successive impressions of the final plate of *Jerusalem*—is that we pay attention to observations concerning technical matters of production and the material specificities of the illuminated books (and the differences among them) as "a useful propaedeutic to set down what one sees as clearly as possible before attributing to it purpose and meaning." The point of this, he says, is "to set forth the technological matrix in which forms and their meanings evolve." But, he adds, there is one further crucial step in "building a foundation for interpretation—an understanding of each impression not simply as a separate and alternative version of an image but as a stage in the continuous evolution of a graphic form."[75] What we should attend to, Essick concludes, is the *logic* of that evolution as revealed by the pattern of changes between one version of an illuminated book and another; for elaborations of the logic and the pattern of changes and repetitions among the books are ultimately more productive for interpretations of the books than an exhaustive attempt to catalog one by one the manifestations of those changes in different copies of different plates of different books. He insists, however, that this evolution should not be considered the result of the author's unilateral will or intentions prior to the act of execution: concept and material practice develop together.[76]

I would like to add to Essick's cogent account the possibility that the significance of variations among versions of the illuminated books may not be symbolic or iconographic at all, but rather conceptual. That the variability of Blake's mode of production problematizes the concepts of stability dependent upon repeatability may be not a problem for meaning generation, but a meaning *in itself*. The disruption of identity precisely through the process of repeatability may be exactly what is significant about the illuminated books as a mode of production—not the only significant thing, to be sure,

CHAPTER FOUR

but nevertheless a point of significance that must be taken seriously on its own, or in conjunction with other meanings. Hence, our recognition of the changes that take place with the repetition of a single image may be seen as an interpretation in its own right, not merely a path leading to something more significant.

What this suggests, then, is that the different versions of particular plates or books can be read not necessarily as stages in a progressive development, let alone as autonomous units, but rather as reiterations in which some of the traces of difference have assumed a material form. Meaning, in the approach that I propose here, can be seen to be generated and amplified through repetition, rather than threatened by it; and hence, the process of repetition itself directly generates meanings, rather than merely supplying the preconditions for meaning. Because of the importance of this production of meaning through repetition, I also think that we should pay attention to the *similarities* and *continuities*—that is, the repetitions—between the versions of the same plate or same book or different books, since what we must trace is the way in which similarities *become* differences, and the way in which what is repeated, even if it is apparently identical, can become different precisely by virtue of repetition (since what is repeated has to be the same at some level, since otherwise it obviously cannot be a repetition). Instead of taking those similarities for granted as a kind of continuous base on or against which differences can be registered, measured, and made relevant for interpretation, we should also question them and take their significance into account.

What I am suggesting here, in other words, is that we should not try to derive the "meaning" of the illuminated books solely in symbolic or iconographic readings. For such readings would have to be based on what Viscomi refers to as "the relation among the signs that constitute the verbal-visual system of an illuminated poem."[77] My point here is not to contest Viscomi's distinction between differences "in kind," which he says "alter the reading experience," and differences "in degree," which he says do not usually alter that experience. It is, rather, to open up the highly circumscribed notion of meaning that Viscomi's approach seeks to authorize. For, Viscomi argues, "the idea that variants may alter or prompt new readings of an image or a poem is not in question; what is questionable are the ideas that Blake willfully produced variants within editions for the purpose of making each copy of the edition a unique version of the book, that he believed variants within editions altered the book's meaning, and that variations express a conscious desire to rebel against engraving, uniformity, or the 'aristocracy and commercial bourgeoisie.'"[78] Viscomi's argument clearly has a polemical edge, which is to problematize critical inferences about the possible "ideological" significance of the differences between Blake's necessarily heterogeneous and variable mode of production and those of a rather more homogeneous production process. Viscomi concludes that we should be wary of investing Blake's method of production with "ideological" significance.

And yet, even if we were to agree with Viscomi that it would be difficult to ascribe interpretive significance to the specific differences, such as the addition or deletion of specific features, between, for example, particular copies of *America*, we should not be too quick to dismiss the interpretive significance—that is, the broad cultural and political significance—of the variability built into Blake's printing process. Blake developed a mode of production that *necessarily* produced heterogeneous products at precisely the historical moment when manufacturers—and not just those in the art world—were seizing on the potential offered by another mode of production that would, in order to spew out a stream of identical products, ultimately reorient not only the ways in which people work but the entire cultural and political organization of societies all over the world. Moreover, we should be wary of placing too much empirical emphasis on the *products* of a production process in order to determine the significance of its *logic*. There will be variability among the products emerging from even the most efficient factory production line, but that is not to say that we should disregard the fact that the logic of such an assembly line is to produce identical commodities, however much it may fail to do so in practice. When Babbage seized upon copperplate engraving as a kind of ur-form of the factory system, he was more concerned with its conceptual logic than with the flawed products actually emerging from a commercial engraving house.

For what it is worth, Blake himself consistently refused to distinguish between artistic concerns and political ones. Many people are familiar with his declaration in the last year of his life that "a Line is a Line in its Minutest Subdivision Strait or Crooked It is Itself & Not Intermeasurable with or by any Thing Else," which is clearly an intervention in the world of art history and the realm of aesthetics. But it is worth remembering the continuation of the very same sentence, which I have already had occasion to quote elsewhere: "but since the French Revolution Englishmen are all Intermeasurable one by Another Certainly a happy state of Agreement to which I for one do not Agree. God keep me from the Divinity of Yes & No too The Yea Nay Creeping Jesus from supposing Up & Down to be the same Thing as all Experimentalists must suppose."[79] Evidently, the question of intermeasurability and the concepts of exchange, reproduction, and equality from which it cannot be meaningfully separated are simultaneously matters of religion, politics, economics, philosophy, and technology, and not just art. Clearly, material practices never take place outside "ideology," or outside a system of meanings and beliefs and values.

The distinctions between production and reproduction, originality and duplication, singularity and reproducibility, heterogeneity and homogeneity, identity and multiplicity, the exchangeable and nonexchangeable, the intermeasurable and nonintermeasurable, the average and exceptional, the equal and different—all of which do play a significant role in Blake's illuminated books—were, through the 1790s and beyond the turn of the century, *also* the conceptual bases—indeed, the ideologemes, the basic conceptual and ideological building blocks[80]—of the argument of the advocates of liberty against those of the ancien régime. They were, furthermore, the ideologemes of an emergent industrial mode of production which, as we saw in the previous chapter, regarded itself as quite incompatible with those scattered and heterogeneous modes of production, or even work practices and cultural norms of temporality and compensation, deemed to be too irregular, too erratic, too inefficient, too unquantifiable, too unmeasurable, too wasteful, too unpredictable to conform to the requirements of a modern age (see chapter 3). I hope to have demonstrated in the previous two chapters, and parts of this one as well, the extent to which these questions are of great structural and thematic importance in the illuminated books, as well as in the political, economic, and cultural context from which they emerged. For in the illuminated books, Blake was tinkering with and disrupting the core ideologemes of industrial production and the free market: the concepts that would be put together to form the "language" of industrialization and liberal democracy appear in Blake's work as a kind of slang which to the dominant language could appear only as perverse or meaningless gabble.

For Blake, the distinction between the material and the conceptual does not hold: it is as false an opposition as that between the soul and the body, or the subject and the object, or the visible and the invisible, or the physical and the spiritual—or the very distinction between conception and execution, which, as we saw in the previous chapter, had become essential not only to the art of engraving but to industrial production in general. These were, of course—not at all coincidentally—the very questions that the reviewers of his illustrations for the *Grave* most took him to task for, accusing him of being a hallucinating visionary for his unwillingness to distinguish the body and the soul, the visible and the invisible, the material and the immaterial, "confounding," as Hunt proclaimed, questions that should be kept distinct.

But however exceptional Blake may have been by 1809–10, in historical perspective he was hardly so exceptional at all, as he was one among tens of thousands who sought to question these transformations and their underlying narratives of "progress" and "development" through the seventeenth and eighteenth centuries.

CHAPTER FIVE

Blake and Romantic Imperialism

> When the Arabs had no trace of literature or science, they composed beautiful verses on the subjects of love and war. The flights of the imagination, and the laboured deductions of reason, appear almost incompatible.
> —Mary Wollstonecraft

> Every accumulation of knowledge, and especially such as is obtained by social communication with people over whom we exercise a dominion founded on the right of conquest, is useful to the state.
> —Warren Hastings

> The Oriental generally acts, speaks, and thinks in a manner exactly opposite to the European.
> —Lord Cromer

> We ourselves and the things pertaining to us come and go, pass and repass; there is nothing of our own which may not become foreign to us, and nothing foreign to us which may not become our own.
> —Giordano Bruno

1. Introduction

At that momentous historical turning point, toward the end of the eighteenth century, in which almost every attempt to represent otherness seemed to slip into the exoticizing political aesthetic that would enable and justify imperial conquest, it was a matter of some urgency to be able to think of the foreign without resorting to (or sliding into) the language and figures of exoticism. What I want to suggest in this chapter is that Blake drew on and reformulated for the exigencies of his own time a heterogeneous underground tradition that stressed the continuity of European and Afro-Asiatic cultures, rather than the sharp differentiation between Europe and its others which would prove essential to modern imperialism. For, as we shall see, Blake's interest in certain mystical currents which had plunged deep underground long before his own time offered him a way to articulate a logic of cultural heterogeneity that refused the discourse of exoticism. Indeed, his simultaneously political and aesthetic stance on otherness must be seen to enable a carefully articulated position on the cultural politics of imperialism, as well as a discourse of freedom contesting the internal imperialism of the state. Or, rather, Blake's elaboration of a form of religious and political freedom that would defy what he called "state religion" was also an elaboration of a form of political and cultural freedom from the discourse and practice of imperialism. In the following pages I will elaborate Blake's position with reference to the greatest imperial exoticism of all—Orientalism—to try to explain why his position has not been adequately recognized by most earlier scholarship, and to suggest what significance all this has for our understanding and interpretation of the rest of Blake's work in relation to 1790s radicalism and the culture of modernization that emerged with it. What I want to propose is that through this investigation of Blake's anti-imperialism we will discover how he found a way to produce a critique for his own time, rather than as a quasi-reactionary attempt to return to some lost original fullness, both of the ancien régime and of the bourgeois radicalism which attacked it—a way to refuse the logic of the state and of the discourse of sovereign power itself in the name of what he would call "Immortal Joy."[1]

2. Romantic Orientalism

Few English writers or artists of the 1790s with an interest in the "foreign" were able to approach, or even to imagine, foreignness in terms other than exoticism (whether superficial or extravagant, critical or adulatory), which tended to magnify difference into the mark of insurmountable alienation. Of all the exoticisms that blossomed in the two decades before and after 1800, Orientalism had the greatest cultural and political significance. For in those years Orientalism began to take on new significance as Britain's imperial project slowly reemerged (following the debacles of the 1770s and 1780s, and in particular the sensational trial of Warren Hastings) in a properly modern form and with a new set of approaches—informed and sustained by the emergent cultural logic of modernization—to colonized and subject peoples.[2] Especially given these changes, and given the emergence of an altogether new imperial mission fully coinciding with a modern worldview developing in the 1790s, it is in terms of the Orient that we can

CHAPTER FIVE

most clearly locate Blake's divergence from the emergent culture of modernization as that culture was articulated both in romanticism and in the radical movement alongside which it appeared. The Orient and Orientalism provide us with an important index of the distance between the aesthetic and political position articulated by Blake and the one being elaborated by other writers of the 1790s, including Tom Paine, Constantin Volney, Mary Wollstonecraft, John Thelwall, and William Wordsworth.

The hegemonic radical critique of the ancien régime and its "traditional culture" of despotism, patronage, ritual, corruption, and privilege helped to define an emergent culture of modernization based on a universalist discourse of rights and duties, rather than inherited privileges; a discourse of merit, rather than religious inspiration; and, above all, a discourse of sturdy rational frugality, control, virtue and regulation, rather than emotional (let alone sensual) excess. By 1800 the Orient would be definitively recognized as the imaginary locus par excellence of the culture of excess—despotic, enthusiastic, sensual, exotic, erotic—that was the target of bourgeois radicalism. Hence, it served as the ideal surrogate target for radical critique, an imaginary space on which to project all the supposed faults of the old regime and then subject them to attack, scorn, condemnation, repudiation—a cultural and ideological process that cannot meaningfully be separated from the simultaneous change in paradigms of imperial rule, which were already preparing the way for the enormous expansion of imperial activity later in the nineteenth century. Perhaps the single clearest example of this can be seen in the work of Constantin Volney, who had enormous influence on English radicalism in the 1790s and afterward, and whose *Travels in Syria and Egypt* (1787) and *Ruins of Empires* (1791) may almost be thought of as handbooks for imperial conquest. According to Edward Said, Napoleon's invasion of Egypt in 1798—which marked the beginning of the new modern phase of imperial rule—was partly inspired by Volney's writings, and indeed Napoleon discusses Volney's work in his *Campagnes d'Egypte et de Syrie*.[3] Modern scholars have not yet fully explored the striking, at times almost comprehensive, overlap between 1790s radicalism and the new imperialism. Indeed, romanticist scholarship generally—and Blake scholarship in particular—has been blinded by a tendency to take the hegemonic form of radicalism at its word and to associate it with a vision of freedom for all, whereas in fact it was from its origins associated with the emergence of a new form of imperial power, and of what we ought today to recognize as Eurocentric culture. Volney, whose imperial attitudes were inextricable from his radicalism, was hardly a unique case, if only because of his influence: E. P. Thompson points out (without mentioning Volney's impressive imperial credentials) that *The Ruins* was published in cheap pocket-book form, certain chapters were frequently circulated as tracts, and the book itself "remained in the libraries of many artisans in the 19th century."[4]

As we have seen in previous chapters, the dominant radical political culture of the 1790s, with its Enlightenment pedigree, emphasized highly regulated individual consumer and political choice against both the despotism of the ancien régime (which, without regard to merit or reason, excluded all but a tiny minority from a public sphere which it kept under strict control) and the vulgarity, conformity, and potentially catastrophic excess of the "swinish multitude," from whom many radicals were as eager as their aristocratic enemies to distance themselves. For, as Jon Mee observes, the radical "Enlightenment appeal to critical reasoning as constitutive of the public sphere, while potentially democratic, was always defined in terms of certain minimum requirements that guaranteed the exclusion of the unlearned and unlettered," with all their potential for dangerous enthusiasm.[5] Radicals such as Tom Paine and John Thelwall and Volney himself—with all their distrust of enthusiasm and their contrary faith in skepticism, doubt, and evidence—repeatedly stressed the role of rational knowledge and inquiry as the appropriate tools for political reform (even though they could at times also mingle certain forms of mysticism with their frugal rationality).[6] In so doing, they appealed to a rational location equidistant from the emotional appeals of Edmund Burke on the one hand and, on the other hand, what Paine would call the "class of people of that description which in England is called the '*mob*,'" who, according to Paine, "are rather the followers of the camp than of the standard of liberty, and have yet to be instructed how to reverence it."[7] 1790s radicalism, at least in its hegemonic formulation, must be understood as a project to locate and articulate a middle-class sensibility as against the unruly excesses of both higher and lower orders. Indeed, as Anna Clark argues, this tendency to articulate middle-class values would eventually abandon radicalism as "the 'progressive and improving' middle class distanced itself even more from both the 'effete aristocracy and the licentious rabble,' using Evangelicism to justify obedience to the established order as well as to serve as a means of moral reform."[8] In warning of the dangers of excess, and particular the unruly excess of the enthusiastic lower orders—the "mob"—the dominant radicals of the 1790s would repeatedly point to the Orient as the prime example, the clearest illustration, of what they meant. Thus, in addition to serving the radical cause as the imaginary locus of so-called traditional culture or feudal despotism, the Orient also served as the imaginary locus of the worst excesses of plebeian dangerous enthusiasm—truly the worst of both worlds.

CHAPTER FIVE

As we shall see, the writers of the 1790s significantly realigned the Oriental vision of earlier writers, such as Montesquieu, whose work had enormous influence on both the American Revolution and the later radical struggle inspired by it. However, although it would be modified, Montesquieu's vision of Oriental despotism, which first appeared in *Persian Letters* (1721) and was later elaborated in *The Spirit of Laws* (1747), played a major role in 1790s Orientalism. Like his followers in the 1790s, of course, Montesquieu was ultimately more concerned with European politics than with Eastern ones. His vision of despotism serves not as a depiction of an "actual" Orient but rather as a warning to European elites of their own tendency toward corruption and the rule of the passions. For despotism in Montesquieu's work, as Althusser has pointed out, is not a matter of one man's rule—the imposition of his will—over others. After all, Usbek in *Persian Letters* is a total failure in this respect, and so are his eunuchs, since the power dynamics of the harem are far from straightforward and operate instead in what the First Eunuch calls an "ebb and flow of authority and submission."[9] Rather, for Montesquieu, despotism involves the unregulated moment-by-moment rule of the passions, both the violent passions of Usbek and his eunuchs and the lustful passions of the harem women—passions which succeed each other in an "ebb and flow" of power. As Althusser points out, this is a vision of despotism as the dissolution of regularity, succession, stability, and the reduction of all politics to the highly turbulent rule of momentary passions, and indeed to a "regime of the moment." Moreover, and much more seriously, Althusser argues, for Montesquieu, pure despotism "leaves the people to their passions," and "when passions dominate, the people, who are passion, always win in the end."[10] This, according to Althusser, is precisely what Montesquieu seeks to warn his readers of: a vision of despotism—in which "all men are equal,"[11] in which "the people hurried away of themselves, push things as far as they can go,"[12] in which "the disorders they commit are all extreme"[13]—precisely as a "regime of popular revolution."[14] As we shall see, popular and Oriental extremism and enthusiasm would invariably be linked together in much of the political discourse of the 1790s. However, at the same time, albeit somewhat paradoxically, the image of Oriental enthusiasm and despotism would also be mobilized by the hegemonic radical movement in its confrontation with what it took to be an equally extremist and emotional ancien régime. Against the luxurious and superficial showiness of the established order, the hegemonic radical movement sought to bring into being, by appealing to it, a sober, rational, frugal "middle," subject to neither the corruption of the upper class nor the enthusiasm of the lower class.

Nowhere is the radical appeal to a rational, sober, reasoning, instructing (and relentlessly productive) middle more clearly made than in Mary Wollstonecraft's *Vindication of the Rights of Woman*, which explicitly addresses itself to women in the middle class, "because they appear to be in the most natural state," as opposed to either the presumably mindless (let alone swinish) multitude or an upper class made up of "weak, artificial beings, raised above the common wants and affections of their race," who, "in premature unnatural manner, undermine the very foundation of virtue, and spread corruption through the whole mass of society."[15] Both the vocabulary and the underlying concepts (corruption, contagion, disease, debauchery, idleness, weakness, unnaturalness, degeneration, effeminacy) of such accusations were carefully and exactly lifted from the list of charges which were being made at the very same time—by Wollstonecraft among others—against all those Oriental despots supposedly luxuriating in their decaying seraglios.

In this context it is especially striking that scholars (as far as I know) have yet to take seriously, or to make much of, the fact that Blake was basically the *only* major poet of the late eighteenth and early nineteenth centuries who categorically refused to dabble in recognizably Orientalist themes or motifs. Certainly, each of the other major romantic poets had at least a passing interest in Orientalism—if not a full-blown Orientalist phase. For many writers and artists of the period the Orient provided not just an important point of reference for cultural or political difference, but an essential scene in the formation of a literary or artistic career. Consider the array of Orientalist publications from even the early part of the period—including, to name only a few cases, Sir William Jones's translations from (and imitations of) poetry in Arabic, Persian, and Sanskrit, William Beckford's *Vathek*, Robert Bage's *Fair Syrian*, Samuel Taylor Coleridge's *Kubla Khan*, Robert Southey's *Thalaba the Destroyer*; Cornelia Knight's *Dinarbas*, Walter Savage Landor's *Gebir*; Richard Johnson's *Oriental Moralist*, Elizabeth Hamilton's *Letters of a Hindoo Raja*, and Charlotte Dacre's *Zofloya*, not to mention the virtually endless matrix of references to "Oriental despotism" in the surge of political pamphlets in the 1790s, almost exclusively in the work produced by radicals, to all of which would be added in later decades the somewhat redefined Orientalism of, for example, Byron's Turkish tales, *Childe Harold*, and *Don Juan*, Thomas Moore's *Lalla Rookh*, Percy Shelley's *Ozymandias, Revolt of Islam*, and *Alastor*; the Oriental tableaux of Delacroix and Gérôme, and the opium-munching Malay of De Quincey's *Confessions of an English Opium-Eater*.

Certainly, the later Orientalism of Byron, Shelley, and De Quincey, or Delacroix and Gérôme, has attracted much more scholarly interest than the

CHAPTER FIVE

Figure 18. Eugène Delacroix, French, 1798-1863, *The Combat of the Giaour and Hassan*, 1826, oil on canvas, 59.6 × 73.4 cm, Gift of Mrs. Bertha Palmer Thorne, Mrs. Rose Movius Palmer, Mr. and Mrs. Arthur M. Wood, and Mr. and Mrs. Gordon Palmer, 1962.966. The Art Institute of Chicago. All Rights Reserved.

earlier material.[16] But although the earlier period was already all-pervasively obsessed with the East, nowhere in Blake's work from that period (or later for that matter) do we see the turbans, harems, genies, seraglios, sultans, viziers, eunuchs, slave girls, janissaries, snake charmers, fakirs, and imams made familiar by two or three generations of European Orientalist mythmaking and found irresistible by most of Blake's romantic contemporaries.

Marilyn Butler reminds us that the scope and variety of romantic Orientalism prevented it from becoming as monolithic as Edward Said in his seminal study sometimes suggests Orientalism can be.[17] Butler's main concern is to demonstrate the variety of positions on the Orient in romantic-period Britain, not all of them critical of Eastern culture. As I suggest in *Romantic Imperialism*, however, the variety of romantic and preromantic Orientalist positions along a spectrum from the quasi-sympathetic (William Jones,

Figure 19. Eugène Delacroix, *La Mort de Sardanapale*. Reproduced by kind permission of the Louvre, Paris.

Lady Sydney Morgan, Byron, Mary Wortley Montagu) to the downright hostile (Robert Southey, Charles Grant, Thomas Maurice, Mary Wollstonecraft, Percy Shelley) should not be mistaken for a range of positions "for" and "against" imperialism. Rather, these different modes of Orientalism correspond to different and highly specifiable moments in Britain's (and the East India Company's) imperial project—in which the romantic period marks a moment of transition—and hence to different approaches and strategies for successful colonial rule.[18]

After all, Warren Hastings's profound interest in the culture and literature of India was as essential to imperial policy in the 1780s as Thomas Macaulay's notorious contempt for non-European cultures and literatures ("A single shelf of a good European library...") would be in the 1830s. Their respective knowledge and ignorance were ultimately matters of state, not merely of personal taste. In any case, however heterogeneous they may be, and whether they valorize or excoriate the East, what all forms of Orientalism have in common, according to the definition developed by Edward

CHAPTER FIVE

Said, is an underlying structural logic distinguishing the same from the different, Occident from Orient, self from other. Even if not all writers found or even sought ways of "realizing an alienness that was imaginatively almost impossible to cope with,"[19] and even if the alien can be presented with either a positive or a negative valence, such a discourse of differentiation, whether absolute or relative, defines and structures romantic approaches to the East.

It has been over half a century since Raymond Schwab argued that the emergence of romanticism itself had been inspired by the European "discovery" of the East in what he calls the Oriental Renaissance of the late eighteenth century—a claim that has had surprisingly little impact on the way romanticist literary scholarship conceives of its object of study.[20] A wave of translations of Eastern texts opened up whole new vistas of the imagination for European artists and writers. The European "discovery" of the East helped to define Europe's dramatically changing relationship with its newly invented others.[21] This relationship both determined and was determined by the political and cultural exigencies of European empire-building projects, of which, of course, the most extensive was the British—over one hundred and fifty million people were brought under British imperial control between 1790 and 1830. The imperial relationship between Europe and its others sometimes inspired and sometimes compelled European writers to articulate what it was that made Europe different from its others. That is, it prompted the emergence of a new sense of imperial European subjectivity against the Afro-Asiatic objects of European rule—a process that was at times exhilarating and at times threatening. In this sense, Orientalism can be thought of as a collective version of the highly personalized individual experience of the sublime.[22] Just as the experience of the sublime, in the realm of aesthetics and philosophy, enables the constitution of an individual phenomenological self as against some profound force (natural or otherwise), Orientalism enables the constitution of a collective cultural and political identity, the definition of an imperial culture as against its civilizational others. This suggests the possible nature of the relationship between the newly developing Orientalist experience of the East and the more specifically *individual* experience of the sublime that we ordinarily associate with Wordsworthian romanticism. Romanticism may, in effect, be thought of as the discourse emerging from and articulating both encounters (collective and individual) at once.[23] Or, more broadly speaking, it may be recognized as a discourse of otherness which comprehends Orientalism along with other forms of exoticism.[24]

The nature of the relationship between, on the one hand, the civilizational encounter of West and East and, on the other hand, the individual encounter of self and other in arenas often far removed from the Orient itself must be elaborated at a conceptual level. For it seems unlikely to have been merely a coincidence that the romantic period witnessed the consolidation of both bourgeois individualism—the cornerstone of modern cultural politics and political culture—and a new modern imperial project. On the one hand, the consolidation through the romantic period of the solitary self as the dominant cultural, aesthetic, and political category owed as much to the changing nature of the large-scale European encounter with "other" cultures as it did to small-scale individual encounters with the romantic otherness of, for example, Nature, working-class mobs, the Scottish Highlands, or foreigners. And, on the other hand, all these forms of domination—in which the dialectic of self and other functioned in essentially the same way—would have been impossible, or would have taken an entirely different form, without the cultural, aesthetic, and political category of the solitary self. Thus, we might argue that the imperial politics of otherness in the romantic period were as essential to the construction and consolidation of the bourgeois sense of self as the latter was to them, for it was in the sovereignty of the empire that the sovereignty—the empire—of the self reached its apotheosis. The change of mission and self-understanding of Britain's imperial project in the romantic period, in other words, would not have been possible, or at least it would not have taken the shape it did, without the category of the subject, or the self; and the subject, or the self, would not have made sense, would not have taken the shape *it* did, without that change in mission and the dramatic alteration of Britain's relationship with its colonial others, above all in the Orient. Thus, the articulation, through the 1790s, of the discourse of self-determination, was often an explicitly imperialist discourse; and, as we shall see, attempts to resist that discourse often took on an anti-imperialist stance.

We must therefore keep in mind that that version of Orientalism which emerged in the 1790s and would be significantly altered only after 1815 or so (with the work of Byron and Shelley, as discussed by Nigel Leask and others) cannot meaningfully be separated from highly politically charged discussions of the status and rights of the individual, and from an ontological and epistemological process of self-definition that extended far beyond the "anxieties of empire" that Leask has elaborated specifically in terms of the Orient itself. This process would ultimately enable the constitution of a transcendental viewing subject from whose philosophical, aesthetic, and phenomenological standpoint the culture of (Western) modernity could be understood and defined for better or for worse—as against, for example, the sublime panoramas of Oriental splendor and/or decay that emerged in

CHAPTER FIVE

Montesquieu and Antoine Galland, accelerated through the work of Jones and Johann von Herder, were realigned by Volney and Southey, and would reach a kind of crisis in Byron and De Quincey (to mention only a few of the dozens of writers experimenting with Orientalist themes through the eighteenth century and on into the romantic period). Leask's "anxieties of empire" are not, in other words, limited to the East itself. Especially in the 1790s, these are the anxieties attendant upon the constitution of the bourgeois subject, a process whose primary concern was ultimately not the other, but rather the politicization of the self, the citizen, the subject, at a moment in which aesthetic, political, and philosophical discourses converged in that explosion of activity that characterized the 1790s—an explosion in which the Orient was only one laboratory, however important and, indeed, essential it may have been.

3. Radical Orientalism

What we can distinguish as a specifically 1790s form of Orientalism—which provides the context for the emergence of Blake's own critique of exoticism—is therefore characterized not merely by certain "anxieties of empire," but by a simultaneously ontological, epistemological, phenomenological, and philosophico-political obsession with the self, the citizen, the subject. At the same time, the explosion through the 1790s of writing on self-determination and the rights of the sovereign individual was also an Orientalist discourse. Of course, 1790s radicalism, especially in the hands of writers like Paine, Thelwall, or Wollstonecraft, was not nearly as interested in the Orient "as such" as it was in the self from whose standpoint the East could (and would) ultimately be viewed and controlled. Here once again we must push Schwab's point farther than he wanted to take it. For almost all, if not quite literally all, British Orientalism in the 1790s (Wollstonecraft's, for example, or Paine's) had literally nothing to do with the experience of the East, whether personal or collective, let alone with the actual cultures and civilizations of that part of the earth whose fate it was to be gathered under the rubric of "the Orient." The Orient was important to the dominant form of 1790s radicalism, and hence to the Wordsworthian romanticism which emerged alongside and in dialogue with it, not because of its (genuine or perceived) civilizational otherness, and not because of any experience of that otherness, but because it could be mobilized as an imaginary site on which to project all those political and ideological modes of being—forms of subjectivity—incompatible with the hegemonic radical tendency.

Of all those modes of being, despotism, idleness, femininity, and luxury, as well as a certain brand of enthusiasm, were by far the most incompatible with what writers such as Paine, Volney, Thelwall, and (again most clearly) Wollstonecraft were proposing. Moralism, and particularly that species of moralism linking so thoroughly together the work of the hegemonic radicals of the 1790s with that of their supposed enemies—the archconservative evangelical crusaders (notably Wilberforce and More)—in a common attack on aristocratic indolence, undoubtedly had a role to play here. However, despotism, idleness, femininity, and luxury were excoriated by the radicals not simply on the basis of moralism, but rather on far more urgent conceptual and philosophical grounds. And it was the elaboration of these grounds that would ultimately mark the distinction between the 1790s radicals and their conservative evangelical counterparts, with whom they otherwise have so much in common.[25]

It is in Wollstonecraft that we find the clearest and most carefully and thoroughly articulated exposition of the relationship between 1790s radicalism and Orientalism. *A Vindication of the Rights of Woman* is haunted by a fear of the seraglio. However, for Wollstonecraft the seraglio is not just a kind of prison for women, but rather the most appropriate synecdoche for the Orient as a locus of despotism, idleness, femininity, and luxury, those great scourges of the decent, virtuous, sober, and "manly" citizen—male and female—whose rights she aims to vindicate. For the rights of the manly citizen are shown to be incompatible with the seraglio, and with the East in general, for the same reason that they are incompatible with an aristocratic economy also supposedly characterized by "unnatural" despotism, idleness, and luxury. Over and over again, Wollstonecraft deploys the trope of Asiatic despotism (and the seraglio in particular) in order to articulate her argument in favor of the manly rights of what could now be recognized—for the first time—as a specifically Western mode of citizenship. This mode of citizenship is not only incompatible with the East, but structurally at odds with it. Wollstonecraft's articulation of the rights and duties of citizenship (couched, of course, in the language of natural universalism with which the West, or this West at any rate, has always privileged its own culture, as opposed to the unnatural and degenerate cultures of the East, which it excludes from all claims to the universal) rests upon a unyielding contrast with the "unnatural" contagion threatened from the East.

In fact, what we see throughout the corpus of 1790s radicalism—Wollstonecraft's text is only the clearest and most thoroughly consistent case—is a conflation of the enemies of the liberal-radical cause, the aristocratic enemy and the Oriental enemy, in which the faults of the former are rewritten and overcoded in terms of the faults of the latter, and the faults of both are gendered as feminine. In other words, the supposed characteristics of Oriental society and culture are projected onto the aristocratic enemies of the radical cause ("the proud and polished, the debauched, effeminate, and luxurious," as John Thelwall put it)[26] while at the same time the Orient becomes the topos of aristocratic degeneration, and the Oriental seraglio the dark cousin of the aristocratic palace, both literally oozing degeneration, corruption, and filth into the society at large. "The dissipation and luxury that reign uncontrolled," William Godwin warned, "have spread effeminacy and irresolution everywhere."[27] Indeed, such a link between the Oriental and the aristocratic would hardly have been original in Wollstonecraft, Thelwall, or Godwin, of course: the great Cagliostro had already given expression to that convergence in himself in the 1780s, and Philip de Loutherbourg had embellished Beckford's seat at Fonthill precisely by further Orientalizing it; moreover, as John Barrell and Nigel Leask point out, pseudo-Oriental style continued to be enjoyed among the fashionable elite (even if as what Barrell calls an "inoculating" gesture).[28] But in Wollstonecraft the convergence is elevated from the merely naughty or fashionable to a dire threat to social order and propriety; in Wollstonecraft, the connection of the aristocratic and the Oriental is gendered, saturated with a discourse of femininity, and elaborated as a threat not only to a specifically masculine-gendered virtue, but to the very possibility of constituting a bourgeois subject, a masculine-gendered citizen (whether male or female does not really matter, as in Wollstonecraft's account gender as a social construction quite comprehensively overwrites sex as a matter of mere physiology).

Consider, for example, the question of style. At the very beginning of *A Vindication*, Wollstonecraft dismisses "those pretty feminine phrases" and "that weak elegancy of mind, exquisite sensibility, and sweet docility of manners, supposed to be the sexual characteristics of the weaker vessel." She insists that she will disdain to "cull" her phrases or "polish" her style, and, aiming "at being useful," and hoping "rather to persuade by the force of my arguments than to dazzle by the elegance of my language," she says that she will not waste her time "in rounding periods, or in fabricating the turgid bombast of artificial feelings." She declares that she "shall be employed about things, not words!" and hence that she will do her best "to avoid that flowery diction which has slided from essays into novels, and from novels into familiar letters and conversations."[29] It soon becomes abundantly clear that for Wollstonecraft the preeminent and most notorious source of that flowery diction, that dazzling (but bewildering and entrapping) elegance, that weak, effeminate language, those "pretty superlatives, dropping glibly from the tongue," which "vitiate the taste, and create a kind of sickly delicacy that turns away from simple unadorned truth," that "deluge of false sentiments and overstretched feelings, stifling the natural emotions of the heart," which "render the domestic pleasures insipid, that ought to sweeten those severe duties, which educate a rational and immortal being for a nobler field of action" is, of course, the Orient. And it is worth pondering why it would have been so important to Wollstonecraft to specify at such length and in such detail her stylistic distance from the Orient in the opening pages of her *Vindication*.

Oriental tales, stories, poems, and histories—and all their proliferating European imitations, of which Beckford's *Vathek* would have been only one recent example among dozens of others—are so defined by such language as to make them, from the sober, objective, rational standpoint being claimed by Wollstonecraft, at best doubtful sources of genuine knowledge (let alone truth), and at worst dangerous repositories of "those emotions which disturb the order of society, and engross the thoughts that should be otherwise employed."[30] By the 1790s, as Martha Conant observes, the stock pseudo-Oriental tale had a fairly stable set of components, including slight characterization, vaguely Asiatic scenery, and "a picturesque background of strange Eastern customs, sometimes enriched by allusions to religious or philosophical beliefs, often by lavish use of magic and enchantment." Oriental or pseudo-Oriental nomenclature, Conant adds, "aids in producing the desired effect of remoteness," and the language would usually have been "coloured by oriental phraseology," frequently "figurative and inflated."[31] By the end of the eighteenth century, however, the norms of exoticism had changed considerably (which is the main reason Conant chooses to end her survey before 1800), and few, if any, successful romantic Orientalist texts threatened to drown their readers in the unfathomable and unnavigable mysteries of grotesque Oriental style (the kind of drowning that would later haunt De Quincey in his opium-fueled Asiatic nightmares).

Nigel Leask has argued that the most successful Orientalist tales or pictures in the romantic period depended upon a sometimes jarring discrepancy between, on the one hand, the work's quasi-Oriental allusions, styles, images, and themes and, on the other hand, a distancing apparatus consisting of notes or ironic qualifications and subversions of the supposedly Oriental material, which would pull the reader back to a secure location, "away from a dangerous proximity to the image, in order to inscribe him/her in a position of epistemological power; nothing other than the commanding vision of imperialist objectivity."[32] In this context, and given the prominence that it has, Wollstonecraft's denunciation of overembellished language and style, flowery diction, and artificial bombast can hardly be a rejection simply of the usefulness of such a style. An integral element in her overall argument, it is, rather, a rhetorical move designed to emphasize her perspective of what Leask rightly identifies as "imperialist objectivity," her distance from the turgid bombast of Eastern manners typically associated with the Oriental tale, and her location in an objective, rational—and newly-invented—*Western* discourse of rights, in which artificiality and excessive figural language have no place. In Wollstonecraft's *Vindication*, however, Oriental artificiality and excess are also overcoded in terms of feminine seductiveness. Here, virtually for the first time, the despotic and an altogether new conception of femininity (which might otherwise seem at odds with despotism) are merged in a discourse of seductiveness whose primary locus would of course be the seraglio—a space in which the despotism and the soft languid femininity of the East become inseparable.[33]

The "arts of seduction" have no place in Wollstonecraft's argument, she says, since the manifest clarity of what she has to say in opposing despotism obviates the need for seduction. However, "in a seraglio," Wollstonecraft writes, "all these arts are necessary; the epicure must have his palate tickled, or he will sink into apathy." It is in this crucial rhetorical move that Wollstonecraft articulates the continuity of feminine and Oriental artificiality and seductiveness, urging that women in particular distance themselves from the potential of any association with Asiatic languor and pleasure. For, she goes on to ask, "have women so little ambition as to be satisfied with such a condition? Can they supinely dream life away in the lap of pleasure, or the languour of weariness, rather than assert their claim to pursue reasonable pleasures, and render themselves conspicuous by practising the virtues which dignify mankind? Surely she has not an immortal soul who can loiter life away merely employed to adorn her person, that she may amuse the languid hours, and soften the cares of a fellow-creature who is willing to be enlivened by her smiles and tricks, when the serious business of life is over."[34] If for Wollstonecraft a reliance upon flowery and figurative language would weaken the mind and corrupt a woman's virtues so far as to render her "only fit for a seraglio,"[35] it would surely incapacitate her own argument. If, according to the position that Wollstonecraft articulates, Islam denies women souls, the West would restore the promise of an immortal soul in the next life, as long as it is earned by hard work in this one.

Of course, Wollstonecraft is bringing to the radical cause a question—women's rights—that, for the most part, did not much concern other radicals. For this reason she is more heavily invested in matters of gender than most of her comrades, since she aims to vindicate the rights of women in addition to those of the unrepresented in general. Given the condition of women in late-eighteenth-century England, Wollstonecraft's intervention in the radical cause was essential. The problem with her intervention, however, is that, while it addresses the question of gender, it turns a blind eye to the question of race: while pointing to the constructedness of gender, and arguing that gender roles can and should be changed to improve the status of women, it takes for granted various essential racial or cultural differences between peoples. Wollstonecraft seeks to rescue (Western) women from the charge of irrationality, potential enthusiasm, excess, and so on by projecting all these negative qualities on a newly invented Oriental space to which "our" others must belong. Thus, she rescues (Western) women from charges of Oriental luxury by redirecting those charges and confining them to the Orient. It becomes clear, in any case, that Wollstonecraft does not think that such charges are absurd in themselves; on the contrary, they carry enormous rhetorical weight for her. The East is made to pay the price for her "vindication" of women, which is in fact their Westernization.

For in Wollstonecraft the dualisms of feminine and masculine, languid and virtuous, artificial and natural, seductive and forthright, weak and strong, unfree and free are, in a word, transfigured into the all-determining dualism opposing West and East. In so doing, however, Wollstonecraft contributes to the fabrication of a new Orient, which will make an entirely appropriate object for an altogether new project in imperialism. Thus, Wollstonecraft elaborates the dualism of East and West into the crucial determining structure of her argument, thereby distinguishing the defenders of the seraglio (like Burke) from its attackers, and the languid, soft, delicate, artificial, seductive, wasteful, degenerate pleasures of a now thoroughly feminized East from the hard, sober, manly duties and virtues of the rational, masculine West (which Western women ought to be able to participate in). Such dualisms would continue to dominate writing in the romantic period, and in a perverse sense Wollstonecraft is, of course, absolutely right, even prescient, to warn of the potential dangers to Western women of the supposed connection between the Oriental and the feminine, although this is ironically a self-fulfilling prophecy, since it is a connection that she was among the very first to articulate.

For what we see in *A Vindication* is an almost entirely new conception both of the East and of its antagonistic opposite, the West. Eastern despotism, and the East in general, had not previously been thought of in particularly feminine terms. Much of the seventeenth- and earlier-eighteenth-century English writing in the East seems purely pragmatic and commercial, quite uninterested in political and cultural matters, and barely interested at all in contemporary Oriental life (Lady Mary Wortley Mon-

CHAPTER FIVE

tagu's Turkish Embassy letters are the notable exception). Henry Maundrell, for example, who traveled to the Levant at the end of the seventeenth century, described the Arabs and Turks he encountered in terms of ferocious barbarism—filthy and bestial—rather than soft and wily seductiveness wrapped in the guise of elegant languor.[36] But if for Maundrell "Lust, Arrogance, Covetousness and the most exquisite Hypocrisy compleat their Character," he could at least admit that one thing he could commend in Muslims "is the outward Decency of their Carriage, the profound Respect they pay to Religion and to every thing relating to it, and their great Temperance and Frugality."[37] Nowhere in such pre-Orientalist texts can we find the seductive seraglio masters of the romantic political imagination. On the contrary, it is precisely the *lack* of "art and design" that defines Eastern culture for Maundrell. "Dirt and Nastiness"[38] rather than elaborate artificiality, crude bestial lust rather than the arts of seduction, characterize native life, reflecting the primitive earthiness—even naturalness—that in the seventeenth century were taken to be characteristic of Eastern culture. Thus, "art and design" signify civilization for Maundrell and other seventeenth-century writers, and their absence signifies barbarism, which is precisely the opposite argument from that which would be produced by 1790s radicals such as Wollstonecraft. In any case, he is explicitly uninterested in contemporaneous Eastern culture. He writes that he and his fellow European merchants avoid all unnecessary contact with the local culture whenever possible. "As to our living amongst them," he notes in reply to a query, "it is with all possible quiet and safety: And that's all we desire, their Conversation being not in the least entertaining. Our Delights are among our selves: and here being more than forty of Us, we never want a most Friendly and Pleasant Conversation."[39] And in navigating his way through the Levant, Maundrell relies on an imaginary map provided by biblical and Greek or Roman sources. Even the illustrations accompanying his volume are entirely devoid of any living human presence: the native homes, for example, are hardly more than blank rectangles, unembellished by the often enhanced Oriental scenery that we will see in the work of later European artists, such as Thomas, William, and Samuel Daniell, William Hodges, or Luigi Mayer (see fig. 20).

Even for Montesquieu—one of the greatest Orientalist writers of the eighteenth century—Eastern despotism and the pleasures of the seraglio are two quite different things, not thought of in the way that the 1790s radicals would conjure up in their associations. For Montesquieu, the seraglio is the locus of harsh and vicious despotism, not of the "arts of seduction." When, toward the end of *Persian Letters*, Usbek writes to his assistants back

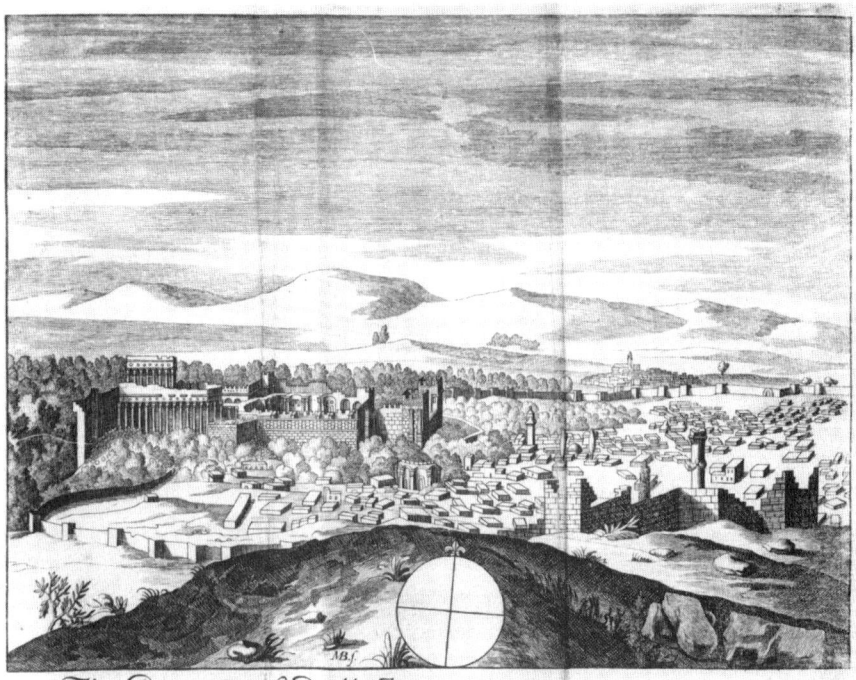

Figure 20. Prospect of Balbeck, in Henry Maundrell, *A Journey from Aleppo to Jerusalem* (Oxford, 1740). Reproduced by kind permission of the University of Chicago Library.

home to reassert his authority in the harem, he insists to them that "fear and terror should be your companions; go with all speed to punish and chastise in room after room; everyone must live in dread, everyone must weep before you . . . exterminate the criminals, and strike dread into those who contemplated becoming so."[40] This attempted reassertion of a tyrannical order is unable to stop the harem women from snatching, as they had all along, brief moments of pleasure, thereby turning, as Roxana writes to Usbek, "your terrible seraglio into a place of delightful pleasures."[41] By the end of Montesquieu's text, however, Roxana is dead, and it is clear that delightful pleasures should never be associated with the seraglio. It is clear that Oriental despotism, for Montesquieu, is the result of degeneration and decay, the result of unnatural weakness which is here symbolized by the eunuchs. This is a theme that Montesquieu would elaborate further in *The Spirit of Laws*, which would inspire both the United States Constitution and the 1790s radicals in London.

It is worth bearing in mind here that one of the few Europeans to witness

CHAPTER FIVE

anything like the inside of a seraglio, Lady Mary Wortley Montagu, had little to say about either the arts of seduction or Asiatic despotism. Montagu's first visit to a Turkish bath surprises her, and she is charmed by the receptiveness, politeness, and propriety of the goings-on inside. She reflects on the community of women enabled by the social space of the bath and is impressed by seeing "so many fine women naked, in different postures, some in conversation, some working, others drinking coffee or sherbot, and many negligently lying on their cushions, while their slaves (generally pretty girls of seventeen or eighteen) were employed in braiding their hair in several pretty fancies. In short, 'tis the womens coffee-house, where all the news of the town is told, scandal invented, &c."[42] Particularly with the metaphorical transposition to the coffeehouse, the nakedness of the women in the bath is rendered banal. The most interesting thing about Montagu's reflections is the way in which patriarchal oppression is configured, if anything, as Western rather than Eastern. "I was at last forced to open my shirt, and shew them my stays," she writes, "which satisfied them very well; for, I saw, they believed I was locked up in that machine, and that it was not in my own power to open it, which contrivance they attributed to my husband,—I was charmed with their civility and beauty, and should have been very glad to pass more time with them."[43] How it could be that she is able to "see" what the Turkish ladies "believed" and "attributed" remains unexplained, and presumably this says something about the way in which Montagu projects her own feelings about being imprisoned in her stays onto the Turkish women, with whom she could not have actually exchanged more than a few signs and gestures.

Even in British writing from as late as the middle of the eighteenth century there is still a strong distinction between the subtle femininity of the arts of seduction and the Orient itself, which the 1790s radicals would collapse into each other. In his monumental tome on the ruins at Palmyra, in Syria, Robert Wood is, like Maundrell, quite explicitly uninterested in the contemporaneous East. Also like Maundrell, Wood and his fellow travelers set out for the East armed with a library of Greek and biblical sources, for what they were seeking for were Greek and Roman ruins, not the living cultures of the East. "The various countries we went through, furnish, no doubt, much entertainment of different sorts," Wood notes; "But however we might each of us have some favorite curiosity to indulge, what engaged our greatest attention was rather their antient than present state."[44] While this did not prevent them from buying as many manuscripts in Syriac and Arabic as they could find ("we chose rather to bring home a great many bad things, than run the risk of leaving any thing curious in languages we did not

Figure 21. Fallen ruins, in *Ionian Antiquities*. Reproduced by kind permission of the University of Chicago Library.

understand"), their attitude toward living Arabs was one of nearly total lack of interest. A similar attitude would be reflected in the text and illustrations of the 1769 edition of *Ionian Antiquities*, where we see native Orientals lounging around on the fallen memorials of ancient Greece, totally oblivious, presumably, to the awesome majesty of the broken and scattered ruins (see fig. 21). Some of the latter illustrations, incidentally, were produced in the workshop of Blake's master, Basire.

However, Wood reflects at some length on the heroism of Queen Zenobia, the local ruler who resisted (and was ultimately destroyed by) the Roman Empire and who remains something of a folk figure in the contemporary Arab world. Far from being a supine and languorous harem girl, this great Asiatic heroine is portrayed as "a woman of extraordinary beauty," with dark skin, "black sparkling eyes of an uncommon fire," and great mental and physical stamina. If, Wood continues, "we add to this uncommon strength, and consider her excessive military fatigues; for she used no carriage, generally rode, and often marched on foot three or four miles with the army: And if we, at the same time, suppose her haranguing her soldiers, which she used to do in a helmet, and often with her arms bare, it will give us an idea of that severe character of masculine beauty, which puts one more in mind of Minerva than Venus."[45] Ultimately, however, Wood sees no contradiction between Zenobia's military and political leadership and abilities, on the one hand, and the fact, on the other hand, that she is described as "graceful and genteel beyond imagination." Her knowledge of several languages, history, politics, and warfare, her ability to outdrink her Persian and Armenian counterparts (though she was "generally moderate in her use of liquor") are not seen to be at odds with her rich and bejeweled dress, her "female fondness of shew and magnificence."[46] Thus, in Wood's account, the showy splendor of the East is far from incompatible with political skill, martial valor, and what Wollstonecraft would call "manly virtue."

Wollstonecraft's intervention in Orientalist discourse—and especially her feminization of the East—does not, however, have much to do with the East itself, of which her knowledge was extremely limited, and generally defined by the prejudices of her day, although, as we shall see, like Paine and others, she succeeded in amplifying some of those prejudices and carrying them to a new level, in effect paving the way for a new generation of imperialists. For one thing, identification with the soft, languid dissipation of the East is not a problem only for women, according to Wollstonecraft: she says that we can see another pressing danger to manly Western virtue in, for example, the European officer class, made up of "idle superficial young men, whose only occupation is gallantry, and whose polished manners render vice more dangerous, by concealing its deformity under gay ornamental drapery."[47] If for Robert Wood "fondness of shew and magnificence," however "female" a tendency it might have been, could readily be reconciled with the "severe character of masculine beauty" that he associates with Queen Zenobia, for Wollstonecraft such "shew and magnificence" is definitively and calamitously a token of that languorous femininity linking together the East and the degenerate aristocracy of the West.

Though she may have perfected it, such a link is certainly not unique to Wollstonecraft's *Vindication*. It has long been recognized, for example, that just such a move is an essential component of Paine's attack on Burke in *Rights of Man*.[48] In arguing that Burke "is not affected by the reality of the distress touching his heart, but by the showy resemblance of it striking his imagination," that Burke "pities the plumage, but forgets the dying bird," Paine is able to reconfigure his opponent as a fawning servant of kings and priests, for whom "shew and magnificence" are a kind of substitute reality, an imaginative world to be accessed via hippogriffs and flying sentry boxes. "Accustomed to kiss the aristocratical hand that hath purloined him from himself," Paine writes of Burke, "he degenerates into a composition of art, and the genuine soul of nature forsakes him. His hero or his heroine must be a tragedy-victim expiring in show, and not the real prisoner of misery, sliding into death in the silence of a dungeon."[49] Here Paine prepares the way for the climactic moment of his argument against Burke a few pages later, where he refuses "to follow Mr Burke through a pathless wilderness of rhapsodies, and a sort of descant upon governments, in which he asserts whatever he pleases, on the presumption of its being believed, without offering evidence or reasons for so doing." As against such emotional assertions, Paine insists that "before anything can be reasoned upon to a conclusion, certain facts, principles, or data, to reason from must be established, admitted, or denied," and that Burke's flowery, imaginative, and hence pseudo-Oriental discourse is not compatible with such reasoning (though in following Paine this far we are given no choice, in order to accept his argument, but to take it on just the sort of unfounded faith of which he accuses Burke, that "God said, Let us make man in our own image,"[50] and that the resulting image, and hence the basis of all right, is of an individual man).

However moralistic their critiques of Burke may also be, for both Paine and Wollstonecraft the real problem with those "polished manners" that "render vice more dangerous, by concealing its deformity under gay ornamental drapery," is not merely a matter of morality (which is the overriding concern of evangelicals like Hannah More). The problem with such false showiness is, in other words, not simply that it substitutes the "plumage" for the "dying bird," the "showy resemblance" for the "reality of distress," the "tragedy-victim dying in show" for the "real victim of misery," or, in a word, a pretend reality (of "art," "show," and "tragedy") for genuine reality (the reality of "facts, principles, and data"). Rather, the problem is that artificiality and show corrupt the "genuine soul of nature," and allow an individual to be "purloined" from himself. "Vice," according to Wollstonecraft, is rendered "more dangerous, by concealing its deformity under gay ornamental drapery," not just because it is more difficult for others to recognize in us, but above all because it is more difficult for us to recognize in ourselves (which is essentially also what Paine is accusing Burke of). Showy style, elaborate forms of writing, excessive figuration, inflated phraseology—in short, the essential elements not just of Burke's *Reflections* as read by Paine and Wollstonecraft, but above all of Oriental and pseudo-Oriental style, since at least the time of *Vathek* the ultimate "pathless wilderness of rhapsodies"—are bad not just because they prevent us from engaging with "facts, principles, and data"; they are bad because they prevent genuine self-knowledge, self-awareness, and self-control. Art is to be distinguished from reality by the same mechanisms which allow us to distinguish excess from simplicity, idleness from vigor, unfounded assertion from reasoned argument, the artificial from the natural, the useless from the useful, the unmanly from the manly, and hence, ultimately, the East from the West—our others from our selves. This, of course, is a very different notion of the relation of art and nature than that proposed by Maundrell, who had, as we have seen, a radically different notion of the East.

As it is elaborated by Paine and Wollstonecraft, then, the question of style is an immediately political question, and not merely an aesthetic one. Or rather, aesthetics and politics are collapsed into each other. Style here is not so much an expression of an underlying political position; it occupies and defines a location on a political terrain constructed in and through language. According to Wollstonecraft and Paine, self-control and self-knowledge—and hence self-affirmation, self-constitution, self-determination—are rendered equally impossible by despotism, which denies it, and by excess, which precludes it (as Malthus would argue at around this time, scarcity rather than abundance is the key to self-control and ultimately to an accompanying political economy based on self-restraint).[51] And this holds true as much in a stylistic or aesthetic sense as it does in a practical one: genuine self-expression, self-knowledge, self-control are stifled or precluded as much by turgid and bombastic—or pretty and superlative—prose as they are by the effects of political dictatorship or military hierarchy. This is because for Wollstonecraft and Paine the contours of individual freedom must be defined by voluntary self-regulation, self-limitation, self-denial—a rejection of figurative and verbal, as well as bodily and sensual, excess—rather than by externally enforced regulation, limitation, and denial.

While Wollstonecraft's lengthy excursus on style, and in particular her refusal of "polish" and "art" in the name of natural simplicity and forthright "manly" honesty, is, at face value, a rejection of the politics of feudalism and aristocracy as represented by Burke, it is articulated as a systematic repudiation of the excess, luxury, and idleness of the East. In order to mobilize her critique of the ancien régime represented by Burke, in other words, she must dismiss Oriental style, with all its "turgid bombast of artificial feelings," and embrace, by defining it virtually for the first time, a new conception of Western style, which aims at being "useful" rather than "elegant," which concerns "things, not words!"[52] This paramount concern with "things" rather than "words" enables, for Wollstonecraft, an honesty based on things, things being, of course, clear, obvious, manifest, unencumbered by signifying capacity, whereas words are not to be trusted, loose signifiers apparently incapable of offering the incontrovertible permanence of thing-like signifieds. (Another half century would elapse before Marx would provide his account of commodity fetishism: for Wollstonecraft the commodity is pure use value).

Wollstonecraft's Orient is not only a repository of loose, ungrounded words, excess signifiers unattached to solid things. It is also, and as a result, at once the place where one cannot be oneself—for it threatens one's very being—and the place essential to one's being, reminding the West of what it is not, serving as the "vice" against which Western "virtue" can be understood. In practical terms, "virtue" is for Wollstonecraft the product of achieving mental authority over bodily inclinations, so that we can learn self-control only by learning to restrain and discipline our desires, to "sharpen the senses, form the temper, regulate the passions as they begin to ferment," as Wollstonecraft would amply illustrate in her *Original Stories from Real Life; with Conversations Calculated to Regulate the Affections and Form the Mind to Truth and Goodness*.[53] In stylistic terms, we achieve virtue—and hence define our selves through discourse—by restraining our prose, avoiding the "soft phrases, susceptibility of heart, delicacy of sentiment, and refinement of taste," which are "almost synonymous with epithets of weakness," and which are of course absolutely synonymous with Oriental style.[54] Wollstonecraft dismisses "those pretty feminine phrases, which the men condescendingly use to soften our slavish dependence," and "that weak elegancy of mind, exquisite sensibility, and sweet docility of manners," not just because they are "supposed to be the sexual characteristics of the weaker vessel," but also, as she announces in the very opening sentences of *A Vindication*, because they conform to the "true style of Mahometanism."[55]

Ultimately, what becomes clearer and clearer as one reads Wollstonecraft is that the Mahometanism, the Orient, and the seraglio that haunt every page of *A Vindication* haunt it because they represent for Wollstonecraft the locus of the body, and all the sensual drives and desires, against which the virtuous West must struggle to define itself. "A moderate quantity of proper food," says the matronly Mrs. Mason to one of her overindulging charges in Wollstonecraft's training manual for small children, which was subversively illustrated by Blake (see figs. 22, 23),[56] "recruits our exhausted spirits, and invigorates the animal functions; but, if we exceed moderation, the mind will be oppressed, and soon become the slave of the body, or both grow list-

Figure 22. Blake, *Oeconomy and Self Denial*, in Mary Wollstonecraft, *Original Stories from Real Life* (London, 1791). Reproduced by kind permission of the University of Chicago Library.

Figure 23. Blake, frontispiece, in Mary Wollstonecraft, *Original Stories from Real Life* (London, 1791). Reproduced by kind permission of the University of Chicago Library.

less and inactive."[57] If the Orient is the locus of the "fastiduous sensualist" and the "luxurious monster,"[58] that is because it is the site where the desires function without discipline, where passions run amok, and where the mind is the slave to the body. The West, on the other hand, is the site where "the night of sensual ignorance"[59] comes to an end, and where "true civilization"[60] can finally be brought about, by, among other things, the elimination of the excessive (and unproductive) pleasures of the seraglio, and their replacement by the productive (i.e., reproductive) bourgeois family unit, whose success must rest on the elimination not only of carnal lust, but of love itself. Indeed, Wollstonecraft argues, "in order to fulfil the duties of life, and to be able to pursue with vigour the various employments which form the moral character, a master and mistress of a family ought not to continue to love each other with passion. I mean to say that they ought not to indulge those emotions which disturb the order of society, and engross the thoughts which should otherwise be employed."[61] Here, society in general functions like a collective individual: just as the individual subject must achieve virtue by learning to regulate his or her own bodily and sensual desires, the society as a whole—that is, Western society—achieves virtue by assuring collective control over those "thoughts" and "emotions" which should be otherwise employed, and, indeed, by concerning itself above all with "things," with duties, employments, regulations, rules, and the demands of a life geared toward, oriented around, systematically taken over and dominated by hard, sober, honest, clean, manly, vigorous *work*—in short, society dominated by "stern demands of Right & Duty instead of Liberty."[62]

Thus, Wollstonecraft in *A Vindication* or Paine in *Rights of Man* must be seen to be articulating, virtually for the first time, the modernizing ideology that would propel British imperialism in the East through the nineteenth century and on into the twentieth. In their condemnation of Oriental style, dissipation, luxury, weakness, inarticulateness, deceitfulness, wiliness, seductiveness, and so on, the hegemonic radicals of the 1790s must be recognized as the antecedents of James Mill (that able servant of the East India Company), who would condemn Oriental culture on exactly the same grounds ("such, in many of them, is their imbecility of mind; so faint are the traces of their memory; so vivid the creations of their imagination; so little are they accustomed to regard truth in their daily practice; so much are they accustomed to mingle fiction with reality in all they think, and all they say; and so inaccurate is their language, that they cannot tell a true story, even when they are without any inducement to deceive").[63] They must be recognized as the antecedents of Lord Cromer, England's man in Egypt from

1882 to 1907, who would argue that "want of accuracy, which easily degenerates into untruthfulness, is, in fact, the main characteristic of the Oriental mind," so that, if, on the one hand, "the European is a close reasoner," whose "statements of fact are devoid of ambiguity," who is "by nature sceptical and requires proof before he can accept the truth of any proposition," whose "trained intelligence works like a piece of mechanism," who is "bursting with superfluous energy, active in mind, inquisitive about everything he sees and hears," the Oriental, on the other hand, "like his picturesque streets, is eminently wanting in symmetry," since "his reasoning is of the most slipshod description"; and since Orientals "are often incapable of drawing the most obvious conclusions from any simple premises of which they may admit the truth," they are "devoid of energy and initiative, stagnant in mind, wanting in curiosity about matters which are new to [them], careless of waste of time and patient under suffering."[64] They must be seen as the antecedents of T. E. Lawrence ("of Arabia"), who would write of "his" Arabs that they are "a dogmatic people, despising doubt, our modern crown of thorns," a "limited, narrow-minded people," inhabiting "superlatives," whose "inert intellects lay fallow in incurious resignation," whose imaginations are "vivid, but not creative," and who are, all in all, entirely lacking in "organization of mind or body."[65] They must be seen as the antecedents of Lord Balfour (author of the notorious 1917 declaration carrying his name), who would justify European intervention in the East by arguing that "You may look through the whole history of the Orientals in what is called, broadly speaking, the East, and you never find traces of self-government . . . conqueror has succeeded conqueror; one domination has followed another; but never in all the revolutions of fate and fortune have you seen one of those nations of its own motion establish what we, from a Western point of view, call self-government."[66]

There is presumably no need here to reiterate at any great length the well-known central argument of Said's *Orientalism* (where all of these concepts, and some of these very passages, are discussed in systematic detail) concerning the integral relationship between such Orientalist representations of the East and the actual practice of British imperialism in the nineteenth century. Orientals cannot tell fact from fiction; they are not in a position to acquire knowledge of themselves, let alone of us; we, on the other hand, do have knowledge, and especially knowledge of them; our knowledge of them is synonymous with our power over them; they, unorganized, dishonest, inept, inefficient, weak, incapable, pathetic as they are, fundamentally *need* us to rule them; and indeed, as Balfour says, they have never been capable of self-rule (neither in the individual sense nor in the collec-

CHAPTER FIVE

tive), so it is, alas, our duty to show them how to go about organizing themselves (both individually and collectively).⁶⁷ My point here is not simply to single out Wollstonecraft or Paine from among the jostling crowd of 1790s liberal-radicals as the only antecedents for a Victorian imperialism whose rallying cries would be honesty, simplicity, clarity, manliness, vigor, productivity, employment, cleanliness, sobriety, and so forth. Nor do I mean to suggest that there is a direct, literal, causal relationship between Wollstonecraft's or Paine's theories in particular and the imperial practice of Cromer or Balfour.

My point, rather, is to recall the extent to which Cromer's and Balfour's understanding of the East, and hence their understanding of Britain's imperial mission—which they served so ably—would crucially depend on the structure of feeling mobilized around the binary opposition of Eastern and Western ("on every point," as Cromer puts it, "they are the poles asunder").⁶⁸ And, in turn, this opposition would hinge, above all, on the rigid contrast between the rational, vigorous, manly, honest, articulate, sober, active, organized Western subject and the irrational, inarticulate, lazy, weak, degenerate, deceitful, disorganized, effeminate, overindulging Eastern object of his rule. Without this contrast—and without the apparently seamless logical continuity between the sovereignty and organization of the individual and the sovereignty and organization of the people, the state, the nation—nineteenth-century British imperialism would not have worked, or it would have taken an entirely different form from the one that it actually did (both ideologically and materially). And such an opposition is not to be found in British (or for that matter French) Orientalism—in a significantly consistent, coherent and sustained way—until the 1790s, when it was brought into being by the radical advocates of "liberty," who, precisely in the name of the sovereignty of the self, mobilized it in their attack on the ancien régime.⁶⁹

4. Orientalist Romanticism

If the concept of the sovereign self would prove essential to the work of the empire builders of the nineteenth century, it was as a concept to be put to use for a greater cause, namely, the empire itself. This would be especially true for the empire seen as a project whose avowed aim was to help and instruct that slovenly Eastern object to learn to become a subject himself.⁷⁰ For the struggles of the liberal-radicals of the 1790s, however, the liberty of the sovereign individual self—his liberation from excess and despotism—*was* the objective. Moreover, the knowledge and power of the self would also serve as the central cognitive orienting node for a political and aesthetic project that was already emerging and becoming clear as the radicals proclaimed their mission—a project not so much in the field of politics in the narrowest sense as in the field of aesthetics and cultural production, which enables and sustains political action ("Empire follows Art & Not Vice Versa," Blake once pointed out).[71] Especially in the 1790s, it was already abundantly clear that there is, as Wordsworth puts it, a continuity between "Poetry" and "moral relations," so that, in order to discover the extent to which "language" and "the human mind" act and react on one another, it is essential to retrace "the revolutions not of literature alone but likewise of society itself."[72]

In proposing a new aesthetic form in *Lyrical Ballads*, Wordsworth was therefore, of course, also proposing an explicitly political intervention, in which style serves at once as an auxiliary for the aesthetic and political project and as an analogue for it. Just as Wollstonecraft and Paine had done a few years earlier (which is hardly a coincidence), Wordsworth needed to preface his "revolutionary" poems with some account of the politics of their style. For if, he writes in the "Preface," "there will be found in these volumes little of what is usually called poetic diction," that is because Wordsworth rejects that diction and the style associated with it. Just as Wollstonecraft had denounced "that flowery diction which has slided from essays into novels, and from novels into familiar letters and conversations," Wordsworth refuses to indulge in the "arbitrary and capricious habits of expression" which are used by certain unmentionable Poets "in order to furnish food for fickle tastes and fickle appetites of their own creation." Instead of the "gross and violent stimulants" provided by fashionable literature, by those "frantic novels, sickly and stupid German Tragedies, and deluges of idle and extravagant stories in verse" (of which the Oriental tale, then at the peak of its popularity, was the prime example), which, with their "false refinement or arbitrary innovation," offer nothing but "outrageous stimulation," Wordsworth offers poems written in "a plainer and more emphatic language," relying on "simple and unelaborated expressions," and appealing as much as possible to "greater simplicity."[73]

The majority of the poems in *Lyrical Ballads*, Wordsworth explains, "are to be considered as experiments. They were written chiefly with a view to ascertain how far the language of conversation in the middle and lower classes of society is adapted to the purposes of poetic pleasure. Readers accustomed to the gaudiness and inane phraseology of many modern writers," he adds, "will perhaps frequently have to struggle with feelings of strangeness and aukwardness: they will look round for poetry, and will be induced

CHAPTER FIVE

to enquire by what species of courtesy these attempts can be permitted to assume that title."[74] Wordsworth claims to revert to the language of the middle and lower classes (though by "lower class" he means, of course, not the urban proletariat but rather the sturdy yeomen farmers of a mythical English countryside that he was helping to invent) for the same reason that Wollstonecraft addresses her *Vindication* primarily to them. This class of people, as Wollstonecraft puts it, free of the "false refinement, immorality, and vanity" of the aristocracy, is "in the most natural state," a state in which, as Wordsworth would add, "the passions of men are incorporated with the beautiful and permanent forms of nature."[75] Here and indeed throughout the "Preface"—and in exactly the same way we have already seen in Wollstonecraft and Paine—art is contrasted with nature, falsehood with truth, meaningless excess with rigorous simplicity, unmanly gaudiness with manly vigor. Here, in other words, Wordsworth is reactivating the very same matrix of dualisms so thoroughly explicated by Wollstonecraft only a few years earlier in *A Vindication*, and for precisely the same purpose: the necessarily simultaneous political and aesthetic project of "redeeming" (i.e., bringing into being by articulating) the sovereign self.

To counteract the state of affairs in this fallen world, in which manly vigor is threatened by excessive figuration, by "idle and extravagant stories in verse," by "false refinement or arbitrary innovation," by "outrageous stimulation," the aesthetic and political project that Wordsworth launches in *Lyrical Ballads* aims to reincorporate the "passions of men" with those permanent forms of nature. The key to success in this project is to frame those passions, to discipline and control them, to mobilize them for a purpose, and in so doing to ensure that the mind is allowed to control the passions, rather than being overwhelmed by them, or in other words to assert self-identity through self-control, particularly in language, where the difference between "inane and gaudy phraseology" and "a plainer and more emphatic language" is precisely the difference between the surrendering and the reassertion of self-control.

Such discipline is nowhere clearer than in the experience of the sublime, in which the "cultivated imagination" confronts—primarily and, for Wordsworth, almost exclusively, in a visual register—some force or power which rouses it "to a sympathetic energy and calls upon the mind to grasp at something towards which it can make approaches but which it is incapable of attaining—yet so that it participates [in] the force which is acting upon it."[76] The experience of the sublime emerges from feeling that participation. Actually, it *is* that feeling of participation, and it requires a particularly disciplined mind because a "lesser" mind would be overwhelmed by passion, by a feeling of physical terror, and by a rush to surrender mental equipoise to bodily impulse. In a properly prepared mind, however, such bodily passion can be brought under mental control, so that the sense of terror would give way to that of the sublime, to a sense of controlling rather than being overwhelmed, to a sense of power rather than powerlessness, and specifically to that sense of power enabled by self-control, and more specifically still to that sense of power enabled by the control of the cultivated, disciplined, vigorous, "manly" mind over the irrational, capricious, and impulse-driven "unmanly" body.

This, Wordsworth explains, is why "the capability of perceiving these qualities, and the degree in which they are perceived, will of course depend upon the state or condition of the mind, with respect to habits, knowledge, and powers, which is brought within the reach of their influence."[77] For all the talk of naturalness, such qualities are not innate. Like taste, they must be developed and cultivated. For, according to Wordsworth, taste itself—in the aesthetic and political meaning of the word—is not a passive sense; it is active, and hence it requires investment, training, preparation, development. Wordsworth is of course fully aware of the extent to which, as he himself says, "every author, as far as he is great and at the same time *original*, has had the task of *creating* the taste by which he is to be enjoyed."[78] This process of creating taste is precisely the task that Wordsworth has set himself in *Lyrical Ballads*, as he makes clear. He acknowledges, however, that if taste, like imagination itself, "is a metaphor, taken from a *passive* sense of the human body, and transferred to things which are in their essence *not* passive,—to intellectual *acts* and *operations*,"[79] then to create taste would clearly be an immensely difficult task in a society confronted on all sides by "a multitude of causes unknown to former times," which "are now acting with a combined force to blunt the discriminating powers of the mind, and unfitting it for all voluntary exertion to reduce it to a state of almost savage torpor."[80]

Wordsworth's struggle is therefore to rescue poetry from being merely "a matter of amusement and idle pleasure," as though a taste for poetry were "as indifferent as a taste for Rope-dancing, or Frontiniac or Sherry."[81] It is a struggle, in the face of "idleness and unmanly despair,"[82] to create an explicitly "manly" style,[83] in order to show the reader how to equip himself with the kind of "sound and vigorous mind"[84] ultimately required for fully appreciating Wordsworth's own poetry. For, though it derives from them, great poetry is not simply "the spontaneous overflow of powerful feelings," of which the most powerful is the experience of the sublime. Rather, "it takes its origin from emotion recollected in tranquillity: the emotion is contemplated till by a species of reaction the tranquillity gradually disappears, and an emotion, similar to that which was before the subject of contemplation, is gradually produced, and does itself actually exist in the mind."[85] Emotion and excitement, on their own, suggest "an unusual and irregular state of the mind," in which "ideas and feelings" do not "succeed each other in accustomed order"; and in powerful poetry "there is some danger that the excitement may be carried beyond its proper bounds." However, Wordsworth adds, "the co-presence of something regular," that is, meter and rhyme, "cannot but have great efficacy in tempering and restraining the passion by an intertexture of ordinary feeling."[86] The rigorous new style that Wordsworth seeks to create, then, draws its rigor and power precisely from the fact that, because of rhyme and meter, it is "regular and uniform, and not, like that which is produced by what is usually called poetic diction, arbitrary and subject to infinite caprices upon which no calculation whatever can be made." In the latter, Wordsworth explains, "the Reader is utterly at the mercy of the Poet respecting what imagery or diction he may choose to connect with the passion," whereas in the former—his own poetry—the meter obeys certain laws, "to which the Poet and Reader both willingly submit because they are certain."[87]

The kind of poetry to which Wordsworth aspires is one that would allow for the greatest expression of emotion, while at the same time keeping that emotion firmly regulated and uniform, under strict linguistic control. Such poetry is a celebration of self-control, of the capacity of an elevated mind to assert, through the highly regulated language of "good" poetry, control over what would otherwise be merely disorganized feelings, however powerful ("bad" poetry, on the other hand, is bad because it surrenders such self-control in a gush of "gross and violent stimulants"). Powerful poetry thus reenacts in language the experience of the sublime. It is, in other words, a celebration of the substitution of raw natural emotion for a reproduced emotion whose condition of possibility is self-control. Thus, it is a celebration, a "calling forth" and "communication," of *power*.[88]

But, as Wordsworth would explicitly add in the "Essay, Supplementary to the Preface," for all the poet's own power and capacity for linguistic self-control, for all his skill at expressing pathos and sublimity, "without the exertion of a co-operating *power* in the mind of the Reader, there can be no adequate sympathy with either of these emotions: without this auxiliary impulse, elevated or profound passion cannot exist."[89] To be moved by passion, Wordsworth continues, requires an effort on the part of the reader, which is why he must be of "sound and vigorous mind." If the genius of the poet represents "an advance, or a conquest," Wordsworth asks, "is it to be supposed that the reader can make progress of this kind, like an Indian prince or general—stretched on his palanquin, and borne by his slaves? No; he is invigorated and inspired by his leader, in order that he may exert himself; for he cannot proceed in quiescence, he cannot be carried like a dead weight." Therefore, Wordsworth concludes, "to create taste is to call forth and bestow power, of which knowledge is the effect; and *there* lies the difficulty."[90] The difficulty, in other words, lies in creating not just a new kind of taste, but an altogether new kind of reader, an explicitly *Western* reader, who—unlike an Indian general or any other Oriental potentate addicted to an easy life lounging around the harem, being carried about by slaves from one easy delight to another, unable to tell fact from fiction, lazy, inertia bound, despotic, soft, languorous, and so on—is capable of the vigorous self-organization and self-discipline that Wordsworth says his poetry requires, and, indeed, calls forth as an expression of "power, of which knowledge is the effect."

Ultimately, Wordsworth's argument most clearly dovetails with Wollstonecraft's on the question of self-control and on the extent to which that self-control is necessarily synonymous with power, and hence knowledge. In both cases, the power and knowledge of the subject is contrasted with the world of objects surrounding him, over which he seeks to gain control and mastery precisely by being able to express it, know it, represent it. Especially given the visual register which so dominates Wordsworth's passages on aesthetic philosophy, as well as his poetry, the subject's power and knowledge is exerted over a landscape whose primary defining feature is that it is outside him, *exotic* at once in the sense that it is alien and in the sense that it is external, its externality and alienness being, in fact, mutually constitutive, dialectically enabling the constitution of the viewing subject. This is why, as I suggested in *Romantic Imperialism*, there is such a startling continuity between romantic landscape aesthetics and the emergent cultural politics of imperialism. Why else, in describing his nature poetry, would Wordsworth find himself obliged to fall back on the otherwise seemingly inappropriate political and military vocabulary of "conquest," in which the reader too must participate, must be interpellated, if the conquest is to be successful?

Poetry, for Wordsworth, is the highest form of knowledge; and hence, it expresses the highest form of power. In his hands, poetry becomes explicitly an imperial discourse. The poet's power over the landscape, over an exotic object world, over the visual field in general, is synonymous with his ability to know and to represent it, just as, for the great prophets of nineteenth-century British imperialism, the empire's power over its colonies would be precisely synonymous with its knowledge of them. Whereas, for Cromer, for Lawrence, for Balfour, the knowing subject can demonstrate his knowledge and power through his ability to construct and elaborate a reasoned argument, the object of his vision, and hence of his rule, is incapable of such argument and has to rely instead on impulse, caprice, wiliness, seduction, assertion, mere persuasion. The poet, for Wordsworth, must express not raw emotion, not "the spontaneous overflow of powerful feelings," with the attendant danger of unbounded excitement—for *that* is the hallmark of the enthusiastic Oriental, not to mention the enthusiastic plebeian—but rather, "emotion recollected in tranquillity," that is, emotion reconstructed, reconsidered, re-presented trough the controlling, restraining regularity of law-obeying rhyme and meter.

Here the power and knowledge of the self-controlling, self-knowing, self-representing sovereign subject confronting an exotic landscape is precisely analogous to the power and knowledge of the empire, whose sovereignty is derived from its ability to know, to control, and to represent its others. If, as Nigel Leask reminds us, the most successful Orientalist art and literature of the romantic period would combine exposure to otherness with a turn back toward a position of "imperialist objectivity," guaranteed by control over the forms of representation (linguistic or visual or both), Wordsworth's poetry works in precisely the same way. It expresses deep emotions but keeps them under control at the same time; it always has recourse to a position of "objectivity" grounded in the subject (that is, in the subject's control over the object world). This is why it involves a celebration of the power of the observing subject. In the sovereign subject emerging in the 1790s, romantic aesthetics and political ideology—particularly but not exclusively the emergent ideology of a new form of imperialism, one of whose driving forces would be the capacity to represent otherness—become quite inseparable. The future imperialism would rely at its most basic level on the structure of dualistic otherness that emerged in the 1790s in the discourse of radicalism and in the Wordsworthian romanticism that emerged alongside it.

5. Blake and the Politics of "Immortal Joy"

> An Angel came to me and said O pitiable foolish young man! O horrible! O dreadful state! consider the hot burning dungeon thou art preparing for thyself to all eternity, to which thou art going in such career.
> I said. perhaps you will be willing to shew me my eternal lot & we will contemplate together upon it and see whether your lot or mine is most desirable.
> So he took me thro' a stable & thro' a church & down into the church vault at the end of which was a mill; thro' the mill we went, and came to a cave. down

the winding cavern we groped our tedious way till a void boundless as a nether sky appeard beneath us, & we held by the roots of trees and hung over this immensity, but I said, if you please we will commit ourselves to this void, and see whether providence is here also, if you will not I will? but he answerd, do not presume O young-man but as we here remain behold thy lot which will soon appear when the darkness passes away

So I remaind with him sitting in the twisted root of an oak, he was suspended in a fungus which hung with the head downward into the deep;

By degrees we beheld the infinite Abyss, fiery as the smoke of a burning city; beneath us at an immense distance was the sun, black but shining round it were fiery tracks on which revolv'd vast spiders, crawling after their prey; which flew or rather swum in the infinite deep, in the most terrific shapes of animals sprung from corruption. & the air was full of them, & seemd composed of them; these are Devils. and are calld Powers of the air, I now asked my companion which was my eternal lot? he said, between the black & white spiders.

But now, from between the black & white spiders a cloud and fire burst and rolled thro the deep blackning all beneath, so that the nether deep grew black as a sea & rolled with a terrible noise: beneath us was nothing now to be seen but a black tempest, till looking east between the clouds & the waves. we saw a cataract of blood mixed with fire and not many stones throw from us appeard and sunk again the scaly fold of a monstrous serpent. at last to the east, distant above three degrees appeard a fiery crest above the waves slowly it reared like a ridge of golden rocks till we discovered two globes of crimson fire. from which the sea fled away in clouds of smoke, and now we saw, it was the head of Leviathan, his forehead was divided into streaks of green & purple like those on a tygers forehead: soon we saw his mouth & red gills hang just above the raging foam tinging the black deep with beams of blood, advancing toward us with all the fury of a spiritual existence.

My friend the Angel climb'd up from his station into the mill: I remain'd alone, & then this appearance was no more, but I found mys[e]lf sitting on a pleasant bank beside a river by moonlight hearing a harper who sung to the harp. & his theme was, The man who never alters his opinion is like standing water, & breeds reptiles of the mind.[91]

If the driving force of a Wordsworthian landscape is the tension between the viewing subject and the viewed object, over which power is sought, the Blakean landscape of *The Marriage of Heaven & Hell* lacks that tension because it lacks the all-determining structural and structuring opposition of subject and object. But if the vertiginous landscapes visited by the narrator

CHAPTER FIVE

of *The Marriage* and his angelic enemy/friend do not exist in an objective sense, that is not because they are merely the idealistic projections of a viewing subject, for the subject himself does not exist as such, either (which is what prevents Blake from sliding into an idealism predicated on a viewing subject). Whereas the relation of spectator and spectacle in Wordsworth is one of essential alterity (enabling the mutual dialectical constitution of self and other), in Blake one cannot speak of a spectator that is in any way essentially different from the spectacle being viewed. The "landscapes" being viewed and the "subject position" from which they are viewed are both as unstable as the wildly unbalanced poetry, prose, and art constituting Blake's notoriously unstable text. The point here is not, of course, to contrast an "unstable" text with some fantasy of a normative textual "stability." It is, rather, to consider the ways in which Blake's text plays on—exaggerates—its own instability; and in particular to consider the political implications of this instability in the historical context of the 1790s, when such instability was considered by the hegemonic radical movement to be not only a bad thing, but the worst and most dangerous thing, the telltale warning sign of dangerous plebeian enthusiasm, aristocratic indulgence, feminine licentiousness, Oriental seductiveness, wiliness, treachery.

The impossible landscapes traversed by the many narrators of *The Marriage* are—like the verbal and visual material form which they constitute—incompatible with a self-centered viewing subject. As we have seen, the explicit task of the highly regulated and law-obeying language of Wordsworth's poetry is to "temper" and "restrain" the possibility of an "unusual and irregular state of the mind," in which "ideas and feelings" do not "succeed each other in accustomed order," so that excitement can be prevented from being "carried beyond its proper bounds."[92] Similarly, the explicit task of Wollstonecraft's or Paine's polemical prose is to be "useful" rather than "elegant," to be concerned with "things, not words!" and hence to manifest a forthright "manly" honesty grounded on the incontrovertible security of clear, obvious, manifest *things*, supposedly unencumbered by any dangerously excessive signifying capacity.[93] On the other hand, "That which can be made Explicit to the Idiot," as Blake wrote, "is not worth my care," and indeed the task of the insanely excessive language of Blake's composite art involves an unleashing of signifying potential in as many different forms (verbal, visual, material, spiritual) as possible, bypassing, we might say, the individual consciousness and instead "rouzing" the sub- or trans- or meta-individual "faculties to act."[94] If, for Paine, Wollstonecraft, and Wordsworth—and then later on Cromer, Balfour, and company—rhetorical or linguistic stability serves as an analogue for the stability of the sovereign subject, for Blake linguistic and visual instability undermine the false stability of any solitary subject position. But, more than that, they also require an entirely new way of conceiving being and belonging; that is, they require a radically different aesthetic mode—call it a "style"—and a political stance appropriate to it. Without recognizing this, Blake cannot be understood: his work will look like the gibberish so many people have found it to be.

For the hegemonic radicals, as we have seen, self-knowledge and self-determination depend upon, among other things, one's capacity to construct an elaborate argument by "establishing, admitting, or denying" certain "facts, principles, or data to reason from" rather than merely asserting whatever one pleases, "on the presumption of its being believed, without offering evidence or reasons for so doing," which is what Paine accuses Burke of—and which, in their own time, Cromer and Balfour would accuse Indians and Arabs of. Blake, on the contrary, pushes us to consider how or to what extent such "Perswasion" actually *does* produce reality ("Does a firm perswasion that something is so, make it so?" the narrator of *The Marriage* asks Isaiah, who replies, "All poets believe that it does, & in ages of imagination this firm perswasion removed mountains").[95] As we see here and throughout Blake's prophetic books, this kind of "Perswasion," whose dangers Locke had explicitly tried to ward off in the chapter on enthusiasm which he added to the *Essay on Human Understanding*,[96] is not, however, the prerogative of the individual subject or the lonely artist, but rather a collective endeavour, whose potential is amplified by the ever greater joining together of bodies and minds.

For what Blake calls "poetic genius" can be understood—if it can be understood at all—only as a collective process. If language and art here offer lines of flight away from the apparent certainty of knowledge grounded in the viewing subject, they do so by allowing an approximation of the "poetic genius," whose true "subject-position" could be occupied only by that infinite being in common which Blake calls God. This is why throughout his work Blake would contrast, on the one hand, the subject-grounded "philosophic and experimental" knowledge of "man" as a "natural organ subject to sense," that is, man as a "natural body," with, on the other hand, man as a "spiritual body" defined by that capacity for the infinite opened up by poets and prophets activating the "poetic genius."[97] The former, experimental knowledge, is produced through controlled and disciplined discourse. It involves not simply the confrontation of a knowing mind with a material object world over which it seeks "power, of which knowledge is the effect,"[98] as Wordsworth puts it, but also, ultimately, the subjection of that mind to a set of material circumstances which are understood as given once and for all time, determining a human mind which is understood to be equally given once and for all time—hence Wordsworth's project to reconnect the "indestructible" human mind with the "great and permanent objects that act upon it, which are equally inherent and indestructible."[99]

Although Blake himself is often thought of in terms of Napoleonic, Byronic, or Wordsworthian romantic genius and was certainly notoriously prone to angry bouts of paranoia—which were not always unjustified—it is important to remember the extent to which he relentlessly removed himself as the grounding authority, even the author figure, in his own texts. For on his own account, his work is little more than dictation inspired by Jesus Christ, or John Milton, or "the eternals," or fairies (like the one who dictated *Europe*), or his dead brother Robert, with whom Blake claimed to "converse daily & hourly in the Spirit," and who, supposedly appearing to Blake in a vision, taught him how to combine words and pictures in the special method for which he is now known.[100] Blake's work may in this sense be said to have been collectively authored. At the very least, this approach pushes us to bear in mind the extent to which all work is ultimately a collective endeavor rather than the accomplishment of an individual genius—though, as we shall see, the individual and the collective, like the body and the soul, or the material and immaterial, are not opposed for Blake in the way we ordinarily think of them.

Many scholars are familiar with those lines in his annotations on Wordsworth in which Blake writes that "Natural Objects always did & do now Weaken deaden & obliterate Imagination in Me," adding that Wordsworth's supplementary "Essay" seems to have been written not by a true poet but by a "Landscape Painter."[101] For, Blake insists, the imagination "is the Divine Vision not of The World nor of Man nor from Man as he is a Natural Man but only as he is a Spiritual Man."[102] Thus, as against the "philosophic and experimental" knowledge of Paine or Wordsworth, with its class- and race-defined requirements for what we can now recognize as a stable Western subject (adequately learned, prepared, disciplined, and "cultivated"), and with its quest for moral virtue and domination over the other, Blake proposes the prophetic power precisely of the unlearned, of his "fellow labourers,"[103] and especially of children, who, he tells Trusler, "have taken a greater delight in contemplating my Pictures than I even hoped."[104] Jesus, Blake writes, "supposes every Thing to be Evident to the Child & to the Poor & Unlearned Such is the Gospel." For, he adds, "the Whole Bible is filld with Imaginations & Visions from End to End & not with Moral virtues that is the baseness of Plato & the Greeks & all *Warriors* The Moral Virtues are continual Accusers of Sin & promote Eternal Wars & *Domineering over others*."[105] Thus, rather than the imperial "warrior" discourse of Wordsworth and the hegemonic liberal-radicals—a discourse obsessed with sovereign power and domination of the other—Blake proposes an opening out away from the discourse of sovereign power and toward the mode of being in common appropriate to the spiritual man—that is, a mode of being which recognizes that "God is Man & exists in us & we in him."[106] Infantilization, and especially the infantilization of women, is the disaster that Wollstonecraft seeks to avert, but for Blake, we might say that infantilization—for example, the unity of body and mind that we see in young children, whose impulses Wollstonecraft seeks to bring under control in her training manual for children—actually presents a mode of power precluded by the cultural politics of sovereignty. But Blake's is a radically different conception of power—and his brand of Ranterish plebeian enthusiasm would have made Paine or Wollstonecraft uncomfortable (to say the least). And indeed Blake had occasion elsewhere to apologize for his "Enthusiasm which I wish all to partake of Since it is to me a Source of Immortal Joy."[107] In the remainder of this chapter, I wish to explore not only what Blake meant by this "Immortal Joy," but to consider what a politics built on such joy might look like in an age already dominated by the political aesthetics of empire. Before we can return explicitly to the Orient as the site of imperialism, however, I need to clarify a few more conceptual issues.

First of all, the distinction between "spiritual" and "natural" is not proposed by Blake as an absolute opposition. The spiritual and the natural are, rather, two different sides of the same coin, or to use Spinoza's language, two different modes of the same substance. In fact, according to Blake, it is the reification of this opposition (as in the binary polarization of body and soul) that is the great source of error in his own day: as he says in *The Marriage*, "Man has no Body distinct from his Soul for that calld Body is a portion of Soul discernd by the five Senses, the chief inlets of soul in this age."[108] Ultimately, for Blake, an absolute distinction between the material and the spiritual does not hold ("A Spirit and a Vision are not, as the modern Philosophy supposes," he writes, "a cloudy vapour or a nothing: they are organized and minutely articulated beyond all that the mortal and perishing nature can produce").[109] It would be as false an opposition as that between the soul and the body, or the subject and the object, or the visible and the invisible: the essential oppositions of the dualistic philosophy inherited from Locke, which Blake condemned at every opportunity.

As it happens, this would be the very issue for which the "polite" reviewers of Blake's illustrations for the Cromek edition of Blair's *Grave*, as well as Blake's 1809 exhibition, would most take him to task. For, as we saw in the previous chapter, they would accuse him of being an enthusiast, a hallucinating visionary, because of his unwillingness to distinguish the body and the soul, the visible and the invisible, the material and the immaterial, "confounding," as Robert Hunt proclaims, matters that should be kept distinct.[110] Interestingly, and not at all coincidentally, a similar "confounding," an "attempt to describe spiritual existences by terms and images which appertain to corporeal forms," was the only serious "blemish" that Warren Hastings, then the governor-general of Bengal, had found in the Bhagavad Gita, which was translated into English for the first time by Charles Wilkins in 1785, under the auspices of the East India Company: a blemish, which, according to Hastings, "will scarcely fail to make its own impression on every correct mind."[111] Hastings, however, had implored English readers to "exclude, in estimating the merit of such a production, all rules drawn from the antient or modern literature of Europe, all references to such sentiments or manners as are become the standards of propriety for opinions and action in our own modes of life, and equally all appeals to our revealed tenets of religion, and moral duty." Wilkins, shown translating the *Gita*, is the subject of *The Bramins*, one of the paintings in Blake's 1809 exhibition which would be excoriated by Hunt, who found the artist "an unfortunate lunatic," and the *Descriptive Catalogue* of his exhibition "a farrago of nonsense, unintelligibleness, and egregious vanity, the wild effusions of a distempered brain." Clearly, Hunt's liberal-radical sentiment toward other cultures—imbued with the aggressive protoimperial cultural logic also seen in Wollstonecraft and Shelley—was not nearly as generous as that of Hastings.

What is most interesting for our purposes, however, is that Hunt recognizes Blake's "confounding" precisely as an Oriental tendency. He argues that Blake, in his art and writing, tries "to perform impossibilities, to convert the pencil into a magical wand, and with it to work wonders, surpassing any recorded in the Tales of the Genii."[112] Hunt's Blake is little better than a depraved Oriental storyteller. The distinction between East and West—and hence self and other, material and immaterial—that would prove so essential both to radical writing and to Wordsworthian romanticism, have no role to play in Blake's work. The latter, if it cannot be said to be Western (which it surely is not, in any meaningful sense of that term), must, by the logic of a Hunt or a Wollstonecraft, be Eastern instead, there being no room for other alternatives in such a highly dualistic worldview. This Blake, then, is all the more a freak: a crazy "distempered" Oriental in Cockney guise: a magic-carpet salesman, a vendor of crazy picture books.

But however exceptional Blake may have seemed by 1809, he was only one among thousands and millions who sought to question the supposed truths held as sacred by "correct minds," and the great narrative of "progress" and "development" running through the seventeenth and eighteenth centuries and culminating in the explosion of radical writing and activism in the 1790s, in which the opposition of material and immaterial was as essential as the opposition of vice and virtue, manly and unmanly, East and West. As we saw in chapter 3, a mill, for example, is for Blake not just a kind of workplace or a technical machine, but also, together with all its "complicated wheels," a mode of thought, deadening to the imagination because it operates in terms of mechanistic and dualistic paradigms derived from Newton and Locke. Hence, it pertains to what Blake distinguished as "the Philosophic & Experimental" from the "Poetic or Prophetic character," without which the former "would soon be at the ratio of all things & stand still, unable to do other than repeat the same dull round over again."[113] Here Blake asserts a distinction between the finite, the bounded, the limited on the one hand, and the infinite on the other. And if the inability to grasp abstraction and classification would be identified as among the great shortcomings of the Oriental races, a refusal of such abstraction would be enough to mark Blake as a degenerate Orientalist enthusiast. However, what Blake proposes, both materially and politically, need not involve an escape into a fantasy world of a private lunacy; it requires, rather, a reorientation of seeing and belonging in an altogether new dimension, which would allow us to see and transform the world in ways otherwise quite literally unimaginable.

6. Blake's Orient

It was not just the conquerors, explorers, pirates, and grocers who mounted journeys to faraway lands: Blake, too, had an Oriental expedition. In the *Descriptive Catalogue* of his 1809 exhibition. Blake compares his work not to the earliest European classics of Greece and Rome, but rather to Persian, Indian, and Egyptian art. The traces of those ancient arts are, he says, still preserved on monuments, "being copies from some stupendous originals now lost or perhaps buried till some happier age. The Artist having been taken in vision into the ancient republics, monarchies, and patriarchates of Asia, has seen those wonderful originals called in the Sacred Scriptures the Cherubim, which were sculptured and painted on walls of Temples, Towers, Cities, Palaces, and erected in the highly cultivated states of Egypt, Moab, Edom, Aram, among the Rivers of Paradise, being originals from which the Greeks and Hertrurians copied Hercules, Farnese, Venus of Medicis, Apollo Belvidere, and all the grand works of ancient art."[114] Just a few years after Blake wrote these lines, Shelley would famously proclaim in *Hellas*,

CHAPTER FIVE

"we are all Greeks. Our laws, our literature, our religion, our arts have their roots in Greece. But for Greece—Rome, the instructor, the conqueror, or the metropolis of our ancestors, would have spread no illumination with her arms, and we might still have been savages and idolaters; or, what is worse, might have arrived at such a stagnant and miserable state of social institution as China and Japan possess."[115]

Shelley's rhetoric, of course, has not only an aesthetic motive, but also a very clearly articulated political one as well. It serves to distinguish an emergent European world of modernity from a premodern world of savages, barbarians, and Orientals, all of whom were much in need of "our" glorious civilization.[116] Shelley, in other words, consolidates in *Hellas* an imperial worldview that had only begun to emerge in the radical discourse of the 1790s—and would be transmitted to the Cromers and Balfours of coming generations, serving, in making its all-important distinction between Europe and its others, as one of the crucial ideological underpinnings of nineteenth-century British imperialism. What is being marked here is the transition, explored at length by Martin Bernal, toward a Hellenocentric model of Western European identity, which involves the repudiation and denial of the Afro-Asiatic sources of the earliest European cultures.[117]

Blake's position, on the other hand, involves something more than merely a rhetorical disdain for "the silly Greek & Latin slaves of the sword" and dismissal of "the Stolen and Perverted Writings of Homer & Ovid: of Plato & Cicero, which all Men ought to contemn."[118] For if Blake refuses the Hellenocentric move, he does so not only in order to stress the Afro-Asiatic origins of European culture (a notion also stressed, for quite different purposes, by East India Company officials including William Jones and Thomas Maurice as well as artists like Luigi Mayer), but also in order to emphasize the of *all* human cultures. Such a notion of sharing and being in common—notwithstanding important differences—must be seen to be quite drastically at odds with the imperialist rhetoric both of his own time and of the coming decades. In his work of the 1790s, Blake contests the political aesthetics of empire which were emerging in Wordsworthian romanticism as well as in the liberal-radical writings of Paine and Wollstonecraft, and which would pit self against other, West against East.

Whereas the political aesthetic of empire is predicated on the dialectics of otherness, what Blake attempts in his work is the resurrection of a lost common being which might reunify humankind *along with* all its differences. We can see this political aesthetic at work, for example, in *A Divine Image* in *Songs of Innocence*:

246

To Mercy Pity Peace and Love,
All pray in their distress:
And to these virtues of delight
Return their thankfulness.

For Mercy Pity Peace and Love,
Is God our father dear:
And Mercy Pity Peace and Love,
Is Man his child and care.

For Mercy has a human heart
Pity, a human face:
And Love, the human form divine,
And Peace, the human dress.

Then every man of every clime,
That prays in his distress,
Prays to the human form divine
Love Mercy Pity Peace.

And all must love the human form,
In heathen, turk or jew.
Where Mercy, Love & Pity dwell,
There God is dwelling too.

Written at a moment of intense political and military interest in foreign cultures, these lines present a radical challenge to the emergent cultural politics of British imperialism. Only through the most superficial and banal of readings, which have often been proposed, could this expression of Blake's intense antinomian faith—and its underlying political stance—be assimilated into the ideology of the established church. Indeed, although Blake bound the plates constituting the various copies of *Songs of Innocence and of Experience* in widely divergent and seemingly random sequences, one of the rare consistencies among the different editions is that in the majority he paired *A Divine Image* with either *Holy Thursday* or *The Chimney Sweeper*.[119] All three of these songs share a highly critical attitude toward the religious conventions of the established church, which Blake identified elsewhere in unambiguous terms as the "state religion" that he associated with such notorious "state tricksters" as the bishop of Llandaff, and, moreover, with that version of the Bible which had been repeatedly deployed as "a State Trick, thro which tho' the People at all times could see they never had the power to throw off."[120] Nor, for that matter, could *A Divine Image* rightly be seen as anything like an approximation of the supposed "humanism" of evangelical abolitionists such as William Wilberforce or Hannah More. The evangelical challenges to the slave trade were quite readily compatible with highly repressive attitudes regarding domestic politics and an aggressively proimperial stance on foreign affairs, both of which would have been profoundly offensive to Blake.[121]

In *A Divine Image*, the orthodox Christianity of the established church and state (as articulated for example in Isaac Watts's fervent lines, "Lord, I ascribe it to thy Grace / And not to Chance, as others do, / That I was born of *Christian* Race, / And not a *Heathen*, or a *Jew*")[122] is challenged by Blake's affirmation that all religions are one, a position that he had already elaborated in his first work in illuminated printing the year before (1788): "As all men are alike (tho' infinitely various) So all Religions."[123] Here it is precisely the infinite variety of humankind that makes it "alike," and constitutes its essential unity, as well as the unity of God and the human form divine. "Essence is not Identity," Blake had written in his scornful annotations to the work of Emanuel Swedenborg at around the same time as he was working on *All Religions are One*, "but from Essence proceeds Identity & from one Essence may proceed many Identities as from one Affection may proceed many thoughts." If, he added, "the Essence was the same as the Identity there could be but one Identity. Which is false. Heaven would upon this plan be but a Clock but one & the same."[124]

In the less explicitly philosophical language of *A Divine Image*, the essential being in common of Christian, Heathen, Turk (i.e., Muslim), and Jew is constituted by their *heterogeneity*, rather than by their *sameness*. The relationship of essence and identity formulated by Blake is something like the relationship of substance and mode in Spinoza. In both cases, essential unity is sharply differentiated from homogeneity, and, as we have seen, in both cases this opens up the possibility of a kind of freedom that is far less constraining than the emergent discourse of "liberty" constructed around the position of a supposedly transcendent bourgeois subject, whose freedom could be worked out only in a network of relations with "others" who are more or less free. Especially in the context of empire (which is the context in which the 1790s advocates of liberty were working) these others would generally have been less free rather than more free.

In Blake's account, there is no contradiction between being "infinitely various" and being "alike," no contradiction between one essence and many identities, or, to use Spinoza's language, one substance and many modes. Rather, the "alike" for Blake is perfectly consistent with infinite variety: "As all men are alike in outward form, So (and with the same infinite variety) all are alike in the Poetic Genius," he writes in *All Religions are One*. Indeed, such variety and infinity in Blake's antinomian conception are what *immanently* define being, and what define God: "the desire of Man being infinite the possession is Infinite & himself Infinite," he writes in another early copy engraving; "Therefore God becomes as we are, that we may be as he is." What would threaten our infinite and ever-differentiated being is, on the contrary, constant identity, conformity, nullity, and death, since "the same dull round even of a univer[s]e would soon become a mill with complicated wheels."[125] Infinite variety is in other words what makes being possible and desirable, while a uniform identity (turning all difference into sameness, all others into the self, and indeed hardening the self itself into an atom-like monad) would turn the world into a predictable mechanism like a clock or a mill.

If what I am calling the political aesthetic of empire distinguishes one person from another, one culture from another, Blake's religio-political aesthetic is an attempt to resurrect a lost immanent unity—identified in those "stupendous originals now lost or perhaps buried till some happier age"—without placing one culture in a position superior to that of another. "The antiquities of every Nation under Heaven," he writes, "are the same thing as Jacob Bryant, and all antiquaries have proved." For, he adds, "all had originally one language, and one religion, this was the religion of Jesus, the Everlasting Gospel."[126] Here the everlasting gospel—the central organizing concept in the underground antinomian tradition going back at least to the seventeenth century—is sharply distinguished from the Judeo-Christian tradition of the established state religion, which would so ably serve the imperial culture of the nineteenth century as a way to distinguish savages from civilized men.

Blake must be seen here to be articulating his own autodidactically cobbled-together and highly radicalized version of a very old tradition of pantheistic thought, which claimed its origins in pre-Christian antiquity, when all humankind is supposed to have shared one language and one religion (Blake's "everlasting gospel"), which was copied, appropriated, and perverted by later religions and cultures. According to Martin Bernal, we can trace this tradition "past Spinoza to Bruno and beyond, to the Neo-Platonists and Egypt itself."[127] This tradition claimed to have its origins in the work of the mythical figure of Hermes Trismegistos (Blake, like Milton, called him "thrice great Hermes,"[128] though he also makes an appearance in *The Song of Los* simply as "Trismegistus"),[129] and, through the Hermetic tradition, various Gnostic and neo-Platonist currents—invigorated after the thirteenth century with strands of Muslim and Kabbalistic mysticism emerging from the ruins of Arab Spain—can be traced to medieval and Renaissance mystics such as Joachim of Fiore, Jakob Böhme, Paracelsus, and Giordano Bruno (burned at the stake by the Catholic Church in 1600).[130] In varying degrees, these currents of thought had considerable influence on later writers, not least Spinoza and Blake (who claimed that Paracelsus and Böhme, among others, appeared to him in visions).[131]

Blake, however, would have inherited this tradition—whose lineage was traced as long ago as the 1950s by A. L. Morton,[132] but seemingly forgotten by Blake scholars—after its regeneration in the middle of the seventeenth century, when, following Isaac Casaubon's repudiation of the antiquity of the Hermetic texts, the Hermetic tradition went underground and was highly radicalized during England's revolutionary years. From then on, the Hermetic tradition can be seen to have diverged, one line of thought leading to an elitist notion of hidden knowledges and mysteries, which would be most fully elaborated in Rosicrucianism and Freemasonry, and the other line of thought plunging deeper underground in a lineage of antinomian dangerous enthusiasm, one of whose end points would be William Blake, who stood out in his own time as a freak, a crazy Orientalized Cockney, trying to sell crazy picture books. Christopher Hill reminds us that after the middle of the seventeenth century Hermeticism would appeal both to elitists and to lower-class radicals: "not all Hermeticists were radicals, by a long way," Hill argues, "but most radicals were Hermeticists."[133] What Frances Yates identifies, for example, as they key themes of Giordano Bruno's version of Hermeticism, the worship of "God in things," the recognition that "God as a whole . . . is in all things," the belief in "one simple divinity which is in all things, one fecund nature, mother and preserver of the universe, shines forth in diverse subjects, and takes diverse names, according as it communicates itself diversely,"[134] would be more or less exactly replicated in the radical antinomian writers of the middle of the seventeenth century, who in turn had enormous influence on Blake. Jacob Bauthumley writes, for example, that "God is in all creatures, Man and Beast, Fish and Fowle, and every green thing, from the highest Cedar to the Ivey on the wall," for, Bauthumley writes, "Every Creature and thing having that Being living in it . . . there is no difference betwixt Man and Beast."[135] Put back in this context, from which it emerged, one of the lines that is repeatedly reiterated in Blake's illuminated books—"every thing that lives is holy"—suddenly takes on new meaning, for we are reminded that Blake was not alone in his beliefs, however bizarre they may have seemed in his own time, let alone in our own. He was part of a long tradition of what appears from the standpoint of the dominant dualistic philosophical and political tradition deriving from Locke as a series of "savage anomalies."[136]

However, in the context of the 1790s, Blake's reactivation and rearticulation of the old panthetistic and antinomian tradition takes on particular political significance. Somewhere in the hidden core of this tradition was the belief that European civilization is not essentially different from Afro-Asiatic civilization, or, in other words, the belief that, in spite of all their differences, "All Religions are One." Modern imperialism could emerge really only with, or after, the recognition that Europe was essentially different from its others, that is, with the recognition of an insurmountable distinction between East and West ("East is East and West is West"). Blake's emphasis on the common essential unity of humankind would, quite clearly, have been radically incompatible with the emerging imperialist worldview, including the version of that worldview which we can see in the work of evangelical writers who sought to affirm a common humanity by turning all cultures into the same. For Blake, as we have seen, essential unity was quite readily compatible with enormous heterogeneity and difference.

In tracing a lost being in common, of course, Blake sometimes runs the risk of seeming to collapse all cultures into each other. Whereas the Oriental scenes of Montesqiueu, Byron, or Southey are structured in terms of radical difference from some Western norm, the kings and counselors of "Asia" in *The Song of Los*, for example, look and sound rather like their European counterparts, seeming particularly indistinguishable when they seek "to fix the price of labour" and "to cut off the bread from the city, / That the remnant may learn to obey," charges which were frequently levelled at the Pitt regime in England all through the 1790s.[137] Various critics have pointed to the reference to the "darkness of Asia" awaiting the "thick-flaming, thought-creating fires of Orc" in *The Song of Los*, suggesting that Blake here participates in Eurocentric or Orientalist discourse in a depiction of Oriental ignorance awaiting Western enlightenment.[138] Yet *all* the continents of Blake's 1790s prophecies are described (for whatever such "descriptions" are worth) as "dark," including revolutionary America itself, which is repeatedly shown wrapped in "thick clouds and darkness."[139]

If anything, all the continents and all the peoples of Blake's world are equally subject to the same forces of oppression, all together waiting for the fires of freedom and deliverance from a common enemy—the Urizenic codes, which take on different forms in different places but nevertheless share underlying continuities. For, just as Blake traced an original language and religion immanently and heterogeneously uniting humankind via "the poetic genius" (since "the Religions of all Nations are derived from each Na-

CHAPTER FIVE

tions different reception of the Poetic Genius"), the perversion of the common poetic genius and its usurpation by a hierarchizing state is also shown to be a universal occurrence, manifested differently from place to place. Thus in *The Song of Los* there is an ongoing systematic relationship between the "Abstract Philosophy" given to "Brama in the East," the "abstract Law" given to "Pythagoras, Socrates & Plato," the "loose Bible" given to "Mahomet," the "Code of War" given "in the North, to Odin," and the "Philosophy of Five Senses" which Urizen places in the hands of "Newton & Locke."[140] So while Blake's great idol Milton had declared—like many of the radicals of Blake's own time—that "the people of Asia" are "much inclinable to slavery,"[141] Blake's Asians are neither more nor less servile than his Europeans, and they certainly do not seem particularly different. Actually, their appearance never really registers as an issue, and in this context we should bear in mind Blake's tendency to de-exoticize as much as possible many of the images of otherness that were involved in his commissioned work. Robert Essick and Bernard Smith point out, for example, the extent to which Blake seems to have added a measure of dignity in the bearing and stature of the South Pacific natives he engraved after a drawing by the lieutenant-governor of Norfolk Island (see fig. 24).[142] The Pacific Islanders and Asian peoples illustrated by Blake for Daniel Fenning and Joseph Collyer's *New System of Geography*, as well as the figures of the black slaves in Blake's illustrations for Stedman's *Narrative*, are similarly enhanced (see fig. 25).[143]

It has recently been suggested, however, that Blake's representation of non-Europeans amounts to a denial of cultural difference. For example, Blake's *Little Black Boy* in *Songs of Innocence* is in many copies of the plate indistinguishable from the little white boy with whom he appears (though, as Morris Eaves points out, too few readings of *Little Black Boy* pay sufficient attention to that plate's relationships to *The Chimney Sweeper*, in which skin color has nothing to do with matters of race or culture). Anne Mellor sees this as evidence that, although in his visual artwork (including his commissioned work, notably the Stedman illustrations) Blake may indeed have made an effort to portray African or Asian bodies as more noble and heroic by making them seem more "European," this is because he "participated in a cultural erasure of difference between races and individuals that gave priority to Western, white models."[144] As further evidence for her claim, Mellor points to Blake's engraving of the Stedman drawing, *Europe supported by Africa and America* (see fig. 26), and argues that we should recognize the "racism and sexism" of the image, not only because the three women are physiologically similar, but also because "the women of color support the white woman, not vice versa," which suggests that "their labor is used to shore up

252

Figure 24. Blake after King, *A Family of New South Wales*. Collection of Robert N. Essick. Reproduced with the kind permission of Robert N. Essick.

Figure 25. Blake, *The Execution of Breaking on the Rack*, from John Gabriel Stedman, *Narrative of a Five Years Expedition Against the Revolted Negroes of Surinam* (London, 1796). Collection of Robert N. Essick. Reproduced with the kind permission of Robert N. Essick.

Figure 26. Blake, *Europe Supported by Africa and America*, from John Gabriel Stedman, *Narrative of a Five Years Expedition Against the Revolted Negroes of Surinam* (London, 1796). Collection of Robert N. Essick. Reproduced with the kind permission of Robert N. Essick.

CHAPTER FIVE

the central and superior European female, who wears a jeweled necklace, the overt sign of the wealth they produce, while the women of color wear arm bands reminiscent of the fetters of the slave."[145] Similarly, Mellor argues that "neither the verbal nor the visual representations of sex, violence, and slavery in *Visions of the Daughters of Albion* contests the racist or sexist dimensions of the Enlightenment discourse of Anglo-Africanism Blake inherited."[146]

It is not clear, however, how much of Blake's own thoughts and intentions we can read into that particular image (quite apart from the fact that it was a commissioned piece after Stedman's sketch, so that Blake must be seen to have been operating under professional constraints). Even taken at face value, the fact that "Africa" and "America" are in chains need not be read as evidence that Blake supported slavery.[147] On the contrary, the image could easily be read instead as a critique of a world system based on inequality and brutal exploitation, such as the "Universal Empire . . . rattling with clanking chains" whose baleful effects we see throughout Blake's work. In any case, in examining texts and images from the late eighteenth and early nineteenth centuries, we need to be careful to distinguish between, on the one hand, attitudes toward other cultures and, on the other hand, positions on imperialism. As I mentioned earlier, Warren Hastings and William Jones admired Indian culture as much as Thomas Macaulay and James Mill would revile it—but all of them were committed imperialists. The problem is that they were committed to quite different imperialist projects, or perhaps to different moments of the same imperialist project. In the late eighteenth and early nineteenth centuries it was therefore possible to mobilize what we would today recognize as racist arguments in order to oppose imperialism, just as it was also possible to justify one's support for the empire's civilizing mission on the basis of one's profound and genuinely felt concern for other peoples and cultures, one's sense of their desperate need for the "gift" of what has been called civilization. Indeed, such contradictions persist into our own time. While, for example, it is easy enough to recognize that Victorian imperialists tended to express hostility toward what they regarded as inferior cultures, we sometimes have to pinch ourselves to remember the extent to which, for all its celebration of "otherness" and "difference," twenty-first century multiculturalism—in an era of truly globalized capitalism—is in fact a by-product of the most aggressively acquisitive exploitation of other cultures in the history of the world.

For similar reasons, the suppression—rather than the emphasis—of racial and cultural difference need not, in itself, be taken as evidence of the visual discourse of modern European colonialism.[148] At certain moments in its history, as we have seen, European colonialism itself celebrated difference and otherness; at others it denigrated them. The mere suppression or expression of racial difference, in themselves, therefore do not automatically indicate positions for and against colonialism itself. It has, in fact, been the central argument of the present chapter that by the end of the eighteenth century a sense of radical cultural difference (real, exaggerated, or otherwise) would provide the new form of the British imperialist project that began to emerge during the 1790s with one of its essential ideological underpinnings, which is why, even in its most benign guise, the period's widespread interest in—or really obsession with—exoticism would have such an immediately political character. In this context, Blake's systematic avoidance of such exoticism suggests a very different attitude toward other cultures and peoples than the ones rising to dominance at the dawn of the nineteenth century.

If "the Religions of all Nations are derived from each Nations different reception of the Poetic Genius," what that suggests is not that "all Religions are One" in the sense that they are all homogeneous, but rather that "all Religions are One" in the sense that they are all quite different. From the normative notion of identity and difference evoked by Mellor, this proposition could amount to little more than a flat contradiction in terms. But for Blake this proposition offers a line of flight away from the normative discourse of "warrior" aesthetics. The work of Jacob Bryant, to which Blake often refers, is a monumental attempt to chart out the common ancestry of humankind, to locate in every distinct cultural tradition "some shattered fragments of original history; some traces of a primitive and universal language."[149] The "Jewish & Christian Testaments," Blake writes in *All Religions are One*, "are An original derivation from the Poetic Genius."[150] But each religion, each nation, each people, has its own version of the same—but immanently differentiated—lost original, which was the object of Bryant's enquiry. "The Religions of all Nations," Blake writes, "are derived from each Nations different reception of the Poetic Genius which is every where call'd the Spirit of Prophecy."[151] Blake is able to avoid collapsing all nations and peoples into a bland homogeneous sameness, while at the same time he is able to preserve each nation's distinctiveness, since each nation's distinct identity does not prevent it from sharing in a common essence. Blake here must be seen to be trying to preempt or perhaps subvert the monadic politics of sovereign power—which, as he could already see, was threatening to reduce the world to a homogeneous machine and to preserve the possibility of the political aesthetics based on "immortal joy."

Blake's refusal of Orientalism, in offering an escape from the models of normative self-regulating subjectivity, proposes not only a different way of regarding otherness, however, but above all a different way of living, sharing, belonging, loving, being in common. All of this is not to say, though, that Blake was unique in his disengagement with Orientalism. To find his nearest equivalents, however, we have to look not among the canonical romantic poets but rather among the many appeals to working people around the world issued by members of the insurrectionary underground of the 1790s, especially those members of the underground who were more concerned with fighting the state than with insinuating themselves into it, such as Thomas Spence, or Daniel Isaac Eaton, who—in response to Burke's reference to "a swinish multitude"—wrote in one issue of his *Politics for the People* that "we, the swine of Great Britain, have no right to esteem ourselves superior, in the scale of beings, to the swine of France, or any other country; we regard our brethren, whether they be found in the East or Western Indies, or on the burning plains of Africa, with true fraternal affection."[152] The common cause among the peoples of Africa, Asia, America, and Europe in Blake's Lambeth books—including *The Song of Los*—must be understood in this context: it requires much more adaptation, and a great sacrifice of its political significance, to fit it into the Eurocentric discourse of romantic Orientalism.

Nor, clearly, were all radicals as quick as, say, Paine or Wollstonecraft or Thelwall to reject the charge of belonging to the "swinish multitude," or to try to lay claim to respectability and moral superiority over others. However subversively, Eaton, Spence, and many others eagerly embraced Burke's dismissive epithet in their stories and publications ("Pig's Meat," "Salmagundi for Swine," "Swineherd's Remonstrance," "Advice to Swine," etc.). Without conforming to the agenda of either Eaton or Spence, Blake—whose library, as Frederick Tatham pointed out, included many "mystical" titles[153]—was also interested in an altogether different kind of political culture from the one so zealously championed by the hegemonic radicals. It is no coincidence that Oriental exoticism held little interest for him as he tried to imagine a world in which the all-important distinctions between Orient and Occident—or self and other—had no role to play, and in which supposedly essential distinctions among the continents were put to one side rather than mobilized as the explanation and indeed the root cause of all cultural and political differences among people.

Blake must be seen to be trying to rescue against all odds the possibility of a political aesthetic of immortal joy, which we can understand as an affirmation of joyous unity and collective freedom. This amounts to a refusal of the very logic of domination, of warrior power over others. More precisely, the quest for such immortal joy can be seen to involve two distinct components: first, a struggle against transcendence and domination in all of their political and religious and military forms, and second, a struggle for a form of being in common that would not require authorization by a transcendental principle such as the king, or the state, or the transcendent god of the established church. In the next chapter we will take this tentative discussion of immortal joy a little further and explore the full potential of Blake's illuminated books.

CHAPTER SIX

Impossible History and the Politics of Life

I am like an atom
A Nothing left in darkness yet I am an identity
I wish & feel & weep & groan Ah terrible terrible
—William Blake

I contain multitudes.
—Walt Whitman

Adieu then to striving against the stream, since the readiest way to get to port is to go with it. So here goes, my boys, for an estate and vassals to bow to me! Who would not be a gentleman and live without care! Especially a democratic gentleman without a king. Avaunt rights of man! I am henceforth a democrat, but no leveller!
—Thomas Spence

1. Introduction

And his world teemd vast enormities
Frightening; faithless; fawning
Portions of life; similitudes
Of a foot, or a hand, or a head
Or a heart, or an eye, they swam mischevous
Dread terrors! delighting in blood[1]

Blake's Urizen books reveal a fallen world. The only apparent salvation from the "petrific abominable chaos"[2] of the fall seems to be the imposition of Urizenic despotism, an attempt to realize Urizen's dream to bring all life under the control of "One command, one joy, one desire, / One curse, one weight, one measure, / One King, one God, one Law."[3] Urizen's despotic fantasy turns out to be an impossibility, of course, and, sickened, he curses "Both sons and daughters; for he saw / That no flesh nor spirit could keep /

His iron laws one moment."[4] Even when it inevitably falls short of the Urizenic absolute, however, life in the fallen world is, or threatens to become, regulated life. For the basis of all power in this fallen world (including the very power that constitutes Urizen) is the regulation of life itself. Such regulation attempts to obtain power over—literally by giving form to—the "hurtling bones,"[5] "cataracts of blood,"[6] "fibres of blood, milk and tears,"[7] "disease on disease, shape on shape,"[8] in short, the "*life in cataracts,*"[9] that vomits forth, tumbles, cascades, and flows nightmarishly and nauseatingly through the Urizen books.

To be kept from lapsing uncontrollably into "formless unmeasurable death,"[10] such "similitudes," such "portions of life," and hence life itself, must be formed, regulated, organized, disciplined by an external regulative power. That is, the limitless potential of eternal life must be organ-ized: formed into branchy "finite inflexible organs" which can be assigned tasks and functions and linked to each other in productive machines and organized bodies. Such bodies are abstracted from life itself, life lived as limitless potential—that is, the "eternal life"[11] in which imagination determines form, creatively, immanently, freely. Organ-ization and formation take place in the disciplinary apparatuses, the "Churches: Hospitals: Castles: Palaces" that operate according to a "Philosophy of the Five Senses," and that proliferate through the fallen world "Like nets & gins & traps to catch the joys of Eternity."[12] Here—with the logic of Bacon, Newton, and Locke, the "Philosophy of the Five Senses," taken to its ultimate extreme, the organized body's finite organic perception becomes a solely material process, one in which the body's regulated organs allow access to the five senses that they themselves define, senses according to which life can be perceived, defined, and understood. Thus, the limitless potential of life is parceled out into limited forms, which "no more" can "rise at will / In the infinite void," but are "bound down / To earth by their narrowing perceptions."[13] Here, what can and cannot be perceived, what can and cannot be sensed, is determined by the material forms that make perception possible in the first place.

Indeed, it is precisely in accepting that what can be perceived defines what is possible, and that what is possible defines what can be perceived, that the fall takes place, every day. The fall, in other words, does not constitute a reality. Rather, it constitutes a certain highly circumscribed ontology of perception and of being—a mode of perceiving which is precisely what makes reality real to the limited forms of life appropriate to it. The latter, stripped of the capacity for imagination, and "bound down / To earth by their narrowing perceptions," regard this fallen world as the only world, this reality as the only possible reality, themselves as the only possible forms of

CHAPTER SIX

being, and hence their history as the only possible (that is, legally sanctioned) history. Thus, perception and being are collapsed into one another in such a way that ontological limitations are manifested as epistemological, representational, and conceptual limitations. The legally sanctioned "history of the possible" must take these limitations for granted as its very basis, its point of departure. "Impossible history," on the other hand, refuses such assumptions; its impossibility consists precisely in its refusal to take for granted that which the law mandates as "possible" and "necessary."

However, the Urizen books do not merely reveal the stark choices made available by such a world. Even in the darkest and bleakest moments of their revelation, Blake's works reach toward "love," which "Always is to joy inclind, / Lawless wingd & unconfind / And breaks all chains from every mind."[14] What I want to explore in this chapter and the next one is the possibility that we can see Blake's illuminated books constituting a new kind of body, and anticipating a new kind of being, one no longer subject to the law, and especially to the laws of necessity and of regulation. Instead, these books can be seen to open out and away from the limiting continuum of regulated desire, regulated being, and regulated life itself—and hence the legally-sanctioned history of the possible (whose exponents have unsurprisingly failed to understand them)—and toward what Blake called the eternal, a state in which thought and life, body and mind, are unified and coextensive, strengthening and reaffirming each other. For by flying "lawless wingd & unconfind" from the continuum of finitude and of regulated life, Blake's books do not claim to lead to chaos or formless anarchy (such as "the unorganized Blots & Blurs of Rubens & Titian"),[15] but rather to a way of being with which an imposed logic of regulation would be incompatible, unnecessary, redundant: a form-of-life which does not recognize the existence of the law.[16] This is Blake's ontological antinomianism: an ontology that is immediately and inseparably aesthetic, religious, philosophical and political, that refuses the basic requirements of the history of the possible and as a result has never made sense in it.

It should come as no surprise to us that it is in art that such a form-of-life should be anticipated and articulated. For Blake it is precisely in art that God, the "eternal body of man" of which we are all members, is immanently produced; in other words, it is in art that humanity creates itself as God. "In his creative activity," Northrop Frye explains in his elaboration of Blake's political and aesthetic stance, "the artist expresses the creative activity of God."[17] Thus, art for Blake is not an isolated, abstract, and idealized activity, but rather an ensemble of material practices, makings, beings, thoughts, images, and imaginations that constitute and define life itself. "Practice is Art," he writes; "if you leave off you are Lost."[18] Art for Blake is, in other words, a creative and an *ontological* activity, rather than simply a representational or epistemological one (which unfortunately is the rather more limited sense in which Blake's art is often understood by his students and critics, many of whom have gone so far as to think of Blake—that most comprehensively materialist artist—as a free-floating idealist, simply because they cannot recognize Blake's form of materialism for what it is, in sharp distinction from that other kind of materialism, which Blake associated with Bacon, Newton, and Locke).

If art and imagination ought to constitute life, a world in which "the arts" are abstracted from a wider set of material and mental practices threatens to confirm the separation of body and mind, thought and practice, reality and representation, conception and execution—in short, a division of life and of labor, or rather of life into labor—which for Blake it would be sheer folly to accept without resistance. If, on the contrary, "the whole Business of Man is the Arts . . . ," a new form of art presupposes a new way of making the world; and if "the whole Business of Man is the Arts *& All Things Common*,"[19] a new form of art presupposes a new way of sharing, of loving, of living, of being, *in common*.

2. The Production of Life

The Urizen books are concerned with one thing and one thing only: production—the production of time; the production of space; the production of worlds, of earth, of animals, of humans, of organs, of organisms, of language, of religion, of images, of meaning, of books; the production of production; the production of life itself. Life *is* production, both material and immaterial. Think of all the *making* that goes on in the three books, where you can barely go a line without bumping into some kind of making, some kind of production. Think, most obviously, of all those hammers, anvils, bellows, tongs; think of all the measuring, stretching, pulling, cutting, fracturing, compassing (a term whose simultaneous material and immaterial meaning assumed great significance during the 1790s, when the defendants in the treason trials were accused of "compassing or imagining the death of the king"). Think of the "enormous labours," "perplex'd labring," "incessant labour"; think of all the breeding, brooding, generation, regeneration. Think of what a noisy environment it is: all that "howling," "sund'ring, dark'ning, thund'ring!" "groaning! gnashing! groaning!" all those "hurtlings & clashings & groans," "throbbings & shootings & grindings." It is not without reason that Robert Essick says that Blake "may be our noisiest

Figure 27. Blake, *Laocoön*. Robert N. Essick Collection. Copyright © 2001 the William Blake Archive. Used with permission.

poet," sometimes so noisy that "the noises cluster together and overwhelm all other senses. 'The howlings gnashings groanings shriekings shudderings sobbings burstings / Mingle together to create a world for Los,' and a cacophony for the reader, in Night the Sixth of *The Four Zoas.*"[20] Significantly, noise in Blake's work is invariably ontological, associated with making—literally *creating* a world for Los, as in Essick's example—and in particular with the making of life itself. Los howls "in a dismal stupor, / Groaning! gnashing! groaning," when he tumbles into being; "A shriek" runs "thro' Eternity: / And a paralytic stroke; / At the birth of the Human shadow," when Orc emerges from the recapitulative production process of Enitharmon's womb; "Howling, the Child with fierce flames / Issu'd from Enitharmon." Thiriel appears "Weeping! wailing!" and "astonish'd at his own existence." Utha and Grodna emerge "lamenting" and "howling," and it is, finally, to the accompaniment of "throbbings & shootings & grindings" that the Inhabitants of the world of Urizen are produced, their nerves and marrow hardening, shrinking, contracting, limiting, as they are "bound down / To earth by their narrowing perceptions." (And yet, strangely, once they are made, once they are alive, once they have "form'd laws of prudence, and call'd them / The eternal laws of God," these inhabitants lose their very sense of production, of themselves as products, as their ears grow "wither'd & deafen'd, & cold.")

The noise level in Blake is something like an index, a barometer—perhaps a speedometer—of making, and especially of the making of life. Given all this, if we can agree with Essick that Blake is "our noisiest poet," we may have little choice but to accept that he is also the poet most obsessed with making, and in particular with the making of life—life as endless making, life as the convergence of being and becoming, of production and constitution. At once political and ontological, we may think of Blake's aesthetic and material practice in terms of what Cesare Casarino has identified as "philopoesis."[21] For the question that Blake pushes us to ask is not whether life is made, but how, and under what circumstances; whether that making, and life itself, are to be sorrowful—a matter of lamenting, shrieking, howling, gnashing—or rather a matter of joy, celebration, piping, and singing; whether life is to be dominated by "happy chear" which we "weep with joy to hear," as in the introduction of *Songs of Innocence*, by the "bells chearful sound" of *The Ecchoing Green*, by the "tender voice" of the lamb, by *The Laughing Song's* "sweet chorus of Ha, Ha, He," or instead by the howlings and shriekings of life perverted, abstracted, and stolen: the harlot's curse, the soldier's sigh, the chimney sweeper's "weep, weep, in notes of woe!"

Chapter Six

The question, in other words, is whether life is to be the instrumental and reified life of the organized organism (whose making we explored in chapter 3) or, on the contrary, the joyous life of "the prolific," indefinite, open, reaching out toward an infinitely prolific number of re-makings, re-connections, re-imaginations—life as pure potential, life as constituent, rather than constituted, power.[22] "Some will say, Is not God alone the Prolific? I answer, God only acts & Is, in existing beings or Men."[23] Far more than being merely law breaking and transgressive, Blake's antinomianism is positive, affirmative, prolific, creative. If "the Eternal Body of Man is THE IMAGINATION. that is God himself," the "Divine Body" of which "we are his Members,"[24] our collective life is—or ought to be—a life of endlessly proliferating creation, a life of ontological power. Freedom in this sense is not, as it is for the liberal tradition, a negative matter of freedom from external restraint (that is, the kind of freedom recognized and validated by the market). For, recognizing no externality, this is a creative, affirmative, positive freedom, the freedom of a life of creative *power*. Freedom here is the power to constitute "the eternal body of man"; it is the power to imagine, and to create through imagining; it is the power to participate in an infinite being in common called God; it is the power to affirm life as being in common, life as the making of that "divine body" of which "we are his members."

Blake's concept of the imagination is, hence, far from idealist—which is a point that we modern students, readers, and scholars have been far too slow to recognize, mostly because, in our approach to his work, we have been so crippled by our indoctrination into a political philosophy inherently hostile to Blake's; a political philosophy against which he waged an unceasing struggle. For Blake's concept of the imagination unifies body and mind, thought and action, material and immaterial, not in the sense that it mediates between them, but in the sense that it marks the deployment of pure creative ontological power on both a mental and a material plane. It is, in other words, the expression of a materialist ontology.[25] Once we have freed ourselves of our own political, philosophical, and aesthetic limitations, this really, in all honesty, ought to come as no surprise. Even as late as the 1790s, the imagination still conveyed a sense of potential that we should not lose sight of—and Blake's concept of imagination has a heritage far older than the 1790s. After all, the defendants in the 1790s treason trials were accused of—and indeed, Colonel Despard would later be hanged for—"compassing or imagining the death of the king," a charge that recognizes no meaningful distinction between a supposedly "immaterial" thought and a material action, since to imagine or compass the death of the king was tantamount to actually murdering him; indeed, it is worth remembering that this charge, which carried the sternest punishment in English law, recognized imagination, and thought itself, as highly politicized and immediately material activities, to an extent that we, because of our own limitations, may find it difficult to recognize.[26]

In Blake, then, the imagination defines an absolute unity of material and immaterial, mental and bodily activity—an absolute unity of the principles that by Blake's time, as we have seen in previous chapters, had been distinguished from one another as *conception* and *execution*. If "every thing possible to be believ'd is an image of the truth,"[27] such images—and the truth itself—do not exist abstractly; they must be continually re-imagined, and hence reproduced. Imagination here is the process by which such images of truth are produced: it is the process by which lived, experienced reality is brought into being. The freedom to imagine is the power to create the world, and here that power is human rather than divine (or rather such divine power is here recognized as inherently human: "God is Man & exists in us & we in him"). In other words the ultimate political power (of creation, of making, of production) rests with humanity rather than with abstract gods and rules, with systems of nature, with unquestionable divine principles, with "the laws of nature and of nature's God,"[28] which we must all be made to obey precisely as though they had been divinely or naturally ordained, among those things, as Burke puts it, "with which we shall in vain contend."[29]

Blake's conception of the imagination is very close to, if not the same as, the sense of fancy or imagination that we see at work in certain seventeenth-century writers such as James Harrington and Spinoza, for whom, as Antonio Negri has argued, "fancy and imagination do not simply mediate between the concrete and the abstract—they are not epistemological functions; on the contrary, they are ontological and constitutive functions."[30] Thus, to say that the imagination produces the world should not be mistaken (as it so often has by scholars) for an idealist argument. We have to take seriously the affirmation that "a firm perswasion that a thing is so, makes it so,"[31] or in other words, that "perswasion" possesses ontological, creative power, for, as Michael Hardt points out, "a positive, materialist ontology is above all an ontology of power."[32] There is an extremely important caveat to all this, of course: imagination in this full creative sense is necessarily a *collective*, rather than an *individual*, power, which is precisely why Blake invokes it as the prerogative not of one man but of that "divine body" of which "we are his members." For to say that "the imagination" *is* God is to say that it is pure creativity, and that the image itself—far from being reified and stable, fixed and determinate—expresses creative power. And to say that "Man is all Imagination God is Man & exists in us & we in him"[33] is to

Chapter Six

affirm that the power of the imagination is a collective human power, that humanity in the collective sense, not God in the abstract sense (as in God & Priest & King), possesses and defines ontological power.

In the world of Urizen, however, life is regulated by a very different mode of power, and if life is nevertheless a matter of production, it is a kind of production that is carefully controlled, instrumentalized, directed. As we saw in chapter 3, this amounts to a life in which the powers of conception and of execution have been separated, and in which the the imagination has been abstracted and seen as an independent supervening power, the prerogative of an omnipotent creative God distinct from his creations. In laying claim to "Nature's wide womb,"[34] Urizen lays claim to the foundation of production itself—the *fons et origo* of all makings, the primal factory of life as production:

> And a roof, vast petrific around,
> On all sides He fram'd: like a womb;
> Where thousands of rivers in veins
> Of blood pour down the mountains to cool
> The eternal fires beating without
> From Eternals; & like a black globe
> View'd by sons of Eternity, standing
> On the shore of the infinite ocean
> Like a human heart strugling & beating
> The vast world of Urizen appear'd.[35]

The world of Urizen—the world as a planet, the world as a heart, the world as an organ, the world as a globe, the world as an inhabited space—is itself "like" the primal site of production, a womb. There is actually nothing genuinely *primal* about this site, however, since this virtual womb itself has to be produced and "fram'd." That is, production itself must be produced, it is not just naturalized, and it does not just happen all by itself. This is one of the many things that ought to prevent us from turning Blake's work into an expression of abstract and ethereal mythology, into a story of psychical drives and essences of the sort that various Blake scholars seem to be in search of. In a world in which everything is produced, no form of life, no form of being, can be taken for granted. Blake provides us with a kind of ontological materialism, a materialism whose ontological plenitude has for too long gone un- or at least underrecognized by scholars. Ontological matters are here seen to prefigure, even to preempt, the writing of history. If, in order to be written, the legally sanctioned history of the possible must assume and take for granted a certain ontological (as well as temporal) framework, as well as certain definite subjective forms, part of what makes "impossible history" impossible is that it does not take being for granted, just as it refuses to take for granted that time exists in a stream of empty homogeneous units.

Essick has pointed out the way in which Blake's language in this passage slides through and between a series of figural and metaphorical categories, a slippage which undermines the lexical stability of language itself. Here, for example, we slide from architectural to biological to geophysical frames, none of which contain the verbal movement. Essick suggests that "the very act of transgressing categorical distinctions presupposes the existence of such categories as the primary ground of the figural."[36] Hence, he reads this passage as an example of Blake's violating the rules of Urizenic language. But it might be possible to think of this movement in positive rather than negative terms. Here we can think of Blake's art as immediately creative, in the sense that it produces new images and forms as it flies between visual, verbal, and aural registers. "The moment I have written," Blake once admitted to Crabb Robinson, "I see the Words fly about the room in all directions."[37] And in a sense we can think of Blake's restlessly productive language flying from one category to the next in a creative and a positive (rather than transgressive) movement, a flow of associations, ideas, concepts, thoughts, images that does not heed Urizenic categories, or even categorical thought as such, not so much because it is transgressing them as because it does not even know what they are. Blake's language, as Essick writes, can in this sense be seen as "prolific activity in which the desire to act encompasses, but overflows, the desire to mean."[38] I would add that here we can see the desire to *create* encompassing and overflowing all other desires. Language in this sense is pure becoming, pure creative activity, pure joy, pure life.[39]

Such life and such joy are incompatible with the fallen world, in which life is regulated, controlled, constituted, directed, and hence stunted, limited, confined into crude materiality (crude in the sense of being stripped of imagination), and alienated, made subordinate to, a supervening intellectual, imaginative, and creative power, the expression of a crass and reductive form of materialism quite incompatible with Blake's own ontological materialism.[40] And we see such confinement over and over again in the Urizen books—the organization of life in a process in which, however, Urizen is as much a victim as a villain. Confronted by the "formless unmeasurable death,"[41] for example, Los rushes to organize and "imbody" Urizen. Through each of the seven ages of "dismal woe," and "Numb'ring with links, hours, days & years,"[42] Los transforms disorganized elements and matter into the body of Urizen, beginning by "inclosing" Urizen's "fountain

CHAPTER SIX

of thought." Then, heaving his tongs and bellows, he works his way through the other major organs and body parts—spine, ribs, central nervous system, eyes, ears, nostrils, throat, tongue, arms, legs, and feet. Once Urizen is "inclosed," that is, "embodied," in this organized form, he is cut off from "All the myriads of Eternity: / All the wisdom & joy of life," which "Roll like a sea around him, / Except what his little orbs / Of sight by degrees unfold."[43] Thus, "his eternal life / Like a dream was obliterated."[44] No sooner has Los finished his work than he is horrified and begins to pity Urizen. Once again the process of making a limited body begins: the "life in cataracts" flowing through and in Los conglobes into a "round globe of blood," a "globe of life blood trembling," which soon branches "out into roots; / Fib'rous, writhing upon the winds; / Fibres of blood, milk and tears."[45] Ultimately, these conglobed fibers "imbody" a female form, Enitharmon. And yet again the process of organization begins, as Los and Enitharmon produce Orc, who grows from a worm or serpent through "many forms of fish, bird & beast," to become a "Human shadow."[46]

Or at least that is how the story goes in *The Book of Urizen*. In *The Book of Ahania* and *The Book of Los* we see different accounts of "conglobing," "imbodiment," "outbranching," the linking together of glands, organs, muscles, limbs, "organizing the Human / Into finite inflexible organs."[47] As we saw in chapter 4, however, it is worse than useless to try to reduce these verbal, visual, and aural hypertexts to a kind of narrative, let alone a consistent narrative. Indeed, to try to pin them to a narrative form, as tellings or retellings of more or less the same story, is precisely to try to confine and delimit them in much the same way as Los limits Urizen. In any case, there is finally no way to reduce these narrative strands to a consistent account: even from line to line and from word to word—let alone in the proliferating gaps between words and images—there are too many contradictions, erasures, conflicts, too many changes of scale and time, tone, mode of language, discursive register—biological, psychological, geological, political, religious.

Pointing out the extent to which both *The Book of Ahania* and *The Book of Los* "seem to rework sections of the narrative of *The Book of Urizen* in ways which offer not only a different perspective on the events described but substantial and even contradictory differences," Jon Mee argues that such variations (in addition to the many self-contradictions of *Urizen* itself, some of whose copies have *two* chapter 4s, not to mention two or three conflicting accounts of the creation) "undermine the deep-rooted critical notion that there is some kind of prior Blakian myth articulated in each of his poetic performances."[48] Blake's poetic practice, Mee argues, refuses such fidelity to an originary moment, an antecedent text, a prior fixed and hence re-presentable truth which it ought to be our job as critics to faithfully rediscover. The act of representation here collapses into the represented event; the act of execution into that of conception. Mitchell argues, similarly, that Blake's sense of time pushes us to "see creation not as an event which occurred in the remote past, but as something which continually recurs in time, as if the cosmos were being redesigned with each passing moment."[49] The books of *Urizen*, *Ahania*, and *Los* do not, in other words, recount a single definite event, a single creation/fall that happened once and can be subsequently re-presented according to the history of the possible. Among other things, this rules out the possibility of a return to a prelapsarian moment. Eternity is not something we can go back to: it is something we have to *make*. Eternity is the experience of ontological affirmation; it is the expression of imagination as ontological power. For in insisting that all life must be located on an immanent plane of production, Blake's books are grounded, and hence ground us, not in the misty realms of "myth," but rather in production itself, a production whose "history" we *make*, though not necessarily under conditions of our own choosing.

In the illuminated books, Blake produces not legally sanctioned history, but rather an "impossible history," an antinomian ontology of the present that preempts the present's own laws of constitution, production, narrative, and time, all of which are essential to conventional histories, legally sanctioned histories of the *possible*—those histories of fixed and definite forms in which radical reformism meet conservative reaction on a rhetorical battleground whose very existence and terms of reference Blake in effect sidesteps. It is precisely on this rhetorical battleground that most of our own histories of the 1790s have been written. To pursue Blake's "impossible history" requires that we leave this stable representational ground and consider the ontological struggles by which it is constituted, as well as the ontological alternatives to it. However, such a concern with ontology is not a feature of most historical accounts of the period (nor, as Dipesh Chakrabarty reminds us, of historicism itself),[50] most of which bracket off any discussion of the philosophical and conceptual politics of ontology and take being and ontological form for granted. Blake does not fit into, does not make sense in, most of our historical accounts of the 1790s. But if we can agree that Blake's works are primarily ontological in nature, and hence concerned above all with the relationship between being and form, it is little wonder that they neither fit in—nor have they been understood by—most conventional historical accounts of the 1790s, which, as their own condition of possibility, have to take being and form for granted in a way that Blake's work refuses to do.

CHAPTER SIX

Blake's perpetual critique, through all his 1790s books, of the "philosophy of the five senses" can be understood only in simultaneously political, economic, philosophical, religious, and aesthetic terms—that is, in a sense which unifies these various discourses, whose splitting apart Blake vehemently opposed. This need for a comprehensive approach really should come as no surprise, given that, according to Locke, the body's physicosensory limitations impose limitations on the mind's capacity for thought, and given that, for Blake, deliverance from such limitation—both immaterial and material—must be possible. As we saw in chapter 2, this is the kind of freedom he promises at the end of *America* and in *The Marriage of Heaven & Hell*. Such deliverance would amount to the construction of new kinds of minds and bodies, a new kind of thought, a new experience of being as affirmative joy.

"This world is a world of imagination and vision," Blake wrote to Dr. Trusler in 1799; "I see every thing I paint in this world, but every body does not see alike. . . . as a man is so he sees." He added, "You certainly mistake when you say that the Visions of Fancy are not to be found in This World. To me This World is all One continued Vision of Fancy & Imagination & I feel flatterd when I am told so."[51] This assertion of the ontological power of the imagination—and its seventeenth-century associate, fancy—runs exactly contrary not only to Trusler's objections to Blake's work, but to the arguments proposed in the 1600s by Blake's greatest enemy, Locke, which were uncritically inherited by most of the London radicals of the 1790s.

According to Locke, each individual must orient himself and navigate his way through the world by deciphering a stream of external sensory inputs which are passively absorbed through organs of perception. Passive sensory perception, Locke argued, is the basis of all knowledge. "It is not in the Power of the most exalted wit, or enlarged Understanding," he writes, "to invent or frame one new simple Idea in the mind," not taken in by the perceptions through the five senses.[52] Thus, for Locke the five senses, which are given once and forever, permanently establish both how we can see and indeed who we are: they are "the Windows by which light is let into this dark Room" of the self.[53] "The infinite wise Contriver of us, and all things about us," writes Locke, "hath fitted our Senses, Faculties, and Organs, to the conveniences of Life, and the Business we have to do here. We are able, by our senses, to know, and distinguish things; and to examine them so far, as to apply them to our Uses, and several ways to accommodate the Exigencies of this Life." But, he adds, "it appears not, that God intended, we should have a perfect, clear, adequate knowledge of them: that perhaps is not in the

Comprehension of any finite Being. We are furnished with Faculties (dull and weak as they are) to discover enough in the Creatures, to lead us to the Knowledge of the Creator, and the Knowledge of our Duty; and we are fitted well enough with Abilities, to provide for the Conveniences of living: These are our Business in this World."[54] Here each finite individual is defined by his sensory apparatus: one's capacity as a perceiving machine not only establishes the limits of one's thought; it establishes the limits—indeed, the finitude—of one's being as a fixed and definite form—a form defined by the Creator. What is at issue for Locke is therefore one's necessarily limited "knowledge" of an already-created outside world (a world created by an external, superhuman power), rather than any human ontological potential, any human capacity for making (or remaking) the world and its forms, or even transgressing the proper limits of knowledge. Hence, knowledge and duty go together; they are the knowledge and duty of the created, rather than of the creator; they describe a closed circuit in which the creative and indeed deviant, deviating impulses of imagination and what both Locke and Blake call "Perswasion" have no role to play.

As we have seen, this predetermined, finite, sensory closed circuit ultimately provided the basis for the Lockean version of liberal democracy which was inherited by the 1790s radicals: because we all perceive in the same ways, because we each inhabit the same fixed and definite form, we are equivalent (and even interchangeable) beings, and hence we are all entitled to the same set of rights and duties. For Locke, moreover, stable, predetermined external reality can best be measured by the stable rational individual who achieves self-control by regulating his reactions to the stream of sensory inputs constantly bombarding him from the outside and who, moreover, learns to use reason to limit the ontological potential of his own imagination, that is, his capacity for what he calls perswasion. "Every Conceit that thoroughly warms our Fancies must pass for an Inspiration, if there be nothing but the Strength of our Perswasions, whereby to judge of our Perswasions," he writes; "if *Reason* must not examine their Truth by something extrinsical to the Perswasions themselves; Inspirations and Delusions, Truth and Falshood will have the same Measure, and will not be possible to be distinguished."[55] Reason here functions as a self-imposed limit on one's capacity for thought, and in particular it functions as a limit on the creative and ontological power of thought, of the imagination. Paradoxically, one's capacity to reason, to limit and regulate oneself, is what defines one's freedom—precisely as a freedom *from* ontological power.

Indeed, as we saw in previous chapters, for most of the radicals of the 1790s, individual self-control was the very key to liberty. We can be free, they argued, only when we are free to exercise control over ourselves, rather than having that control imposed on us by a tyrannical government ("let us exert over our own hearts a virtuous despotism," the radical Coleridge writes, "and lead our own Passions in triumph, and then we shall want neither Monarch nor General").[56] From such a perspective, freedom is that condition under which we move from external regulation to internal regulation, a condition in which our creative desires are kept under the strict control of our reason, so that virtue can be understood as "the conquest of Passion by Reason."[57] As we saw in chapter 5, this is the source of the virulent Orientalism inherent in much of 1790s radicalism, which would be inherited by nineteenth- and twentieth-century liberalism and imperialism. Desire here, it should be noted, is externally defined as the experience of lack, or as Locke puts it, an experience of "uneasiness," which he says, for better or for worse, is "the chief if not only spur to humane [i.e., human] Industry and Action."[58] This uneasiness gives rise to desires which must be regulated; the primal condition of life is therefore one of scarcity and of permanent "unease"—that is to say, a condition of permanent *finitude* which we are powerless to correct—an account which, it should be noted, would be adopted not only by the 1790s radicals but also by writers such as Burke and Malthus.

However, anyone who has ever read *The Marriage of Heaven & Hell* will immediately recognize that for Blake such self-control is not only misleading: it is even more oppressive than enforced obedience to a tyrannical government. For Blake, freedom meant freedom *to*, not freedom *from*—not moving from one disciplinary regime to another, from state regulation to self-regulation. The priests in black gowns walking their rounds and binding with briars our joys and desires in *The Garden of Love* are figures for all forms of repression, "internal" as much as "external." For Blake, desire is not an enemy to be brought under control (as all those "Proverbs of Hell" remind us), nor is it negatively understood, a response to some external lack or unease caused by the world's hopeless finitude. On the contrary, for Blake, desire is understood in positive rather than negative terms.

Far more than any other single issue, this is what sharply distinguishes Blake's position from that of the Paineite radicals, for whom desire was a scourge to be resisted and contained at all costs. If for Blake we are defined by our desire, then by "restraining" it we diminish our own capacity not merely for affecting and being affected, but also for being, for our being is here understood in terms of our desire, rather than in terms of the limitations of our physical sensorium. "Mans perceptions are not bounded by organs of perception. he perceives more than sense (tho' ever so acute) can discover." More than that, "The desire of Man being infinite," man is "himself infinite."[59] More even than that, "He who sees the Infinite in all things sees God. He who sees the Ratio sees himself only. Therefore God becomes as we are, that we may be as he is."[60] Our infinite desires define our infinite being, our collective participation in "the Eternal Body of Man," that is, "THE IMAGINATION," or, in a word, "God himself," the "Divine Body" of which "we are his Members." For Blake, then, as for Spinoza, desire is our very essence.[61] Indeed, Spinoza's understanding of desire may help us to clarify Blake's very closely related use of this concept, which, perhaps because it (misleadingly) seems so obvious, has never really received the critical attention it deserves. Both Blake and Spinoza participated in a kind of materialist ontological tradition which developed a positive and an affirmative notion of being—and, after all, Crabb Robinson was not and is not the only one to see "Spinozism" at work in Blake.[62]

How, then, are we to explain such utterances, which seem so alien, nonsensical, even insane, to the modern sensibilities according to which we have too often tried to read Blake?

Perhaps the best way to consider all these questions is to try to think through the extent to which, both for Blake and for his opponents, aesthetic, philosophical, religious, psychological, economic, and political principles function as an ensemble. As Frye pointed out, if we attempt to frame Blake's aesthetic principles with Lockean political or philosophical principles we will never be able to account for them, and they will appear to us (as they have to so many others) as sheer insanity, pure unintelligibility.[63] What we need, then, is to consider the way in which aesthetics and politics, economics and philosophy, religion and psychology work together, or in other words the way in which a certain understanding of form is immediately joined to a certain understanding of God, to a certain understanding of aesthetics, to a certain understanding of production, and hence to a certain understanding of imagination, freedom, joy, life—or perhaps to their "contraries," knowledge, confinement, duty, death.

In fact, Locke's philosophico-politico-religious argument crucially hinges on a certain understanding of form, particularly the form of images, and on a certain understanding of image production, and hence aesthetics. And Blake's refusal of Locke's philosophy, religion, and politics is inseparable from his rejection of Lockean aesthetics and of Locke's understanding of form and image production, with all of which Blake was altogether at odds. For Locke, the most elementary cognitive process is sensation, through which a store of simple ideas is built up, which can later be reflected upon for the production of more complex ideas. Sensation and reflection,

CHAPTER SIX

he argues, furnish us with our finite stock of ideas—really, our mental capital—and we can have nothing in our mind which was not impressed upon it first by sensation and then by reflection.[64] Locke thinks of the mind as a surface upon which ideas are *imprinted* just as images are printed on a page, that is, in the supposedly simple and mechanical process by which images are transferred from the realm of conception to the realm of execution.

There are two important points here. First, idea reception for Locke is limited by its formal affinity to image printing, and specifically to the exactly mimetic printing of images as identical copies of already-created external objects (or, in the case of higher-order reflections, of images produced in the mind itself as a result of accumulating and reflecting on images already "imprinted" through sensation). For Locke, "the *Understanding* is meerly *passive*," since "the Objects of our Senses, do, many of them, obtrude their particular Ideas upon our minds, whether we will or no." Hence, "these *simple Ideas*, when offered to the mind, the Understanding can no more refuse to have, nor alter, when they are imprinted, nor blot them out, and make new ones in it self, than a mirror can refuse, alter, or obliterate the Images or *Ideas*, which, the Objects set before it, do therein produce. As the Bodies that surround us, do diversly affect our Organs, the mind is forced to receive the Impressions; and cannot avoid the Perception of those *Ideas* that are annexed to them."[65] The second important point here, then, which follows from the first, is that all ideas and forms are necessarily conditioned by a predetermined external object world, over whose reality we have no control, over which we can exercise no creative power, "The Dominion of Man, in this little World of his own Understanding, being muchwhat the same, as it is in the great World of visible things, wherein his Power, however managed by Art and Skill, reaches no farther, than to compound and divide the Materials, that are made to his Hand; but can do nothing towards the making the least Particle of new Matter, or destroying one Atome of what is already in Being."[66] Here, Locke's understanding of religious and political potential (or lack thereof) arises from his understanding of image production, and particularly his understanding of form as expressed in images, and vice versa.

Thus, for Locke images cannot be *created*, they can only be *copied*. The imagination as a creative and an ontological power—creating images, creating forms, creating life—has no role to play in Locke's argument. Rather, the imagination is explicitly marked and cordoned off by Locke as the potential source of enthusiasm, should it be allowed to slide from its proper receptive and mimetic duties into creative ones. Indeed, the chapter on enthusiasm that Locke, for political reasons, felt compelled to add to the *Essay on Human Understanding* is explicitly a rejection of the ontological power of the imagination. Enthusiasts are dangerous, Locke says, because their arguments—being unrestrainedly affirmative and creative—recognize no limits. "What readier way can there be to run our selves into the most extravagant Errors and Miscarriages," he asks, than to "set up phancy for our supreme and sole Guide, and to believe any Proposition to be true, any Action to be right, only because we believe it to be so? The strength of our Perswasions are no Evidence at all of their own rectitude."[67] Rather than give way to open-ended enthusiasm (with all its creative potential), Locke concludes, we must learn to recognize that our ideas and hence our thoughts are limited and finite, defined by a finitude that is directly tied to the limited and finite collections of forms and images constituting our thought, and of forms and objects constituting the external world. Northrop Frye points out that what Blake protests against in Locke is "the implication that man is material to be formed by an external world and not the former or imaginer of the material world."[68] For Locke, then, the form of our being is defined by an external creator, and our "business in this world" is to accept, rather than to create; the only power we possess is the power of choice; the only freedom we can imagine is the freedom to reason and compare, and then to choose as best we can from the things made available to us by an external creative power.[69]

"I will not Reason & Compare; my business is to Create."[70] Los's often-quoted cry at the beginning of *Jerusalem* may push us to think through Blake's understanding of the ontological power of the imagination. As we saw in chapter 4, image production for Blake has nothing to do with the copying and faithful reproduction of prior external images onto a receptive surface. Rather, image production is for Blake a creative act. In itself, this should come as no surprise, since as Essick argues, the image produced on Blake's printed page is not—and was never supposed to be—a faithful materialization of an ideal concept. Rather, in Blake's art the material process and the mental process work together; both are driven by the imagination's power to create. In refusing any sharp distinction between ideal (conception) and material (execution), let alone the subjection of the material to the ideal, Blake's mode of aesthetic production (as we have explored at length in chapter 4) keeps the process of conception alive through each stage of execution. According to Essick, Blake's basic aesthetic position is based on the unity of conception and execution, and hence, the insistence that "there can be no conception without a medium of execution to conceive in," a position that would be violated by "either a belief in concepts (Blake would call them 'abstractions') that transcend all media, or by processes (such as reproductive engraving) that try to suppress eruptions of new conceptions within acts of execution."[71] Thought and the production of ideas for Blake therefore do not involve—as they do for Locke—simply the translation of internal (mental) images into external (material) images; rather, thought as imagination involves the production of all these images, those we think as well as those we inhabit and experience. In other words, thought is for Blake a thoroughly material activity ("Thought is Act. Christs Acts were Nothing to Caesars if this is not so").[72]

Indeed, Blake understands form, and being itself, as an open-ended process of becoming; hence his interest not only in living forms but in form as the expression of life. For Blake, it is not form that defines life, it is life that defines form—and goes on defining it. This explains why he places such extraordinary emphasis on the creative impulse in art, and indeed on art as creation, as creativity, as "unceasing practice." This also explains why he makes such a strong distinction between buying and selling art (as finished goods, things, objects, forms) on the one hand, and *making* art on the other. "Where any view of Money exists Art cannot be carried on, but War only,"[73] Blake writes. War in this sense does not just suggest military activity, but rather a social order based on regulation, competition, and exchange, on accumulation and acquisition as opposed to creativity; a social order based on law as opposed to love. "A warlike State never can produce Art," Blake insists; "It will Rob & Plunder & accumulate into one place, & Translate & Copy & Buy & Sell & Criticise, but not Make."[74] If art in this sense is making, freedom must be understood as the freedom to make, and to keep making, and for people to make as they choose, rather than the freedom simply to buy and sell what has been already made, or to be told to make in particular ways under particular circumstances as determined by external contingencies (necessity, law, regulation) or some extrinsic patriarchal power (God & Priest & King). For we must remember that for Blake art does not simply refer to a collection of aesthetic objects: it is, rather, an expression of the ontological power of the imagination. If "practise is Art," if "Art is the Tree of Life," the capacity to *create* and to practice is what defines a life of ontological freedom and power.

"All of us on earth are united in thought," Blake writes, "so it is impossible to know God & heavenly things without conjunction with those who know God & heavenly things." Knowing God here means *becoming God*, participating in that common "divine body" of which "we are his members"; and this unity of thought and making in the imagination is the fullest vision of freedom, in which our "conjunction" in a common power is precisely what sets us all free, because we possess and inhabit power, we are no longer subject to abstract power manifesting itself to us as an external force. What defines freedom here, then, is the capacity and the power to affect and be affected by as many others as possible, through and with whom we think and experience. "We cannot experience pleasure but by means of others," Blake writes, "who experience either pleasure or pain thro us."[75] For our capacity to think and to experience is actually affirmed, rather than contradicted and blocked by, the capacity to think of all others with whom we are joined—joined in such a way that thought and being work together so that a unity in thought is coextensive with a unity in being.

From such a Blakean perspective, we can see how in Locke the law's chains of subordination must take as their basis a limited, organized, subjectified form, given once and for all time as the fixed "image" of a transcendent creator, in relation to whom our business, as his material creations, is that of "duty" and obedience. Hence Locke's argument that "The infinite wise Contriver of us, and all things about us, hath fitted our Senses, Faculties, and Organs, to the conveniences of Life, and the Business we have to do here." For in this version of things it is the transcendent creator who possesses and defines constituent power as he constitutes his creatures in his image, and our business as his creatures is to obey his law. If, however, we refuse to separate conception from execution, body from mind, manual labor from mental direction, the governed from their governors, and hence the creatures from their creator, constituent power is wrested from above and becomes a common creative power. This is what Blake is getting at when he insists, against Locke and the Deists, that "the whole Business of Man is the Arts & all things Common," it being understood that art is "Unceasing Practice," it is creativity itself, it is "the Tree of Life," it is the positive affirmation of what Henri Bergson would later call "*elán vital.*"[76]

What we learned in chapter 3 was that Blake was by no means alone in the 1790s in thinking through the organized—indeed, thoroughly *organismic*—distinction between mental and material, ruler and ruled, boss and worker. Unlike most commentators, however, he was not so willing to accept the argument that, as one conservative pamphlet put it, "each person is but an engine in the great mechanism of circulation."[77] Again, this is what should prevent us from accepting scholarly claims about Blake's interest in universal psychic essences, drives, and so on. "God only acts or is, in existing beings or Men": in seeking to reunify conception and execution, body and mind, creatures and creator, Blake is not merely opposing what was being consolidated—both among the hegemonic radical tendency and among conservatives and reactionaries—as the dominant way of thinking; he is also proposing a positive, affirmative, ontological alternative. Indeed, Blake resists the regulative language of the 1790s precisely in positive (rather than negative) terms, which is perhaps why his resistance has so often not been recognized as a critique in the first place.

3. Power and Life

The law, as we have seen, is for Blake a code that in the fallen world enables and determines sociopolitical and economic reproduction as well as psycho-bio-political reproduction. In the fallen world, the law's rule over life is expressed in the way in which legally sanctioned forms constitute, determine, control, enclose, and regulate life, rather than leaving life free to determine its own ever-changing forms. We must understand this process of formation and constitution as manifested simultaneously in a variety of different discursive levels or fields: in aesthetic terms as the subordination of execution to conception, in economic terms as the subordination of manual labor to intellectual direction (or as Marx puts it, "the separation of the intellectual faculties of the production process from manual labour, and the transformation of those faculties into powers exercised by capital over labour," that is, the separation by which the machinery of a factory "confronts the worker during the labour process in the shape of capital, dead labour, which dominates and soaks up living labour-power"),[78] in political terms as the subordination of the governed to their governors, and in religious terms as the subordination of (to use Locke's language) creatures to creator. Such a sense of discursive simultaneity, by which an economic process or discourse could merge with a political or a religious discourse, was not unique to Blake. Andrew Ure, for example, would attribute a quasi-divine power, not mere anthropomorphism, to capital in the post-Arkwright factories of the 1790s and later. As we saw in chapter 3, Ure detects in such factories not merely "portions of inert matter . . . resembling organized beings," but, more specifically still, an "intelligent agency" infused "into forms of wood, iron and brass," an awesome intelligent power who "summons around him his myriads of willing menials, and assigns to each the regulated task, substituting for painful muscular effort on their part, the energies of his own gigantic arm."[79] In manufacture, "the workers are the parts of a living mechanism," Marx would note only a little later in a similar convergence of economic and biological discourses; "in the factory we have a lifeless mechanism which is independent of the workers, who are incorporated into it as its living appendages." This is why, he adds, "factory work exhausts the nervous system to the uttermost; at the same time, it does away with the many-sided play of the muscles, and confiscates every atom of freedom, both in bodily and in intellectual activity."[80] However, the capacity for discursive simultaneity that Ure and later Marx made use of in their discussions of the principles of economic production was already present in 1790s discourses on politics, theology, and aesthetics, and we might say psychology as well, or rather that concatenation of psychology, biology, and neurology that so interested (and appalled) Blake.

What makes matters confusing for us in reading Blake, however, is that in his work the logic of formation, constitution, organization, and regulation not only fuses together different discourses, but also operates seamlessly on a variety of different scales, so that, for example, the organization and formation of the individual body is shown to be directly and immediately related to the organization and formation of a larger social body—and in Blake's work we can slip insensibly from one level and one discourse to another, easily losing our way. For what is at stake for Blake is the *logic of form* itself, and even more specifically what Foucault would later call the principle of *governmentality*, rather than the particular scale or mode in which such formal organization—the process by which a psycho-bio-political body is organ-ized to fit a particular form—happens to unfold in any given instance.[81] And what confuses us in Blake's pursuit of governmentality is his continuous shifting between different discursive fields, registers, and scales, from epidemiology to politics, from aesthetics to biology, from religion to physics, from individual to collective organized bodies and forms of organization. In tracing these shifts, Blake is in effect tracing the seamlessness of the law's operation on all aspects of life, its attempt to appropriate life's endlessly proliferating creative energies and to confine being into limited forms.

Having overcome our initial sense of confusion and disorientation, what becomes clearer and clearer for us is that in Blake's concept of freedom—as endless striving, creativity, making—what is at stake is freedom from the logic of organization, regulation, constitution, and economy, regardless of the scale (social or individual) on which it takes place. This is precisely what pushes Blake beyond the vision of freedom articulated by the liberal-radicals, who sought to escape the old regime's organ-ization of the social body but based their vision on a form of governmentality and organ-ization operating on an individual scale instead, that is, on the individual selfhood that we may from a Blakean perspective recognize precisely as the product—literally the embodiment—of power itself.

Paine's discourse of liberty offers freedom from the tyranny of the social body, by linking liberated individual bodies into an open network; but this is a network whose nodes are made up of individual atomistic units, of self-regulated organized bodies, whose origins and constitution Paine resolutely takes for granted; and so his vision does not offer freedom from the limitations of organ-ization and definite form itself, or from the kind of power that constitutes such forms and subjects in the first place. From Blake's perspective, then, the problem with Paine's argument is that it does not go far enough toward liberating the creative capacities and energies of the imagination, and hence our ontological power. Thus, the problem that Blake's work forces us to confront is the logic of form and of organization itself, and hence the very technologies of regulation that produced the individual selfhood whose supposed "freedom" constituted the core of the liberal-radical struggle.

The problem facing us in reading Blake is therefore not just to discover an alternative notion of freedom, but rather to imagine a different concept of being (and of form) from the one proposed by either the conservatives or the liberal-radicals. For if we understand freedom as a life of imagination, a life of creative ontological power, and if we understand the imagination as "the eternal body of man . . . that is God himself," the "divine body" of which "we are his members," freedom must be understood in ontological terms, rather than in the representational terms pursued by the liberal-radicals who took our being, our nature, our form for granted. Engaging with Blake's notion of freedom therefore requires us to imagine an alternative understanding of form, and of the relationship of body to form, in such a way that form can become liberating rather than confining; in such a way that our ontological power can be freed, and directed by love rather than the law. But how can we produce a concept of freedom—of that notion of joyous striving also celebrated by Spinoza—that, while delivering us from the Scylla of state tyranny asserted by the conservatives, does not crash us into the Charybdis of individual finitude, limitation, subjectification, even objectification asserted by the hegemonic radicals? Michel Foucault argues that "the political, ethical, social, philosophical problem of our days is not to try to liberate the individual from the state, and from the state's institutions, but to liberate us both from the state and from the type of individualization linked to the state. We have to promote new forms of subjectivity through the refusal of this kind of individuality that has been imposed on us for several centuries."[82] Spinoza is very rightly a major source of inspiration for such alternative, liberating forms of ontology, not just in the work of Foucault but in that of other recent or contemporary philosophers—Deleuze, Negri, Giorgio Agamben, Louis Althusser, Étienne Balibar, and others. But it seems to me that the work of Blake, too, pushes, requires, inspires us to try to imagine alternative forms of being and ontology, situated as it is at the very historical moment when the form of the individual selfhood, the individual subject whose existence started to be taken for granted as the point of departure for so many arguments, was being consolidated as the focal point of political, cultural and economic life, really its defining form.

Blake was not alone even in the London of his own time in trying to think through such questions. In seeking for an alternative form of being, moreover, Blake was drawing on traditions going back at least to the seventeenth century, if not longer—and to British and indeed transatlantic as well as Continental sources, of which the Continental line of thought running roughly from Spinoza to Deleuze, Félix Guattari, and Negri has not taken account, though it would enrich that line of thought immeasurably (as would the consideration of Blake, for that matter).[83] For in the "impossible history" of the British and the anti-imperial transatlantic experience, we can find something like an equivalent of Spinoza's rarified Latin thought experiments, not only in philosophy, but also in poetry, in painting, in printmaking, in song, and in revolutionary struggle, including experimentations with new forms of social and individual and formal organization, most or all of which seem to have been purged from the Continent as early as the sixteenth century, following the eradication or expulsion of the followers of Henry Niclaes and Thomas Müntzer, the Familists, and the Anabaptists, whose energies, multiplied and intensified, were transplanted to Britain as well as its far-flung and genuinely multicultural transatlantic empire, where an underground millenarian and sometimes communist tradition continued to flourish—in between decades of repression and persecution—through the seventeenth and eighteenth centuries and on into the nineteenth.[84] One such moment of flourishing took place in the 1790s; another took place in that fleeting moment of political (and publishing) freedom in the middle of the seventeenth century, and it is worth briefly considering the latter moment to see what it might teach us about the continuity of this tradition, its later manifestations, and its relationship to what Peter Linebaugh and Marcus Rediker have recently termed "the hidden history of the revolutionary Atlantic."

4. Form and Life, Form of Life

1. That which gives the being, the action and the denomination to a creature or thing, is the form of that creature or thing.

2. There is in form something that is not elementary but divine.

3. The contemplation of form is astonishing to man, and has a kind of trouble or impulse accompanying it that exalts his soul to God.

4. As the form of a man is the image of God, so the form of a government is the image of man.

In these lines from *A System of Politics*, which he was working on through the 1660s, James Harrington opened up the question of the ontology of form in a way whose potential would soon afterward be refused by what would become the bourgeois tradition of political philosophy.[85] For this potential lies in the possible relationships that these lines articulate between being and form. Here, although Harrington says that form determines being (including the being of man, society, government, people), he understands form itself as a kind of image and, in the case of man in particular, as the image of God. What has become a conventional reading of these lines would see here the suggestion that the "form" of man is fixed and defined as a fixed and definite image of a fixed and definite God, and hence, that a fixed and definite set of rights and duties goes along with the fixed and definite form and image of man. This is precisely the argument that Tom Paine would make in *Rights of Man*, and though Paine makes the argument without explicit reference to Harrington, the similarity is hardly a coincidence:

> Every history of the creation, and every traditional account, whether from the lettered or unlettered world, however they may vary in their opinion or belief of certain particulars, all agree in establishing one point, *the unity of man;* by which I mean, that men are all of *one degree*, and consequently that all men are born equal, and with equal natural right, in the same manner as if posterity had been continued by *creation* instead of *generation*, the latter being only the mode by which the former is carried forward; and consequently, every child born into the world must be considered as deriving its existence from God. The world is as new to him as it was to the first man that existed, and his natural right is of the same kind.
>
> The Mosaic account of the creation, whether taken as divine authority, or merely historical, is full to this point, *the unity or equality of man*. The expressions admit of no controversy. "And God said, Let us make man in our own image. In the image of God created he him; male and female created he them." The distinction of sexes is pointed out, but no other distinction is even implied. If this be not divine authority, it is at least historical authority, and shows that the equality of man, so far from being a modern doctrine, is the oldest upon record.[86]

Paine's argument hinges, clearly, on a very particular understanding of images and of image production. There are two strands to his argument. First, man was created in the image of God, and not just the first man, but all people ever since, since, as Paine argues, reproduction (generation) should be thought of as the endless repetition of the same original act of creation, or in other words, the endless reprinting of the same and forever identical image. We have already seen that Locke's philosophy hinges on a similar understanding of image production, since for Locke our ideas are imprinted on the mind in such a way that "the Understanding can no more refuse to have, nor alter [them], when they are imprinted, nor blot them out, and make new ones in it self, than a mirror can refuse, alter, or obliterate the Images or *Ideas*, which, the Objects set before it, do therein produce." And the imagination as a creative and an ontological power—creating images, creating forms, creating life—has no more role to play in Paine's argument than it does in Locke's: again, its role is that of a receptive faculty, a built-in printing press that automatically receives and reproduces forms and images. Where Paine differs from Locke, however, is that, whereas the latter thinks of image copying as a "meerly passive" activity, the former thinks of this copying process as itself a form of production, albeit one that is essentially reproductive. This is a kind of reproduction shorn of conception—exactly the form of production, that is, the repeated re-production of an identical image (prototype) that according to Babbage, as we saw in chapter 3, would define the modern assembly line. For, according to Paine, once the image has been conceived (by God) its form must remain unchanged even as it is faithfully reproduced through the ages. Thus, the second strand of Paine's argument follows immediately from the first: since the form of man is defined once and forever by God, it is not only an immutable image, but expresses a kind of "unity," by which Paine means a combination of self-identity and immutability, and it is from this "unity" that Paine derives his concept of rights. Hence, he says, our equality is derived from our status as identical images of the same identical form, and since we are all interchangeable products of the same image factory, we are all equal, entitled to the same sets of rights and duties.

Such a line of argument is certainly quite compatible with one way of reading what Harrington says in those lines from *A System of Politics*. But another possibility is inherent in Harrington's propositions, one that represents a path not taken by either Paine or Locke, which is that, although form expresses a kind of divine power, and although the contemplation of form is "astonishing to man" because it compels him to recognize this divine power, man may himself be capable of defining and inventing forms, and hence capable of that kind of divine ontological image-making power otherwise ascribed to God. If the contemplation of form astonishes us and troubles us, exalting our soul to God, perhaps that is because in contemplating form we recognize our own creative and ontological potential, and hence our own "divinity." For Harrington, form is defined in terms of ontological potential: "form is not elementary but divine," that is, it expresses not a fixed material property or a certain arrangement of elements, but rather a creative *capacity*, a capacity to generate images, and hence a capacity to endow being with life and vitality. For Harrington, then, the imagination is an ontological power. The possibility that his political project hinges on, indeed, is that such imaginative and ontological capacity is properly human, and hence, images and forms are not, in his system of politics, handed down once and forever by an external, transcendent, divine authority, but are rather subject to reinvention, alteration, reconception, redefinition, according to human—and hence social, political, and cultural—needs and desires.

This may explain why, in certain respects, and despite many essential differences, Harrington's political philosophy resembles that of Hobbes, for both understood politics as intimately creative and ontological, and both likened the formation of the state to the generation of a human being, literally to a making-human. For Hobbes, the generation of a commonwealth involves the creation of an "Artificiall Person" from the multitude—not just a mere act of "representation" that could somehow be distinguished from "reality" (for in a sense we are all "artificiall persons" for Hobbes, and the opposition to "naturall persons" is somewhat misleading),[87] but rather the immediate organic creation of a new reality, "a reall Unitie of them all, in one and the same Person, made by Covenant of every man with every man." Hence, Hobbes's notion of government is also ontological (though ontology for Hobbes assumes an immediately mechanico-physical quality).[88] This "multitude united in one Person," the Leviathan, may be thought of in divine terms, as an artificially fabricated "*Mortall God*, to which wee owe under the *Immortal God*, our peace and defence," and hence such an act of formation clearly involves a certain degree of hubris, of meddling with the divine power of generation and formation.[89] Thus, for Hobbes humans, in forming a commonwealth, do indeed create an artificial person and endow it with life, since commonwealths, he says, require "procreation" and "nutrition" just like any natural body. For Harrington, too, the formation of a government is not just a matter of devising a mechanics of representation, but it instead involves a formidable creative and ontological capacity, "an infusion of the soul or faculties of a man into the body of a multitude."[90] Such a democratic result may be very different from (in fact, exactly the opposite of) the multitude formed into unity that defines Hobbes's Leviathan, but it shares with it the sense of awesome ontological power. In Harrington, then, the creation of life-endowing forms and images is shown to be a thoroughly human activity, even if it is an activity that approaches that of the divine. And hence, forms of life are not merely to be "copied" from some immutable master image, given once and forever; they are to be invented and reinvented according to human needs and desires. While such an understanding either of forms or of images would be denied by Locke and later on by Paine, it flourished in the seventeenth century and carried with it certain political possibilities which would become much more difficult to imagine later on. Harrington was drawing on these possibilities even while seeking to reformulate them in his own brand of democratic politics.

Here I am referring not so much to the struggle of the Levellers as to the more "extremist" elements of the English revolutionary period, whose creative potential would be suppressed by Cromwell and Parliament long before the Restoration, and who would dive deep underground in Britain—and across the Atlantic. In fact, as the mid-seventeenth-century Putney debates made abundantly clear, even the program of the Levellers was already too much for the representatives of the new power in Britain. The Levellers based their vision of democracy on a solid foundation of private property and self-propriety—indeed, on the relationship of private property and property-in-self as "natural rights" (an argument that would be resuscitated almost verbatim in the program of the liberal-radicals of the 1790s). "To every individual in nature is given an individual property by nature not to be invaded or usurped by any," write the authors of *An Arrow Against all Tyrants* (1646); "For every one, as he is himself, so he has a self-propriety, else could he not *be* himself. . . . Mine and thine cannot be, except this be."[91] Here the direct correlation between private property and the very being of the individual self is made quite clear: *being* and *having* are absolutely tied together, two sides of the same coin. What is more interesting for our purposes, however, is that the Levellers' argument here is also predicated on a very particular understanding of the mimetic printing process through which images are supposedly produced:

> I may be but an individual, enjoy my self and my self-propriety and may right myself no further than my self, or presume any further; if I do, I am an encroacher and an invader upon another man's right—to which I have no right. For by natural birth all men are equally and alike born to like propriety, liberty and freedom; and as we are delivered of God by hand of nature into this world, every one with a natural, innate freedom and propriety—as it were writ in the table of every man's heart, never to be obliterated—even so are we to live, every one equally and alike to enjoy his birthright and privilege; even all whereof God by nature has made him free. . . . And from this fountain or root

all just human powers take their original—not immediately from God (as kings usually plead their prerogative) but mediately by hand of nature, as from the represented to the representers.[92]

The Leveller argument anticipates the positions of Locke and later of Paine in several important ways. The image taken from an external original and "writ in the table of every man's heart, never to be obliterated," is an image of God mediated by the biological process through which we are actually brought into the world. However mediated, though, we are still "representers" of an original, immutable "represented" image, and it is in this that our being and hence our rights and duties consist, insofar as our being is understood as a representation—a re-presentation—of an original image, stamped, printed, "writ," once and forever. "For it is a standing rule in nature," they add, "*omne simile generas simile:* every like begets its like."[93] Thus, according to the Leveller argument, we can trace our rights back to the "original" which lives on in us all as a constant form, defining our very being, and hence clearly also our rights, within the narrow confines of that being, that self within whose compass we may be allowed to enjoy our rights.

The Leveller argument was, of course, suppressed by those whom the revolution and Civil War brought to power (the Putney debates were only an anticipation of later difficulties), and, as we saw in chapter 2 and elsewhere, it would remain suppressed until it reemerged, sometimes almost point for point, in the program of liberty proposed by the liberal-radicals of the 1790s and again by the Chartists in the early nineteenth century. But in mid-seventeenth-century England, this was not the only conception of rights, or the only conception of being. Gerrard Winstanley, for example, launched the communist project of the True Levellers, or Diggers, with an explicit rejection of the politics of representation, and with a renunciation of the "selfish love" that pitches one against another while differentiating what is mine from what is yours. "What a man sees or hears to-day, may be gone to-morrow," writes Winstanley in *The New Law of Righteousness* (1649); "all outward glory that is at a distance from the five senses, and taken in by a representation, is of a transient nature; and so is the heaven that your preachers tell you of."[94] Instead of the heaven that is promised to us in the transient image of a future world if we work hard and suffer in this one, Winstanley calls for an apocalypse now—opening the "now" out into an immanent plane of time—that would abolish the rigid distinction between one self and another, one property and another, that had been foundational for the Levellers earlier in the 1640s and that would be foundational again for Paine and the liberal-radicals in the 1790s. What Winstanley and the

Diggers sought instead involved the abolition of private property, the abolition of selfish power, and hence the sharing of the earth and its fruits among all men and women, so that "none shall lay claim to any creature and say, This is mine, and that is yours, This is my work, and that is yours. But every one shall put to their hands to till the earth and bring up cattle, and the blessing of the earth shall be common to all."[95] Moreover, their project involved above all a sense of being in common of which, for Winstanley, sharing in common was only the logical expression (just as private property was seen by the Levellers as the logical expression of individual being). Equally important, this being in common would itself be the expression—the immediate image—of a collective human potential, the "Rising up" of a "universal power," a "universal spreading of the divine power, which is Christ in mankind."[96] Such an apocalypse in the here and now—a disruption of the stream of progressive time, a reconstitution of the ground of history itself—would take place in the expansive moment when "the Lord Christ do spread himself in multiplicities of bodies, making them all of one heart and one mind, acting in righteousness to one another. It must be one power in all."[97] It is important to note that such a divine being in common does not involve a homogeneous integration of multiplicity into one smooth undifferentiated body. Christ is spread precisely in "multiplicities of bodies," and hence the divine power communicated by Winstanley's communist project is understood in immanent rather than transcendent terms, as a joining together of multiple and ever-differentiated bodies in a common joy:

> There shall be no buying nor selling, no fairs nor markets, but the whole earth shall be a common treasury for every man, for the earth is the Lord's. And mankind, thus drawn up to live and act in the law of love, equity and oneness, is but the great house wherein the Lord himself dwells, and *every particular one a several mansion*. And as one spirit of righteousness is common to all, so the earth and the blessings of the earth shall become common to all; for now all is but the Lord, and the Lord is all in all. Eph. iv 5, 6.[98]

Clearly, however, such a joyful unity has to be based on the already immanent existence of divine power in humanity; a power that would find its fulfillment rather than its origins in the apocalyptic communism of which Winstanley is writing. In other words, the Lord is always already the all in all. Thus, Winstanley's argument is *not* about abstract natural rights; it is an ontological argument about how we are to live, and about how we are to imagine time, how we are to conceive of life itself. If it would require an act of divine intervention to bring about the state of which Winstanley is writing, the point that he is trying to make is that that power is already human,

CHAPTER SIX

and it is or ought to be available in an immediate sense, rather than in the transient representations of some future world which the great ones of the earth always seem keen to perpetually defer away from the "common people."

Winstanley deploys a particular reading of the New Testament (especially parts of Corinthians and Ephesians) to ground his communist beliefs in the notion that humans can share "one power in all" to constitute themselves as an all in all. Christ or God in this sense may be thought of not as transcendent forces but rather as the immediate expressions of an immanent human power. For, according to this mode of thought and of power, not only does God exist in all creatures: God has no existence *apart* from the creatures (or, as Blake would express exactly this point little over a century later, "God only acts & Is, in existing beings or Men"). Such a notion of God—and of human ontological power—flourished briefly in seventeenth-century England, before plunging underground only to reappear in the 1790s (a story that has been told elsewhere).[99] In *The Light and Dark Sides of God*, for example, the antinomian Jacob Bauthumley argues not only that God "is the subsistence [i.e., substance] and Being of all Creatures and things, and fills Heaven and Earth and all other places," but also that God "hath his Being no where else out of the Creatures." Thus, Bauthumley concludes, all the creatures in the world "are not so many distinct Beings, but they are one intire Being, though they be distinguished in respect of their formes; yet their Being is but one and the same Being, made out in so many formes of flesh, as Men and Beast, Fish and Fowle, Trees and Herbes."[100] Being is here clearly differentiated from form. Form serves merely as the location or manifestation or actualization of being (indeed, we may think of this notion of form in Bergsonian terms as an actualization of a being that exists virtually).[101] Thus, not only does form not constitute the fixed image or copy of a prior being (as Paine or Locke would argue), but all being is made up of such images, which are always being created, re-created, re-invented, actualized in a continual process, the *élan vital* of which life consists. The image here is far from a copy of some prior reality; rather, the image proliferates, multiplies, reaches out, evolves; the image constitutes reality; the image is life itself. For if there is only one virtual being, and if it exists only in transitory actualizations in forms or images, form is determined by being, rather than the other way around. And the one virtual being—in "multiplicities of bodies"—can determine an infinite number of actual forms. In its power to define and articulate form, being thus conveys a limitless ontological and creative potential: it always produces (and exists in) new images.

If, moreover, we understand human life—and not just human life, but the whole *élan vital* of which humanity is but one part—in terms of a common participation in an infinite virtual being, rather than as a series of finite and intermeasurable forms (or fixed and circulating, accumulable and intermeasurable images), then we have arrived at a very different foundation of politics, aesthetics, and social being from the one that would propel Locke and Paine—a foundation in which relations, associations, connections, and affects carry much greater significance than mere transitory form. For now we might think of our being not in terms of fixed and definite units (forms) but rather in terms of ever-changing bundles of relations and affects temporarily condensing in particular forms on particular occasions but always continuing to participate in an infinite common being; and hence, we might think of our being in terms of our infinite desire to keep making connections and forming new lines of affect, generating new images, and indeed to think of the essence of our being *as* just such making, desiring, forming, changing, *striving*. As we have seen, this is a very different notion of being—essential not only to Winstanley but also to the heterogeneous antinomian, Behmenist, Paracelsian, Hermetic, Brunian traditions which Blake himself would later tap into—from the one entertained by most of the radicals of the 1790s.

In the seventeenth century, such a concept of being received perhaps its most striking formulation in the work of Abiezer Coppe, much of which constitutes a restless series of experiments with the relationship of being and form. Coppe launches his project with a call "to arise out of Flesh into Spirit, out of Form into Power, out of Type into Truth, out of Signes into the thing Signified."[102] While some, Coppe says, "cannot live without Shadows, Signs, Representations," and see only the world of "Signes, Vails, Glasses, Formes, Shaddows, &c," he promises his readers access to the true vitality of "a naked God . . . uncloathed of *flesh* and *forme*," or in other words the spiritual world that exists here and now (not just in a happy afterlife), from which our investment in fixed signs, forms, and representations distracts us.[103] Like Winstanley, Coppe is not interested in transient representations taken in through the five senses. Like Winstanley too, Coppe's claim is that the ability to bypass the chain tying signifier to signified, the ability to access reality in an immediate sense, also constitutes an ability to participate in the creation of that reality rather than merely "reading" its manifest signs and forms. An end to the aesthetics and politics of fixed form, in other words, would allow access to truth in an immediate sense—to the "truth" (i.e., the immediacy) of our own being—and hence to what Coppe calls "power."

I mention Coppe's project, however, not out of antiquarian theological curiosity but because of the way in which it demonstrates how a certain theological or philosophical conception of being enables a certain understanding of form in both an aesthetic and a political sense. For Coppe, the liberation of the narrator or author from the confines of his own form allows him to speak in a variety of tongues, to abandon or escape his own narrow selfhood and assume the voice of the Lord precisely as a common power:

> Behold, behold, behold, I the eternall God, the Lord of Hosts, who am that mighty Leveller, am coming (yea even at the doores) to Levell in good earnest, to Levell to some purpose, to Levell with a witness, to Levell the Hills with the Valleyes, and to lay the Mountaines low. . . . And as I live, I will plague your Honour, Pompe, Greatnesse, Superfluity, and confound it into parity, equality, community; that the neck of horrid pride, murder, malice, and tyranny, &c. may be chopt off at one blow. And that my selfe, the Eternall God, who am Universall Love, may fill the Earth with universall love, universall peace, and perfect freedome.

This amounts to something more than merely an argument for "moral renewal inspired by God's spiritual informing of individuals," which is how J. C. Davis sees it.[104] In *A Second Fiery Flying Roule*, this spreading of universal love is further refined in terms of what Coppe calls "Blood-life-spirit-communion," or in other words a community of bodies and being—at once a spiritual and a material community—that expresses even less patience with the "mine and thine" possessiveness of individual selfhood and private property than Winstanley's version of communism:

> Howl, howl, ye nobles, howl honourable, howl ye rich men for the miseries that are coming upon you. For our parts, we that hear the APOSTLE preach, will also have all things common; neither will we call any thing that we have our own. Do you (if you please) till the plague of God rot and consume what you have. We will not, wee'l eat our bread together in singlenesse of heart, wee'l break bread from house to house.[105]

Clearly, the "we" that constitutes the authorial or narrative voice of Coppe's rolls is hardly identifiable with, or reducible to, Abiezer Coppe himself. For at such moments Coppe, as an authorial fiction, ceases to claim any influence at all on the direction the writing takes. "For the Ranters," Nigel Smith argues, "the presence of God within the individual threatens to obliterate the self, so that the persona speaks with the identity of God." Such writing, as Smith points out, constitutes "the denial of self in the presence of the divine."[106] It should come as no surprise, then, that in Coppe's rolls we hear the voice of God, or that of the disenfranchised and dispossessed; or perhaps (most frighteningly) we hear the disenfranchised and the dispossessed speaking through and as God. Indeed, according to Clement Hawes, such "manic enthusiasm" offers "a particular strategy for speaking and writing with an authority otherwise unavailable to those assigned a lowly social identity. What makes manic writing deviant," Hawes adds, "is not merely 'pathology,' as if the subjective crisis it dramatizes were finally merely a matter of individual misfortune. It is, rather, the formal projection of an oppositional, sometimes subversive ideology at the level of the subject."[107] Hawes is, I think, quite right to see the "form" of the subject—the individual selfhood—as a kind of ideological battleground; and, as we have seen, the kinds and "formes" of subjectivity mobilized by Coppe go far beyond the individual subject.

In such moments, then, the "authorial" voice seeks its authorization in a community of those who share, belong, and *are* together, in the blood-life-spirit-communion, and in the common power that such a communion constitutes. For in calling on the rich to "give, give, give, give up, give up your houses, horses, goods, gold, Land, give up, account nothing your own, have ALL THINGS common,"[108] Coppe retains—but inverts—the link established by the Levellers between being and having, at once doing away both with having and with being in an individual sense and tying together having and being in a collective sense, in community. The end of private property, the end of self-propriety: such self-annihilation is precisely what Coppe is writing about; but such an escape from form, sign, and representation is here constituted as a movement of absolute strength, pure affirmation, infinite being, which is why such self-annihilation is actually a positive and an affirmative proposition, the expression of common being and common power.

5. The Wild Effusions of Distempered Brains

What Coppe and other antinomian writers of the middle of the seventeenth century—as well as Winstanley and the Diggers—elaborated is a concept of being in common, a sense of common participation in a unity made up of infinite heterogeneity ("distinction, diversity, variety"). Thus, they elaborated a sense of common, shared power as the proper basis for political and aesthetic form. They understood freedom in terms of the creative ontological capacity of this common power, rather than in terms of a set of abstract given "rights" appropriate to a fixed and intermeasurable form. In other words they understood freedom in terms of a collective human capacity to create and keep creating the images of which life is constituted—a sense of creation predicated on a concept of time as simultaneously repeating and differing from itself—rather than accepting as inevitable the mere replication through empty homogeneous time of a "permanent" image handed down by an external, transcendent, divine power at the beginning of time. For they recognized no transcendent power or authority—no divinity, no king, no god—outside or beyond the immanently constituted collective power in which all can participate both equally and differently. Here, religion, politics, philosophy, and aesthetics are inextricably fused into the same (but highly vertiginous and heterogeneous) set of concepts, which mark interventions at one and the same time in philosophical discourse, in religious discourse, and in political discourse. In response to such threats, and pushed on no doubt by publications such as Thomas Edwards's *Gangraena*, England's revolutionary Parliament (having won the war and executed the king, and thus finding itself better able to dispense with undesirable elements in the army) in August of 1650 passed the Blasphemy Act, which made it a punishable offence to claim to be God, or equal to God. Most of the "enthusiasts," as they became known, were silenced or driven underground.[109]

Clearly, the antinomian, Ranter, or Digger visions of heterogeneous equality were sharply at odds with the notion of power and right founded on the logic of private property and self-propriety, and the opposing sense of politico-religious commitment, which was developed both by the spokesmen of the emergent state and their best-known opponents, the Levellers, both of whom would dismiss and renounce "enthusiasts" and their visions of "impracticable equality." The notion of civil and political rights acknowledged by the leaders of the new state was restricted to property holders, those with a "permanent interest in the land," a formulation that would be retained and formalized by the settlement of 1688 and would remain intact until the Reform Act of 1832. Indeed, we can detect a line of argument, one based on the sanctity of property, particularly the property of great landholders, running more or less uninterrupted from General Henry Ireton in the 1640s to Edmund Burke in the 1790s. And, against this, we can detect another line of argument running more or less without interruption from Thomas Rainborough and the Levellers, via Tom Paine and the leadership of the American Revolution (not to mention other routes of transmission, such as the one running through Rousseau to the French Revolution), to John Thelwall and the London Corresponding Society.

Thus, although the Levellers themselves, following their defeat by Parliamentary forces at Burford and the arrest or assassination of their leadership, have been counted among the "losers" of history, their arguments in favor of parliamentary democracy, manhood suffrage, universal rights, and political equality based on those rights would be continually propagated, and would attain many remarkable victories, through the seventeenth and eighteenth centuries and into the nineteenth and twentieth. The irony, of course, is that the very notion of "levelling," in the social and economic sense, was never part of the Leveller program, and not just they, but also those who adopted their arguments in favor of individual political rights, consistently repudiated the term by which the Levellers are today remembered.[110] Meanwhile, as we saw in chapter 2 and elsewhere, their propertied opponents developed an argument that would endure long after the demise of the Levellers themselves and would last from the time of Cromwell and Ireton to that of Burke and Colquhoun, namely, the argument that the struggle for political equality was merely a kind of cover for plebeian dangerous enthusiasm, and that political equality would inevitably lead to social and economic levelling (such arguments persisted until it became clear, in the nineteenth century, that an extension of the franchise could actually safeguard property rights rather than undermine them). Even though the London Corresponding Society consistently denounced levelling ("since last November," says a communiqué of July 1793, for example, "false and calumnious aspersions have been circulated, and those who would restore the House of Commons to a state of independence have been labelled levellers"),[111] well over one hundred publications denouncing "levelling" and "levellers" appeared in the 1790s alone, many of them, of course, the work of the Association for the Preservation of Liberty and Property from Republicans and Levellers and most of them warning in one way or another that the 1790s might turn into a replay of the 1640s, and hence that England was in critical danger of being overrun by the "wildest phrenzies of Fanaticism, Superstition, and Enthusiasm."[112] Thus William Hamilton Reid, describing the "infidel societies" of London in the 1790s from the relatively secure standpoint of 1800, argued that if anyone had truly believed "that a Parliamentary Reform was the *real object*, and not merely the *stalking-horse* of these societies, their want of information is really to be pitied. They must have known very little of the hatred borne to all the privileges of birth or acquirements, or of the frenzy, which sometimes raged in the brains of their humble friends in the city, and eastern suburbs."[113]

It has too often been assumed by modern and postmodern scholars that, if the Levellers themselves were eradicated after 1650, the Diggers, Ranters, and various antinomian tendencies must also have vanished. And yet even as late as the end of the eighteenth century there was clearly a lingering sense that somewhere there still remained the danger that had once been

CHAPTER SIX

posed by the explosion of plebeian enthusiasm in the seventeenth century: that moment when members of the "lower orders... not only turned preachers, but likewise prophets," as William Hurd noted with some alarm in 1785; "some pretended to foretel future events; others said they were apostles risen from the dead; while a third sort had the assurance to assert, that they were some of those persons who had been prophesied of in the book of Revelation."[114] The English revolution of 1648 would come to be "widely regarded as the product of religious enthusiasm run riot," Jon Mee points out; "a historical memory, however vague and imprecise, of uneducated prophets and tub preachers rushing into print to announce the rule of the Saints remained the apotheosis of enthusiasm for the century which followed."[115] Even the very late eighteenth century, according to Mee, "retained a firmer and more detailed memory of the prophets of the Civil War as examples of the dangers posed to the stability of church and state by popular religious enthusiasm than is often allowed." Indeed, "enthusiasm" came to name a general condition, the potentiality of the multitude to be swept by what their superiors regarded as fanatical crazes—to yield to the "frenzy" that still "raged in their brains," as Reid put it. And in a still more general sense, Mee adds, "the recurrent and sustained interest in the term 'enthusiasm' indicates that it was foundational to the mentality of the long eighteenth century," an enduring threat to the respectable, rational subject and the rational bourgeois public sphere.

"Enthusiasm," in other words, came to name not merely a particular religious tendency, but rather the creative political potential of the multitude, its fearsome capacity to generate other modes of social, economic, cultural, aesthetic, religious, and political organization than the ones recognized and valorized by either established authorities or bourgeois reformers. For both statesmen and reformers ultimately—and certainly by the time of the Reform Act—came to share a discourse predicated on the dual sanctity of, on the one hand, the rational, sovereign, Western bourgeois subject, and, on the other hand, private property, both of which would be challenged by plebeian enthusiasm. "Enthusiasm," in short, threatened the sanctity, the stability, the sovereign imperviousness of the unitary subject, just as it threatened the sanctity of private property and the political norms and orders of the state. It came to stand not merely for religious passion but in a far more general sense for all that is excluded from the realm of properly bourgeois aesthetics, bourgeois subjectivity, bourgeois politics and economics, and bourgeois history itself—whose very articulation depended in part on their opposition to enthusiasm. This is precisely why enthusiasm, which refuses the logic of time as a triumphant march of progress, came to be identified with others: with the mad prophets of the 1640s, with the plebeian preachers of the 1790s, with the mob, the multitude, the Orient; with dangerous excess, unruly passions; with egregious vanity, wild effusions of distempered brain; with vendors of magic carpets, crazy stories, and picture books.

Much of Jon Mee's history of enthusiasm in the long eighteenth century is concerned with the role of enthusiasm as a theoretical or philosophical problem to be dealt with in what he calls the discourse of regulation—both the self-regulation of the private subject and also the regulation of the bourgeois public sphere. However, Mee's project is also concerned with tracing the development of an inverted "public sphere" of enthusiasm right through the eighteenth century. "Habermas's notion of the bourgeois public sphere, with its newspapers being discussed in coffee houses and clubs, its periodicals encouraging the circulation of sound knowledge, and significantly banning disputation in religion from its pages," Mee writes, "had an alter-ego in the chapels, field meetings, and the huge circulation of popular religious pamphlets and sermons where disputation thrived." Indeed, Mee has alerted us to the persistence of the "public sphere of enthusiasm" in the eighteenth century, which exploded into the open once again in the 1790s, leading many to compare the events of that decade to the trauma of the 1640s, as a moment when plebeian excess once again threatened to merge religious fervor and political potential in a challenge to bourgeois politics, economics, subjectivity, and history.[116]

Indeed, we are now in a position to recognize the reappearance of "enthusiasm" in the turbulent and revolutionary 1790s as what was at the time only the latest manifestation of a long tradition going back to at least the middle of the seventeenth century. This was a tradition of plebeian struggle whose religious and political and philosophical components were inextricable from each other (that is, they constituted a unity more integral than is allowed by A. L. Morton's account of it as the expression of "political ideas in a religious form," since for the Ranters or Winstanley—or Blake—the distinction between "politics" and "religion" would have been nonsensical).[117] It was a tradition that had been there all along, even if it had been repeatedly defeated and driven back underground or overseas by various political, military, and religious authorities over the intervening decades. "Even during the Republic," Morton points out, revolutionary "enthusiasts," as they would come to be known, "were often persecuted, and after the restoration of the Monarchy in 1660 they were driven underground, preserving their faith in little, obscure conventicles, treasuring subversive pamphlets in old cupboards, holding the ideas of the revolution, as it were, in suspension, until towards the end of the eighteenth century, the world seemed ready for them again."[118] In their recent book, *The Many-Headed Hydra*, Peter Linebaugh and Marcus Rediker reveal the extent of this transatlantic and ultimately global tradition, which was more active than even Morton allows. They demonstrate how we must understand it as the hidden underbelly of the long and bloody process of globalization (a process which has reached its apotheosis only in our own time, though its origins go back to the beginning of the transoceanic empires). We must understand it, in other words, as a constituent feature of the formation of what Blake himself would call the "universal empire," which came into the world with "groans" and "rattling with clanking chains," with children "sold to trades / Of dire necessity still labouring day & night," with "slaves in myriads in ship loads," burdening "the hoarse sounding deep."[119]

Linebaugh and Rediker trace the resistance to the imposition of this global system of production and circulation through virtually every stage, moment, and location of that process. Thus, they trace the successive sites of struggle from the English commons—including the sites of the first Digger communes, which were broken up and dispersed by force—to the slave plantations of the West Indies, to the ships that tied the empires together and burdened "the hoarse-sounding deep," and finally to the space of the modern factory (where, as we saw in chapter 3, children, along with men and women, were indeed sold to trades and forced to labor day and night). And if they agree with Marx that the imposition of factory discipline has been a "Herculian enterprise," they remind us that the global workmasters have long likened those who resisted their rule to a many-headed hydra, a monster of different races, shapes, sexes, and colors, with "heads" that, once they have been lopped off in one location, pop up in others. "The emphasis in modern labor history on the white, male, skilled, waged, nationalist, propertied artisan/citizen or industrial worker," they argue, "has hidden the history of the Atlantic proletariat of the seventeenth, eighteenth, and early nineteenth centuries. That proletariat was not a monster, it was not a unified cultural class, and it was not a race." They continue:

> This class was *anonymous, nameless*. Robert Burton noted in *The Anatomy of Melancholy* (1624), "Of 15000 proletaries slaine in battle, scarce fifteene are recorded in history, or one alone, the General perhaps, and after a while his and their names are likewise blotted out, the whole battle it selfe is forgotten." It was *landless, expropriated*. It lost the integument of the commons to cover and protect its needs. It was *poor*, lacking property, money, or material riches of any kind. It was often unwaged, forced to perform the unpaid labors of capitalism. It was often hungry, with uncertain means of survival. It was *mobile*,

transatlantic. It powered industries of worldwide transportation. It left the land, migrating from country to town, from region to region, across the oceans, and from one island to another. It was *terrorized, subject to coercion*. Its hide was calloused by indentured labor, galley slavery, convict transportation, the workhouse, the house of correction. Its origins were often traumatic: enclosure, capture, and imprisonment left lasting marks. It was *female* and *male*, of *all ages*. (Indeed, the very term *proletarian* originally referred to poor women who served the state by bearing children). It included everyone from youth to old folks, from ship's boys to old salts, from apprentices to savvy old masters, from young prostitutes to old "witches." It was *multitudinous, numerous* and *growing*. Whether in a square, at a market, on a common, in a regiment, or on a man-of-war with banners flying and drums beating, its gatherings were wondrous to contemporaries. It was *numbered, weighed*, and *measured*. Unknown as individuals or by name, it was objectified and counted for purposes of taxation, production, and reproduction. It was *cooperative* and *laboring*. The collective power of the many rather than the skilled labor of the one produced its most forceful energy. It moved burdens, shifted earth, and transformed the landscape. It was *motley*, both dressed in rags and multiethnic in appearance. Like Caliban, it originated in Europe, Africa, and America. It included clowns, or cloons (i.e., country people). It was without genealogical unity. It was *vulgar*. It spoke its own speech, with a distinctive pronunciation, lexicon, and grammar made up of slang, cant, jargon, and pidgin—talk from work, the street, the prison, the gang, and the dock. It was *planetary*, in its origins, its motions, and its consciousness. Finally, the proletariat was *self-active, creative*; it was—and is—alive; it is onamove.[120]

According to Linebaugh and Rediker, the discontinuous struggles of the multitude took place on and off all through the seventeenth and eighteenth centuries and into the nineteenth. The eruption of antinomian and Digger "enthusiasm" in the revolutionary decades of the seventeenth century was only one moment of what they identify as a much longer tradition of proletarian struggle. Other moments in the discontinuous struggle traced by Linebaugh and Rediker—a struggle whose very untranslatability into history is suggested by those moments in their book when their prose itself begins to mutate—include slave rebellions in the West Indies, mutinies in the Royal Navy, various episodes of transatlantic piracy, Tacky's Revolt in Jamaica, the opening stages of the American War of Independence (whose energies were appropriated by what they call the "American Thermidor" led by the so-called Founding Fathers), the Haitian Revolution, and the explosion of revolutionary activism in the late 1780s and 1790s, not just in France, but also in the many struggles, armed and unarmed, in England, Scotland, Ireland, and Wales, and all across the Atlantic. Not all these struggles and episodes of revolutionary upheaval were explicitly related to each other, of course, much less tied together into a systematic continuous history. There were, however, a number of relays between different revolutionary moments. Think, for example, of the ties linking the early stages of the American Revolution to the French Revolution, to 1790s London, to the divisions of the London Corresponding Society; with strands and lines of activity splitting off from there to the foiled attempt to arm with pikes, to the 1797 mutiny in the Royal Navy fleets at Spithead and the Nore, to the United Irishmen—many of them ex-LCS men—and thence to the 1798 uprising in Ireland, and so across the seas with exiled Irish sailors, soldiers, and mutineers—and back again in the abortive coup d'état planned by the Irish colonel Edward Despard (who had served in the British army in colonial Jamaica), a plot which the presiding judge at Despard's trial condemned as "a wild scheme of impracticable equality"[121] and which ended with the execution of Despard and six of his comrades in London in 1803, among the few men in history to be charged, found guilty, and executed on the basis of having imagined the death of their king.[122] However discontinuous and heterogeneous all these struggles may have been,[123] Linebaugh and Rediker argue that in most of them we can detect some recurring themes: an emphasis on common power, on sharing and community as the appropriate bases for social, economic, political, and religious organization, on the use of revolutionary violence where need be, and on the need to resist at all costs brutality, inequality, and exploitation, whether political or economic, to refuse the extraction of private profits from the collective labor power of the multitude, and to confront an elite culture of private learning and exclusionary ("learned," "prepared," "cultivated") discourse with the art, music, writing, and songs of the unlearned and untutored, of the unlicensed and unrespectable, of laborers, of prophets and children, of pipers and bards.

6. "Wild and Impracticable"

As we have seen in the preceding chapters, the explosion of politico-religious "enthusiasm" (real and imagined) in 1790s London took place within the wider context of an enormously heterogeneous and disunited radical movement. We must be careful, however, not to let our scholarly concern with heterogeneity and complexity obscure the fact that, within the radical movement, we can discern two tendencies, which, no matter how intertwined they sometimes seemed, would ultimately prove contradictory and incompatible. To be more precise, there were two tendencies, one of which, in its bid for respectability and acceptability—that is, for a location within what would ultimately be recognized as the disenchanted and progressive history of modernity—desperately tried to rid itself of the other, or rather *its* other, which for its part summoned forth a world of visionary prophecies and divine interventions, a world in which duration unevenly folds in on and differentiates itself from itself, in which eternity always *is*, in which time always renews itself heterogeneously—a world, in short, in which "eternity is in love with the productions of time."[124]

For, on the one hand, there emerged in the radical struggle of the 1790s the tendency that I have heuristically identified as the hegemonic strand of radicalism—that is, the movement whose ultimate dominance of the radical field (by the early nineteenth century) would allow later historians to conclude that "'radicalism' at the end of the eighteenth century primarily meant a wish to reform a corrupt parliament and to extend the franchise."[125] Even when it was (paradoxically) articulated by members of the dying artisan class, or in other words even when it had not yet risen to political and cultural dominance, this tendency was committed to and driven by a properly bourgeois discourse of rights, duties, rational subjectivity, and reasoned argument. This strand of radicalism limited itself to a demand for parliamentary reform, an extension of the franchise, the political equality of citizens, and the recognition of individual rights.[126] It was generally articulated by the leading radical intellectuals—Paine, Thelwall, Coleridge, and others—and hence, at least until 1796–97, by the leadership of organizations such as the London Corresponding Society or the Society for Constitutional Information. This tendency unequivocally denounced the possibility of demanding greater socioeconomic equality, which not only statesmen and magistrates but also activists like Thelwall recognized as "wild" and "impracticable."[127] It sharply differentiated the reasoned expostulations of "that small but glorious band, whom we may truly distinguish by the name of thinking and disinterested Patriots," from the specter, the "wild justice," the "wilder features," of "the multitude"—those who, as Coleridge put it, "listen only to the inflammatory harangues of some mad-headed Enthusiast, and imbibe from them Poison, not Food; Rage, not Liberty," those who, according to Paine, "are rather the followers of the camp than of the standard of liberty, and have yet to be instructed how to reverence it."[128] And hence, it renounced not only "levelling" in particular but also the whole mantle of "enthusiasm" in general, with which levelling had come to be identified by the end of the eighteenth century (Thelwall, for example, was very keen to distinguish his own "peacable diffusion of knowledge" from "the rant of inconsiderate enthusiasm," which he associated with the 1640s).[129] It did so not just because such "levelling doctrines" are, as Thelwall argued, "impracticable," but also because "the vain attempt to execute so wild a scheme, must plunge the world into yet unheard-of horrors; must send forth the pretended reformer, armed with the dagger in one hand, and the iron crow in the other, to pillage, murder and destroy; and, after all, to no better end, than to transfer all property from the proud and polished, the debauched, effeminate and luxurious, to the brutal, the ignorant, and the ferocious."[130] As against such "wild" schemes, this strand of radicalism was articulated on behalf of, and restricted itself to, the individual political rights of rational men (and in a few cases women) of all classes, though it frequently distinguished those capable of speaking to those rights ("Pure Ones and uncorrupt," as Coleridge called them)[131] from those who, *in principle*, ought one day—once they had been properly prepared, instructed, illuminated—to have a right to enjoy them; hence, it often saw that its duty was "to plead *for* the Oppressed, not *to* them."[132] Even the less "cultivated" LCS leaders, and the LCS membership in general, differentiated themselves from "the people" and aimed to dispel their "ignorance and prejudice as far as possible, and instill into *their* minds by means of the press a sense of *their* rights as freemen, and of *their* duties to *themselves*,"[133] and even attempting like sorcerers to breathe life into "the great body of the people,"[134] calling out, "we conjure you. . . ."[135] The tendency expressed by the leading intellectuals condemned and repudiated Burke's famous epithet ("swinish multitude") precisely because the phrase obscured the differences in talent and ability among individuals, because it refused to recognize the disenfranchised as rational individuals endowed with the individual rights and duties of citizenship, because it reduced independent sovereign selves to an undifferentiated mass, as though they were an Oriental horde, rather than "free-born Englishmen." What it found objectionable in Burke's epithet, in other words, was not so much the "swinish" part of the phrase—which was merely insulting—but rather that of the "multitude," which it took to be properly injurious.

This was, in short, an argument for the political rights of the individual, and it was thoroughly grounded on and driven by bourgeois concepts of subjectivity, identity, and property, very much as opposed to the collective power and being in common of "the multitude," which it had to deny and disavow at every step.

On the other hand, there were those who gladly embraced Burke's phrase, and not only in an ironic or rhetorical way. There were countless references to pigs and swine among a certain strand of radical writers and activists (e.g.,

"Old Bristleback," "Hog's Wash," "Pigs Meat," "A Spare Rib," "Gruntum Snorum," "The Rights of Swine," "A Liberty Pig," "The Stye of Oppression") who sought for a way to express their own opposition to the form of power and sovereignty for which Burke stood but who nevertheless articulated a very different kind of opposition from the one represented by the leading intellectuals or the early leadership of the LCS. This alternative form of opposition drew its own sense of power and authority *precisely* from the creative ontological and political potential of the "swinish multitude," with which it happily identified. And it was often either implicitly or explicitly critical of the stance of the leading radical intellectuals, though it was also perfectly willing to cooperate with them when necessary, and, as Jon Mee and Iain McCalman remind us, to mingle as needed certain components of rational critique with its own brand of multitudinous enthusiasm. The plans—real, fabricated, exaggerated, fantastical, or otherwise—to arm and prepare for a mass urban uprising were surely an element of this tendency (as we saw in chapter 2). Indeed, all the discussions and preparations for ordering pikes from Sheffield for a general uprising in London, for example (discussions which took place not just during the secret drills at Spence's house, but also in the pages of Eaton's *Politics for the People*), stressed the role of pikes as *the people's weapon:* cheap to make, easy to use—and effective only when deployed by a multitude, that is, by the people armed and mobilized as a mass, as the "proper counterpoise to the enormous power of their standing armies."[136]

Moreover, in addition to possible or rumored arming (in defiance of the radical intellectual leadership's exhortations that "riot, tumult and violence are not the fit means of obtaining a redress of grievances"),[137] this tendency within 1790s radicalism was partly fueled by the reemergence of "enthusiasm," and hence by certain concepts of power, community, and temporality of which the dominant radical intellectuals so sternly disapproved and which they banished to the margins. Thus, as Reid points out, in addition to the Deists and Atheists constituting the leadership of the radical movement, "a number of straggling auxiliaries might be reckoned upon, who were drawn together by the noise and alarm of the Field-Disputants. These consisted of a variety of Mystics, Muggletonians, Millenaries, and a variety of eccentric characters of different denominations."[138] Of the latter, he writes, "the visionary expectation of a new order of things, it is presumed, often vibrated from the imaginations of the leading members to their fingers ends."[139] Although Reid's account is at times exaggerated to the point of hysteria, the relationship he exposes between radical activism and the resurgence of millenarian enthusiasm was, as we saw in chapter 2, of grave concern both to the government and to the spokesmen of the hegemonic radical tendency, who sought to distance themselves from the contagion of enthusiastic "brain-phrenzy," and to stick to their plans for orderly rational reform amid the swirl of prophetic and millenarian ecstasy all around them, which threatened at times to drown them out.

However exaggerated it may have been, then, Reid's account reflects the extent to which enthusiasm had resurfaced in 1790s London and provided a number of links to the seventeenth century heretics, antinomians, and communists, as well as to the long, discontinuous tradition of plebeian struggle explored by Linebaugh and Rediker.[140] The links had been fortified and sustained all through the eighteenth century by the republication of seventeenth-century antinomian, Ranter, and millenarian tracts, many of them officially banned or burned (and their authors arrested, imprisoned, and punished), which one might have otherwise thought had vanished from the earth or indeed laid hidden in cupboards. These included Richard Coppin's *Advancement of all things in Christ* (reprinted in 1763), *A Blow to the Serpent* (reprinted in 1764), and *Truth's Testimony* (reprinted in 1768); John Reeve and Ludovick Muggleton's *Joyful News from Heaven* (reprinted in 1752), *Acts and Witnesses of the Spirit* (reprinted in 1764), and *Stream from the Tree of Life* (reprinted in 1758); William Erbery's *Scourge for the Assirian* (reprinted in 1770); and the collected works of James Nayler (reprinted in 1716), who had preached revolution and jubilee until he was sentenced under the Blasphemy Act in 1656 and punished with 310 lashes and having his forehead branded and a hole bored through his tongue with a red-hot iron (the same punishment meted out to the Ranter Jacob Bauthumley).[141] To these reprints were added a new wave of republications during the 1790s themselves, including John Saltmarsh's stridently antinomian tract *Free Grace: or, the Flowings of Christ's Blood Freely to Sinners* (reprinted in 1792), which proclaimed that "Christ is the second Adam, in whom all that are alive do live," that "there is no sin past, present, or to come, which Christ did not pay down the price of his blood for upon the cross," that "those that are under grace revealed, are no longer under the law," and hence that "the Spirit of Christ sets a believer as free from hell, the law, and bondage, here on earth, as if he were in heaven";[142] Muggleton's *True Interpretation of the Witch of Endor* (reprinted in 1793) and *Remonstrance from the Eternal God* (reprinted in 1793); the collected works of Tobias Crisp, in *Christ Alone Exalted* (reprinted in 1791); Samuel Cobbler How's *Sufficiency of the Spirit's Teaching* (reprinted in 1792); and the salacious *Anarchy of the Ranters and other Libertines*, by the seventeenth-century heresiographer Robert Barclay, which was reprinted in London in 1790.

Figure 28. Garnet Terry, frontispiece, in *Prophetical Extracts*, no. 5 (British Library shelfmark 3187.d42.TP). By permission of the British Library.

Antinomianism and enthusasm did not merely resurface in 1790s London in the form of republications from the previous century, however. For in addition to the wave of reprints and the anthologies filled with visionary and prophetic material—such as George Ribeau's *God's Awful Warning* (1795) and Garnet Terry's series of *Prophetical Extracts* (1794–95)—a new wave of prophetical and enthusiastic writing swept through the radical

CHAPTER SIX

movement and much farther afield as well: as Reid points out, "prophecies, relative to the destruction of almost every kingdom and empire in the world, teemed from the British press."[143] Moreover, the 1790s witnessed the publication or republication of several politically and culturally—as well as religiously—motivated attacks on antinomianism, including *Antinomianism Explained and Exploded* (1790) and *Antinomianism Unmasked and Refuted* (1791). In this context we must situate the work not only of Richard Brothers, the "mad prophet" whose political influence on radical circles the government deemed dangerous enough to have him locked up more or less permanently, but also the work of people such as Thomas Spence, Richard Lee, and many others, who combined a commitment to the radical struggle against aristocratic despotism with a powerful sense of the continuity of the plebeian struggle initiated in the seventeenth century—with, in other words, a powerful sense of deep and heterogeneous time as constituted and reconstituted by and through human, divine, and supernatural activity. Such activists, writers, and prophets frequently claimed divine vision, divine authority, and divine and collective power as the basis for their radical political aims. And as Jon Mee points out, they "printed from different premises (under threat from Church and King thugs), threw together anthologies of other people's writing, and inserted their own verses wherever they were able. They appeared to offer no coherent body of work," Mee adds, and "they seemed to be at one moment willing to dispense entirely with the 'author function,' cutting up and reassembling whatever was at hand, while at another moment making shockingly presumptuous claims for the divine basis of their inspiration."[144] The publications of Richard Lee (including the one-page *King Killing* as well as volumes of poetry such as *Songs from the Rock*) and also journals such as Spence's *Pigs' Meat* exemplify this tendency in radicalism.

Pigs' Meat, after all, not only provided nourishment to the swinish multitude of the 1790s; it represented the choicest "cuts" from those who had participated in the revolutionary struggles of the previous one or two hundred years as well as those of the 1790s. Hence, like Terry's prophetical extracts, it helped to provide a sense of time as a time of discontinuous struggle. The authority it claimed was in this sense genuinely collective, and we might say transhistorical, even divine, rather than limited to the persona of Thomas Spence. For in its pages we not only read the most radical selections (carefully edited to sharpen their edge) from Barlow, Paine, Godwin, Frend, Erskine and Volney, we also hear again the voices of Harrington, of the Neapolitan revolutionary Masaniello, of slave maroons, of Native American "communists," and of revolutionary sailors; we read "A Lamentation for the Oppressed," "A Song to be sung at the Commencement of the Milenium," "The glorious prospect of better Times, which are fast approaching," "The Marseilles March, or Hymn," "On the Government of Hell," "Rights of the Devil," "Rights of Swine," "The impossibility of commencing Tyrant over an armed Nation convinced of the universal Equality of Mankind," and "Popular Assemblies understand only their own Interest."[145] And through the whole journal there is the constant reminder that the best way to resist oppression is for the multitude to work together, to draw on its power as a multitude, and hence to be as genuinely *swinish* as possible. For, we learn, whereas humans vary enormously according to their individual wealth, so that "some are like to burst with fat and satiety, while others appear like shadows, and frequently die of want, and diseases flowing from scarcity, or unwholsome diet," on the other hand "swine living together are all alike, either all fat or all lean." Hence the great falsehood of Burke's epithet, this ironic passage continues playfully, since real swine, unlike people in their current state, "will not quietly suffer want on any account, much less by the encroachments of their fellow-creatures. If any great hog offer to thrust them from the trough, they will scream most sediciously, and will, without regard to consequence, insist on having their noses in, on one side or the other."[146]

This tendency—and not only as it is exemplified in *Pigs' Meat*—differed from hegemonic radicalism in that it would prove incompatible with bourgeois values and bourgeois history, a problem of which its claim for divine inspiration rather than rational expostulation may be taken as exemplary, as may its interest and investment in the "swinish multitude," the threat it poses to private property, its evocation of a divine being in common, and indeed its frequent explicit call for armed struggle and "king killing" rather than merely rational expostulation and thoughtful petitioning as the means to deliverance from the common enemy. Richard Lee's poem "Let us Hope to See Better Times," which was included in *Songs from the Rock*—one of the publications for which Lee would be dragged before the Treasury Solicitor's Office for interrogation in October of 1795—is perhaps indicative of all these tendencies:

LET US HOPE TO SEE BETTER TIMES
I.
Ye "Rabble" and Multitude "swinish" and base,
Who suffer and smart beneath Tyranny's Sway;
Let Hope yield a Balm for your present Distress,
For you shall ere long, see a happier Day.

CHAPTER SIX

II.
Even now it is dawning; I see its bright Rays,
Reflected from Nations once wretched as we;
From Nations who feel its meridian Blaze,
And reap NATURE'S BLESSINGS unpaid for and free.

III.
O! let it enliven the Hearts of the Poor,
While Tyrants shall tremble and sink in Despair;
The Reign of Oppression is but for an Hour,
'Till all the wide World sweet FREEDOM shall share.

IV.
No more shall they sell us the Light of the Sun,
And claim as their own, the Earth, Rivers, and Seas,
For LIBERTY governs, and now has begun,
To execute Heav'n's all-gracious Decrees

V.
Yon Palace that now is the guilty Abode,
Of Luxury and her degenerate Sons;
Shall (crush'd with the Weight of the Vengeance of GOD)
Soon mingle its Ruins with Tyranny's Thrones.

VI.
The Earth, and the Sea, and the Stream shall resign,
To ALL undistinguish'd, whate'er they contain;
The Light of the Day on our Dwellings shall shine,
As freely as Heav'n first gave it to Men.*

*The Heaven, even the Heavens are the LORD's, but the Earth hath he given to the Children of Men. PSAL. CXV. 16[147]

Lee's poetry is evocative of the antinomian writers of the seventeenth century, and Winstanley as well—but we would be blinded by our own modern prejudices to think of this as either nostalgia or anachronism, since for Lee (and for many others at the time) there really did exist an urgent sense that a "new day" was coming, and its bright and happy rays could already be seen. Driven by this sense of divine inspiration, Lee mingles a Winstanleyan communism founded on sharing—not merely equal representation in parliament—as the basis of liberty ("all the wide world sweet freedom shall share") with a Ranterish sense of divine embodiment in God or Christ as a collective power. Hence, Lee marks his millenarian vision of liberty not as a moment when all will have a right to vote in annual elections (the main LCS demand) but rather as a moment when private property will end and all will share the earth and its produce equally, or in other words as a moment when all will share in a divine sense of being in common, a moment when, as Lee puts it in another poem, "'JESUS the GOD is universal KING!' / And crowns with FREEDOM all the Sons of Men."[148] (Spence, for his part, would anticipate a similar millennium, "when there shall be neither lord nor landlords, but *God and man will be all in all*").[149] Indeed, throughout Lee's work, just as in Winstanley's or Coppe's, we detect the sense that God is not merely a transcendent power up in heaven, but rather the immanently constituted expression of the power of the multitude, alive and active both in the here and now and in the lived and experiential sense of deep heterogeneous time, loving and sharing when possible, armed and dangerous when necessary. The violence of this collective power in seeking vengeance against tyrants and rulers, tumbling "the Blood-Built Thrones of Despots down"—"overturning, overturning, overturning," as Coppe might have put it—is perhaps nowhere clearer than in Lee's poem "The Rights of God."[150]

Thomas Spence would publish "The Rights of God" in one of the editions of *Pigs' Meat* (for which he was frequently in trouble with the government, and arrested and imprisoned several times). In fact, Jon Mee observes that Spence and Lee may have had a mutually radicalizing effect on each other.[151] Like Lee, Spence based his vision of freedom in divine authority and in the power of the multitude. He combined in equal measure revolutionary pragmatism and the quasi-biblical language of prophetic enthusiasm and redistributive jubilee, claiming, for example, both that his plan for destroying and overturning the power of the rich and sharing the wealth of the land equally could be effected by "a few thousands of hearty determined fellows well armed"[152] and that "if ever there be a millennium or heaven upon earth, it can only exist under the benign 'System of Spensonia.'"[153] The vision of Spensonia was originally laid out in, among other publications, Spence's allegory of the "marine republic," founded on a desert island, whose citizens "declared the property of the island to be the property of them all collectively."[154] It is essential, however, to bear in mind the extent to which Spence's communist vision was—unlike the secularized communism of the nineteenth century which would follow it—the product of what would at the time have been recognized as "enthusiasm," conveying a sense of imminent apocalypse and immediate divine intervention. We can see such enthusiasm spanning Spence's work from as early as his 1782 "SONG, to be sung at the end of oppression, or the commencement of the political millennium, when there shall be neither lord nor landlords, but God and

309

CHAPTER SIX

man will be all in all" (in which Spence evokes the biblical concept of jubilee[155] to set "all at liberty"), to *Fragment of an Ancient Prophecy* of 1796, in which Spence condemns the "specious, but partial Rights of Man" celebrated by the Paineite radicals, who believe in "the false tree of Liberty composed of heterogeneous materials as if part iron, part clay, part liberty, and part tyranny, capable of shedding the influence of liberty and independence only on the wealthy, the shadow merely falling on the poor who are still to groan under oppression." As against this "false" notion of liberty, Spence, speaking as a prophet—and in a tone reminiscent of Blake's *America*—anticipates instead the coming day of genuine freedom: "Then shall the whole earth, as Isaiah saith, be at rest and in quiet, and shall break forth into singing; and they shall say, Now we are free indeed! Our lands which God gave us to dwell upon are now our own: Our governments now free from aristocracy are easily supported with a small proportion of our rents; and the remainder being our own, we spend in parochial business and divide among ourselves. Amen."[156]

What particularly distinguishes Spence's work from that of the hegemonic radical tendency, then, is his willingness to embrace armed struggle and the language of prophecy, and above all his willingness to speak both to and on behalf of the disenfranchised and the dispossessed—the swinish multitude—rather than either an actual or a would-be elite. To the multitude he offered a vision of freedom with much broader reach than the "partial" vision of liberty offered by Thelwall, Paine, and the liberal-radicals (who, as Spence put it caustically, "have no chance of being kings; but many of them are already, and the rest foolishly and wickedly hope to be sometime or other, landlords, greater or lesser").[157] And hence, as we have seen, instead of offering writings to the public that inhabit the authorial voice of the rational Enlightenment man, we find in Spence's publications (as in Lee's, and for that matter Coppe's) the voice of God, the swinish multitude, the poor, the illiterate, the uneducated, and, in what is perhaps his most radical piece—*The Rights of Infants*—women and children, who challenge the voice of aristocratic authority with a disavowal of the limited demand for rights made by and for men, "who are not to be depended upon" (i.e., Paine and his limited "rights of man," which Spence tirelessly denounced for its limitations), and who proclaim instead the rights of *all* to receive and share the bounty of the earth, "the natural fruits of the earth being the fruits of our undoubted common."[158] Spence's vision of communist jubilee would, as Linebaugh and Rediker point out, be echoed only a little later by Robert Wedderburn in *Axe Laid to the Root* (a publication whose biblical title itself had a long revolutionary heritage) and by Thomas Evans and the nineteenth-century Spenceans.[159]

No matter how many connections—personal or institutional—there were between the different strands of radicalism, what I am distinguishing as the spokesmen of the hegemonic tendency in radicalism had to work hard to keep their more enthusiastic comrades at bay and to try to maintain arguments in favor of reason, expostulation, evidence, and enlightenment amid the din of voices calling for overturning, levelling, divine inspiration, and jubilee. "If one is claiming a right to participate in the public sphere on the basis of the universality of reason, as Thelwall was," Jon Mee argues, "it is not very helpful to have as an ally someone claiming to be directly empowered by a divine vision, confirming Burke's worst predictions about popular frenzy and religious dissent."[160] What is remarkable, however, is not just the way in which someone like Thelwall worked to deny the sense of vitality and power conveyed by 1790s enthusiasm, but rather the way in which modern historians have tended to replicate Thelwall's liberal move, denying the legitimacy (and ultimately even the voice and the presence) of a way of seeing and imagining the world that was very much at odds not only with the ancien régime but also with the hegemonic radical tendency itself, which had to work so hard to impose a kind of order on the radical struggle and would not really succeed until the consolidation of a certain variety of liberal reformism in the early nineteenth century.

Historians arriving on the scene, such as William Hamilton Reid, and those writing long since, have generally shared Thelwall's indictment of the enthusiasts and his epistemological foundation, which allowed no room for visions, dreams, and divine inspiration or messages. Jon Mee cautions us that for modern historians to replicate Thelwall's discomfort with regard to enthusiasm "and to regard Lee as a lunatic or an anachronism is profoundly unhistorical."[161] Perhaps inevitably, however, the modern historian or critic feels as excluded as did William Hamilton Reid when he described the enthusiastic and antinomian tendency within 1790s radicalism, a tendency in which, according to Reid, "human learning was declaimed against, as one of the greatest enemies to human happiness or the improvement of the intellect, and dreams, visions, and immediate revelations, were recommended as a substitute! The faculty of foretelling future events was also insisted upon; the discernment of spirits, by the physiognomy, the voice, the gait, &c. together with the possibility of conversing with departed souls. In fact, those pretences were carried so far, that any visitor, not in the habit of hearing supernatural voices, or not informed of the common occurrences of the day,

CHAPTER SIX

by the ministration of Angels, would have been treated as a novice and a disciple of the lowest form."[162] For our modern disciplinary tools, apparatuses, discourses, and methodologies—many or all of which emerged precisely in opposition to the sorts of revelations, foretellings, and supernatural pretenses exposed in Reid's account—actually bar us from accessing or even taking seriously the culture of a world not yet desacralized, a world not yet stripped of the sense that "every thing that lives is holy."[163] That we find ourselves, by virtue of our own disciplinary and ideological categories, barred from such a culture accounts perhaps for the sense of distortion that takes place when scholars try to appropriate Blake's work by translating it into—and making it accountable to—our own conceptual categories. Almost as a matter of definition, this difficulty makes it virtually impossible to adequately "historicize" the culture of late-eighteenth-century enthusiasm without attempting to reconsider how we distinguish the historical from the ahistorical, the real from the unreal, the possible from the impossible.

CHAPTER SEVEN

Conclusion: Striving

"Since the French Revolution," Blake wrote toward the very end of his life, "Englishmen are all Intermeasurable One by Another, certainly a happy state of Agreement to which I for One do not Agree."[1] As we have seen, Blake was not alone in his refusal of the cultural, political, philosophical, religious, and aesthetic consensus—the "happy state of Agreement"—which emerged through the 1790s and was essential to the hegemonic strand of radical thought in the period. This consensus privileged the sovereign, independent self, the "intermeasurable" citizen, as the appropriate basis for all political, aesthetic, economic, and cultural practice in the desacralized time of modernity. The heterogeneous radical struggle of the 1790s may indeed have been crushed, whether as a result of its own contradictions, the enormous repression of the state, a residual conservatism that was more widespread even if less strongly voiced than radicalism, or some combination of all three and perhaps other factors as well. Ultimately, however—and certainly by the time of Blake's approaching death in the 1820s—the premodern concept of society as an enormous organism whose individual organs play highly differentiated and necessarily unequal roles in the sustenance and regulation of the social, political, and economic system as a whole would be replaced by this new consensus, which, as we have seen, received its most elaborate development in what I have heuristically identified as the hegemonic tendency in 1790s radicalism.

This emergent consensus was driven by a faith in the atomistic equality, and hence the intermeasurability, of the self-regulating units of which society is composed, on a potentially universal scale (since, as Paine argues, "by the same rule that nature intended the intercourse of two, she intended that

CHAPTER SEVEN

of all").[2] Freedom, according to the new consensus, involved the ability of each atomistic unit—each monadic self—to regulate itself as an independent organism rather than being regulated by external forces and located as a dependent organ in a larger social organism. For Blake, however, such self-regulation represented simply a different form of confinement and restriction from the one central to the conservative vision: an imposition of the logic of governmentality on an even more efficient scale. Hence, as we have seen, it represented for him not true freedom, but rather a leap from the frying pan into the fire.

In trying to imagine and sustain alternatives to this emergent consensus, Blake was able to draw on the long—albeit discontinuous and heterogeneous—tradition of antinomian enthusiasm, which survived well into his own time. The language of revolution, as A. L. Morton notes, had changed in the passage from the seventeenth century to the eighteenth, "and the old ideas were barely intelligible to the men who listened to Paine and Thelwall, and mere crazy nonsense to the more sophisticated followers of Bentham." Nevertheless, "they did provide a means of communication for a great poet: Blake's tragedy was that he was speaking a language which was already becoming obsolete," Morton continues; "he was the greatest English Antinomian, but also the last."[3] Thanks to the work of Jon Mee and others, however, we now know that Blake was not the last antinomian, that enthusiasm was alive and well during his own lifetime, and that it posed a vital threat to the happy consensus that emerged through the 1790s. However much it may have superseded the residual conservative concepts of society, whose political and cultural foundations it challenged through the romantic period, this consensus could really be consolidated and assume its dominance of the public sphere only once the last traces of enthusiasm had been eradicated or perhaps aestheticized into romanticism, or otherwise absorbed into the legally sanctioned "possible history" of modernity.[4] Thus, by the 1790s the language of antinomian enthusiasm may indeed have been "obsolete," as Morton says, but only in the sense that it was allowed no room in the historicist discourse of modernity, which had to work hard to purge itself of any enthusiastic tendencies, to de-Orientalize itself as much as possible, as we have seen in the writing of radicals such as Paine and Wollstonecraft.

Late-eighteenth-century enthusiasm refused the concept of empty homogeneous time which would prove foundational not just for modernity, but for the very sense of history according to which—as I argued in *Romantic Imperialism*—other cultures, peoples, narratives can be seen as "obsolete." Enthusiasm, in other words, had to be kept not only out of the progressive revolutionary narratives developed by Paine and Thelwall and others, but also out of the narratives that have been inherited and sustained by subsequent historians and literary critics, whose disciplines lack the conceptual capacity and even the language with which to ascribe genuine agency to the "multitude" as such, let alone to give much credence—other than in terms of individual psychosis, which misses the point altogether—to divinely inspired visions or prophecies, to a sense of time as fractured and heterogeneous, to a decentered and hyperdifferentiated sense of being. From a modern historical standpoint, such other cultures—indeed, such other worlds—seem impossible, inexplicable, dangerous, laughable, or perhaps simply insane. And hence, insofar as they are essentially untranslatable into a modern idiom, such other worlds seem consignable to the heap of "minority pasts" that according to Dipesh Chakrabarty cannot be admitted to modern historical discourse, or even to history itself.[5] Or perhaps they may be assigned a location in an emergent bourgeois political unconscious, a location that needs to be kept under strict control, monitored as a potentially problematic source of quasi-Orientalized plebeian enthusiasm (see chapter 5).

Crabb Robinson's meeting with Blake in December of 1825 represents just such an encounter between a skeptical modern consciousness and a mode of life and being, a culture, that remains inadmissible to modernity and to the history of the possible. According to Robinson, Blake "spoke of his paintings as being what he had seen in his visions—and when he said *my visions* it was in the ordinary unemphatic tone in which we speak of trivial matters that every one understands & cares nothing about—In the same tone he said—repeatedly 'the Spirit told me'—I took occasion to say You use the same word as Socrates used—What resemblance do you suppose there is between your spirit & the spirit of Socrates? The same as between our countenances—He paused & added—I was Socrates. And then as if correcting himself: A sort of brother—I must have had conversations with him—So I had with Jesus Christ—I have an obscure recollection having been with both of them."[6] Blake added, "We are all coexistent with God—Members of the Divine body—We are all partakers of the divine nature." When Robinson asked Blake what he thought of the divinity of Christ, Blake said, "*He is the only God*—But then he added—And so am I and so are you." Clearly, there is no way of corroborating this particular story of an encounter with Blake, which left Robinson struggling to "fix Blake's station between Christianity Platonism & Spinozism."[7] However, it is consistent with many other reports concerning Blake's seeing visions and deriving inspiration from the spirits, from the first time he reported seeing a tree full of angels, their "bright angelic wings bespangling every bough like stars,"

CHAPTER SEVEN

for which he only narrowly avoided receiving a thrashing by his father for "telling lies,"[8] to his claim that his dead brother Robert appeared to him in a night vision to reveal the technique of relief etching,[9] to his terrifying vision "of the 'Ancient of Days' at the top of his staircase in Hercules Buildings," to his seeing a ghost, "scaly, speckled, very awful," which so frightened him that he ran into the street to get away from it (he would later paint just such a figure in *The Ghost of a Flea*).[10] Moreover, the sense of Blake that we get from Robinson's account is squarely consistent with the conceptual bases of antinomian enthusiasm, which we see throughout Blake's work, in an extrabiographical sense: a belief in the divinity of humanity, in a common joyous participation in an infinite being called God, a sense of being in common in an uneven, disjointed and infinitely heterogeneous plane of time.

Indeed, right through those years of revolutionary crisis, when enthusiasm, with all its wild and dangerous seventeenth-century connotations, was being excoriated on all sides—among reformers and conservatives alike—Blake, for his part, consistently and defiantly identified himself as an enthusiast. He did so not just in the playful farewells of his letters ("nothing can withstand the fury of my Course among the Stars of God & in the Abysses of the Accuser," he concludes a letter to Thomas Butts; "my Enthusiasm is still what it was only Englarged and confirmd"),[11] but also in his various annotations (as against Reynolds's suggestion that "enthustiastick admiration seldom promotes knowledge," for example, Blake insists that "Enthusiastic Admiration is the first principle of Knowledge & its last"),[12] and even in the preface to *Jerusalem*, where he confesses "The Enthusiasm of the following Poem" and expresses his hope that "the Reader will be with me, wholly One in Jesus our Lord, who is the God [*of Fire*] and Lord [*of Love*] to whom the Ancients look'd and saw his day afar off, with trembling & amazement."[13] Indeed, on more than one occasion Blake identified enthusiasm as a "source of immortal joy" and as the very foundation of his work.[14] In a letter of October 1804, for example, Blake asks William Hayley to "excuse my enthusiasm or rather madness, for I am really drunk with intellectual vision whenever I take a pencil or graver into my hands."[15]

Such enthusiasm, the source of the "madness" and "drunkenness" of intellectual vision, is precisely what drives Blake away from the discourse of rational enlightenment, the language of the learned elite, and hence away from the figure of the rational Enlightenment man—morally virtuous and superior to all others—who plays what I would argue is *the* pivotal role in much of the radical writing of the 1790s, and who continues to play the leading role in almost all the histories of the period, displacing other figures to the margins and beyond. Rather than seeking the validation and respectability offered by arguments founded on rational enquiry and cool methodical knowledge—with the sort of sobriety, patience, temperance, moderation, modesty, self-control, and intellectual frugality summoned forth by the Paines and Wollstonecrafts of the 1790s, who as Blake himself pointed out, worked miracles without even knowing it[16]—Blake's work seeks to ground itself in a creative capacity that is held in common not among the learned elite (who renounce it), but among children, among the poor and unlearned, the illiterate and dispossessed, "my fellow laborers," the swinish multitude, the wretched of the earth. Thus, against Thornton's assertion that the Bible "is the *most difficult* book in the world to *comprehend*, nor can it be understood at all by the *unlearned*, except through the aid of CRITICAL and EXPLANATORY notes," Blake insists that "Christ & his Apostles were Illiterate Men," whereas "Caiphas Pilate & Herod were Learned"; and he adds that "the Beauty of the Bible is that the most Ignorant & Simple Minds Understand it Best."[17] In this sense, Blake rejects systems of knowledge whose decipherment and interpretation require training, preparation, and rational examination, require the aid of just the kind of scholarly weaponry which Thornton praises, require the virtuous moral superiority celebrated by Paine and Wollstonecraft, and for that matter require the "sound and vigorous mind" that Wordsworth says his own poetry demands.[18]

But if the poor and illiterate and children have easier access to the Bible than learned scholars and Enlightenment gentlemen—with their "sound and vigorous minds"—that is so, according to Blake, not simply because "the Whole Bible is filld with Imaginations & Visions from End to End," rather than the "Moral Virtues" of "Plato & the Greeks & all Warriors" (whose imperialist version of power and knowledge, as well as its reincarnation in 1790s romanticism and radicalism, we explored in earlier chapters), but precisely because, as Blake adds in a subsequent note, "Man *is All Imagination* God is Man & exists in us & we in him."[19] As we have seen in the previous chapter, vision and imagination are not receptive faculties for Blake. They are creative powers: they are, to be precise, creative ontological powers, endowing us not only with a mode of *seeing* but with a mode of *creating*, which is to say, a mode of *being*. The "everlasting gospel" of the antinomian tradition empowers us not because it allows us to read, but because through reading it allows us to create, and in creating, to be, to become. It allows us to become aware of our own divine power, and our participation in God. Northrop Frye brilliantly captures this sense of ontological power in Blake. For Blake, "we do not perceive God," Frye explains in *Fearful Symmetry*; "we perceive *as* God." This is why, he says, for Blake "Man in his creative acts and perceptions is God, and God is Man."[20] Thus, for Blake the "visions and imaginations" of which the Bible is full, which are more readily accessible to the poor, to children and the illiterate than to the learned and the powerful, are not to be understood simply in epistemological or representational terms, but rather in ontological and creative terms. We access the Bible's "visions and imaginations" not when we read them as scholars, historians, and critics—as fixed texts whose supposedly inert and hidden meanings and messages we ought to discover and revere—but when we draw upon them to transform perception into creation, to create, to be, to become, and to live a life of imagination, a life of affirmative and creative *power*.

What Blake seeks to articulate, then, is just this sense of common vision, common knowledge, common power—a sense of divine prophecy and revelation not as gifts handed down from on high but rather as a common power possessed by all. "The worship of God is. Honouring his gifts in other men each according to his genius," says one of the revolutionary devils in *The Marriage of Heaven & Hell*; "those who envy or calumniate great men hate God. for *there is no other God*."[21] This infuriates the Angel, defender of the established order; for, hearing the devil's assertion, he becomes "almost blue but mastering himself he grew yellow, & at last white pink & smiling, and then replied, 'Thou idolater, is not God One? & is not he visible in Jesus Christ? and has not Jesus Christ given his sanction to the law of ten commandments and are not all other men fools, sinners & nothings?'" The devil then points out the extent of Christ's transgression of the Old Testament's moral law and concludes, "I tell you, no virtue can exist without breaking these ten commandments: Jesus was all virtue, and he acted from impulse: not from rules."[22] In fact, it is no coincidence that this is the most strikingly antinomian passage of *The Marriage*.

For we are reminded that what Blake seizes on in the language and figures of antinomian enthusiasm is its sense of the possession of a common creative power. In so doing, Blake rejects the narrow, confined "knowledge" of the narrow, confined, solitary self—along with the limited claims to circumscribed "rights" and "duties" appertaining to the sovereign self, all of which serve only to articulate the life of the reified organism ("barr'd and petrified against the infinite"), the fixed and definite form that exists as the product and locus, the very ground, of state power. And he affirms on the contrary the joyous life of the prolific—life as an infinitely prolific number of re-makings, re-imaginations, re-becomings, the joyous life of pure potential, of endless striving, of *élan vital*. For Blake, as we have seen, our being is defined by our desire: we exist not in definite "rights-endowed" forms created once and forever and then tediously and faithfully reprinted according to the principle *omne simile generas simile*—but rather as ever-changing bundles of relations articulated by our infinite desires. Being no longer involves the atom-like existence of the monad, it no longer consists in a fixed set of properties—or in some supposedly "natural" capacity for private property and self-propriety—but rather in our infinite *striving*. As I argued in previous chapters, what is preserved in this being in common is precisely the *minute particularity* that is actually threatened to the point of extinction by the logic of homogeneous production that links together the sovereign subject and the reified commodity as two sides of the same coin, "intermeasurable" according to the "happy consensus" with which Blake found it impossible to agree.

For Blake, all being exists in "minute particulars." All forms of being involve an immanent sharing, an ongoing dynamic rearticulation, of the minute particulars making us who we are. It is in this sense that we can be understood to exist in, and as, a dynamic, regenerating network of relations—a unity of minute particulars, some or all of which may at different times be shared with others—rather than as static hardened selfhoods; as ever-changing composites, rather than as a stream of interchangeable monads "unable to do other than repeat the same dull round over again." Thus, the infinite being in common called God can be seen to be constituted *immanently* by all the minute particulars of which it is composed—each of which is itself constituted by its own combinations of minute particulars—rather than as a transcendent force or power standing outside or beyond them. Nothing, including the minute particular, exists as a fixed form; rather, life and being consist in creative combinations and recombinations, in creating and striving. If Northrop Frye is right to say that "in his creative capacity the artist expresses the creative activity of God,"[23] that is so because Blake understood art as creativity and practice; in other words life and art are (or ought to be) the same thing for Blake.

"Freedom" here is no longer the restricted freedom of the bourgeois self, but rather the kind of freedom that is enabled by sharing and immanent being in common, in which the more we are connected, the more we share, the more we are open to others, the more we love, the freer we become. What Blake pushes toward is an immanent as opposed to a transcendent sublimity, which removes us from our selfhoods—hence the "self-annihilation" of *Milton* and *Jerusalem*—rather than strengthening our own sovereign sense of power over others. This, again, is something like the sublimity that we encounter in Spinoza, for whom our being also involves a sharing of parts ("the human body, to be preserved, requires a great many other bodies, by which it is, as it were, continually regenerated"). As we saw in the previous chapter, Spinoza had been influenced by Bruno, according to whom "the material and substance of things is incorruptible and must in all its parts pass through all forms," a notion echoed by seventeenth-century antinomian enthusiasts like Coppe and Bauthumley and reiterated by Blake a century later. "And we ourselves and the things pertaining to us come and go, pass and repass," Bruno writes; "there is nothing of our own which may not become foreign to us, and nothing foreign to us which may not become our own."[24] For Spinoza, an ever greater opening out, an ever greater connection to other bodies and minds, is precisely the condition of an ever greater proliferation of freedom, in both a mental and a physical sense.[25] The bond that ties together bodies and minds—the parts of which we are composed—is desire; since our striving depends on our ability to affect and be affected by others, our freedom and our very being are expressed by our desires.

For Blake, too, as we have seen, our relations with other human beings provide the basis of our common belonging in God. If "the most sublime act is to set another before you," the effect of sublimity is to remove you from your selfhood and to force you to consider the extent to which you share with—love—these others, whose existence is essential to your own being not in that they are opposed to you, but in that you share with them, in that your being immanently merges with theirs, each retaining its minute particularity even while participating in an infinite being in common. For modern and postmodern readers, this is undoubtedly the most difficult concept we encounter in Blake. His understanding of freedom, the freedom offered by our being in common, is an infinite capacity for particularity—not *individuality*, which for Blake is a form of confinement and limitation, but *particularity*, always becoming anew, tracing and retracing different trajectories of actualization, existing in and as and through *striving*, but at the same time mixing in and with and through others, allowing our own striving to be affirmed and strengthened by the striving of others with and through whom we immanently participate in being.

This is what allows us to understand Blake's enormous emphasis on "minute particularity" in a political, economic, and philosophical sense as well as the aesthetic sense in which it is ordinarily understood in scholarship. In his annotations to Reynolds, Blake insists, against the latter's emphasis on general views and general knowledge, that "All Sublimity is founded on Minute Discrimination," and that "singular & Particular Detail is the Foundation of the Sublime." "What is General Knowledge is there such a Thing," Blake asks; "all Knowledge is Particular."[26] What he is expressing here is not the perfectionist's relish for detail (anyway, Blake was hardly a perfectionist) but rather the far more profound sense that generality need not be opposed to particularity, much less privileged over it, since the particular immanently constitutes the general. "He who wishes to see a Vision; a perfect Whole," Los proclaims in *Jerusalem*, "Must see it in its Minute Particulars."[27] He goes on to attack the ruler of the established warlike order: "You accumulate Particulars, & murder by analyzing, that you / May take the aggregate; & you call the aggregate Moral Law: / And you call that Swelld & bloated Form; a Minute Particular. / But General Forms have their vitality in Particulars: & every / Particular is a Man; a Divine Member of the Divine Jesus."[28] For the ultimate horizon of our affective relations and our infinite desires—and hence the ultimate horizon of our being—is not a narrow, rights-endowed selfhood but rather our participation in the common body of God, the "divine body" of which "we are his members." It is no coincidence then that Blake's emphasis on minute particularity, his insistence that "all Knowledge is Particular," is reminiscent of Spinoza's claim that "the more we know particular things the more we know God."[29] Knowledge, love, and life consist in the particular, the source of vitality and striving. This is why freedom for Blake has to be understood as the ability to persevere in our desire to pursue particularity, to live life as continuous striving.

The most powerful and vital image of such a life of affects and connections that is to be found in Blake's illuminated books is not, however, to be found in a specific moment or passage but rather in the form of being that the books themselves embody: an image composed of many images, an image composed of a ceaseless bundle of relations between and among other images (both verbal and visual). Again we might allow ourselves to be guided by Spinoza, for whom there is a relationship between, on the one hand, the principle that "The more the body is capable of affecting, and being affected by, external bodies in a great many ways, the more the mind is capable of thinking," and on the other hand the principle that "The more an image is joined with other images, the more often if flourishes."[30] For as I argued in earlier chapters, we must think of the illuminated books—both internally and in their open and expansive relationship to each other—not as fixed and definite forms but rather as bundles of images, and in particular as an expansive network of relations among images. That each image exists in and as part of this open network enables it to flourish: the more it is joined with the other images, the more it flourishes. Thus, the illuminated books constitute a body made up of minute particulars, each of which flourishes in and through its relationship to all the others; they constitute a body of differentiated and infinitely proliferating "identities" that share a common essence; they constitute a body of striving elements whose "meanings" consist not in formal unities but rather in the networks of relations between them.

CHAPTER SEVEN

If in their material form the illuminated books undermine the distinction between copy and original, between production and reproduction, then, as I argued in chapter 4, this challenge must be considered not a *precondition* of their meaning, but a constituent element in the broader challenge that the illuminated books present to the conceptual, political, religious, and economic orthodoxy—and the basic ideologemes—of the Lockean tradition, whose greatest exponents in the 1790s were not Burke and the landed gentry of the ancien régime but rather Paine and the rising commercial and industrial order that sought to redefine social and political institutions in terms of the life, liberty, and pursuit of happiness of the property-owning individual. From an antinomian perspective, the latter can be seen to be caught in the "same dull round" of finite individuality elaborated by Locke and celebrated by Paine, cut off from the infinite variability opened up by antinomian belief, in which there is no contradiction in saying that "all men are alike (tho' infinitely various)" precisely because all human beings together immanently and heterogeneously constitute the infinite which is God. It seems obvious, then, that if we are to read the illuminated books from a Lockean or Paineite perspective, we either are going to read them reductively and turn them into something that they are not (narratives of the discourse of bourgeois liberty, or simply a collection of beautiful images reduced to the status of simple commodities) or are not going to "understand" them at all, because they will look like untranslated gibberish, with no apparent sense of temporal, subjective, or narrational order. "Hostile critics," as W. J. T. Mitchell points out, "have always recognized this quality in Blake's major prophecies when they indicted them for being 'impossible to follow.' That is precisely the point."[31]

In a world in which "Englishmen are all Intermeasurable one by Another," in which there is "one law for the lion and the ox," in which "Commerce Cannot endure Individual Merit its insatiable Maw must be fed by What all can do Equally well," in which the monopolizing trader "manufactures Art by the Hands of Ignorant Journeymen till at length Christian Charity is held out as a Motive to encourage a Blockhead & he is Counted the Greatest Genius who can sell a Good for Nothing Commodity for a Great Price," identity becomes a form of finite individuality. This in turn enables a process of exchange that relies for its very existence on some version of homogeneous computational equivalence. Apart from everything else, what most clearly and systematically emerges from these often angry comments is a sense, which I remarked upon in previous chapters, that the logic of equivalence and exchange in the world of objects necessarily correlates to a certain logic of equality in the world of subjects, and hence that there is some ongoing relationship between the constitution of subjects and of objects in which both are reduced to fixed, definite, exchangeable, intermeasurable, reified units. Ultimately, the "good for nothing Commodity" and the "Intermeasurable Englishman," both scorned by Blake, are two sides of the same coin, the constituent elements of a social order whose basis can only be quantifiable homogeneity.

However, as we saw in chapter 2, the antinomian tradition with which Blake engaged locates in its faith in the eternal and the infinite—that is, in God—a concept of particularity that cannot be reduced to a single, definite, and reified—and hence quantifiable, measurable, and interchangeable—form, even though it is "infinitely various." Blake's defense of "Individual Merit" against the homogenizing "Maw of Commerce," an expression that has often been read reductively as a celebration of bourgeois ideology, should be understood not as a vindication of the reified form of consciousness associated with bourgeois individualism, but rather, as we saw in chapter 3, as a last-ditch defense of just that form of infinite variability evoked by Oothoon, which makes no sense in the dualistic spatiotemporal continuum of bourgeois philosophy because it is quite incompatible with it. However, as we saw in chapter 4, it is only in these terms that we could imagine a world in which one "joy" cannot "absorb" another, not because each is finite and discrete—which would return us to the categories of bourgeois philosophy—but precisely because each is "Holy, eternal, infinite." And it is only in these terms that, as we saw in chapter 5, that we could speak of all people being both "alike" and "infinitely various," a conjunction that would, again, produce an irresolvable contradiction according to the categories of bourgeois philosophy, in which the infinite can only be understood as the opposite of the particular, the eternal as the opposite of the unique, the "same" as the opposite of the "different," and the smooth flow of linear time as the opposite of the eternally returning and repeating time of the infinite.

Alike though infinitely various; the same though perpetually different; infinite, though minutely particularized; eternal, though endlessly repeated: for Blake these terms define all forms of existence. But do they not also define the kinds of images constituting the illuminated books, and indeed the books themselves? Such a suggestion does not quite seem unwarranted. Blake wrote in one of his notebook entries:

Reengravd Time after Time
Ever in their Youthful prime
My Designs unchangd remain
Time may rage but rage in vain

CHAPTER SEVEN

> For above Times troubled Fountains
> On the Great Atlantic Mountains
> In my Golden House on high
> There they Shine Eternally[32]

If these lines are read in Blakean terms, there is absolutely no contradiction between the eternal and unchanging existence of the illuminated books, on the one hand, and, on the other hand, their dazzling and heterogeneous variability and multiplicity. They are the same even though they change: they constantly change even though they are "reengravd Time after Time." Indeed, the sense of heterogeneous, uneven, and fractured time, always folding and refolding on itself, that we have explored in Blake's work, is here shown to be both a time of change and a time of unity, both of the moment and of all eternity, both particular and infinite, precisely like the reiterations by which, as Blake writes in *A Descriptive Catalogue*, "we see the same characters repeated again and again." I am certainly not trying to reintroduce a logic of authorial intention here. I am trying to point out a consequence of reading the illuminated books with a different set of conceptual and interpretive categories from the ones that govern the world we presently inhabit.

And what did Blake introduce into this world? He sold his books and other prints as commodities, to be sure; maybe not "good for nothing Commodities," but commodities all the same. However, those books offer images that articulate a desire to be "Holy, eternal, infinite," precisely in their very particularity; they speak of a joy that must remain incompatible with the quantifiable world of exchange; and above all they speak to beings and to a community based on joy and on giving and on love, rather than on "selling into waste." Yes, there is an incommensurability between Blake's illuminated works and the world we live in. And if they were never regarded as much more than bizarre oddities, however beautiful, it is not because Blake was a bad businessman; it is because he was making art for an audience that literally did not exist, that no longer existed—or that does not yet exist.

 NOTES

Chapter 1

1. William Blake, *A Descriptive Catalogue*, in *The Complete Poetry and Prose of William Blake*, ed. David Erdman (New York: Doubleday, Anchor Books, 1988), E543. Unless otherwise noted, all references to works by Blake are to this edition, identified by the letter *E* preceding the page number.
2. Blake, *Marriage of Heaven & Hell*, E40.
3. Blake, *Laocoön*, E273.
4. Thompson, *Witness against the Beast: William Blake and the Moral Law* (New York: New Press, 1993), p. 20.
5. See Saree Makdisi, *Romantic Imperialism: Universal Empire and the Culture of Modernity* (Cambridge: Cambridge University Press, 1998).
6. Blake, *Public Address*, E580.
7. Blake, annotations to Berkeley, E664. Emphases added.
8. Blake, annotations to Berkeley, E664, and *Divine Image*, in *Songs of Innocence and of Experience*, E13.
9. Fredric Jameson, *Postmodernism* (Durham, N.C.: Duke University Press, 1990), p. 15.
10. In this context, it is interesting to note that Robert Graves, Siegfried Sassoon, and others carried editions of Blake's poetry with them into the trenches of the Western Front.
11. See Mary Wollstonecraft, *A Vindication of the Rights of Woman* (1792; reprint, Harmondsworth: Penguin, 1992), p. 115.
12. Blake, *There is No Natural Religion* [b], E3.
13. Gilles Deleuze, *Spinoza: Practical Philosophy*, trans. Robert Hurley (San Francisco: City Lights, 1988), pp. 123–27.
14. Blake, annotations to Watson, E618.
15. Ibid., E619.
16. See Fredric Jameson, *The Political Unconscious* (Ithaca, N.Y.: Cornell University Press, 1981), pp. 87–88.
17. In an earlier publication, of which the present study forms a kind of extension, I argue that Blake's work contests this notion of history as the history of development. See *Romantic Imperialism*.
18. G. W. F. Hegel, *Introduction to the Philosophy of History*, trans. Leo Rauch (Indianapolis: Hackett, 1986), pp. 88–90.
19. Blake, *No Natural Religion*, 2d ser., E2.
20. Blake, *Descriptive Catalogue*, E543.
21. Blake, *Marriage of Heaven & Hell*, E36.

Chapter 2

1. Henry Crabb Robinson, "William Blake, Artist, Poet, and Religious Mystic," in *Blake Records*, ed. G. E. Bentley (Oxford: Oxford University Press, 1969), p. 454.

2. Alan Cunningham, selection from *Lives of the Most Eminent British Painters, Sculptors, and Architects*, in Blake Records, p. 503.

3. Alexander Gilchrist, *The Life of William Blake* (1863; reprint, Mineola, N.Y.: Dover, 1998), pp. 109–13.

4. Most recent accounts of *America* are derived in one way or another from David Erdman's magnificent study *Blake: Prophet against Empire* (Princeton, N.J.: Princeton University Press, 1977). According to Erdman, *America* tells the story of the American War of Independence and celebrates the goals of the American Revolution and the American Declaration of Independence. John Howard questions Erdman's reading of the significance of Barlow's *Visions of Columbus* as a source for *America* but confirms Erdman's argument that Blake's prophecy "recounts the struggle in America of the contrary forces during the 1770s." See John Howard, *Infernal Poetics: Poetic Structures in Blake's Lambeth Prophecies* (Cranbury, N.J.: Associated University Presses, 1984). Also see Stephen Behrendt, *Reading William Blake* (New York: St. Martin's Press, 1992), and "History When Time Stops: Blake's *America, Europe*, and *The Song of Los*," *Papers on Language and Literature* 28, no. 4 (1992); Michael Ferber, *The Social Vision of William Blake* (Princeton, N.J.: Princeton University Press, 1985), and "Blake's *America* and the Birth of Revolution," in *History and Myth: Essays on English Romantic Literature*, ed. S. Behrendt (Detroit: Wayne State University Press, 1990); Nicholas Williams, *Ideology and Utopia in the Poetry of William Blake* (Cambridge: Cambridge University Press, 1998); and James Swearingen, "William Blake's Figural Politics," in *ELH*, vol. 59 (1992). Other critics have questioned the extent to which *America* can be read simply as a celebration of the War of Independence: Minna Doskow questions such optimistic readings, as does James McCord. See Minna Doskow, "William Blake's *America:* The Story of a Revolution Betrayed," *Blake Studies* 8, no. 2 (1978); and James McCord, "West of Atlantis: William Blake's Unromantic View of the American War," *Centennial Review* 30, no. 1 (1986).

5. See Doskow, "William Blake's *America*," pp. 169–77. Nicholas Williams argues that "the apocalyptic joy of the poem must always be read in the light of this historical deconfirmation, not indeed as an exercise in pessimism but as a way of suggesting that the promises of that earlier struggle have yet to be fulfilled, a fulfillment that they will find only in the medium of history, as Blake's continuation of the line from *America* to *Europe* . . . eventually serves to show." See Nicholas Williams, *Ideology and Utopia*, pp. 116–17.

6. Critics interested in politics often pay more heed to *America* and its sister prophecies from the mid-1790s than to the later works, while those interested in psychic themes generally do the opposite. Erdman's work continues to be the reference point for politically and historically oriented scholarship on Blake. *Blake: Prophet against Empire*, Jackie DiSalvo argues, "definitively established" Blake's place in the political struggles of the era of the French Revolution (though DiSalvo herself is one of the critics who have taken the study of Blake's politics beyond *America*). There is a prevailing consensus, even among such thoroughgoing critics as Helen Bruder, that the task of historicizing Blake in the political context of the 1790s "has been largely completed." See Jackie DiSalvo, *War of Titans: Blake's Critique of Milton and the Politics of Religion* (Pittsburgh: University of Pittsburgh Press, 1983), p. 12; and Helen Bruder, *William Blake and the Daughters of Albion* (New York: St. Martin's Press, 1997), p. 91.

7. Indeed, in *Dangerous Enthusiasm*, one of the most thorough studies of Blake's radicalism, Jon Mee argues that *Prophet against Empire* may ironically have led scholars astray to the extent that its engagement with *America's* politics makes the other prophetic books seem less political by contrast. Since, Mee points out, "Erdman tends to identify political poetry with the representation of historical events," an absence of such explicit representation, as for example in *The Book of Urizen*, "has to signify either a retreat from the political domain or some kind of shadowing of history by an allegorical mythopoesis." See Jon Mee, *Dangerous Enthusiasm: William Blake and the Culture of Radicalism in the 1790s* (Oxford: Oxford University Press, 1994).

8. Blake, annotations to Watson, E618.

9. See David Worrall, "Blake and 1790s Plebeian Radical Culture," in *Blake in the Nineties*, ed. Steve Clark and David Worrall (New York: St. Martin's, 1999); and Jon Mee, "The Strange Career of Richard 'Citizen' Lee: Poetry, Popular Radicalism and Enthusiasm in the 1790s," forthcoming.

10. See Jon Mee, "Is There an Antinomian in the House? William Blake and the After-life of a Heresy," in *Historicizing Blake*, ed. S. Clark and D. Worrall (New York: St Martin's Press, 1994).

11. See Morton Paley, "William Blake, the Prince of the Hebrews, and the Woman Clothed with the Sun," in *William Blake: Essays in Honour of Sir Geoffrey Keynes*, ed. M. Paley and M. Phillips (Oxford: Oxford University Press, 1973).

12. See W. R. H. Trowbridge, *Cagliostro: The Splendour and Misery of a Master of Magic* (London: Chapman and Hall, 1910). I am indebted to Iain McCalman's discussion of Cagliostro in the paper he presented at the "Romantic Metropolis" conference held at the Huntington Library in January 1999.

13. See Mee, *Dangerous Enthusiasm*, p. 5.

14. Iain McCalman, *Radical Underworld: Prophets, Revolutionaries and Pornographers in London, 1795–1840* (Cambridge: Cambridge University Press, 1988), p. 1; also see McCalman, "The Infidel as Prophet: William Reid and Blakean Radicalism," in Clark and Worrall, *Historicizing Blake*.

15. William Hamilton Reid, *The Rise and Dissolution of the Infidel Societies of this Metropolis* (London, 1800), p. 1.

16. See A. L. Morton, *The Everlasting Gospel: A Study in the Sources of William Blake* (London: Lawrence and Wishart, 1958); Michael Ferber, *The Social Vision*; and E. P. Thompson, *Witness against the Beast: William Blake and the Moral Law* (New York: New Press, 1993).

17. The concept of the "everlasting gospel" is invoked both by Blake and the Ranters. See Blake, *Everlasting Gospel*, E518–25; also see Abiezer Coppe, *A Fiery Flying Roll* (1649), reprinted in *A Collection of Ranter Writings from the Seventeenth Century*, ed. Nigel Smith (London: Junction Books, 1983).

18. Iain McCalman, "Introduction," in *The Horrors of Slavery and Other Writings by Robert Wedderburn*, ed. Iain McCalman (New York: Marcus Wiener, 1991), p. 11.

19. See Craig Calhoun, *The Question of Class Struggle: Social Foundations of Popular Radicalism during the Industrial Revolution* (Chicago: University of Chicago Press, 1982).

20. John Thelwall, "The Second Lecture on the Causes of the present Dearness and Scarcity of Provisions, delivered Friday, May 1st, 1795," in *The Politics of English*

Jacobinism: Writings of John Thelwall, ed. G. Claeys (University Park: Pennsylvania State University Press, 1995), pp. 208–9.

21. See James Chandler, *England in 1819* (Chicago: University of Chicago Press, 1998), p. 15.

22. Günther Lottes, "Radicalism, Revolution and Political Culture: An Anglo-French Comparison," in *The French Revolution and British Popular Politics*, ed. Mark Philp (Cambridge: Cambridge University Press, 1991), p. 80. Also see C. B. Macpherson, *The Political Theory of Possessive Individualism: Hobbes to Locke* (Oxford: Clarendon Press, 1963).

23. See Christopher Hill, *The World Turned Upside Down: Radical Ideas during the English Revolution* (Harmondsworth: Penguin, 1991), esp. pp. 344–86, and *Liberty against the Law: Some Seventeenth Century Controversies* (Harmondsworth: Penguin, 1997); and A. L. Morton, *The World of the Ranters: Religious Radicalism in the English Revolution* (London: Lawrence and Wishart, 1970). Kevin Gilmartin notes that "early English radicalism plagued the house of the 'swaggering aristocrat' rather than the shop of the mercantile capitalist, and it only slowly and searchingly formed a labor theory of value that would make capital rather than hereditary privilege the antagonist of the 'useful and productive' classes." See Gilmartin, *Print Politics: The Press and Radical Opposition in Early Nineteenth-Century England* (Cambridge: Cambridge University Press, 1996), p. 102.

24. See Hill, *World Turned Upside Down*, pp. 13–16.

25. London Corresponding Society, *Address to the Nation*, 24 May 1792, in *Selections from the Papers of the London Corresponding Society*, ed. Mary Thale (Cambridge: Cambridge University Press, 1982), p. 10.

26. See Mee, "The Strange Career of Richard 'Citizen' Lee." Also see Reid, *Rise and Dissolution*, p. 6.

27. Thomas Spence, *The End of Oppression* (London, c. 1796).

28. Francis Place, "Notes for a biography of Thomas Spence," Place Collection, British Library (Add. MSS 27,808).

29. See Iain McCalman, "Introduction," p. 12.

30. Blake, annotations to Thornton, E667.

31. According to Etienne Balibar, "the key philosophical notions which are still in use today when dealing with individual rights and personality were actually invented or systematized by Locke." Thus, Balibar says, "we may suggest that the best way of reading Locke is not to characterize him as a 'forerunner' of any of the particular modern ideologies which have become projected into the past (for example, as a supporter of 'possessive individualism,' in a Marxist paradigm, or as a representative of 'natural political virtue,' in a conservative-liberal paradigm), but rather to understand how he made all these different ideologies possible, by creating their common ground." See Etienne Balibar, "What Is 'Man' in Seventeenth-Century Philosophy? Subject, Individual, Citizen," in *The Individual in Political Theory and Practice*, ed. J. Coleman (Oxford: Oxford University Press, 1996), p. 215–41, esp. pp. 233–39.

32. See Lottes, "Radicalism, Revolution and Political Culture," p. 85.

33. See Craig Calhoun, *The Question of Class Struggle: Social Foundations of Popular Radicalism during the Industrial Revolution* (Chicago: University of Chicago Press, 1982).

34. *The Contrast* (n.d., but c. 1795).

35. See E. P. Thompson, *The Making of the English Working Class* (New York: Vintage, 1966), pp. 177–78; Gwyn Williams, *Artisans and Sans-Culottes: Popular Movements in France and Britain during the French Revolution* (London: Edward Arnold, 1968), p. 71–73; and Mark Philp, "The Fragmented Ideology of Reform," in Philp, *The French Revolution*.

36. Calhoun, *The Question of Class Struggle*, p. 36.

37. Calhoun argues that "The relatively elite artisans who formed the core of the LCS were excluded from the main corridors of political power. The artisans called for the opening of these corridors to all sane, noncriminal men. They did not call for an abolition of the particular privileges which they enjoyed. A generation later it would be unthinkable for common workers to cooperate with elite groups which did not include at least a semblance of an appeal to economic reform and equality in their programs." See Calhoun, *The Question of Class Struggle*, p. 36; also see pp. 3–59 more generally.

38. Here I disagree with Dror Wahrman's argument that radical rhetoric such as Paine's was incompatible with the language of a middle class inasmuch as "the language of natural rights was in its essence universal." For Wahrman, Paine represents one end of a binary opposition between "rich" and "poor," an opposition that would set the stage for the emergence of a respectable "middle" in someone like Christopher Wyvill. As I will discuss later on (especially in chap. 5), however, I see radicals like Paine and Wollstonecraft laying claim to a potentially universal middle ground between the enthusiastic mob on the one hand and the debauched aristocracy on the other; and if there seems to be a contradiction in trying to imagine a potentially universal middle, that is precisely the point. See Dror Wahrman, *Imagining the Middle Class: The Political Representation of Class in Britain, 1780–1840* (Cambridge: Cambridge University Press, 1995), pp. 36–41.

39. Blake, *There is No Natural Religion*, E2–3.

40. Blake, *Everlasting Gospel*, E520.

41. Blake, *No Natural Religion*, E2–3. Compare this with the line from *The Marriage of Heaven & Hell*: "God only Acts & Is, in existing being or Men" (E40).

42. Ferber, *The Social Vision*, p. 14. Ferber's book, following through the doors opened by Morton, does an excellent job of enumerating and elaborating many of Blake's political and religious distinctions from the hegemonic form of radicalism. But it ultimately does not complete the transition from thematic explication to an elaboration of Blake's illuminated books on a conceptual level. This is probably due to the fact that Ferber had to postpone more intense conceptual readings to a second book, as he indicates in his preface. My task, following Morton and Ferber and now also Mee, Worrall, and Thompson, is much easier than the one facing Ferber in the mid-1980s. In a sense, what I propose here amounts to a continuation of Ferber's study.

43. Thompson, *Witness against the Beast*, p. 128.

44. See Robert Essick, "William Blake, Thomas Paine, and Biblical Revolution," *Studies in Romanticism* 30 (1991): 199.

45. See Ferber, *The Social Vision*, p. 31.

46. See Richard Price, *Discourse on the Love of our Country* (London, 1789). Also

see Joel Barlow, *Advice to the Privileged Orders, in the Several States of Europe, Resulting from the Necessity and Propriety of a General Revolution in the Principles of Government* (London, 1792).

47. *America*, plate 11 (E55).

48. Thomas Paine, *Rights of Man* (1790–92; reprint, Harmondsworth: Penguin, 1985), p. 210. Also see Chandler, *England in 1819*, pp. 532–54.

49. Paine, *Rights of Man*, p. 162. Constantin Volney had his own version of this. See Volney, *The Ruins of Empires* (1792; reprint, Baltimore: Black Classics Press, 1991), p. 59.

50. See Blake, *King Edward the Third*, E423–38.

51. Behrendt, "History When Time Stops," pp. 382–83. Emphases added.

52. See Ferber, *The Social Vision*, p. 74.

53. See Bruder, *William Blake*, pp. 123–28; and Howard, *Infernal Poetics*, p. 115.

54. See W. J. T. Mitchell, *Blake's Composite Art* (Princeton, N.J.: Princeton University Press, 1978), p. 28.

55. See Northrop Frye, "Poetry and Design in William Blake," in *Discussions of William Blake*, ed. John Grant (Boston: Heath, 1961).

56. See Mitchell, *Blake's Composite Art*, pp. 25, 31.

57. See Nicholas Williams, *Ideology and Utopia*, p. 122.

58. See Peter Middleton, "The Revolutionary Poetics of William Blake," *Oxford Literary Review* 6, no. 1 (1983): 41; and Vincent DeLuca, "Proper Names in the Structural Design of Blake's Myth-Making," *Blake Studies* 8, no. 1 (1978): 9.

59. See, for example, the 24 May 1792 *Public Address* of the London Corresponding Society, or the article denouncing the landing of foreign troops in England in *Politics for the People: Or, A Salmagundy for Swine*, no. 7 (London, 1794).

60. Ferber, *The Social Vision*, p. 125.

61. Erdman sees this plate as Blake's poetic paraphrase of the Declaration of Independence. See Erdman, *Blake*, p. 25.

62. When he wrote those lines, of course, Jefferson himself owned hundreds of slaves.

63. See H. T. Dickinson, *Liberty and Property: Political Ideology in Eighteenth-Century Britain* (New York: Holmes and Meier, 1977), p. 235.

64. See chaps. 5 and 6 for more on Blake and moral virtues.

65. Interestingly enough, the language here comes quite close to the passage in *The Ruins* in which Volney depicts revolution as a mass phenomenon, "a numberless people, rushing in all directions, pour through the streets and fluctuate like waves in the public places." See *The Ruins*, p. 63.

66. Blake, *America*, E57.

67. Paine, *Rights of Man*, pp. 58–59.

68. See Gilchrist, *Life of William Blake*, pp. 36–37; and Peter Linebaugh, *The London Hanged: Crime and Civil Society in the Eighteenth Century* (Cambridge: Cambridge University Press, 1992), pp. 368–70.

69. George Rudé, *The Crowd in the French Revolution* (Oxford: Oxford University Press, 1957), p. 237. Peter Linebaugh shows that the crowd that broke into Newgate freed members of the propertyless class, most of whom were being held for crimes against property. See Linebaugh, *The London Hanged*, pp. 333–70; and George Rudé, *The Crowd in History: A Study of Popular Disturbances in France and England, 1730–*

1848 (London: Lawrence and Wishart, 1981), pp. 183–227, and *Hanoverian London, 1714–1808* (Berkeley: University of California Press, 1971), pp. 47–65.

70. See Erdman, *Blake*, pp. 7–11. Essick has recently suggested that this inscription dates to sometime after 1800, and possibly as late as 1820.

71. Erdman, *Blake*, p. 10.

72. Robert Essick, *William Blake, Printmaker* (Princeton, N.J.: Princeton University Press, 1980), p. 74.

73. Edmund Burke, *Reflections on the Revolution in France* (1790; reprint, Harmondsworth: Penguin, 1986), pp. 193–94.

74. Blake, *America*, E57.

75. From a printed declaration of the Association of Weavers to the public in Bolton, 13 May 1799 (PRO, HO 42/47).

76. See John Lilburne, "An Agreement of the Free People of England" (1649), reprinted in *The English Levellers*, ed. Andrew Sharp (Cambridge: Cambridge University Press, 1998), p. 169.

77. See Richard Overton, "An Arrow Against all Tyrants, shot from the Prison of Newgate into the Prerogative Bowels of the arbitrary House of Lords and all other usurpers and tyrants whatsoever," in Sharp, *English Levellers*, p. 55; and Paine, *Rights of Man*, p. 144 and elsewhere.

78. As long ago as *The Piper and the Bard* (1959), Robert Gleckner argued that in Blake's concept of salvation, "the denial of self, the reachievement of imaginative vision, and the descent and resurrection of Christ are all merged." Gleckner's insight, echoed more recently by Leopold Damrosch, has not yet been adequately taken into account in political and historical examinations of Blake, which tend to place greater emphasis on the history of political events than they do on the history of the *concepts* that we rely upon to understand those events. See Robert Gleckner, *The Piper and the Bard* (Detroit: Wayne State University Press, 1959). Also see David Aers, "Blake: 'Active Evil' and 'Passive Good,'" in *Romanticism and Ideology*, ed. D. Aers et. al. (London: Routledge, 1981). "Rather than seeing history (or the cosmos) as a nightmare from which we are trying to awake," Leopold Damrosch argues, "Blake sees ourselves as the nightmare." See Damrosch, *Symbol and Truth in Blake's Myth* (Princeton, N.J.: Princeton University Press, 1980), p. 139.

79. Blake, *Europe*, E63.

80. Blake, *Book of Ahania*, E88.

81. Blake, *Book of Los*, E92.

82. Blake, *Book of Ahania*, E87.

83. Ibid., E87.

84. Blake, *Europe*, E60.

85. Blake, *Book of Urizen*, E83.

86. Blake, *Song of Los*, E67–68.

87. Blake, *Book of Ahania*, E88.

88. Blake, *America*, E58.

89. Blake, *Marriage of Heaven & Hell*, E34–35.

90. Ibid., E39.

91. See Gilmartin, *Print Politics*, p. 102.

92. Mary Wollstonecraft, *A Vindication of the Rights of Woman* (1792; reprint, Harmondsworth: Penguin, 1992), p. 114.

93. See Wollstonecraft, *A Vindication*, p. 115.

94. Wollstonecraft, *A Vindication*, p. 114. Emphasis added.

95. See Volney, *The Ruins*, pp. 37–38. One of the recurring themes among the conservative writers in the 1790s was that the luxurious lifestyle of the rich and famous employed so many poor people. See, for example, John Bowles, *Dialogues on the Rights of Britons, Between a Farmer, a Sailor, and Manufacturer* (London, 1792), pt. 2, p. 6; and William Paley, *Reasons for Contentment; Addressed to the Labouring Part of the British Public* (London, 1792), p. 5.

96. Volney, *The Ruins*, p. 38.

97. Neil McKendrick argues that "Wedgwood was no mere Gradgrind. He moved in a society of liberal improvers—men who read and gave him to read the works of Priestley, Price, Paine, Rousseau, Cartwright, Howard and Malthus." See Neil McKendrick, "Josiah Wedgwood and Factory Discipline," *Historical Journal* 4, no. 1 (1961): 50.

98. A century after Blake, Oscar Wilde would reiterate similar disgust with the productive efficiency of what would by then be called the bourgeoisie. See *The Complete Works of Oscar Wilde* (New York: Harper and Row, 1989), pp. 1084, 1206.

99. See Peter Linebaugh and Marcus Rediker, *The Many-Headed Hydra: Sailors, Slaves, Commoners, and the Hidden History of the Revolutionary Atlantic* (Boston: Beacon Press, 2000), pp. 211–47; I quote from p. 238. Also see Seth Cotlar, "Radical Conceptions of Property Rights and Economic Equality in the Early American Republic: The Trans-Atlantic Dimension," in *Explorations in Early American Culture*, vol. 4 (2000); Gordon Wood, *The Radicalism of the American Revolution* (New York: Knopf, 1992); and Alfred Young, *Beyond the American Revolution: Explorations in the History of American Radicalism* (De Kalb: Northern Illinois University Press, 1993). Also see Ray Raphael, *A People's History of the American Revolution: How Common People Shaped the Fight for Independence* (New York: New Press, 2001).

100. Alfred Young, *The Shoemaker and the Tea Party: Memory and the American Revolution* (Boston: Beacon Press, 1999), pp. 92–94.

101. See Linebaugh and Rediker, *The Many-Headed Hydra*, p. 240.

102. This is nowhere clearer than in the *Federalist Papers*, which influenced to the framing of the U.S. Constitution in the 1780s. The framers of the U.S. Constitution shared with the hegemonic radicals of London a deep distrust of what we may call "fierce rushing." The author (either Alexander Hamilton or James Madison) of *The Federalist*, no. 62, writes, "It may be suggested, that a people spread over an extensive region cannot, like the crowded inhabitants of a small district, be subject to the infection of violent passions, or to the danger of combining in pursuit of unjust measures." There are, the same author writes, "particular moments in public affairs when the people, stimulated by some irregular passion, or some illicit advantage, or misled by the artful misrepresentations of interested men, may call for measures which they themselves will afterwards be the most ready to lament and condemn. In these critical moments, how salutary will be the interference of some temperate and respectable body of citizens, in order to check the misguided career, and to suspend the blow meditated by the people against themselves, until reason, justice, and truth can regain their authority over the public mind." The author (probably Madison) of *The Federalist*, no. 10, argues that "a pure democracy, by which I mean a society consisting of a small number of citizens, who assemble and administer the government

in person, can admit of no cure for the mischiefs of faction. A common passion or interest will, in almost every case, be felt by a majority of the whole; a communication and concert result from the form of government itself; and there is nothing to check the inducements to sacrifice the weaker party or an obnoxious individual. Hence it is that such democracies have ever been spectacles of turbulence and contention; have ever been found incompatible with personal security and the rights of property; and have in general been as short in their lives as they have been violent in their deaths." The same author concludes, respecting the difference between the form of republicanism that he advocates as opposed to the popular democracy that he dreads, "the effect of the first difference, is, on the one hand, to refine and enlarge the public views, by passing them through the medium of a chosen body of citizens, whose wisdom may best discern the true interest of their country, and whose patriotism and love of justice will be least likely to sacrifice it to temporary or partial considerations. Under such a regulation, it may well happen that the public voice, pronounced by the representatives of the people, will be more consonant to the public good than if pronounced by the people themlselves." See Alexander Hamilton, John Jay, and James Madison, *The Federalist: A Commentary on the United States Constitution* (1787; reprint, New York: Modern Library, n.d.), pp. 164–65, 410.

103. See John Keegan, *A History of Warfare* (New York: Vintage, 1993), pp. 329–34.

104. See the discussion of pikes in Eaton, *Politics for the People*, 2:297–98, 325–31, 359–61. I quote from p. 326.

105. See the affidavit given on 18 May 1794 by Edward Gosling, one of the many government spies infiltrating the LCS (PRO, PC/2/140).

106. Actually, there seems to have been considerable overlap between the two armed factions, since some of the same people attended drill sessions both in Holborn and in Lambeth. See the interrogation of John Philip Franklow on 23 May 1794, PRO, PC/2/140. Another member of the LCS who participated in military drill, the gun engraver Samuel Williams, testified that "They were for a reform of Parliament, and if they could not obtain it in any other way, it was to be by force of Arms. This he recollected from their conversations, particularly from the Language held by Orr at various times—some actually agreed to this, as Williamson—others by their silence." From the interrogation of Samuel Williams, 24 May 1795, PRO, PC/2/140. Spence, for his part, denied involvement in the Lambeth association, though he admitted knowing Franklow and seeing him at his (Spence's) house. See the interrogation of Thomas Spence, 23 May 1795, PRO, PC/2/140. The draft transcript of all these interrogations can be found under PC/1/22/36A in the PRO. In his testimony on 22 May 1794 (PC/2/140), the spy Nodder said that he first went to Spence's house because he had heard that people were drilling there.

107. In its article (13 May 1794) covering the arrest of Thomas Hardy, the secretary of the London Corresponding Society, the *Times* writes that "Hardy, in person, is a tall thin man; much marked in the face with the small pox; his manners low and vulgar: and in dress and habit quite a *Sans Culotte*." In a later article, concerning the treason trials of Hardy and the other LCS leaders (10 October 1794), the *Times* declares that the ideas of the apprehended Jacobins and their allies still at large "extend to a complete subversion of all order and government; aping the manners of the French Convention."

108. See Clive Emsley, "The London 'Insurrection' of December 1792: Fact, Fiction, or Fantasy?" *Journal of British Studies*, 17, no. 2 (spring 1978); Malcolm Thomis and Peter Holt, *Threats of Revolution in Britain, 1789–1848* (London: Archon Books, 1977), pp. 5–28; and Roger Wells, *Insurrection: The British Experience, 1795–1803* (Gloucester: Alan Sutton, 1983), and "English Society and Revolutionary Politics in the 1790s: The Case for Insurrection," in Philp, *The French Revolution*..

109. See David Worrall, *Radical Culture: Discourse, Resistance, and Surveillance, 1790–1820* (New York: Harvester Wheatsheaf, 1993).

110. Wells, *Insurrection*, p. 258.

111. Wells, "English Society and Revolutionary Politics," p. 206.

112. See Emsley, "The London 'Insurrection' of 1792," p. 86.

113. See Paine, *Rights of Man.*, pp. 58–59. Also see Wahrman, *Imagining the Middle Class*, pp. 40–41.

114. See Gwyn Williams, *Artisans and Sans-Culottes*, p. 71–73; and J. Ann Hone, *For the Cause of Truth: Radicalism in London, 1796–1821* (Oxford: Clarendon Press, 1982), p. 20.

115. A perfect example is the pamphlet *Revolutions without Bloodshed; Or, Reformation Preferable to Revolt*, published by Daniel Isaac Eaton in 1794 (PRO, TS/24/3/153).

116. For example, the first public address of the LCS (on 2 April 1792) concludes with a resolution "that this Society do express their *Abhorrence* of Tumult and Violence, and that, as they aim at Reform, not Anarchy, Reason, Firmness, and Unanimity are the only Arms they themselves will employ, or persuade their Fellow-Citizens to exert, against *Abuse of Power.*" And in defence of themselves and to fend off accusations against them of fomenting riots, their 1794 pamphlet *Reformers No Rioters* declared that "One of the fundamental principles of this Society, and a lesson that we have ever industriously inculcated is, that riot, tumult and violence are not the fit means of obtaining a redress of grievances" (London Corresponding Society, *Selections from the Papers*).

117. Testimony of the spy Gosling, PRO, PC/2/140. He goes on to say that the arming members asked themselves "Is there any one who believes a Parliamentary Reform is all we want,—no not one."

118. See McCalman, "Introduction," p. 14. Also see John Belchem, *Industrialization and the Working Class: The English Experience, 1750–1900* (London: Scolar Press, 1990), p. 70.

119. See Wells, *Insurrection*.

120. See Thompson, *Making of the English Working Class*, pp. 177–78.

121. See Kathryn Sutherland, "'Events . . . Have Made Us a World of Readers:' Reader Relations 1780–1830," in *Penguin History of Literature: The Romantic Period*, ed. D. Pirie (Harmondsworth: Penguin, 1994); also see Olivia Smith, *The Politics of Language, 1791–1819* (Oxford: Clarendon Press, 1984), p. 70.

122. See Olivia Smith, *The Politics of Language*, p. 64.

123. Anonymous letter to the solicitor general, PRO, TS/11/978/3560.

124. See *The Trial of Daniel Isaac Eaton for Publishing a Supposed Libel, Intutled Politics for the People; or Hog's Wash: at Justice Hall in the Old Bailey, February 24th, 1794* (London, 1794).

125. See Barlow, *Advice to the Privileged Orders*, p. 20.

126. Anonymous letter from a spy to Joseph Banks, dated 22/4/94, in PRO, TS/11/953/3497. The author of another anonymous letter, to the *Sun*, dated 29 March 1794, writes: "I cannot suggest a better channell than yourself to point out to the Guardians of our Laws, one J Thelwall No 3 New Compton Street Soho, who delivers a sort of Lecture every Friday—This advertisement in the Morning Chronicle . . . led me to attend it, with the view of speaking in defence of our happy Constitution—but about 8 o clock at night I found a small room quite full, & himself only addressing an Audience who violently applauded every stroke of sedition—As he professed more to instruct the lower class than appeal to the reflecting part, the Poison of his Doctrine is more likely to be extensively propagated, & I assure you the vehemence of his Zeal & bitterness, not altogether destitute of coarse Wit, cause a great sensation among his hearers, & render him in My Mind a Most dangerous member of Society" (PRO, TS/11/953/3497).

127. See Worrall, *Radical Culture*, p. 23.

128. Michael Phillips, *William Blake: The Creation of the Songs, from Manuscript to Illuminated Printing* (London: British Library, 2000), p. 112.

129. Blake, memoranda from the notebook, E694.

130. See Keri Davies, "Mrs. Bliss: A Blake Collector of 1794," in Clark and Worrall, *Blake in the Nineties*.

131. Phillips, *Creation of the Songs*, p. 112. Also see Phillips, "Blake and the Terror, 1792–93," *Library* 16, no. 4 (1994): 290–95.

132. See D. W. Dörbecker, "Innovative Reproduction: Painters and Engravers at the Royal Academy," in Clark and Worrall, *Historicizing Blake*, p. 138.

133. See Essick, "William Blake, Thomas Paine," p. 190. Also see Mee, *Dangerous Enthusiasm*, pp. 220–23.

134. Mee, *Dangerous Enthusiasm*, p. 220–21.

135. Essick, "William Blake, Thomas Paine," p. 212.

136. Terry Eagleton, *Criticism and Ideology* (London: Verso, 1988), p. 153.

137. See Gregory Claeys, *Thomas Paine: Social and Political Thought* (Boston: Unwin Hyman, 1989), p. 76.

138. Thomas Paine, *Rights of Man, Part II*, pp. 182–83.

139. Paine, *Rights of Man II*, p. 184.

140. Paine, *Rights of Man II*, p. 213.

141. Paine, *Rights of Man II*, p. 212.

142. See Claeys, *Thomas Paine*, p. 99.

143. By the time of *Agrarian Justice* (1797), Paine would dilute his commercial optimism with a stronger redistributive mechanism, for which Spence—whose own *Rights of Man* had stressed the importance of economic as well as political equality—congratulated him. Even then, Paine's new scheme, as Spence pointed out, called for the redistribution of some 10 percent of the land; Spence favored redistributing 100 percent. See Claeys, *Thomas Paine*, p. 207.

144. John Thelwall, letter dated 13 February 1794, PRO, TS/11/953/3497.

145. See John Thelwall, "The Connection between the Calamities of the Present Reign, and the System of Borough-Mongering Corruption—Lecture the Third.—The Connection between Parliamentary Corruption and Commercial Monopoly; with Strictures on the West-India Subscription, &c. Delivered Wednesday, Oct. 14, 1795," in Claeys, *The Politics of English Jacobinism*, p. 283.

146. See Thompson, *Making of the English Working Class*, pp. 159–60.

147. See John Thelwall, "Rights of Nature, Against the Usurpations of Establishments. A Series of Letters to the People, in Reply to the False Principles of Burke," in Claeys, *The Politics of English Jacobinism*, p. 478.

148. John Thelwall, "Second Lecture on the Causes of the present Dearness," p. 188.

149. Ibid., p. 195.

150. See Philp, "Fragmented Ideology," p. 52.

151. "Commerce, uncorrupted by monopolizing speculation, is one of the greatest advantages that result from social union. It is by this that the comforts and accomodations of each quarter of the globe are transplanted to every other, and that every individual spot of the universe might be benefited by the knowledge of all the rest. A fair and liberal spirit of commerce has a considerable tendency to inform the understanding of mankind, to increase the progress of intelligence, and above all, to do away the ridiculous and destructive principles of nationality.—The intercourse of man with man, and nation with nation, of the trader of one country with the trader of another, if conducted on liberal and equal principles, must certainly remove the delusive idea that humanity and virtue are the attributes of a particular soil, and convince us that we ought to extend the narrow sphere of our affections, and in all our schemes of justice and policy, to regard alike the happiness and welfare of the whole universe; because all the inhabitants of the universe are but one family." See Thelwall, "The Connection . . . Lecture the Third," pp. 285–86.

152. See Thelwall, "Second Lecture on the Causes of the present Dearness," pp. 208–9.

153. John Thelwall, *Sober Reflections on the Seditious and Inflammatory Letter by the Right Hon. Edmund Burke, to a Noble Lord* (London, 1796), pp. 33–34.

154. Philp, "Fragmented Ideology," p. 56.

155. See the published pamphlet *The Restorer of Society to its Natural State*, by Spence (London, 1801), found in the Place Collection (Add. MSS 27,808; 254–78) in the British Library.

156. See Jon Mee, "Is There an Antinomian in the House?"

157. See Morton Paley, "William Blake," pp. 281–83. Also see Crabb Robinson's story about Blake's refusing to join Brothers; "such men as Blake are not fond of playing the second fiddle," Robinson notes (quoted in Bentley, *Blake Records*, p. 235).

158. See Philp, "Fragmented Ideology," p. 55.

159. Lynn Lees, *The Solidarities of Strangers: The English Poor Laws and the People, 1700–1948* (Cambridge: Cambridge University Press, 1998), p. 82.

160. See the first public declaration of the London Corresponding Society, April 1792 (London Corresponding Society, *Selections from the Papers*).

161. It was undoubtedly a major turning point in English political history when, at its first meetings, the LCS members resolved in the affirmative the debate over whether "we who are Treadsmen—Shopkeepers and mechanicks have any right to seek to obtain a parliamentary reform?" (from Hardy's account of the beginnings of the LCS; Add. MSS 27814 in the British Library).

162. See Anna Clark, *The Struggle for the Breeches: Gender and the Making of the British Working Class* (Berkeley: University of California Press, 1995), pp. 141–57.

163. "An Explanation of the Word 'Equality'" (London, 1793). Emphases in

original. Also see the remarkably similar pamphlet "The Perverse Definition Imposed on the Word Equality" (London, 1792). At the LCS General Committee Meeting on 10 January 1793, there was "A Motion for printing an Excellent explanation of the word equality—but cautious of not running the Society into debt—it was negatived—but each of the delegates agreed to subscribe and have it printed and distributed at their own expence." See London Corresponding Society, *Selections from the Papers*, pp. 41–42.

164. According to an LCS handbill of 29 November 1792, "*Difference of Strength, of Talents, and of Industry, do and ought to afford proportional Distinctions of Property, which,* when acquired and confirmed by the Laws, *is sacred and inviolable.*" See London Corresponding Society, *Selections from the Papers*, p. 32. Eaton argued that in a reformed political system private property (and hence gradations of wealth) would be allowed but insisted that extremes of wealth and poverty would be reduced. See Daniel Isaac Eaton, "An Essay on the Influence of some Human Institutions on Human Happiness," *Philanthropist*, December 1795, pp. 2–3.

165. See Dickinson, *Liberty and Property*, pp. 235–36.

166. See Clark, *Struggle for the Breeches*, pp. 146–47.

167. Ibid., p. 146.

168. Blake, annotations to Berkeley, E664.

169. See Christopher Hobson, *Blake and Homosexuality* (New York: Palgrave, 2000).

170. Burke, *Reflections*, p. 271; also see pp. 140–41.

171. Thelwall, "Rights of Nature" p. 478. Also see Burke, *Reflections*, p. 311.

172. See Burke, *Reflections*, p. 271. Also see Edmund Burke, *Thoughts and Details on Scarcity, Originally Presented to the Rt. Hon. William Pitt, in the Month of November, 1795* (London, 1800), p. 13.

173. See George Dyer, *The Complaints of the Poor People of England* (London, 1793), p. 84.

174. See Thomas Malthus, *An Essay on the Principle of Population* (London: Joseph Johnson, 1798).

175. Gregory Claeys, *Machinery, Money and the Millennium: From Moral Economy to Socialism, 1815–1860* (Princeton, N.J.: Princeton University Press, 1987), pp. 20–21.

176. See, however, Roger Wells on the connection between radical societies and trade unionism in London ("English Society and Revolutionary Politics," esp. pp. 203–7).

177. Belchem, *Industrialization and the Working Class*, pp. 61–62.

178. Letter from Thomas Bayley and Henry Norris to Henry Dundas, 19 July 1792, PRO, HO 42/19.

179. Letter from Henry Blundell to William Pitt, 14 April 1792, PRO, HO 42/20.

180. Letter from Henry Blundell to Henry Dundas, 27 May 1792, PRO, HO 42/20.

181. Letter from Col. De Lancey to the secretary of war, 13 June 1792, PRO, HO 42/20.

182. Letter from Capt. George Monro to Henry Dundas, 9 August 1792, PRO, HO 42/22.

183. Letter from Henry Blundell to Henry Dundas, 1 October 1792, PRO, HO 42/22.
184. Letter from Edmund Lacon to the Marquess Townshend, 30 October 1792, PRO, HO 42/22.
185. Letter from Thomas Powditch to William Pitt, 3 November 1792, PRO, HO 42/22.
186. See, for example, the printed declaration of the Association of Weavers to the public in Bolton, 13 May 1799, PRO, HO 42/47.
187. A clipping dated 16 Dec 1799 in the microfilm series of the Place Collection in the British Library (reel 10). Note how close the wording of this working people's declaration comes to Blake's language in his annotations to Reynolds and his *Public Address* (E635–56; E571–81).
188. See Wells, "English Society and Revolutionary Politics," p. 205.
189. Orders issued by Admiral Adam Duncan to the captain of HMS *Vestal*, 26 May 1797, PRO, ADM 1/524.
190. Letter from Admiral Adam Duncan to Evan Nepean, 17 June 1797, PRO, ADM 1/524.
191. There are countless examples of this. Hannah More produced many pamphlets and dialogues whose constant theme was that political republicanism would inevitably lead to economic catastrophe, a message summed up in the seal in the preface to *Village Politics*, which contrasts "French Liberty" and "British Liberty" and asks, "Which is best? French Liberty: Atheism. Perjury. Rebellion. Treason. Anarchy. Murder. Equality. Madness. Cruelty. Injustice. Treachery. Ingratitude. Idleness. Famine. National & Private Ruin. Misery... British Liberty: Religion. Morality. Loyalty. Obedience to the Laws. Independance. Personal Security. Justice. Inheritance. Protection. Property. Industry. National Prosperity. Happiness." See Hannah More, *Village Politics: Addressed to all Mechanics, Journeymen, and Day-Labourers in Great Britain* (Durham, 1793). Also see *A New Dialogue Between Monsieur Francois and John English, on the French Revolution* (London, 1793); John Bowles, *Dialogues on the Rights of Britons* (London, 1792); *Political Dialogues upon the Subject of Equality* (London, 1792); *A Few Plain Questions, and a Little Honest Advice, to the Working People of Great Britain* (London, 1792); Richard Hey, *Happiness and Rights* (London, 1792); and William Playfair, *Better Prospects to the Masters and Manufacturers of Great Britain* (London, 1793).
192. The often panicked letters by justices of the peace and other respectable citizens to Pitt or Dundas in the Home Office Papers provide some of the best evidence of this. See PRO, HO 42/20–22.
193. See, for example, the denunciation of republicans and levellers by an anonymous author in 1793, in *A Caution Against the Levellers* (London, 1793), p. 13.
194. See Blake, annotations to Reynolds, E635–56.
195. Richard Watson, *A Defence of Revealed Religion, in Two Sermons* (London, 1797), p. 2.
196. Also see William Huntington, *A Watchword and a Warning from the Walls of Zion* (London, 1798).
197. Burke, *Thoughts and Details on Scarcity*, p. 4.
198. Blake, *The Chimney Sweeper*, from *Songs of Experience*, E22.
199. See William Wordsworth, "A Letter to the Bishop of Llandaff," written in

1793 but published posthumously in 1876, in *William Wordsworth: Selected Prose*, ed. John Hayden (Harmondsworth: Penguin, 1988), pp. 139–60.

200. Blake, annotations to Watson, E611–20. Gilbert Wakefield was sentenced to two years in prison for his supposedly libelous attack on the bishop. See Gilbert Wakefield, *A Reply to Some Parts of the Bishop of Llandaff's Address to the People of Great Britain* (London, 1798).

201. Blake, annotations to Watson, E612. Even Gilbert Wakefield, who attacked Watson for the latter's comparison of society to a building with several levels, admits in his own pamphlet that, "with respect to rank and riches . . . it follows, I think, most unquestionably, that no distinctions in society should prevail, but what arise from personal merit and public services." See Wakefield, *A Reply*, pp. 16, 38.

202. See Thompson, *Witness against the Beast*, p. 52.

203. Blake, annotations to Watson, E611.

204. Ibid., E618.

205. Ibid., E616.

206. Ibid., E614.

207. See Ferber's chapter on religious and political liberty in *The Social Vision*, pp. 116–30.

208. See DiSalvo, *War of Titans*, esp. pp. 274–86.

209. See William Hurd's *New Universal History of the Religious Rites, Ceremonies and Customs of the Whole World* (1785), p. 639.

210. E. P. Thompson, *Witness against the Beast*, p. 19.

211. See Mee, *Dangerous Enthusiasm*.

212. Thompson, *Witness against the Beast*, pp. 62–63.

213. Ibid., p. 106.

214. Hurd, *New Universal History*, p. 669.

215. *The Advantage of a National Observation of Divine and Human Laws: A Discourse in Defence of our Admirable Constitution by a Layman in the County of Suffolk* (London, 1792), p. 9.

216. Burke, *Reflections*, p. 194.

217. Huntington, *Watchword*, p. 41.

218. Ibid., pp. 74–75.

219. Maria de Fleury, *Antinomianism Unmasked and Refuted; and the Moral Law Proved from the Scriptures of the Old and New-Testament* (London, 1791), p. 13.

220. *Antinomianism Explained and Exploded* (Coventry, 1790), p. 9.

221. Hurd, *New Universal History*, p. 640.

222. See Mee, *Dangerous Enthusiasm*, pp. 49–57.

223. Hurd, *New Universal History*, pp. 640–41.

224. Blake, *The Little Vagabond*, E26.

225. *Essay on Trade and Commerce* (London, 1770), p. 52.

226. Ibid., p. 56.

227. See Dickinson, *Liberty and Property*, p. 246.

228. See Belchem, *Industrialization and the Working Class*, pp. 85–86.

229. See Jon Mee, *Romanticism, Enthusiasm and Regulation* (Oxford: Oxford University Press, forthcoming).

230. Thompson, *Witness against the Beast*, p. 128.

231. Karl Marx, *Capital* (1857; reprint, New York: Vintage, 1977), 1:926.

232. Thompson, *Witness against the Beast*, p. 111.
233. Jacob Bronowski and Bruce Mazlish discuss the ways in which such institutions as the Lunar Society mediated the relations between the liberal-radicals of the American independence movement and those of 1790s England. See Jacob Bronowski and Bruce Mazlish, *The Western Intellectual Tradition* (New York: Harper, 1960), pp. 307–35.
234. Blake, *Four Zoas*, E355.
235. Gilchrist, *Life of William Blake*, p. 111.

Chapter 3
1. Blake, *Book of Urizen*, E75.
2. Ibid., E78.
3. Ibid., E81.
4. Ibid., E82.
5. Blake, *Book of Ahania*, E88.
6. Blake, *Book of Los*, E93.
7. F. B. Curtis, "William Blake and Eighteenth-Century Medicine," *Blake Studies* 8, no. 2 (1979): 188.
8. See Robert Essick, *William Blake's Commercial Book Illustrations* (Oxford: Clarendon Press, 1991), p. 61.
9. See Stefani Engelstein, "Organs of Meaning: The 'Natural' Human Body in Literature and Science of the Late Eighteenth and Early Nineteenth Centuries" (Ph.D. diss., University of Chicago, 2001).
10. See Essick, *William Blake's Commercial Book Illustrations*, pp. 45–49.
11. John Locke, *Essay Concerning Human Understanding* (Oxford: Oxford University Press, 1979), pp. 162–63.
12. Here I do not intend that concept proposed by Deleuze and Guattari (though I think they have something similar in mind). See Gilles Deleuze and Félix Guattari, *Anti-Oedipus: Capitalism and Schizophrenia* (Minneapolis: University of Minnesota Press, 1983).
13. "There are two meanings of the word 'subect,'" Foucault argues: "Subject to someone else by control and dependence, and tied to his own identity by a conscience or self-knowledge. Both meanings suggest a form of power that subjugates and makes subject to." See Michel Foucault, "The Subject and Power," trans. Robert Hurley et al., in *Essential Works of Michel Foucault, 1954–1984*, vol. 3: *Power*, ed. Paul Rabinow (New York: New Press, 2000), p. 330.
14. According to the OED, "organization" originally referred to "the action of organizing, or condition of being organized, as a living being; also, the way in which a living being is organized; the structure of an organized body (animal or plant), or of any part of one; bodily (*rarely* mental) constitution."
15. *A Dialogue Between a Gentleman and a Mechanic* (London, 1800), pp. 4–7.
16. Andrew Ure, *The Philosophy of Manufactures; Or, an Exposition of the Scientific, Moral, and Commercial Economy of the Factory System of Great Britain* (London, 1835), pp. 13–14.
17. See Fredric Jameson, *The Political Unconscious* (Ithaca, N.Y.: Cornell University Press, 1981), pp. 87–88.
18. Blake, *America*, E53.

19. Hence, perhaps, the striking similarity to the antinomian projects of the seventeenth century. See, e.g., Abiezer Coppe, *Some Sips, of Some Sweet Spirituall Wine*, in *A Collection of Ranter Writings from the Seventeenth Century*, ed. Nigel Smith (London: Junction Books, 1983), p. 51.

20. I will use the term "organs" here to refer to body parts in general, sacrificing medical accuracy in order to keep the distinction between organ and organism in full view.

21. Blake, *Jerusalem*, E165.

22. Frederick Morton Eden, *The State of the Poor: Or, An History of the Labouring Classes in England* (London, 1797), vol. 1, pp. 421–22. Also see John Fielden, *The Curse of the Factory System* (London, 1836).

23. See Stephen Behrendt, *Reading William Blake* (New York: St. Martin's Press, 1992), p. 127.

24. See Helen Bruder, *William Blake and the Daughters of Albion* (New York: St. Martin's Press, 1997), pp. 55–99, esp. pp. 73–99.

25. Ibid., pp. 77–78.

26. Ibid., p. 57.

27. Blake, *Visions of the Daughters of Albion*, E49–50.

28. Recall the "Proverb of Hell" "Brothels are built with bricks of religion" in *The Marriage of Heaven & Hell*, E36.

29. See Laurence Clarkson, *A Single Eye*, in Smith, *A Collection of Ranter Writings*, p. 169.

30. Blake, *Visions of the Daughters of Albion*, E50.

31. Ibid., E47.

32. Clarkson, *A Single Eye*, pp. 172–73.

33. Blake, *Visions of the Daughters of Albion*, E49.

34. Blake, *America*, E52.

35. Lynn Lees, *The Solidarities of Strangers: The English Poor Laws and the People, 1700–1948* (Cambridge: Cambridge University Press, 1998), p. 108.

36. See Patrick Colquhoun, *A Plan for the Purpose of Affording Extensive Relief to the Poor* (London, 1795).

37. *Essay on Trade and Commerce* (London, 1770), p. 60.

38. Ibid., p. 52.

39. See Patrick Colquhoun, *The State of Indigence, and the Situation of the Casual Poor, in the Metropolis, Explained* (London, 1799), p. 11.

40. Colquhoun, *State of Indigence*, p. 18. When Colquhoun expanded this study into his even more systematic *Treatise on Indigence* in 1806, his sentiments would become even clearer: "*Poverty* is therefore a most necessary and indispensable ingredient in society, without which nations and communities could not exist in a state of civilization. It is the lot of man—it is the source of wealth, since without poverty there would be no *labour*; and without *labour* there could be no *riches*, no *refinement*, no *comfort*, and no *benefit* to those who may be possessed of wealth—inasmuch as without a large proportion of poverty surplus labour could never be rendered productive in procuring either the conveniences or luxuries of life." See Patrick Colquhoun, *A Treatise on Indigence; Exhibiting a General View of the National Resources for Productive Labour* (London, 1806), pp. 7–8.

41. Colquhoun, *State of Indigence*, p. 18.

NOTES TO PAGES 102–104

42. See Peter Linebaugh, *The London Hanged: Crime and Civil Society in the Eighteenth Century* (Cambridge: Cambridge University Press, 1992), p. 427.

43. See Lees, *The Solidarities of Strangers*, p. 107.

44. Thomas Ruggles, *The History of the Poor: Their Rights, Their Duties, and the Laws Respecting them* (London, 1797), p. 59.

45. *Report of the Philanthropic Society, Instituted September 1788, for the Prevention of Crimes, and the Reform of the Criminal Poor, by the Encouragement of Industry, and the Culture of Good Morals, among those Children who are now training Up to Vicious Courses, public Plunder, Infamy and Ruin* (London, 1790), p. 3.

46. See Robert Young, *The Undertaking for the Reform of the Poor, of which a Principal Branch is the Asylum for Industry* (London, 1792), pp. 4–5.

47. I. Wood, *Some Account of the Shrewsbury House of Industry* (Shrewsbury, 1795), p. 9.

48. Edward Wilson, *Observations on the Present State of the Poor, and Measures Proposed for its Improvement* (Reading, 1795), p. 7–8

49. *Letters on the Utility and Policy of Using Machines to Shorten Labour; Occasioned by the Late Disturbances in Lancashire* (London, 1780), p. 2

50. Patrick Colquhoun, *An Account of the Rise, Progress, and Present State of the Charity School for the Education of Boys in the Parish of St Leonard, Shoreditch* (London, 1793), p. 19

51. *Report of the Philanthropic Society*, p. 4

52. Wood, *Some Account*, p. 9.

53. *Account of the Foundling Hospital in London* (London, 1799), p. 65

54. *A Brief Account of the Charity School at St. Pancras for Instructing, Cloathing, Qualifying for Useful Servants, and Putting out to Service, the Female Children of the Industrious Poor* (London, 1795), p. 4

55. *An Abstract from the Account of the Asylum, of House of Refuge, Situated in the Parish of Lambeth, for the Reception of Friendless and Deserted Orphan Girls* (London, 1794), pp. 4–5. Emphasis in original.

56. See Fielden, *The Curse of the Factory System*, pp. 6–7.

57. Thomas Simons, *A Letter to Every Housekeeper in London, on Behalf of Parochial Industry Schools* (London, 1792), p. 13.

58. Wilson, *Observations on the Present State of the Poor*, p. 25.

59. See, for example, J. H. Plumb, "The Commercialization of Leisure," in *The Birth of a Consumer Society*, ed. N. McKendrick, J. Brewer, and J. Plumb (London: Europa, 1982).

60. Richard Dienst argues that this long-sought-after dream would be accomplished at least in part with the development of television: "If the machine system of large-scale industry radically collectivized and redistributed social labor time according to capitalist imperatives, the television system now performs the same function for other segments of time: pleasure time, public or community time, household time, parenting time, childhood time, even animal and vegetable time. In a word, some share of what used to be called 'disposable time' is put at the disposal of television, so that non-work time becomes subject to the same kinds of antagonisms that cut across labor time." See Richard Dienst, *Still Life in Real Time: Theory after Television* (Durham, N.C.: Duke University Press, 1994), p. 59.

61. *Essay on Trade and Commerce*, p. 153.

62. William Young, *Considerations on the Subject of Poor-Houses and Work-Houses* (London, 1796), p. 16.

63. George Dyer, *The Complaints of the Poor People of England* (London, 1793), p. 61.

64. William Young, *Considerations*, pp. 20–21; also see pp. 24, 32.

65. See Edmund Bott and Francis Const, eds., *Decisions of the Court of King's Bench, Upon the Laws Relating to the Poor* (London, 1793).

66. See David Porter, *Considerations on the Present State of Chimney Sweepers* (London, 1792); and J. P. Andrews, *An Appeal to the Humane, on Behalf of the Most Deplorable Class of Society, the Climbing-Boys Employed by the Chimney-Sweepers* (London, 1788).

67. Porter writes, in a passage that anticipates of Blake's treatment of the chimney sweeper in *Songs of Innocence and of Experience*, "If we would see this poor apprentice as he really is, let us view him in a wintry morning exposed to the surly blast or a falling snow, trudging the streets half naked, his sores bleeding, his limbs contracted with cold, his inhuman maser driving him beyond his strength, whilst the pitious tears of hunger and misery trickle down his cheek, which is, indeed, the only means he has to vent his grief; follow him home, and view him in his gloomy cell, and there will be found misery unmasked: we shall see this poor boy in a cellar, used as a foot warehouse on one side, and his lodging room on the other; I would have said his bed-room, but he has seldom any other bed than his sack, or any other covering than his foot cloth: in this comfortless state he shiveringly sleeps, or rather passes over the chilly hours of night. It would be some consolation to the boy if in six days of misery he could anticipate the seventh as a respite, not only from his sooty labours, but his gloomy cell, to be washed from his filth so as to be admitted into society and the public worship of his God; but alas! his whole wardrobe is a ragged shirt and tattered breeches, both of the sable hue. From those disadvantages he is banished from society, and can associate only with the companions of his own misery." See Porter, *Considerations on the Present State of Chimney Sweepers*, pp. 30–31.

68. J. Howlett, *Examination of Mr Pitt's Speech in the House of Commons, on Friday, February 12, 1796, Relative to the Conditions of the Poor* (London, 1796), p. 2.

69. Eden, *The State of the Poor*, 1:421–22.

70. Deborah Valenze, *The First Industrial Woman* (Oxford: Oxford University Press, 1995), esp. pp. 85–127; Anna Clark, *The Struggle for the Breeches: Gender and the Making of the British Working Class* (Berkeley: University of California Press, 1995), esp. pp. 13–24.

71. See E. P. Thompson, *The Making of the English Working Class* (New York: Vintage, 1966), pp. 269–313.

72. See Richard Guest, *A Compendious History of the Cotton-Manufacture* (Manchester, 1823).

73. See David Erdman, *Blake: Prophet against Empire* (Princeton, N.J.: Princeton University Press, 1977), pp. 329–40.

74. See Guest, *A Compendious History*, p. 47.

75. See "On the Employment of Children in Cotton and other Factories" (London, 17 August 1825), in the Place Collection in the British Library.

76. In his book *The Curse of the Factory System* (London, 1832), the MP for Oldham John Fielden recalls from his own boyhood (in the late 1790s and early 1800s),

working seventy-one hours per week in a factory that was trying to catch up with competitors who made their hands work eighty-four hours a week, until an act in 1819 stopped that. Fielden notes that the new machines actually led to increased work and work-time: "Here, then, is the 'curse' of our factory-system: as improvements in machinery have gone on, the 'avarice of masters' has prompted many to exact more labour from their hands than they were fitted by nature to perform." See Fielden, *The Curse of the Factory System*, p. 34.

77. See John Belchem, *Industrialization and the Working Class: The English Experience, 1750–1900* (London: Scolar Press, 1990), p. 46.

78. Colin Campbell, *The Romantic Ethic and the Spirit of Modern Consumerism* (Oxford: Basil Blackwell, 1987), p. 25.

79. See Plumb, "The Commercialization of Leisure"; and Neil McKendrick, "The Consumer Revolution of Eighteenth-Century England," and "The Commercialization of Fashion," in McKendrick, Brewer, and Plumb, *The Birth of a Consumer Society*.

80. Fernand Braudel, *Capitalism and Material Life, 1400–1800* (New York: Harper and Row, 1973), p. 33.

81. See David Green, *From Artisans to Paupers: Economic Change and Poverty in London, 1790–1870* (London: Scolar Press, 1995), p. 82.

82. John Thelwall, "Rights of Nature, Against the Usurpations of Establishments. A Series of Letters to the People, in Reply to the False Principles of Burke," in *The Politics of English Jacobinism: Writings of John Thelwall*, ed. Gregory Claeys (University Park: Penn State University Press, 1995), p. 478.

83. *Hints Respecting the Distresses of the Poor* (London, 1795), pp. 3–5.

84. See Peter Ackroyd, *Blake* (London: Minerva, 1996), pp. 130–31.

85. Society for the Diffusion of Useful Knowledge, *The Working-Man's Companion: The Results of Machinery, Namely, Cheap Production and Increased Employment, Exhibited; Being an Address to the Working-Men of the United Kingdom* (London, 1831), p. 180.

86. Colquhoun, *A Plan for the Purpose of Affording Extensive Relief*, p. 1.

87. See E. P. Thompson, "Time, Work-Discipline and Industrial Capitalism," in *Customs in Common*, (New York: New Press, 1993). Also see Richard Biernacki, *The Fabrication of Labour* (Berkeley: University of California Press, 1997), pp. 351–85.

88. See Neil McKendrick, "Josiah Wedgwood and Factory Discipline," *Historical Journal* 4, no. 1 (1961): 38.

89. See Gerhard Dohrn–Van Rossum, *History of the Hour: Clocks and Modern Temporal Orders* (Chicago: University of Chicago Press, 1997), p. 279.

90. See Linebaugh, *The London Hanged*, pp. 371–441.

91. River work employed perhaps a third of the London workforce. See Linebaugh, *The London Hanged*, pp. 417–18.

92. See Samuel Bentham, *Report to the Royal Navy Concerning Dockyard Labour System* (London, 1800), pp. 5, 10–11, 15. Also see Linebaugh's marvelous chapter "Ships and Chips: Technological Repression and the Origin of the Wage," in *The London Hanged*, pp. 371–401, which is largely concerned with Bentham's project.

93. John Thelwall, *The Natural and Constitutional Right of Britons to Annual Parliaments, Universal Suffrage, and the Freedom of Popular Association; Being a Vindication of the Motives and Political Conduct of John Thelwall, and of the London Corresponding So-*

ciety in General, Intended to have been Delivered at the Bar of the Old Bailey, in Confutation of the Late Charges of High Treason (London, 1795).

94. Published circular by committee of mechanics in Glasgow, 1811, in the Place Collection in the British Library, microfilm set, reel 10.

95. Edmund Burke, *Thoughts and Details on Scarcity, Originally Presented to the Rt. Hon. William Pitt, in the Month of November, 1795* (London, 1800), p. 13.

96. Ibid., p. 18.

97. Ibid., p. 26. Also see Wilson, *Observations on the Present State of the Poor*, p. 12.

98. Marx, of course, has another way of expressing what happens when the laws of commerce produce an unacceptable result. With regard to the working day, he writes: "Leaving aside certain extremely elastic restrictions, the nature of the commodity itself imposes no limit to the working day, no limit to surplus labour. The capitalist maintains his rights as a purchaser when he tries to make the working day as long as possible, and, where possible, to make two working days out of one. On the other hand, the peculiar nature of the commodity sold implies a limit to its consumption by the purchaser, and the worker maintains his right as a seller when he wishes to reduce the working day to a particular normal length. There is here therefore an antinomy, of right against right, both equally bearing the seal of the law of exchange. Between equal rights, force decides. Hence, in the history of capitalist production, the establishment of a norm for the working day presents itself as a struggle over the limits of that day, a struggle between collective capital, i.e., the class of capitalists, and collective labour, i.e., the working class" (Karl Marx, *Capital* [1857; reprint, New York: Vintage, 1977], 1:344).

99. Thelwall, "Rights of Nature," pp. 398–99.

100. Thelwall, "Third Lecture on the Causes of the Present DEARNESS & SCARCITY of PROVISIONS, delivered Wednesday, May 6th, 1795," in Claeys, *The Politics of English Jacobinism*, p. 194.

101. See Thelwall, "Rights of Nature," p. 477.

102. Blake, *Book of Urizen*, E83.

103. See, for example, the report in the *Statesman*, 22 June 1811, of the Committee of the House of Commons on the petition of the weavers. From the Place Collection in the British Library, microfilm set, reel 14.

104. Marx, *Capital*, 1:456–57.

105. Ibid., 1:448–49.

106. See Green, *From Artisans to Paupers*, pp. 80–102.

107. See Clark, *Struggle for the Breeches*, pp. 25–41.

108. Craig Calhoun, *The Question of Class Struggle: Social Foundations of Popular Radicalism during the Industrial Revolution* (Chicago: University of Chicago Press, 1982), p. 12.

109. Burke, *Thoughts and Details on Scarcity*, p. 16.

110. Blake, *Public Address*, E573.

111. Burke, *Thoughts and Details on Scarcity*, p. 10.

112. "Thinking itself, in this age of separations," he adds, "may become a peculiar craft." See Adam Ferguson, *History of Civil Society* (Edinburgh, 1767), pp. 280–81.

113. See Morris Eaves, *The Counter-arts Conspiracy: Art and Industry in the Age of Blake* (Ithaca, N.Y.: Cornell University Press, 1992). I will return to this important

book, and to these issues, at greater length in the next chapter. The following references to Blake's *Public Address* are from E571–82.

114. Blake, "Now Art Has Lost Its Mental Charms," E479.
115. Blake, *Public Address*, E580–81.
116. Blake, annotations to Watson, E618.
117. William Hurd, *A New Universal History of the Religious Rites, Ceremonies, and Customs of the Whole World* (London, 1785), p. 640.
118. Maxine Berg cautions against producing a binary opposition between a mythical romantic artisan on the one hand and the factory of large-scale industry on the other. See Maxine Berg, *The Age of Manufactures, 1700–1820: History, Innovation and Work in Britain* (London: Routledge, 1994), pp. 189–279, esp. pp. 194–95.
119. Marx, *Capital*, 1:460.
120. See Johannes Fabian, *Time and the Other* (New York: Columbia University Press, 1986). This is also a question that I discuss at length in different contexts within my own *Romantic Imperialism: Universal Empire and the Culture of Modernity* (Cambridge: Cambridge University Press, 1998).
121. See Ure, *The Philosophy of Manufactures* p. 7.
122. Quoted in Marx, *Capital*, 1:352.
123. See Moishe Postone, *Time, Labor, and Social Domination: a Reinterpretation of Marx's Critical Theory* (Cambridge: Cambridge University Press, 1993).
124. Fielden notes the proliferation of twenty-four-hour production with day and night shifts. See Fielden, *The Curse of the Factory System*, p. 6.
125. Sir James Philip Kay, *Moral and Physical Conditions of the Operatives Employed in the Cotton Manufacture in Manchester* (London, 1832), p. 24.
126. Sir James Philip Kay, quoted in Fielden, *The Curse of the Factory System*, p. 37. Emphasis in original. Also see Ure, *The Philosophy of Manufactures*, pp. 7–8; and, for a more sympathetic account, J. L. Hammond and Barbara Hammond, *The Town Labourer, 1760–1832* (1917; reprint, London: Allen Sutton, 1995), pp. 18–19.
127. Charles Babbage, *On the Economy of Machinery and Manufacture* (London, 1832), p. 133.
128. Ibid., p. 153.
129. Ibid., p. 136.
130. McKendrick, "Josiah Wedgwood and Factory Discipline," pp. 32–33.
131. Josiah Wedgwood, quoted in McKendrick, "Josiah Wedgwood and Factory Discipline," p. 32.
132. See Babbage, *On the Economy of Machinery*, p. 132.
133. Marx, *Capital*, 1:458. "As against this, however," he adds, "constant labour of one uniform kind disturbs the intensity and flow of a man's vital forces, which find recreation and delight in the change of activity itslf" (p. 460).
134. Babbage, *On the Economy of Machinery*, pp. 137–38.
135. Ibid., p. 173.
136. Jeremy Bentham, *Panopticon; Or, the Inspection-House* (Dublin, 1791), p. 76.
137. Babbage, *On the Economy of Machinery*, p. 136.
138. Marx, *Capital*, 1:450.
139. Quoted in McKendrick, "Josiah Wedgwood and Factory Discipline," p. 41. The Hammonds quote the table of fines from a spinning mill near Manchester in Blake's time. "We have to remember," they note, "that the population that was flung

into the brutal rhythm of the factory had earned its living in relative freedom, and that the discipline of the early factory was particularly savage. To understand what this discipline meant to men, women, and children, we have to remember too that poor people rarely had a clock in the house. Sadler said that you could year the feet of children pattering along the dark streets long before the time for the mills to open." See Hammond and Hammond, *The Town Labourer*, pp. 19–21.

140. From *Reports of the Inspectors of Factories for the Half Year, October 1856*, quoted in Marx, *Capital*, 1:350. Also see Dohrn–Van Rossum, *History of the Hour*, pp. 289–321.

141. Ure, *The Philosophy of Manufactures*, p. 20.

142. Ibid., p. 20.

143. Josiah Wedgwood, quoted in McKendrick, "Josiah Wedgwood and Factory Discipline," p. 34. Marx argues that "what is lost by the specialized workers is concentrated in the capital which confronts them. It is a result of the division of labour in manufacture that the worker is brought face to face with the intellectual potentialities [*geistige Potenzen*] of the material process of production as the property of another and as a power which rules over him" (Marx, *Capital*, 1:482).

144. Ure, *The Philosophy of Manufactures*, p. 20.

145. Hammond and Hammond, *The Town Labourer*, p. 19.

146. Jeremy Bentham, *Panopticon*, p. 76.

147. Blake, *Four Zoas*, E355.

148. Marx, *Capital*, 1:549. "Owing to its conversion into an automaton," Marx adds, "the instrument of labour confronts the worker during the labour process in the shape of capital, dead labour, which dominates and soaks up living labour-power."

149. See Belchem, *Industrialization and the Working Class*, p. 46.

150. Marx, *Capital*, 1:465.

151. Ferguson, *History of Civil Society*, p. 280.

152. See Babbage, *On the Economy of Machinery*, p. 153.

153. Jeremy Bentham, *An Introduction to the Principles of Morals and Legislation* (1789; reprint, New York: Hafner Press, 1948), p. 3. Emphases in original.

154. Ure, *The Philosophy of Manufactures*, pp. 13–14.

155. Marx, *Capital*, 1:466.

156. Ibid., 1:469.

157. For more on Schiller and the play-drive, see Friedrich Schiller, *Letters on the Aesthetic Education of Man*, trans. Elizabeth Wilkinson and L. A. Willoughby (Oxford: Oxford University Press, 1986).

158. See Gilles Deleuze and Felix Guattari, *Anti-Oedipus: Capitalism and Schizophrenia*, trans. Robert Hurley et al. (Minneapolis: University of Minnesota Press, 1983), pp. 1–50.

159. Babbage, *On the Economy of Machinery*, pp. 22, 48, 51.

160. McKendrick, "The Commercialization of Fashion," p. 56.

161. McKendrick, "The Consumer Revolution," p. 21.

162. See, among others, J. H. Plumb, "The Acceptance of Modernity," in McKendrick, Brewer, and Plumb, *The Birth of a Consumer Society*; and Ann Bermingham and John Brewer, eds., *The Consumption of Culture, 1600–1800* (London: Routledge, 1995).

163. Wilson, *Observations on the Present State of the Poor*, pp. 10–11.

164. See Bill Brown, *The Material Unconscious: American Amusement, Stephen Crane, and the Economies of Play* (Cambridge, Mass.: Harvard University Press, 1996).

165. Blake, *Marriage of Heaven & Hell*, E40.

166. Marx, *Capital*, 1:477.

167. Thelwall, "Rights of Nature," p. 407.

168. A similar argument is presented by Colin Campbell in *The Romantic Ethic and the Spirit of Modern Consumerism*.

169. Here I disagree with Dror Wahrman's understanding of the middle class. See Dror Wahrman, *Imagining the Middle Class: The Political Representation of Class in Britain, 1780–1840* (Cambridge: Cambridge University Press, 1995).

170. Edmund Burke, *Reflections on the Revolution in France* (1790; reprint, Harmondsworth: Penguin, 1986), p. 311.

171. *A Dialogue Between a Gentleman and a Mechanic* (London, 1800), pp. 4–7.

172. *A Word in Season to the Traders and Manufacturers of Great Britain* (London: Association for the Preservation of Liberty and Property from Republicans and Levellers, 1793), p. 13.

173. From the published *Proceedings* of the Association for the Preservation of Liberty and Property from Republicans and Levellers, 20 November 1792, p. 3.

174. John Bowles, *Dialogues on the Rights of Britons, Between a Farmer, a Sailor, and Manufacturer* (London, 1792).

175. Richard Hey, *Happiness and Rights* (London, 1792), p. 20.

176. *A Word in Season*, p. 15.

177. William Playfair, *Better Prospects to the Masters and Manufacturers of Great Britain* (London, 1793), p. v.

178. *A Word in Season*, p. 15.

179. Association for the Preservation of Liberty and Property from Republicans and Levellers, *Association Papers* (London, 1793), pp. v–vi.

180. William Hamilton Reid, *The Rise and Dissolution of the Infidel Societies of this Metropolis* (London, 1800), p. 113.

181. See Jeremy Bentham, "Panopticon versus New South Wales: Or, The Panopticon Penitentiary System, and the Penal Colonization System, Compared," in *The Works of Jeremy Bentham*, ed. John Bowring (Edinburgh: William Tait, 1843), 4:176. I am grateful to Tom Ford for bringing this essay to my attention.

182. Burke, *Reflections*, p. 120.

183. Ibid., pp. 193–94.

184. Ibid., pp. 194–95.

185. Fredric Jameson, *The Political Unconscious* (Ithaca, N.Y.: Cornell University Press, 1981), p. 20.

186. Babbage, *On the Economy of Machinery*, p. 48.

187. Ibid., p. 52.

188. It may be useful to bear in mind the ways in which modern and postmodern production techniques have also tended to dematerialize as much as possible the prototype. The new Boeing 777, for example, made aviation (and production) history because it was conceived and developed as a "prototype" only on the company's computers: the first 777 to come off the assembly line was a "copy" with no material

precedent, but it was also a fully functional flying machine essentially ready for delivery into airline service.

189. See Morris Eaves, "Blake and the Artistic Machine: An Essay in Decorum and Technology," *PMLA* 92 (1977): 903–9.

190. See Robert Essick, *William Blake, Printmaker* (Princeton, N.J.: Princeton University Press, 1980), p. 121.

191. Josiah Wedgwood, quoted in McKendrick, "Josiah Wedgwood and Factory Discipline," p. 38.

192. See Eaves, *The Counter-arts Conspiracy*, p. 68.

193. James Barry, *An Inquiry into the Real and Imaginary Obstructions to the Acquisition of the Arts in England* (1775; reprint, New York: Garland, 1972), p. 140.

194. Blake, *Public Address*, E571–82.

195. See Eaves, *The Counter-arts Conspiracy*, pp. 157–75.

196. "For as many as thirteen hours a day, Blake the apprentice labored at the many tasks necessary for transforming a bare piece of metal into a print" (Essick, *William Blake, Printmaker*, p. 26).

197. Ibid.,, p. 27.

198. Eaves, "Blake and the Artistic Machine," p. 907.

199. See chap. 2.

200. Essick, *William Blake, Printmaker*, p. 26.

201. In *Society of the Spectacle* Debord may perhaps be seen as articulating a more critical version of Babbage's own association of the commodity with the image.

202. Jacob Bronowski, *William Blake: Man without a Mask* (London: Secker and Warburg, 1943), p. 3.

203. See Calhoun, *The Question of Class Struggle*, pp. 45, 55.

204. Blake, annotations to Reynolds, E636.

205. Ibid., E636.

206. See Essick, *William Blake, Printmaker*, p. 159.

207. Blake, *Descriptive Catalogue*, E541.

208. Essick, *William Blake, Printmaker*, p. 73.

Chapter 4

1. I am deeply indebted here to Walter Benjamin's discussion of historical time in "Theses on the Philosophy of History," in *Illuminations*, trans. Harry Zohn (New York Schocken, 1985).

2. The use of "aspire" to indicate breathing was already archaic in Blake's time, but, as suggested also by the rhyme, it clearly works here as a complement to the primary meaning of the word, an indication of the youth's projected desire.

3. Blake, annotations to Watson, E612–16.

4. Blake, annotations to Berkeley, E664.

5. Blake, letter to Dr. Trusler, E702–3.

6. See W. J. T. Mitchell, *Blake's Composite Art* (Princeton, N.J.: Princeton University Press, 1978), p. 35.

7. Ibid., pp. 3–39.

8. See Morris Eaves, "On Blakes We Want and Blakes We Don't," *Huntington Library Quarterly* 58, nos. 3, 4 (1997): 413–39, esp. 428–39.

9. Blake, *America*, E52; *Song of Los*, E68.
10. Blake, *Marriage of Heaven & Hell*, E53, 45.
11. See Blake, *Marriage of Heaven & Hell*, and *Visions of the Daughters of Albion*, E45, 54, 51.
12. See Robert Essick, *William Blake, Printmaker* (Princeton, N.J.: Princeton University Press, 1980), p. 27. See also pp. 118–19, 136–64.
13. Blake, *Milton*, E95–96.
14. See Jacques Derrida, *Limited Inc* (Evanston, Ill.: Northwestern University Press, 1988).
15. See Robert Essick, "William Blake, William Hamilton, and the Materials of Graphic Meaning," *ELH* 52 (1985): 852.
16. Jerome McGann, *The Beauty of Inflections: Literary Investigations in Historical Method and Theory* (Oxford: Oxford University Press, 1988), pp. 119–20. Emphases in original.
17. McGann's account, and such an approach to Blake's work more generally, has been questioned on materialist grounds by Essick and Joseph Viscomi. See, for example, Joseph Viscomi, *Blake and the Idea of the Book* (Princeton, N.J.: Princeton University Press, 1993), pp. 163–76.
18. See McGann, *The Beauty of Inflections*, p. 120. Paul Mann makes a similar point, arguing that "freed of the machinery of [literary and artistic] production, Blake unintentionally and ironically freed himself of the audience in its custody" (Paul Mann, "Apocalypse and Recuperation: Blake and the Maw of Commerce," *ELH* 52, no. 1 [1985]). More recently, Michael Phillips has proposed an important alternative consideration of Blake's relationship to his market and audience, which I will discuss a little later on. See Michael Phillips, "Blake and the Terror, 1792–93," *Library* 16, no. 4 (1994).
19. See Friedrich Schiller, *On the Aesthetic Education of Man*, trans. Elizabeth Wilkinson and L. A. Willoughby (Oxford: Oxford University Press, 1986), p. 43, from the sixth letter.
20. Morris Eaves, *William Blake's Theory of Art* (Princeton, N.J.: Princeton University Press, 1982), p. 72. Also see pp. 176–77. See Mann's very useful discussion of Eaves's version of Blake, esp. "Apocalypse and Recuperation," pp. 3–5.
21. Eaves continues: "Blake's vision of the alternative is itself, from what we can tell, classless, but the imagined state of classlessness is a projection from the middle. Insofar as the *Public Address*'s trenchant criticisms of divided labor are criticisms of the class structure itself, they point toward reintegration at a newly legitimated middle that would eliminate the need for any other class. That classlessness returns to us the question of originality in its personal form, individuality, for the kind of classlessness implicated in the *Public Address* seems to resolve itself in the integrated individual, capable of the kind of merit excluded by commerce. Blake's middle-class dream of integrated action takes the form of a robust individualism." Eaves concludes by saying that "it is tempting to label this, even at the risk of anachronism, a *bourgeois* individualism." But he also admits that "it would be rash to conclude that his [Blake's] nonconformist individualism spurns community." See Morris Eaves, *The Counter-arts Conspiracy: Art and Industry in the Age of Blake* (Ithaca, N.Y.: Cornell University Press, 1992), pp. 165, 169–70; and pp. 158–272 more generally. Also see

Eaves's important essay "Blake and the Artistic Machine: An Essay in Decorum and Technology," *PMLA*, vol. 92, (1977).

22. Blake, *Public Address*, E576–77. "Original art is an act of imagination in a community where any one expression of individuality complements or coexists with many other expressions of individualities," writes Eaves. See *William Blake's Theory of Art*, p. 78.

23. See, Eaves, *The Counter-arts Conspiracy*, pp. 175–82.

24. Laura Rigal, *The American Manufactory: Art, Labor, and the World of Things in the Early Republic* (Princeton, N.J.: Princeton University Press, 1998), p. 12. Also see chap. 3, above.

25. Viscomi cautions that this approach tends to romanticize Blake's position. See Viscomi, *Blake and the Idea of the Book*, pp. 173–75 and elsewhere.

26. Eaves, *William Blake's Theory of Art*, p. 176.

27. Eaves, *The Counter-arts Conspiracy*, p. 172.

28. Ibid., pp. 148, 151.

29. Ibid., p. 151.

30. Ibid., p. 174.

31. Mitchell, *Blake's Composite Art*, p. 22.

32. See Mann, "Apocalypse and Recuperation," p. 11.

33. Blake, *America*, E55.

34. Blake, *Human Abstract*, E27. The tree of mystery receives its fullest treatment in *Book of Ahania*.

35. The distinction between arborescent and rhizomatic is at the heart of Deleuze and Guattari's project in *A Thousand Plateaus*. "Any point of a rhizome," they write, "can be connected to anything other, and must be. This is very different from the tree or root, which plots a point, fixes an order." Thus, they add, "there are no points or positions in a rhizome, such as those found in a structure, tree or root. There are only lines." This, of course, comes uncannily close to Blake's privileging of the *line* as the measure of all art. See Gilles Deleuze and Félix Guattari, *A Thousand Plateaus: Capitalism and Schizophrenia*, trans. Brian Massumi (Minneapolis: University of Minnesota Press, 1988), pp. 7–8.

36. We should be careful of course not to read these proverbs without the proper degree of irony; after all, "if the lion was advised by the fox. he would be cunning."

37. Blake, *Tiriel*, E285.

38. Nelson Hilton, *Literal Imagination: Blake's Vision of Words* (Berkeley: University of California Press, 1983), p. 11; and Mann, "Apocalypse and Recuperation," p. 2.

39. See Robert Essick and Morton Paley, eds., *Robert Blair's* The Grave, *Illustrated by William Blake: A Study with Facsimile* (London: Scolar Press, 1982), pp. 68–69; and Essick, *The Separate Plates of William Blake: A Catalogue* (Princeton, N.J.: Princeton University Press, 1983), pp. 49–52.

40. See Mitchell, *Blake's Composite Art*, pp. 14–39.

41. Hilton, *Literal Imagination*, p. 3.

42. W. J. T. Mitchell, *Picture Theory* (Chicago: University of Chicago Press, 1994), p. 147.

43. Ibid., pp. 147–50, and pp. 144–45 n. 56.

44. Ibid., pp. 148–49 n. 61.

45. See chap. 3.

46. See Henri Bergson, *Matter and Memory* (New York: Zone Books, 1991); also see Gilles Deleuze, *Cinema 2: The Time-Image* (Minneapolis: University of Minnesota Press, 1989). "Matter," Bergson writes, "is an aggregate of 'images.' And by 'image' we mean a certain existence which is more than that which the idealist calls a *representation*, but less than that which the realist calls a *thing*—an existence halfway between the 'thing' and the 'representation.'" See Bergson, *Matter and Memory*, p. 9.

47. See Hilton, *Literal Imagination*, p. 11. Mitchell also argues that Blake's composite art is antipictorial as well as antinarrational. See Mitchell, *Picture Theory*, pp. 20–30.

48. Derrida, *Limited Inc*, p. 7.

49. "The traits that can be recognized in the classical, narrowly defined concept of writing, are generalizable," according to Derrida; "they are valid not only for all orders of 'signs' and for all languages in general but moreover, beyond semiolinguistic communication, for the entire field of what philosophy would call experience." Every sign, he adds, "linguistic or nonlinguistic, spoken or written (in the current sense of this opposition), in a small or large unit, can be cited, put between quotation marks; in so doing it can break with every given context, engendering an infinity of new contexts in a manner which is absolutely illimitable. This does not imply that the mark is valid outside of a context, but on the contrary that there are only contexts without any center or absolute anchoring. This citationality, this duplication or duplicity, this iterability of the mark is neither an accident nor an anomaly, it is that (normal/abnormal) without which a mark could not even have a function called 'normal.'" See *Limited Inc*, pp. 9–12.

50. See Mitchell, *Blake's Composite Art*, pp. 107–64. Also see Essick, *William Blake, Printmaker*, pp. 145–46.

51. See Essick, *William Blake, Printmaker*, pp. 8–28; and Viscomi, *Blake and the Idea of the Book*, pp. 47–142, for much more comprehensive accounts of Blake's etching and printing techniques and their relationship to commercial developments.

52. Blake, *Marriage of Heaven & Hell*, E39.

53. This point is stressed repeatedly by Viscomi. See Viscomi, *Blake and the Idea of the Book*, pp. 32, 44.

54. Essick, *William Blake, Printmaker*, p. 118.

55. Blake's relief etching, as Essick has argued, allowed him to break down the rigid distinctions between the medium and its content, between conception and execution, and between craftsman and artist. See Essick, *William Blake, Printmaker*, pp. 80, 120.

56. Essick, "Materials," p. 836.

57. See Essick, *William Blake, Printmaker*, pp. 147–49.

58. Ibid., pp. 136–64; Viscomi, *Blake and the Idea of the Book*, pp.103–18; Essick, "Materials," pp. 865–57.

59. See Viscomi, *Blake and the Idea of the Book*, pp. 372–73.

60. Ibid., p. 175. Also see Essick, "Materials," pp. 840–41 and elsewhere.

61. See Dennis Read, "The Rival Canterbury Pilgrims of Blake and Cromek: Herculean Figures in the Carpet," *Modern Philology* 86, no. 4 (1988); and Aileen Ward, "Canterbury Revisited: The Blake-Cromek Controversy," *Blake: An Illustrated Quarterly* 22, no. 4 (1988/89).

62. See, for example, Essick and Paley, *Robert Blair's* The Grave.

63. See Dennis Read, "The Context of Blake's 'Public Address': Cromek and the Chalcographic Society," *Philological Quarterly* 60, no. 4 (1981). Chalcography is the art of engraving on copperplates.

64. G. E. Bentley, ed., *Blake Records* (Oxford: Oxford University Press, 1969), p. 172.

65. Ibid., p. 174.

66. Ibid., 195–97.

67. Ibid., 200–205.

68. Ibid., 215–16.

69. See Eaves, *The Counter-arts Conspiracy*, pp. 175–269. I quote from p. 178.

70. Ibid., p. 266. Eaves concludes, "Blake's egalitarianism, like Thomas Paine's, operates very much in the service of a meritocracy, conceived as the liberation of real distinction from the absurdities of a 'hereditary system' of discrimination 'repugnant to human wisdom' as Paine says." See p. 269.

71. Ibid., p. 173.

72. Not, of course, that these technical differences could somehow account for all the differences between these copies of the prophecy.

73. See Viscomi, *Blake and the Idea of the Book*, pp. 32–44.

74. See Essick, "Materials."

75. Essick, "Materials," p. 849.

76. Thus, Essick argues that meaning develops as an integral part of the process of execution.

77. See Viscomi, *Blake and the Idea of the Book*, p. 182.

78. Ibid., p. 183.

79. Blake, letter to Cumberland, 12 April 1827, E783.

80. See Fredric Jameson, *The Political Unconscious* (Ithaca, N.Y.: Cornell University Press, 1981), pp. 87–88.

Chapter 5

1. Blake, letter to Hayley, 6 May 1800, E705.

2. This is a point that I discuss at much greater length in *Romantic Imperialism: Universal Empire and the Culture of Modernity* (Cambridge: Cambridge University Press, 1998).

3. See Edward Said, *Orientalism* (New York: Vintage, 1979), p. 81.

4. See E. P. Thompson, *The Making of the English Working Class* (New York: Vintage, 1966), pp. 98–99.

5. Jon Mee, "Anxieties of Enthusiasm: Coleridge, Prophecy, and Popular Politics in the 1790s," *Huntington Library Quarterly* 60, nos. 1, 2, pp. 179–203; I quote from p. 188.

6. See Jon Mee, *Dangerous Enthusiasm: William Blake and the Culture of Radicalism in the 1790s* (Oxford: Oxford University Press, 1994), p. 5.

7. Thomas Paine, *Rights of Man* (1790–92; reprint, Harmondsworth: Penguin, 1985), pp. 58–59.

8. Anna Clark, *The Struggle for the Breeches: Gender and the Making of the British Working Class* (Berkeley: University of California Press, 1995), p. 152.

9. Montesquieu, *Persian Letters* (1721; reprint, Harmondsworth: Penguin, 1993), letter 9, p. 51.

10. Louis Althusser, *Montesquieu: La politique et l'histoire* (Paris: Presses Universitaires de France, 1969), pp. 85–96.

11. Montesquieu, *The Spirit of Laws* (1757, reprint, Berkeley: University of California Press, 1977), p. 156.

12. Montesquieu, *Spirit*, p. 142.

13. Montesquieu, *Spirit*, p. 142.

14. Althusser, *Montesquieu*, p. 96.

15. Mary Wollstonecraft, *A Vindication of the Rights of Woman* (1792; reprint, Harmondsworth: Penguin, 1992), p. 81.

16. See Nigel Leask, *British Romantic Writers and the East: The Anxieties of Empire* (Cambridge: Cambridge University Press, 1992); also see John Barrell, *The Infection of Thomas De Quincey: A Psychopathology of Imperialism* (New Haven, Conn.: Yale University Press, 1991). The recent excellent collection edited by Tim Fulford and Peter Kitson, *Romanticism and Colonialism: Writing and Empire, 1780–1830* (Cambridge: Cambridge University Press, 1998) has helped to redress this imbalance. Also see the venerable but very useful study by Martha Conant, *The Oriental Tale in the Eighteenth Century* (New York: Columbia University Press, 1908).

17. See Said, *Orientalism*; also see Marilyn Butler, "Orientalism," in *The Romantic Period*, ed. David Pirie (Harmondsworth: Penguin, 1994).

18. See my *Romantic Imperialism*, esp. chaps. 5, 6.

19. Butler, "Orientalism," pp. 418–19.

20. Raymond Schwab, *The Oriental Renaissance* (New York: Columbia University Press, 1984).

21. See, however, Martin Bernal, *Black Athena: The Afroasiatic Roots of Classical Civilization* (New Brunswick, N.J.: Rutgers University Press, 1987).

22. See Schwab, *The Oriental Renaissance*, p. 18. Here it becomes essential to bear in mind Edward Said's critique of Schwab, and the political and historical corrective he applies to Schwab's argument. See Said, *Orientalism*, pp. 5–6.

23. Schwab, *The Oriental Renaissance*, hints at such an understanding of romanticism; see p. 18.

24. Or so I argue in *Romantic Imperialism*.

25. See Kevin Gilmartin's recent essay on Hannah More, forthcoming in *ELH*.

26. John Thelwall, "Rights of Britons" (1795), reprinted in *The Politics of English Jacobinism: Writings of John Thelwall*, edited by Gregory Claeys (University Park: Pennsylvania State University Press, 1995), p. 473.

27. William Godwin, *A Defence of the Rockingham Party*, quoted in Clark, *Struggle for the Breeches*, p. 148.

28. See Leask, *British Romantic Writers*; and Barrell, *The Infection of Thomas De Quincey*, on Oriental style and inoculation.

29. Wollstonecraft, *Vindication*, pp. 82–83.

30. Ibid., p. 114.

31. See Conant, *The Oriental Tale in the Eighteenth Century*, pp. 226–27.

32. Nigel Leask, "'Wandering through Eblis': Absorption and Containment in Romantic Exoticism," in Fulford and Kitson, *Romanticism and Colonialism*, pp. 164–88.

33. For more on Wollstonecraft's reorientation of an emergent discourse of femininity and a woman's role in society, see Mary Poovey, *The Proper Lady and the Woman Writer* (Chicago: University of Chicago Press, 1984), esp. pp. 48–81.

34. Wollstonecraft, *Vindication*, p. 113.
35. Ibid., p. 83.
36. Henry Maundrell, *A Journey from Aleppo to Jerusalem, at Easter, AD 1697* (London, 1697), p. 39.
37. Ibid., pp. 147–48.
38. Ibid., p. 9.
39. Ibid., p. 148.
40. Montesquieu, *Persian Letters*, letters 148 and 153, pp. 271, 274.
41. Ibid., letter 161, p. 280.
42. [Lady Mary Wortley Montagu], *Letters of the Right Honourable Lady M—y W—y M—e; written during her Travels in Europe, Asia, and Africa, to Persons of Distinction, Men of Letters, &c. in different Parts of Europe, Which contain, among other Curious Relations, Accounts of the Policy and Manners of the Turks. Drawn from Sources that have been inaccessible to other Travellers* (London, 1790), p. 68. Note that this edition of the *Letters* was published just before Wollstonecraft's *Vindication*.
43. Montagu, *Letters*, p. 68.
44. Robert Wood, *The Ruins of Palmyra, otherwise Tedmor, in the Desart* (London, 1753), p. ii.
45. Ibid., pp. 7–8.
46. Ibid., pp. 8–9.
47. Wollstonecraft, *Vindication*, p. 97.
48. See, for example, Olivia Smith, *The Politics of Language, 1791–1819* (Oxford: Clarendon Press, 1984).
49. See Paine, *Rights of Man*, p. 51.
50. Ibid., pp. 66–67.
51. See Thomas Malthus, *An Essay on the Principle of Population* (1798; reprint, Oxford: Oxford University Press, 1993).
52. See Wollstonecraft, *Vindication*, p. 82.
53. Ibid., p. 102.
54. Ibid., pp. 81–82.
55. Ibid., pp. 82, 80.
56. I agree with Anne Mellor that Blake was attacking and subverting Wollstonecraft's training manual for children in his illustrations. See Anne Mellor, "Sex, Violence, and Slavery: Blake and Wollstonecraft," *Huntington Library Quarterly* 58, nos. 3, 4 (1997): 345–70; also see Morris Eaves's response to Mellor, in his article in the same issue of *Huntington Library Qaurterly*, called "On Blakes We Want and Blakes We Don't," pp. 413–39.
57. Mary Wollstonecraft, *Original Stories from Real Life; with Conversations Calculated to Regulate the Affections and Form the Mind to Truth and Goodness* (London, 1791), pp. 78–79.
58. Wollstonecraft, *Vindications*, p. 99.
59. Ibid., p. 99.
60. Ibid., p. 99.
61. Ibid., pp. 99, 114.
62. Blake, *Four Zoas*, E301.
63. James Mill, *The History of British India* (1836; reprint, Chicago: University of Chicago Press, 1975), p. 567.

64. "Endeavour to elicit a plain statement of fact from an ordinary Egyptian," Cromer continues; "His explanation will generally be lengthy, and wanting in lucidity. He will probably contradict himself half-a-dozen times before he has finished his story. He will often break down under the mildest process of cross-examination" (The Earl of Cromer, *Modern Egypt* [New York: Macmillan, 1908], 2:146–48).

65. T. E. Lawrence, *Seven Pillars of Wisdom: A Triumph* (1926; reprint, New York: Anchor Books, 1991), pp. 38–39.

66. Quoted in Said, *Orientalism*, pp. 32–33.

67. Ibid., esp. pp. 31–110.

68. Cromer, *Modern Egypt*, p. 144.

69. Certain elements of this opposition had been proposed earlier by Montesquieu in *The Spirit of Laws* and later echoed by Gibbon, but they would really be systematically integrated into a new theory of the East—as a justification for British imperialism—only from the 1790s onward. Of course, the 1790s radicals saw themselves as reviving *The Spirit of Laws* and fulfilling Montesquieu's arguments for their own time.

70. And how, Cromer asks, was the lone Englishman to accomplish that mission; "was he, in his energetic, brisk, northern fashion, to show the Egyptians what they had to do, and then to leave them to carry on the work by themselves? This is what he thought to do, but alas! he was soon to find that to fulminate against abuses, which were the growth of centuries, was like firing a cannonball into a mountain of mud" (Cromer, *Modern Egypt*, p. 124).

71. Blake, annotations to Reynolds, E636.

72. William Wordsworth, "Preface," in *Lyrical Ballads*, by William Wordsworth and Samuel Taylor Coleridge (1800; reprint, London: Routledge, 1991), pp. 242–43.

73. Wordsworth, "Preface," pp. 244–47.

74. William Wordsworth, "Advertisement" (1798), reprinted in Wordsworth and Coleridge, *Lyrical Ballads*, p. 7.

75. Wordsworth, "Preface," p. 245.

76. See William Wordsworth, fragment on the sublime, in *Selected Prose* (Harmondsworth: Penguin, 1988), pp. 263–74.

77. Wordsworth, fragment on the sublime, pp. 266–67.

78. William Wordsworth, "Essay, Supplementary to the Preface," in *Selected Prose*, pp. 387–413, quotation on p. 408. Emphasis in original.

79. Wordsworth, "Essay," p. 409. Emphasis in original.

80. Wordsworth, "Preface," p. 249.

81. Ibid., p. 257. This passage is from the 1802 edition.

82. Ibid., p. 257. This passage is from the 1802 edition.

83. Ibid., p. 263.

84. Ibid., p. 266.

85. Ibid., p. 266.

86. Ibid., p. 264.

87. Ibid., p. 262.

88. See Wordsworth, "Essay," p. 410.

89. Ibid., p. 409. Emphasis in original.

90. Ibid., pp. 409–10. Emphasis in original.

91. Blake, *Marriage of Heaven & Hell*, E41.

92. See Wordsworth, "Preface," p. 264.
93. See Wollstonecraft, *Vindication*, p. 82.
94. Blake, letter to Dr. Trusler, 23 August 1799, E702.
95. Blake, *Marriage of Heaven & Hell*, E38–39.
96. Jon Mee's current work on enthusiasm addresses, among many other things, the significance of Locke's warning for 1790s enthusiasm and romanticism itself.
97. See Blake, *There is No Natural Religion*, E2–3.
98. Wordsworth, "Preface."
99. Ibid., pp. 249–50.
100. See G. E. Bentley, ed., *Blake Records* (Oxford: Oxford University Press, 1969), pp. 32–33, 406; also see Blake, letter to Hayley, 6 May 1800, E705.
101. See Blake, annotations to Wordsworth, E665–66.
102. Ibid., E666.
103. Blake, *Public Address*, E580.
104. Blake, letter to Dr. Trusler, E703.
105. Blake, annotations to Berkeley, E664. Emphases added.
106. Ibid., E664.
107. Blake, letter to Hayley, E705.
108. Blake, *Marriage of Heaven & Hell*, E34.
109. Blake, *Descriptive Catalogue*, E541.
110. See Bentley, *Blake Records*, 195–97.
111. Warren Hastings, introductory letter to *The Bhagvad-Geeta, or Dialogues of Kreeshna and Arjoon*, trans. Charles Wilkins (London, 1785), p. 10.
112. Bentley, *Blake Records*, 195–97.
113. Blake, *No Natural Religion*, E2–3.
114. Blake, *Descriptive Catalogue*, E531.
115. Shelley, preface to *Hellas*.
116. I discuss this at length in the chapter on Byron and Shelley in *Romantic Imperialism*.
117. Bernal, *Black Athena*, esp. pp. 161–308.
118. Blake, *Milton*, E95.
119. In *Songs of Innocence*, copies A–H and K–M, *Chimney Sweeper* and *Divine Image* appear together on facing pages; in copies I, O, P, Q, and S, *Divine Image* and *Holy Thursday* appear together; in the complete *Songs of Innocence and of Experience*, in copy A, all three appear in sequence, and then in copies B–F, I, M, and P, *Divine Image* is paired with or appears sequentially after either *Holy Thursday* or *Chimney Sweeper*. See G. E. Bentley, *Blake Books: Annotated Catalogues of William Blake's Writings in Illuminated Printing, in Conventional Typography, and in Manuscript* (Oxford: Oxford University Press, 1977), pp. 375–80.
120. See Blake's annotations to the bishop of Llandaff's *Apology for the Bible* (E612–16). Of course, as Blake points out in *The Everlasting Gospel*, "Both read the Bible day & night, / But thou readst black where I read white." See Blake, *Everlasting Gospel*, E524.
121. The abolitionist movement's object of concern was the slave as an individual ("am I not a man and a brother?"), and in particular the slave as a potential Christian, rather than the slave as a representative of a particular alien culture. In other words, the slave was deemed worthy of reform to the extent that he or she could be

converted to "our" religion and way of life. Wilberforce's stance on the slave trade, for example, did not seem at odds with his position on India, where—informed by Orientalist doctrine—he was in favor of ever greater British domination, particularly in cultural and religious affairs. See the recent work of Kevin Gilmartin, to whom I am grateful for many suggestions.

122. Isaac Watts, *Divine Songs*, quoted in the editor's notes in the Blake Trust edition of *Songs of Innocence and of Experience*, ed. Andrew Lincoln (Princeton, N.J.: Princeton University Press, 1991), p. 159.

123. Blake, *All Religions are One*, E2.

124. Blake, annotations to Swedenborg, E604.

125. Blake, *No Natural Religion*, 2d ser., E2.

126. Blake, *Descriptive Catalogue*, 543.

127. Bernal, *Black Athena*, p. 27.

128. See Blake's descriptions of his illustrations to Milton, E685.

129. Blake, *Song of Los*, E67.

130. See Norman Cohn, *The Pursuit of the Millennium* (New York: Oxford University Press, 1970); Frances Yates, *Giordano Bruno and the Hermetic Tradition* (Chicago: University of Chicago Press, 1979); Elaine Pagels, *The Gnostic Gospels* (New York: Vintage Books, 1989).

131. See Blake's letter to Flaxman, 12 September 1800, E707.

132. See A. L. Morton, *The Everlasting Gospel: A Study in the Sources of William Blake* (London: Lawrence and Wishart, 1958).

133. Christopher Hill, *Milton and the English Revolution* (London: Faber and Faber, 1977), p. 76.

134. Bruno, quoted in Yates, *Giordano Bruno and the Hermetic Tradition*, pp. 211, 213, 242.

135. Jacob Bauthumley, *The Light and Dark Sides of God* (1650), reprinted in *A Collection of Ranter Writings from the 17th Century*, ed. Nigel Smith (London: Junction Books, 1983), p. 232.

136. See Antonio Negri, *The Savage Anomaly: The Power of Spinoza's Metaphysics and Politics*, trans. Michael Hardt (Minneapolis: University of Minnesota Press, 1991).

137. See Blake, *Song of Los*, E68–69.

138. See, for example, Butler, "Orientalism," esp. pp. 408–9. Also see Blake, *Song of Los*, E68.

139. Blake, *America*, E54.

140. See Blake, *Song of Los*, E67–68.

141. John Milton, *The Tenure of Kings and Magistrates*, in *John Milton: Critical Edition of Major Works* (Oxford: Oxford University Press, 1991), p. 279.

142. See Robert Essick, *William Blake's Commercial Book Illustrations* (Oxford: Clarendon Press, 1991), pp. 64–65; and Bernard Smith, *European Vision and the South Pacific* (New Haven, Conn.: Yale University Press, 1985), pp. 159–87.

143. See Essick, *William Blake's Commercial Book Illustrations*.

144. See Mellor, "Sex, Violence, and Slavery," esp. pp. 350–59.

145. Ibid., pp. 357–58.

146. Ibid., p. 368.

147. Morris Eaves also questions Mellor's argument on a basic interpretive level. See Eaves, "On Blakes We Want and Blakes We Don't," pp. 428–39.

148. Mellor, "Sex, Violence, and Slavery," p. 359.

149. Jacob Bryant, *A New System, or Analysis of Ancient Mythology; wherein an Attempt is made to divest Tradition of Fable; and to reduce the Truth to its Original Purity* (London, 1774).

150. Blake, *All Religions are One*, E1.

151. Ibid., E1.

152. Daniel Isaac Eaton, ed., *Politics for the People: Or, A Salmagundy for Swine*, no. 5 (London, 1794), p. 60.

153. See Bentley, *Blake Records*, p. 41 n. 4.

Chapter 6

1. Blake, *Book of Urizen*, E81
2. Ibid., E71.
3. Ibid., E72.
4. Ibid., E81.
5. Ibid., E74.
6. Ibid., E73.
7. Ibid., E78.
8. Blake, *Book of Ahania*, E87.
9. Blake, *Book of Urizen*, E77. Emphasis added.
10. Ibid., E74.
11. Ibid., E83.
12. Blake, *Song of Los*, E67.
13. Blake, *Book of Urizen*, E83.
14. Blake, "Love to Faults is Always Blind," E472.
15. Blake, *Public Address*, E576.
16. With his concept of a "form-of-life," Giorgio Agamben pushes us to think of "a life that can never be separated from its form," or "a life for which what is at stake in its way of living is living itself," a specifically human life "in which the single ways, acts, and processes of living are never simply facts but always and above all possibilities of life, always and above all power (potenza)." See Giorgio Agamben, "Form-of-Life," trans. Cesare Casarino, in *Radical Thought in Italy: A Potential Politics*, ed. Michael Hardt and Paolo Virno (Minneapolis: University of Minnesota Press, 1996).
17. Northrop Frye, *Fearful Symmetry: A Study of William Blake* (Princeton, N.J.: Princeton University Press, 1969), p. 30.
18. Blake, *Laocoön*, E274.
19. Ibid., E273.
20. Robert Essick, *William Blake and the Language of Adam* (Oxford: Oxford University Press, 1989), p. 173.
21. See Cesare Casarino, *Modernity at Sea: Melville, Marx, Conrad in Crisis* (Minneapolis: University of Minnesota Press, 2002).
22. Antonio Negri, *Insurgencies: Constituent Power and the Modern State* (Minneapolis: University of Minnesota Press, 1999).
23. Blake, *Marriage of Heaven & Hell*, E40.

24. Blake, *Laocoön*, E273.
25. See Michael Hardt, *Gilles Deleuze: An Apprenticeship in Philosophy* (Minneapolis: University of Minnesota Press, 1993).
26. See John Barrell's new book, *Imagining the Death of the King* (Oxford: Oxford University Press, 2000).
27. Blake, *Marriage of Heaven & Hell*, E37.
28. The United States Declaration of Independence.
29. Edmund Burke, *Thoughts and Details on Scarcity, Originally Presented to the Rt. Hon. William Pitt, in the Month of November, 1795*. (London, 1800), p. 13.
30. Negri, *Insurgencies*, pp. 120–21.
31. Blake, *Marriage of Heaven & Hell*, E38–39.
32. See Hardt, *Gilles Deleuze*, p. 115.
33. Blake, annotations to Berkeley, E664.
34. Blake, *Book of Urizen*, E72.
35. Ibid., E73.
36. See Essick, *William Blake and the Language of Adam*, pp. 157–58.
37. See G. E. Bentley, ed., *Blake Records* (Oxford: Oxford University Press, 1969), p. 547.
38. Essick, *William Blake and the Language of Adam*, p. 159.
39. James Chandler points out the way in which Blake's poetry both invites and defeats the reader and spectator's impulse to circulate among subject positions, the kind of "moving" sympathy that became essential to the language of sentiment. "Blake's poetry is not a medium for an imaginative exchange of places of the sort that builds sentiment," Chandler argues; "The kind of crossing of terms we see in *The Mental Traveler*—its distinctive Blakean chiasmus—is a part of the grammatical structure that defines his medium as exactly not a facilitator of sentiment. It resists the commonality of sense in the name of its own forms of sense making and unmaking" (James Chandler, "Blake and the Syntax of Sentiment," lecture presented at the conference "Blake, Nation and Empire" at Tate Britain, December 2000).
40. "Materialism should never be confused with a simple priority of body over mind, of the physical over the intellectual," argues Michael Hardt; "rather, materialism repeatedly appears in the history of philosophy as a corrective to idealism, as a denial of the priority of mind over body. Spinoza corrects Descartes just as Marx corrects Hegel. This materialist correction is not an inversion of the priority, but a proposition of an equality in principle between the corporeal and the intellectual. Deleuze makes clear that this refusal of the priority of the intellect serves to point toward and reinforce the priority of being equally over all its attributes (thought, extension, etc.). From this perspective, the only true ontology must be materialist.... The intellectual and the corporeal are equal expressions of being: this is the fundamental principle of a materialist ontology" (Hardt, *Gilles Deleuze*, p. 74).
41. Blake, *Book of Urizen*, E74.
42. Ibid., E75.
43. Ibid., E77.
44. Ibid., E77.
45. Ibid., E78.
46. Ibid., E79.
47. Blake, *Book of Los*, E92.

48. Jon Mee, *Dangerous Enthusiasm: William Blake and the Culture of Radicalism in the 1790s* (Oxford: Oxford University Press, 1994), p. 164.
49. W. J. T. Mitchell, *Blake's Composite Art* (Princeton, N.J.: Princeton University Press, 1978), p. 127.
50. See Dipesh Chakrabarty, *Provincializing Europe: Postcolonial Thought and Historical Difference* (Princeton, N.J.: Princeton University Press, 2000).
51. Blake, letter to Trusler, E702.
52. John Locke, *Essay Concerning Human Understanding* (1689; reprint, Oxford: Oxford University Press, 1979), pp. 119–20.
53. Ibid., pp. 162–63.
54. Ibid., p. 301.
55. Ibid., p. 704.
56. Samuel Taylor Coleridge, "Lectures on Revealed Religion: Lecture 6" (1795), reprinted in *Collected Works*, ed. Kathleen Coburn and Bart Winer (Princeton, N.J.: Princeton University Press, 1969), 2:229.
57. See Mary Wollstonecraft, *A Vindication of the Rights of Woman* (1792; reprint, Harmondsworth: Penguin, 1992), p. 115.
58. Locke, *Essay Concerning Human Understanding*, p. 230.
59. Blake, *There is No Natural Religion* (b), E3.
60. Ibid., 2d ser., E2–3.
61. Spinoza, *Ethics*, IIIP9S.
62. See Bentley, *Blake Records*, p. 324.
63. This, obviously, is why Frye begins *Fearful Symmetry* with "The Case against Locke."
64. See Locke, *Essay Concerning Human Understanding*, 105–6.
65. Ibid., p. 118. Emphases in original. See all of 104–18.
66. Ibid., p. 120.
67. Ibid., p. 703.
68. See Frye, *Fearful Symmetry*, p. 23.
69. See Locke, *Essay Concerning Human Understanding*, 244–45.
70. Blake, *Jerusalem*, E151.
71. Essick, *William Blake and the Language of Adam*, p. 163.
72. Blake, annotations to Bacon, E623.
73. Blake, *Laocoön*, E275.
74. Blake, *On Virgil*, E270.
75. Blake, annotations to Lavater, E600.
76. According to Deleuze, *élan vital* for Bergson is "always a case of a virtuality in the process of being actualized, a simplicity in the process of differentiating, a totality in the process of dividing up." Thus, being exists as a vrtual totality that is actualized through a process of differentiation. "When the virtuality is actualized, it differentiates, is 'developed,' when it actualizes and develops its parts, it does so according to lines that are divergent, but each of which corresponds to a particular degree in the virtual totality," Deleuze explains; "there is no longer any coexisting whole; there are merely lines of actualization." Thus, differentiation for Deleuze and Bergson is "essentially positive and creative" (see Gilles Deleuze, *Bergsonism*, trans. Hugh Tomlinson and Barbara Habberjam [New York: Zone, 1988], pp. 94–103; also see Hardt, *Gilles Deleuze*, pp. 14–19).

77. *A Dialogue between a Gentleman and a Mechanic* (London, 1800).
78. Karl Marx, *Capital* (1857; reprint, New York: Vintage, 1977), 1:548.
79. See Andrew Ure, *The Philosophy of Manufactures; Or, an Exposition of the Scientific, Moral, and Commercial Economy of the Factory System of Great Britain* (London, 1835), pp. 2, 9, 18.
80. Marx, *Capital*, 1:548.
81. See the discussion of governmentality in *Essential Works of Michel Foucault, 1954–1984*, vol. 3: *Power*, ed. Paul Rabinow (New York: New Press, 2000).
82. Foucault, *Power*, p. 336.
83. In *Insurgencies*, Negri provides an exhilarating reading of Harrington against the background of the English revolution. But some of what Negri seeks to extract from Harrington seems forced, especially when Negri might have derived similar arguments—without having to push the limits of his reading—from (more or less) contemporaries of Harrington's, such as Winstanley or Coppe, in whose work we may locate an explicit spiritual-material communism without trying to read it against the grain.
84. See Norman Cohn, *The Pursuit of the Millennium* (Oxford: Oxford University Press, 1970); Christopher Hill, *The World Turned Upside Down* (Harmondsworth: Penguin, 1991); and Peter Linebaugh and Marcus Rediker, *The Many-Headed Hydra: Sailors, Slaves, Commoners and the Hidden History of the Revolutionary Atlantic* (Boston: Beacon, 2000).
85. See James Harrington, "*The Commonwealth of Oceania*" and "*A System of Politics*," ed. J. G. A. Pocock (Cambridge: Cambridge University Press, 1996), p. 273.
86. Thomas Paine, *Rights of Man* (1790–92; reprint, Harmondsworth: Penguin, 1985), pp. 66–67.
87. In fact Hobbes repeatedly blurs the distinction between "artificiall" and "naturall" persons; for, he says, one's very status as a *person* goes beyond one's mere bodily existence. "A *Person*," he writes, "is the same that an *Actor* is, both on the Stage and in common Conversation; and to *Personate*, is to *Act*, or *Represent* himself, or another" (Thomas Hobbes, *Leviathan* [Cambridge: Cambridge University Press, 1996], p. 112. Emphases in original).
88. That is, for Hobbes, one's bodily organization may be understood in mechanical and hence "artificial" terms. "For seeing life is but a motion of Limbs, the begining whereof is in some principall part within; why may we not say, that all Automata (Engines that move themselves by springs and wheeles as doth a watch) have an artificiall life? For what is the *Heart*, but a *Spring*; and the *Nerves*, but so many *Strings*; and the *Joynts*, but so many *Wheeles*, giving motion to the whole Body, such as was intended by the Artificer?" Thus, Hobbes goes on to compare the Sovereign to the Soul of the Leviathan; the magistrates to its joints; and reward and punishment to its nerves (Hobbes, *Leviathan*, p. 9. Emphases in original).
89. Ibid., pp. 120–21.
90. Harrington, "*The Commonwealth of Oceania*" and "*A System of Politics*," p. 273.
91. Richard Overton, "An Arrow Against all Tyrants and Tyranny, shot from the Prison of Newgate into the Prerogative Bowels of the arbitrary House of Lords and all other usurpers and tyrants whatsoever," in *The English Levellers*, ed. Andrew Sharp (Cambridge: Cambridge University Press, 1998), p. 55. Emphasis in original. Actually, in this respect it must be said that Cromwell and Ireton had a more consistently

historical foundation for their own arguments in defense of their "rights" (especially to property) than that of the Levellers, who assumed such rights to be naturally given, in language that anticipates the U.S. Declaration of Independence as well as the 1790s London radicals. Ireton, for example, makes no such natural or divine claim, basing his defense of property on entirely practical, historical, and constitutional grounds. "The Law of God does not give me property, nor the law of nature" Ireton says; "but property is of human constitution. I have a property and this I shall enjoy. Constitution founds property." See "Extracts from the Debates at Putney," in Sharp, *The English Levellers*, p. 119.

92. Overton, "Arrow," p. 55.
93. Ibid., p. 64.
94. Gerrard Winstanley, *The New Law of Righteousness*, in *Gerrard Winstanley: Selections from his Works*, ed. Leonard Hamilton (London: Cresset Press, 1944), p. 27.
95. Ibid., p. 20.
96. Ibid., p. 18.
97. Ibid., p. 20.
98. Ibid., p. 20. Emphasis added.
99. See Hill, *The World Turned Upside Down;* and A. L. Morton, *The World of the Ranters: Religious Radicalism in the English Revolution* (London: Lawrence and Wishart, 1970).
100. Jacob Bauthumley, *The Light and Dark Sides of God*, in *A Collection of Ranter Writings from the Seventeenth Century*, ed. Nigel Smith (London: Junction Books, 1983), pp. 232–33.
101. Bergson distinguishes virtual being from actualized being, which is always differentiating itself from virtual being in the process of *élan vital*. This process of actualization or differentiation lies at the heart of Deleuze's reading of Bergson. "The central constructive task of Deleuze's reading of Bergson," according to Michael Hardt, "is to elaborate the positive movement of being between the virtual and the actual that supports the necessity of being and affords being both sameness and difference, both unity and multiplicity." Thus, being consists at once in heterogeneously differentiated actuality and in an immanently constituted virtual whole (see Hardt, *Gilles Deleuze*, p. 14). This is almost exactly the understanding of being that we see at work in Giordano Bruno or Bauthumley—or Blake himself.
102. Abiezer Coppe, *Some Sweet Sips, of Some Spirituall Wine*, in Smith, *A Collection of Ranter Writings*, p. 43.
103. Coppe, *Some Sweet Sips*, p. 49.
104. J. C. Davis, *Fear, Myth and History: The Ranters and the Historians* (Cambridge: Cambridge University Press, 1986), p. 51. Davis makes some good points in his exploration of the genealogy of a particular form of historiography. It must be said, however, that on methodological grounds alone his deconstruction of Ranterism could equally be applied to any group, movement, school, or organization, even ones far more consistent and coherent than the Ranters. In any case, in compensating for left-leaning accounts of the Ranters, Davis goes out of his way to understate the social and political nature of their intervention. See Nigel Smith, *Perfection Proclaimed: Language and Literature in English Radical Religion, 1640–1660* (Oxford: Clarendon Press, 1989); and Clement Hawes, *Mania and Literary Style: The Rhetoric of Enthusiasm from the Ranters to Christopher Smart* (Cambridge: Cambridge University Press, 1996).

105. Abiezer Coppe, *A Second Fiery Flying Roule*, in Smith, *A Collection of Ranter Writings*, pp. 112–13.
106. Smith, *Perfection Proclaimed*, p. 24.
107. Hawes, *Mania and Literary Style*, p. 28.
108. Coppe, *A Second Fiery Flying Roule*, p. 101.
109. See Cristopher Hill, *The World Turned Upside Down*, and *Liberty against the Law: Some Seventeenth Century Controversies* (Harmondsworth: Penguin, 1997); and Morton, *The World of the Ranters*.
110. See William Walwyn et al., "A Manifestation," in Sharp, *The English Levellers*, p. 161.
111. London Corresponding Society, *Address to the Nation*, 8 July 1793, in *Selections from the Papers of the London Corresponding Society, 1792–1799*, ed. Mary Thale (Cambridge: Cambridge University Press, 1982), p. 75.
112. Association for the Preservation of Liberty and Property from Republicans and Levellers, *Association Papers* (London, 1793), p. 4.
113. William Hamilton Reid, *The Rise and Dissolution of the Infidel Societies of this Metropolis* (London, 1800), p. 93. Emphases in original.
114. William Hurd, *A New Universal History of the Religious Rites, Ceremonies, and Customs of the Whole World* (London, 1785), p. 669.
115. Jon Mee, *Romanticism, Enthusiasm and Regulation* (forthcoming from Oxford University Press). I quote from the unpublished manuscript.
116. See Jon Mee, *Dangerous Enthusiasm*, "The Strange Case of Richard 'Citizen' Lee: Poetry, Popular Radicalism, and Enthusiasm in the 1790s," in *Radicalism in British Literary Culture, 1650-1830: From Revolution to Revolution*, ed. Timothy Morton and Nigel Smith (Cambridge: Cambridge University Press, 2002), and "Anxieties of Enthusiasm: Coleridge, Prophecy, and Popular Politics in the 1790s," *Huntington Library Quarterly* 60, nos. 1–2.
117. A. L. Morton, *The Everlasting Gospel: A Study in the Sources of William Blake* (London: Lawrence and Wishart, 1958), p. 36. See also Chakrabarty, *Provincializing Europe*.
118. Morton, *The Everlasting Gospel*, p. 36.
119. Blake, *Four Zoas*, Night the Seventh, E361. See Linebaugh and Rediker, *The Many-Headed Hydra*.
120. Linebaugh and Rediker, *The Many-Headed Hydra*, pp. 332–33. Emphases in original.
121. Quoted in Linebaugh and Rediker, *The Many-Headed Hydra*, p. 251.
122. See David Worrall's discussion of Despard in *Radical Culture: Discourse, Resistance, and Surveillance, 1790–1820* (New York: Harvester Wheatsheaf, 1993).
123. See Linebaugh and Rediker, *The Many-Headed Hydra*, p. 327.
124. Blake, *Marriage of Heaven & Hell*, E36.
125. Gregory Claeys, *Machinery, Money and the Millennium: From Moral Economy to Socialism, 1815–1860* (Princeton, N.J.: Princeton University Press, 1987), p. 21.
126. Here I strongly disagree with Dror Wahrman's reading of the "middle-class" rhetoric of the 1790s, which he associates with quietist reformers such as Wyvill, as against activists like Paine, who were driven by "universal" arguments. Wahrman does not sufficiently distinguish among radicals, and hence he tends to collapse writers like Thelwall and Paine in with the multitude from whom they

were, I believe, quite anxious to distinguish themselves. Although I agree with Wahrman that Paine and Thelwall deployed a universalist rhetoric, I do not see how that is incompatible with a certain concept of the "middle class," which, as I argued in previous chapters (see chap. 5, for example), the radicals sought to rescue from lounging aristocrats on the one hand and rushing multitudes on the other. To make such a "middle" universal was precisely Paine's point; and if this seems like a self-contradictory, paradoxical, oxymoronic ambition—well, why should that be particularly surprising? See Dror Wahrman, *Imagining the Middle Class: The Political Representation of Class in Britain, 1780–1840* (Cambridge: Cambridge University Press, 1995).

127. See, for example, John Thelwall, "The Rights of Nature, Against the Usurpations of Establishments. A Series of Letters to the People, in Reply to the False Principles of Burke" (1796), reprinted in *The Politics of English Jacobinism: Writings of John Thelwall*, ed. Gregory Claeys (University Park: Pennsylvania State University Press, 1995), p. 472. Thelwall uses *precisely* the terms—"wild and impracticable"—that the judge who would later condemn Despard to death would use to describe any form of "levelling."

128. Samuel Taylor Coleridge, *Conciones ad Populum* (1795), reprinted in *The Collected Works of Samuel Taylor Coleridge*, ed. Lewis Patton (London: Routledge and Kegan Paul, 1970), 1:38; Paine, *Rights of Man*, pp. 58–59.

129. Thelwall, *Political Lectures* of 1795, quoted in Mee, "Anxieties of Enthusiasm," p. 197.

130. Thelwall, "Rights of Nature," pp. 472–73.

131. Coleridge, *Conciones*, p. 43.

132. Coleridge again. See *Conciones*, p. 43.

133. London Corresponding Society, *Selections from the Papers*, p. 6. Emphases added.

134. Ibid., p. 65.

135. Ibid., p. 76.

136. See the discussion of pikes in Daniel Isaac Eaton, ed., *Politics for the People: Or, A Salmagundy for Swine*, no. 2 (London, 1794), pp. 297–98, 325–31, 359–61. I quote from p. 326.

137. London Corresponding Society, *Reformers no Rioters* (London, 1794).

138. Reid, *Rise and Dissolution*, p. 16.

139. Ibid., p. 12.

140. See Mee, *Dangerous Enthusiasm*; Iain McCalman, "The Infidel as Prophet: William Reid and Blakean Radicalism," in *Historicizing Blake*, ed. Steve Clark and David Worrall (New York: St. Martin's Press, 1994); and E. P. Thompson, *Witness against the Beast: William Blake and the Moral Law* (New York: New Press, 1993).

141. See Linebaugh and Rediker, *The Many-Headed Hydra*, pp. 94–97; and A. L. Morton, *The World of the Ranters: Religious Radicalism in the English Revolution* (London: Lawrence and Wishart, 1970), esp. pp. 70–112.

142. John Saltmarsh, *Free Grace; or the Flowings of Christ's Blood Freely to Sinners* (London: Garnet Terry, 1792), pp. 143, 147, 154.

143. Reid, *Rise and Dissolution*, p. 2. For a thorough discussion of 1790s enthusiasm, see Mee, *Dangerous Enthusiasm*, esp. pp. 20–74.

144. Mee, "The Strange Case of Richard 'Citizen' Lee."

145. These are some of the pieces in the first edition of the journal.
146. See Thomas Spence, *Pigs' Meat* (London, 1794–95),2:263.
147. Richard Lee, "Let us Hope to see Better Times," in *Songs from the Rock, to Hail the Approaching Day* (London, 1795), pp. 9–10.
148. Richard Lee, "God a Refuge in times of Persecution and Oppression," in *Songs from the Rock*, pp. 15–16.
149. See Thomas Spence, "A SONG . . . ," in *The Political Works of Thomas Spence*, ed. H. T. Dickinson (Newcastle: Avero, 1982), p. 38. Emphasis added.
150. Richard Lee, "The Rights of God," in *Songs from the Rock*, pp. 17–18.
151. See Mee, "Anxieties of Enthusiasm," p. 189.
152. Thomas Spence, "The End of Oppression," in *The Political Works of Thomas Spence*, p. 36.
153. Thomas Spence, "A Further Account of Spensonia," in *The Political Works of Thomas Spence*, p. 33.
154. Thomas Spence, "The Marine Republic," in *Pigs' Meat*, 1:68–72.
155. See Linebaugh and Rediker, *The Many-Headed Hydra*, on the question of jubilee and its role in plebeian struggle, pp. 290–96 and elsewhere.
156. Thomas Spence, "A SONG . . . ," and "A Fragment of an Ancient Prophecy," in *The Political Works of Thomas Spence*, pp. 38, 46.
157. Spence, "The End of Oppression," p. 35.
158. See Thomas Spence, *The Rights of Infants*, in *The Political Works of Thomas Spence*, pp. 48–53.
159. See Linebaugh and Rediker, *The Many-Headed Hydra*, pp. 287–326.
160. Mee, "The Strange Case of Richard 'Citizen' Lee," p. 17.
161. Ibid., p. 17.
162. Reid, *Rise and Dissolution*, p. 91.
163. See Chakrabarty, *Provincializing Europe*, esp. pp. 97–113.

Chapter 7
1. Blake, letter to Cumberland, 12 April 1827, E783.
2. Thomas Paine, *Rights of Man* (1790–92; reprint, Harmondsworth: Penguin, 1985), p. 213.
3. A. L. Morton, *The Everlasting Gospel: A Study in the Sources of William Blake* (London: Lawrence and Wishart, 1958), p. 36.
4. One of Jon Mee's arguments in *Romanticism, Enthusiasm and Regulation* is that a certain strand of enthusiasm ends up being domesticated in the romanticism of Wordsworth and Coleridge.
5. See Dipesh Chakrabarty, *Provincializing Europe: Postcolonial Thought and Historical Difference* (Princeton, N.J.: Princeton University Press, 2000).
6. G. E. Bentley, ed., *Blake Records* (Oxford: Oxford University Press, 1969), p. 310.
7. Bentley, *Blake Records*, p. 311.
8. Alexander Gilchrist, *The Life of William Blake* (1863; reprint, Mineola, N.Y.: Dover, 1998), p. 7.
9. Ibid., p. 71.
10. Bentley, *Blake Records*, p. 54.
11. Blake, letter to Thomas Butts, 22 November 1802, E720.

12. Blake, annotations to Reynolds, E647.
13. Blake, *Jerusalem*, E145. Words in italics and brackets were deleted from later copies.
14. Blake, letter to William Hayley, 6 May 1800, E705.
15. Blake, letter to William Hayley, 23 October 1804, E757.
16. See Blake's annotations to Watson.
17. Blake, annotations to Thornton, E667. Emphases in original.
18. William Wordsworth, "Preface," in *Lyrical Ballads*, by William Wordsworth and Samuel Taylor Coleridge (1800; reprint, London: Routledge, 1991), p. 266.
19. Ibid., E664. Emphasis added.
20. Northrop Frye, *Fearful Symmetry: A Study of William Blake* (Princeton, N.J.: Princeton University Press, 1969), pp. 30, 32.
21. Blake, *Marriage of Heaven & Hell*, E43. Emphasis added.
22. Ibid., E43.
23. Frye, *Fearful Symmetry*, p. 30.
24. Giordano Bruno, quoted in Frances Yates, *Giordano Bruno and the Hermetic Tradition* (Chicago: University of Chicago Press, 1979), p. 242.
25. Spinoza, *Ethics* IV, appendix XXVII. "The more the body is capable of affecting, and being affected by, external bodies in a great many ways, the more the mind is capable of thinking," Spinoza writes in *Ethics* VP13. This, again, is why Deleuze argues that, if we are true Spinozists "we will not define a thing by its form, nor by its organs and its functions, nor as a substance or a subject"; rather, we will define it "by the affects of which it is capable." See Gilles Deleuze, *Spinoza: Practical Philosophy*, trans. Robert Hurley (San Francisco: City Lights, 1988), p. 127.
26. Blake, annotations to Reynolds, E643–48.
27. Blake, *Jerusalem*, E251.
28. Ibid., E251.
29. Spinoza, *Ethics* VP24.
30. Ibid., IV, appendix XXVII.
31. W. J. T. Mitchell, *Blake's Composite Art* (Princeton, N.J.: Princeton University Press, 1978), p. 35.
32. See David Erdman, ed., *The Notebook of William Blake: A Photographic and Typographic Facsimile* (Oxford: Oxford University Press, 1973), p. N87.

BIBLIOGRAPHY

Works by Blake
Blake, William. *The Complete Poetry and Prose of William Blake*. Edited by David Erdman. New York: Doubleday, Anchor Books, 1988.

Unpublished and Manuscript Sources
London Corresponding Society (LCS) Papers. Add. MSS 27814. British Library.
Place, Thomas. *Notes for a Biography of Thomas Spence*. n.d. Add. MSS 27,808. British Library.
Place Collection. Microfilm. Reel 10. British Library.
PRO. HO 42/47, HO 42/19, HO 42/20, HO 42/21, HO 42/22, HO 42/47, PC/2/140, PC/1/22/36A, TS/24/3/153, TS/11/978/3560, TS/11/953/3497, ADM 1/524.

Works Originally Published before 1850
An Abstract from the Account of the Asylum, of House of Refuge, Situated in the Parish of Lambeth, for the Reception of Friendless and Deserted Orphan Girls. London, 1794.
Account of the Foundling Hospital in London. London, 1799.
Adams, Rev. J. *A View of Universal History, from the Creation to the Present Time*. London, 1795.
The Advantage of a National Observation of Divine and Human Laws: A Discourse in Defence of our Admirable Constitution by a Layman in the County of Suffolk. London, 1792.
Advice to the Labourer, the Mechanic, and the Parent. London, 1800.
Andrews, J. P. *An Appeal to the Humane, on Behalf of the Most Deplorable Class of Society, the Climbing-Boys Employed by the Chimney-Sweepers*. London, 1788.
Anstie, John. *Observations on the Importance and Necessity of Introducing Improved Machinery into the Woollen Manufactory*. London, 1803.
Antinomianism Explained and Exploded. Coventry, 1790.
Association for the Preservation of Liberty and Property from Republicans and Levellers. *Publications Recommended to the Perusal of the Public*. London, 1792.
———. *Association Papers*. London, 1793.
Babbage, Charles. *On the Economy of Machinery and Manufacture*. London, 1832.
Barlow, Joel. *Advice to the Privileged Orders, in the Several States of Europe, Resulting from the Necessity and Propriety of a General Revolution in the Principles of Government*. London, 1792.
Barry, James. *An Inquiry into the Real and Imaginary Obstructions to the Acquisition of the Arts in England*. 1775. Reprint, New York: Garland, 1972.
Bauthumley, Jacob. *The Light and Dark Sides of God*. 1650. Reprinted in *A Collection of Ranter Writings from the Seventeenth Century*, edited by Nigel Smith. London: Junction Books, 1983.

BIBLIOGRAPHY

Baxter, J. *Resistance to Oppression*. London, 1795.
Behmen, Jacob. *Works, in 3 Volumes*. London, 1764.
Bentham, Jeremy. *An Introduction to the Principles of Morals and Legislation*. 1789. Reprint, New York: Hafner Press, 1948.
———. *Panopticon; Or, the Inspection-House*. Dublin, 1791.
———. "Panopticon Versus New South Wales; Or, the Panoption Penetentiary System and the Penal Colonization System Compared." In *Works of Jeremy Bentham*, edited by John Bowring. Edinburgh: William Tate, 1843.
Bentham, Samuel. *Report to the Royal Navy Concerning Dockyard Labour System*. London, 1800.
The Best Use of Bad Times; Or, Friendly Hints to Manufacturers and Mechanics, on their present Distresses. London, 1793.
Bott, Edmund, and Francis Const, eds. *Decisions of the Court of King's Bench, Upon the Laws Relating to the Poor*. London, 1793.
Bowles, John. *Dialogues on the Rights of Britons, Between a Farmer, a Sailor, and Manufacturer*. London, 1792.
A Brief Account of the Charity School at St. Pancras for Instructing, Cloathing, Qualifying for Useful Servants, and Putting out to Service, the Female Children of the Industrious Poor. London, 1795.
Brothers, Richard. *A Revealed Knowledge of the Prophecies and Times*. London, 1794.
———. *A Description of Jerusalem*. London, 1801.
Bryant, Jacob. *A New System, or Analysis of Ancient Mythology; wherein an Attempt is Made, to divest Tradition of Fable; and to reduce Truth to its Original Purity*. London, 1774.
Burke, Edmund. *Reflections on the Revolution in France*. 1790. Reprint, Harmondsworth: Penguin, 1986.
———. *Thoughts and Details on Scarcity, Originally Presented to the Rt. Hon. William Pitt, in the Month of November, 1795*. London, 1800.
A Caution Against the Levellers. London, 1793.
Charter and Act of Parliament for Establishing the Hospital for the Maintenance and Education of Exposed and Deserted Young Children. London, 1799.
Clarke, Richard. *Jesus the Nazarene*. London, 1795.
Clarkson, Laurence. *A Single Eye*. Reprinted in *A Collection of Ranter Writings from the Seventeenth Century*, edited by Nigel Smith. London: Junction Books, 1983.
Coleridge, Samuel Taylor. "Conciones ad Populum." 1795. Reprinted in *The Collected Works of Samuel Taylor Coleridge*, edited by Lewis Patton. London: Routledge and Kegan Paul, 1970.
———. "Lectures on Revealed Relgion: Lecture 6." 1795. Reprinted in *Collected Works*, edited by Kathleen Coburn and Bart Winer. Princeton, N.J.: Princeton University Press, 1969.
Colquhoun, Patrick. *Case of the British Cotton Spinners and the Manufacturers of Piece-Goods*. London, 1790.
———. *An Account of the Rise, Progress, and Present State of the Charity School for the Education of Boys in the Parish of St Leonard, Shoreditch*. London, 1793.
———. *A Plan for the Purpose of Affording Extensive Relief to the Poor*. London, 1795.

———. *The State of Indigence, and the Situation of the Casual Poor, in the Metropolis, Explained.* London, 1799.
———. *A Treatise on Indigence; Exhibiting a General View of the National Resources for Productive Labour.* London, 1806.
The Contrast. London, c. 1795.
Coppe, Abiezer. *A Fiery Flying Roll.* 1649. Reprinted in *A Collection of Ranter Writings from the Seventeenth Century*, edited by Nigel Smith. London: Junction Books, 1983.
———. *Some Sweet Sips, of Some Spirituall Wine.* Reprinted in *A Collection of Ranter Writings from the Seventeenth Century*, edited by Nigel Smith. London: Junction Books, 1983.
Cunnhingham, Alan. From *Lives of the Most Eminent British Painters, Sculptors, and Architects.* Reprinted in *Blake Records*, edited by G. E. Bentley. Oxford: Oxford University Press, 1969.
de Fleury, Maria. *Antinomianism Unmasked and Refuted; and the Moral Law Proved from the Scriptures of the Old and New-Testament.* London, 1791.
A Dialogue Between a Gentleman and a Mechanic. London, 1800.
Dyer, George. *The Complaints of the Poor People of England.* London, 1793.
Eaton, Daniel Isaac. *Revolutions without Bloodshed; Or, Reformation Preferable to Revolt.* London, 1794.
———. "An Essay on the Influence of some Human Institutions on Human Happiness." *Philanthropist*, December 1795.
———, ed. *Politics for the People: Or, A Salmagundy for Swine.* London, 1794.
———, ed. *The Philanthropist.* London, 1795.
Eden, Frederick Morton. *The State of the Poor: Or, An History of the Labouring Classes in England.* London, 1797.
Essay on Trade and Commerce. London, 1770.
Estlin, John. *Evidences of Revealed Religion.* London: Joseph Johnson, 1796.
An Explanation of the Word "Equality." London, 1792.
Ferguson, Adam. *History of Civil Society.* Edinburgh, 1767.
A Few Plain Questions, and a Little Honest Advice, to the Working People of Great Britain. London, 1792.
Fielden, John. *The Curse of the Factory System.* London, 1836.
Gast, John. *Calumny Defeated.* London, 1802.
Godwin, William. *Political Justice.* London: Joseph Johnson, 1793.
Guest, Richard. *A Compendious History of the Cotton-Manufacture.* Manchester, 1823.
Hamilton, Alexander, John Jay, and James Madison. *The Federalist: A Commentary on the Constitution of the United States.* 1787. Reprint, New York: Modern Library, n.d.
Harrington, James. *"The Commonwealth of Oceania" and "A System of Politics."* Edited by J. G. A. Pocock. Cambridge: Cambridge University Press, 1996.
Hastings, Warren. "Introductory Letter." In *The Bhagvad-Geeta, or Dialogues of Kreeshna and Arjoon*, translated by Charles Wilkins. London, 1785.
Hegel, G. W. F. *Introduction to the Philosophy of History.* Translated by Leo Rausch. Indianapolis: Hackett, 1986.
Hey, Richard. *Happiness and Rights.* London, 1792.

Bibliography

Hints Respecting the Distresses of the Poor. London, 1795.
Hobbes, Thomas. *Leviathan.* Cambridge: Cambridge University Press, 1996.
Howlett, J. *Examination of Mr Pitt's Speech in the House of Commons, on Friday, February 12, 1796, Relative to the Conditions of the Poor.* London, 1796.
Huntington, William. *The Lying Prophet Examined, and his False Predictions Discovered; Being a Dissection of the Prophecies of Richard Brothers.* London, 1795.
———. *A Watchword and a Warning from the Walls of Zion.* London, 1798.
Hurd, William. *A New Universal History of the Religious Rites, Ceremonies, and Customs of the Whole World.* London, 1785.
Kay, James. *Moral and Physical Conditions of the Operatives Employed in the Cotton Manufacture in Manchester.* London, 1832.
Lee, Richard. *King Killing.* London, 1795.
———. *Songs from the Rock, to Hail the Approaching Day.* London, 1795.
Letters on the Utility and Policy of Using Machines to Shorten Labour; Occasioned by the Late Disturbances in Lancashire. London, 1780.
Lilburne, John. "An Agreement of the Free People of England." 1649. Reprinted in *The English Levellers*, edited by Andrew Sharp. Cambridge: Cambridge University Press, 1998.
Locke, John. *Essay Concerning Human Understanding.* 1689. Reprint, Oxford: Oxford University Press, 1979.
London Corresponding Society. *Public Address, 2 April 1792.* London, 1792.
———. *Address to the Nation, 24 May 1792.* In *Selections from the Papers of the London Corresponding Society*, edited by Mary Thale. Cambridge: Cambridge University Press, 1988.
———. *Reformers no Rioters.* London, 1794.
Malthus, Thomas. *An Essay on the Principle of Population.* London: Joseph Johnson, 1798.
Maundrell, Henry. *A Journey from Aleppo to Jerusalem, at Easter, A.D. 1697.* Oxford, 1740.
Mill, James. *The History of British India.* 1836. Reprint, Chicago: University of Chicago Press, 1975.
Milton, John. "The Tenure of Kings and Magistrates." In *John Milton: Critical Edition of Major Works.* Oxford: Oxford University Press, 1991.
Montagu, Lady Mary Wortley. *Letters of the Right Honourable Lady M——y W——y M——e; written during her Travels in Europe, Asia and Africa.* London, 1790.
Montesquieu. *Persian Letters.* 1721. Reprint, Harmondsworth: Penguin, 1993.
———. *The Spirit of Laws.* 1757. Reprint, Berkeley: University of California Press, 1977.
Moral Annals of the Poor, and Middle Ranks of Sociey, in Various Situations of Good and Bad Conduct. London, 1792.
More, Hannah. *Village Politics: Addressed to all Mechanics, Journeymen, and Day-Labourers in Great Britain.* Durham, 1793.
A New Dialogue Between Monsieur Francois and John English, on the French Revolution. London, 1793.
On the Employment of Children in Cotton and Other Factories. London, 1825.
Overton, Richard. "An Arrow Against all Tyrants, shot from the Prison of Newgate into the Prerogative Bowels of the arbitrary House of Lords and all other

usurpers and tyrants whatsoever." In *The English Levellers*, edited by Andrew Sharp. Cambridge: Cambridge University Press, 1998.

Paine, Thomas. *Rights of Man*. 1790–92. Reprint, Harmondsworth: Penguin, 1985.

———. *Agrarian Justice*. London, 1796.

———. *The Decline and Fall of the English System of Finance*. London, 1796.

Paley, William. *Reasons for Contentment; Addressed to the Labouring Part of the British Public*. London, 1792.

The Perverse Definition Imposed on the Word Equality. London, 1792.

Place, Francis. "Notes for a Biography of Thomas Spence." British Library, Add. MSS 27,808, n.d.

A Plan for the Purpose of Affording Extensive Relief to the Poor. London, 1795.

Playfair, William. *Better Prospects to the Masters and Manufacturers of Great Britain*. London, 1793.

Political Dialogues upon the Subject of Equality. London, 1792.

Porter, David. *Considerations on the Present State of Chimney Sweepers*. London, 1792.

Price, Richard. *Discourse on the Love of our Country*. London, 1789.

Reid, William Hamilton. *The Rise and Dissolution of the Infidel Societies of this Metropolis*. London, 1800.

Report of the Philanthropic Society, Instituted September 1788, for the Prevention of Crimes, and the Reform of the Criminal Poor, by the Encouragement of Industry, and the Culture of Good Morals, among those Children who are now training Up to Vicious Courses, public Plunder, Infamy and Ruin. London, 1790.

Robinson, Henry Crabb. "William Blake, Artist, Poet, and Religious Mystic." In *Blake Records*, edited by G. E. Bentley. Oxford: Oxford University Press, 1969.

Ruggles, Thomas. *The History of the Poor: Their Rights, Their Duties, and the Laws Respecting them*. London, 1797.

Saltmarsh, John. *Free Grace; or the Flowings of Christ's Blood Freely to Sinners*. London: Garnet Terry, 1792.

Schiller, Friedrich. *Letters on the Aesthetic Education of Man*. Translated by Elizabeth Wilkinson and L. A. Willoughby. Oxford: Oxford University Press, 1986.

A Short but Serious Address to the Manufacturers, Yeomanry, and Tradesmen of Great Britain and Ireland. London, 1791.

Simons, Thomas. *A Letter to Every Housekeeper in London, on Behalf of Parochial Industry Schools*. London, 1792.

Society for the Diffusion of Useful Knowledge. *The Working-Man's Companion: The Results of Machinery, Namely, Cheap Production and Increased Employment, Exhibited; Being an Address to the Working-Men of the United Kingdom*. London, 1831.

Spence, Thomas. *The Real Rights of Man*. London, 1793.

———. *Pigs' Meat: Or, Lessons for the Swinish Multitude*. London, 1794–95.

———. *The End of Oppression*. London, c. 1796.

———. *Spence's Recantation of the End of Oppression*. London, c. 1796.

———. *The Restorer of Society to its Natural State*. London, 1801.

———. "A Fragment of an Ancient Prophecy." In *The Political Works of Thomas Spence*, edited by H. T. Dickinson. Newcastle: Avero, 1982.

———. "A Further Account of Spensonia." In *The Political Works of Thomas Spence*, edited by H. T. Dickinson. Newcastle: Avero, 1982.

Bibliography

———. "The Marine Republic." In *The Political Works of Thomas Spence*, edited by H. T. Dickinson. Newcastle: Avero, 1982.

———. "The Meridian Sun of Liberty." In *Pigs Meat: The Selected Writings of Thomas Spence*, edited by G. I. Gallop. Nottingham: Spokesman, 1982.

———. "The National Debt." In *Pigs Meat: The Selected Writings of Thomas Spence*, edited by G. I. Gallop. Nottingham: Spokesman, 1982.

———. "The Rights of Infants." In *The Political Works of Thomas Spence*, edited by H. T. Dickinson. Newcastle: Avero, 1982.

———. "The Rights of Man." In *Pigs Meat: The Selected Writings of Thomas Spence*, edited by G. I. Gallop. Nottingham: Spokesman, 1982.

———. "A SONG . . ." In *The Political Works of Thomas Spence*, edited by H. T. Dickinson. Newcastle: Avero, 1982.

Stedman, John Gabriel. *Narrative of a Five Years' Expedition Against the Revolted Negroes of Surinam*. 1796. Reprint, Baltimore: Johns Hopkins University Press, 1988.

Thelwall, John. "The Connection between the Calamities of the Present Reign, and the System of Borough-Mongering Corruption—Lecture the Third.—The Connection between Parliamentary Corruption and Commercial Monopoly; with Strictures on the West-India Subscription, &c. Delivered Wednesday, Oct. 14, 1795." 1795. Reprinted in *The Politics of English Jacobinism: Writings of John Thelwall*, edited by Gregory Claeys. University Park: Pennsylvania State University Press, 1995.

———. *The Natural and Constitutional Right of Britons to Annual Parliaments, Universal Suffrage, and the Freedom of Popular Association; Being a Vindication of the Motives and Political Conduct of John Thelwall, and of the London Corresponding Society in General, Intended to have been Delivered at the Bar of the Old Bailey, in Confutation of the Late Charges of High Treason*. London, 1795.

———. "Rights of Britons." 1795. Reprinted in *The Politics of English Jacobinism: Writings of John Thelwall*, edited by Gregory Claeys. University Park: Pennsylvania State University Press, 1995.

———. "The Second Lecture on the Causes of the present Dearness and Scarcity of Provisions, delivered Friday, May 1st, 1795." 1795. Reprinted in *The Politics of English Jacobinism: Writings of John Thelwall*, edited by Gregory Claeys. University Park: Pennsylvania State University Press, 1995.

———. "Third Lecture on the Causes of the Present Dearness and Scarcity of Provisions, delivered Wednesday, May 6th, 1795." Reprinted in *The Politics of English Jacobinism: Writings of John Thelwall*, edited by Gregory Claeys. University Park: Pennsylvania State University Press, 1995.

———. "Rights of Nature, Against the Usurpations of Establishments. A Series of Letters to the People, in Reply to the False Principles of Burke." 1796. Reprinted in *The Politics of English Jacobinism: Writings of John Thelwall*, edited by Gregory Claeys. University Park: Pennsylvania State University Press, 1995.

———. *Sober Reflections on the Seditious and Inflammatory Letter by the Right Hon. Edmund Burke, to a Noble Lord*. London, 1796.

The Trial of Daniel Isaac Eaton for Publishing a Supposed Libel, Intutled, Politics for the People; *or* Hog's Wash: *at Justice Hall in the Old Bailey, February 24th, 1794*. London, 1794.

United Irishmen of Dublin. *Address of the United Irishmen of Dublin to the Friends of the People in London.* London, 1792.
Ure, Andrew. *The Philosophy of Manufactures; Or, an Exposition of the Scientific, Moral, and Commercial Economy of the Factory System of Great Britain.* London, 1835.
Vincent, Dr. *Short Hints Upon Levelling.* London, 1792.
Volney, Constantin. *The Ruins of Empires.* 1792. Reprint, Baltimore: Black Classics Press, 1991.
Wakefield, Gilbert. *A Reply to Some Parts of the Bishop of Llandaff's Address to the People of Great Britain.* London, 1798.
Walwyn, William, et al. "A Manifestation." In *The English Levellers*, edited by Andrew Sharp. Cambridge: Cambridge University Press, 1998.
Watson, Richard. *A Defence of Revealed Religion, in Two Sermons.* London, 1797.
Wedderburn, Robert. "The Horrors of Slavery." In *The Horrors of Slavery and Other Writings by Robert Wedderburn*, edited by Iain McCalman. New York: Marcus Wiener, 1991.
———. "Truth Self-Supported; Or a Refutation of Certain Doctrinal Errors." In *The Horrors of Slavery and Other Writings by Robert Wedderburn*, edited by Iain McCalman. New York: Marcus Wiener, 1991.
Wilson, Edward. *Observations on the Present State of the Poor, and Measures Proposed for its Improvement.* Reading, 1795.
Winchester, Elhannan. *A Course of Lectures on the Prophecies that Remain to be Fulfilled.* London, 1789.
———. *A Defence of Revelation.* London, 1796.
Winstanley, Gerrard. *The New Law of Righteousness.* In *Gerrard Winstanley: Selections from his Works*, edited by Leonard Hamilton. London: Cresset Press, 1944.
Wollstonecraft, Mary. *Original Stories from Real Life; with Conversations Calculated to Regulate the Affections and Form the Mind to Truth and Goodness.* London: Joseph Johnson, 1791.
———. *A Vindication of the Rights of Woman.* 1792. Reprint, Harmondsworth: Penguin, 1992.
Wood, I. *Some Account of the Shrewsbury House of Industry.* Shrewsbury, 1795.
Wood, Robert. *The Ruins of Palmyra, otherwise Tedmor, in the Desart.* London, 1753.
A Word in Season to the Traders and Manufacturers of Great Britain. London: Association for the Preservation of Liberty and Property from Republicans and Levellers, 1793.
Wordsworth, William, and Samuel T. Coleridge. *Lyrical Ballads.* 1800. Reprint, London: Routledge, 1991.
———. "A Letter to the Bishop of Llandaff." In *William Wordsworth: Selected Prose*, edited by John Hayden. Harmondsworth: Penguin, 1988.
Wyvill, Christopher. *A Defence of Dr Price, and the Reformers of England.* London: Joseph Johnson, 1792.
Young, Robert. *The Undertaking for the Reform of the Poor, of which a Principal Branch is the Asylum for Industry.* London, 1792.
Young, William. *Considerations on the Subject of Poor-Houses and Work-Houses.* London, 1796.

Works Published after 1850

Ackroyd, Peter. *Blake*. London: Minerva, 1996.
Aers, David. "Blake: 'Active Evil' and 'Passive Good.'" In *Romanticism and Ideology*, edited by David Aers et al. London: Routledge, 1981.
Agamben, Giorgio. "Form-of-Life." Translated by Cesare Casarino. In *Radical Thought in Italy: A Potential Politics*, edited by Michael Hardt and Paolo Virno. Minneapolis: University of Minnesota Press, 1996.
Althusser, Louis. *Montesquieu: La politique et l'histoire*. Paris: Presses Universitaires de France, 1969.
Altizer, Thomas. *History as Apocalypse*. Albany, N.Y.: SUNY Press, 1985.
Ault, Donald. *Visionary Physics: Blake's Response to Newton*. Chicago: University of Chicago Press, 1974.
Balibar, Étienne. "What Is 'Man' in Seventeenth-Century Philosophy? Subject, Individual, Citizen." In *The Individual in Political Theory and Practice*, edited by Janet Coleman. Oxford: Oxford University Press, 1996.
——. *Spinoza: From Individuality to Transindividuality*. Delft: Uitgeverij Eburon, 1997.
Barrell, John. *The Infection of Thomas de Quincey: A Psychopathology of Imperialism*. New Haven, Conn.: Yale University Press, 1991.
Becker, Carl. *The Declaration of Independence: A Study in the History of Political Ideas*. New York: Vintage, 1970.
Behrendt, Stephen. "History When Time Stops: Blake's *America*, *Europe*, and *The Song of Los*." *Papers on Language and Literature* 28, no. 4 (1992).
——. *Reading William Blake*. New York: St. Martin's Press, 1992.
Belchem, John. *Industrialization and the Working Class: The English Experience, 1750–1900*. London: Scolar Press, 1990.
Benjamin, Walter. "Theses on the Philosophy of History." In *Illuminations*, translated by Harry Zohn. New York: Schocken, 1985.
Bentley, G. E., ed. *Blake Records*. Oxford: Oxford University Press, 1969.
——, ed. *Blake Books: Annotated Catalogues of William Blake's Writings in Illuminated Printing, in Conventional Typography, and in Manuscript*. Oxford: Oxford University Press, 1977.
Berg, Maxine. *The Age of Manufactures, 1700–1820: History, Innovation and Work in Britain*. London: Routledge, 1994.
Bergson, Henri. *Matter and Memory*. New York: Zone Books, 1991.
Bermingham, Ann, and John Brewer, eds. *The Consumption of Culture, 1600–1800*. London: Routledge, 1995.
Bernal, Martin. *Black Athena: The Afroasiatic Roots of Classical Civilization*. New Brunswick, N.J.: Rutgers University Press, 1987.
Bidlake, Steven. "Blake, the Sacred, and the French Revolution." *European Romantic Review* 4, no. 1 (1992).
Biernacki, Richard. *The Fabrication of Labour*. Berkeley: University of California Press, 1997.
Bindman, David. *William Blake: His Art and Times*. New Haven, Conn.: Yale Center for British Art, 1982.
Blackburn, Robin. *The Overthrow of Colonial Slavery, 1776–1848*. London: Verso, 1988.

Braudel, Fernand. *Capitalism and Material Life, 1400–1800.* New York: Harper and Row, 1973.
Brewster, Glen. "'Out of Nature': Blake and the French Revolution Debate." *South Atlantic Review* 56, no. 4 (1991).
Bronowski, Jacob. *William Blake: Man Without a Mask.* London: Secker and Warburg, 1943.
———. *William Blake and the Age of Revolution.* New York: Harper Colophon, 1969.
Bronowski, Jacob, and Bruce Mazlish. *The Western Intellectual Tradition.* New York: Harper, 1960.
Brown, Bill. *The Material Unconscious: American Amusement, Stephen Crane, and the Economies of Play.* Cambridge, Mass.: Harvard University Press, 1996.
Bruder, Helen. *William Blake and the Daughters of Albion.* New York: St. Martin's Press, 1997.
Butler, Marilyn. "Orientalism." In *The Romantic Period,* edited by David Pirie. Harmondsworth: Penguin, 1994.
Calhoun, Craig. *The Question of Class Struggle: Social Foundations of Popular Radicalism during the Industrial Revolution.* Chicago: University of Chicago Press, 1982.
Campbell, Colin. *The Romantic Ethic and the Spirit of Modern Consumerism.* Oxford: Basil Blackwell, 1987.
Casarino, Cesare. *Modernity at Sea: Melville, Marx, Conrad in Crisis.* Minneapolis: University of Minnesota Press, 2002.
Chakrabarty, Dipesh. *Provincializing Europe: Postcolonial Thought and Historical Difference.* Princeton, N.J.: Princeton University Press, 2000.
Chandler, James. *England in 1819.* Chicago: University of Chicago Press, 1998.
Claeys, Gregory. *Machinery, Money and the Millennium: From Moral Economy to Socialism, 1815–1860.* Princeton, N.J.: Princeton University Press, 1987.
———. *Thomas Paine: Social and Political Thought.* Boston: Unwin Hyman, 1989.
Clark, Anna. *The Struggle for the Breeches: Gender and the Making of the British Working Class.* Berkeley: University of California Press, 1995.
Clark, Steve, and David Worrall. "Introduction." In *Historicizing Blake,* edited by Steve Clark and David Worrall. New York: St Martin's Press, 1994.
———, eds. *Historicizing Blake.* New York: St. Martin's Press, 1994.
Cohn, Norman. *The Pursuit of the Millennium.* New York: Oxford University Press, 1970.
Conant, Martha. *The Oriental Tale in the Eighteenth Century.* New York: Columbia University Press, 1988.
Cotlar, Seth. "Radical Conceptions of Property Rights and Economic Equality in the Early American Republic: The Trans-Atlantic Dimension." *Explorations in Early American Culture,* vol. 4 (2000).
Cromer, Earl of. *Modern Egypt.* New York: Macmillan, 1908.
Curtis, F. B. "Blake and the Booksellers." *Blake Studies* 6, no. 2 (1975).
———. "William Blake and Eighteenth-Century Medicine." *Blake Studies* 8, no. 2 (1979).
Damon, S. Foster. *A Blake Dictionary: The Ideas and Symbols of William Blake.* New York: Dutton, 1971.
Damrosch, Leopold. *Symbol and Truth in Blake's Myth.* Princeton, N.J.: Princeton University Press, 1980.

Bibliography

Daniels, John. *The Early English Cotton Industry.* London, 1920.
Davies, Keri. "Mrs. Bliss: A Blake Collector of 1794." In *Blake in the Nineties,* edited by Steve Clark and David Worrall. London: Macmillan, 1999.
Debord, Guy. *Society of the Spectacle.* New York: Zone, 1995.
Deleuze, Gilles. *Bergsonism.* Translated by Hugh Tomlinson and Barbara Habberjam. New York: Zone, 1988.
———. *Spinoza: Practical Philosophy.* Translated by Robert Hurley. San Francisco: City Lights, 1988.
———. *Cinema 2: The Time-Image.* Minneapolis: University of Minnesota Press, 1989.
Deleuze, Gilles, and Félix Guattari. *Anti-Oedipus: Capitalism and Schizophrenia.* Minneapolis: University of Minnesota Press, 1983.
———. *A Thousand Plateaus: Capitalism and Schizophrenia.* Translated by Brian Massumi. Minneapolis: University of Minnesota Press, 1988.
DeLuca, Vincent. "Proper Names in the Structural Design of Blake's Myth-Making." *Blake Studies* 8 no. 1 (1978).
Derrida, Jacques. *Limited Inc.* Evanston, Ill.: Northwestern University Press, 1988.
Dickinson, H. T. *Liberty and Property: Political Ideology in Eighteenth-Century Britain.* New York: Holmes and Meier, 1977.
Dienst, Richard. *Still Life in Real Time: Theory after Television.* Durham, N.C.: Duke University Press, 1994.
DiSalvo, Jackie. *War of Titans: Blake's Critique of Milton and the Politics of Religion.* Pittsburgh: University of Pittsburgh Press, 1983.
Dohrn-Van Rossum, Gerhard. *History of the Hour: Clocks and Modern Temporal Orders.* Chicago: University of Chicago Press, 1997.
Dörbecker, D. W. "Innovative Reproduction: Painters and Engravers at the Royal Academy." In *Historicizing Blake,* edited by Steve Clark and David Worrall. New York: St. Martin's Press, 1994.
Doskow, Minna. "William Blake's *America:* The Story of a Revolution Betrayed." *Blake Studies* 8, no. 2 (1978).
———. "William Blake and the Wheels of Compulsion." In *History and Myth: Essays on English Romantic Literature,* edited by Stephen Behrendt. Detroit: Wayne State University Press, 1990.
Eagleton, Terry. *Criticism and Ideology.* London: Verso, 1988.
Eaves, Morris. "Blake and the Artistic Machine: An Essay in Decorum and Technology." *PMLA,* vol. 92 (1977).
———. *William Blake's Theory of Art.* Princeton, N.J.: Princeton University Press, 1982.
———. *The Counter-arts Conspiracy: Art and Industry in the Age of Blake.* Ithaca, N.Y.: Cornell University Press, 1992.
———. "On Blakes We Want and Blakes We Don't." *Huntington Library Quarterly* 58, nos. 3, 4 (1997).
Emsley, Clive. "The London 'Insurrection' of December 1792: Fact, Fiction, or Fantasy?" *Journal of British Studies* 17, no. 2 (spring 1978).
Erdman, David. *Blake: Prophet against Empire.* Princeton, N.J.: Princeton University Press, 1977.

Essick, Robert. *William Blake, Printmaker.* Princeton, N.J.: Princeton University Press, 1980.

———. *The Separate Plates of William Blake: A Catalogue.* Princeton, N.J.: Princeton University Press, 1983.

———. "William Blake, William Hamilton, and the Materials of Graphic Meaning." *ELH,* vol. 52 (1985).

———. *William Blake and the Language of Adam.* Oxford: Oxford University Press, 1989.

———. *William Blake's Commercial Book Illustrations.* Oxford: Clarendon Press, 1991.

———. "William Blake, Thomas Paine, and Biblical Revolution." *Studies in Romanticism,* vol. 30 (1991).

Essick, Robert, and Morton Paley, eds. *Robert Blair's* The Grave, *Illustrated by William Blake: A Study with Facsimile.* London: Scolar Press, 1982.

Fabian, Johannes. *Time and the Other.* New York: Columbia University Press, 1986.

Ferber, Michael. *The Social Vision of William Blake.* Princeton, N.J.: Princeton University Press, 1985.

———. "Blake's *America* and the Birth of Revolution." In *History and Myth: Essays on English Romantic Literature,* edited by Stephen Behrendt. Detroit: Wayne State University Press, 1990.

———. *The Poetry of William Blake.* Harmondsworth: Penguin, 1991.

Foucault, Michel. *Essential Works of Michel Foucault, 1954–1984.* Vol. 3, *Power.* Edited by Paul Rabinow (New York: New Press, 2000).

Franklin, Caroline. "'Some Samples of the Finest Orientalism': Byronic Philhellenism and proto-Zionism at the time of the Congress of Vienna." In *Romanticism and Colonialism: Writing and Empire, 1780–1830,* edited by Tim Fulford and Peter Kitson. Cambridge: Cambridge University Press, 1998.

Frye, Northrop. "Poetry and Design in William Blake." In *Discussions of William Blake,* edited by John Grant. Boston: Heath, 1961.

———. *Fearful Symmetry: A Study of William Blake.* Princeton, N.J.: Princeton University Press, 1969.

Fulford, Tim, and Peter Kitson, eds. *Romanticism and Colonialism: Writing and Empire, 1780–1830.* Cambridge: Cambridge University Press, 1998.

Garrett, Clarke. *Respectable Folly: Millenarians and the French Revolution in France and England.* Baltimore: Johns Hopkins University Press, 1975.

Gilchrist, Alexander. *The Life of William Blake.* 1863. Reprint, Mineola, N.Y.: Dover, 1998.

Gilmartin, Kevin. *Print Politics: The Press and Radical Opposition in Early Nineteenth-Century England.* Cambridge: Cambridge University Press, 1996.

Gleckner, Robert. *The Piper and the Bard.* Detroit: Wayne State University Press, 1959.

Green, David. *From Artisans to Paupers: Economic Change and Poverty in London, 1790–1870.* London: Scolar Press, 1995.

Hammond, J. L., and Barbara Hammond. *The Skilled Labourer, 1760–1832.* 1919. Reprint, London: Allen Sutton, 1995.

———. *The Town Labourer, 1760–1832.* 1917. Reprint, London: Allen Sutton, 1995.

Hardt, Michael. *Gilles Deleuze: An Apprenticeship in Philosophy.* Minneapolis: University of Minnesota Press, 1993.
Hardt, Michael, and Antonio Negri. *Empire.* Cambridge, Mass.: Harvard University Press, 2001.
Hawes, Clement. *Mania and Literary Style: The Rhetoric of Enthusiasm from the Ranters to Christopher Smart.* Cambridge: Cambridge University Press, 1996.
Hill, Christopher. *Milton and the English Revolution.* London: Faber and Faber, 1977.
———. *The Experience of Defeat.* New York: Viking, 1984.
———. *The World Turned Upside Down: Radical Ideas during the English Revolution.* Harmondsworth: Penguin, 1991.
———. *Liberty against the Law: Some Seventeenth Century Controversies.* Harmondsworth: Penguin, 1997.
Hilton, Nelson. *Literal Imagination: Blake's Vision of Words.* Berkeley: University of California Press, 1983.
———. *Essential Articles for the Study of William Blake.* Hamden: Archon, 1986.
Hobson, Christopher. *Blake and Homosexuality.* New York: Palgrave, 2000.
Hone, J. Ann. *For the Cause of Truth: Radicalism in London, 1796–1821.* Oxford: Clarendon Press, 1982.
Howard, John. *Infernal Poetics: Poetic Structures in Blake's Lambeth Prophecies.* Cranbury, N.J.: Associated University Presses, 1984.
Jameson, Fredric. *The Political Unconscious.* Ithaca, N.Y.: Cornell University Press, 1981.
———. *Postmodernism.* Durham, N.C.: Duke University Press, 1990.
Keegan, John. *A History of Warfare.* New York: Vintage, 1993.
Lawrence, T. E. *Seven Pillars of Wisdom: A Triumph.* 1926. Reprint, New York: Anchor Books, 1991.
Leask, Nigel. *British Romantic Writers and the East: The Anxieties of Empire.* Cambridge: Cambridge University Press, 1992.
———. "'Wandering through Eblis': Absorption and Containment in Romantic Exoticism." In *Romanticism and Colonialism: Writing and Empire, 1780–1830,* edited by Tim Fulford and Peter Kitson. Cambridge: Cambridge University Press, 1998.
Lees, Lynn. *The Solidarities of Strangers: The English Poor Laws and the People, 1700–1948.* Cambridge: Cambridge University Press, 1998.
Linebaugh, Peter. *The London Hanged: Crime and Civil Society in the Eighteenth Century.* Cambridge: Cambridge University Press, 1992.
Linebaugh, Peter, and Marcus Rediker. *The Many-Headed Hydra: Sailors, Slaves, Commoners, and the Hidden History of the Revolutionary Atlantic.* Boston: Beacon Press, 2000.
London Corresponding Society. *Selections from the Papers of the London Corresponding Society, 1792–1799.* Edited by Mary Thale. Cambridge: Cambridge University Press, 1982.
Lottes, Günther. "Radicalism, Revolution and Political Culture: An Anglo-French Comparison." In *The French Revolution and British Popular Politics,* edited by Mark Philp. Cambridge: Cambridge University Press, 1991.
Macpherson, C. B. *The Political Theory of Possessive Individualism: Hobbes to Locke.* Oxford: Clarendon Press, 1963.

Makdisi, Saree. *Romantic Imperialism: Universal Empire and the Culture of Modernity*. Cambridge: Cambridge University Press, 1998.
Mann, Paul. "Apocalypse and Recuperation: Blake and the Maw of Commerce." *ELH* 52, no. 1 (1985).
Marx, Karl. *Capital*. 1857. Reprint, New York: Vintage, 1977.
McCalman, Iain. *Radical Underworld: Prophets, Revolutionaries and Pornographers in London, 1795–1840*. Cambridge: Cambridge University Press, 1988.
———. "Introduction." In *The Horrors of Slavery and Other Writings by Robert Wedderburn*, edited by Iain McCalman. New York: Marcus Wiener, 1991.
———. "The Infidel as Prophet: William Reid and Blakean Radicalism." In *Historicizing Blake*, edited by Steve Clark and David Worrall. New York: St Martin's Press, 1994.
McCord, James. "West of Atlantis: William Blake's Unromantic View of the American War." *Centennial Review* 30, no. 1 (1986).
McGann, Jerome. *The Beauty of Inflections: Literary Investigations in Historical Method and Theory*. Oxford: Oxford University Press, 1988.
McKendrick, Neil. "Josiah Wedgwood and Factory Discipline." *Historical Journal* 4, no. 1 (1961).
———. "The Commercialization of Fashion." In *The Birth of a Consumer Society*, edited by Neil McKendrick et al. London: Europa, 1982.
———. "The Consumer Revolution of Eighteenth-Century England." In *The Birth of a Consumer Society: The Commercialization of Eighteenth-century England*, edited by Neil McKendrick, et al. London: Europa, 1982.
———. "Josiah Wedgwood and the Commercialization of the Potteries." In *The Birth of a Consumer Culture*, edited by Neil McKendrick, et al. London: Europa, 1982.
Mee, Jon. "The Radical Enthusiasm of Blake's *The Marriage of Heaven & Hell*." *British Journal of 18th Century Studies* 14, no. 1 (1991).
———. *Dangerous Enthusiasm: William Blake and the Culture of Radicalism in the 1790s*. Oxford: Oxford University Press, 1994.
———. "Is There an Antinomian in the House? William Blake and the After-life of a Heresy." In *Historicizing Blake*, edited by Steve Clark and David Worrall. New York: St Martin's Press, 1994.
———. "The Strange Case of Richard 'Citizen' Lee: Poetry, Popular Radicalism, and Enthusiasm in the 1790s." In *Radicalism in British Literary Culture, 1650–1830: From Revolution to Revolution*, edited by Timothy Morton and Nigel Smith. Cambridge: Cambridge University Press, 2002.
———. *Romanticism, Enthusiasm and Regulation*. Oxford: Oxford University Press, 2003.
———. "Anxieties of Enthusiasm: Coleridge, Prophecy, and Popular Politics in the 1790s." *Huntington Library Quarterly* 60, nos. 1, 2.
Mellor, Anne. "Sex, Violence, and Slavery: Blake and Wollstonecraft." *Huntington Library Quarterly* 58, nos. 3, 4.
Middleton, Peter. "The Revolutionary Poetics of William Blake." *Oxford Literary Review* 6, no. 1 (1983).
Mitchell, W. J. T. *Blake's Composite Art*. Princeton, N.J.: Princeton University Press, 1978.

Bibliography

———. *Picture Theory*. Chicago: University of Chicago Press, 1994.
Morton, A. L. *The Everlasting Gospel: A Study in the Sources of William Blake*. London: Lawrence and Wishart, 1958.
———. *The World of the Ranters: Religious Radicalism in the English Revolution*. London: Lawrence and Wishart, 1970.
Negri, Antonio. *The Savage Anomaly: The Power of Spinoza's Metaphysics and Politics*. Translated by Michael Hardt. Minneapolis: University of Minnesota Press, 1991.
———. *Insurgencies: Constituent Power and the Modern State*. Minneapolis: University of Minnesota Press, 1999.
Otto, Peter. *Constructive Vision and Visionary Deconstruction: Los, Eternity and the Productions of Time in the Later Poetry of William Blake*. Oxford: Oxford University Press, 1991.
Pagels, Elaine. *The Gnostic Gospels*. New York: Vintage Books, 1989.
Paley, Morton. *Energy and the Imagination: A Study of the Development of Blake's Thought*. Oxford: Clarendon Press, 1970.
———. "William Blake, the Prince of the Hebrews, and the Woman Clothed with the Sun." In *William Blake: Essays in Honour of Sir Geoffrey Keynes*, edited by Morton Paley and Michael Phillips. Oxford: Oxford University Press, 1973.
Peterfreund, Stuart. *William Blake in a Newtonian World*. Norman: University of Oklahoma Press, 1998.
Phillips, Michael. "Blake and the Terror, 1792–93." *Library* 16, no. 4 (1994).
———. *William Blake: The Creation of the Songs, from Manuscript to Illuminated Printing*. London: British Library, 2000.
Philp, Mark. "The Fragmented Ideology of Reform." In *The French Revolution and British Popular Politics*, edited by Mark Philp. Cambridge: Cambridge University Press, 1991.
Plumb, J. H. "The Acceptance of Modernity." In *The Birth of a Consumer Society*, edited by Neil McKendrick et al. London: Europa, 1982.
———. "The Commercialization of Leisure." In *The Birth of a Consumer Society*, edited by Neil McKendrick, J. Brewer, and J. Plumb. London: Europa, 1982.
Poovey, Mary. *The Proper Lady and the Woman Writer*. Chicago: University of Chicago Press, 1984.
Postone, Moishe. *Time, Labor, and Social Domination: a Reinterpretation of Marx's Critical Theory*. Cambridge: Cambridge University Press, 1993.
Raphael, Ray. *A People's History of the American Revolution: How Common People Shaped the Fight for Independence*. New York: New Press, 2001.
Read, Dennis. "The Context of Blake's 'Public Address': Cromek and the Chalcographic Society." *Philological Quarterly* 60, no. 4 (1981).
———. "The Rival Canterbury Pilgrims of Blake and Cromek: Herculean Figures in the Carpet." *Modern Philology* 86, no. 4 (1988).
Rigal, Laura. *The American Manufactory: Art, Labor, and the World of Things in the Early Republic*. Princeton, N.J.: Princeton University Press, 1998.
Rothenberg, Molly Anne. *Rethinking Blake's Textuality*. Columbia: University of Missouri Press, 1993.
Rudé, George. *The Crowd in the French Revolution*. Oxford: Oxford University Press, 1957.

———. *Hanoverian London, 1714–1808*. Berkeley: University of California Press, 1971.
Rudé, George. *The Crowd in History: A Study of Popular Disturbances in France and England, 1730–1848*. London: Lawrence and Wishart, 1981.
Said, Edward. *Orientalism*. New York: Vintage, 1979.
Schwab, Raymond. *The Oriental Renaissance*. New York: Columbia University Press, 1984.
Smith, Bernard. *European Vision and the South Pacific*. New Haven, Conn.: Yale University Press, 1985.
Smith, Nigel. *Perfection Proclaimed: Language and Literature in English Radical Religion, 1640–1660*. Oxford: Clarendon Press, 1989.
Smith, Olivia. *The Politics of Language, 1791–1819*. Oxford: Clarendon Press, 1984.
Stevenson, W. H. "Death's Door." *Blake Newsletter*, vol. 4 (1970).
Sutherland, Kathryn. "'Events . . . Have Made Us a World of Readers': Reader Relations, 1780–1830." In *Penguin History of Literature: The Romantic Period*, edited by David Pirie. Harmondsworth: Penguin, 1994.
Swearingen, James. "William Blake's Figural Politics." *ELH*, vol. 59 (1992).
Thomis, Malcolm, and Peter Holt. *Threats of Revolution in Britain, 1789–1848*. London: Archon Books, 1977.
Thompson, E. P. *The Making of the English Working Class*. New York: Vintage, 1966.
———. "Time, Work-Discipline and Industrial Capitalism." In *Customs in Common*. New York: New Press, 1993.
———. *Witness against the Beast: William Blake and the Moral Law*. New York: New Press, 1993.
Trowbridge, W. R. H. *Cagliostro: The Splendour and Misery of a Man of Magic*. London: Chapman and Hall, 1910.
Trumpener, Katie. *Bardic Nationalism: The Romantic Novel and the British Empire*. Princeton, N.J.: Princeton University Press, 1997.
Valenze, Deborah. *The First Industrial Woman*. Oxford: Oxford University Press, 1995.
Viscomi, Joseph. *Blake and the Idea of the Book*. Princeton, N.J.: Princeton University Press, 1993.
Wahrman, Dror. *Imagining the Middle Class: The Political Representation of Class in Britain, 1780–1840*. Cambridge: Cambridge University Press, 1995.
Walvin, James. "Abolishing the Slave Trade: Anti-slavery and Popular Radicalism, 1776–1807." In *Artisans, Peasants and Proletarians, 1760–1860*, edited by Clive Essler and James Walvin. London: Croom-Helm, 1985.
Ward, Aileen. "Canterbury Revisited: The Blake-Cromek Controversy." *Blake: An Illustrated Quarterly* 22, no. 4 (1988/89).
Wells, Roger. *Insurrection: The British Experience, 1795–1803*. Gloucester: Alan Sutton, 1983.
———. "English Society and Revolutionary Politics in the 1790s: The Case for Insurrection." In *The French Revolution and British Popular Politics*, edited by Mark Philp. Cambridge: Cambridge University Press, 1991.
Wilde, Oscar. *The Complete Works of Oscar Wilde*. Edited by Richard Ellman. New York: Harper and Row, 1989.
Williams, Eric. *Capitalism and Slavery*. London: Andre Deutsch, 1964.

Williams, Gwyn. *Artisans and Sans-Culottes: Popular Movements in France and Britain during the French Revolution.* London: Edward Arnold, 1968.

Williams, Nicholas. *Ideology and Utopia in the Poetry of William Blake.* Cambridge: Cambridge University Press, 1998.

Wilson, Mona. *The Life of William Blake.* London: Rupert Hart-Davis, 1948.

Winstanley, Gerrard. *The Works of Gerrard Winstanley.* Edited by George Sabine. Ithaca, N.Y.: Cornell University Press, 1941.

Wood, Gordon. *The Radicalism of the American Revolution.* New York: Knopf, 1992.

Worrall, David. *Radical Culture: Discourse, Resistance, and Surveillance, 1790–1820.* New York: Harvester Wheatsheaf, 1993.

———. "Blake and 1790s Plebeian Radical Culture." In *Blake in the Nineties*, edited by Steve Clark and David Worrall. New York: St. Martin's, 1999.

Yates, Frances. *Giordano Bruno and the Hermetic Tradition.* Chicago: University of Chicago Press, 1979.

Young, Alfred. *Beyond the American Revolution: Explorations in the History of American Radicalism.* De Kalb: Northern Illinois University Press, 1993.

———. *The Shoemaker and the Tea Party: Memory and the American Revolution.* Boston: Beacon Press, 1999.

Zinn, Howard. *A People's History of the United States.* New York: Harper, 1995.

INDEX

Ackermann, Rudolph, 117, 147
aesthetics, 170, 171, 196, 198, 201, 226; and politics, 38, 132, 151, 214, 225–27, 233–38, 240, 243–46, 249, 262–63, 265, 272, 275, 291–92, 297, 319; and subjectivity, 171–74
Agamben, Giorgio, 282, 359 n. 16
Age of Reason (Paine), 24
Ahania, 81
Althusser, Louis, 208, 282
America. *See* United States
antinomianism, 3, 8, 10, 11, 20, 21, 23, 28, 29, 47, 53–54, 58–59, 70–75, 95, 97, 119–20, 193, 196, 247, 249, 250, 251, 262, 266, 271, 280, 291, 293, 296, 304–5, 308, 314, 318, 320, 322–23, 340 n. 19; and the multitude, 74; and otherness, 75; and work discipline, 70–75. *See also* enthusiasm
art. *See* aesthetics
artificiality, 224
artisan class, 22, 53, 115, 301; and radicalism, 22, 28
Association for the Preservation of Liberty and Property from Republicans and Levellers, 66, 138–39, 295
authoritarianism, 124, 126–29, 131–32, 135, 137–43
automaton, 127–29, 132, 137

Babbage, Charles, 9, 10, 87, 122–23, 126–28, 133, 143, 146–49, 167–68, 187, 190, 192, 197, 201, 285
Bacon, Sir Francis, 147, 261, 263
Bage, Robert, 209
Balfour, Arthur, 231–32, 237, 240–41, 246
Balibar, Etienne, 282, 328 n. 31
Barlow, Joel, 30, 31, 33, 34, 50, 306
Barrell, John, 216
Barry, James, 148, 150
Basire, James, 223
Baudrillard, Jean, 87
Bauthumley, Jacob, 95, 250, 290, 304, 320
Beckford, William, 209, 216–17, 226
Beethoven, Ludwig von, xii
Behmen, Jakob, 250, 291
Behrendt, Stephen, 30–31, 92
being, 7, 40, 93, 97, 132, 243, 249–50, 261–62, 265, 268–69, 272–73, 278, 282, 287–93,

315, 317, 319–21, 360 n. 40, 361 n. 76, 363 n. 101, 367 n. 25; and desire, 7, 24; and form, 7, 69, 97, 271, 284, 290–94; and image, 291, 294; virtual, 290–91, 361 n. 76, 363 n. 101
being in common, 1, 2, 5, 6, 7–8, 95, 97, 243, 248, 250–51, 257, 259, 263, 266, 278–79, 289, 291–94, 307, 309, 315–16
Belchem, John, 49, 64, 74, 87, 107, 110, 127
Benjamin, Walter, 349 n. 1
Bentham, Jeremy, 74, 85, 86, 100, 123, 126–28, 141, 314
Bentham, Samuel, 100, 111
Bentley, G. E., 194
Bentley, Thomas, 20
Berg, Maxine, 87, 346 n. 118
Bergson, Henri, 187, 279, 290, 352 n. 46, 361 n. 76, 363 n. 101
Bernal, Martin, 246, 249
biology, 38, 40, 41
Blair, Robert, xii, 151, 183; *The Grave*, xii
Blake, Catherine, 190
Blake, Robert, 209, 242
Blake, William: 1809 Exhibition, 193–95, 243–45; and aesthetics, 132, 150–51, 172–74, 196, 201, 242, 262–63, 265, 278, 317, 319, 351 n. 35; and American War of Independence, 33–46, 155–56, 158, 326 n. 4, 330 n. 61; and antinomianism, 3, 8, 10, 11, 21, 29, 53–54, 67–75, 95, 119, 124, 193–94, 196, 247, 249–51, 266, 315, 318, 320, 322; and art (*see* Blake, and aesthetics); and authoritarianism, 103, 118–20, 124, 126, 129, 131, 143, 242, 261–62; and being, 7–9, 40–41, 95, 249, 251, 260–63, 265, 268, 271–75, 278, 283, 317, 319–21; and being in common, 1, 2, 5, 6, 7–8, 95, 97, 243, 248–51, 257, 263, 266, 278–79, 319–24; and books, 164, 175; and children, 4, 53, 103, 105, 162–63, 242, 317–18, 355 n. 56; and class, 19, 25, 26, 53–54, 74, 116, 143–44, 150–51, 172–74, 197, 317–18, 322, 350 n. 21, 353 n. 70; and color printing, 170; and commercial engraving, xi–xii, 135, 148–51, 154, 189–90, 193–97, 201, 252, 256, 349 n. 196; and the commodity, 148–51, 171, 319, 322–23; and communism, 29, 196, 283; and

385

Index

Blake, William (*continued*)
community, 74, 97–99, 120, 173–74; and consumer culture, 5–6, 8–9, 135–48, 150–51; critique of commerce, 76, 115–20, 150–54, 197 (*see also* Blake, and the "Maw of Commerce"); critique of discourse of liberty, 19–21; 28–33, 39, 40, 41, 42, 43, 44, 45, 52–54, 62, 67–68, 74–77, 82, 90, 107, 113, 144–46, 151–59, 178, 181, 185, 193, 202, 281–82, 314; critique of modernity, 87, 150, 202; critique of moral virtue, 67–75, 318; critique of patriarchy, 71, 93, 124, 137; critique of radicalism, 17–21, 25–26; 28–31, 34, 39, 40, 41, 42, 43, 44, 45, 52; and desire, 7–8, 40, 42–44, 95, 98, 132, 249, 274–75, 319, 321; and engraving, 168, 170–71, 182, 185–86, 188, 191–94; and enthusiasm, 53–54, 243–45, 316, 320; and eternity, 262; and excess, 240; and exoticism, 204–5, 214, 240, 249; and form, 67, 81, 89, 97, 260–62, 271, 275, 278, 281–82; and freedom, 8–9, 11, 14, 15, 20, 28, 29, 52, 67, 69, 74, 76–77, 81, 89, 96–98, 101–2, 106, 153–54, 158–59, 181, 205, 248, 258–62, 266–67, 274, 278, 281–83, 314, 319–20; and gender, 92–97, 256; and globalization, xiv, 256, 298; and God, 28, 95, 97, 248–50, 266–67, 275, 278, 282, 316–18, 321–23; and hermeticism, 250; and history, sense of, xiv, 1–2, 155–56, 158, 315, 326 n. 5; illuminated books, 2, 6, 8, 9, 20, 28, 29, 53, 79–81, 83, 85, 87, 103, 114, 120–21, 128, 130, 132–33, 136, 143, 162–64, 166, 168–69, 175, 186–92, 197–200, 202, 250, 257, 259, 271, 321–22, 324; and image, 87, 148–49, 185–91, 267, 275, 277, 278, 324; and imagination, 1–2, 132, 153, 241, 262–72, 275, 277–78, 282, 317; and imperialism, xiv, 204–5, 242–59, 257; and individuality (*see* Blake, and subjectivity); and industrial production, 100, 116–20, 124, 126, 128–29, 131–33, 148–51, 187, 189–92, 197, 201–2; and infinite, 132; and joy, xiii, 8, 28, 95, 98, 103, 209, 238, 258–59, 269, 272, 323, 342; and labor, 77, 85, 90, 100, 101, 103, 105–7, 117, 119, 120, 129, 131–33, 135, 146, 148–49, 153, 160, 173, 187, 197; and language, 160, 186–88, 240–42, 269, 360 n. 39; and law, 280–81, 321; and life, 260–72, 278, 280–81, 319–21; and love, xiii, 2, 74, 98, 120, 262, 320–21, 324; material form of work, 7, 121, 147, 162, 170–75, 181–82, 186–93, 197–203, 321–23; and the "Maw of Commerce," 173, 322–23 (*see also* Blake, critique of commerce); and the mill, 90–92, 99, 107, 152–54, 245, 249; mode of production, 189–202; and modernization, 150, 156, 202–6, 315; and the multitude, 34, 38, 39, 40, 46, 258, 317; and narrative, 32, 155–60, 162–63, 168; network of texts in, 7, 92, 157, 162–71, 181–82, 185–92, 198–200, 321–23; and ontology, 95–96, 100–102, 107, 113, 260–65, 268–71, 275, 277–79, 282, 318–19; open text in, 162–69; and organ-ization, 85, 97, 120, 128–29, 131, 133, 143, 148, 282; and Orientalism, 4, 194, 204–5, 209–10, 214, 244–45, 257–58; and otherness, 205, 240, 242–43, 247–49, 252, 256–57; and politics, xiv, 1, 7, 17–20, 34, 38, 40, 41, 52, 74, 75–76, 193–94, 201, 326 n. 4, 327 n. 6; and power, 239, 243, 257, 259, 266, 268, 271, 277, 279–80, 318; and printmaking, 189–91; and progressivism, 31–32, 77, 157–58, 203; and power, 1, 4; and race, 252, 256–57; and radicalism, 4–6, 8–9, 17–21, 25–26, 28–31, 39, 53–54, 62, 67–68, 71, 74–77, 82, 90, 107, 113, 144–46, 155–58, 181, 193, 205–6, 227, 243–44, 258, 282, 317, 322, 326 nn. 4, 6, 329 n. 42; and reading, 162–63; and regulation, 227, 241, 260–61, 281, 314; and religion, 193–94, 196, 247, 249, 251; and resentment, xi–xii, 106, 150–51, 196–97; and revolution, 38; and romanticism, 173, 206; and sexuality, 92–98; and state religion, 67–71, 74, 76, 119, 162, 205, 248–49; and striving, 281, 319–21; and subjectivity, 38–43, 77, 80, 82, 95–100, 113, 132, 172–74, 177–79, 181, 197, 239–41, 249, 282, 319, 322–23; and time, 32, 39, 77, 155–60, 162–63, 316, 323, 324; verbal-visual interplay in, 7, 29, 162–65, 321; and work discipline, 76, 106, 117–20, 126, 151

Blake, William, commercial illustrations: advertisement for Moore & Co., 109 (fig. 7); illustration for Blair's *Grave*, xii, 150–57, 157, 183–85, 193–97, 202, 243; illustration for Darwin's *Botanic Garden*, 80; illustration for Stedman's *Narrative*, 252, 254 (fig. 25), 255 (fig. 26); illustration for Wollstonecraft's *Original Stories*, 228–29 (figs. 22, 23), 355 n. 56; illustrations of South Pacific islanders, 252, 255 (fig. 24)

Blake, William, works: annotations to Thornton, 317; *The Accusers of Theft, Adultery, Murder*, 37 (fig. 3), 38; *All Religions are One*, 199, 248–49, 251, 257; *America: A Prophecy*, 6, 7, 11, 12, 13, 14, 16–17, 18 (fig. 1), 19–20, 29–42, 53, 77, 80–81, 88–99, 131–33,

Index

149, 151–52, 155–61, 164, 168, 170, 175–77, 182–85, 189, 194, 198, 272, 326 n. 4; *Book of Ahania*, 13, 41, 191, 270–71; *Book of Los*, 13, 41, 80, 92, 190, 270–71; *The Book of Urizen*, 6, 13, 41, 80, 82 (fig. 5), 84 (fig. 6), 189, 260–71; *The Bramins*, 244; *Canterbury Pilgrims*, 193; *Chimney Sweeper*, 164–65, 247, 252, 265, 357 n. 119; *Dance of Albion*, 35, 36 (fig. 2), 38, 153–54; *Death's Door*, 183, 194; *Descriptive Catalogue*, 151, 196, 244, 245, 324; *Divine Image*, 179, 246–48, 267, 357 n. 119; *Ecchoing Green*, 265; *Europe*, 16, 31, 41, 71, 81, 92; *Everlasting Gospel*, 196; *Four Zoas*, 16, 76–77, 96, 117, 120, 140, 265; *The French Revolution*, 17; *The Garden of Love*, xiii, 98, 274; *Gates of Paradise*, 183; *Ghost of a Flea*, 316; *Holy Thursday*, 247; *The Human Abstract*, 178; *Jerusalem*, xiii, 32, 77, 90, 105, 170, 183–84, 199, 277, 316, 321; *King Edward the Third*, 30; *Laocoon*, 264 (fig. 27); *Laughing Song*, 265; *Little Black Boy*, 164–65, 166 (fig. 8), 167 (fig. 9), 252; *A Little Girl Lost*, xiii; *Little Vagabond*, 73; *London*, xiii, 184, 265; *The Marriage of Heaven and Hell*, 6, 7, 11, 13, 41, 43, 44, 51 (fig. 4), 52, 81, 92, 95, 99, 119, 151, 157, 168, 170, 176, 180, 183–85, 198, 239, 241, 243, 272, 274, 318; *Milton*, 32; *No Natural Religion*, 153; *Our End is Come*, 38, 52; *A Poison Song*, xiii; *Public Address*, xi, 116–18, 120, 131, 171, 193, 195, 197, 350 n. 21; *Song of Liberty*, 168, 176; *Song of Los*, 31, 41, 103, 168, 170, 190, 249, 251–52, 258; *Songs of Innocence and of Experience*, 6, 32, 103, 157, 159, 164–65, 166 (fig. 8), 167 (fig. 9), 169–70, 198, 246–47, 252, 265, 357 n. 119; *Sun-Flower*, xiii, 159–61; *Tiriel*, 180; "To the Public," 52; *Visions of the Daughters of Albion*, xiii, 6, 7, 13, 41, 81, 92–99, 131–32, 134, 152–53, 157, 168, 170, 176–80, 185, 198, 256, 323
body, 227, 230, 235, 242, 244, 261–63, 279, 281, 290, 292
book, idea of, 191–92, 200
Boulton, Matthew, 134
Bowles, John, 139
Boydell, John, 117, 147–48, 172
Braudel, Henri, 108
Bromion, 176, 180
Bronowski, Jacob, 34, 150, 340 n. 233
Brothers, Richard, 59, 70, 306
Brown, Richard, 86
Bruder, Helen, 31, 93, 326 n. 6
Bruno, Giordano, 204, 249–50, 291, 319

Bryant, Jacob, 249, 257
Burke, Edmund, 19, 20, 29, 39, 47, 49–50, 62–63, 67, 71, 111, 115–16, 121, 124–26, 137, 141–44, 207, 219, 224–26, 241, 258, 267, 274, 294–95, 302–3, 307, 311, 321
Burton, Robert, 298
Butler, Marilyn, 210
Byron. *See* Gordon, George

Cagliostro, 216, 327 n.12
Calhoun, Craig, 26, 27, 115, 150, 329 n. 37
Campbell, Colin, 108
Casarino, Cesare, 265
Cesaire, Aimé, 159
Chakrabarty, Dipesh, 271, 315
Chandler, James, 22, 360 n. 39
Chartism, 22, 48, 288
children, 162–63, 317–18; and labor, 86, 102–7
chimney sweeper, figure of, 105–6, 265
choice, culture of, 207
Claeys, Gregory, 54–55, 63
Clark, Anna, 60–61, 86–87, 107, 115–16, 207
Clarkson, Laurence, 21, 95, 97
class, 19, 25–29, 35, 44, 54–56, 74–75, 85, 101–4, 113–16, 135–45, 165, 172–74, 197, 207–9, 215, 226, 233–34, 250, 298, 301, 316, 329 nn. 31, 38, 332 n. 15, 348 n. 169
Coleridge, Samuel Taylor, 209, 274, 301–2
Colquhoun, Partrick, 20, 86, 100–103, 106, 141, 295, 341 n. 40
commerce, 74, 152, 156, 173, 175, 181, 322, 336 n. 151; and radicalism, 30
commodity, 146, 148–50, 153, 156, 172, 175, 180–81, 227, 319, 322, 324
communism, 23, 24, 25, 29, 58, 95, 196, 283, 288–94, 304, 306–10, 335 n. 43, 362 n. 83
community, xiv, 12, 14, 15, 23, 24, 29, 40, 59, 74, 97, 174, 303
Conant, Martha, 217
conception, vs. execution, 28, 116, 118, 135–36, 171, 199, 263, 146, 202, 267–68, 276–79
consumer culture, 2–7, 134–36, 147–50, 171, 197, 201–2, 207; and subjectivity, 134–36, 139, 144, 152–53
Coppe, Abiezer, 21, 95, 97, 291–93, 309–10, 320, 362 n. 83
Coppin, Richard, 304
copy, vs. original, 7, 12, 119, 146–48, 169–71, 189–91, 197–202, 322
copying, and repetition, 134
Crisp, Tobias, 304
criticism: Blake, xiii, 2, 9, 13, 17, 26, 30, 31, 31, 44, 156, 158, 162–63, 188, 193–95, 198, 205–6, 209, 212, 250, 263, 266, 268, 270,

387

INDEX

criticism (*continued*)
  295, 312, 315, 318; fun face of, 20, 53–54, 58, 70, 72
Cromek, Robert, xi, 151, 157, 183, 193–94, 243
Cromer, Lord, 204, 230, 232, 237, 240–41, 246, 356 nn. 64, 70
Cromwell, Oliver, 287, 295, 362 n. 91
Cunningham, Alan, 17
Curtis, F. B., 80

Dacre, Charlotte, 209
Damrosch, Leopold, 331 n. 78
Daniells, Thomas and Samuel, 220
Darwin, Erasmus, 45, 80
Davies, Keri, 52
Davis, J. C., 292, 363 n. 104
Debord, Guy, 87
Declaration of Independence (United States), 6, 33–34
De Fleury, Maria, 72
Delacroix, Eugène, 209–11 figs. 18, 19
Deleuze, Gilles, 7, 87, 187, 282–83, 340 n. 12, 351 n. 35, 360 n. 40, 361 n. 76, 363 n. 101, 367 n. 25
De Loutherbourg, Philip, 216
democracy, 23, 26, 180, 295
De Quincey, Thomas, 209, 214
Derrida, Jacques, 187–88, 352 n. 49
desire, 7, 40, 81, 92–98, 132, 227, 230, 235, 240, 249, 260, 274–75, 286–87, 291, 319–21, 349 n. 2; and being, 7, 81; infinite, 7; and radicalism, 7, 44; regulation of, 7 (*see also* regulation, self-); and subjectivity, 7, 44, 132, 177
Despard, Colonel Edward, 25, 49, 266, 300
despotism, 208–9, 214–15, 218, 232, 237
development, 161, 178, 245. *See also* modernization
Dickinson, H. T., 34, 60, 74
Dienst, Richard, 86, 104, 342 n. 60
Diggers, 288–89, 293–95
Di Salvo, Jackie, 69, 326 n. 6
disciplinary institutions, 86, 100, 102–8
Dohrm-Van Rossum, Gerhard, 111
Doskow, Minna, 326 n. 4

Eagleton, Terry, 54
Eaton, Daniel Isaac, 29, 47, 49, 50, 58, 258, 303, 334 n. 115, 337 n. 164
Eaves, Morris, 118, 147, 149, 171–74, 196, 350 n. 21, 351 n. 22, 353 n. 70, 355 n. 56
Eden, Frederick Morton, 91, 100, 107, 127
Edgeworth, Maria, 45

Edwards, Thomas, 294
effeminacy, fear of, 216
egalitarianism, political vs. economic, 22–24, 60–67, 136, 138–41, 294–95, 335 n. 143, 337 nn. 163, 164, 353 n. 70
Eliot, T. S., 5
empire, political aesthetic of, 246–49
Emsley, Clive, 48
Engelstein, Stefani, 80
engineering, social, 100–106
engraving, 10, 12, 146, 168–70, 182; commercial, xii, 9, 87, 108, 146–49, 169, 185–92, 201; social status of, xii; and repetition, 12
Enlightenment, 39; and radicalism, 19, 39
enthusiasm, 3, 20, 21, 24–26, 45, 53, 70–75, 173, 196, 207, 215, 219, 238, 240, 243–45, 250, 276, 293–303, 308–16, 320, 366 n. 4
Equiano, Olaudah, 25
Erdman, David, 19, 29, 33, 35, 38, 92, 107, 158, 326 nn. 4, 6, 330 n. 61
essence, vs. identity, 248
Essick, Robert, 29, 38, 53, 147, 149, 154, 189–91, 199, 252, 263, 265, 277, 349 n. 196, 350 n. 17, 352 n. 55, 353 n. 76
eternity, 271
Eurocentrism, 206, 231
evangelicism, 207, 215, 251
Evans, Thomas, 49, 59, 311
excess, 207–8, 226, 240, 297
exchange, 113, 175–81, 201–2, 278, 313, 319–20
execution, vs. conception, 28
exoticism, 204–5, 212, 217, 237, 240, 252, 258

factory, as body, 127–28. *See also* industrial production
femininity, fear of, 61–62, 214–27, 230–32, 240
Ferber, Michael, 21, 29, 33, 69–70, 329 n. 42
Ferguson, Adam, 116, 121, 125–27
Fielden, John, 126–27, 343 n. 76
five senses, 41–43, 82, 96–97, 144, 152, 261, 272, 288, 291
form, 261, 269–78, 281–86, 290, 292; and being, 7, 69, 293; and content, 7; and desire, 7; and freedom, 8; and identity, 7–8; and illuminated books, 29; and image, 275–77, 286–91; and life, 261, 268, 283, 287, 359 n. 16; and subjectivity, 80, 106
Foucault, Michel, 86, 281–82, 340 n. 13
Franklin, Benjamin, 33, 34
freedom, 11, 14, 15, 23, 81, 88–90, 94–98, 101, 106, 132, 136, 145, 152, 158, 161, 178, 181, 205, 248, 258–59, 266, 274, 277–78,

388

281–82, 292–93, 308–10, 314, 419–20; and desire, 8, 152; and imagination, 1; and joy, 8
Frye, Northrop, 32, 262, 275, 277, 317, 319
Fuseli, Henry, 80, 194

Galland, Antoine, 214
gender, 215–19, 222–27, 232, 256
Gilchrist, Alexander, 17, 32, 77
Gilmartin, Kevin, 328 n. 23, 358 n. 121
Gleckner, Robert, 331 n. 78
globalization, 75, 201, 256, 298
God, 1, 5, 7, 8, 179, 241, 248–49, 262, 265–66, 268, 278, 282, 284–85, 287–94, 309, 315–23
Godwin, William, 17, 20, 45, 216, 306
Gordon, George (Lord Byron), 209, 211, 213–14, 242, 251
Gordon Riots (1780), 35, 38
governmentality, 281, 314
Graves, Robert, 325 n. 10
Great War, 6
Green, David, 87, 87, 108, 110, 115, 127
Guattari, Félix, 283, 340 n. 12, 351 n. 35

Habermas, Jürgen, 297
Hamilton, Alexander, 332 n. 102
Hamilton, Elizabeth, 209
Hammond, Barbara and J. L., 126, 346 n. 139
Hardt, Michael, 267, 360 n. 40, 363 n. 101
Hardy, Thomas, 49, 333 n. 107
harlot, figure of, 93–97, 106, 265
Harrington, James, 267, 284, 286–87, 306, 362 n. 83
Hastings, Warren, 204–5, 211, 244, 256
Hawes, Clement, 293
Hayley, William, 316
Hegel, G. W. F., 14
hermeticism, 249–50
Hill, Christopher, 23, 250
Hilton, Nelson, 181, 186–87, 192
history: in Blake's work, 1, 14, 41; conceptions of, 156, 161, 262, 268, 289, 297, 299, 300, 312, 314–15, 326 n. 5; of the impossible, 10, 14, 262, 269–71, 312, 315; and law, 1; and narrative, 1; and modernity, 3, 10, 41, 156, 311, 325 n. 17; and modernization, 3, 11, 12; and narrative, 155–56; and possibility, 1, 11; of the possible, 262, 271, 312, 314–16; and regulation, 2; and revolution, 41
Hobbes, Thomas, 130, 286, 362 nn. 87, 88
Hobson, Christopher, 62
Hodges, William, 220
Hone, J. Ann, 48
How, Samuel, 59, 304
Howard, John, 326 n. 4

Hunt, Henry, 22
Hunt, Robert, 193–96, 202, 244
Huntington, William, 71
Hurd, William, 72–73, 120, 296

identity. *See* subjectivity
idleness, 61–62, 73
image, 9, 87–88, 145–46, 162–65, 166, 168–70, 181–87, 191, 198, 200, 225, 263, 267, 276, 279, 284–94, 321–2, 352 n. 46; and commodity, 9, 87–88, 146–50, 168, 172; and copy, 168; and form, 269, 279, 285, 288; and industrial culture, 9, 87–88, 146–49, 192; and industrial production, 146–47, 200; and language, 185–88; and subjectivity, 4, 5–6, 7–8, 11; and time, 12, 184–85
imagination, 92, 132, 153, 171, 186, 234, 245, 261, 263, 266–69, 271–73, 275, 278, 282, 285–86, 318; and history, 1–2; and life, 92; and politics, 1; and power, 1–2, 3
immanence, 179, 192, 249, 254, 257, 261, 271, 289–90, 309, 319–20
imperialism, xiv, 3, 44, 45, 90, 141, 204–6, 212, 217–20, 224, 230–32, 237–38, 243, 246, 248, 251, 256–57, 283; culture of, 205, 211, 217, 237, 243–44, 247, 249, 256–57, 314; and exoticism, 213, 217; and subjectivity, 4, 212, 213
individual: rights of, 22–23, 27, 29, 39, 40, 45, 52–63, 75, 77, 101, 136–38, 145, 152, 156, 172, 178, 180–81, 207, 213, 218, 285, 287, 288, 295, 301–2, 310, 313, 318; sovereign, 39–43, 45, 53–60, 63, 80, 95–98, 106, 130–37, 143–45, 150–58, 171–74, 178, 180, 213, 226, 232, 289, 292, 314, 319
"Individual Merit," 130–31, 173, 322–23, 350 n. 21
industrial culture, 9, 75, 116, 146, 202
industrial production, 9, 11, 89–90, 100, 108, 110–11, 108, 116–29, 131, 134–35, 146–49, 168, 170, 172, 180, 197, 201–2, 280, 298, 344 n. 76; and subjectivity, 11, 86, 100, 125, 127, 129–38, 140, 153; and time, 90, 110–11, 120, 122–23, 133
infinite, 42–43, 132, 145, 177–79, 181, 316, 323
intellectuals, and radicalism, 19, 22
Ionian Antiquities, 223 (fig. 21)
Ireton, Henry, 294–95, 362 n. 91

Jacobinism, 64–65, 72
Jameson, Fredric, 5, 87, 145
Jefferson, Thomas, 33, 46, 330 n. 62
Joachim of Fiore, 250

389

Index

Johnson, Joseph, 17, 19, 52–54, 63, 80
Jones, Sir William, 209–10, 214, 246, 256
joy, xiii, 8, 28, 43, 81, 98, 132, 152, 176–79, 205, 238, 243, 258–60, 265, 269, 272, 275, 289, 323, 324
Joyce, James, 5

Kay, James, 126
Knight, Cornelia, 209

labor, 33, 45, 63, 78, 88–92, 98–135, 149, 152–53, 159, 161, 173, 178–79, 180, 185, 187, 197, 263, 298, 322, 341 n. 40, 344 n. 76, 345 n. 98, 346 nn. 133, 139, 347 nn. 143, 148; and industrial production, 86, 119–25, 131–33, 149, 153; mental vs. manual, 116–28, 135–39, 144, 147–48, 279–80; and ontology, 100–114, 132, 136, 153–54; and subjectivity, 129, 131–32, 152–54, 171–73; and time, 90–91, 104, 110, 111, 159–60; and work discipline, 122–24
labor power: alienation of, 107–8, 111–24, 300; quantification of, 114–17, 120–27, 146, 149
Landor, Walter Savage, 209
Landseer, John, 148
language, 160, 186–88, 217–18, 224–25, 234, 269, 352 n. 49, 360 n. 39; and self-regulation, 225–41
law, 80–81, 94, 176, 260–62, 278–81, 321; and organ-ization, 42
Lawrence, 231, 237
Leask, Nigel, 213, 216–18, 238
Lee, Richard, 24, 29, 58, 70, 306–9
Lees, Lynn, 59, 100–101, 104
Levellers, 287–88, 293, 295, 301, 362 n. 91
levelling, 23, 26, 28, 48, 57–58, 60, 65–66, 141, 295, 302
Lewis, Wyndham, 5
liberalism, 2, 5, 130, 180, 266, 311; and consumer culture, 6
liberty: and commercial freedom, 54–58, 74, 76, 136–39, 145, 151–52, 180; and consumer culture, 6; discourse of, 3, 6, 14, 17–60, 64, 67, 76, 90, 99–103, 106, 136–39, 144–45, 152–58, 176, 180–81, 202, 230, 232, 248, 273, 281, 283, 301, 308, 310; and imperialism, 232; and narrative, 31, 77, 90; and private property, 40, 60–63, 74–75; and self-regulation, 226, 232; and sovereign individual, 22, 27, 29, 40, 54–61, 73–75, 99, 101, 136–37, 144–45, 152, 226, 232; and subjectivity, 180–81, 232; and time, 158

life, 92, 154, 176, 261, 265, 268–71, 278, 280–85, 289, 291, 293, 315, 319, 321, 322, 359 n. 16; production of, 263; regulation of, 261–69
Lillburne, John, 40
Linebaugh, Peter, 87, 102, 283, 298–99, 304, 310, 330 n. 69
Locke, John, 9, 26, 28, 34, 39, 42, 43, 44, 75, 81–82, 96, 147, 153, 156, 173–75, 197, 241, 245, 251–52, 261, 263, 272–80, 284, 287–88, 290–91, 322, 328 n. 31, 357 n. 96
London, 16, 19–20, 27, 30, 34–35, 45, 47–48, 50, 63–64, 70–71, 77, 86, 100, 103–11, 134, 150, 155, 157
London Corresponding Society, 19, 21, 22, 23, 24, 30, 34, 46, 47, 48, 49, 58–65, 77, 172, 294–95, 300–303, 329 n. 37, 330 n. 59, 333 nn. 106, 107, 334 nn. 116, 117, 336 n. 161, 337 nn. 163, 164
Los, 265, 277, 321
Lottes, Günther, 23, 26
love, xiii, 2, 93–95, 97, 152, 262, 278, 292, 309, 320–32, 324
Lunar Society, 45

Macaulay, Thomas, 211, 256
machine: human, 121–32; mechanical, 121–30
machinery, 78, 122–27
Macpherson, C. B., 22
Madison, James, 332 n. 102
Makdisi, Saree, 210, 237, 314, 325 n. 17, 346 n. 120
Malthus, Thomas, 55, 63, 74, 226, 274, 332 n. 97
Mann, Paul, 181, 192, 350 n. 18
Marinetti, Filippo, 5
market, culture of, 26, 73, 74, 112, 114, 136–39, 151, 175, 180, 202, 266, 313; freedom of, 62, 74
Marx, Karl, 75, 87, 114, 121–22, 124, 126–29, 135–37, 139, 227, 280–81, 298, 345 n. 98, 346 n. 133, 347 nn. 143, 148
masculinity, 60–62, 74
material, vs. immaterial, 242–43, 266
materialism, 263, 360 n. 46
Maundrell, Henry, 220–21, 226
Maurice, Thomas, 246
Mayer, Luigi, 220, 246
McCalman, Iain, 20, 21, 25, 302, 327 n. 12
McGann, Jerome, 170–71, 350 n. 17
McKendrick, Neil, 122, 134
meaning, 165–67, 175, 181, 192, 199–200, 263, 321, 352 n. 49, 353 n. 76

390

INDEX

Mee, Jon, 20, 21, 24, 29, 53–54, 58, 70, 72, 207, 270, 296–97, 302, 309, 311, 314, 327 n. 7, 329 n. 42, 357 n. 46, 366 n. 4
Mellor, Anne, 252, 256–57, 355 n. 56
Middleton, Peter, 32
mill, as conceptual space, 92, 132, 152–53, 157, 161, 183
Mill, James, 230, 256
Milton, John, 91, 158, 242, 252
minute particularity, 319–23
Mitchell, W. J. T., 32, 175, 186–89, 271, 321
mob, fear of, 26, 34, 35, 46, 47–53, 207–8, 212, 297
modernism, 5–6
modernity, 3, 7, 87, 156, 202, 213, 246, 312–15; and history, 3, 10, 39, 156, 301, 314; ideologemes of, 9, 87; and imperialism, 213, 246; and Orientalism, 246; and time, 39, 121, 156
modernization, 10, 87, 150, 158, 203, 205–6; conceptual language of, 11; cultural logic of, 2, 3; culture of, 9, 13; and history, 3; and "Universal Empire," 10, 12
Montagu, Mary Wortley, 211, 219–21
Montesquieu, 208, 214, 220, 220–21, 250, 356 n. 69
Moore, Thomas, 209
moralism. See virtue, moral
More, Hannah, 20, 66, 100, 215, 225, 248, 338 n. 191
Morton, A. L., 21, 78, 250, 297–98, 314, 329 n. 42
Muggleton, Ludowick, 304
Muggletonians, 71, 303–4
multitude, 34, 45–53, 74, 162, 207–8, 258, 286, 296–310, 314, 317, 364 n. 126
Munch, Edward, 5
mutinies, in Royal Navy (1797), 49, 58, 65, 300

Napoleon, 206, 242
narrative, 88, 120–21, 158–63, 168, 182, 270; and progressivism, 31–32, 158–59; and time, 32, 157–58, 162
necessity, 8, 68, 80, 145, 153, 262
Negri, Antonio, 267, 282–83, 362 n. 83
network, virtual. See text, virtual
Nietzsche, Friedrich, xi
Newgate Prison, 35, 48
Newton, Sir Isaac, 42, 147, 245, 252, 261, 263
noise, 263–65

ontology, 26, 39, 41, 80–83, 94–100, 152, 213, 261–62, 265, 271, 273, 284, 286, 289–94, 318, 361 n. 76, 363 n. 101, 367 n. 25; materialist, 262–78, 285–86, 360 n. 40, 363 n. 101; social, 100–104
Oothoon, 92–99, 131–32, 152–53, 176–79, 323
Orc, 31, 98, 182, 265
organ, vs. organism, 79–82, 86, 89, 96–100, 107, 119, 128–48, 152, 261, 263, 266, 318, 341 n. 20
organ-ization, 41, 42, 80–85, 97, 107, 120, 128–31, 140–43, 261, 269–70, 279, 281, 282, 314, 340 n. 14; and industrial labor, 107, 130, 140, 148; and law, 42, 80–81; and narrative, 85; and subjectivity, 41, 42, 85–86, 100, 140, 261
Orientalism, 4, 62, 194, 204–59, 274, 302, 314–15, 354 n. 22, 356 nn. 64, 69, 70; and class, 208; and exoticism, 212, 218–24, 231, 244; and language of regulation, 4, 62; and radicalism, 4, 12, 30, 44–45, 62; and romanticism, 4, 12, 212; and sexuality, 216–18; and subjectivity, 4, 62, 212–20, 238
otherness, 4, 5, 6, 204–5, 212–18, 222–26, 242–43, 247, 251, 297, 301; domination of, in radicalism, 4; domination of, in romanticism, 4
Overton, Richard, 40, 42, 362 n. 91
Owen, Wilfred, 1

Paine, Tom, 3, 4, 5, 8, 16–17, 19, 20, 21, 29, 30, 31, 33, 34, 35, 39, 40, 43, 44, 45, 48, 49, 50, 54–59, 63, 67–68, 71–72, 74–77, 80, 82, 86, 96, 136, 156, 172, 193, 206–7, 215, 224–26, 230, 274, 281–82, 284–85, 287–88, 290–91, 294, 301, 306, 310, 313–14, 317, 321, 329 n.38, 332 n. 97, 335 n. 143, 353 n. 70, 364 n. 126
Paley, Morton, 59
Palmer, Samuel, xii
particularity, vs. individuality, 177–79, 320
patriarchy, 66–67, 71, 115–16, 138, 278
perception, ontology of, 261–65, 272–77, 317
Peterloo Massacre, 22
Phillips, Michael, 52
philopoesis, 265
philosophy, and politics, 22, 23, 24, 28, 29, 30, 38, 39, 243
Philp, Mark, 20, 58–59
Place, Francis, 24
Plato, 242, 246
pleasure, politics of, 44–45, 61–62, 94–97, 133, 218, 221, 230, 235
plebeian subculture, 21–27

391

INDEX

poetry, and regulation, 233–38
politics: and aesthetics, 38; conceptual, 38, 41; and economics, 83–87, 120; and philosophy, 22, 23, 24, 28, 29, 30, 38, 39, 243
Poovey, Mary, 354 n. 33
power, 236–43, 257, 261, 266, 269–71, 278–82, 286, 289–93, 303, 307, 317, 359 n. 16; ontological, 271, 277–79, 282, 285, 290, 293, 317–18, 359 n. 16
Price, Richard, 30, 31, 33, 45, 332 n. 97
Priestley, Joseph, 17, 45, 332 n. 97
printing, color, 190–91
production: as reproduction, 179, 322; socioeconomic vs. psychobiological, 81–86, 100–101, 113, 120, 131
progressivism, 156–59, 168, 194, 202, 207, 245, 296, 314; in Blake criticism, 31–32; and radicalism, 31–33, 156
property, private, 23, 24, 26, 46, 55, 60, 63, 287, 289, 296, 307; and discourse of liberty, 40, 46, 55, 63, 75; and subjectivity, 40, 60, 75, 287–96, 302, 309

race, 165, 253, 256–57, 298
radicalism, 2, 3, 5, 17–77, 172, 238, 245–46, 272, 291, 329 n. 37; absence of economic questions in, 54–58, 65–66, 77, 136, 139; and aesthetics, 38; and American War of Independence, 33–34, 90, 93, 155–58, 221, 340 n. 233; and armed struggle, 47–50, 54, 333 nn. 104, 106; and artisan class, 22, 28; and commercial liberalism, 24, 30, 45, 54–58, 64, 74–75, 77, 85, 111–14, 136–37, 180; and consumer culture, 5–6, 136–37; and desire, 7–8, 44–45, 61, 227, 230, 234, 274; and Enlightenment, 19; and enthusiasm, 20–21, 24, 25, 27, 58, 74–75, 207; and exoticism, 205–9, 214–19, 224–26, 244, 258; femininity, fear of, in, 61–62, 209, 215–19, 224–27, 230, 240; freedom, 23; and French Revolution, 48–49; hegemonic position in, 11, 58–65, 72, 75, 82, 90, 99, 101, 106, 111, 113, 136–37, 155, 155–58, 172, 206–7, 215, 232, 240–43, 281–82, 287–88, 301–7, 310–14; hegemonic strand of, 21–30, 33, 34, 39, 41, 48; heterogeneity of, 20–29, 54, 58–59, 300–316; and imperialism, 4, 12, 44, 45, 205–7, 214–15, 224, 230, 232, 248, 258, 274; and industrial culture, 85, 136–37; and intellectuals, 19, 22, 23; and labor, 85, 101, 106, 111–14, 136–37; in London, 19, 20, 22, 34; and modernization, 205–7; and multitude, 207–8, 258; and narrative, 158–59; and Orientalism, 4, 7, 12, 44–45, 62, 205–10, 214–19, 221, 224–27, 230, 232–33, 240, 244, 258, 274; and progressivism, 31–33, 155–59, 215; and property, private, 63, 75; and race, 4; respectable vs. plebeian, 21–27; and romanticism, 3, 206; and secularism, 19, 20; and self-regulation, 7–8, 44–45, 60–63, 136, 225–30, 234, 240–41, 274; and subjectivity, 4, 5, 6, 7–8, 11, 26, 28, 38, 41, 44–45, 60–62, 77, 80, 99–101, 106, 113, 135–39, 153, 180–81, 215–18, 232, 234; and time, 156–59; and virtue, moral, 60–63, 74, 207–8, 215, 218, 224–30

Rainborough, Thomas, 294
Ranters, 292, 294–95, 297, 304, 308, 363 n. 104
Read, Dennis, 193
Rediker, Marcus, 283, 298–99, 304, 310
Reeve, John, 304, 320
regulation, 269, 278, 280, 282, 297; self-, 4, 5, 8, 44, 45, 60–63, 144, 224–37, 241, 243, 261–62, 273, 281, 314, 317, 355 n.56
Reid, William Hamilton, 21, 24, 141, 295–96, 303–4, 306, 311–12
reification, 175, 192; and subjectivity, 95–99, 106, 114, 130, 132, 144, 152–53, 176–77, 180–81
religion, and politics, 2, 43, 66–76, 112, 119, 132, 193, 205, 244, 247, 249, 296–97
repetition, 133–34, 146, 148, 157, 161, 164–69, 189; and meaning, 169, 175; and transformation, 168–76, 181, 185–200
representation, 201, 288, 293, 352 n. 46; political, 22–23, 29, 55, 63, 65, 68, 85, 286
reproduction, sexual, 93–99, 134, 152
republicanism, 2, 5, 8, 27, 141; and consumer culture, 5–6; and subjectivity, 7–8
Revolution, English (seventeenth century), 23, 24, 27, 46, 95, 270, 287, 294, 296
Revolution, French, 19, 26, 30, 48, 144, 181, 294, 300, 313
Reynolds, Sir Joshua, xi, 147, 150, 156, 196, 316
Ribeau, George, 305
Rigal, Laura, 172
rights, individual, 5, 6, 7–8, 22–23, 26, 28, 29, 39, 45; representational, 21, 24, 26, 27, 28
Robinson, Henry Crabb, 16, 269, 275, 315–16
Romantic Imperialism, 3, 13
romanticism, 3, 4, 171–74, 206, 210–12, 233–42, 244, 314; and class, 207–9, 215–16, 226, 233–34; and exoticism, 210–14, 219, 233; and imperialism, 3, 12, 206, 212–14, 217, 219, 246; and language, 233–34, 236; and Orientalism, 4, 12, 206, 209, 211–14, 217,

219, 232–33, 236–38, 246, 258; and race, 4; and radicalism, 3, 12, 206, 213–14, 233–34, 238; and regulation, 233–38; and style, 233; and subjectivity, 171, 174, 212–13, 217, 234–38
Rousseau, Jean-Jacques, 39, 294
Royal Academy of Art, xii; and engraving, xii
Rudé, George, 35

Said, Edward, 206, 210–12, 231, 354 n. 22
Saltmarsh, John, 59, 304
Sassoon, Siegfried, 325 n. 10
Schiavonetti, Louis, xi, 183, 193–94
Schiller, Friedrich, 133, 171, 174
Schwab, Raymond, 212, 214, 354 n. 22
secularism, and radicalism, 19
selfhood, individual. See subjectivity
selfishness, 94–97. See also individual, sovereign
sexuality, 38, 39, 60–62, 92–98, 152, 216
Sharp, William, 20
Shee, Martin, 117, 148
Shelley, Percy, 30, 209, 211, 213, 244–46
slavery, 33–34, 88–99, 131, 152–59, 161, 248, 256, 330 n. 62, 357 n. 121
Smith, Adam, 63
Smith, Bernard, 252
Smith, Nigel, 292
society: as body, 128, 136–44, 313; as factory, 106–7, 136–42
Society for Constitutional Information, 58, 301
solitude, 177
Southcott, Joanna, 59
Southey, Robert, 209, 211, 214, 251
sovereignty, 205, 232, 234, 240, 357, 303
Spence, Thomas, 20, 24, 25, 29, 46, 47, 49, 58, 258, 260, 303, 306–7, 309–10, 335 n. 143
spies, 47–50
Spinoza, 7, 8, 155, 243, 248–50, 267, 275, 282, 315, 319, 320–21, 360 n. 40, 367 n. 25
State, 8, 47–52, 59, 67–68, 252
State Religion, 8, 19
Stedman, John Gabriel, 34, 252, 256
Stein, Gertrude, 5
Stothard, Thomas, 193, 196
Strange, Robert, 118
striving, 281, 291, 319–21
struggle, armed, 47–52
style, 216–27, 233–41
subjectivity, 2, 5, 6, 11, 12, 13, 14, 29, 38, 39, 43, 44, 45, 60–62, 75, 77, 81, 88, 95–99, 113, 130–58, 172–81, 197, 212–17, 225–30, 235–48, 281–82, 293, 296–97, 313, 322,

328 n. 31, 340 n. 13; and biology, 40; and desire, 7; and exchange, 176–79; 181, 202; and history, 41; and imperialism, 4, 212–14; and industrial production, 11, 100, 113, 127, 130, 133–37, 141; and labor, 99, 106, 113, 127–37; and organ-ization, 41–42, 86, 99, 135–37, 139, 144, 362 nn. 87, 88; and perception, 81 (see also perception, ontology of); and private property, 40; in radicalism, 4, 5–6, 7–8, 26, 28, 38, 39, 60–62, 77, 83; and revolution, 38, 39; and time, 88, 99, 132, 180
sublime, the, 212, 234–36, 320, 331 n. 78
Swedenborg, Immanuel, 248

Tatham, Frederick, 258
Terry, Garnet, 20, 58–59, 70, 305
text: open, 169–71; virtual, 163–75, 183–88; visual, 189
textuality, 162–70, 240
Thelwall, John, 3, 4, 16, 22, 24, 49–50, 54–58, 60, 62–63, 74, 111–13, 136, 206–7, 214–16, 258, 294, 301–2, 310–11, 314, 335 n. 126, 336 n. 151, 364 n. 126
Thompson, E. P., 2, 20, 21, 29, 55, 70, 75, 86, 206, 329 n. 42
time, 78, 132, 158–60, 182–83, 263, 271, 288, 342 n. 60; clock, 110–11, 156 (see also time, linear); cyclical, 160, 168; diachronic, 160–61 (see also time, linear); discipline, 110–11; economy of, 78; heterogeneous, 1, 156–61, 184–85, 294, 301, 306, 309, 315–16, 323–24; homogeneous, 3, 121–22, 132, 156–61, 269, 294; and image, 12; and industrial production, 12, 78, 90–91, 120–22, 149; and labor, 90–91, 104, 110–11, 120–21; linear, 5, 39, 88, 155–68, 179, 184–87, 323; and modernity, 39, 121, 313; and narrative, 1, 31–32, 121, 160–62; and progressivism, 31–32, 156, 168, 289; and subjectivity, 180; 110–11, 121–28, 149; synchronic, 160–61
Tiriel, 180
Tooke, John Horne, 59
treason trials, 59, 263

United Britons, 49, 65
United Englishmen, 49
United Irishmen, 49, 58, 65, 300
United States, 14, 30–47, 58, 61, 88, 93, 155, 157, 172, 182, 221, 332 n. 102
"Universal Empire," xiv, 16, 75–76, 118, 298
Ure, Andrew, 85, 125, 128–29, 143, 147, 280–81

INDEX

Urizen, 41, 66, 71, 76, 80, 113, 116–19, 126–29, 132, 139–40, 176–77, 251, 260–63, 265, 268–70

Valenze, Deborah, 87, 107
van Gogh, Vincent, 5
virginity, and subjectivity, 93–97
virtue: and masculinity, 60–62; moral, 4, 30, 31, 34, 44, 45, 59, 63, 67–68, 73, 75, 207, 209, 215–18, 224–33, 245, 318; and Orientalism, 4, 30, 44, 45, 62, 215; and otherness, 4, 30, 60–62
Viscomi, Joseph, 189–90, 192, 200–201, 350 n. 17
visual/verbal interplay, 162–70, 181–91, 199, 240, 270
Volney, Constantin, 24, 29, 44, 45, 55, 205–7, 214–15, 306, 330 n. 65

Wahrman, Dror, 329 n. 38, 364 n. 126
Wakefield, Gilbert, 339 nn. 200, 201
Walwyn, William, 40
War of Independence, American, 14, 16, 19, 30–47, 53, 58, 61, 155–57, 182, 208, 294, 299, 300, 340 n. 233
Washington, George, 32, 33, 34, 41, 46, 70
Watson, Richard, Bishop of Llandaff, 66–69, 71, 74, 162, 247
Weber, Max, 74, 174
Wedderburn, Robert, 20, 25, 310

Wedgwood, Josiah, 45, 110–11, 122, 124–27, 134, 147, 332 n. 97
Wells, Roger, 47, 65
Whitman, Walt, 260
Wilde, Oscar, 332 n. 98
Wilkins, Charles, 244
Williams, Gwyn, 48
Williams, Nicholas, 326 n. 5
Winstanley, Gerrard, 24, 29, 196, 288–93, 297, 308–9, 362 n. 83
Wollett, William, 118
Wollstonecraft, Mary, 3, 17, 19, 20, 44, 45, 61, 62, 204–5, 209, 211, 214–20, 224–27, 230, 232–34, 237, 240, 242, 244, 246, 258, 314, 317, 354 n. 33, 355 n. 56
women, 34, 60, 61, 107, 134, 152, 209, 216, 219, 221–23, 354 n. 33; rights of, 61, 209–21
Wood, Robert, 222–24
Woolf, Virginia, 5
Wordsworth, William, 4, 12, 67, 205, 212, 214, 233–46, 366 n. 4
work discipline, 45, 72, 77, 86, 109–11, 119–25
World War I, 6
Worrall, David, 20, 47, 50, 58, 329 n. 42, 361 n. 122
Wyvill, Christopher, 48, 56, 329 n. 38, 364 n. 126

Yates, Frances, 250
Young, Alfred, 46

394